TRAVEL AND LODGING LAW

TRAVEL AND LODGING LAW
Principles, Statutes, and Cases

by

John R. Goodwin, JD
Professor of Business Law
West Virginia University

and

James M. Rovelstad, Ph.D.
Program Director and Professor of
Travel and Tourism Administration
Graduate School of Management and Urban Professions
The New School for Social Research
New York City

Grid Publishing, Inc., Columbus, Ohio

Library of Congress Cataloging in Publication Data

Goodwin, John R   1929-
     Travel and lodging law.

     (Grid series in law)
     Includes index.
        1.   Hotels, taverns, etc. — Law and legislation —
United States.   2.   Tourist trade — Law and
legislation — United States.   3.   Restaurants,
lunch rooms, etc. — Law and legislation — United
States.   I.   Rovelstad, James M., joint author.
II.   Title.
KF951.G66   343′,73′078   79-12189
ISBN 0-88244-188-4

To

Shawn Michael Paugh
From a Grandfather who could not be
prouder,

and
Amy and Connie
From a Father who could not be
prouder.

Contents

PREFACE

1 THE TRAVEL AND LODGING (HOSPITALITY) INDUSTRY   1

The Impact of Travel and Tourism; Institutions and Organizations; Definition of a Traveler; Inns, Hotels, and Motels; Lodging at Places Other than Hotels; The Traveler's Need for Special Legal Attention; The Legal Environmental Mix; Liability of Those Delivering Recreation Services, Facilities, and Products; Over-regulation by Government of the Private Sector; Concessions Nationwide Recreation Plan; Questions; Endnotes

2 LAW   19

Today; Sources of Law; History; Written Law; Common Law; Administrative Law; Questions; Endnotes

3 CLASSIFICATIONS OF LAW   33

Legal and Administrative Law; Common Law and Statutory Law; Common Law and Civil Law; Public Law and Private Law; Substantive Law and Procedural Law; Contract Law and Property Law; Tort Law and Contract Law; Law and Equity; Questions

4 LAWYERS, JUDGES AND JURIES 45

Lawyers; Services of Lawyers; Fees; Judges; Juries; Questions; Endnotes

5 HOSPITALITY CASES IN COURT 57

Third Meaning; Reporter System; Legal Research; Statutes; Courts; Questions

6 HOSPITALITY CONTRACTS—CONVENTIONAL 73

Definition; Classifications; The Statute of Frauds; Form of Contract; Requirements of a Binding Contract; Performance and Breach; Specific Performance; Implied Contract; Illegal Contracts; Contracts Against Public Policy; Questions; Endnotes

7 HOSPITALITY SALES CONTRACTS 91

Key Terms; Formation of a Sales Contract; Offer and Acceptance; Obligations of the Parties; Sellers Right to Cure; Passing of Title; Risk of Loss; Recapture Rights; Miscellaneous Sales Contracts Cases; Questions; Endnotes

8 HOSPITALITY AGENTS AND INDEPENDENT CONTRACTORS 107

Agency; Formation of the Relationship; Scope of Agent's Authority; Rights, Duties and Liabilities; Notice; Termination of the Relationship; Independent Contractors; Mechanics' and Laborers' Liens; Truth in Lending Disclosures; Summary; Questions; Endnotes

9 HOSPITALITY EMPLOYEE RELATIONS 121

Equal Employment Opportunity Act; Changes in Title VII; Questions; Endnotes

10 HOSPITALITY COMMERCIAL PAPER 131

Some History; What Is Commercial Paper? Types of Commercial Paper; Requirements of Negotiability; Mis-

cellaneous Preliminary Matters; Transfer and Negotiations;
Types of Indorsements; Holders in Due Course; Checks in
Use; Warranties; Notes in Use; Certificates of Deposits in
Use; Bills of Exchange in Use; A Hotel Check; Questions;
Endnotes

11 INFORMAL HOSPITALITY ORGANIZATIONS   151

Proprietorships; Partnerships; Types of Partnerships;
Terms and Definitions; Interpretation of Knowledge and
Notice; Partnership Property; Relations of Partners with
Third Parties; Relation of Partners to Each Other; Dis-
solution; Limited Partnerships; Questions; Endnotes

12 FORMAL HOSPITALITY BUSINESS ORGANIZATIONS   173

A Definition; Classifications; Types and Terminology;
Corporate Formation; How to Incorporate; Questions;
Endnotes

13 HOSPITALITY PROPERTY   189

How Is Property Defined? Property Terms; Obtaining and
Transfering Ownership of Property; Questions; Endnotes

14 OWNERSHIP, CONTROL AND MANAGEMENT OF HOSPITALITY PROPERTY   207

Forms of Property Ownership; Control of Property;
"Zoning"; Liens and Encumberances; Questions; Endnotes

15 HOSPITALITY CONSTRUCTION AND MORTGAGE FINANCING   223

Facts; Realtors' Role; Bank's Role; Advertising for Bids;
Time Is Running; Lawyer's Role; Title Search; "Title
Chain"; Adversing the Chain; Closing; Recording; Bids;
Back to the Bank; Construction Begins; Foreclosure;
Questions

16 DUTIES OF INNKEEPERS AND GUESTS 247

Public Duties; Duty to Receive Guests; To Receive
Goods; Invited Nonguests; Suitable Accommodations;
Standard of Care; Courteous Treatment; Phone Calls and
Messages; Holding Mail; Duties of Guests; Public Health
Duties; Hotels and Restaurants; Questions; Endnotes

17 RESERVATIONS AND CHECK-IN 269

Reservations; Contract Counterpart; Excuse; Advance
Payment; Acceptable Condition; Late Arrivals; False
Registration; Overbooking; Breach of Traveler; Set
Periods; Recovery; Questions; Endnotes

18 RIGHTS OF INNKEEPERS AND GUESTS 289

Assigning New Rooms; Entry of Rooms; Effect of Emer-
gencies; Ejecting Guests; The Opposite Sex; Lock Outs;
Criminal Sanctions; Ejection of Nonguests; Innkeepers'
Lien; Rights of Guests; Questions; Endnotes

19 PROPERTY OF GUESTS AND THIRD PARTIES 305

Limitations on Liability; Examples; Property of Guests;
Goods from Third Parties; Banquets and Other Activities;
Tenants; Bailment; Excuses from Liability; Questions;
Endnotes

20 LIABILITY FOR THE AUTOMOBILES OF GUESTS 325

Loss v. Damage; Bailment; Loss of Items Inside Vehicles;
Limiting Liability; Statutory Limitations in the United
States; Questions; Endnotes

21 INJURY TO GUESTS AND OTHERS 335

Safe Premises; Outside of the Inn; Contributory Negli-
gence; Swimming Pools; Protecting from Employees;
Protecting from Third Persons; Falling Objects; Questions;
Endnotes

22 TRAVEL AGENCIES 353

Some Basics; "Sale" or Not?; Standard of Care; Prior
Experience; Duty to Accept; Not an Insurer; Regulation
of the Industry; Agents or Not? Dual Agents; As Independent Contractors; Measure of Damages; Disclaimers;
Questions; Endnotes

23 RESTAURANTS AND BARS 373

Case Definition; Definition by Statute; Restaurant v. Inn;
Liability of Restaurateur; Duties; Taverns; Questions;
Endnotes

24 CARRIERS 387

Cruise Ships; Reservations—Airlines; Questions; Endnotes

APPENDIX A 401

APPENDIX B 419

APPENDIX C 429

APPENDIX D 439

INDEX TO CHARTS, FIGURES, AND STATUTES 445

INDEX TO CASES 446

INDEX TO WORDS AND TOPICS 450

Preface

During 1978, the authors made a survey of course content and books available for use in college level courses in travel and lodging law. From this study certain conclusions were drawn. First, it was discovered that most of the books available were almost 100% case presentations or were treatises on the subject of the laws of innkeepers—not travel. While these books are useful depending upon how they are used, they all fall short of what the authors believe is needed in a basic course in the laws of travel and lodging. Next, it was discovered that because of the limited scope of these books, many teachers are forced to resort to traditional business law texts, thus requiring two books to do what one should do. Finally, it was realized that if one was to be exposed to the laws of both travel *and* lodging, a *third* book might be required. This was due to the fact that the available books dwell uniformly on the laws of hotel and innkeepers, with little or no coverage being given to the laws of travel and travel agents.

It was concluded that there is a need for a single book that would couple relevent portions of the laws of business with those of both travel and lodging. This book is the result of that conclusion and is a contraction of what in the past has required two or three books to accomplish in the classroom.

The format used in its creation was basically simple: applicable principles of law are presented and then tied directly to the facts and circumstances of the travel and lodging industry. This enables the reader to directly relate these principles to those facts and circumstances. This format is followed throughout the book.

One who studies from this book will gain an understanding of the nature of law as it is encountered in the travel industry. This awareness will follow from the text presented as well as the cases that illustrate the material. The book represents a blending of almost two decades of study and teaching of undergraduate students and should fill a void in the field to which it is directed: a void that exists perhaps because of mistaken understandings of modern times as they relate to older times.

To illustrate, it is difficult for one today to relate modern travel by jet, auto, train, ship and other means, including space travel, to systems that our minds tell us existed a hundred years ago—and to what we feel must have existed thousands of years ago. The result is a tendency for one to assume that our present day rapid and mass travel is unique to our times. But when one realistically considers what history tells us, we have to be aware that this assumption is wrong. One can easily be misled when thinking of the *form* of travel as related to the *need* for it, the latter being more important than the former.

From the earliest times of recorded history, an extended system of travel, although not so rapid, has in fact been a part of each civilization of the world. Indeed, the advancement of civilization itself has had as a basic requirement, the need for extended movement within each society. This is true because of the need to promote development of remote areas; to allow an orderly exchange of ideas and information; for recreational purposes, and to simply bind a people together in a national spirit.

Therefore, then, as well as now, in order to facilitate an extensive system of travel, it was and is necessary for suitable accomodations be made available for use by travelers. Further, reliable transportation is required to permit the travel itself to be realized. Finally, such a system needs the cohesion that comes from orderly regulation of all of those who take part in the system itself. This is true because of the need for *certainty* of transportation and lodging, as well as for reasons of safety for the traveler. These regulations or controls must by necessity, come from law in some form.

It is the overall purpose of *Travel and Lodging Law*, to examine in detail, the laws of travel and lodging as they have evolved historically and as they exist today. The undertaking of this study can be both rewarding and interesting, something that cannot be said about every study of the laws of business.

If this book permits the student to advance his or her knowledge of the laws of travel and lodging in an orderly, understandable and beneficial manner, then the effort that it has taken to produce it will have been most worthwhile.

John R. Goodwin
James M. Rovelstad

The Travel and Lodging (Hospitality) Industry

This book is directed to those who work in businesses and publically owned organizations that serve the traveler, or who plan to do so in the future. Specifically, it focuses on the legal rights, responsibilities, and obligations between the traveler and the travel business. But, before this legal interface is explored, it is important to establish for the reader, a common ground of understanding as to what the "travel industry" is, and to define who or what is a traveler, or tourist. The purpose of this chapter is to provide this framework, plus an insight into the unique characteristics of the travel industry and the facets of its legal environment.

THE IMPACT OF TRAVEL AND TOURISM

For those not directly involved, and in fact for many who are, the travel and tourism industry may be one of the best kept secrets in the United States. This is so even though the industry by most measures is larger than more familiar ones such as steel, automobiles, and coal mining, leading one of the authors to describe it as the *invisible giant.*[1] A few facts will help to put this statement in perspective.

Travel and tourism in the United States, both by its own citizens and by foreign visitors, produced over $100 billion in annual sales revenues in 1976, and employed over four million Americans.[2] Although most of the travelers in the United States are its own citizens, there is a large number of foreign visitors. The United States Travel

Service reports that 17.5 million persons from other nations visited us during 1976, and that they spent $5.8 billion on goods and services while here, plus an additional $1.0 billion on transportation from U.S. flag carriers.[3] Figure 1-1 shows the countries from which these economic impacts come.

Most of the other nations of the world have given recognition to the travel industry as a major factor in their economies. A measure of its world-wide significance is provided by the Organization for Economic Cooperation and Development (OECD). It reports that international tourism receipts by member countries rose by 250 percent between 1968 and 1974, when international travelers spent $28.8 billion.[4] This does not include the amounts spent by travelers in their own countries.[5]

Looking at the travel industry on a more disaggregated level, it has been found to be among the largest three business sectors in most of

FIGURE 1-1
Economic Impact of Foreign Travelers to the U.S.

RECEIPTS
$5.8 billion (est.)
(Excluding Transportation)

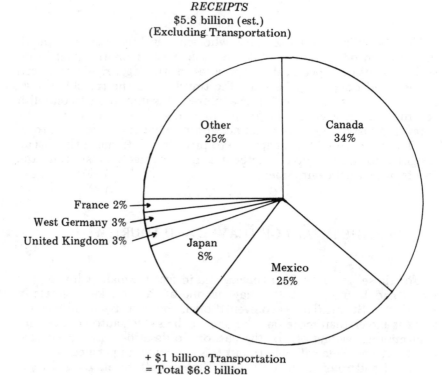

+ $1 billion Transportation
= Total $6.8 billion

From: U.S. Department of Commerce, United States Travel Serivce, Research and Analysis Division, *Summery and Analysis of International Trade to the U.S., 1976*, p. 7.

the states in the U.S. For example, in the relatively small state of West Virginia, known more for its coal mining industry, travelers spent over $640 million in 1976, and this provided 37,000 full-time jobs.[6] Coal mining, by contrast, provided about 70,000 jobs.[7] In Florida, a well known travel destination, travel is the number one industry, producing $7.2 billion in sales in 1975 and employment for 261,000 persons [8]

The significance and importance of travel and tourism in the U.S. is, at last, beginning to be recognized. The United States Travel Service has been given a mission to foster the improvement of domestic travel, and the U.S. Congress has initiated action that should lead to the formulation of a national tourism policy. Thus, the near future should see not only far greater visibility of this industry, but also an acceleration in its already rapid growth. These conditions make an understanding of the legal environment in which travel businesses must operate even more important.

INSTITUTIONS AND ORGANIZATIONS

The key to understanding the travel industry is its diversity. Certain businesses are easily recognized as major participants because a large portion of their operations are dedicated to serving travelers. These include hotels, motels, campgrounds, airlines, buslines, and travel agencies. However, these account for less than one-third of all traveler expenditures. Automobile services and fuel take another twenty percent of the traveler's expenditures. But, over fifty cents of every dollar of travel expenditure goes for food, entertainment, recreation, gifts and the like, as shown in Figure 1-2.[10] Much of the latter is provided by businesses that derive most of their sales from local residents and may not even consider themselves to be participants in the travel industry. One result of this is that the industry tends to be highly fragmented with few accepted industry-wide spokesmen.

Although most of the U.S. travel industry is made up of private businesses, federal, state and local governments also play an important role. This comes in the form of local, state, and national parks, man-made lakes for recreation, museums, theaters, and of course all commercial airports. In other nations, the national government often plays an even more active role. For example, most of the world's international airlines are wholly or partly owned by national governments. Many go further—for example, Aer Lingus, the Irish national airline owns several hotels. The United States is more the exception than the rule in the degree of private vs. public ownership of travel industry facilities.

There also is a hybrid form of travel facility that is a mix of private and public enterprise. Many publicly developed properties provide for leasing out portions for operation by private business per-

4

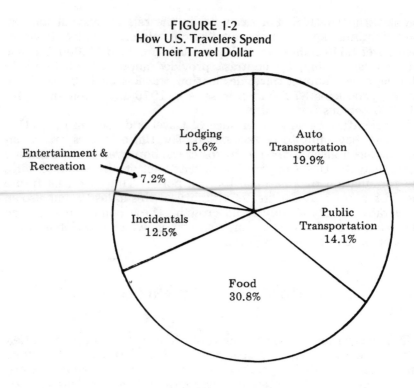

FIGURE 1-2
How U.S. Travelers Spend
Their Travel Dollar

Lodging
15.6%

Auto
Transportation
19.9%

Entertainment &
Recreation

7.2%

Public
Transportation
14.1%

Incidentals
12.5%

Food
30.8%

From: U.S. Travel Data Center, *The Impact of Travel on State Economies: 1974*, p. 7.

sons, called "concessionnaires." Although the specific mechanisms vary from situation to situation, these arrangements commonly call for the private business to pay a fee based on gross business receipts to the governmental unit owning the facility. The business also agrees to abide by specified operating procedures established by the government agency. These mixed enterprises are common in places such as state and national parks, U.S. Army Corps of Engineers water impoundments, and airports. Of course, concessionnaires also are found in many non-travel related government facilities, but nevertheless they do play a significant role in the travel industry.

Finally, there is a group of special travel industry institutions that are organizations formed by groups of businesses, organizations and individuals that share common interests or problems. Some of these have powers delegated to them by their members, or governmental agencies. For example, the International Air Transport Association (IATA) is delegated authority to set international air transport fares for its members. Some organizations serve as focal points to bring the concerns of their members before governmental bodies at the state and national level. Examples of each include the Travel Industry Association in West Virginia, and the Discover America Travel Organization (DATO). These organizations also serve other needs, especially in promotion and marketing, for their members. Internationally, the European Travel Commission serves this function for its twenty-three member countries.

The other principal category of special institution is that which provides a common forum for its members to share ideas. The Travel Research Association (TTRA) is typical of this type in North America. And of course, many of the institutions serve multiple purposes as in the case of ETC. A comprehensive identification of all of these institutions is not needed for the purposes of this overview, but table 1-1 identifies a few of them.

TABLE 1-1
Selected Tourism Related Organizations

Name	Abbreviation
American Automobile Association	AAA
Association of American Railroads	AAR
Association of Bank Travel Bureaus	ABTB
Association of Caribbean Tour Operators	ACTO
American Hotel and Motel Association	AHMA
Association of Retail Travel Agents	ARTA
American Society of Travel Agents	ASTA
Air Transport Association of America	ATA
Academic Internationale du Tourism	AIT
British Tourist Authority	BTA
Cruise Liner International Association	CLIA
Caribbean Travel Association	CTA
Discover America Travel Organization	DATO
European Travel Commission	ETC
Hotel Sales Management Association	HSMA
International Air Transport Association	IATA
International Civil Aviation Organizations	ICAO
Institute of Certified Travel Agents	ICTA
International Hotel Assocation	IHA
Organization for Economic Cooperation and Development	OECD
Pacific Area Travel Association	PATA
United States Travel Data Center	USTDC
United States Travel Service (Federal Agency)	USTS
World Tourism Organization	WTO
West Virginia Travel Industry Association	WVTIA

Adapted from: Robert W. McIntosh, *Tourism: Principles, Practices, Philosophies,* 2nd Ed., (Columbus, Ohio: Grid, Inc., 1977.) pp. 275-77.

DEFINITION OF A TRAVELER

Although it may not be obvious at this point, there is substantial disagreement among the experts as to exactly who or what constitutes a "traveler" (or tourist). The U.S. Bureau of the Census, which conducts a national travel survey every five years, defines a trip (and therefore, a traveler), as one more than 100 miles, one-way, from one's principal place of residence, except for trips to commute to and from work, or to go to school, i.e. the college student traveling between home and campus.

The U.S. Travel Data Center defines a trip/traveler as, "—all overnight trips away from home, and day trips to places 100 miles or more away from the traveler's origin."[11] Meanwhile, the OECD and the ETC prefer definitions which distinguish between *tourists*—those crossing international boundaries, and staying overnight, *excursionists*—those crossing an international boundary, but staying less than 24 hours, and *domestic holiday makers*—those traveling in their own country of residence.[12] Moreover, there is in some cases a distinction drawn as to whether the traveler is a tourist on a pleasure trip, or a business traveler. For purposes of developing promotional strategy, the latter is sometimes not counted.

There are a variety of good reasons for these differences. When the purpose is to measure the size or impact of the tourism/travel industry, and when the trips are recorded through questionnaires issued at some time substantially later than the trip was taken, people have more difficulty remembering the shorter trip than the longer ones. Or, international organizations may be interested only in those trips in which international boundaries are crossed. And, the business trip is for the most part not influenced by advertising or other promotion, while pleasure trips do have an advertising elasticity of demand.

For the purposes of this book, however, it matters little what the reason is that a person is traveling, how far away from home he/she is, or whether an international boundary is crossed. Legally, all are the same. It may be true that a stranger to an area has, potentially, less familiarity with local law and custom, so the degree of "foreignness" may in turn affect the degree of likelihood that legal problems will develop. Nevertheless, this book defines any person who behaves as a traveler/tourist, and does the things travelers/tourists do, to be a traveler/tourist. The following, drawn from state statutes, may help to provide perspective on this, and at the same time point up the potential for confusion and misinterpretation in definition.

INNS, HOTELS AND MOTELS

The words "inns" "hotels" and "motels" today are synomous for most legal purposes, although this has not always been so. These lodging facilities are regulated closely by statute, as will be appropriately examined as we proceed.

Definitions will vary from state to state, but the following are typical.

MOTEL

This word is a product of the last 25 years and is a contraction of "motorist" and "hotel". As the motel industry began to develop, notably in the 1950's, the word identified a small hotel type structure with rooms for hire by the day, with only a minimum amount of services being provided by management.

Today, the word motel is associated with some of the most luxurious travel accommodations on the face of the earth. It has been noted recently that some of the larger motel chains are advertising their units as "hotels."

HOTEL

Under Virginia law, a hotel is an inn or public lodging house that can accommodate five or more transient guests. A "transient guest" is one who puts up for less than one week.[13]

Hotels normally supply food for pay, while "restaurants", in the strict legal sense, do not furnish lodging and are distinguished in that manner.

Restaurants are quite often part of the hotel or motel, yet a different body of rules has developed in reference to them. As a general rule, one who uses a restaurant within a hotel or motel, but who is not a lodging guest, can claim no greater duty on the part of the innkeeper than that person could claim against the operator of a restaurant only.

GUEST

One who is a "guest" at lodging facilities is given by law greater rights and increased duties from the innkeeper. To determine if one is in fact a "guest" in the innkeeping sense, the courts will look to the intention of the parties. An innkeeper and a "guest" may form a "boarding house", or "landlord and tenant" relationship. If this happens, the "guest" is not a "guest" in the strict innkeeping sense. A townsperson who stops at the cigar stand in the lobby to buy a newspaper, would not be a guest and could not expect to hold the innkeeper to duties and liabilities available to true guests. Therefore, the intention of the parties must be examined to determine if one is a "guest."

BOARDING HOUSE

While the term has had other meanings attached to it in the past, a boarding house is a public house, although not to the extent of

8

hotels and motels. A "boarder" is accepted at such a house on a contract basis between the parties, and not from any obligation to so accept the guest. Thus there would be no innkeeper-guest relationship between a "boarder" and a boarding house.

HOTEL, ANOTHER DEFINITION:

"Every building where food and lodging are usually furnished to guests and payment required therefore shall be deemed a hotel . . . ""But these provisions shall not apply"" . . . to any hotel known as a 'summer hotel' which is not open for guests from November fifteenth to May fifteenth".[14]

LODGING AT PLACES OTHER THAN HOTELS

There are other forms of lodging available to those who travel, including rooming houses, boarding-houses, lodginghouses, condominium rentals, apartment houses and others. In some of these, maid and linen service, desk and bellhop service and other motel-like services may be available. In the absence of a state law that provides otherwise, innkeepers' liability does *not* extend to those who are keepers of such lodging facilities.

THE TRAVELER'S NEED FOR SPECIAL LEGAL ATTENTION

As suggested earlier, a traveler is by nature a person who has placed himself in an unfamiliar situation. Indeed, for the typical tourist, this is one of the main objectives of the trip. But by so doing, the person has exposed himself or herself to more risks than the local resident. For some travelers, being out of their normal and familiar environment may raise the level of caution. But for others, it means that they are more prone to errors in judgement, inadvertent exposure to physical changes, and even to breaking the law or going beyond the protection provided by local laws when different than those at home.

These problems are further compounded when the travelers come from a foreign country. Although small in proportion to all travelers in the United States, they numbered 17.5 million in 1976.[15] As shown in Figure 1-3, the majority (64%) were from Canada, a coun-

FIGURE 1-3
Origins of International Travelers to the U.S.

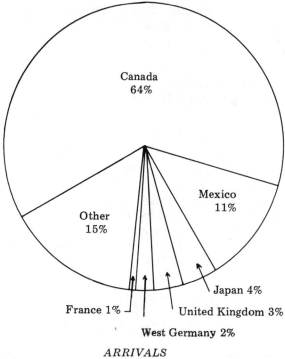

Canada
64%

Other
15%

Mexico
11%

France 1%

United Kingdom 3%

Japan 4%

West Germany 2%

ARRIVALS
17.5 million

From: U.S. Department of Commerce, United States Travel Service,
Research and Analysis Division, *Summary and Analysis of
International Trade to U.S., 1976*, p.7.

try with customs, laws, and physical environment more or less similar to much of the United States. But that leaves 6.3 million persons
traveling about the U.S. during the year who may have total lack of
understanding of many of the things U.S. citizens take for granted,
especially in the area of legal rights and obligations.

These uncertainties are compounded, for both U.S. citizens and
foreign or domestic travelers, by the fact that there is a propensity
in all of us, while visiting new places, to seek out new and adventure-
some experiences—one of the reasons we take vacation trips. This
may range from visiting parts of cities with high crime rates, to
taking physical risks such as white-water trips through river rapids, to
trying out unusual or exotic foods and beverages. While these are a
normal part of the excitement and interest in taking a trip, they also
increase the possibility that something will happen that could lead to
a legal dispute between the travel business and the traveler.

In general, the law in the U.S. does not place much credit in the argument that a person in violation of the law was not aware of the existance of the law. Thus, travelers are assumed to know the rules wherever they visit, whether they come from an adjacent state or from across the Atlantic. In general, U.S. business people and the residents of an area tend to sympathize and assist visitors, especially foreign visitors, to their communities—if they recognize a person as a visitor. But for the most part, visitors look like ordinary people, and therefore go about largely unrecognized. To this extent, the visitor may unwittingly get into difficulty.

Travel related businesses tend to have more person-to-person contact with their customers because they are service-oriented businesses. This, too, contributes to the potential legal risk, because the "product" is a variable. That is, the business operator cannot fully control, as in the case of a manufactured product, the condition of the product when it is accepted and consumed by the customer, because the employee delivering the service becomes an integral part of the total product received by the customer. Moreover, interpersonal behavior between customer and employee can cause the employee, reacting with human emotion, to do something which may transgress the legal rights of the customer.

THE LEGAL ENVIRONMENTAL MIX

All of the preceeding provides a background for interpretation and understanding of the special legal environment within which the travel business must operate. Most of the laws which apply to other businesses apply here, to which must be added the laws that apply particularly to some or all travel businesses. These include criminal law, commercial law, regulatory law, tax law, administrative law, and of course the laws of tort. Moreover, these may generate from local, state, or federal governments, and involve a myriad of agencies. In fact, a study by the National Tourism Resources Review Commission disclosed that there are over 100 Federal Programs and over 50 Federal agencies dealing with tourism and tourism-related matters.[16]

An even more serious situation appears to be developing, however. Just as liability actions are increasingly more troublesome for professionals such as doctors and lawyers, they also affect many travel businesses. The following is a statement received by the United States Department of Interior, Heritage Conservation and Recreation Service (HCRS) for consideration in developing the 1978 Nationwide Recreation Plan.[18]

LIABILITY OF THOSE DELIVERING RECREATION SERVICES, FACILITIES, AND PRODUCTS

STATEMENT OF ISSUE:

The liability problem facing business in the recreation and sports areas is rapidly reaching crisis proportions. Proliferating liability suits and attendant costs for defense and resulting increases in the cost of insurance are threatening the very existence of some firms at worst and are being passed on to consumers in substantially higher prices at best.

BACKGROUND INFORMATION:

The report of the Federal Government Interagency Task Force on Product Liability, issued in November, 1977, cited a 280% increase in product liability insurance premiums for all industries. While this is considerable, it does not touch the tip of the iceberg in the experiences of recreation and sporting goods businesses. In a 1976 survey of the Sporting Goods Industry, one member's insurance premiums went from $1,000 to $225,000; another's, from $16,000 to $297,000; and still another's from $75,000 to $400,000. And in camping, one company's insurance jumped from $392 to $55,000 in two years. Another camping manufacturer's insurance was canceled and this, with no history of suits. In Dayton, Ohio, Outdoor Sports Headquarters, a wholesaler, had a premium jump from $6,000 to $62,000. Just last month it was announced that intercollegiate football was being dropped at Los Anglees State University after 26 years because of the expenses of insurance and overall inflation.

No more than 5 years ago, there were 14 U.S. manufactureres of football helmets. Now there are only 8 manufacturers. The helmet industry has suits approximating $175 million, which is six times the size of the industry. Examples of what is happening are in our press daily, such as a jury award of a $1.2 million settlement to a 12-year old boy who caught his foot on a tree root on a field trip and suffered brain damage. Of several camping equipment manufacturers reporting problems at the Senate Small Business hearings in September 1976, one has ceased to exist, another has sold out to a larger company, and both actions are directly attributable to the product liability crisis.

These are just samples taken from our files that bulge with letters from manufacturers, wholesalers, and retailers, and from newspaper accounts.

In the ski industry, whereas in the past it was considered that the skier assumed the risk of tumbling down the slopes, recent lawsuits have been based on the assertion of increasing the responsibility of the ski area operators. Thus, for example, a Vermont court recently made an award of $1.5 million for injuries suffered in a fall while skiing down a slope. As a result of the increasing threat of litigation, insurance premiums in the past two years increased an average of 200%; there are now only two companies writing such insurance in all of the northeast, and they are threatening to pull out. Thus, the continued availability of insurance at any cost is of serious concern.

CURRENT EFFORTS TO RESOLVE ISSUE:

Product Liability Reform Legislation is pending in the U.S. Congress and in many State Legislatures to provide for changes in tort laws and insurance programs. However, we are not extremely optimistic that the reform needed to turn the problem around will be enacted in the foreseeable future. The Department of Commerce recently announced that plans are underway to create an office to deal with product liability problems and possibly other accident compensation matters, and that a detailed liability paper with specific proposals for change based on the Interagency Task Report will be prepared. However, we believe that a government study specifically geared to recreation and sports is urgently needed.

In certain states legislation has been introduced and is under consideration which, if enacted, would define the responsibilities of both ski area operators and skiers. Such remedial legislation may be of some help, but it will not stop the increasing aggressiveness of certain elements of the public in bringing lawsuits, with the result that the availability of insurance at affordable rates will still be a problem. It is submitted that this problem could affect all forms of recreation, not solely skiing, where the public [is participating] in outdoor sports when skill and risk are involved. In these circumstances, it is submitted that consideration be given to a government program of reinsurance, or some other form of guaranteed assistance, to help assure the availability of insurance at reasonable rates to the suppliers of public recreation opportunities.

The confusing, and often contradictory, roles of the many government agencies regulating or affecting the travel industry was noted earlier. The HCRS received the following statement regarding this issue.

OVER-REGULATION BY GOVERNMENT
OF THE PRIVATE SECTOR

STATEMENT OF ISSUE:

Regulatory confusion and over-regulation of the private sector of outdoor recreation.

BACKGROUND:

Government and public sector should encourage and assist the private sector in the provision of outdoor recreation opportunities, programs, and services to meet the nation's highest priority needs. To aid in this objective existing problems that limit the effectiveness of the private sector in playing a greater role in the provision of recreation opportunities need to be identified and solved.

The impact of government legislation and regulation is felt by the private sector when the initial planning of an enterprise begins and continues right on through the development and operational phases. Private recreation enterprises of any size and scope are subject to a myriad of regulations and requirements administered by a great number of governmental agencies. It is often difficult to know which regulations and agencies apply to a particular project since the agencies do not even know. This is usually an extremely frustrating process which can easily discourage all but the most determined and well financed enterprises.

What started out as relatively simple procedures to cover a program or regulation are continuously revised and fussed with so that over a period of time they become unduly and unnecessarily complex. The frustrating factors are usually not related to a basic act or program but to the resultant regulations and "red tape" involved in obtaining permits, licenses, inspections, etc.

ACTION NEEDED:

Business interests need reliable rules and regulations in order to achieve certainty and predictability in their operations. Because business people, including those in the recreation business, are involved in planning and allocating considerable resources, they can rarely afford to take action that might later be curtailed or prohibited.

The government created problems in the regulatory area, as perceived by recreation enterprises, include inadequate understanding and frequent misinterpretation of legislative intent, conflicting regulations between agencies or between adjoining jurisdictions, and arbitrary enforcement. The private sector feels that it does not have input into legislation, or an opportunity to work with regulatory agencies through advisory committees, or any other means for meaningful participatory opportunities.

As a final example, the mixed public/private businesses (the concessionnaires that operate businesses on public lands), are concerned about the regulations that govern their operations. HRRS received the following input from this group.

CONCESSIONS NATIONWIDE RECREATION PLAN

STATEMENT OF ISSUE:

Current concession policy needs to be improved to ensure maximum utility of our scarce resources.

BACKGROUND INFORMATION ON ISSUE:

The way in which Federal agencies and commercial outdoor recreation oriented organizations promote, develop, operate, and maintain facilities and services on public lands, is inadequate. Studies indicate that Federal agencies have neglected their contract administrative responsibilities, have imposed undue restrictions, rules and regulations on concession operations, and have either discouraged or have been antagonistic towards commercial developments. Other reports state that commercial operations have neglected their contractual responsibilities, have provided inadequate services and facilities for their guests and have maintained substandard working conditions for their employees. In each document, recommendations have been proposed but few have been accepted or acted upon.

Responsibility for this situation rests with the public, the business community, and the Federal Government. Because of the public's lack of concern, their elected representatives have failed to influence protective legislation, to appropriate adequate administrative, operation and maintenance funds, or to participate in government (agency) administrative policy decision making activities. Agencies have consistently resisted legislative intents to designate resources to assist the concession operators, or to develop adequate citizen participation programs. Business itself has, in some cases, secured unrealistic legislation, overly promoted their capabilities and become inflexible in their attitudes towards the future welfare of the political, cultural, economic, and ecological resource complex in which they must operate.

Three basic problems have contributed to the situation. They are: (1) the general public's lethargic attitude; (2) the agencies' antagonistic posture and (3) the business community's self-centered attitude toward public lands and commercial ventures. The general public lack of understanding has contributed to the growth of complacency in accepting the decisions and standards of others without question. This is often to their detriment rather than their benefit. Management by default has become the rule rather than the exception. In addition, agencies' antagonistic attitudes have stifled development by imposing unrealistic and prohibitive policies, rules, and operating procedures; a detriment to the business community and the public as well. The business community, in turn, has become self-centered and single-purpose oriented. This, in itself, has stagnated the industry and has hampered effective policy decision-making processes.

CURRENT EFFORTS TO RESOLVE THE ISSUE:

Efforts to resolve the issue have met with little success. Public hearings and studies have brought the problem to light but have done little to resolve the conflicts. All parties appear to be ignoring the proposals and recommendations. Each, instead is pursuing his own course of action; the concessionnaires by promoting their own interests, the Federal agencies by providing recreation opportunities for special interest groups, and the public by not raising its voice in dissent.

RECOMMENDATIONS AND SOURCES OF INFORMATION:

To improve the development, operation, and maintenance of facilities and services on public lands, the following three recommendations are presented: Foremost is a national policy of developing the public's recreation resources in a fair and equitable manner, to assure equal protection of the individual's rights. Congress should review all Federal legislation to determine whether or not it (a) promotes the orderly growth and development of resources between agencies, (b) promotes undue restraints or advantages to the business sector working within these laws, and (c) provides consistent enabling guidelines for each sector of the economy so that each may profit equally well within the legislatures' intent.

Second, policies reflecting legislative intent must be standardized within and between agencies. Rules, regulations, and reporting programs must be critically evaluated. Unnecessary or prohibitive programs must be eliminated. Attitudes must be reviewed and changed to reflect current thinking.

Third, new goals and directions must be formulated to protect both public and business interests. The public must be assured of adequate accommodations and services. Businesses, in turn, must be able to receive a fair return on their investments in order to survive and serve the public.

It is now imperative that all contractual parties—business, Federal agencies, and the public—cease viewing each other with suspicion and animosity. The development, operation, and management of commercial outdoor recreation facilities and services on public lands has become an integral part of the Nation's economic and social welfare. Without this sector of the economy, goods and services as currently provided would not be available to the traveling public on these public lands.

The above provide just a few insights into the size and variety of impacts that the law may have on a travel business. They should be sufficient to suggest the importance to these business owners and managers of having a comprehensive understanding of the legal environment in which they must operate.

QUESTIONS

1. How would you explain the fact that the United States is one of the few countries in the world that does not have an integrated national tourism policy?
2. Why should businesses serving travelers have to look at their legal environment any differently than any other type of business?
3. Give examples for each level of government of specific activities, or facilities that they operate, which are part of the travel industry.
4. List as many of the kinds of businesses you can in your community which might be traveler-serving businesses.
5. Try to remember and list all of the times in the past year that you have been a traveler/tourist:
   a. Under the U.S. Bureau of the Census definition.
   b. Under the U.S. Travel Data Center Definition.
   c. Under the E.T.C. definition.
   d. Under the broad definition described in this chapter.
6. For each of the following businesses, make up a story that might realistically take place that could develop into a legal problem for the business:
   a. Restaurant.
   b. Airport ticket counter.
   c. Travel agency.
   d. Motel.
   e. Car rental agency.

ENDNOTES

1. James M. Rovelstad, *Behavior-Based Marketing Strategies for Travel and Tourism: The West Virginian Model* (Morgantown, West Virginia; Bureau of Business Research, West Virginia Univ., 1975) p. 1.
2. U.S. Travel Data Center, *Travel Printout* Vol. 7, No. 2 (February 1978), p. 1.
3. U.S. Department of Commerce, United States Travel Service, *Summary and Analysis of International Travel to the U.S. in 1976* (Washington, D.C.: U.S. Department of Commerce, 1977) p. 6.
4. Organization for Economic Cooperation and Development, *Tourism Policy and International Tourism in OECD Member Countries* (Paris: OECD, 1975)
5. O.E.C.D. members are: Aі stralia, Austria, Belgium, Canada, Denmark, Finland, France, the Federal Republic of Germany, Greece, Iceland, Ireland, Italy, Japan, Luxembourg, the Netherlands, New Zealand, Norway, Portugal, Spain, Sweden, Switzerland, Turkey, the United Kingdom and the United States.
6. *West Virginia Travel, 1976-77* (Morgantown, West Virginia: Bureau of Business Research, West Virginia Univ., 1978) p. 2.
7. U.S. Department of Labor, Bureau of Labor Statistics, "BL8790 Monthly Report on Employment, House and Earnings for West Virginia, "December 1977", p. 2.
8. U.S. Travel Data Center, *The Import of Travel on State Economies: 1975* (Washington, D.C.: U.S. Travel Data Center, 1977), pp. 14 and 29.

9. U.S. Senate, Committee on Commerce and National Tourism Policy Study, "A Conceptual Basis for the National Tourism Policy Study" (Washington, D.C.: U.S. Government Printing Office, 1976).
10. U.S. Travel Data Center, *The Impact of Travel on State Economies: 1974:* (Washington, D.C.: U.S. Travel Data Center, 1975) p. 7.
11. *The Impact of Travel on State Economics,* p. 2.
12. OECD, *Tourism Policy—,* pp. 7-11.
13. Section 35-1, Code of Virginia, (1950).
14. W. Va. Code. Ch. 16 Art. 6 Sec. 3. (1966).
15. U.S. Department of Commerce, United States Travel Service, *Summary and Analysis of International Travel to the U.S.,* 1976, p. 7.
16. *Destination U.S.A.:* Report of the National Tourism Resources Review Commission (Washington, D.C.: 1973).
17. 563 P.2d 635 (1977).
18. The three statements are taken from a letter from HCRS to the Nationwide Plan, Work Group V, dated January 30, 1978.

2

Law

The American Law Institute (ALI) defines law as " . . . that body of rules, customs and usages that are enforceable in courts." From this definition several preliminary conclusions can be drawn. First, "law" is more than rules because it encompasses customs of a people as well as usages. Next, the word "usage" denotes a variety of matters and tells us that more than rules and customs are involved. Finally, we see that for something to be "law", it must be a matter that can be enforced in a court. Conversely, something that cannot be enforced in a court is not law. As we will learn, there is no place other than a court that law *can* be enforced. A lawyer may read a principle of law and give a client an opinion of what it means; a legislature may enact laws of all types; the people in turn are affected by these laws—yet it is only in a court that law can be enforced.

The ALI definition falls short of what the law is in fact because law never exists in a vacuum. It must in some manner involve the will of the people, and in addition, other forces must come to bear upon it. Justice Oliver Wendell Holmes alluded to this when he defined law as " . . . a statement of the circumstances in which the public force will be brought to bear through the courts."[1]

TODAY

In modern usuage, "law" means a variety of things to various people. To a lawyer, it is the subject matter of a respected profession. To a judge, it is the rulings that he or she makes in court. To a

19

librarian, it is the hundreds of thousands of volumes in a law library. To a court reporter, it is the testimony offered at trial and reduced to written form. To a city council, it is the ordinances that it passes. To a police officer, it is the city traffic code, and to the citizen, it is often a police officer—"the law." The law is all of these and much more. Thus we see that the "law" is at best difficult to define in a succinct, positive manner. Rather than make a further effort to define law, it is best now to examine the sources of it.

SOURCES OF LAW

There are four primary sources of law; history, written law, common law, and rulings of administrative agencies.

HISTORY

"History" in the simplest sense, is what has been done in the past; a record of humanity; what has been done by others in prior centuries. Thus the rulings of the Pharoah in ancient Egypt; procedures followed in the early Greek and Babylonian courts; the practices of lawyers following the Norman Conquest; the actions of the abritrators in Colonial times in America, are all sources of law. One who studies legal history constantly finds modern rules or principles of law that have their roots in antiquity. As a striking example of this, the modern definition of a partnership is almost word for word the same as that found in the Code of Hammurabi.

Thus what has gone before us in the courts, in law offices, in ancient law making bodies, is a primary and ongoing source of law. Most of our modern principles of property law can be traced to early centuries in England.

A second source of law is that which is referred to as being "written" to contrast it with law that is "spoken".

WRITTEN LAW

Law that is written is law that at the time of its inception, is placed in written (today, printed) form. There are two broad categories of written law: "constitutions" and their amendments, and "statutes". The word "statute" refers to formal law created in a prescribed manner, by a properly constituted law making body. As we use the word here, it will be synomous with "ordinances" created at the municipal level.

Constitutions will be examined first and then we will take a look at statutes.

CONSTITUTIONS

A constitution is the supreme law of the state or nation for which it was created. It follows that amendments to constitutions, supplement or alter the basic law of the state or the nation, as the case may be, and become part of that supreme law.

Today in the United States, we have 51 constitutions; one U.S. Constitution and 50 state constitutions. The U.S. Constitution has been amended 26 times, with one amendment, the Equal Rights Amendment, (ERA), pending. The number of amendments in our state constitutions will vary from state to state and with the age of the state itself.

Each constitution is supreme in its own area of "jurisdiction." But this statement is qualified in reference to our states. The U.S. Constitution provides "This Constitution and the laws of the United States which shall be made in pursuance thereof, and all treaties made, or which shall be made under the authority of the United States, shall be the supreme law of the land; and the judges of every state shall be bound thereby, anything in the Constitution or laws of any state to the contrary notwithstanding,"[2]. Thus it is clear that state laws and constitutions must be subordinate to the U.S. Constitution. With this exception, each state constitution is supreme within the state itself and all other laws of the state must in turn, conform to it. For example, a city cannot create an ordinance that would violate the state constitution. And in turn, a state legislature cannot create a law that would violate the U.S. Constitution or its amendments. Perhaps it isn't precise to say that such laws "cannot be created." It is better to say that if they are created, they are "unconstitutional" and are subject to being struck down by a court.

Thus we see an anomoly: a law may be placed in effect that is unconstitutional, but until it becomes a subject matter of a court action, it is "law." After one is arrested under that law, or once one brings a lawsuit to challenge it, a court can then pass on the constitutionality of it. Judges cannot unilateraly act upon any law. They must wait for "justiciable controversies."

CREATE THE STATE

Constitutions are supreme because they emanate from a people and thus create the "state" itself. Thus the U.S. Constitution created the United States, and each state constitution created each state. Examine Figure 2-1. In this diagram we first see "a people" who have evolved over some span of time, bringing with them their customs, usages and history. By organizing these people, such as was done in the Continental Congress in the 1700's, a constitution can be drafted and ratified or adopted by representatives of the people. In this manner the state is created. The state then consists of the three branches of government: the executive, legislative and judicial. Now a workable political entity exists that can begin carrying out the functions of government. From the diagram, we see that "administrative agencies" come into being from the legislative branch. These agencies carry out the day to day functions of running a government for the people—and as we shall see, these agencies also create law.

FIGURE 2-1

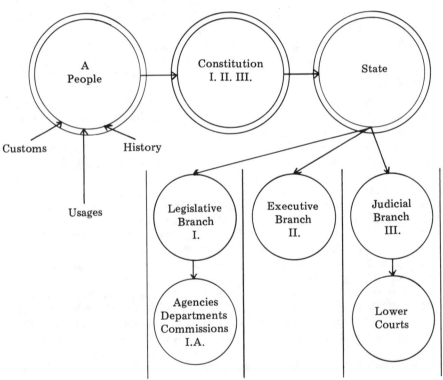

Separation of Powers

The executive branch can issue executive orders and operates under the "executive privilege"—which in the past included the power to declare war. The legislative branch not only creates agencies but in turn, creates new laws called "statutes." The judicial branch provides the forum where the constitutionality of these new statutes (laws) can be tested; it is here that controversies can be litigated, and as we shall see, the judicial branch can also create law.

Thus, by tracing a political entity backwards, we come to the constitution, and beyond this document, we find the people themselves. If it should become desirable to amend the constitution, it cannot be done by a unilateral act of a law making body, nor by executive order, nor by court ruling. It can only be done by the people through the constitutional ratification process.

However, we must point out that a court can *interprete* constitutional provisions and by doing so, place new meanings on the words. This power of the courts was recognized by John Marshall in 1819 an opinion of the U.S. Supreme Court in which he wrote; "We must never forget that it is a constitution that we are expounding, intended to indure for ages to come, and consequently to be adapted to the various crises of human affairs."[3] Since that time our courts have called upon this thought to place new meanings upon the old words of our constitution.

In the trilogy of government, executive, legislative, and judicial, we see the "separation of powers" principle. No one division is superior over any other. "The doctrine of the separation of powers was adopted by the Convention of 1787, not to promote efficiency but to preclude the exercise of arbitrary power. The purpose was, not to avoid friction, but, by means of the inevitable friction incident to the distribution of the governmental powers among three departments, to save the people from autocracy."[4] The principle has worked well in the United States for two centuries.

Statutes come from the legislative branch of government.

STATUTES

Written laws created by law making bodies are called statutes, and make up the largest body of written law. The word encompasses city ordinances, acts of state legislatures (legislation) and acts of Congress. Statutes can be "standard" or they may be "uniform."

STANDARD STATUTES

A constant need arises to place new regulations upon businesses, individuals and others within our society. For example, a city may find it necessary to pass a law forbidding the consumption of alcholic beverages on city streets. Almost all college towns have had to pass such laws. The state may see a need for a new law to regulate the insurance industry. The federal government may find it necessary to create a new law in the credit industry. As these needs arise, laws are created to meet them. Thus we have a constantly increasing body of statutory laws that regulates business; sets standards of personal conduct of citizens, and provides new regulatory measures in an ever changing variety of situations. Many of these laws will effect business and are thus "business laws." Some will affect the travel and lodging industry. All are important and require constant awareness of the ongoing creation of the usual or standard statutory law.

The second kind of statutes that we encounter are "uniform" in nature. Uniform laws represent a significant advance, especially those that relate to business.

UNIFORM STATUTES

In the past, the law making bodies of our states acted independently of one another. No state ever concerned itself about what the lawmakers were doing in other states. Because of this, we wound up with 48 separate codes of laws—and today with the addition of Hawaii and Alaska, 50. No particular harm resulted from this so long as business and industry remained on a purely local basis. When Holiday Inn had one motel in Memphis, the manager had to be concerned with one body of state law. But with almost 2000 inns today, the opposite is the truth for that corporation. Thus, as all forms of business began to expand, such as we have seen since World War II, the need for uniformity in laws, especially the laws of business, became apparent.

NATIONAL COMMISSIONERS

A National Conference of Commissioners on Uniform State laws was created. Their job was to modernize, update and make uniform the various bodies of business law; to draft uniform acts, and to encourage the state legislatures to adopt them after they were created.

The most important accomplishment of the National Commissioners was the creation and subsequent adoption of the Uniform Commercial Code (UCC) by 49 of our 50 states. The sole holdout is Louisiana which it had its own commercial code. The UCC replaced the Uniform Sales Act and the Negotiable Instruments Law (NIL), which were pioneer efforts in uniform laws. A new uniform draft recently completed by the Commissioners is the Uniform Land Transfer Act (ULTA). The success of this draft, as far as uniform adoption by the states, is uncertain at the moment.

Unfortunately, each state legislature maintains a true independence, even with uniform laws, and often makes substantial changes in the uniform drafts. As a result, even in the case of the UCC, it in fact varies from state to state. In spite of this, the effort being made with uniform laws is a vast improvement over the situation that existed 25 years ago. When Congress enacts a law, it comes close to true uniformity since it is a single law that binds 50 states as one. Uniformity could be achieved by adopting the UCC as a *federal* law. There is no indication, however, that this will be done in the near future.

The next source of law is found in law that is "common" to all citizens of a single state, called the "common law."

COMMON LAW

This phrase has two meanings. The first is that body of law that was brought to the American Colonies from England in the 1600's. This was the "English Common Law" and much of it is with us today. For example, any rule of law found in an American Colony in 1650 that has not been altered, or replaced, is still the law today of the state that developed from that Colony.

The second meaning of the phrase "common law", and the one that we are concerned with here, is law created by court decisions as contrasted with law created by law making bodies.

AN EXAMPLE

A motel developer diverts surface water from its natural dispersion pattern, which causes it to flow onto the land of an adjoining property owner where it causes damage. The injured party files suit seeking a sum of money to be paid by the motel developer for the damages done.

Assume that this occurs in a state that has no statutes directed to such a problem, and that this is a "case of first impression" — there has never been a case like it in that state. Assume further that after trial by jury, a verdict is returned in favor of the injured property owner in the sum of $10,000. This happened because the jury found that a developer who diverts water is responsible for the damages caused by that diversion.

Once this verdict is entered in the court records, it becomes a "judgment" and an appeal period begins to run. If the ruling is overturned by an upper court, the case is normally returned for a new trial. If it is upheld, or if an appeal is not taken, the verdict stands and the case becomes part of the "common law." In this manner, "precedent" is created and the case can be looked to by others in that jurisdiction when similar circumstances arise in the future. The case would then tend to regulate the activities of other developers. It is a general principle of the common law to let such decisions or cases stand once they are created — that is, to follow such cases in the future and not disturb them.

"STARE DECISIS"

Let the decision stand" said the oldtime judges. "It is not so important that a matter be decided correctly as it is that it simply be decided." The doctrine of stare decisis is very much a part of our common law system today and its existence tends to encourage others to tailor their affairs to fit within existing common law rules.

A legislature may pre-empt a common law area by passing a statute to cover it, but until that happens, the decision will stand until some reason is shown to a court why it should no longer be a rule of common law in that state.

REJECTING STARE DECISIS

If a common law principle becomes "too old" or if it no longer serves a rational purpose, a court can reject it. Courts are reluctant to do this however, since this upset matters that have already been settled. Yet, the power remains. However, in the area of "public law," the doctrine is frequently ignored. This often happens in cases involving prior interpretations of a constitution.

"A judge looking at a constitutional decision may have compulsions to revere past history and accept what was once written. But he remembers above all else that it is the Constitution which he swore to support and defend, not the gloss which his predecessors may have put on it. So he comes to formulate his own views, rejecting some earlier ones as false and embracing others. He cannot do otherwise unless he lets men long dead and unaware of the problems of the age in which he lives do his thinking for him.

"This reexamination of precedent in constitutional law is a personal matter for each judge who comes along. When only one new judge is appointed during a short period, the unsettling effect in constitutional law may not be great. But when a majority of a Court is suddenly reconstituted, there is likely to be substantial unsettlement. There will be unsettlement until the new judges have taken their positions on constitutional doctrine. During that time — which may extend a decade or more — constitutional law will be in flux. That is the necessary consequence of our system and to my mind a healthy one. The alternative is to let the Constitution freeze in the pattern which one generation gave it. But the Constitution was designed for the vicissitudes of time. It must never become a code which carries the overtones of one period that may be hostile to another.

"So far as constitutional law is concerned *stare decisis* must give way before the dynamic component of history. Once it does, the cycle starts again. Today's new and startling decision quickly becomes a coveted anchorage for new vested interests. The former proponents of change acquire an acute conservatism in their new *status quo*. It will then take an oncoming group from a new generation to catch the broader vision which may require an undoing of the work of our present and their past . . . "[5]

The final source of law that we will discuss is found in rulings of administrative bodies.

ADMINISTRATIVE LAW

First, it is helpful to distinguish an administrative function from a legal one. The determination of liability for the water run-off situation that we just discussed, was a legal matter. The "law" and a court were involved. On the other hand, regulation of the common carriers in a state would be an administrative function — not a legal one. It is the latter type of activity that we will examine briefly, because here we find another and relatively new, source of law.

A hundred years ago, the population of the United States was a fraction of what it is today. Business was agriculture-oriented and localized for the most part. Our nation was only partially settled and life still had a rural, local, personal atmosphere to it. All of this changed with the coming of the first war "to end all wars."

An industrial expansion started that has never ceased in growth. Life changed to one of ever increasing complexities, and perhaps something was lost in the process. The courts and law were caught up in the change. While the courts had been adequate to regulate society in that other age of one hundred years ago, it became increasingly evident that they could no longer fill this role in such changing times.

When this came to pass, large gaps existed in the regulations needed to make certain that an orderly process of business and life itself, would be available to our society today and tomorrow. A hundred years ago, one could challenge a business practice, or seek protection by bringing a law suit and then patiently waiting for the legal process to run its course. But today, it would be impossible for our courts to regulate the growing airline, hotel, motel, travel, radio, television and other industries that have had their inceptions in relatively recent times. The courts would never be able to catch up with the growing regulatory needs of such businesses. Something else was needed to provide such regulation.

SOLUTION

The device selected appeared at first to be a simple one, and it had its beginning when legislative bodies began to enact laws that were designed to create "administrative agencies." These laws would grant certain powers to a "commission," the membership of which would then be filled by the executive officer. The commission would first create basic rules for its conduct, and would then draft rules and regulations to be followed by those that were to be regulated. These rules in turn became an important source of law.

TODAY

At the federal level, we find the Federal Trade Commission (FTC), Interstate Commerce Commission (ICC), and numerous other "alphabet agencies." At the state level we find public service commissions, departments of public safety, banking commissions, insurance commissions and others. At the municipal level we find water and sanitation commissions, parking authorities and police forces.

As a practical matter, the day-to-day impact of such agencies and commissions is much greater than that of the courts, and they play a direct and important part in the conduct of business. When an administrative agency creates regulations, these must be observed. When they issue rulings after holding hearings, these rulings are "law" and must be obeyed.

Administrative agencies and their rulings have been challenged as an unconstitutional extension of the three-part separation of powers. But the courts uphold them as an extension of the legislative power since it is there that they are created in the first instance.

These agencies are versatile in practice and have powers to investigate, advise, supervise, adjudicate, make rules — and even prosecute if the circumstances warrant it. In the following case, we see an appeal that had been taken from the ruling of an administrative agency. It involves an application for a liquor license which was refused. A close reading of the case provides insight into the functions of such agencies, as well as the tendency of our courts to uphold the rulings of them.

MARKANTONATOS v. OREGON LIQUOR CONTROL COMMISSION
Or. App. 562 P. 2d 570 (1977)

THORNTON, Judge.

Petitioners seek judicial review of the Oregon Liquor Control Commission's

(OLCC) refusal to grant them a Dispenser Class "A" (DA) license for their restaurant, Zorba the Greek. Petitioners assert that the OLCC's findings of fact and ultimate findings of fact are not supported by substantial evidence and that therefore the conclusions of law, on which the license refusal ultimately depends, are unsupported. Additionally, petitioners assert that it was error for the hearings officer to have access to an OLCC file detailing evidence in a previous case in which petitioners were denied a license where the file was not introduced into evidence and that it was error for the commissioners to issue a final order without hearing the case or considering the record.

Petitioners at the hearing before the hearings officer introduces, in support of their application for a DA license, a petition signed by about 650 supporters, various documents indicating that petitioners' credit is sound, photographs of the decor of the restaurant, an Economic Analysis of the Portland Downtown Guidelines Plan conducted by a Portland consulting firm, a letter from the mayor of Portland indicating a need for more downtown liquor licenses and testimony be eight favorable witnesses. OLCC presented evidence in opposition in the form of testimony by three witnesses and the results of an informal survey.

After a hearing the hearings officer recommended denial of a DA license. At the hearing before OLCC, the denial was affirmed based on the following ultimate findings of fact, which are generalized restatements of findings of fact, and conclusions of law:

"ULTIMATE FINDINGS OF FACT

"1. There is some opposition in the community to the issuance of the license, and there is likewise some support.

"2. The area in which applicants' outlet is located is heavily saturated with DA outlets, with seven in a radius of 1½ blocks. These outlets offer reasonably adequate service to the public. Applicants' witnesses referred in significant numbers to the shortcomings of only three of the outlets, and a generalized statement to the effect that 'all the outlets' in the area have similar problems does not adequately demonstrate that the witness was in fact aware of the existence of each of the seven outlets' names. The fact that three outlets in the area have replaced seven previously licensed is as indicative of lack of demand leading to the closure of the other outlets, as it is an opportunity for additional licenses in the area. Issuance of licenses to Rian's and L'Omelette was made on the basis of saturation at that time, together with all other factors present, and these outlets are more centrally located.

"3. A gross volume of food sales averaging approximately $60 a day is indicative of the lack of demand at the location, and the adequacy of present outlets to meet the public demand. A change of menu may possibly increase food sales, but the fact and extent of this change cannot be determined on the present record.

"4. Demand for Dispenser outlets in the downtown Portland core area in general may well continue to be present and increase in the future, but there is no basis in the record that this demand requires an additional DA outlet at this time, or if so, such demand exists at applicants' specific location. The testimony of a small number of witnesses is not persuasive on the issue of demand by the entire public, especially when the sales of the establishment indicate that large numbers of persons choose not to partronize the outlet.

"5. The fact that the number of DA licenses in downtown Portland exceed its ratable allocation indicates that the citizens of the state would be better served by issuance of the license to establishments better able to serve a greater number of the citizens of the community and state.

"From the foregoing Findings of Fact, the following Conclusions of Law are entered:

"CONCLUSIONS OF LAW

"1. Seven premises licensed to serve liquor by the drink are available within a radius of 1½ blocks from applicants' premises, [10 — 715(1)].

"2. Applicants' low gross food sales indicate a lack of demand at that location, and the adequacy of the seven outlets mentioned previously to provide service to the public, [10 — 720(5)].

"3. The granting of a Dispenser license to applicants' outlet would not be a judicious use of the limited number of such licenses available statewide, [10 — 715(10)].

" * * * ."

Since the actual grounds for denial of the license in this case are the conclusions of law, findings of fact not relevant to those conclusions are superfluous and we need not consider them on appeal.

Petitioners maintain that the findings of saturation in the area and that other outlets adequately serve the public are not based on substantive evidence. The evidence is uncontroverted that there are seven DA licensed outlets within one and one-half blocks of applicants' premises. Applicants and six of their supporting witnesses testified that other establishments in the area generally provided bad service, were overcrowded and charged high prices. The OLCC found that the applicants had failed to establish that the other outlets were inadequate and gleaned the opposite conclusion from the testimony, i. e., the fact that the witnesses patronized the other establishments was evidence that the prices were not too high and the service was adequate. The applicants in this case did not introduce specific evidence tending to establish the inadequacy of other outlets in the area. The OLCC's conclusions that there is a heavy saturation in the area and that these outlets offer reasonably adequate service to the public, are rationally supported by the evidence.

Petitioners challenge the OLCC's findings on food sales but do not contend that they are not based on the evidence. They maintain that the average per day food sales figure is misleading because petitioners are only open six days a week and not seven days a week. The commission's arithmetical method may have been questionable, but that does not affect the operative fact that the applicants' food sales are low and that fact led the OLCC to conclude that there is a lack of demand for a DA license at the subject location. The finding that applicants' food sales are low is supported by the evidence.

Petitioners also object to the commission's rejection of their argument that present food sales are not pertinent since petitioners intend to change their menu to offer specialty Greek cuisine which would, according to their testimony, increase food sales by 100 percent to 400 percent. The OLCC need not accept petitioners' speculative predictions.

Contrary to petitioners' argument, the OLCC's third conclusion of law referred to above was not a holding that the 1:2000 ratio (ORS 472.110(4)) precludes issuance of the license, but that issuance of the license to these applicants would not be judicious given low food sales and a saturation in the immediate area.

Prior to the hearing, petitioners were told by the referee that he had access to the entire file of the OLCC, including material relevant to a refusal of a prior application by petitioners for a DA license. Petitioners assign as error the consideration of this material in violation of ORS 183.-450(2). As petitioners were fully apprised that the referee had access to the prior material and that material did not form the basis for the commission's decision in this case, the error of the OLCC was not prejudicial. Annotation.

In their third assignment of error, petitioners maintain that the decision of the OLCC must be reversed because the members of the commission did not personally hear the case or consider the record, contrary to the provisions of former ORS 183.-460. That portion of former ORS 183.460 on which petitioners rely was deleted from the statute by Oregon Laws 1975, ch. 759, § 13, p. 2092, effective October 8, 1975. The final order in this proceeding was issued November 18, 1975. The requirement that the OLCC members personally consider the record before issuing a final order does not, therefore, apply in this case.

Affirmed.

QUESTIONS

1. How would *you* define law after having read this chapter. Write it out.
2. Explain how some modern rules of law could be over 1000 years old.
3. Explain how something can be unconstitutional.
4. Explain how something could be unlawful but not unconstitutional.
5. Why must a judge wait for a justiciable controversy before a matter can be declared unconstitutional?
6. Give an example of law-making in each of the three branches of the federal government.
7. Give an example of how interpretation by a court may change a statute. (Make up a ficticious statute. "It shall be unlawful to . . . ")
8. Why do we have so few uniform laws when compared with all of the laws that we do have?
9. Make up a ficticious court ruling to show how common law is created.
10. T. or F. In the area of public law, the doctrine of stare decisis is seldom ignored.

ENDNOTES

1. *American Banana Co. v. United Fruit Co.* 213 U.S. 347, (1909).
2. U.S. Constitution, Article VI.
3. *McCullough v. Maryland, Wheat* 316, 407 (1819).
4. *Myers v. United States,* 272 U.S. 52, 240, 293.
5. Justice William O. Douglas, Eighth Annual Benjamin Cardozo Lectures.

3

Classifications of Law

Once law is created, it will be of a certain type or will fit into a category and can thus be classified. These classifications are important because one must understand where law of one type stands in relation to another. To assist in gaining this understanding, we will examine eight classifications of law with the objective of learning the relationship of these with each other. The eight classifications are (A.) legal and administrative law, (B.) common law and statutory law, (C.) common law and civil law, (D.) public law and private law, (E.) substantive law and procedural law, (F.) contract law and property law, (G.) tort law and criminal law, and finally (H.) law and equity.

LEGAL AND ADMINISTRATIVE LAW

Many things that become the subject matter of court action, involve matters that are "legal" in nature. That is, they come from law as it is created in constitutions, statutes and by common law rulings. Administrative "law" has as its source, an agency that exists outside of the normal legal system. Thus we have "legal law" and we have an "administrative law." These classifications can be understood if one reflects on our discussion of administrative law in Chapter 2.

COMMON LAW AND STATUTORY LAW

Again, these classifications were previously identified and discussed at length. The former is created by court rulings, the latter by acts of law making bodies. A classification of the common law that varies from this however, is found in the next category.

COMMON LAW AND CIVIL LAW

While the former exists because of court decisions, the latter exists because of legislative acts. Where we find a civil law system, ancient Roman law has had an influence on that system. The law of Europe and South America is civil — a statutory or "codified" system as contrasted with one that uses precedent from case decisions to create new law. Thus a civil law system operates primarily on statutes — a common law system operates on case precedent.

Louisiana, Texas, California, and a few other states, follow a civil law system. If any common law state would reduce all of its law to a "code" (codification), than that state would be a civil law state.

PUBLIC LAW AND PRIVATE LAW

Public law is law that affects us collectively as a "people". This heading can be subdivided into constitutional law, administrative law, and criminal law.

Private law, on the other hand, is made up of those branches of law that relate directly to legal relationships between one individual and another. Examples of private law include contract, tort and property. These will be examined under classifications that follow.

A ruling of a Public Service Commission is a public law ruling. An interpretation of a constitutional principle — even if it concerns only one person, is also public. This is true since that interpretation will affect society *en masse* just as the constitution itself does. If A kills B, that act is public in nature even though it is a highly personal matter to B. If C enters into a contract with D, or if E injures F in a car accident, those acts are private between C and D, and E and F.

SUBSTANTIVE LAW AND PROCEDURAL LAW

"Substantive" law is the substance of the law itself. It may be a statutory or civil law rule of law. It may be a common law precedent. It is the law itself. Statutes that set forth health regulations for lodging facilities, are substantive. (See page 257 for an example). So are case decisions that establish liability standards for innkeepers. Likewise, rulings of an administrative agency are substantive since they are part of the matrix or substance of the law.

Procedural law, on the other hand, concerns matters of our legal system *other* than substantive law. Here we encounter the methods by which lawsuits are started; the way that wages are attached and countless other matters of procedure.

Thus, one must look to substantive law to determine if a "cause of action" exists — the right to use a court in an attempt to obtain relief. If a cause of action does *not* exist, or if in the opinion of a lawyer it does not exist, then in most instances the matter ends there. If a cause of action does exist, or if in the opinion of a lawyer there is at least a fair chance of success, then one can begin to use procedural law in a court.

Procedural law includes filing suits, serving papers, calling jurors, serving subpoenas on witnesses, taking testimony in court, enforcing judgments and all of the other functions carried out by courts and administrative bodies. Procedural law may be thought of as the "machinery" of the courts.

The next classifications of contract and tort, and tort and crime, involve substantive law, since these topics are part of the principles of law itself.

CONTRACT LAW AND PROPERTY LAW

Two age-old categories of substantive law, and ones that will be the subject matter of coming chapters, are "contract" and "property."

Contract law is that body of law that regulates the creation of private agreements between individuals and firms. These agreements almost always arise from promises. These promises may be to build a motel, to remodel a restaurant, or to serve as a manager in a travel agency. The promises may be to supply materials, to construct specially designed equipment or to pave a parking lot. There is no end to the matters that can be the subject matter of contract.

The principal feature of a contract is that two persons, firms, or any combination of persons and firms, have voluntarily brought into play an obligation on the part of each side that had no existence before the contract was made. Thus a contract is a voluntary relationship since one can never force a contract upon another — or if it is in fact forced, a court will not enforce it.

By the use of the contract, we can buy buildings, construct restaurants, hire employees, buy and sell stock, have a bank account, and do the endless everyday matters that become involved in travel and lodging functions. The contract will be examined in detail in Chapters 6 and 7.

"Property" in the simplest sense, is the earth and everything permanently affixed to it, and all other items that are loose upon the earth or which are recognized as being property at law. A motel is affixed to the earth "permanently" (although it may be removed at some future time) and is "real property." An automobile is loose upon the earth and is "personal property." Property can be invisible, such as a debt obligation that one owes another. A debt is a "property right" of the one to whom it is owed.

Property is perpetually the subject matter of contract for it is by the contract that property is acquired. It is by the contract that property is sold and transferred. It is by the contract that property is constructed in the first place. Therefore, contract and property are inseparable in the private and business community. The law of contract sets forth the rules for owning, transferring, improving and doing a thousand other things with property. Property law, on the other hand, provides the rules of ownership, title, rights and duties of possession of property. The principles of property law will be examined in detail in Chapters 13, 14 and 15.

TORT LAW AND CONTRACT LAW

Outside of the study of law, one seldom encounters the word "tort". Rather, one will read of an automobile accident case in which A and B were injured, or will learn that C was arrested because of a physical assault upon D. Both of these incidents, involve "torts". A tort is a negligent, careless or deliberate act of one person that results in injury to another person, or the other person's property, or both.

The word evolved from the French word "torquere" which means "twisted" or wrong. A tort can be distinguished from a contract because it will seldom involve a voluntary act by *both* parties. In addition, the parties normally do not intend for a tort to come into being, while they do intend to bring into being the contracts that they create. Therefore the one is involuntary — the other voluntary. An exception exists when one *intends* to harm another. In a deliberate assault by C on D, it can be assumed that C intended to injure D or the assault would not have occured. But regardless of the intention, the assault or attack is a tort. In addition, since the act was deliberate, it would also be a "crime".

A crime then is some conduct that, due to standards of society, is recognized as being undesireable to society collectively. Therefore, the law of crime — criminal law — involves duties that are owed to the state. It is for this reason that the state prosecutes those who commit crimes.

In the absense of intention to commit harm, torts are treated as violations of duties owed to the injured party. Thus they are private between those parties. A owes a duty to the state not to rob B with a gun. C owes a duty to D not to operate his (C's) car in such a careless manner as to injure D. Thus tort and crime can be distinguished by the duties owed. Tort liability can arise in a variety of ways.

Negligence is the most common basis upon which tort actions are based. "Negligence" is the failure to use due care in doing an act, such as driving a car. Or it can be the failure to do something that a reasonable person should have done under the same circumstances. An example would be the failure to replace burned out lights in a motel hallway.

Tort liability can also arise from the maintenance of a "nuisance." The smoke and smell from an outdoor incinerator that disturbs neighbors would form the basis of a tort action. Failure to pave a truck loading area which results in dust blowing upon adjacent property would also give rise to a tort action.

There are other grounds for tort actions and these will be discussed at appropriate places in the following chapters. It is sufficient for the moment to recognize that some acts can be both a tort and a crime if the intent to commit harm is present. When this happens, one can be prosecuted for the crime and at the same time be sued for the tort. A tort action is handled in the courts just as other lawsuits. If one can prove liability and damages, a jury can award compensation to the injured party for the loss.

The final classification is that of law as contrasted to "equity".

LAW AND EQUITY

"Law" encompasses all of those matters that have been discussed up to this point. Contract, tort, crime, property, constitutions, statutes, ordinances, common-law rulings and many others are "legal subjects" and thus law. The major portion of this book is concerned with legal matters. One branch of our court system however, is concerned with "equity" as contrasted to "law," and a look at some history will assist us in understanding this.

A thousand years ago, the English courts used a "writ system." This was a procedural arrangement in which one could sue another *provided* that a writ was available to cover the facts. There were writs in contract, tort, property, trespass and other technical areas. These are known today as "common law forms of action." In those times it was mandatory that one keep legal matters within the prescribed bounds. But it occassionally happened that a set of circumstances would arise in which there was no writ available to cover the facts. Because of this, an old saying developed that "if there is no writ, there is no remedy." This meant that if one could not fashion one's case to match a writ, there was no remedy or way that that person could proceed in court.

Thus if A recklessly drove an ox cart through the garden of B causing damage, B could seek a writ against A in tort for the trespass and would, in time, have a remedy. If C negligently struck D with an ax, D would seek a writ in tort for the "trespass viet armis" — with force of arms. If E sold F a painting and delivered it, but F refused to make payment, a writ was available for recovery of the debt. The writ system served well and lasted for centuries, yet it still had a deficiency.

To illustrate, A contracted to sell a certain painting to B. B made a down payment of two cows, with the painting to be delivered in one month. At the end of 30 days, A attempted to return the down payment and refused to deliver the painting. B refused the return of the down payment, and demanded delivery of the painting. Could B use the courts to force delivery? It so happens that for many centuries the answer was "no". There was no legal writ that would force one to perform an *act*. The law could give one compensation for a tort, or it could allow damages for breach of contract. But, as in the painting case, the law could not provide a remedy.

At some point in history, such matters began to come to the attention of the King or Queen who in turn would refer them to the spiritual advisor, the "chancellor."

After consideration of the matter, the chancellor might have said, "Why not order A to deliver the painting since it is the just thing to do." At that point, when the King or Queen began issuing orders based upon such advice, "equity" was born. This then became that side of our courts that deals in what is just or right: in short, what is "equitable."

From the birth of equity until today, equitable actions were handled by the issuance of orders from an appropriate person. Today the same is true and all equitable matters are heard and decided by a judge sitting without a jury. Some examples of modern equity matters include specific performance (ordering one to do an act promised), rescission (cancelling a contract), injuctions (an order to someone to stop doing something) and divorces (reversing the marriage contract).

If one refuses to obey an equitable order, that person can be held in "contempt of court" and may be jailed until the order is obeyed. Many courts today list their equity cases on the "chancery" docket, a modern remembrance of the ancient chancellor who had a hand in the development of equity.

Today, most courts call both legal and equitable cases, "civil actions", yet all modern courts handle equitable matters without a jury.

In the following case, we see a legal action brought because of a "tort" (wrong) committed by one person against the property of another. The case gives us an opportunity to compare this legal action with the administrative case on page 28. It also enables us to see how a court treats "damages" and enables us to see how contracts are enforced.

OWEN v. BURN CONST. CO.,
563 P. 2d 91 (1977).

EASLEY, Justice.

Plaintiffs A. A. Owen and his wife, Rubye, (Owen), owners of a restaurant building in Las Cruces, sued Burn Construction Company, Inc. (Burn) in damages for the negligent destruction of the building. The jury returned a verdict of $3500.00 in favor of Owen. Both parties filed motions for judgment notwithstanding the verdict and both motions were denied by the trial court. Both parties appealed to the Court of Appeals and that court reversed the trial court, directing that judgment be entered in favor of defendant notwithstanding the verdict. Owen petitioned for certiorari. We reverse the Court of Appeals and the trial court.

Burn held a contract with Las Cruces Urban Renewal Agency (Agency) to demolish a two-story hotel building immediately adjacent to Owen's restaurant building. While the work was in progress part of the second story of the hotel toppled onto Owen's structure completely destroying its usefulness. The Agency agreed to complete the demolition of the Owen building and to remove the debris. Part of the agreement was that the action of the Agency in clearing Owen's lot would not prejudice Owen's right to seek damages against Burn for the destruction of the building.

Two months after the hotel collapsed on the Owen structure and after the debris had been removed, the Agency filed suit to condemn the vacant lot. The Agency and Owen stipulated to the entry of judgment whereby Owen would receive $59,072.00 for the vacant lot. The judgment signed by the court specifically set forth that the settlement was based on the value of the lot at the time the condemnation action was filed, i. e. without the building, and that the settlement would in no way affect any claim which Owen might have against Burn for the prior damage to the building.

Owen later filed this case against Burn to recover $26,000.00 in damages for the total destruction of the building. It was undisputed that the damage to the building was the fault of Burn. The evidence was also uncontested that the value of Owen's building at the time the damage occurred was $26,000.00.

On the theory that Owen had already been fully compensated by the Agency for both the lot and the building, Burn induced the trial court to take judicial notice of the entire file in the prior condemnation action. Over Owen's objections and in derogation of the express terms of the judgment entered pursuant to the stipulation of the parties, testimony and written opinions of the court-appointed appraisers were admitted into evidence to attempt to prove that the $59,072.00 appraised value included both the building and the land.

The jury returned a verdict for Owen in the inexplicable amount of $3500.00. Both parties moved for judgment n. o. v. which motions were denied; judgment was entered; both parties appealed.

The Court of Appeals held that the trial court should have entered judgment n. o. v. in favor of Burn, and remanded with instructions to set aside the

$3500.00 judgment for Owen and to enter judgment for Burn. This court granted Owen's petition for writ of certiorari.

Owen makes three contentions: (1) the judgment in the condemnation matter was clear and unambiguous; therefore, it was error for the trial court to permit evidence which varied and contradicted the judgment and it was error for the court to refuse an instruction that the building had not been paid for in the condemnation case; (2) the admission of written appraisals made by persons who were not called as witnesses and were not subject to cross-examination was violative of N.M.R.Evid. 802 [§ 20-4-802, N.M.S.A.1953 (Supp.1975)]; and (3) the Court of Appeals' direction of a verdict for Burn was improper because the record shows that Owen was entitled to that relief.

Owen first contends that the two lower courts were in error in deciding that evidence of the condemnation suit and the appraisals made in conjunction therewith were admissible in this cause for the purpose of proving that Owen had already been paid for his building.

The consent judgment entered by stipulation of the Agency and Owen was in no way ambiguous. It provided:

> The compensation is based upon the value of the premises . . . on the date of the commencement of this action, and such award is not intended to affect any claim which the defendants may have against any person, firm or corporation who may have damaged said premises prior to the commencement of this proceeding, and the stipulation on file herein and this judgment shall not constitute a settlement or release of any claim which the defendants may have by reason of damage that may have occurred to the condemned premises prior to the commencement of this action; . . .

The written stipulation that was filed was even more explicit as to the parties' intent that the $59,072.00 be considered payment for the vacant lot.

However, the trial court permitted testimony and written opinions from the appraisers that their evaluations in the condemnation suit included both the land and the building. The Court of Appeals held that the consent judgment was binding on the Agency and Owen but was not binding Burn, that since the appraisers considered the value of the land and the building in arriving at their evaluations that Owen had already been justly compensated, that assessment of damages is the exclusive function of the jury and that "duplication of damages is not proper." We disagree that these principles of law are dispositive of the case.

It is true, as pointed out by the Court of Appeals, that a stipulated judgment is not considered to be a judicial determination; "rather it is a contract between the parties," *State v. Clark*, 79 N.M. 29, 439 P.2d 547 (1968); but this legal principle is not controlling and does not diminish the legitimacy of the claim or preclude the relief prayed for by Owen.

The rules to be followed in arriving at the meaning of judgments and decrees are not dissimilar to those relating to other written documents. Where the decree is clear and unambiguous, neither pleadings, findings nor matters dehors the record may be used to change or even to construe its meaning. *Chavez v. Chavez* 82 N.M. 624, 485 P.2d 735 (1971).

Considering this consent judgment as a mere contract between Owen and the Agency affords no comfort to Burn. "It is well settled in New Mexico that where the language of a contract is clear and unambiguous, the intent of the parties must be ascertained from the language and terms of the agreement." *Hondo Oil & Gas Co. v. Pan American Petroleum Corp.*, 73 N.M. 241, 245, 387 P.2d 342, 345 (1963). It is not the province of the court to amend or alter the contract by construction and the court must interpret and enforce the contract which the parties made for themselves.

The case of *Vaca v. Whitaker*, 86 N.M. 79, 519 P.2d 315 (Ct.App.1974) involved a malpractice suit in which there had been a prior judgment entered and satisfied and a new claim later filed for additional damages against a second party. The opinion states (86 N.M. at 83—84, 519 P.2d at 319—20):

. . . This involves an examination of the pertinent portions of the record in the prior case. The fact of "prior satisfaction" is to be determined from the record, and not from oral testimony.[1]

[1] When the record in the prior action is silent or ambiguous, so that the record does not show the injuries for which recovery was obtained, we recognized that oral testimony may be introduced. The oral testimony may properly be introduced only to explain the prior record; the oral testimony may not go beyond that record.

See also *Lemon v. Morrison-Knudsen Co.*, 58 N.M. 830, 277 P.2d 542 (1954); 2 Black on Judgments § § 624—625 (2d ed. 1902).

The Court of Appeals in *Vaca*, supra, ruled that medical expenses incurred subseqeunt to the judgment in the prior case were not included among the issues litigated and the subsequent claim was not barred by satisfaction of the prior judgment. *Seven Rivers Farm, Inc. v. Reynolds*, 84 N.M. 789, 508 P.2d 1276 (1973).

In this case the words cannot be misconstrued; they spell out clearly that the parties intended that Owen should have the right to preserve this action against Burn for damages. There can be no legitimate claim of ambiguity; therefore, there was no need for the court to resort to evidence extrinsic to the agreement.

We are confronted with the specious reasoning of Burn, which corporation was not a party to the suit, that we should go behind the judgment and the specific stipulation signed by the parties and adopt unsworn testimony to emasculate these solemn documents. Who would know what was bought and sold and at what price better than the buyer and seller; and how much better can the bargain be sealed than by a lucid stipulation and judgment?

We hold that it was error to admit the evidence dehors the record to vary the terms of the judgment in condemnation; and, as a necessary corollary, we hold that it was error for the court to refuse Owen's instruction that he had not received compensation for his building in the first suit.

Owen claims that the trial court was in error in admitting into evidence written appraisals of the property in question without the appraisers being present for cross-eximination. The trial court held that the evidence was admissible under N.M.R.Evid. 803(6), [§ 20—4—803(6), N.M.S.A.1953 (Supp.1975) as an exception to the hearsay rule because it was a record of a regularly-conducted activity. The rule provides that a report setting forth an opinion in the course of a regularly-conducted activity. "as shown by the testimony of the custodian or other qualified witness," is admissible even though the declarant is not available.

The evidence shows that the written appraisals were prepared for use in the condemnation proceedings, i. e., for purposes of litigation. The Agency did not prepare them but engaged outside parties, whom they did not supervise, to make the appraisals. The Agency would not vouch for the accuracy of the reports and did not know what factors were considered by the appraisers. The evaluation of one of the appraisers was based on the erroneous assumption that the building was forty years old rather than ten years old. There was no opportunity for Owen to cross-examine, the appraisers not being present at the trial.

Owen claims that the circumstances under which the appraisals were prepared and presented provide none of the circumstantial guarantees of trustworthiness which are normally required to justify an exception to the hearsay rule. We agree.

N.M.R.Evid. 801(c), [§ 20—4—801(c), N.M.S.A.1953 (Supp.1975)] defines "hearsay" as "a statement, other than one made by the declarant while testifying at the trial or hearing, offered in evidence to prove the truth of the matter asserted." Unless the written appraisals fall within the protection of the exception asserted by Burn, the evidence is patently hearsay, since the plain object of offering the evidence was to prove the truth of the assertions in the written opinions that both the building and the land were included in the evaluation.

In *Lahr v. Lahr*, 82 N.M. 223, 478 P.2d 551 (1970) this court held that a husband's opinion as to the value of community real estate was admissible in evidence; however, the court ruled that the accountant employed by the husband could not testify by deposition regarding statements by the husband to the accountant as to the husband's opinion regarding the value of community realty. The court stated (82 N.M. at 225, 478 P.2d at 553):

> . . . Even if these values are those of the defendant as well as the appraiser, the accountant's deposition testimony remains hearsay because it is the testimony of a witness as to out-of-court statements of a declarant who was not a witness as to that specific subject matter. *Chiordi v. Jernigan*, 46 N.M. 396, 129 P.2d 640 (1942).

In *Chiordi* this court explained the basis of its exclusion of certain testimony as hearsay by stating (46 N.M. at 402, 129 P.2d at 644):

> . . . That it is not subject to the tests which ordinarily can be applied to ascertain its truthfulness by cross-examination of the declarant; and because not given under the sanctity of an oath, and because the declarant is not subject to the penalties of perjury.

The prejudice inherent in the admission of such hearsay evidence is readily apparent. It is even questionable, although we need not decide, that the evidence qualifies as a "record of a regularly conducted activity."

Therefore, even if Burn had the legal right to challenge the efficacy of the judgment in question, the entire evidentiary basis of his challenge was inadmissible hearsay. The trial court and the Court of Appeals were in error in holding otherwise.

(3) Owen's third issue on appeal is that the two lower courts were in error in failing to hold that Owen's motion for judgment n.o.v. should have been granted, and was in error in giving the same relief to Burn. We agree. The issues as to Burn are heretofore set forth. There is no rational basis to support the $3500.00 verdict awarded by the jury. Furthermore, as to Burn's liability and the amount of $26,000.00 as the damages suffered by Owen there are no issues of material fact disclosed by the record.

In a case such as this where the evidence on an issue of fact is undisputed, and the inferences to be drawn therefrom are plain and not open to doubt by reasonable men, the issue is no longer one of fact to be submitted to the jury, but becomes a question of law. If reasonable minds cannot differ, then a directed verdict is not only proper but the court has a duty to direct a verdict.

We have no hesitancy in holding that reasonable minds could not differ as to the liability of Burn or as to the amount of damages, since there literally is no evidence disputing either of these factual issues. The same holding pertains to the wholly-unsubstantiated award of damages in the verdict of the jury.

It necessarily follows that we dismiss the cross-appeal of Burn, reverse the Court of Appeals and the trial court on issues above indicated, affirm the Court of Appeals' decision ordering that the award to Owen of $3500.00 be set aside, and direct that judgment be entered, notwithstanding the verdict, awarding Owen $26,000.00 in damages plus his costs.

IT IS SO ORDERED.

McMANUS, C. J., and SOSA and PAYNE, JJ., concur.

In the following casino gambling case, we see the role that "public policy" can play in court cases.

CONDADO ARUBA CARIBBEAN HOTEL v. TICKEL
Colo. App. 561 P. 2d 23 (1977).

ENOCH, Judge.

Plaintiff, Condado Aruba Caribbean Hotel, N.V., appeals a judgment denying relief on their claim for $14,500 against defendant, Bill Tickel. We affirm.

The facts are undisputed. Plaintiff hotel loaned defendant $20,000 for gambling at its casino in Aruba, Netherlands Antilles. Gambling is legal in Aruba. Defendant wrote two checks to repay the debt, each of which was returned for insufficient funds. Defendant subsequently paid $5,500 of the debt, and plaintiff brought this action to recover the remainder.

Plaintiff contends that the trial court erred in holding that the gambling debt was enforceable. We disagree.

Plaintiff concedes that gambling debts have been held unenforceable in Colorado, *see, e.g., National Surety Co. v. Stockyard National Bank,* 84 Colo. 563, 272 P. 470, but asserts that this refusal to enforce such debts was based on a statute, C.R.S.1963, 40—10—13, which has now been repealed. Colo.Sess.Laws 1971, ch. 121, sec. 1. Therefore, plaintiff urges, collection of gambling debts incurred where gambling is legal is no longer against public policy in Colorado, and such debts should now be enforced. This contention is without merit.

Contrary to plaintiff's assertion, the policy of refusing to enforce gambling debts in Colorado has not been based solely on statutory grounds. In the early case of *Eldred v. Malloy,* 2 Colo. 320, the court ruled that enforcement of gambling debts was against sound public policy, and so ruled without reference to the statutory prohibition in effect at the time.

Even in the absence of grounds independent of the statutory prohibition against the enforcement of gambling debts, repeal of C.R.S.1963, 40—10—13, does not necessarily evidence an intent by the legislature to change the existing policy. The current legislative declaration relating to the criminal statutes regarding gambling declares that it is the policy of the general assembly:

to restrain all persons from seeking profit from gambling activities in this state; to restrain all persons from patronizing such activities when conducted for the profit of any person; [and] to safeguard the public against the evils induced by common gamblers and common gambling houses . . . Section 18—10—101, C.R.S.1973.

This declaration evidences a continuation of the policy against gambling for profit in Colorado, and we therefore conclude that gambling debts owed to a for-profit gambling business are still unenforceable in this state.

Furthermore, we find no indication in this declaration which would support plaintiff's contention that, although gambling is illegal and against public policy when it occurs in Colorado, it would not be contrary to public policy to enforce gambling debts incurred where gambling is legal. To the contrary, we find in the above legislative declaration a policy restraining any activities related to gambling conducted for profit, when not specifically sanctioned by statute, including collection of any gambling debts.

Plaintiff also claims that because defendant drew a check to pay a debt that was legal where incurred, he is liable on the check, even if the underlying debt is unenforceable. We disagree.

Even if we were to assume plaintiff was a holder in due course, it does not take the instrument free of defenses of any party to the instrument with whom it had dealt. See § 4—3—305(2), C.R.S.1973.

Finally, plaintiff contends that since defendant paid a portion of the debt, he has reaffirmed it, and is therefore liable for the remainder.

While there may be certain situations where the action of a party who issues a negotiable instrument for a gambling debt may be estopped to deny the validity of the instrument, here there is neither an innocent third party, see *Sullivan v. German National Bank*, 18 Colo.App. 99, 70 P. 162, nor a change of position by plaintiff as a result of defendant's partial payment which could make the doctrine of estoppel applicable. See *Ayer v. Younker, 10 Colo.App. 27, 50 P. 218.*

Judgment affirmed.

RULAND and KELLY, JJ., concur.

QUESTIONS

1. Give an example of "substantive" law and "procedural" law.
2. What does a "cause of action" mean?
3. Explain why a contract has to be voluntary.
4. Give five examples of personal property — five of real property.
5. Historically tort grew out of crime. Explain why.
6. Give an example of a "nuisance" not mentioned in this chapter.
7. What did "no writ no remedy" mean 900 years ago?
8. In the *Owen* case, page 39, why did the court set aside the verdict of $3,500?
9. In the *Condado* case, page 43, is there anything that can be done to collect the gambling debt?
10. Give another example of how "public policy" could have an effect on a court action.

4

Lawyers, Judges and Juries

LAWYERS

A lawyer is a person who is learned in the law: ". . . who for fee or reward, prosecutes or defends causes in court of records or other judicial tribunals of the United States, or of any of the states, or whose business it is to give legal advice in relation to any cause or matter whatever."[1] Thus we see at the outset that lawyers function both in and out of court. In England, lawyers are divided into two categories: solicitors and barristers. The former confine their legal activities to their offices and are rarely seen in court. The latter specialize in trial work. It is common in England for solicitors to prepare cases for the barristers who then present the cases to judges and juries.

While there is no such formal distinction in the United States, as a practical matter we have "office lawyers" and we have "trial lawyers." Many of our 450,000 plus lawyers engage in both activities — others specialize in office consultation and some in trial work. A few have gained national reputations for criminal defense work. Some are recognized for their abilities in airline tort work and other forms of personal injury cases.

About one-half of the American lawyers belong to the American Bar Association (ABA), and all practicing lawyers are members of their respective state bar assocations. Some states have more than one association. In addition, all states have local bar associations. Through these organizations, standards of conduct are established and rules of court procedure are developed. Thus, practicing lawyers tend to be a close-knit group and quite liberal in their beliefs and attitudes. In addition, they tend to be a highly intelligent group collectively, although they have not been spared criticism in the past or at the present time.

LEGAL PROFESSION UNDERFIRE

In recent years, the profession has been subjected to closer scrutiny than ever before by the public as well as by the courts. For example, the U.S. Supreme Court has ruled that fee schedules used by local bar associations are a form of price fixing and thus illegal.[2] In addition, many of the practices of the profession have been successfully challenged, and this can be expected to continue in the future. After all, lawyers engage in a form of public trust as they represent others, so the rights of the public must be respected by lawyers. Although there has been considerable publicity directed toward lawyers who have plundered estates, or who have been held to be incompetent in the courts, the vast majority of American lawyers are intelligent, honest, hard working men and women, who give value for the fees that they are paid.

The principal code of conduct for our lawyers, is found in the *Code of Professional Responsibility*.

CODE OF PROFESSIONAL RESPONSIBILITY

While there have been other codes of conduct for lawyers, the primary one that is followed today, is the *Code of Professional Responsibility*. This *Code* was based upon older "canons of ethics" and is an update of the old canons. Set forth in the *Code* are detailed guidelines establishing standards of conduct for lawyers. While the *Code* is a product of the ABA which represents only about 50% of American lawyers, it is understood that all lawyers must comply with its standards. The supreme courts of most of our states, have approved the *Code*, in effect making it state law.

Failure to so comply can result in disciplinary action, such as a reprimand, or, in severe cases, disbarment of the offending lawyer. A detailed discussion of the *Code* is beyond the scope of this book, but suffice it to say, any person who feels that he or she has a complaint against a member of the legal profession, should make that complaint known. The place to begin is with an informal complaint to the President of the local bar association. Bar associations, as a rule, are prompt and strong in the application of the standards of the *Code* and will take action against lawyers who do not measure up to those standards.

It is next important to become acquainted with the services that the legal profession provides. Lawyers provide services in their offices, in the courts and before administrative agencies.

SERVICES OF LAWYERS

The greatest part of a practicing attorney's time is spent in the office, because it is here that consultation takes place. Consulting touches all phases of business activities and is perhaps the most important service that the legal profession can provide. Proper legal advice, timely sought and wisely given, can avoid the necessity of going to court.

Lawyers also do court work, and many specialize in this. But lawyers who consult with business persons will admit that the necessity of using the courts often means that something went wrong along the line. Of course, if one's business is sued, it is necessary to use the courts for defensive purposes. As part of the court function, lawyers will prepare the papers needed to start and defend lawsuits; research and prepare trial briefs; prepare witnesses and develop evidence to be produced at trial; present and defend cases before judges and juries and file appeals if they are warranted. When a lawyer engages in the trial function a tremendous amount of skill, effort and knowledge must be placed into use. Many "office" lawyers refer trial work to those who specialize in this activity.

Related to court work is the handling of matters before administrative bodies. Perhaps a client has been cited for an OSHA or on ECOA violation that the client wants to defend against. The lawyer will prepare the forms and see that they are timely filed. At appropriate times, testimony may be required before the agency. These proceedings are similar to court proceedings. Records are made, transcripts are prepared, and appeals are taken as required. As a general rule, administrative procedures are much more informal than court proceedings. The technical rules of evidence do not apply and paper work is carried out by the exchange of notices and letters. It is the practice of administrative agencies to issue their rulings in opinion form in which the facts, findings and conclusions are set forth.

PARALEGAL MOVEMENT

As on off-shoot of the activities of lawyers, the paralegal movement should be mentioned. There has been a growing tendency in recent years to delegate "lawyer like" duties to legal assistants. These persons are *not* secretaries, but persons trained to handle routine legal matters. They must, however, work under the supervision of a licensed practitioner. They are frequently business trained persons with no formal legal training. Instead, they are provided special training by the law firms in order to enable them to carry out their duties. They are being used to make investigations; to prepare corporate minutes and resolutions; to handle routine filing work in the courts, and to do the countless routine legal matters that have become a drain on the lawyers time. They do not try cases; prepare suits, nor do any type of legal work that requires professional training. They operate much like paramedics, who have proven their worth in recent years.

One who contemplates the use of legal services, will naturally be interested in what those services are going to cost.

FEES

Before the *Goldfarb* case, it was a nationwide practice for local bar associations to publish and circulate "minimum bar fee schedules." The fees set forth were the least that could be charged for the services listed. For example, a name change might be listed at $100, a will at $25 and a deed at $20. Now, because of the *Goldfarb* decision, lawyers charge what they feel the clients will bear, which is often *higher* than the minimum fees. However, a vestige of the minimum fees remain in "flat fees."

FLAT FEES

In all bar associations, certain legal services tend to become standardized so that each lawyer may charge a flat fee for those routine services. This is true in adoption, divorce and title search fees. These fees remain uniform in spite of the striking down of the fee schedules.

As another way of charging fees, many lawyers work on an hourly basis.

HOURLY FEES

Many lawyers and legal firms, provide legal services on a straight hourly rate basis. Minimum contact, such as a 5 minute phone call, is logged as ¼ hour. Longer times are logged accordingly. At appropriate times, the hours are billed at a rate that may begin at $30 per hour or may exceed $250 per hour. Surprisingly enough, this is often the cheapest way that legal fees can be provided. The client can obtain a constant stream of lawyer contact, split into a series of relatively short time periods, that may add up to only an hour or two. The total bill is frequently reasonable when one considered that the services may have been provided over a long period of time. Administrative matters, such as OSHA or EEOC complaints, or workmens compensation matters, are best handled on an hourly basis. In addition, the hourly fee is desirable from the lawyers point of view, since the next half hour or hour after giving advice to one client can be devoted to providing services to other clients.

Some business persons, however, prefer to place lawyers on general, or special "retainers."

RETAINERS

A "retainer" is the . . . "act of a client in employing his attorney or counsel, and also denotes the fee which the client pays when he retains the lawyer to work for him, and thereby prevents him from acting for his adversary."[3] Retainers can be general or special.

GENERAL RETAINERS

A "general retainer" gives one the right to expect legal services when requested but none that is not requested. It binds the one retained not to take a fee from another that would be contrary to that retainer.[4]

SPECIAL RETAINERS

A "special retainer" is an engagement of the services of a lawyer for a designated purpose, such as to defend one on a criminal charge.[5]

Annual general retainers may run into the hundreds of thousands of dollars, or be as low as $100 in local, small business situations. Their value is in the gaining of the assurance that the services of a particular lawyer or firm will be available if needed. If services are provided, the client will be expected to pay for services rendered beyond the amount of the retainer. In criminal defense work, it is the usual practice for a flat retainer to be paid at the outset. Most lawyers refuse to invoice clients for criminal defense services, just as some lawyers require that divorce fees be paid in advance.

Many legal fees are based upon the "contingency of recovery".

Contingent Fees It has not been uncommon to find legal fees being taken from recoveries obtained in court on behalf of a client. This was the nationwide practice in personal injury cases, most of which arose from automobile accidents. An agreement would be reached initially, in which the lawyer was to be paid a percentage of any recovery realized in or out of court. Typical percentages were 25% for out of court settlements before suit was filed; 33-⅓% after suit was filled; and 50% if a verdict was appealed from and sustained by an appelate court.

Thus if Attorney Zero brought a personal injury case on behalf of Client Zippo, who had been injured by Defendant Zilch, and if $100,000 was recovered after trial, the legal fee was $33,333.33. The balance, after expenses were deducted, belonged to the client. The advent of no-fault insurance and its spread to 23 states as of 1978, severly reduced this lucrative way of charging legal fees in automobile personal injury cases.

One final way that fees are charged is by use of "prepaid legal service plans."

PREPAID PLANS

These plans are the product of the 1970's. When they are in operation, covered employees contribute so much per hour, week, or month worked, toward a prepaid legal service plan. This is matched by employer contributions.

To implement these plans, prearrangements are made with lawyers in "closed plans" or the general bar in "open plans." The scope of the services then available per year are spelled out, such as 6 hours office consultation, one will, one contested court action. As an employee draws upon his or her plan, the fees are paid out of the fund. Some plans have deductibles which require that the employee pay the first $10, $30, $50 or whatever the plan calls for.

These plans have found wide acceptance in just a few years and can now be bargained for collectively just as other fringe benefits. This has been permitted by a specific act of Congress.

In the following case, a woman who was injured in a hotel lost her cause of action due to the carelessness of her lawyer. Such an occurance is rare — but not unheard of. The injured person would now have a cause of action against her lawyer for his negligence.

BRADY v. DURAN
372 A. 2d 283 (New Hampshire 1977).

KENISON, Chief Justice.

This is an appeal from the denial of the plaintiff's motion for late entry. In her suit she seeks damages for personal injuries allegedly sustained while she was a guest at the defendants' hotel. The plaintiff's writ of summons was issued on July 17, 1974, returnable the first Tuesday of September 1974. The defendants were properly served and made a special appearance on the September 1974 return day. The plaintiff's counsel, however, did not file the writ with the clerk of court on the return day as required by RSA 496:2. In fact, he did not enter the writ nor pay the court entry fees until February 25, 1976, nearly eighteen months later. At that time he also filed a motion for late entry. After a hearing on the matter, *Johnson, J.*, denied the motion, and the plaintiff appealed. All questions of law were reserved and transferred to this court.

The superior court is empowered to allow the late entry of any writ, process or appeal. RSA 496:2. The question is whether the court properly refused to do so in this case. The preface to the Superior Court Rules states that "[r]elief from failure to comply with the provisions of any rule may be granted on such terms as the Court may order, where, due to accident, mistake or misfortune and not through neglect, justice so requires." Other statutes similarly excuse noncompliance with procedural requirements because of accident, mistake or misfortune. E. g., RSA 567-A:5 (Supp.1975), RSA 281:42, RSA 74:8. Recently we stated: "The words 'accident, mistake or misfortune' ' "ordinarily import something outside of the petitioner's own control, or at least something which a reasonably prudent man would not be expected to guard against or provide for." ' " *Pelham Plaza v. Pelham*, N.H., 370 A.2d 638 (1977).

In this case the plaintiff's counsel failed to enter the writ seasonably because of a clerical error which was caused by a change in personnel at his office. At the hearing, he stated "we obviously forgot about filing our Writ . . . " A long line of New York cases holds that such excuses as loss or misplacement of files, changes in personnel and clerical errors are not permissible justifications for delinquency in filing or serving papers during the pleadings stage of litigation. E. g., *Kahn v. Samson Management Corp.*, 44 A.D.2d 571,353 N.Y.S.2d 227 (1974).

In our own cases we have often strictly adhered to deadlines and other procedural requirements and have denied relief to delinquent parties whose excuses for noncompliance were more meritorious than the excuses offered in the present case. E. g., *Pelham Plaza v. Pelham*, N. H., 370 A.2d 638(1977). A client whose attorney negligently fails to prosecute a civil claim in a timely fashion is generally denied relief from the consequences of his attorney's neglect. Mazor, *Power and Responsibility in The Attorney Client Relation*, 20 Stan.L.Rev. 1120, 1125 (1968). We hold that the trial court could find that inexcusable neglect accounted for the late entry. Accordingly, under the preface to the Superior Court Rules, the superior court properly denied relief.

There was some discussion in oral argument, although not in the briefs, as to whether the plaintiff could bring a second suit under RSA 508:10 in the event that we sustained the denial of the motion for late entry. The question is not actually before us, and the answer to it is not readily apparent to us at this time. Under these circumstances, a decision would not be proper unless and until such time as the plaintiff actually files a second suit and the parties give the superior court an opportunity to decide the question.

Plaintiff's exception overruled.

GRIMES, J., dissented; the others concurred.

JUDGES

At Roman law, the "judex" was a private person appointed by the praetor (a judicial magistrate of the City of Rome). to hear and decide a cause of action brought before him. The praetor furnished the judex with a written formula that set forth the legal principles to be applied in arriving at the decision. The proceedings before the judex were "in judicio."

Today the judex, our judge, functions in much the same manner as in early Roman times. Judges exist to hear and decide disputes and to apply the law in rendering their decisions as well as in guiding the decisions of juries. Thus judges decide the law today, and as we shall see, juries decide the facts.

At Roman law, a "judex ad quem" was one to whom an appeal was taken from the ruling of a lower judex. Today, such a judge is an "appellate judge."

CREATE LAW

"Judge-made law" results from the decisions handed down by judges. Such decisions may be interpretations of statutes and constitutions, or they may be rulings on matters of "first impression."

ORDERS AND JUDGMENTS

While judges can never bring matters before themselves by unilateral action, once a controversy is there, they can hold hearings, issue orders and render judgments.

When a court enters an "order", it must be obeyed unless a timely appeal is taken from it. Failure to obey court orders permit judges to issue contempt citations in both legal and equitable matters.

A "judgment" has been defined as "the official and authentic decisions of a court of justice upon the respective rights and claims of the parties to an action or suit therein litigated and submitted to its determination."[6] "The conclusion (of the judge) is a syllogism having for its major and minor premises issues raised by the pleadings and the proofs thereon."[7]

FORMS OF JUDGMENTS

Various forms of judgments are found in our courts, and a few will be mentioned. A "confession of judgement" means that one admits the truth of the charges against him or her. A "consent judgment" is one the terms of which the parties agree upon. A "default judgment" is one entered by a court when one of the parties fails to defend. A "deficiency judgment" is one in which repossessed collateral does not bring enough to settle the debt thus the debtor is sued for the balance and judgment is entered for that balance. A "final judgment" puts an end to a lawsuit: an "interlocutory judgment" is of a preliminary, temporary nature.

JUDGMENT TERMS

A "judgment book" is where judgments are recorded and indexed. A "judgment debtor" is one who has had judgment entered against him or her. A "judgment creditor" is the one to whom the judgment debt is owed. Judgments can be "in personam"—against the person, or "in rem"—against a particular thing or subject matter. The latter would take the form of a "judgment lien" against the property once the judgment is placed on record.

Turning from forms and terms of judgments, it is important to look at qualifications of judges and the legal reasoning applied by them in the courts.

QUALIFICATIONS OF JUDGES

The qualifications of judges will vary from state to state, but most state constitutions set minimum age and residency requirements. In most states it is *not* a requirement that judges be lawyers. At the federal level, since judges must be nominated by the President and confirmed by the U.S. Senate; it is mandatory that they be lawyers.

The way that judges *think* can have direct bearing upon their decisions.

SCHOOLS OF THOUGHT

Some judges are influenced by historical thought and give weight to the evolutionary process of ideas and prior case decisions. They tend to be influenced by custom and prior usuages, and frequently do *not* exercise independent judgment. Rather, they rely upon what other judges have done in the past.

Other judges are "natural law" thinkers. Such persons view humanity as a grouping of persons who seek ideal rights and justice and such a judge is concerned about "good" and "evil". Law rests on reason and is something more than human-made law. The latter may be held by such a thinker to be unfair, unjust or unreasonable. One who thinks this way, may find ways to circumvent such laws when rendering decisions.

An "analytical thinker," views law as something that is made up of those rules and principles that the *state* feels is mandatory for its citizens-even if those rules may seem unjust or unreasonable to the judge. For one influenced by this type of thinking, there is a need for certainty, and law is considered to be a series of commands or orders from the state. Under such thinking, the less control by law, the wider latitude those in business have in which to conduct their affairs. If the state does not consider certain acts to be unjust, the judge will not interfere with those acts. Such judges often say, "If that should be the law, then it is for the legislature to say so, not me." Out of such thinking developed the Nineteenth Century ideas of freedom of competition and contract. Governmental control took a backseat to business.

Other judges are "sociological thinkers." Law to them is a means to an end—it is a matter of striking a balance between conflicting interests. Law thus becomes a generalization and is based on experience. Such a judge attempts to examine the affected areas of society in order to determine what the law shall be and how is should develop.

Many judges are, of course, affected by different combinations of the above "schools of legal thought," and even a mixture of them, as different facts are confronted by them in different cases. This tells us that the "law" can be what a judge says it should be. In practice, some judges become identified with certain forms of thinking, and are sought by some litigants for that reason. Other litigants avoid certain judges for the same reason. It is similar to the process encountered in undergraduate schools where certain teachers are sought—and others are avoided.

A frequent companion of judges in the court room, are "juries."

JURIES

The word "jurata" in old English law, referred to those persons chosen by their peers to hear and decide questions of *facts* in court. After being sworn to "truly try the facts" (jurata), they would hear evidence from all parties and then "declare the truth" of the matter before them. The term "jury" today includes grand juries, trial or petit juries, coroners juries and others.

A jury is selected by jury commissioners and the parties to the suit, and at common law was made up of 12 persons. Today the 6 person jury is in evidence in Florida and in the federal courts in civil matters. In time, the jury may be reduced to 3—or even one person.

A counterpart of the one-person jury is found in modern-day arbitration.

TRIAL BY JURY

This phrase means a trial by the designated number of ". . . competent men, disinterested and impartial not of kin, nor personal dependents of either of the parties, having their homes within the jurisdictional limits of the court, drawn and selected by officers free from all bias in favor of or against either party, duly empaneled and sworn to render a true verdict according to the law and the evidence."[8]

A "grand jury" is one that hears preliminary evidence in a pending criminal case and decides if "probable cause" has been shown that one has committed a crime. If so the jury can return an "indictment" against that person. These juries *do not* decide questions of fact. A petit or trial jury is the fact finding body, and these are used in civil and criminal cases. They are not encountered in administrative proceedings, although they are seen at times in Justice of the Peace and state Magistrate courts.

JURIES IN COURT

Once juries are selected, empaneled and sworn, they will hear the evidence of the trial as it is given to them by the testimony of witnesses. They will examine photos, and other documents that the judge allows to "come into evidence."

One of the functions of the judge is to make certain that all evidence that comes to the jury is proper and relevant. "Objections" to proposed evidence raised by lawyers in court, require a ruling by the judge on the admissibility of that evidence.

Jury service is an essential part of our court system and it is a duty of our citizens to respond when called upon to serve. Yet jury duty is quite often a frustrating experience. One of the main reasons for this is the requirement of holding hearings on objections out of their hearing. Yet the judges must make certain that prejudicial, "contaminated." or irrelevant evidence does not come to the minds of the jury. If it does, the verdict of the jury may be set aside on appeal.

FACT FINDERS

The role of our petit juries as "finders of fact" presents an interesting situation. If A claims that facts UV&W control the contract that he has entered into with B, but if B claims that facts XY&Z control, then a finding must be made of the "true facts". This is done by the filing of suit and presentation of evidence. After this, the court (judge) will "instruct" the jury of the applicable law. After giving the case to the jury, they must render a decision. This decision is called a "verdict." Once it is announced, it becomes the determination of what the facts in controversy were. If a case is presented fairly to an impartial jury, an upper court will seldom set aside their verdict.

QUESTIONS

1. Do American lawyers have anything in their legal system that compares to Englands' barristers and solicitors?
2. Why is the *Code of Professionals Responsibility* a completely rewritten draft rather than an update of the old "canuns"?
3. T. or F. Paralegals are trained to make legal decisions on their own.
4. Give an example of a special retainer—a general retainer.
5. Give one reason why a plaintiff might complain about a contingent fee arrangement.
6. Give an example of how one could become a "judgment debtor."
8. Distinguish a grand from a petit jury.
9. T. or F. Trial juries are triers of the law—not the facts.
10. Why do appellate courts tend to refuse to meddle with jury verdicts—in the absense of clear error?

ENDNOTES

1. Act of July 13, 1866, sec. 9, 14 St. at Large 121.
2. *Goldfarb v. Virginia State Bar.* 421 U.S. 773 (1975).
3. *Bright v. Turner*, 205 Ky. 188, 265 S.W. 627, 628.
4. *Rhode Island Exch. Bank v. Hawkins* 6 R.I. 206.
5. *Agnew v. Wolden*, 84 Ala. 502, 4 So. 672.
6. *Bullock v. Bullock*, 52 N.J. Eq. 561, 30 A. 676, 27 L.R.A. 216.
7. *Barlow v. Scott*, Mo. Sup., 85 S.W. 2d 504, 517.
8. *Shafer Motor Freight Service*, 4 N.Y.S. 2d 526, 167 Misc. 681.

Hospitality Cases in Court

As each cause of action goes into our judicial system, it becomes known as a "case" or lawsuit. A court has said that ". . . the word 'case' or 'cause' means a judicial proceeding for the determination of a controversy between parties wherein rights are enforced or protected, or wrongs are prevented or redressed."[1]

The phrase "cases and controversies" is found in the United States Constitution: It means ". . . controversy of a justiciable nature, excluding advisory decrees on hypothetical facts."[2] A "case sufficient to go to a jury" is one that ". . . has proceeded upon sufficient proof to that stage where it must be submitted to jury and not decided against the state (or other) as a matter of law."[3]

Thus the word "case" has a precise meaning at law. It also has a common meaning, such as a box or container in which something is packed. Further, it has a third meaning that we should understand.

THIRD MEANING

At some trial court levels, and at the appellate level of most state and all federal courts, case decisions are reduced to printed form. This is done in typewritten form by the judges as they arrive at their rulings. Afterwards, these decisions are placed into printed volumes, as will be explained in a moment. Once in printed form, they are available to the public and wide use is made of them by law schools, business schools, lawyers, agencies, judges and others. Thus the "case study" of law is one that makes use of the decisions found in printed volumes, a "reporter system."

REPORTER SYSTEM

West Publishing Company has divided the United States into "reporter regions." This company accumulates the decisions from all major courts in these regions and places them in bound volumes. Their reporter areas are as follows:

ATLANTIC

(A) Connecticut, Delaware, District of Columbia, Maine, Maryland, New Hampshire, New Jersey, Pennsylvania, Rhode Island and Vermont.

NORTHEASTERN

(NE) Illinois, Indiana, Massachusetts, New York and Ohio.

NORTHWESTERN

(N.W.) Iowa, Michigan, Minnesota, Nebraska, North Dakota, South Dakota and Wisconsin.

PACIFIC

(P) Alaska, Arizona, California, Colorado, Hawaii, Idaho, Kansas, Montana, Nevada, New Mexico, Oklahoma, Oregon, Utah, Washington and Wyoming.

SOUTHEASTERN

(SE) Georgia, North Carolina, South Carolina, Virginia and West Virginia.

SOUTHWESTERN

(SW) Arkansas, Kentucky, Missouri, Tennessee, and Texas.

SOUTHERN

(S) Alabama, Florida, Louisiana and Mississippi.

In addition to these, New York has the "New York Supplement" (NYS) and California the "California Reporter" (Cal. Rep.) These extra reporters were created because of the volume of litigation carried out in those two states.

FEDERAL REPORTERS

At the federal level are found the *Federal Supplement* (F. Supp) that reports some, but not all, of the decisions of the federal district courts; the *Federal Reporter* which reports cases in the 10 U.S. Courts of Appeal and the *Supreme Court Reporter*, whose name tells us what cases it contains.

To make use of this immense body of cases, which grows larger each day, one must understand something about legal research.

LEGAL RESEARCH

As one begins to search for relevant cases, it is necessary to identify areas in which the search should be conducted. This is done by the use of the "TAP" rule: "things," "acts" and "places." To illustrate, A is injured by a dog kept in an adjoining room of a motel. A seeks legal advice and the lawyer wants to know if the innkeeper is liable. "Things" would include, "pets," "animals," "injury to motel guest," and others. "Acts" would include "animals in motel rooms," "boarding of animals," "innkeepers liability" and others. Places would include "motels," "hotels," "inns," and "lodging facilities." Armed with these terms, the lawyer can use the indexes to cases, reporters, and other legal treaties to establish the extent of liability— if any, as developed by prior case law.

In this process, items may be found that lead to different sources. In the end, a skillful researcher will have complied perhaps only one or two relevant case citations, or citations to appropriate statutes. But that is often all that is required.

Legal research is one of the arts of the legal profession and an in-depth discussion of it is beyond our scope here. We do need how-ever, to understand how to read case citations.

A CASE CITATION EXAMPLE

Examine the following case citation: *Gray v. Zurick Insurance Co.*, 65 Cal. 2d 263. 419 P. 2d 168, 54 Cal. Rep. 104 (1966).

The title tells us the names of the parties to the lawsuit. It does *not* tell us who was the plaintiff or defendant since the names may be reversed depending upon who takes the appeal. The case can be found in the *California* reports. Second Series, volume 65, beginning on page 263. It can also be found in the *Pacific Reporter, Second Series*, volume 419 beginning on page 168, as well as in the *California Reporter*, volume 54 beginning on page 104. The case was decided in 1966.

This citation refers to three sources, some only refer to two. In a few instances, particularly with older state cases, the citation may be to the state report only.

Armed with this information, one can obtain the entire case from the appropriate reporter and make use of it as required.

CASE EXAMPLE

To become further acquainted with what is in a case, examine the decision of *Page* v. *Sloan* 12 N.C. App. 433, 183 S.E. 2d 813 (1971) that follows. Here a man lost his life in a motel explosion. The case is reported in volume 183 *South Eastern Reporter, Second Series*, beginning on page 813.

PAGE v. SLOAN

Plaintiff, Administratrix C.T.A. of the Estate of Channing Nelson Page, Insti-tuted this action on 4 February 1966, to recover for the wrongful death of Channing Nelson Page, who was killed on 29 August 1964, by the explosion of an 82 gallon electric hot water heater located in an utility room of the Ocean Isle Motel in Brunswick County, North Carolina. She alleged that Mr. Page was a paying guest in said motel which was owned and operated by the defendants as co-partners and that Mr. Page was assigned a corner room which adjoined the utility room which contained the motel's hot water heater. This electric hot water heater was installed, used, and operated by defendants for the purpose of furnishing hot water to the various guest rooms of the Ocean Isle Motel. She alleged that the explosion of the electric hot water heater was the direct and proximate cause of the death of Page and that at all times the said water heater was in the exclusive possession and control of the defendants. She further alleged that the explosion of said electric hot water heater was caused by, or due to, the actionable negligence of the defendants.

Defendants answered admitting allegations of residence, the death of Channing Nelson Page, their ownership and operation of Ocean Isle Motel, their acceptance of Page as a paying guest and assigning him a corner room adjoining the utility room containing the electric hot water heater, the water heater serving the function of furnishing hot water to various guest rooms in the said motel, and said electric hot water heater exploding at the alleged time and place. However, the defendants specifically denied negligence on their part.

Pursuant to the provisions of Rule 16 of the Rules of Civil Procedure and Rule 7, General Rules of Practice in the Superior and District Courts, a final pretrial conference was held in this action on the 7th day of January, 1971. It was stipulated that all the parties were properly before the court, and that the court had jurisdiction over the parties and the subject matter. The parties stipulated and agreed with respect to the following salient facts:

"(i) This hot water heater unit installed by Shallotte Hardware Company at Ocean Isle Motel remained in operation and use in the new units at that place from approximately April, 1962, until the explosion in August, 1964.

* * * * * * *

"(k) In June or July, 1964, George Sloan and Rea Sloan had Olaf Thorsen check the hot water unit here in question due to a complaint of no hot water or insufficient hot water by motel guests. Olaf Thorsen removed the lower heating element of the water heater and obtained a replacement from Shallotte Hardward Company. The original heating element was of the size of 2500 watts. After the explosion it was determined that the lower heating element in the heater at the time of the explosion was an element of 4500 watt size.

"(l) The water heater in question was rated by an inscription on a plate attached thereto at 3000 watts for the upper element, at 2500 watts for the lower element, and at 3000 watts maximum.

* * * * * * *

"(p) Olaf Thorsen was a licensed plumber in Brunswick County, North Carolina.

* * * * * * *

"(r) The 82 gallon electric hot water heater was manufactured by State Stove and Manufacturing Company and installed in the Ocean Isle Motel by Shallotte Hardware Company and worked on by Olaf Thorsen and was the hot water heater which exploded in the utility room adjacent to the motel room occupied by Channing Nelson Page.

* * * * * * *

"(s) There was no inspection of the installation of the hot water heater at the time of its installation in 1962 by the N. C. Department of Labor Boiler

Inspection Division as required by North Carolina General Statutes. The installation was inspected by the Brunswick County inspector who was not with the Department of Labor."

In addition to the foregoing stipulations, several depositions were considered by the trial judge at the hearing on motion for summary judgment. These depositions, which were considered by consent, included depositions of each of the defendants, the deposition of Olaf Thorsen (the plumber-repairman), and the depositions of each of the three partners in Shallotte Hardware (the original installer of defendants' electric hot water heater).

The deposition of Olaf Thorsen tends to show that he is a licensed plumber, and that he has no license or experience as an electrician. It tends to show that defendants called him to adjust or repair the electric hot water heater because there was no hot water. It tends to show that he removed a 2500 watt heating element and replaced it with a 4500 watt element, and reset the thermostat to a higher temperature reading. The stipulations show that the water heater was rated for a 2500 watt heating element, and a maximum of 3000 watts. The deposition of Alton Milliken, a licensed electrician, tends to show that the introduction of a 4500 watt heating element would heat the water faster and would draw a larger current through the thermostat which would tend to cause its points to melt and thereby freeze the thermostat so that it would no longer control the temperature. The deposition of Glenn Williamson tends to show that the tank of defendants' electric hot water heater was blown some two hundred to three hundred feet by the explosion.

Defendants' motion for summary judgment was heard during the 18 January 1971 Session of Superior Court held in Moore County. It was stipulated that Judge Long might enter judgment out of the District and after expiration of the Session. After consideration of the pleadings, depositions, and stipulations, Judge Long by judgment filed 31 March 1971 found that there was no genuine issue of any material fact as to liability and that defendants' motion for summary judgment should be granted. Plaintiff appeals.

BROCK, Judge.

Plaintiff-appellant insists that the doctrine of *res ipsa loquitur* is applicable in this case and, being entitled under that doctrine to have the case submitted to the jury, that summary judgment for defendant was error. We agree.

Summary judgment is proper only where movant shows that there is no genuine issue as to any material fact and that he is entitled to judgment as a matter of law. Application of the doctrine of *res ipsa loquitur* recognizes that common experience sometimes permits a reasonable inference of negligence from the occurrence itself. In other words, the application of the doctrine of *res ipsa loquitur* recognizes a genuine issue as to the material fact of defendants' actionable negligence and precludes summary judgment for defendants.

The rules governing the application of the doctrine of *res ipsa loquitur* in North Carolina have been stated as follows: "When a thing which causes injury is shown to be under the exclusive management of the defendant and the accident is one which in the ordinary course of events does not happen if those in control of it use proper care, the accident itself is sufficient to carry the case to the jury on the issue of defendant's negligence."

In this case the evidence before the trial judge clearly shows that the electric hot water heater was under the exclusive management and control of defendants, and that they had undertaken the maintenance of it. It is a matter of common knowledge that electric water heaters are widely used to fill the hot water requirements of residential, commercial, and industrial users. When in a safe condition and properly managed, electric hot water heaters do not usually explode; therefore, in the absence of explanation, the explosion of an electric hot water heater reasonably warrants an inference of negligence.

A hotel or motel keeper, from the nature of his occupation, extends an invitation to the general public to use his facilities. When a paying guest goes to a hotel or motel the very thing he bargains for is the use of safe and secure premises for his sojourn. Although the hotel or motel keeper is not an insurer of the guest's personal safety, he has the duty to exercise reasonable care to maintain the premises in a reasonably safe condition; and if his negligence in this respect is the proximate cause of injury to a guest, he is liable for damages.

Defendants argue that *res ipsa loquitur* does not apply because the evidence leaves the cause of the explosion a matter of conjecture. The depositions of the two defendants which were before the trial judge indicated that a thunderstorm was in the area during the night preceding the explosion of the electric hot water heater. This testimony may constitute evidence for consideration by the jury as a possible explanation of the cause of the explosion, but its probative value is for jury determiniation and it does not remove the more reasonable inference that the cause of the explosion was negligence of defendants in the management and control of the electric hot water heater.

Defendants further argue that they lack the knowledge and skill to inspect and regulate the heater, that they reasonably relied upon an independent contractor for proper installation, and that they reasonably relied upon an independent contractor for repairs. The evidence before the trial judge discloses that defendants hired one Olaf Thorsen to adjust and repair the electric hot water heater. The evidence before the trial judge discloses that Olaf Thorsen is not a licensed electrician and is not experienced as an electrician, but is licensed and experienced only as a plumber. The evidence before the trial judge further discloses that the repair and maintenance on the electric hot water heater required working with, installing, and adjusting electrical wiring, electrical heating elements, and a thermostat to control the flow of electrical current. At the time of the accident in question. G.S. § 87-43 provided in part as follows: "No person, firm or corporation shall engage in the business of installing, maintaining, altering or repairing within the State of North Carolina any electric wiring, devices, appliances or equipment unless such person, firm or corporation shall have received from the Board of Examiners of Electrical Contractors an electrical contractor's license: * * *."

Plumbers who are answerable only for the result of their work are generally regarded as independent contractors. The general rule is that an employer or contractee is not liable for the torts of an independent contractor committed in the performance of the contracted work. However, a condition prescribed to relieve an employer from liability for the negligent acts of an independent contractor employed by him is that he shall have exercised due care to secure a competent contractor for the work. Therefore, if it appears that the employer either knew, or by the exercise of reasonable care might have ascertained that the contractor was not properly qualified to undertake the work, he may be held liable for the negligent acts of the contractor. "An employer is subject to liability for physical harm to third persons caused by his failure to exercise reasonable care to employ a competent and careful contractor (a) to do work which will involve a risk of physical harm unless it is skillfully and carefully done, or (b) to perform any duty which the employer owes to third persons." Restatement, Second, Torts, § 411. The evidence of the repairs and maintenance performed on the electrical system of defendants' electric hot water heater by Olaf Thorsen tends to affirm the incompetence of defendants' independent contractor as an electrician.

This evidence before the trial judge tends to show a specific act of negligence on the part of defendants in failing to secure the services of a competent independent contractor and tends to strengthen the inference that the cause of the accident was defendants' negligence. The application of the doctrine of *res ispa loquitur* to this case should not be denied because the evidence tends to show a specific act of negligence on the part of defendants.

The entry of summary judgment was error.

Reversed.

VAUGHN and GRAHAM, JJ., concur.

OUR USE OF CASES

In the following chapters "cases", as we have been discussing them, have been inserted to illustrate points and should be read carefully as they are encountered. To assist in understanding them it is good policy to create a "case brief" for each. An example follows.

CASE BRIEFS

As each case, or portion of a case is encountered, "brief" it, answering the following questions:

1. What was the citation of the case?
2. What state or federal court was it decided in?
3. Briefly state the facts of the case—how or why did it get into court.?
4. What was the decision of the court?
5. How would you summarize this decision so it could be stated as a point of law in one short sentence?

If you care to do so, the briefing can be carried out by underlining the text, using the margins for notes.

In addition to cases, we will also make use of statutes.

STATUTES

To illustrate what a statute looks like, and to see how some of them are used in the lodging industry, examine Figure 5-1 closely.

FIGURE 5-1

THE RATE PER DAY OF THIS ROOM

Room No. **213**

For 1 Person **21 00**   For 3 Persons **30 00**

For 2 Persons **26 00**   For 4 Persons **34 00**

NOTICE
Check-Out Time Is 12 Noon

Kindly Notify The Office If Your Departure Will Be Delayed.

CODE OF VIRGINIA

Sec. 35-10—Duties of Inn-Keepers; Limitation of Liability

It shall be the duty of keepers of hotels, inns, and ordinaries to exercise due care and diligence in providing honest servants and employees, and to take every reasonable precaution to protect the person and property of their guests and boarders. No such keeper of hotel, inn or ordinary shall be held liable in a greater sum than three hundred dollars, for the loss of any wearing apparel, baggage or other property not hereinafter mentioned, belonging either to a guest or boarder, when such loss takes place from the room or rooms occupied by said guest or boarder, and no keeper of a hotel, inn or ordinary shall be held liable for any loss by any guest or boarder of jewelry, money or other valuables of like nature belonging to any guest or boarder if such keeper shall have posted in the room or rooms occupied by guests or boarders in a conspicuous place, and in the office of such hotel, inn or ordinary a notice stating that jewelry, money and other valuables of like nature must be deposited in the office of such hotel, inn or ordinary unless such loss shall take place from such office after such deposit is made. The keeper of any such hotel, inn or ordinary shall not be obliged to receive from any one guest for deposit, in such office, any property hereinbefore described, exceeding a total value of five hundred dollars.

Sec. 35-11—Liability Where Guest Failed to Lock or Bolt Doors

If the keeper of such hotel, inn or ordinary shall provide suitable locks or bolts on the doors of the sleeping rooms used by his guests, and suitable fastening on the transoms and windows of said rooms, and shall keep a copy of this and the preceding section conspicuously posted in each of said rooms, together with a notice requiring said guests or boarders to keep said doors locked or bolted, and transoms fastened, and if said guests or boarders fail to lock or bolt said door or doors, or to fasten said windows and transoms, then the said keeper of such hotel, inn or ordinary, shall not be liable for any property taken from such room or rooms in consequence of such failure on the part of such guest or boarder; but the burden of proof shall be upon such keeper to show that he has complied with the provisions of this section, and that such guest or guests have failed to comply with these requirements. Nothing in this section shall be construed to in any wise exempt the keeper, or keepers, of hotels, inns and ordinaries from being liable for the value of any property of guests taken or stolen from any room therein by any employee or agent of said keeper or keepers.

The principles behind this notice taken from a Holiday Inn in Richmond, Virginia, will be explored in detail in coming chapters. Sections 35-10 and 35-11 of the Virginia Code are quoted in this notice.

Next, let's find out something about the place where cases originate—the courts.

COURTS

A "court" has been defined as " . . . a tribunal officially assembled under authority of law at the appropiate time and place for the administration of justice;"[4] " . . . an agency of the sovereign created by it directly or indirectly under its authority, consisting of one or more officers, established and maintained for the purpose of hearing and determining issues of law and fact regarding legal rights and the alleged violations thereof, and of applying the sanctions of law, authorized to exercise its powers in due course of law at times and places previously determined by lawful authority."[5] A characteristic of courts that must be understood is that "it is a passive forum for adjusting disputes and has no power to investigate facts or to initiate proceedings."[6]

CLASSIFICATIONS OF COURTS

Courts can be "courts of record" or "not of record." In the former, court reporters are found who make transcripts of testimony and proceedings. Courts can be "superior" or "inferior", pointing out that some have powers over those below them. Courts can be "civil," and thus handle civil matters, and others, "criminal" courts. Some are "equity" courts and others "law" courts. In smaller, rural jurisdictions, one court may have many of these classifications. There are many specialized courts such as courts of admiralty, bankruptcy, claims and others.

In the following, you will become acquainted with the constitutional provisions by which courts were established in the Virginias. These provisions are typical of what is found in the constitutions of other states.

ARTICLE VIII
Judicial Department

The judicial power of the State shall be vested in a supreme court of appeals, in circuit courts and the judges thereof, in such inferior tribunals as are authorized.

Supreme Court of Appeals

The supreme court of appeals shall consist of five judges, any three of whom shall be a quorum for the transaction of business. They shall be elected by the voters of the State and hold their office for the term of twelve years, unless sooner removed in the manner prescribed by this Constitution, except that the judges in office when this article takes effect, shall remain therein until the expiration of their present term of office.

Scope of Jurisdiction

It shall have original jurisdiction in cases of habeas corpus, mandamus, and prohibition. It shall have appellate jurisdiction in civil cases where the matter in controversy, exclusive of costs, is of greater value or amount than one hundred dollars; in controversies concerning the title or boundaries of land, the probate of wills, the appointment or qualification of a personal representative, guardian, committee or curator; or concerning a mill, road, way, ferry or landing; or the right of a corporation or county to levy tolls or taxes; and, also, in cases of quo warranto, habeas corpus, mandamus, certiorari and prohibition, and in cases involving freedom or the constitutionality of a law. It shall have appellate jurisdiction in criminal cases where there has been a conviction for felony or misdemeanor in a circuit court, and where a conviction has been had in any inferior court and been affirmed in a circuit court, and in cases relating to the public revenue, the right of appeal shall belong to the State as well as the defendant, and such other appellate jurisdiction, in both civil and criminal cases, as may be prescribed by law.

Binding Authority of Decisions

No decision rendered by the supreme court of appeals shall be considered as binding authority upon any of the inferior courts of this State, except in the particular case decided, unless such decision is concurred in by at least three judges of said court.

Reversal or Affirmance of Judgments

When a judgment or decree is reversed or affirmed by the supreme court of appeals, every point fairly arising upon the record of the case shall be considered and decided; and the reasons therefor shall be concisely stated in writing and preserved with the record of the case; and it shall be the duty of the court to prepare a syllabus of the points adjudicated in each case concurred in by three of the judges thereof, which shall be prefixed to the published report of the case.

Writ of Error, Supersedeas and Appeal

A writ of error, supersedeas, or appeal shall be allowed only by the supreme court of appeals, or a judge thereof, upon a petition assigning error in the judgment or proceedings of the inferior court and then only after said court or judge shall have examined and considered the record and assignment of errors, and is satisfied that there is error in the same, or that it presents a point proper for the consideration of the supreme court of appeals.

Provision for Filling Supreme Court Vacancies

If from any cause a vacancy shall occur in the supreme court of appeals, the governor shall issue a writ of election to fill such vacancy at the next general election for the residue of the term, and in the meantime he shall fill such vacancy by appointment until a judge is elected and qualified. But if the unexpired term be less than two years the governor shall fill such vacancy by appointment for the unexpired term.

Officers of Supreme Court

The officers of the supreme court of appeals, except the reporter, shall be appointed by the court, or in vacation by the judges thereof, with the power of removal; their duties and compensation shall be prescribed by law.

Terms of Supreme Court

There shall be at least two terms of the supreme court of appeals held annually at such times and places as may be prescribed by law.

Circuit Courts

The State shall be divided into thirty-three circuits. For the circuit hereinafter called the first, two judges shall be elected, and for each of the other circuits one judge shall be elected by the voters thereof. Each of the judges so elected shall hold his office for the term of eight years unless sooner removed in the manner prescribed in this Constitution. The judges of the circuit courts in office when this article takes effect, shall remain therein until the expiration of the term for which they have been elected in the circuits in which they may respectively reside, unless sooner removed as aforesaid. A vacancy in the office of a judge of the circuit court shall be filled in the same manner as is provided for in the case of a vacancy in the office of a judge of the supreme court of appeals. During his continuance in office the judge of a circuit court shall reside in the circuit of which he is judge. The business of the first circuit may be apportioned between the judges thereof, and such judges may hold courts in the same county or in different counties within the circuit at the same time or at different times as may be prescribed by law.

Terms of Circuit Court

A circuit court shall be held in every county in the State at least three times in each year, and provisions may be made by law for holding special terms of said court. A judge of any circuit may hold the courts in another circuit.

Circuit Court Jurisdiction

The circuit court shall have the supervisions and control of all proceedings before justices and other inferior tribunals, by mandamus, prohibition and certiorari. They shall, except in cases confined exclusively by this Constitution to some other tribunal, have original and general jurisdiction of all matters at law where the amount in controversy, exclusive of interest, exceeds fifty dollars; of all cases of habeas corpus, mandamus, quo warranto, and prohibition; and of all cases in equity, and of all crimes and misdemeanors. They shall have appellate jurisdiction in all cases, civil and criminal, where an appeal, writ of error or supersedeas may be allowed to the judgment or proceedings of any inferior tribunal. They shall also have such other jurisdiction, whether supervisory, original, appellate, or concurrent, as is or may be prescribed by law.

Rearrangement of State into Circuits

The legislature may rearrange the circuits herein provided for at any session thereof, next preceding any general election of the judges of said circuits, and after the year one thousand eight hundred and eighty-eight, may, at any such session, increase or diminish the number thereof.

Special Terms and Judges of Circuit Courts

The legislature shall provide by law for holding regular and special terms of the circuit courts, where from any cause the judge shall fail to attend, or if in attendance, cannot properly preside.

Commissioning Judges; Salaries and Expenses; Practicing Law; Holding Other Office

All judges shall be commissioned by the governor. The salary of a judge of the supreme court of appeals shall be thirty two thousand two hundred dollars per annum, and that of a judge of the circuit court shall be thirty one thousand eight hundred dollars per annum; and each shall receive the same mileage as members of the legislature: Provided, that Ohio county may pay an additional sum per annum to the judges of the circuit court thereof; but such allowance shall not be increased or diminished during the term of office of the judges to whom it may have been made. No judge, during his term of office, shall practice the profession of law or hold any other office, appointment or public trust, under this or any other government, and the acceptance thereof shall vacate his judicial office. Nor shall he, during his continuance therein, be eligible to any political office.

How Judges May Be Removed

Judges may be removed from office by a concurrent vote of both houses of the legislature, when from age, disease, mental or bodily infirmity or intemperance, they are incapable of discharging the duties of their office. But two thirds of all the members elected to each house must concur in such vote, and the cause of removal shall be entered upon the journal of each house. The judge against whom the legislature may be about to proceed shall receive notice thereof, accompanied with the cause alleged for his removal, at least twenty days before the day on which action is proposed to be taken therein.

Clerks of Circuit Courts

The voters of each county shall elect a clerk of the circuit court, whose term of office shall be six years; his duties and compensation and the manner of removing him from office shall be prescribed by law; and when a vacancy shall occur in the office, the circuit court or the judge thereof in vacation shall fill the same by appointment until the next general election. In any case in respect to which the clerk shall be so situated as to make it improper for him to act, the said court shall appoint a clerk to act therein. The clerks of said courts in office when this article takes effect, shall remain therein for the term for which they were elected, unless sooner removed in the manner prescribed by law.

Courts of Limited Jurisdiction

The legislature may establish courts of limited jurisdiction within any county, incorporated city, town or village, with the right of appeal to the circuit court, subject to such limitations as may be prescribed by law; and all courts of limited jurisdiction heretofore established in any county, incorporated city, town or village shall remain as at present constituted until otherwise provided by law. The municipal court of Wheeling shall continue in existence until otherwise provided by law, and said court and the judge thereof, shall exercise the powers and jurisdiction heretofore conferred upon them; and appeals in civil cases from said court shall lie directly in the supreme court of appeals.

(While the following provision seems useless today, it is still part of the constitution of several of our states.)

Regarding Participation in Civil War

No citizen of this State who aided or participated in the late war between the government of the United States and a part of the people thereof, on either side, shall be liable in any proceeding, civil or criminal; nor shall his property be seized or sold under final process issued upon judgments or decrees heretofore rendered, or otherwise, because of any act done in accordance with the usages of civilized warfare in the prosecution of said war. The legislature shall provide, by general laws, for giving full force and effect to this section.

Parts of Common Law Effective

Such parts of the common law, and of the laws of this State as are in force when this article goes into operation, and are not repugnant thereto, shall be and continue the law of the State until altered or repealed by the legislature. All civil and criminal suits and proceedings pending in the former circuit courts of this State, shall remain and be proceeded in before the circuit courts of the counties in which they were pending.

Not only do state constitutions create a court system as we have seen above, they also contain provisions for administrative bodies, often called "county courts." The provisions of the above state constitution continues:

County Courts

There shall be in each county of the State a county court, composed of three commissioners, and two of said commissioners shall be a quorum for the transaction of business. It shall hold four regular sessions in each year, and at such times as may be fixed upon and entered of record by the said court. Provisions may be made by law for holding special sessions of said court.

Terms of Office of County Commissioners

The commissioners shall be elected by the voters of the county, and hold their office for the term of six years, except that at the first meeting of said commissioners they shall designate by lot, or otherwise, in such manner as they may determine, one of their number, who shall hold his office for the term of two years, one for four years, and one for six years, so that one shall be elected every two years. But no two of said commissioners shall be elected from the same magisterial district. And if two or more persons residing in the same district shall receive the greater number of votes cast at any election, then only the one of such persons receiving the highest number shall be declared elected, and the person living in another district, who shall receive the next highest number of votes, shall be declared elected. Said commissioners shall annually elect one of their number as president, and each shall receive ten dollars per day for his services in court, to be paid out of the county treasury.

Powers of County Courts

The county courts, through their clerks, shall have the custody of all deeds and other papers presented for record in their counties, and the same shall be preserved therein, or otherwise disposed of, as now is, or may be prescribed by law. They shall have jurisdiction in all matters of probate, the appointment and qualification of personal representatives, guardians, committees, curators, and the settlement of their accounts, and in all matters relating to apprentices. They shall also, under such regulations as may be prescribed by law, have the superintendence and administration of the internal police and fiscal affairs of their counties, including the establishment and regulation of roads, ways, bridges, public landings, ferries and mills, with authority to lay and disburse the county levies. Provided, that no license for the sale of intoxicating liquors in any incorporated city, town or village, shall be granted without the consent of the municipal authorities thereof, first had and obtained. They shall, in all cases of contest, judge of the election, qualification and returns of their own members, and of all county and district officers, subject to such regulations, by appeal or otherwise, as may be prescribed by law. Such courts may exercise such other powers, and perform such other duties, not of a judicial nature, as may be prescribed by law. And provision may be made under such regulations as may be prescribed by law, for the probate of wills, and for the appointment and qualification of personal representatives, guardians, committees and curators during the recess of the regular sessions of the county court. Such tribunals as have been heretofore established by the legislature under and by virtue of the thirty-fourth section of the eighth article of the Constitution of one thousand eight hundred and seventy-two, for police and fiscal purposes, shall, until otherwise provided by law, remain and continue as at present constituted in the countries in which they have been respectively established, and shall be and act as to police and fiscal matters in lieu of the county court created by this article until otherwise provided by law. And, until otherwise provided by law, such clerk as is mentioned in the twenty-sixth section of this article, shall exercise any powers and discharge any duties heretofore conferred on, or required of, any court or tribunal established for judicial purposes under the said article and section of the Constitution of one thousand eight hundred and seventy-two, or the clerk of such court or tribunal respectively, respecting the recording and preservation of deeds and other papers presented for record, matters of probate, the appointment and qualification of personal representatives, guardians, committees, curators and the settlement of their accounts, and in all matters relating to apprentices.

QUESTIONS

1. Why are state *trial court* cases not reported in the reporter system?
2. Why do New York and California have extra reporters?
3. "Res ispo loquitur" means "the thing speaks for itself." Why was the plaintiff in the *Sloan* case relying upon this legal doctrine?
4. Why must an innkeeper use care when hiring outsiders to do repair work at the inn?
5. Why are the two Virginia statutes quoted verbatim by the Holiday Inn in Richmond as set out in Figure 5-1?
6. Who decides how many terms a year a given court will have?
7. Where does one look to find the jurisdiction or power of a given court?
8. Why are judges prohibited from practicing law?
9. Why was the Civil War provision written into the state constitution as set out on page 69?
10. Distinguish a "county court" from a "circuit court."

ENDNOTES

1. *Ex Parte Chesser,* 93 Fla. 590, 112 So. 87, 90 (1920).
2. *John P. Agnew Co. Inc. v. Hooge,* App. D.C. 69 App. D.C. 116, 99 F. 2d 349, 351.
3. *State v. McDonough,* 129 Conn. 483, 29 A. 2d 582, 584.
4. *In re Carter's Estate.* 254 Pa. 518, 99 A. 58.
5. *Isbill v. Stoval.* Tex Civ. App. 92 S.W. 2d 1067, 1070.
6. *Sale v. Railroad Commission.* 15 Cal. 2d 612, 140 P. 2d 38, 41.

6

Hospitality Contracts—
Conventional

In this chapter we will examine the basic principles that are found in one of the most extensive and well developed bodies of our substantive law—the law of contract. At the outset however, we must recognize that what is discussed in this chapter must be supplemented by and distinguished from what we will learn in the next chapter about "Sales Contracts." Here we will be concerned with all contracts *other* than those that apply to the *sale* of *goods between merchants*, the subject matter of the next chapter.

In routine day to day purchases of goods by hotel/motel managers and others in the travel industry, the principles of sales contracts as found in the next chapter will find application. In hiring employees, buying land and buildings, contracting for new buildings and making building repairs, the principles of this chapter will apply. The latter contracts will be referred to as "traditional contracts" to distinguish them from "sales contracts" of the next chapter.

A good way to begin is by an examination of the definition of contract.

DEFINITION

A leading authority on the subject tells us that "a contract is a promise, or set of promises, for the breach of which the law gives a remedy, or the performance of which the law in some way recognizes as a duty".[1] This definition points out that a promise or promises are needed and that the "law" is involved in the contract. A contract creates obligations when it comes into being; it usually concerns property or something of value, and it creates rights that can be addressed to a court for enforcement. If the contract requires skill, exercise of special knowledge or judgment, it is a personal service contract. If it concerns property, it is a "property contract."

There are various ways in which traditional contracts can be classified.

CLASSIFICATIONS

Contracts can be joint or several, bilateral or unilateral, executory or executed, express or implied, and void, voidable and unenforceable.

JOINT AND SEVERAL

A joint contract is one in which A and B bind themselves to C so that both are responsible for the obligations assumed. Both must be sued by C if they fail to meet their obligations. A "several contract" is one in which either A or B may be sued for breach, at the election of C. This classification is important when suit becomes necessary. The courts will look to the form of the contract to determine if it is joint or several, and will apply the rules of contract construction in making this determination.

BILATERAL OR UNILATERAL

If A and B enter into a contract and each makes binding promises to the other, the contract is "bilateral"—or two-party. If an "offeror"—the one who makes an offer—receives no promise in return, the situation is "unilateral" and can be dangerous for the other. For example, A says "cut down that tree and carry away all debris and I will pay you $200." This is a promise for an act and does not create a binding obligation on either—at least not at that point. If B cuts down the tree and removes the debris, the act requested is completed and A must pay the sum promised. The danger lies in the fact that A can revoke the offer at anytime before the debris is removed. This could leave B with no way to recover payment for the work done before the offer was revoked.

EXECUTORY AND EXECUTED

An executory contract is one in which one or both parties must yet perform. That is, something remains to be done in reference to the promises made. An executed contract is one that has been fully performed with nothing left for either to do. A promise to sell land is an executory contract. After the deed is transferred and the price paid, the contract is executed.

EXPRESS OR IMPLIED

An express contract is one in which the promises and terms are stated by the parties. Implied contracts arise "from mutual agreement and intent to promise but where the agreement and promise have not been expressed in words. Such contracts are true contracts and have sometimes been called contracts implied in fact."[2]

VOID, VOIDABLE AND UNENFORCEABLE

A void contract is technically no contract at all. It may be a contract that the parties felt was valid but that has been held by a court to be invalid. "Void Contract" is thus a redundacy. A "voidable" contract is one that is valid but has built within it the legal right of one or both of the parties to avoid all obligations under the contract. A, a minor, buys a car from B, an adult. A can avoid the contract because of A's age and B can do nothing about it. However, until A avoids, B is bound to perform with A. Thus a voidable contract may become executed and if not set aside before A reaches majority, or a reasonable time thereafter, it is as valid as any other executed contract.

An unenforceable contract is one that for some reason, cannot be enforced by one against another. A contract may be unenforceable in part and enforceable in the balance. For example, A contracts with B and the written contract contains six provisions. Two of these provisions are illegal but the other four are not. The contract is unenforceable as to the two provisions and valid as to the balance.

Turning from classifications, it becomes necessary to examine the legal requirements of a binding contract.

THE STATUTE OF FRAUDS

Each state has statutes that require that certain contracts be in written form and signed by "the party or parties to be charged." Historically such statues were called "Statutes of Frauds," because they were designed to prevent fraud in the use of contract law, and they are called this now. Examples of contracts that must be in writing and signed include:

1. Contracts involving the sale of real estate or any interest in real estate.
2. Contracts that cannot be performed in one year.
3. Promises of one person to pay the debt of another person.
4. Leases for more than one year.
5. Contracts in which one person promises another money or property if that person will enter into marriage with the other.
6. Promises of those who handle deceased persons estates, to pay the debts of creditors out of their own pocket if there is not enough in the estate for that purpose.

FORM OF CONTRACT

No particular words are necessary to show promises or the intention of the parties as it relates to those promises. With the exception of those contracts that must be in writing under the statute of frauds, oral contracts are as binding as written contracts. For example, a hotel manager can hire an assistant manager orally and the terms agreed upon are binding. Employment contracts are an exception to the statute of frauds-one year provision. Even if the employment may last for ten years, it *could* have ended in the first year by the death of the employee. Therefore it is *not* a contract that *cannot be performed* in one year—a technical point.

Of course, employment contracts should, as a matter of good business practice, be in writing and signed by the parties to the agreement—but they do not have to be.

REQUIREMENTS OF A BINDING CONTRACT

The traditional contract has six requirements: offer, acceptance, mutuality, consideration, competent parties and legality. If all requirements are present a contract comes in being. If one or more is missing the contract fails.

OFFER

An offer is made by the "offeror" and is most often a statement of what that person is willing to do if the other is willing to do what is requested. While an offer is a promise, it is conditional. The promise may lapse if not accepted within a reasonable time, or it may be revoked by the one who made it, provided the revocation comes before an acceptance. It must come to the mind of the offeree—the one to whom it is directed. An offer may be rejected by the offeree, or the offeree may make a "counter-offer" which is treated as a rejection of the offer. Mere silence on the part of the offeree is treated as nothing at law and thus the offer will lapse after the passage of a reasonable time.

An offer must be definite in its terms. If there is an offer and an acceptance, but the terms are so indefinite that they cannot be determined, the court will hold that there is no valid contract.

ACCEPTANCE

An acceptance comes when there is some assent that the offeree wants to be bound in a contract with the offeror. If the offer specifies a time by which acceptance must be made, an acceptance after that time is ineffective. If no time limit is specified, an offer must be accepted within a reasonable time. Acceptance comes too late if an offer lapses, is revoked or rejected. If a dispute arises as to whether or not an offer was accepted within a reasonable time, it becomes a question of fact for a jury to determine.

Just as with the offer, an acceptance must be communicated. If before an acceptance is received the offer is revoked, the acceptance fails.

An acceptance can be made in the form in which an offer is made. That is, if an oral offer is made, the acceptance can be oral. If the offer is in writing, the acceptance *should* be in writing. If an offer is made by mail and acceptance is also made by mail, the acceptance is effective *when mailed*. The law of agency causes this result. The offeror chose the mail, so when the acceptance was mailed it was in the hands of the offeror's agent and thus effective at that time. If the offeror specifies that the acceptance will not be effective until received, then that provision controls. In a face to face situation a nod of the head may be a good acceptance.

An acceptance must conform to the offer, and if it varies the terms of the offer, it will fail. The offer must also be accepted in its totality or not at all. An attempt to accept part, would vary the terms of the offer and is not permitted. If parties exchange letters and the terms in those letters are not on "all fours", there is no contract. The letters are merely proposals of each to contract with the other. The court will treat them as "negotiations." If the terms in the letters agree, a valid contract will result.

MUTUALITY

A contract implies mutual obligations.[3] What "mutuality" means at law will vary with the types of contract situations and the intention of the parties. It at least implies that the parties have agreed to assume obligations that move from each of them to the other. In a situation where there is a promise for a promise, the mutuality is obvious.

CONSIDERATION

"Consideration" has been defined as "a benefit to the party promising or a loss or detriment to the party to whom a promise is made."[4] It is thought of by the court as "reasons for enforcing promises," and it does not need to be expressed in, or equated to economic value. It can be doing nothing if that is what the parties bargain for. For centuries, it has been essential for consideration to be present in traditional contracts (at least Anglo-American contracts) and this will continue to be true in the future. In some states, the applying of a seal to a contract (a formal contract) will supply the consideration. In sales contracts, the law has moved sharply away from consideration, as we shall see.

While consideration must be present, there is no requirement that it be *adequate*. The parties to a contract are considered to be the sole judges of value as it relates to consideration. This assumes that there has been no fraud, mistake, duress or undue influence in the creation of the contract. A promise to sell a million dollar building for $1.00 would be adequate consideration if that is what the parties in fact bargained for. Many a parent has deeded valuable real estate to their children in consideration of "love and affection." In short, contract law does not require that value be given for value, only that consideration in some form, be present. Anything that confers a benefit on the party to whom the promise is made, or loss or inconvenience to the party making the promise, is sufficient. Consideration could be an extenstion of payment on a note—or the giving up of smoking. The consideration does not have to have any interest to the party making the promise. It is sufficient if it affects the interest of the party to whom the promise is made.

As a black letter rule, mutual promises standing alone provides the consideration to support them. However, agreeing to do what one is already bound to do will not supply consideration, since it provides no legal reason to enforce a promise. In addition, something that has occured *before* a promise is made will not support that promise. For example, A does a favor for B in May. In June, A enters into an agreement with B on the strength of the prior favor. That will not support the later promises. Consideration must relate to the present or future.

Other matters that have been held to supply sufficient consideration include support and maintenance, withholding competition and giving up the right to file a lawsuit.

"Failure of consideration" occurs when what is promised does not materialize as agreed. This in turn causes the contract to fail.

In addition to the four items discussed, a binding contract must be between parties of contractual capacity and must have legal purpose.

COMPETENT PARTIES

Both parties to a contract must be of the age of majority, functioning free from duress, fraud or mistake and be under no mental disability that would render one incapable of knowing the nature and consequences of ones act. An incompetent party can cause a contract to be void or voidable depending upon the circumstances. The following are considered to be incompetent to contract; infants, those who are adjudicated insane, intoxicated persons, those under the influence of narcotics, and those who, because of the nature of the surrounding circumstances, are not capable of exercising, normal, rational judgment. For example, a kidnap victim under threat of death would not be competent to contract for the sale of his or her property at that time.

LEGAL PURPOSE

A binding contract must be for a legal purpose. Courts will not force parties to do illegal acts even if they had contracted to do them.

PERFORMANCE AND BREACH

In the countless number of contracts entered into yearly, the largest percentage are fully performed without problems arising. It is to those small percentage of contracts where disputes arise that we will briefly turn.

BREACH

One has the *power* to refuse to keep a contract promise. If this is done, the courts can only compensate the other for any loss that results from the failure to keep the promise. But one does not have a *contractual right* to do this. A breach has been defined as anything so material and important as in truth and fairness will defeat the essential purposes of the parties to a contract.[5]

Where a breach occurs, damages to compensate the other for loss are generally available. However, the other may not be able to prove actual loss and thus can recover nothing.

ANTICIPATORY BREACH

If one party to a contract has made it clear in advance that that person will not perform when the time arises, the other can "anticipate" the breach and sue at once.[6] But one must make certain that the facts are correct, because if they are not, the anticipation may in itself be a breach by that party.

REFUSAL TO PERFORM

If when time of performance arrives, one party refuses to perform, that party is guilty of the first breach and can be held responsible for loss caused by the refusal. But if one refuses to perform a minor part of a contract, this may not excuse the other from performing.

If a breach occurs because of fraud on the part of one party, the injured party may sue in tort or contract. If one proceeds in a contract action for the loss suffered, a later tort action will be barred since an "election" has been made.

DAMAGES RECOVERABLE

What can be recovered because of a breach of contract are damages or loss that fairly, reasonably and naturally should arise in the ordinary course from such breach.[7] One will not be allowed to escape liability where the loss will be substantial but not capable of precise determination. The court will allow a "reasonable standards" measurement to be used with the matter being a question of fact for a jury to determine. A court will not permit one to suffer a wrong without providing a remedy. If proof of damages must be based on pure speculation, however, the proof will fail.

LIQUIDATED DAMAGES

The parties to a contract may agree in advance what the damages will be in the event of a later breach. Such provisions are enforceable provided they bear a reasonable relationship to actual loss and are not in the form of a penalty. The term "liquidated" tells us that the damages are "set" and thus not a subject of speculation or proof.

To illustrate, Motel Zero contracts with Ace Construction to remodel the pool. The price agreed upon is $18,000, which includes all costs and labor. The work to be completed no later than May 31, the customary pool opening time.

The parties agree that if the work is not completed by that date, the construction firm will forfeit $50 for each day the firm is late. Since the motel sells outside pool memberships at $100 per family, the agreed upon damages would appear to be reasonable and would be enforced by the court. If the pool is 30 days late in the completion, the motel can deduct $1,500 from the final payment.

If a liquidated damage clause is not included in a contract, and even if a completion date is spelled out, the passage of that time without completion of the contract will generally *not be held* to be a breach. The exception to this would be if the contract makes "time of the essence."

"TIME IS OF THE ESSENCE"

If these are included in a contract, the courts will treat the date specified as being the precise time by which performance must be completed. Otherwise the completion date will be treated as an approximate date.

In some contract situations, the legal remedy of damages (dollars) may not be sufficent. A second remedy is provided by "equity".

SPECIFIC PERFORMANCE

If the subject matter of a contract is unique, then upon breach by one party the other may ask a judge to specifically require the other to perform. This remedy is frequently used in real estate sales contracts where one refuses to perform as promised. Since each parcel of real estate is unique the remedy is available.

To illustrate, A agrees to sell B a restaurant, together with all fixtures, inventory as of a specified date, and "goodwill." The sales price is to be $750,000 and time has been made of the essence. A then refuses to sell and B goes to court in an attempt to obtain a court order to order A to convey the restaurant and land described in the contract. In the absence of fraud, misrepresentation, or similar acts on the part of B, the court has the power to order A to convey title as agreed, upon tender of the $750,000 by B. If A refuses, the court can hold A in "contempt of court" and can order A jailed until the conveyance is made.

Specific performance cannot be used in personal service contracts or in any situation in which supervision would be needed to carry out the contract. A court cannot place itself in the position of an overseer. The only remedy would be an action for damages in such cases.

To complete our discussion of conventional contracts, we will examine implied contracts, illegal contracts, and contracts that violate public policy. A look will then be taken at some actual cases.

IMPLIED CONTRACT

An express contract must be distinguished from a contract implied in fact and one implied in law. The principle involved in implied contracts is an equitable one that holds that one should not unjustly enrich onself at the expense of another.

A contract implied in fact is a true contract, the terms of which will be inferred from the circumstances. When one confers benefits upon another, which the other knows of and should pay for, the law implies an agreement that such payment will be made. An express contract is thus distinguishable from one implied in fact. In the former, the terms are expressly agreed upon. In the latter, the terms and conditions are implied from the conduct of the parties. For example, B knows that A wants the debris removed from the swimming pool repair site. There is no express agreement on this removal. B removes the debris and A refuses to pay. B has a contract action against A on the implied contract.

Contracts *implied in law* are *not* true contracts and are resorted to by the courts for purposes of remedy only. Such situations are often referred to as "quasi-contracts" and will be created by a court regardless of the intention of the parties. The widest application would be found in situations where, if they were not used, an injustice would occur. The basic requirement is that the obligations involved would be of the type that would have been enforced under common law by a contractual action.

As a general rule, where there is an express contract, an implied contract in fact or in law will never arise. The express contract controls. There is no need to imply a contract where one exists expressly.

ILLEGAL CONTRACTS

An illegal contract is one that has as its object an illegal purpose. As a general rule, an illegal contract is void—not voidable—and can never be the subject of a court action for breach of that contract. There can be no enforcement of it in law or in equity whether the illegality existed at the outset or "intervened" later. For example, a subsequent statute may make the terms of a prior contract unlawful. In addition, "when an illegal modification of a lawful contract is attempted, the modification is a nullity and the contract is unscathed."[8]

An illegal contract should be distinguished, however, from one that is against "public policy."

CONTRACTS AGAINST PUBLIC POLICY

"Public policy" refers to a standard that relates to the requirements of the public welfare. A contract that would violate those requirements would be against that policy. "Whatever tends to injustice or oppression, restraint of liberty, commerce, and natural or legal rights; whatever tends to obstruction of justice, or to the violation of a statute; and whatever is against good morals, when made the object of a contract, is against public policy and therefore void and not susceptible of enforcement."[9] Thus, while a contract against public policy *may be illegal*, it is not so limited.

Whenever a court must look at such a matter, the court will not look for a precise definition of "public policy" and will not hesitate in its practical application to the law of contracts.[10] An example of a contract against public policy would be one in which "a party stipulates for his exemption from liability for the consequences of his own negligence."[11] Such a contract is not permitted at law. Other examples include contracts to influence legislation, the joining of companies to circumvent the effect of restrictive statutes and a contract by a servant promising to release the master before injury occurs to others. (*After* injury occurs, such an agreement may be legal provided the servants have the means to personally meet the obligation).

The following cases illustrate conventional contract principles in three hospitality situations. The first is an old case but would still find application in certain hospitality functions today. The second involves the sale of a restaurant and the third involves a caterer at a banquet.

AARON v. WARD
203 N.Y. 351 (1911).

APPEAL, by permission, from a judgment of the Appellate Division of the Supreme Court in the second judicial department, entered March 21, 1910, affirming a judgment of the Municipal Court of the city of New York in favor of plaintiff.

The nature of the action and the facts, so far as material, are stated in the opinion.

In all cases of breach of contract (breach of promise of marriage excepted) the plaintiff's loss is measued by the benefit to him of having the contract performed, and this is, therefore, the true measure of damages. The cases where actions *ex contractu* have been brought against carriers and transportation companies wherein damages have been allowed for humiliation, indignities and mental suffering or anguish are highly exceptional in their character, and arise altogether out of the peculiar nature and character of the particular contract under consideration.

The business conducted by the defendant was purely private in its nature, and the ticket of admission by the plaintiff was entirely revocable at the pleasure of the defendant, and the latter could, if necessary, expel the plaintiff from the premises with all reasonable force.

The trial court having found for the plaintiff it had a right to award the plaintiff compensatory damages and was not limited to the actual loss of money-sustained which in this case was twenty-five cents, the price of the ticket. The case at bar is analogous to that of a passenger for wrongful treatment by a common carrier and to that of a guest for injuries to feelings by an innkeeper. The claim that the business of keeping bathing houses for hire is not of the same public nature as that of a common carrier or an innkeeper and may be said to be a private enterprise may be sound without, however, affecting the rule as to the measure of damages.

CULLEN, Ch. J. The defendant was the proprietor of a bathing establishment on the beach at Coney Island. The plaintiff, intending to take a bath in the surf, purchased a ticket from the defendant's employees for the sum of twenty-five cents, and took her position in a line of the defendant's patrons leading to a window at which the ticket entitled her to receive, upon its surrender, a key admitting her to a bathhouse. When she approached the window a dispute arose between her and the defendant's employees as to the right of another person not in the line to have a key given to him in advance of the plaintiff. As a result of this dispute plaintiff was ejected from the defendant's premises, the agents of the latter refusing to furnish her with the accommodations for which she had contracted. It is not necessary to discuss the merits of the dispute or narrate its details as the questions of fact involved in that matter have been decided in plaintiff's favor by the Municipal Court, in which she subsequently brought suit, and that judgment has been unanimously affirmed by the Appellate Division. The plaintiff was awarded $250 damages against the defendant's contention that she was not entitled to any recovery in excess of the sum paid for the ticket, and the correctness of the defendant's contention is the only question presented on this appeal.

The action is for a breach of the defendant's contract and not for a tortious expulsion. It is so denominated in the complaint and was necessarily so brought as the Municipal Court has no jurisdiction over an action for an assault. It is contended for the defendant that as the action was on contract, the plaintiff was not entitled to any damages for the indignity of her expulsion from the defendant's establishment. It may be admitted that, as a general rule, mental suffering resulting from a breach of contract is not a subject of compensation, but the rule is not universal. It is the settled law of this state that a passenger may recover damages for insulting and slanderous words uttered by the conductor of a railway car as a breach of the company's contract of carriage. (*Gillespie* v. *Brooklyn Heights R. R. Co.*, 178 N.Y. 347.) The same rule obtains where the servant of an innkeeper offers insult to the guest. (*de Wolf* v. *Ford*, 193 N.Y. 397.) And it must be borne in mind that a recovery for indignity and wounded feelings is compensatory and does not constitute exemplary damages. (*Hamilton* v. *Third Ave. R. R. Co.* 53 N.Y. 25.)

It is insisted, however, that there is a distinction between common carriers and innkeepers, who are obliged to serve all persons who seek accommodation from them, and the keepers of public places of amusement or resort, such as the bathhouse of the defendant, theaters and the like. That the distinction exists is undeniable, and in the absence of legislation the keeper of such an establishment may discriminate and serve whom he pleases. Therefore, in such a case a refusal would give no cause of action. So, also, it is the general rule of law that a ticket for admission to a place of public amusement is but a license and revocable. But granting both propositions, that the defendant might have refused the plaintiff a bath ticket and access to his premises, and that even after selling her a ticket he might have revoked the license to use the premises for the purpose of bathing, which the ticket imported, neither proposition necessarily determines that the plaintiff was not entitled to recover damages for the indignity inflicted upon her by the revocation. We have seen that in the case of a common carrier or innkeeper, a person aggrieved may recover such damages as for a breach of contract, while on the other hand, on the breach of ordinary contracts, a party would not be so entitled, and the question is, to which class of cases the case before us most closely approximates. In several of the reported cases the keeping of a theater is spoken of as a strictly private undertaking, and it is said that the owner of a theater is under no obligation to give entertainments at all. The latter proposition is true, but the business of maintaining a theater cannot be said to be "strictly" private. In *People* v. *King* (110 N.Y.418) the question was as to the constitutionality of the Civil Rights Act of this state which made it a misdemeanor to deny equal enjoyment of any accommodation, facilities and privileges of inns, common carriers, theaters or other places of public resort or amusement regardless of race, creed or color, and gave the party aggrieved the right to recover a penalty of from fifty to five hundred dollars for the offense. The statute was upheld on the ground that under the doctrine of *Munn* v. *Illinois* (94 U.S. 113) theaters and places of public amusement (the case before the court was that of a skating rink) were affected with a public interest which justified legislative regulation and interference. In *Greenberg* v. *Western Turf. Assn.* (140 Cal. 357) a statute making it unlawful to refuse to any person admission to a place of public amusement and giving the person aggrieved the right to recover his damages and a hundred dollar penalty in addition thereto, was upheld on the authority of the cases we have cited—a decision plainly correct, because if the legislature can forbid discrimination by the owners of such resorts on the ground of race, creed or color, it may equally forbid discrimination on any other ground. Our statute has since been amended so as to expressly include keepers of bathhouses. On the other hand, no one will contend that the legislature could forbid discrimination in the private business affairs of life—prevent an employer from refusing to employ colored servants, or a servant from refusing to work for a white or for a colored master. So, it has been held that a bootblack may refuse to black a colored man's shoes without being liable to the penalty prescribed by our statute. (*Burks* v. *Bosso*, 180 N.Y. 341.) Such conduct may be the result of prejudice entirely, but a man's prejudices may be part of his most cherished possessions, which cannot be invaded except when displayed in the conduct of public affairs or quasi public enterprises. That public amusements and resorts are subject to the exercise of this legislative control shows that they are not entirely private. Therefore, though under the present law the plaintiff might have been denied admission altogether to the defendant's bathhouse, provided she were not excluded on account of race, creed or color (*Grannan* v. *Westchester Racing Assn.*, 153, N.Y. 449), the defendant having voluntarily entered into a contract with her admitting her to the premises and agreeing to afford facilities for bathing, her status became similar to that of a passenger of a common carrier or a guest of an innkeeper, and in case of her improper expulsion she should be entitled to the same measure of damages as obtains in actions against carriers or innkeepers when brought for breach of their contracts. The reason why such damages are recoverable in the cases mentioned is not merely because the defendants are bound to give the plaintiffs accommodation, but also because of the indignity suffered by a public expulsion. In a theater or other place of public amusement or resort the indignity and humiliation caused by an expulsion in the presence of a large number of people is as great, if not greater, than in the case of an expulsion by a carrier or innkeeper, as it is the publicity of the thing that causes the humiliation.

Nor can I find that the decision we are making is in conflict with the authorities in this country. We have not been referred to any decision that holds in the case of a wrongful expulsion from a place of public amusement the aggrieved party is not entitled to compensation for humiliation and indignity. In the two Massachusetts cases cited the actions were for assault, which of course could not be sustained if the license was revocable. Indeed the later case (*McCrea* v. *Marsh*) seems to limit the time for the exercise of the right of expulsion. They did not deal with the rule of damages. The same is true of *Horney* v. *Nixon* (*supra*). It dealt simply with the form of the action, which was trespass, and in the opinion it is said that the action should have been brought in assumpsit. In *MacGowan* v. *Duff* (*supra*) by mistake the plaintiff had been sold tickets for the wrong evening and was compelled to surrender the seats he occupied. It was held that the case did not justify an award of exemplary damages, and the learned court expressed a doubt as to the English doctrine declared in *Wood* v. *Leadbitter* (13 Mee. & W. 838) that on a revocation of the license the plaintiff could only recover the amount paid. On the other hand, in *Macgoverning* v. *Staples* (7 Lans. 145) the right to revoke a license and expel from the grounds of an agricultural fair was denied. *Smith* v. *Leo* (92 Hun, 242) is the only authority to which we have been referred on the precise question before us. There the plaintiff having bought an admission to the defendant's dancing school, was admitted thereto but subsequently expelled. It was held that he was entitled to compensation for the indignity and disgrace of his expulsion.

The judgment of the Appellate Division should be affirmed, with costs.

GRAY, WERNER, WILLARD BARTLETT, HISCOCK, CHASE and COLLIN, JJ., concur.

Judgment affirmed.

DUNN v. DEAN VINCENT, INC.,
562 P. 2d 972 (Oregon 1977)

O'CONNELL, Justice Pro Tempore.

This is an action at law by the buyers of a tavern against the seller and his broker for common law fraud. The seller made no appearance, was found in default, and is not a party in this appeal. Plaintiffs allege that defendants represented that the tavern sold 50 kegs of beer per month and was netting an average profit of $1,000 per month, that these representations were false and that they were made by the defendants with the knowledge that they were false or with reckless disregard for their truth. The jury returned a verdict for the plaintiffs in the sum of $9,172.77 general damages and $5,000 punitive damages. Judgment was entered on the verdict and defendant Dean Vincent, Inc., appeals.

Defendant contends that there was insufficient evidence to make out the elements of an action for fraud. There was such evidence.

Defendant next contends that the trial court erred in instructing the jury on the measure of plaintiffs' damages. We agree and therefore must reverse. The instruction was as follows:

"If you find that Dean Vincent is guilty of fraud as I have defined it to you, the measure of damage is the money lost, if any, by the Plaintiffs; and in this case this may include, although you are not bound by it of course, although the allegations do constitute a ceiling beyond which an award cannot be made, and considering the general damage, it may consist of the operating loss of $1,327.77, the loss of $800.00 Plaintiffs paid toward equipment according to their theory, and the down payment of $7,000.00. These three figures together make up the figure of $9,172.22."

It is evident from the transcript that plaintiffs' counsel and the trial judge regarded the three dollar amounts designated in the instructions as constituting plaintiffs' net loss as a result of the purchase of the tavern, and that they fell well within the established principle that in a fraud case a successful plaintiff may recover his "out-of-pocket" loss. It was error to so regard plaintiffs' expenditures because where a purchaser *affirms* the contract (which plaintiffs did here by electing to bring a law action for fraud rather than an equity suit to rescind) he elects to retain whatever came to him under the contract, and the value of what he receives must be deducted from the amount which he paid out in computing his "out-of-pocket" loss. Where the purchaser elects to rescind he must tender back what he receives, and therefore what he pays out as purchase money or in the form of expenditures resulting in a loss are properly regarded as his "out-of-pocket" loss. Similarly, in an action at law to recover damages for a fradulent sale, the purchaser's payment on the purchase price and other losses incident to the purchase may be regarded as "out-of-pocket" loss where the evidence establishes that the property purchased is entirely without value, leaving nothing which the purchase could credit against the loss.

In the present case plaintiffs did not adduce evidence to prove that the interests which they received as a result of the contract of purchase were of no value. In the absence of evidence to the contrary, it is fair to assume that the unexpired term of the lease would have some value. Simply because plaintiffs did not wish to continue the unsuccessful business and the property had no value to them for that purpose, it does not follow that the leasehold would not be sold to someone else for some other purpose. Plaintiffs asserted that they "left" the premises and "abandoned" it, and thus retained nothing to set off against the recited outlay made by them. We do not think that simply by these assertions the interests of the plaintiffs in the property acquired under the contract (which by the present action they affirm) were revested in the seller. If they had proposed to thus divest themselves of their interest in exchange for a recovery of their outlay, they could have done so in an orderly and well recognized legal procedure by filing a suit to rescind. The judgment must therefore be reversed.

Reversed and remanded.

LANDRY v. GILLORY
344 So. 2d 1138 (La. App., 1977).

ROGERS, Judge.

Norris John Landry, d/b/a Royal Catering, instituted this action against Jerry Guillory for $2,047.50 allegedly owed plaintiff by defendant on a contract to provide goods and services. Plaintiff confirmed a default judgment against defendant, and defendant has appealed.

The substantial issue before this court is whether plaintiff's petition states a cause of action.

On June 4, 1976, plaintiff filed suit against defendant alleging a certain sum was due for goods and services provided by plaintiff's business, Royal Catering. Generally, the petition alleges that defendant contracted with plaintiff to cater a banquet on behalf of a candidate for State Commissioner of Insurance.

The arrangements were that the banquet was to be held at the Municipal Auditorium in Lafayette, Louisiana on October 6, 1975; that plaintiff would provide all food, utensils, labor and other incidentals; and that plaintiff would receive $6.50 per person served with a minimum guarantee of $2,047.50. Plaintiff's petition further alleges that he did provide the agreed upon services for the specified event, but that he has never received payment. The petition states that there were less than the required minimum number of persons in attendance, and thus plaintiff is entitled to $2,047.50.

Defendant failed to file an answer, and a default judgment was entered against him on July 2, 1976. On August 6, 1976, a hearing was held, plaintiff presented his case, and the default judgment was confirmed and signed. Defendant thereupon sought a devolutive appeal order which was granted by the trial court on December 9, 1976.

Defendant, in his appeal brief, urges that plaintiff's petition failed to state a cause of action against defendant because plaintiff's petition failed to allege that defendant bound himself personally, or exceeded his authority as agent for the Insurance Commissioner candidate, in contracting with Royal Catering.

Defendant did not file an exception of no cause of action in the district court nor has such a motion been formally filed with this court. The only time this contention has been raised is in defendant's appellate brief. However, an exception of no cause of action, since it is peremptory in nature, may be raised for the first time on appeal, if it is placed at issue, as was done here, prior to the submission of the case for a decision. LSA—C.C.P. art. 2163. Therefore, we find that defendant's exception is properly before this court.

The purpose of the peremptory exception, as has been previously held by this court, is to determine whether any remedy is afforded by law to plaintiff under the allegations contained in his petition. *Fremaux v. Buie*, 212 So.2d 148 (La.App. 3 Cir. 1968).

The law is settled that for purposes of considering the exception, all allegations of the plaintiff's petition are deemed to be true. *Verret v. Traveler's Insurance Co.*, 216 So.2d 379 (La.App. 3 Cir. 1968).

Furthermore, when considering an exception of no cause of action, allegations contained in plaintiff's petition must be construed most favorably to sustain plaintiff's cause of action, and defendant's exception must be overruled unless the allegations exclude every reasonable hypothesis of fact other than those showing that plaintiff could not recover as a matter of law.

Paragraph 5 of plaintiff's petition states as follows:

Defendant at said meeting advised plaintiff that he desired to hold a campaign banquet or dinner for Mr. Barcelona in the City of Lafayette at the Municipal Auditorium on October 6, 1975, and desired to contract with and engage plaintiff as the caterer for said banquet.

Clearly, one reasonable interpretation of this paragraph is that plaintiff contracted with defendant personally for providing these services, and not as the agent for Mr. Barcelona, his campaign committee, or any other party as is now urged by defendant on appeal.

If defendant had wanted to prove that he was acting as agent for another party when he contracted with plaintiff, he should have done so at the district court. Instead, defendant took no action, and allowed a default judgment to be entered against him.

To confirm a default judgment the plaintiff must establish a prima facie case proving his demand. LSA—C.C.P. art. 1702. The court minutes and the signed judgment indicate that such was done.

When having a default judgment confirmed, the plaintiff is not required to have the testimony reduced to writing or to have a note made of the evidence introduced, and on appeal, the defendant has the burden of overcoming the presumption that the judgment was rendered upon sufficient evidence and is correct. Here, no transcript or note of the evidence is found in the record, and thus it is presumed that the judgment of the trial court was rendered upon sufficient evidence and is correct.

For the above given reasons, defendant's exception of no cause of action is dismissed, and the judgment of the trial court is affirmed. All costs are assessed against the defendant-appellant.

AFFIRMED.

QUESTIONS

1. T. or F. A "several" contract is one that can be held to be binding on A and B or A or B.
2. Explain the danger inherent in a unilateral contract situation.
3. Under what legal theory may a court imply a contract at law?
4. What evil was the statute of frauds designed to avoid?
5. T. or F. "Consideration" must always have a dollar and cent value.
6. Why do mutual promises standing alone, provide consideration?
7. Why must one be careful when contemplating anticipating a breach of contract?
8. Explain what "liquidated damages" are.
9. What legal impact do the words "time is of the essence" have on a contract?
10. For an example of how "public policy" will influence a court, see the case on page 83.

ENDNOTES

1. 1. *Williston on Contracts*, sec. 1, p. 1.
2. 1. *Williston on Contracts*, sec. 3. p. 6.
3. *Bott v. Wheeler*, 183 Va. 643, 33 S.E. 2d. 184.
4. *Roller v. McGraw*, 63 W.Va. 462, 60 S.E. 410.
5. *F.A. D'Andrea, Inc., v. Dodge* 15 F. 2d 1003.
6. *Burke v. Shaver*, 92 Va. 345, 23 S.E. 749.
7. *Krikorian v. Dailey*, 171 Va. 16, 197 S.E. 442.
8. *Tearney v. Marmison*, 103 W.Va. 394, 137 S.E. 543.
9. *Williams v. Board of Education*, 45 W.VA. 199, 31 S.E. 985.
10. *O'Dell v. Appalachian Hotel Corp.*, 153 Va. 283, 149 S.E. 487, 68 A.L.R. 629.
11. *Johnson v. Richmond & D.R. Co.*, 86 va. 975, 11 S.E. 829.

Hospitality Sales Contracts

It is essential that one who works in almost any capacity in the hotel, motel and general travel industry has a working understanding of the principles of Article 2, Uniform Commercial Code, called "Sales." All orders for supplies, shipment of goods of all types both to and from a place of business will be covered or affected by this article. Article 2 covers "transactions in goods" and is not limited to "sales", nor is it intended to be.[1] It *does not* apply to sales that are intended to be "secured transactions." In that event, Article 9 controls.

A helpful way to begin is by an examination of key terms encountered in Article 2.

KEY TERMS

A "buyer" is any person who buys or *contracts to buy* goods. (This distinction is important). A "seller" is one who sells or contracts to sell goods. A "merchant" is one who deals in goods and has knowledge or skills of those goods and practices of the transaction. A merchant can also be one who has this skill and knowledge attributed to him or her because of the use of agents and other intermediaries. In short, a merchant is one who knows, or should know, more about the goods than an ordinary, untrained person. An innkeeper ordering food supplies for the restaurant would be a merchant. So would the supplier of those goods. This would be a transaction "between merchants." This brings us to the definition of "goods."

WHAT ARE "GOODS"?

"Goods" means all items *that are movable* at the time they become the subject of a sales contract. The definition includes the unborn young of animals, growing crops, and, in some cases, items attached to real estate that are to be severed from the realty.[2] Goods must be *existing* and *identified* before an interest in them can pass. Goods which are not existing and identified are *future goods* and can only be the subject of a contract to sell — not a present sale.

"Lot" means a parcel or a single article which is the subject matter of a separate sale or delivery, whether or not it is sufficient to perform the contract.[3]

"Commercial unit" means such a unit of goods as by commercial usage is a single whole for purposes of sale and division of which materially impairs its character or value on the market or in use. A commercial unit may be a single article (as a machine) or a set of articles (as a suite of furniture or an assortment of sizes) or a quantity (as a bale, gross, or carload) or any other unit treated in use or in the relevant market as a single whole.[4].

DEFINITIONS: "CONTRACT"; "AGREEMENT"; "CONTRACT FOR SALE"; "PRESENT SALE"; "CONFORMING" TO CONTRACT; "TERMINATION"; "CANCELLATION".

(1) "Contract" and "agreement" are limited to those relating to the present or future sale of goods. "Contract for sale" includes both a present sale of goods and a contract to sell goods at a future time. A "sale" consists in the passing of title from the seller to the buyer for a price. A "present sale" means a sale which is accomplished by the making of the contract.[5]

(2) Goods or conduct including any part of a performance are "conforming" or conform to the contract when they are in accordance with the obligations under the contract.[6]

(3) "Termination" occurs when either party pursuant to a power created by agreement or law puts an end to the contract otherwise than for its breach. On "termination" all obligations which are still executory on both sides are discharged but any right based on prior breach or performance survives.[7]

(4) "Cancellation" occurs when either party puts an end to the contract for breach by the other and its effect is the same as that of "termination" except that the cancelling party also retains any remedy for breach of the whole contract or any unperformed balance.[8]

GOODS TO BE SEVERED FROM REALTY: RECORDING. (1) A contract for the sale of timber, minerals or the like or a structure or its materials to be removed from realty is a contract for the sale of goods if they are to be severed by the seller, but until severance, a purported present sale thereof which is not effective as a transfer of an interest in land is effective only as a contract to sell.

(2) A contract for the sale apart from the land of growing crops or other things attached to realty and capable of severance without material harm thereto but not described in subsection (1), is a contract for the sale of goods whether the subject matter is to be severed by the buyer or by the seller even though it forms part of the realty at the time of contracting, and the parties can by identification effect a present sale before severance.

(3) These provisions are subject to any third party rights provided by the law relating to realty records, and the contract for sale may be executed and recorded as a document transferring an interest in land and shall then constitute notice to third parties of the buyer's rights under the contract for sale.[9]

Turning from terms, it is important to find out how a sales contract is created.

FORMATION OF A SALES CONTRACT

Just as with conventional contracts, sales contracts have a statute of frauds.

STATUTE OF FRAUDS

A contract for the sale of goods for the price of $500 or more requires that there be some writing sufficient to indicate the contract, and it must be signed by the one against whom enforcement is sought. It can be signed by an agent. Such writing is not insufficient if it omits a term agreed upon. If it incorrectly states a quantity of goods, then the writing is not effective beyond that quantity.[10] This statute of frauds is quite flexible. The statute does not apply at all if specially manufactured goods are involved, or if one admits in court that a contract had been made, or if one receives the goods and pays for them. These acts standing alone would be sufficient to prove the contract. If a sales contract is in written form and is then modified, the modification should also be in writing and signed. Article 2 makes it clear that an oral modification *does not* satisfy the statute of frauds, although it may constitute a waiver.[11] But it is not a good idea to rely upon the waiver.[12]

EXAMPLES

Certain Alabama cotton farmers contracted to sell their crop of that year for prices in the 3 cents to 35 cents per pound range. At the time the crop was in, the price was 80 cents on the market and the farmers refused to honor the contract to sell. Since the original contract had been oral, the court ruled that the statute of frauds governed and the farmers were free to sell as they pleased.[13]

In a case that arose in Minnesota, a supplier on the witness stand stated in part " . . . I was interested in buying up to fifty million gallons a year (of heating oil). I said, we were interested in selling the product and we agreed to sell it — or to put it in the singular, I agreed to sell it, subject to credit clearance and other clearances back at the home office." The court held that this admission was sufficient to hold the supplier to the oral sales contract.[14]

AVOIDING STATUTE OF FRAUDS

If one is in a situation in which the other refuses to place anything in writing, can something be done to avoid the statute of frauds problem? Under U.C.C. 2-201(2), if one party sends the other a letter of confirmation of the oral deal, and if the other does not object within 10 days, then that letter meets the requirements of the statute.

As a matter of good business practice, all contracts for the sale of goods of $500 or more should be reduced to writing at the outset or confirmed by a letter that sets forth the terms of the contract. If the one who receives the letter does not want to be bound, that person must say so, in writing, and must do so promptly.

Related to the statute of frauds is the "parol evidence rule."

PAROL EVIDENCE RULE

This rule is based upon the common law principle that when two persons reduce their agreement to writing, neither can vary or alter that agreement later by oral testimony. This rule has been carried into sales contracts in a modified form. What is reduced to writing cannot be altered by oral testimony—but it can be explained by course of dealing, usage of trade and prior performance between the parties. The rule does not prohibit oral testimony as to terms not included in the written contract.

A contract for the sale of goods may be made in any manner sufficient to show agreement, including conduct that recognizes the existence of the contract.[15] But one must not forget the effect of the statute of frauds or parol evidence rule.

The precise time of the making of the contract is not essential[16] and the fact that one or more terms are left open does not cause it to fail for indefinitness.[17] Both of these rules are contrary to conventional contract principles.

OFFER AND ACCEPTANCE

An offer invites acceptance in any reasonable manner. If one offers to buy goods that must be shipped, a prompt shipment or promise to ship will be an acceptance. If the offer indicates that the offer is to be accepted by beginning to perform, and the other person does not begin the performance, the offeror may treat the offer as having lapsed before acceptance.[18]

An offer can become "firm"—that is, cannot be revoked - if a merchant promises another in writing to hold the offer open for a period not to exceed 3 months. Such an offer takes the form of an "option", and no consideration is required.[19]

IF ACCEPTANCE CHANGES OFFER

If one accepts an offer but changes the terms of it, *it may still be a good acceptance.* The additional terms are treated as a proposal to make additions to the contract and become part of the contract unless;

(a) the offer limited the terms of the acceptance,
(b) the changes *materially* alter the offer, and
(c) the other party gives prompt notification of objections to the changes. Silence would allow the contract to come into being as altered.[20]

If the writings of the parties do not establish a contract, yet the parties recognize the existence of one, then the contract will be treated as one that contains the terms upon which there is agreement. The U.C.C. will then provide the lacking terms. Course of performance controls in the latter instance, supplemented by course of dealing and usage of trade.

Article 2 contains provisions for modification, rescission and waiver of a sales contract, and all of these should be reduced to writing.[21]

REVOCATION OF OFFER

One who makes a sales contract offer can revoke it before acceptance. The exceptions would be when it was a "firm offer" or when the other had timely started performance. The U.C.C. does not change prior contract law in this area. Unless displaced by the particular provisions of Article 2, the principles of law and equity, including the law merchant and the law relative to capacity to contract, principal and agent, estoppel, fraud, misrepresentation, duress, coercion, mistake, bankruptcy, or other validating or invalidating cause shall supplement its (Article 2) provisions.[22]

OBLIGATIONS OF THE PARTIES

TENDER OF DELIVERY

The seller has a duty to make a proper tender of delivery under the terms of the contract. This is done by placing conforming goods at the disposal of the buyer and by notifying him or her so the buyer can take delivery. It is important that tender be at a reasonable hour and under reasonable circumstances. The goods must be held by the seller or sellers agent for a reasonable time to give the buyer the opportunity to take possession.

STOPPING GOODS IN TRANSIT

Under certain conditions, a seller can stop goods that are in transit to the buyer. If it is learned that the buyer is insolvent or has missed a payment due the seller, shipment can be stopped. If the goods are in the hands of a common carrier, shipment cannot be stopped unless it is a truckload, carload, or planeload. A seller cannot stop a UPS truck and demand that the driver shift through a thousand packages to find one. The order to stop shipment must be made timely. If it is made after the goods are delivered, it comes too late.

When a proper stop shipment order has been made, the one who has the goods (bailee or shipper) must hold the goods and deliver them according to the instructions of the seller.

The right to stop shipment only applies between seller and buyer. If the buyer has resold the goods to others, those goods cannot be stopped in transit.

In a Missouri case, A sold goods to B, who assigned the shipment to C on a nonnegotiable bill of lading. The check from B to A bounced and A stopped shipment to C. The court held that since C was not a "full blown" bona fide purchaser for value, A could stop the shipment.[23] But if C had been a bona fide purchaser for value, A could not have stopped the shipment. If a stop shipment is unlawful in any respect, the seller must bear the responsibility for any loss to the buyer.[24]

BUYERS RIGHT OF INSPECTION

Once the goods are tendered the buyer has the right to inspect them before accepting them.[25] This must be done at a reasonable time and place and in a reasonable manner. If a buyer waives the right to inspect, that in itself is an acceptance *even if the goods are nonconforming.*

If the parties agree that payment is to be made before inspection, then the buyer must pay before inspection even if the goods are nonconforming. This occurs in C.O.D.[26] payments against documents of title and C.I.F.[27] contracts. The burden is now shifted to the buyer who must pay the price and then sue for any loss. Buyers should resist efforts to make them pay before inspection for this reason.

IMPROPER DELIVERY

If an improper delivery is made, such as a shipment of nonconforming goods, the buyer must do one of three things:

1. reject all of the goods.
2. accept all of the goods.
3. accept any commercial unit or units and reject the rest.[28]

If the buyer decides to do 2, above, prompt notice should be given the seller that the buyer demands an allowance for the failure to conform.[29]

If the buyer decides to reject the goods, two extremely important principles *must be followed*:

1. After prompt inspection, the buyer must notify the seller in a reasonable time that the goods are being rejected.[30] A wait of as long as an hour may be too long in some deliveries. Failure to so notify is treated as an acceptance.[31]

2. If the defects are such that they can be "cured" (corrected), the buyer must also tell the seller what these defects are.[32]

After rejection and notification, the buyer must act reasonably with the goods and follow reasonable instructions from the seller as to their disposal. Such instructions might be to reship to the seller or a third party, or even to sell the goods as salvage. If the goods are perishable, the buyer has a duty to sell them promptly to protect the seller. The buyer is entitled to compensation for services performed with rejected goods.[33] If the seller fails to provide instructions in a reasonable time, the buyer can store, ship or sell the goods for the account of the seller.[34] These are the options of the merchant-buyer. A non-merchant buyer has only the duty to hold the goods for the seller.

In any rejection, the buyer should never do anything that could be construed as the buyer treating the goods as being his or her own property. A court might treat such acts as an acceptance. For example, if a non-merchant buyer rejects an air conditioner, then refuses to allow the seller to pick it up, that would be an acceptance and render the buyer liable for the price.[35]

REVOKING AN ACCEPTANCE

In instances where defects cannot be discovered by an immediate inspection, and where such defects are uncovered later, sometimes years later, is the buyer stuck because of the prior acceptance? No, since the buyer can, in some cases, revoke an acceptance.[36] In an Arkansas case, a court held that a defective air conditioner could be rejected three years after purchase, since it had not worked properly all along and efforts had been made to repair it.[37]

SELLERS RIGHT TO CURE

If a seller makes an improper tender of delivery, the seller has the right to be told why the delivery is improper. For example, a delivery of 1000 cruise ship excursion coupons arrives and it is discovered by the buyer that the name of the ship is wrong. The buyer must reject and tell why. The seller now has the right to "cure" or remedy the defect by delivering new coupons.[38] If the cured goods arrive by the deadline for their use, the contract is complete and the price must be paid. If goods cannot be cured timely, then the defective delivery and the rejection results in no binding contract. If the goods arrive late in the beginning, must the buyer still reject timely and tell the seller why? A Florida case involving 100 jet airliners answered this question "yes".[39] So the two steps of rejection should be made for *any* improper delivery that the buyer does not want to accept-even a delivery that comes too late for use.

PASSING OF TITLE

"Passing of title" was an abstract legal concept that caused many problems prior to the U.C.C. Now, Article 2 does not refer to the passing of title but leaves the various sections of the Code to be used to determine the rights and obligations of the parties. However, the Code does contain specific provisions that regulate "passing of title".

Title cannot pass on goods that are not in existence and identified to the contract.[40] Title cannot pass if goods are to be manufactured until they are made. And even after they are completed, title does not pass until the seller indicates that these goods are intended for the buyer.[41] Subject to such rules as these, the parties are free to agree at which point title is to pass.[42]

RISK OF LOSS

The parties are free to make any agreement between them as to risk of loss.[43] However, the agreement cannot be unconscionable. The risk can be divided if they choose.[44] If a shipment contract is involved, the risk of loss normally passes to the buyer when the goods are delivered to the carrier.[45] Examples of shipment contracts are where the delivery terms are F.O.B.[46] point of shipment F.O.B. vessel or car, F.A.S.[47] C.I.F.[48] or C. and F.[49] : (See the endnotes for definitions).

If the contract is a "destination agreement", then risk of loss shifts to the buyer when a proper tender is made at that point.[50] "F.O.B. destination" is a destination agreement. Common sense tells us that both buyers and sellers must be conscious of risk of loss, because it means just that. If the goods are lost, stolen, damaged by fire or other causality, someone must bear the loss. As a policy matter it is sound business practice to agree on the risk and then buy appropriate insurance.

RECAPTURE RIGHTS

If goods are sold on credit, tender is made, and acceptance follows but the buyer refuses to pay for the goods, can the seller "recapture" the goods? If goods are delivered to a buyer who is found to be insolvent, recapture is limited to the following 10 days unless there is proof of misrepresentation of insolvency, then it is extended to 3 months.[51] What happens after these time periods is that the Code shifts the "goods" to a "debt", leaving the seller the right to take legal action on the debt-not the happiest thing for the seller. This provision of Article 2 caused problems and it has been rewritten in recent drafts.

MISCELLANEOUS SALES CONTRACT CASES

Because of the importance of the law of sales, an examination of a variety of situations in which merchants have found themselves in court because of such contracts, is in order.

STATUTE OF FRAUDS

As we have seen, contracts for the sale of goods over $500 in value must be in writing. If not, and if one of the exceptions does not arise, the contract cannot be unenforced. One court has gone beyond the exceptions and has ruled that where one party has so changed his position in reliance on the oral contract that an unconscionable loss would result to the other, that person should be "estopped" to deny the contract,[52] thus enforcing the oral agreement.

Can a down payment satisfy the statute of frauds if made by check? Article 2 provides that it can only do so with respect to goods for which payment has been made and accepted.[53] It is best not to rely on such payments but rather to use the written contract.

In a Maryland case,[54] a party to an oral contract wound up on the witness stand and then admitted the contract. That satisfied the statute.

Turning from the Statute of Frauds, does the U.C.C. have a "statute of limitations"?

STATUTE OF LIMITATIONS

A glass wall had been installed in 1966. In 1972, a boy fell thru the glass and was killed. The court held that the breach of warranty occured at the time of installation, if it occured at all, and since four years had passed, the manufacturer of the glass had no liability. This left the responsibility squarely on the buyer of the glass.

The U.C.C. normally allows a four year period in which to bring a suit for breach of sales contract.[55] This does not always mean what it says. One Martin Becker bought a car in 1969 and sued for breach of warranty within four years. The California court held that in that state, action for injuries caused by a wrongful act or neglect must be brought in one year.[56] It should be pointed out, however, that there is a split of the courts in such instances. In other words, do other state statutes of limitations supercede those in the U.C.C.? The question has not been settled.

Trade usage can severly shorten the statute of limitations. Thus, since a sales contract not only means what it says, but is supplemented by trade custom and practices, the result can be surprising. A buyer purchased certain glass and insisted on a 100% guarantee against "staining". After resale to others, the glass stained and the buyer refunded the price to *his* buyers. He then turned to the seller for recovery on the guarantee. The court held that it was too late, because in the trade of glass selling, it was customary for such complaints to be made between seven and 30 days. The contract was silent on the period of limitations, so trade practice controlled.[57] Turning from periods of limitations, how definite must a sales contract be?

DEFINITENESS

In a Georgia case, the buyer agreed to buy over $58,000 worth of goods and made a down payment of over $4,000. It was in writing and all seemed in order. However, there was no payment schedule, no time for performance and other terms were lacking. Did it fail for "indefiniteness" when the buyer wanted out? The court said no, pointing out that since the parties had intended to make a contract, that Article 2 will supply the price,[58] decide when payment is due,[59] and provide for the method and place of deliver.[60] Thus the contract did not fail for indefiniteness although these terms were missing.[61]

Next, is there a material difference between a "sales" and a "service" contract?

SALES V. SERVICE

Warranty liability only arises if a "sale of goods" is involved. This requires a merchant to stand behind the goods sold. If a mere "service" is involved, the warranties do not apply-at least so it has been in prior years.

A Michigan electric company installed electrical wiring in a building which was followed by an electrical fire. The installer claimed that this was an installation (service) thus warranties did not apply. The court held that since the installer supplied the goods, which carried the waranties, the court would imply a warranty of fitness as to the manner in which the goods were installed. The old distinction between sales and service is no longer as clear as it was in the past.[62]

After a sales contract comes into being, can it be modified, or changed in some material provision?

MODIFICATION

Article 2 permits modification of a sales contract, so long as the parties both agree.[63] The only requirement is that each act in good faith with the other.

In the following case, the sales statute of limitations is involved.

TAKKO v. PETER PAN SEAFOODS
563 P. 2d 710 (Oregon 1977).

PER CURIAM.

This is an action for breach of a contract for the sale of a fishing boat to defendant. Defendant demurred to the complaint. The court sustained the demurrer and plaintiff appeals

The present action was filed on September 10, 1974. Defendant demurred on the ground that the complaint revealed on its face that the action had not been commenced within the time permitted by statute. The demurrer was sustained on the ground that the four-year limitation period prescribed in ORS 72.7250 barred the action. Plaintiff filed a motion requesting the court to reconsider its ruling on defendant's demurrer.

In support of that motion, counsel for plaintiff did not argue that the four-year limitation period had not run in this case; he contended that the case was controlled by ORS 12.220, which provides as follows:

"Except as otherwise provided in ORS 72.7250, if an action is commenced within the time prescribed therefor and the action is dismissed upon the trial thereof, or upon appeal, after the time limited for bringing a new action, the plaintiff * * may commence a new action upon such cause of action within one year after the dismissal or reversal on appeal; however, all defenses that would have been available against the action, if brought within the time limited for the bringing of the action, shall be available against the new action when brought under this section."

In an affidavit accompanying a motion to reconsider the order sustaining the demurrer, plaintiff revealed that a previous action had been filed in 1972 which terminated in an involuntary nonsuit entered on September 19, 1973. The complaint in the former action reveals that both the former action and the present action involved the same transaction. It also reveals that the two actions were brought on different theories, the first action being for the conversion of the boat and equipment and the present action being for breach of contract.

At the time of the argument on the demurrer, plaintiff asserted that numerous authorities supported her position that under ORS 12.220 it was legally proper to file a contract action within one year after dismissal of a previous tort action based upon the same fact situation, contending that both were based upon the same cause of action. The trial judge expressed his doubt as to the correctness of this assertion but granted plaintiff time to present authorities in support of plaintiff's contention before ruling upon the demurrer.

In denying plaintiff's motion to reconsider, the trial judge, in a letter to counsel, explained the basis of his ruling as follows:

"It should also be noted that the complaint contains nothing regarding the previous action for conversion nor the fact the Judge Bohannon granted a nonsuit. Neither does the complaint herein indicate the character of the previous cause of action as being in tort.

"Based upon the foregoing, it would seem that this motion could be denied on the basis of lack of timeliness, the fact that the face of the complaint in question does not contain any factual pleading supporting plaintiff's contentions, and also the fact that the statute of limitations bars this action. However, I have read the authorities that plaintiff has now submitted in her affidavit supporting her motion to reconsider. These authorities establish nothing more that [sic] the well known legal principle that a plaintiff may file over within one year after an order dismissing her previous proceeding by way of involuntary nonsuit on the same cause of action. It must still be noted however that plaintiff has failed to provide any authorities to indicate that an action on contract is the same cause of action as an action in tort. Therefore, the motion to reconsider will be denied upon the same grounds upon which the Court entered its order sustaining the previous demurrer."

Leaving aside the question of whether either ORS 72.7250 or 12.220 are applicable, we think the trial court properly sustained the demurrer on the ground that she failed to plead facts relating to the previous action, thus leaving the court without anything more than the recitation in plaintiff's motion to reconsider as a basis for making a ruling on the matter.

Judgment affirmed.

QUESTIONS

1. Why must goods be *existing* and *identified* before a legal interest in them can pass to another?
2. Name the three exceptions to the sales statute of frauds.
3. Compare the sales statute of frauds with the conventional contracts statute of frauds on page 75.
4. What must a buyer do who receives nonconforming goods?
5. Under what conditions may one stop goods that are in transit?
6. Under what conditions may one revoke an acceptance?
7. Write out the meanings of F.O.B., F.A.S., C.I.F. and C. and F. What is the importance of knowing which of these controls a contract?
8. Why does the law require that a confirmation be objected to quickly?
9. List three ways in which a sales contract can be accepted.
10. Name one way that custom may become involved in a sales case.

ENDNOTES

1. U.C.C. 2-102.
2. U.C.C. 2-107.

3. U.C.C. 2-104 (5).
4. U.C.C. 2-104 (6).
5. U.C.C. 2-106 (1).
6. U.C.C. 2-106 (2).
7. U.C.C. 2-106 (3).
8. U.C.C. 2-106 (4).
9. U.C.C. 2-107.
10. U.C.C. 2-201.
11. U.C.C. 2-209 (4).
12. *Double E. Sportswear Corp. v. Girard Trust Bank*, 488 F. 2d 292 (3d. Cir. 1973).
13. *Cox v. Cox* 289 So. 2d 609, 14 U.C.C. Rep. 330 (1974).
14. *Oskay Gasoline & Oil Co. v. Continental Oil Co.*, 19 U.C.C. Rep. 61 (1976).
15. U.C.C. 2-204.
16. U.C.C. 2-204 (2).
17. U.C.C. 2-204 (3).
18. U.C.C. 2-206.
19. U.C.C. 2-205.
20. U.C.C. 2-207.
21. U.C.C. 2-209.
22. U.C.C. 1-103.
23. U.C.C. 2-703 (b).
24. *Clock v. Missouri—Kansas—Texas Railroad Co. v. Crawford*, 407 F. Supp. 448 (E.D. Mo. 1976).
25. U.C.C. 2-513.
26. "Cash on delivery"
27. "Cost of goods, insurance and freight".
28. U.C.C. 2-601.
29. U.C.C. 714 (2).
30. U.C.C. 2-602 (1).
31. U.C.C. 2-606.
32. U.C.C. 2-605 (1) (a).
33. U.C.C. 2-603 (2).
34. U.C.C. 2-604.
35. U.C.C. 2-709 (1) (a).
36. U.C.C. 2-608.
37. *Dapierlla v. Arkansas Louisana Gas Co.*, 225 Ark. 150, 12 U.C.C. Rep. 468 (1973).
38. U.C.C. 2-508.
39. *Eastern Airlines, Inc., v. McDonnell Douglas Corp.* 532 F2. 957, 19 U.C.C. Rep. 353 (5th Cir. 1976).
40. U.C.C. 2-401 (1).
41. U.C.C. 2-501.
42. U.C.C. 2-401 (1).
43. U.C.C. 2-509 (4).
44. U.C.C. 2-303.
45. U.C.C. 2-509 (1).
46. F.O.B., "Free on board." (This can be at shipping point or at destination).
47. F.A.S. "Free alongside" referring to shipping vessel or other means of transportation.
48. C.I.F. This means that the quoted price includes the cost of goods insurance to the designated destination, and freight charges to that destination.
49. C&F. This means the quoted price includes costs of goods and freight to destination, but not insurance.
50. U.C.C. 2-509 (1) (b).
51. U.C.C. 2-702 (2).
52. *Dangerfield v. Marhel*, 222 N.W. 2d. 373, 15 U.C.C. Rep. 915 (N.D. 1974).
53. U.C.C. 2-201 (3) (c).
54. *Lewis v. Hughes*, 346 A. 2d. 231, 18 U.C.C. Rep. 52 (Med. App. 1975).

55. U.C.C. 2-725 (1).
56. *Becker v. Volkswagon of Am., Inc.*, 18 U.C.C. Rep. 135 (Cal. App. 1975).
57. *Jazel Corp., v. Sentinel Enterprises, Inc.*, 20 U.C.C. Rep. 837 (N.Y. Sup. Ct. 1976).
58. U.C.C. 2-305 (1).
59. U.C.C. 2-310.
60. U.C.C. 2-309.
61. *Deck House, Inc., v. Scarborough, Sheffield & Gastin, Inc.*, 228 S.E. 2d. 142, 20 U.C.C. Rep. 278, (Ga. App. 1976).
62. *Insurance Co. of North America v. Rodiant Elec. Co.* 222 N.W. 2d 323, 15 U.C.C. Rep. 261 (Mich. App. 1974).
63. U.C.C. 2-209.

8

Hospitality Agents and Independent Contractors

In this Chapter, we will examine the broad spectrum of law that relates to the carrying on of business by the use of the services of others. It has become increasingly necessary for this to be done for many reasons; businesses have gone national and international in their operations; local, privately owned businesses have been on the decline since the turn of this century and control of almost any modern business venture is simply beyond the scope of one person. Because of these factors we must use others to perform services for us; agents to carry out many of our business functions; independent contractors to complete large, usually single-in-scope, projects for us—and employees to carry forth our day-to-day business operations.

A good place to begin is by an examination of the traditional reach and scope of the law of agency. This will be followed by an examination of the laws of independent contractors.

AGENCY

Agency has been defined as the relationship which results from the manifestations of consent by one person to another that the other shall act on his behalf and subject to his control and the agreement by the other so to act. The definition leads itself to an outline:

1. B consents that A shall act for B.
2. A agrees to act for B.
3. A agrees that B shall control A while so acting.

In practice B is called the "principal", A the "agent," and these terms will be used by means of the symbol "P" for principal, "A" for agent. It follows that the acts of the agent will in some manner involve third parties, which we will call "T".

The relationship brings three legal consequences into being:

1. A contract is created between P and A.
2. When A acts with T, a contract may come into being between P and T—even though P did not deal with T personally.
3. When A acts for P, and while so doing causes injury to a third party, P may be held responsible for that injury.

Therefore an agent is one who acts for another; who must account to the other; who binds the other in contract and tort, and who usually does not benefit personally from the act performed. Rather the agent is compensated by the principal for the act, or a continuous series of acts, as is so often the case. Examples of agents include actors, lawyers, bank cashiers, brokers, insurance agents, auctioneers, agents of corporations—and in many instances, employees.

AGENTS AND "SERVANTS" ARE DIFFERENT

An agent, by the very nature of the law of agency, acts with third parties, while a servant performs mechanical or manual acts under the direct control of the principal-master. Servants can create liability upon the master, just as the agent can upon the principal. Many employees would seem to have the characteristics of servants— while others could well act with third parties and thus be agents.

TYPES OF AGENTS

Agents are classed as "special", or "general" agents. The former performs a single act or tries to accomplish a single objective. The latter handles continuing, general affairs of the principal. One authorized to purchase all goods needed to keep a restaurant in operation would be a general agent. One who is authorized to sign one deed for a principal is a special agent.

ANOTHER CLASSIFICATION

A "private" agent may bind the principal even when the agent acts beyond the scope of the authority given to A. A "public" agent, such as the governor of a state, only binds the principal (state) if the acts are within the authority granted. Examples of public agents would include governors, police officers, deputy sheriffs, sheriffs and fire marshalls. Thus one who is injured by a public officer may find the scope of recovery sharply reduced because of the limit of liability upon the state.

AGENTS DISTINGUISHED FROM TRUSTEES

In most instances a trustee has no principal. Such a person handles estates or "powers" and is in a fiduciary (high position of trust) capacity. The agent does have a principal as we have seen.

FORMATION OF THE RELATIONSHIP

An agency relationship is most often formed by a contract between P and A. Such relationships are said to be "express agencies" since they arise from the terms expressed orally or in writing by the parties. In addition, agencies can be "implied" and in rare cases, may arise by estoppel.

EXPRESS AGENCY

The agency contract may be oral or written. There is no specific legal form required in either case other than that there be a clear statement of the authority granted by P and an assent on the part of A to act as an agent. If, however, the authority granted will require a formal legal act by A, such as the execution of a deed for P, then in all states the authority granted must have the same "dignity" as the act to be formed. That is, the grant of authority must also be written and signed by P.[1]

In earlier times, a formal grant of authority to an agent had to be sealed—that is, the word "seal" or "L.S.", had to appear following the signature of P. This requirement has been abolished in most states and under the Uniform Commercial Code as well.[2]

If a court is called upon to construe (decide what the parties intended) a written agency contract, the subject matter of the contract, the acts of the parties and the surrounding circumstances will be examined in determining the intent of the principal and agent.

IMPLIED AGENCIES

As agency may be implied from the conduct of P and A, and from the nature and circumstances of that conduct. This means that an agency may in fact exist even though neither party expressly stated that one was in existence. What the parties call themselves is immaterial. The law will look to the actual relationship between them.[3]

AGENCY BY ESTOPPEL

An estoppel can be used by a court in those instances where one has misled another in an "agency type" situation to a degree that harm will result if the misled party is not provided some legal protection. This protection comes in the form of a court stopping (estopping) the one who misled the other, from denying that the two of them were in fact bound in an agency relationship. In short, a court can "close a persons mouth" in certain situations.

To illustrate, assume that X, in some manner, leads Y to believe that Z is the agent of X. In fact, there is no express or implied relationship between X and Z. If Y is misled, and consequently assumes a position of liability, then X will be "estopped" to deny the agency. The effect of this is, Y can look to X just as though an agency had in fact existed between X and Z. However, if Z leads Y to believe an agency exists between X and Z, and X knows nothing about it, the estoppel principle would have no application.

SCOPE OF AGENT'S AUTHORITY

An agent's authority to act for a principal may be express, implied or "apparent"—sometimes called "ostensible." Express authority presents no problems. It simply involves the doing of those things that P expressly gave A the authority to do. But the law does not stop there. With any grant of express authority, there must also go authority that can be "implied" from the express grant itself. To illustrate, if P grants A the authority to lease apartment units in Zero Condominium, then A would have the implied power to advertise the rentals, enter into lease agreements and collect rent for the benefit of P. Conversely, A would *not* have the implied power to sell the building. A coal mine superintendent would have the implied power to hire employees; an accountant would have the implied power to charge P for the books necessary to carry out the bookkeeping. On the other hand, a bus operator would have no authority to enter into a contract on behalf of the company in the absence of an express grant of such authority.

The duties to be carried out and the nature of the acts and the surrounding circumstances become relevant in determining whether or not implied authority exists on behalf of an agent.

APPARENT AUTHORITY

An implied grant of authority *falls within the real scope of the authority granted.* Apparent, or ostensible authority however, falls outside the express and real scope of the authority granted. Examine Figure 8-1. The test of apparent authority is whether a third party, knowing the usages of business, is justified in supposing that A is authorized to perform the act because of the nature of the known duties.[4] Such a rule is necessary in the laws of agency to cover those fringe matters that may arise in the conduct of duties by an agent.

FIGURE 8-1

AGENTS'

| PRINCIPAL GRANTS | Actual, Express, (Real) Authority | Implied From Express (Real) Authority | Apparent, Ostensible, Authority |

AUTHORITY

THIRD PARTY PERIL

When one deals with an agent, it is that persons duty to determine the nature and extent of the authority of the agent. The law presumes that the third party knows the scope of the authority granted to A. If the third party is wrong in its estimation of the authority of A, then that party must bear the risk of loss. To translate this principle into common sense terms, anyone who deals with any agent and who is in doubt of the authority of that agent, should immediately make inquiry to the principal. If T is confronted by A who is asking that the debt owing to P be paid in cash—not check— T obviously has a duty to make inquiry.

In many instances, an agent will act outside the range of actual, implied or apparent authority. In such instances, upon learning of this, P should repudiate such acts of A. In so doing, P will not be bound by those acts. In other instances, however, P may want to *adopt* such acts of A. Now P must take a different action.

RATIFICATION

If P learns that A has done acts with T that are totally outside of all authority, and if P wants to gain the benefits of such acts, those acts must be "ratified." To accomplish this, the principal must expressly or impliedly adopt these acts. This can be done by express statements; by payment, by retention of goods involved—and even by mere silence. It follows that P cannot ratify acts of A that P in fact knows nothing about. The effect of ratification is that P is now bound to T on the unauthorized acts of A, and conversely T is bound to P. One cannot ratify and thus adopt only beneficial parts of an unauthorized act but rather must adopt all of it or none.

In the agency relationship, a multitude of rights, duties and liabilities arise. These run between the parties involved. Examine Figure 8-2.

FIGURE 8-2
Flow of Duties

P ⎯⎯⎯⎯→ A
A ⎯⎯⎯⎯→ P
P ⎯⎯⎯⎯→ T
T ⎯⎯⎯⎯→ P

RIGHTS, DUTIES AND LIABILITIES

DUTIES OF A TO P

The agent must follow reasonable instructions of P. In the event of emergencies, agents are permitted, and expected, to deviate from instructions. For example, P may expressly tell A "under no circumstances are you to make loans in my name." If P should be absent on vacation, and flood waters have damaged the carpets in the motel of P, A could borrow money in the name of P and do other reasonable acts necessary to correct the problem. In fact, A would, as a matter of law, be *expected* to do such acts.

An agent must exercise a reasonable amount of care, caution and discretion. The "reasonable person" test is applied. If one acts as he or she would have if the subject had been his or her property, that person will generally not be held responsible for subsequent loss.

An agent must act in good faith with the principal and be loyal to P. An agent must not profit personally from the acts done for P. If this were done, such profits would be held by A, in trust, for the benefit of P. An agent must at all times make full disclosures to P and not withhold information of value to P. This disclosure is best carried out by periodic written reports to P.

An agent should never sell the goods of P to himself or herself except upon express authority of P. A position of delicacy arises in such cases and the agent must be careful. There is nothing wrong, however, with one agent buying the goods of P from another agent of the same principal. Most principals insist that this pattern be followed.

It follows that an agent should never represent a second principal so as to be in conflict with the interests of the first principal. Nor should an agent commingle the funds of P with the funds of A. Separate accounts must always be maintained. Collections made by A on behalf of P and deposited into the account of A could conceivably lead to a charge of embezzlement or theft. Care is in order. In instances where A collects and maintains accounts for P, A must be ready at all times to give a full accounting to P.

In retrospect, these duties of A to P are reasonable, designed to strip A of temptations to take advantage, and represent rules that a reasonable person would conclude *should* be the duties of A to P.

DUTIES OF P TO A

The principal has a duty to conpensate A for services rendered. The amount is usually set at the time of creation of the relationship. Further, P has a duty to *reimburse* A for expenses, and advances made by A while carrying out the scope of authority granted. If P fails to compensate or reimburse, A would have a lien (claim) against goods or property of P that are in the hands of A. In such circumstances, legal advice should be sought by A before enforcing the lien against such goods.

DUTIES OF A TO T

Generally an agent is not liable to T on any contract entered into on behalf of P. An agent *may* be bound if the agent intended to be bound, but the presumption is otherwise. If a principal remains hidden, or unknown to T (referred to as an undisclosed principal), the agent would be bound on any contract made with T. This is true even though it had been made for the benefit of P, and it is true for the reason that A is the contracting party in such instances. Once P is disclosed, T can also look to P for performance of the contract.

If an agent acts within the limits of the authority granted and is not aware that an apparent wrong or tort is being caused to others, the principal will be responsible for the tort. If P commands A to commit a tort, such as a trespass, both P and A will share the liability. If A commits a tort knowingly, and without any participation by P, A can be looked to for any loss suffered by T.

DUTIES OF P TO T

As long as an agent acts within the scope of the authority, as discussed previously, the principal has a duty to T to fulfill any and all obligations created by A with T.

In an undisclosed agency, when T enters into a contract with A, not knowing of the existence of P, both A and P have a duty to T on the contract—but only after P is disclosed. T can then look to either for performance—but not both. If T sues P on such a contract, P has a duty not to establish any greater claim against T than A could have. For example, T may have a set-off claim against A. Thus P would be subject to this set-off, and have a duty to extend to T the benefits of this set-off.

P has a duty to compensate third parties who are injured by tortious conduct of A while A is carrying out the scope of the authority granted. It is not material whether the tortious act was in accordance to instructions, only whether it was done in the scope of authority granted.

An exception to these rules is found where injury is caused by the *fraud* of A. In the usual instance, P is not liable to T for lies, untruths or fraudulent statements or deceitful acts of A—unless P in some manner acquiesed or encouraged them.

If A exceeds his or her authority, P has no obligation to discharge A upon the demand of T.

DUTIES OF T TO P

Generally, T has a duty to honor all contracts entered into with A on behalf of P. But as mentioned, fraud, deceit or other such acts of A, would impair to right of P to claim the benefit of a contract that arose out of such acts. These acts would provide T with a legal defense against A—and thus provide a legal defense against P.

NOTICE

An important part of agency law has grown up around the principle of "notice." P is bound by notice or knowledge that A receives while in the conduct of authority granted. This is true whether it is passed on to P or not. The notice or knowledge must bear, however, upon the scope of authority. Agents are expected to pass on relevant notice and knowledge acquired while carrying out their authority.

For example, an agent unloading a shipment of goods, discovers that the goods are non-conforming. The agent fails to pass this along to P and an unreasonable time elapses so that P loses the right to reject. P is bound to pay the price for the goods—even though they are not what P ordered.

Principals must create a system of "notice routing" and train their agents in the use of this system.

TERMINATION OF THE RELATIONSHIP

If an agency is created to last until a specified time, or until a certain act is completed, then it would end at that time. Other agencies are "agencies at will" and continue for indefinite time periods.

MUST GIVE NOTICE

Once an agency is terminated, P must give notice to third parties to make certain that subsequent acts of A do not bind P. Direct notice, such as by letter, should be given to all those with whom A had transacted business on behalf of P. General notice should be given to all others. "We wish to invite the public to stop at our inn and meet our new innkeeper" would be general notice that the prior innkeeper is no longer on the job.

Turning from agency, lets briefly examine a relationship closely related to agency—yet different in its legal consequences.

INDEPENDENT CONTRACTORS

In many business situations, a principal (P) wants specific results to be accomplished but wants these results to be reached by one who is neither an agent or employee. The laws of independent contractors (IC) covers this type of situation.

The test applied to determine if an independent contractor relationship exists, is two-fold:

1. Is the one doing the job being paid a certain price for a completed project?
2. Is there an absence of control over that person or firm by the principal?

If the answer is "yes" to both, then an independent contractor situation is in existence. In determining if this relationship exists, as a general rule, common and not statutory law prevails. If the answer to one of these questions is "no", then in all probability an agency exists.

If under a contract, one can dictate the result and direct the means by which it is reached, it *would not* be an independent contractor situation. But this does not mean that a principal cannot make periodic inspections in person or by agents and employees to make certain that the specifications are being met. This is permitted and expected. Yet one must keep in mind the distinction between mere inspection, and active supervision. The latter may convert an independent contractor relationship to an agency—something that the principal may not want to happen. If it does happen, the principal faces the risk of loss from third parties. This is the main reason for creating the IC relationship in the first place.

Another test often applied by a court is whether or not the principal can terminate the services of the other at will. If so, it is usually a master-servant, principal-agent and not an IC situation.

The method of payment is another test often applied: payment based upon time denotes a master-servant relationship; lump sum payment a principal—independent contractor situation.

LIABILITY OF PRINCIPAL

Normally, if a principal uses care in the selection of an IC, P is not liable for negligent, careless or wrongful acts of the IC. However, if an IC brings into being a situation of which the principal has primary responsibility, P cannot use the IC relationship to escape that responsibility. For example, a hotel must make certain that fire exits are not blocked. If an IC, while doing repair work in the hotel, blocks an exit, the hotel will be responsible for injury or death caused by the blocked exit.

Generally, a principal (often an owner or general contractor) is not liable for injuries suffered by *servants and agents of the IC*. This presumes, of course, that such injuries arise while the injured party is in the services of the IC, and also assumes that the principal in no way contributes to the injury. As a common-sense rule, a principal should treat servants and agents of an IC, just as any other third parties would be treated. Care and caution is always good business.

An IC is not an employee as defined in the workmen's compensation laws, and therefore is not insurable under such laws. It is the responsibility of the IC to subscribe to these funds and to make certain all servants and agents *of the IC* are properly covered. Conversely, the IC is responsible for withholding, fringe benefits and the like for its agents and employees.

LIABILITY OF IC

An independent contractor is responsible to third parties, in contract and tort, for acts of its employees and agents carried out under authority granted. Since ICs must also act through servants and agents, principles of agency applied to them.

MECHANICS' AND LABORERS' LIENS

One risk confronted by owner-principals who contract for services from independent contractors, is the danger of third party suppliers and laborers, gaining the right to file "mechanics" and "laborers liens". These are filed against the real estate of the owner-principal that is improved by materials supplied and labor performed.

All states have laws permitting such liens to be filed provided that they are filed promptly. Usual time periods are 60 or 90 days after the last material was supplied or the last labor performed. When properly perfected, these become a lien against the real estate of the owner-principal.

GUARDING AGAINST

One can guard against such liens by making certain that laborers and suppliers are paid out of proceeds due to the independent contractor. It is practice for principal-owners to require proof of payment before funds are distributed to the IC. Mechanics liens are seldom used where materials are purchased by employees or agents, nor are laborers lien used for work done by them. In these instances, the principal is primarily liable for the materials and labor and must see that these obligations are met.

If real estate is being financed by an FHA mortgage, mechanics' liens will be subordinate to them, unless the lien was fully perfected before the FHA loan was made.[5] Many states require that the improvements be "visible" before the lien will attach. So an engineering firm who drew construction plans and staked out foundation locations, lost out to a mortgage lender because the stakes were not visible in the tall grass.[6]

WAIVERS OF MECHANICS' LIENS

Can an IC, a supplier or a laborer sign an agreement in advance to waive the right to file such a lien later? In 1975, New York state amended section 34 of the New York Lien law so that such waivers would be void as being against public policy. This provision has been applied retroactively in that state.

ARE MECHANICS' LIENS CONSTITUTIONAL?

Does an IC, a supplier or a laborer have to give notice to a principal and provide an opportunity for a hearing before filing a mechanics' or laborers' lien against the principal's property? The answer seems to be "no" since these liens do not deny the property owner the right to use the property after the lien is filed.[7] This particular topic raises constitutional issues—"The taking of property without due process of law"—and is being looked at by the courts in a variety of cases including mechanics liens situations.

TRUTH IN LENDING DISCLOSURES

When an independent contractor buys materials to build a garage for a consumer, does the supplier have to disclose to the consumer that the supplier will have the right to file a mechanics lien against the consumers home if the supplies are not paid for by the IC? "Yes" says some courts, opening up an unexpected variation in the mechanics lien laws. In one case, the consumer canceled the transaction under Section 125 of Truth in Lending and refused to pay. The court held that there was nothing against which the lien could be enforced and the consumer walked free.[8]

SUMMARY

The independent contractor relationship can be used in many instances where specific results are to be achieved. The advantages of the relationship lie in the sharply reduced liability of the principal-owner. Independent contractors have been used to build swimming pools, remodel a motel into a closed-dome recreation area, pave parking lots and build new motels and hotels from the ground up. The most obvious problems arise when an IC is chosen that does shody or undependable work, or fails to pay laborers or suppliers. Such persons and firms must be avoided.

QUESTIONS

1. Distinguish an agency from an independent contractor relationship by using the characteristics of each.
2. What is the distinction between agents, servants and mere employees?
3. Give an example of an agency by estoppel in the motel business.
4. Distinguish implied and ostensible authority.
5. T. or F. An agent can ratify unauthorized acts of another agent, so long as they serve the same principal.
6. Give an example of a set-off that may arise in an undisclosed principal situation.
7. What is the effect on P, of fraud on the part of A to T, that P knows nothing about? Why?
8. What items would you want your salesmen-agents to place on their daily customer call reports?
9. Name three reasons why a motel owner would want work to be done by an independent contractor.
10. T. or F. An IC will use agents to carry forth his or her work.

ENDNOTES

1. *Forrest v. Hawkins* 169 Va. 470, 194 S.E. 721 (1938).
2. U.C.C. 2-203.
3. *Chandler v. Kelley*, 149 Va. 221, 141 S. E. 389 (1928).
4. *Richmond Guano Co. v. E.I. Dupont*, 284 Fed. 803 (4th Cir. 1922).
5. *Bellegarde Custom Kitchens v. United States*, 42 *U.S.L.W.* 2250 (1974).
6. *Lampert Yards v. Thompson-Weterling Constr.*, 223 N.W. 2d 418 (1974).
7. *Central Sec. National Bank v. Royal Homes, Inc.*, 371 F. Supp. 476 (E.D. Mich. 1979).
8. *Hobbs Lumber Co. v. Shedell*, 42 Ohio Misc. 21, 326 N.E. 2d 706 (1974).

9

Hospitality Employee Relations

Legislation had been passed by Congress in the 1940's that was directed toward achieving equality in employee opportunity and against employment discrimination. But it was not until 1963 that the Equal Pay Act became law. This act required all employees who were subject to the Fair Labor Standards Act to provide equal pay for men and women who were performing similar jobs at each work site.

This was followed in 1964 by the Civil Rights Act, Title VII of which prohibited discrimination because of race, color, religion, sex, or national origin, in hiring, firing, promotions, and other job related activities. In 1967 the Age Discrimination Employment Act became law and this prohibited discrimination because of age in reference to those between the age of 40 and 65. It was limited however, to employers of 25 or more persons.

In 1972, the Equal Employment Opportunity Act (EEOA) was passed by congress and this law amended Title VII. This title now covers labor unions with 15 or more members; all private employers of 15 or more persons; all public and private educational institutions; state and local government; and joint labor-management committees for apprenticeship education.

Under the 1972 amendments, the EEO Commission can go directly to the courts to enforce the law. In addition, organizations and individuals can also go to court for the same reason.

EQUAL EMPLOYMENT OPPORTUNITY ACT

The Civil Rights Act of 1964, contained a weakness: it did not give the Equal Employment Opportunity Commission (EEOC) the power to issue "cease-and-desist" orders (stop doing some act) in the federal courts. Attempts were made to give the EEOC this power but they failed.

Instead of asking for cease-and-desist powers, the Nixon Administration suggested that the EEOC be given the power to file suits in federal court and to represent those who had meritorious employment discrimination claims. The commission could only file suit, however, after all steps had been taken to conciliate the matter without court action. This seemed to satisfy the federal lawmakers.

In 1972, the House acted first with the Senate strengthening the bill. President Nixon signed it into law on March 27, 1972, and it became effective at once. This new law was an amendment of Title VII of the Civil Rights Act of 1964. We will examine briefly the changes in coverage of Title VII of the 1964 Act. The Act itself is set out in Appendix A, beginning on page 402. The importance of this law to the travel-lodging manager, speaks for itself. We will then examine two cases that involve other laws in employee relations.

CHANGES IN TITLE VII

STATE LOCAL GOVERNMENT

Under the original act, employees of state and local government were excluded from coverage. They are now covered, subject to the exemptions below.

FEDERAL EMPLOYEES

These employees are not within the power of EEOC, but the 1972 Amendment makes it clear that the Federal Government shall not discriminate in personnel matters by reasons of race, color, sex, religion or national origin. The Civil Service Commission and not the

EEOC, has power to hear federal employment discrimination matters.

NUMBER OF EMPLOYEES

Title VII originally applied to employers with 25 or more employees. This has been reduced to 15. This change became effective March 24, 1973, one year from the date of passage of the act.

JOINT-LABOR MANAGEMENT

Apprenticeship training and retraining programs are now covered. These programs have been administered in the past by joint committees of labor and management. Discrimination cannot be practiced in admission to or administration of these training programs. If discrimination were permitted at the apprentice or training levels, skilled trade jobs would never be available to such persons.

EXEMPTIONS

Teachers and religious corporations or organizations originally exempt from the 1964 Act are now covered. However, a church, for example, can still discriminate on the basis of religion in hiring an employee- but not on the basis of race, color, sex or national origin. As to coverage of state and local governments, *elected* officials are exempt as well as their assistants. They are easily distinguished from full time employees.

USE OF THE COURTS

If the EEOC is unable to reach a conciliation with the employer, union, employment agency, or joint labor-management committee within 30 days after a charge is filed, the federal courts can be used by the Commission. If the Commission fails to act, or if the complaining party is not satisfied with the actions taken by the commission, that person has direct access to the federal courts. If a state or local government is involved, the Attorney General can bring the court action. Once a suit is brought and the complaining party has set up its defense, the judge has two alternatives; hear the case promptly or appoint a "master" within 120 days to hear the case.

These time dead-lines were written into the law to prevent procrastination by the EEOC or the courts—or both.

EMPLOYER'S OBLIGATIONS

An employer cannot discriminate against a job applicant, or against one who is already an employee, on the grounds set forth above. This extends to compensation, pay raises and promotions. Likewise, employees cannot be segregated or classified or deprived employment opportunities on the stated grounds. For example, any test used in hiring or promotion cannot be a general intelligence test; it must relate to the job in question. A cook cannot be required to pass the same test as a cashier at the front desk of a motel.[1]

EXCEPTIONS

Members of the Communist Party or a party-front organization can be discriminated against on that ground. Religious societies can discriminate on the basis of religion as mentioned. If a government program requires security clearance, then one who does not have that clearance classification can be discriminated against. A motel operating on or near an Indian reservation can show preference toward Indians in their hiring practices. If a company has a bona-fide seniority system in operation, or a merit award system based on quality of work, then different compensation can be paid under those conditions. However, one could never set up such programs for the sole purpose of practicing "discreet discrimination." These must be bona-fide "good faith" programs. The question of employee "imbalance" is something that the courts are beginning to clarify. It is clear from the act that imbalances existing as of the date of passage of the law are not affected. The *continuation* of previous imbalances must be guarded against. "Affirmative action plans" (plans to eradicate prior discriminations) for government construction and manufacturing by private contractors have been upheld.[2] Affirmative action plans are now very much in order.

The business manager should create and be able to demonstrate that there is in operation, an affirmative action program that complies with these employment laws. Many businesses hire or appoint someone to carry out this function. In the small business, it can be a part-time job.

When confronted with a charge of violations of the EEOA, one should do the following; seek legal advice; reply at once on Form 131 which will be provided the employer within 10 days of the charge; conduct an independent investigation; and finally, a detailed written report should be drafted and maintained. Such a report can be used in negotiations with the Commission, or in court if one intends to fight the accusation. The filing of an EEOA complaint or charge, is just an accusation. Proof must still be forthcoming.

NOTICES AND RECORD KEEPING

Notices created by the EEOC must be posted as required and records kept as prescribed. However, if an employer is covered by state fair employment practices law, one set of records can meet both requirements. If an employer feels that the record keeping requirements will present an undue hardship, an application for an exemption must be made direct to the EEOC-not to a court as was permitted in the 1964 version. If the request is denied, one can then look to the courts for record keeping relief if there is good cause for it.

The act has specific provisions for employment agencies, unions, the states and for employees. These are specifically set forth in the statute.

Other laws become important in employee relations. In the following cases, two of these additional laws are discussed.

LANTX v. B-1202 CORPORATION
d/b/a/ BONANZA RESTAURANT
429 F. Supp. 421 (1977).

MEMORANDUM OPINION AND ORDER

JOINER, District Judge.

Plaintiffs seek recovery of overtime compensation allegedly due to them under the Fair Labor Standards Act, 29 U.S.C. § § 201 *et seq.* As restaurant employees, they are covered by 29 U.S.C. § 213(b)(8)(A), effective May 1, 1974, which extended the Act's overtime compensation requirements to them.

Presently before the court is a motion to dismiss all claims for overtime pay for the first six hours of overtime in a given workweek. For the reasons set forth below, the court grants the motion, holding that an employer of restaurant employees is not liable for overtime compensation until the 47th hour of work in any given workweek.

Section 213(b)(8)(A) provides, in pertinent part, that overtime compensation need not be paid to:

"any employee . . . who is employed by an establishment which is a
. . . restaurant and who receives compensation for employment in excess of forty-six hours in any workweek at a rate not less than one and one-half times

the regular rate at which he is employed. . . ." 29 U.S.C. § 213(b)(8)(A). This provision creates a partial exemption from the overtime compensation requirement for the first six hours of overtime work. Plaintiffs' position is that the statute sets forth two requirements: (1) that the employee must be a restaurant employee; and (2) that he or she must be paid time-and-a-half compensation for employment in excess of 46 hours in any workweek. Defendants argue that this provision does not make payment at the time-and-a-half rate for more than 46 hours of work a condition precedent to the applicability of the partial exemption.

In support of its position, defendants cite *Usery v. Valhalla Inn*, 79 LC ¶ 33,446 (N.D. Cal. 1976); *Dunlop v. Saga Enterprises*, 22 WH Cases 650 (C.D. Cal. 1975). In both of these cases, the court declined to hold the employer liable for back pay at the overtime rate for hours worked in excess of 40 in a workweek, although the employer in each case had failed to pay overtime compensation to their restaurant employees for hours worked in excess of 48.

These cases support the defendants' position here, although neither stands for the broad proposition asserted in this case. In *Saga*, the court based its holding on the fact that the employer actually paid overtime compensation to its employees for hours worked in excess of forty-eight immediately upon learning of its statutory duty to do so, and "within a reasonable time after the workweek in which such overtime was earned." 22 WH Cases at 653.

The court in *Valhalla Inn* stated:

> "The receipt by restaurant employees of overtime after 48 hours at the next regular pay day for the workweek involved is not a condition precedent to the application of the Sections 13(b)(8)(A) and 13(b)(18) exemptions if otherwise applicable."

This statement, however, was dictum. Valhalla Inn has assured the Department of Labor that it would comply with the overtime provision in the future and that it had adopted a 40-hour workweek; in exchange for these assurances, the Secretary had agreed not to insist upon a back-pay injunction against the employer's overtime violations.

A literal reading of section 13(b)(8)(A) supports the plaintiffs' construction of it, as the language may be read to require actual payment at the overtime rate for work in excess of 46 hours. A construction of the provision as setting forth conjunctive requirements is reflected, as well, in department regulations applicable to similar partial exemptions. See 29 C.F.R. §§ 778.602(e)(2), (5), .603.

There is no indication, however, that Congress intended such a literal interpretation of this provision. The legislative history shows only that Congress construed the partial exemption as nothing more than that: an extension of the overtime threshold to 48 hours—later, 46 hours—for restaurant, employees. See U.S.Code Cong. & Admin.News, pp. 2811, 2813, 2822, 2833, 2849 (93d Cong., 2d Sess. 1974).

The Secretary of Labor's present policy is to refrain from seeking back pay at the overtime rate for the first six hours of overtime work by restaurant employees who have not been paid at the overtime rate for hours worked in excess of 46 in a given workweek. Instead, the Secretary is enforcing section 13(b)-(8)(A) as an unconditional partial exemption from overtime liability for the first six hours of overtime work. The Secretary's position, in this respect, is that the Act provides adequate sanctions for willful or knowing violators, see 29 U.S.C. §§ 255(a), 260, and that it would serve no purpose to subject restaurant employers to a penalty for violations which are not willful, knowing, or lacking in good faith.

Having considered the precedents, the legislative history, and department policy, the court concludes that Congress did not intend restaurant employers to be penalized by a literal and unbending application of the partial exemption. Rather, it appears that Congress, in extending the benefit of an overtime pay requirement to restaurant workers for the first time, established the partial exemption for the purpose of easing the burden of the new requirement on restaurant employers. It would not serve any statutory purpose to subject employers in technical violation of the relatively new requirement to a penalty, absent some evidence of willfulness, bad faith, or knowledge.

In construing provisions of the Fair Labor Standards Act, courts are directed to "look to the legislative purpose . . . and [to] follow that purpose even though a literal reading of the language used would suggest a different conclusion." *Wirtz v. Allen Green & Associates, Inc.*, 379 F.2d 198, 200 (6th Cir. 1967). "[P]ractical consideration, and not technical conceptions, guide us in determining coverage of the Act. . . ." *Brennan v. Wilson Building, Inc.*, 478 F.2d 1090, 1094 (5th Cir. 1973). These principles of construction were recently reiterated by the Sixth Circuit in *Dunlop v. Carriage Carpet Company*, 548 F.2d 139, 144 (1977).

For the reasons stated in court at the hearing on this matter, the motion for certification of a class is denied. Under Rule XXIV, of the local court rules, this court will accept any cases filed by other similarly situated restaurant employees of Bonanza Restaurant and will consolidate all such cases for determination of the common issue or issues. Plaintiffs' motion for an order of this court requiring notice to employees is granted. The defendant employer is directed to post on a bulletin board an appropriate notice to its employees of this pending action and/or to include such notice in any mailing to its employees that is made in the ordinary course of business. Such notice shall include a blank consent form which the employee may sign and return to counsel for plaintiff to indicate his or her willingness to bring suit in this matter.

So ordered.

BARRE v. HONG-KONG RESTAURANT, INC.,
La. App. 346 So. 2d 318 (1977).

BOUTALL, Judge.

Plaintiff, Mary Barre, filed suit for recovery of workman's compensation benefits. From a judgment dismissing her suit she has appealed.

It was stipulated that the plaintiff cut her left hand and little finger during the course of her employment as a cook at the defendant restaurant; that she was unable to work from February 26, 1974 through Aprill 22, 1974 and during that period of disability she was paid weekly benefits of $65.00 per week; that prior to trial the defendant insurer paid an additional sum of $1,355.00, based upon the schedule of permanent partial disability of the hand.

It was also stipulated that in October of 1974 the plaintiff developed pain in her neck, left shoulder and left arm and that such symptoms were the result of thoracic outlet syndrome. This condition was not related to either the accident or injury sustained on February 25, 1974.

At the trial, the plaintiff called Dr. Harold M. Stokes who testified as her treating physician and as an expert in the field of orthopedic surgery. Dr. Stokes testified that the plaintiff was told that she could return to work in April of 1974, even though she could expect to have some discomfort. The doctor could not give an opinion as to the degree of discomfort suffered by the plaintiff, but did note that no pain medication or analgesics applications were required. Dr. Stokes continued to see the plaintiff from time to time and on September 10, 1974 his examination revealed that the plaintiff had excellent range of motion in the finger and that there was a demonstrated sensation with sweat in the finger. The doctor found the impairment to be 5% of the little finger, and when pressed to relate that to the hand computed only ½ of 1%. He considered her problem to involve only her finger and expected only progressive improvement. He did not believe that the pain from the injury was significant enough to prevent the plaintiff from doing her job.

Subsequent to that September examination, the plaintiff began to suffer pain and symptoms diagnosed by Dr. Stokes and Dr. Bert Glass as thoracic outlet syndrome. In December, 1974, the pain became severe enough that the plaintiff stopped working as a cook with the defendant.

In January, 1975, the plaintiff saw Dr. Gordon McFarland, an orthopedist and hand surgeon who reported he expected the finger and hand to get better by itself, and listed her permanent partial disability to be at one percent of the hand.

On February 28, 1975, the plaintiff was examined by a neurologist, Dr. William Martin. Dr. Martin's summary stated:

Electrodiagnostic studies are normal with no evidence of neuropathy, radiculopathy or myopathy. I am unable to explain the patient's pain syndrome on the results of this study.

It is apparent from the evidence detailed above that the trial judge was correct in his determination that plaintiff suffered no disability for which she had not been paid, either because of pain or because of physical impairment. A party alleging disability because of pain must establish the reasonable existence of that condition by a preponderance of the evidence. The mere claim of pain without some proof is not sufficient to prove residual disability substantial enough to prevent claimant from carrying on the same or similar work. *Gros v. Employer's Insurance of Wausau*, La. App., 338 So.2d 986 (1976).

Similarly, a workman's compensation claimant must prove permanent and total disability by a reasonable preponderance of evidence. *Tyler v. Owens-Illinois*, La. App., 289 So.2d 893 (1974).

Our review of the record necessarily leads us to the conclusion that the plaintiff failed to prove her claim of pain or functional disability resulting from the accident of February 25, 1974. The medical reports and testimony demonstrate to us that whatever pain the plaintiff suffers is caused by the thoracic outlet syndrome. Her functional disability is limited to 5% of the little finger of her left hand, and she has been more than adequately paid for this disability,

For the foregoing reasons, the judgment appealed is affirmed.

AFFIRMED.

QUESTIONS

1. T. or F. Many federal employment laws have been enacted since 1960.
2. Give one reason why the number of "jurisdictional employees" was reduced from 25 to 15 persons under EEOA.

3. What was the weakness in the 1964 Civil Rights Act as it related to employment?
4. Give one reason why teachers were exempted from the 1964 act, and one reason why they are included now.
5. Give one example of when it would be lawful to discriminate in employment.
6. Why can't the same employment test be used for all applicants for employment at a motel?
7. What is an "affirmative action plan?"
8. What precise territories does Title VII cover?
9. Name three unlawful employment practices today.
10. Distinguish Title VII from workmen's compensation laws.

ENDNOTES

1. *Griggs v. Duke Power Co.*, U.S. Sup. Ct. 3 FEP Cases 175 (1971).
2. *Contractors Ass'n of Eastern Pa.* v. *Hodgson*, 3rd Cir. 1971, 3 FEP Cases 395; *cert. denied* U.S. Sup. Ct., 3 FEP Cases 1030 (1971).

10

Hospitality Commercial Paper

Perhaps one of the more important legal areas of study for one in the travel-hospitality field, is found in "commercial paper." It is by the use of such paper that inventory is financed; that agents, independent contractors and employees are paid and it is by such paper that most hospitality accounts are paid by the traveling public. Many phases of modern travel-hospitality activities could not operate without commercial paper. It follows that this paper plays a key role in the operation of any hospitality business. While there has been a movement to replace commercial paper with "electronic money", this has not happened to date to any impressive degree. Thus the importance of an understanding of what commercial paper is, and what it is used for, is just as important today as it was in 1900—and 1800 as well.

SOME HISTORY

The roots of commercial paper can be traced back many centuries, and all civilizations have used such paper—in some form—in business transactions. This has been true over a thousand years, with modern-type refinement appearing in the English statutes of the Thirteenth Century. Commercial paper, based upon the principles created in early times, found wide use in the American Colonies as well as during the first century of the life of the United States. As the range and scope of business increased in America, beginning with the migration to Oregon and California, and followed by the first trans-continental railway in 1869, the need for a better defined body of commercial paper became apparent.

The National Conference of Commissioners on Uniform State Laws, proposed and drafted a uniform commercial paper law which they called the Negotiable Instruments Law (NIL). By the end of the first quarter of the present century, all of our states had adopted the NIL or a modified version of it. This marked a milestone in commercial legal history since it represented, for the first time and perhaps the last, a law of business in each state that was the same as or similar to the laws of the other states. Yet it still lacked true uniformity because of modifications made by the states when adopting it.

Because of the lack of uniformity in the NIL and other laws of business, the National Commissioners drafted and offered to the states the Uniform Commercial Code, Article 3 of which is entitled "Commercial Paper." Today, Article 3 is the law of commercial paper in 49 states with Louisiana as the exception. Perhaps that state will never adopt the U.C.C. since it has its own commercial code, and uses the NIL for its law of commercial paper. In this chapter, we will examine the nature, form, and content of Article 3, keeping in mind that these principles are modern versions of ancient rules of law.

WHAT IS COMMERCIAL PAPER?

Commercial paper consists of documents that are "negotiable" in nature and which serve in the market place in one of three ways: First, commercial paper can serve as a substitute for money; second, it can serve as a means of advancing credit, and third, it can serve as a means of saving money. A document that is "negotiable" has the quality of being able to move from one person or firm to another in the marketplace, free from claims, challenges, doubts and restraints. "Negotiability" is a quality of "transferability" and this concept is widely relied upon in the business community. While the negotiability concept has had some restrictions placed upon it in recent years, it will remain an important part of all business transactions in the immediate years ahead.

TYPES OF COMMERCIAL PAPER

Commercial paper under Article 3 is divided into four categories:

1. Checks.
2. Notes.
3. Bills of exchange.
4. Certificates of deposit.

Checks are familar to all adult Americans and represent a substitute for money. Notes are not so familiar, but are just as important as checks, and provide a means by which one who has funds, can make those funds available to others in the form of loans. As we will see later, notes can be "secured" or "unsecured." Bills of exchange are similar to checks, yet there are differences. A bill of exchange and a check are both "orders to pay", but the order does not have to be directed to a bank in the case of a bill of exchange while it must be in the case of a check. Finally, certificates of deposit are devices by which one can leave funds with a bank to draw interest for an agreed period of time. Thus "CD's" are "savings" documents.

Each of the four categories will be examined in detail, but first, it is essential to become acquainted with the requirements of "negotiability."

REQUIREMENTS OF NEGOTIABILITY

To be a negotiable instrument within U.C.C. 3-104, an instrument must:

1. be signed by the drawer (checks and bills of exchange) or maker (notes);
2. contain an unconditional promise or order to pay;
3. be payable in a sum certain in "money";
4. be payable on demand or at a definite time;
5. be payable to order or bearer.

An examination of these requirements follow;

SIGNATURE

There is no formal requirement for a signature. It can be handwritten, printed by a check writer, or, in some cases, typed. In earlier times, the classic "X" was often used as a signature. The word "signed" is defined in U.C.C. 1-201 (39) to include " . . . any symbol executed or adopted by a party with present intention to authenticate a writing." It can even be a thumb print.

PROMISE OR ORDER UNCONDITIONAL

When one writes (draws) a check, that person is a "drawer" and orders the bank to pay. When one makes a note, that person is a "maker" and promises to pay. Both the order and promise must be unconditional. This requirement is met by the use of the words "pay" on checks or by the words "promise to pay" on notes. Observe that the word "pay" is a command and that it is unconditional. If a check said "please pay if you have the time," that would not be an unconditional order or command.

In practice, notations are often placed on the face of negotiable instruments for informational purposes, such as the date each monthly payment is paid. Factual statements of the transaction do not disturb the unconditional requirement. However, any notations inconsistent with the note or that make the promise or order conditional or even appear to be conditional, could disturb the negotiability of the instrument. To illustrate, a $2 million dollar note was executed, and at some point a notation of "9/4" was placed on it by someone other than the maker. The maker used this uncertainty to contest the note claiming that this was a "material alteration." At trial it was determined that a teller had made this as a notation of precomputed interest, and the court found it was not a material alteration.[1] While the maker was held responsible for the value of the note, the negotiable features of it had been seriously disturbed in the meantime. In addition, the holder of the note was placed to the expense in time and money of suing on the note. This must be avoided in the creation and use of commercial paper. Extra words and figures can be dangerous.

SUM CERTAIN

A negotiable instrument must be payable in money or "current funds". One payable in foreign currency is certain because the exchange rate can be determined with precision.

U.C.C. 3-106 (1) states in part, that a sum is certain even though it is to be paid:

(a) with stated interest or by stated installments:

(b) with stated different interest rates before or after default on a specified date;

(c) with a stated discount or addition if paid before or after due date;

(d) with costs of collection or an attorneys fee.

An instrument payable in "an ounce of gold" or "fifty bushels of wheat", would not be a sum certain since neither is "currency." Such an instrument would fail the test of negotiability.

TIME CERTAIN

If an instrument is payable "on demand" or "at sight or presentation", the time of payment is certain in that it must be paid when demand is made. Otherwise, if it is a time instrument, one must be able to examine the face of it and calculate the exact day on which it must be paid. If this can be done, it is payable at a "time certain." Most notes are payable on a set date in the future. If a note or check is silent as to time of payment, it is a "demand" instrument. A check dated ahead would be a "time" instrument, and so would a note.

PAYABLE TO ORDER OR BEARER

The fifth requirement of negotiability, is that the instrument must be payable to "order", or payable to "bearer."

An instrument is *payable to order* when, by its terms, it is payable to the "order" (command) of any person who is specified on the instrument. It can also be payable to that person's assigns, and it can be payable to that person's order. To say it another way, one to whom an instrument is made payable may order the instrument paid to him or her - or to any other person to whom he or she orders the money to be paid.

U.C.C. 3-110 tells us that an instrument may be made payable to:

(a) the maker or drawer;

(b) the drawee;

(c) a payee who is not maker, drawer or drawee;

(d) two or more payees together or in the alternative;

(e) an estate, trust or fund, in which case it is payable to the order of the representative of each estate; trust or fund or his successors;

(f) an office, or an officer (by his title as such), in which case it is payable to the principal, but the incumbent of the office or his successors may act as if he or they were the holder;

(g) a partnership or unincorporated association, in which case it is payable to the partnership or association and may be indorsed or transferred by an authorized person.

An instrument that contains such words as "payable upon return of this instrument properly indorsed" is *not* payable to order and is not negotiable. Between the immediate parties it would be a good contract - but it could not serve in the marketplace as a substitute for money. An instrument made payable "to order or bearer" is payable to order. However, if the bearer word is handwritten or typewritten, the word bearer will control.

An instrument is *payable to bearer* when by its terms it is payable to:

(a) bearer or the order of bearer;

(b) a specified person or bearer;

(c) "cash" or the order of "cash", or any other indication which does not purport to designate a specific payee.

MISCELLANEOUS PRELIMINARY MATTERS

Other preliminary matters that involve the creation of commercial paper, should be examined at this time. These are quoted from the Uniform Commercial Code.

TERMS AND OMMISSIONS

The negotiability of an instrument is not affected by:

(a) the omission of a statement of any consideration or of the place where the instrument is drawn or payable; or

(b) a statement that collateral has been given to secure obligations either on the instrument or otherwise of an obligor on the instrument or that in case of default on those obligations the holder may realize on or dispose of the collateral; or

(c) a promise or power to maintain or protect collateral or to give additional collateral; or

(d) a term authorizing a confession of judgment on the instrument if it is not paid when due; or

(e) a term purporting to waive the benefit of any law intended for the advantage or protection of any obligor; or

(f) a term in a draft providing that the payee by indorsing or cashing it acknowledges full satisfaction of an obligation of the drawer; or

(g) a statement in a draft drawn in a set of parts (Section 3-801) to the effect that the order is effective only if no other part has been honored.[3]

INCOMPLETE INSTRUMENTS

(1) When a paper whose contents at the time of signing show that it is intended to become an instrument is signed while still incomplete in any necessary respect, it cannot be enforced until completed, but when it is completed in accordance with authority given it is effective as completed.

(2) If the completion is unauthorized, the rules as to material alteration apply, even though the paper was not delivered by the maker or drawer; but the burden of establishing that any completion is unauthorized is on the party so asserting.[4]

INSTRUMENTS PAYABLE TO TWO OR MORE PERSONS

An instrument payable to the order of two or more persons

(a) if in the alternative is payable to any one of them and may be negotiated, discharged or enforced by any of them who has possession of it;

(b) if not in the alternative is payable to all of them and may be negotiated, discharged or enforced only by all of them.[5]

If a check or note is drawn or made to "A or B," it is payable to either (U.C.C. 3-116 (a)). A note or check payable to "A and B" is payable to both, not either (U.C.C. 3-116 (b).) But what if it is payable to "A and/or B."? A Colorado court ruled that 3-116 (a) applies, *and either can be paid.* The court looked to the official Comments of the U.C.C. which contains an observation on this point. *Lohf v. Warner* 495 P. 2d 241, 10 U.C.C. Rep. 850. For a case in which a court held that when a note is made payable to "A or B", and the note goes into default, *either may bring suit* on it even though the other objects, see *McDonald v. McDonald,* 232 Ga. 199, 205 S.E. 2d. 850 (1974).

An insurance company made a check payable to "claimant and claimant's lawyer." The lawyer indorsed it, forged the clients signature and then cashed it. What now? The court applied the U.C.C. 3-116 (b) rule and held that since both signatures were required, and since only one signed, the bank had to make good the loss.

INSTRUMENTS PAYABLE WITH WORDS OF DESCRIPTION

An instrument made payable to a named person with the addition of words describing him

(a) as agent or officer of a specified person is payable to his principal but the agent or officer may act as if he were the holder;

(b) as any other fiduciary for a specified person or purpose is payable to the payee and may be negotiated, discharged or enforced by him;

(c) in any other manner is payable to the payee unconditionally and the additional words are without effect on subsequent parties.[6]

AMBIGUOUS TERMS AND RULES OF CONSTRUCTION

The following rules apply to every instrument:

(a) Where there is doubt whether the instrument is a draft or a note the holder may treat it as either. A draft drawn on the drawer is effective as a note.

(b) Handwritten terms control typewritten and printed terms, and typewritten control printed.

(c) Words control figures except that if the words are ambiguous figures control.

(d) Unless otherwise specified a provision for interest means interest at the judgment rate at the place of payment from the date of the instrument, or if it is undated from the date of issue.

(e) Unless the instrument otherwise specifies two or more persons who sign as maker, acceptor or drawer or indorser and as a part of the same transaction are jointly and severally liable even though the instrument contains such words as "I promise to pay."

(f) Unless otherwise specified, consent to extension authorizes a single extension for not longer than the original period. A consent to extension, expressed in the instrument, is binding on secondary parties and accommodation makers. A holder may not exercise his option to extend an instrument over the objection of a maker or acceptor or other party who tenders full payment when the instrument is due.[7]

Turning from the creation of negotiable paper, it becomes necessary to examine the principles surrounding the transfer and negotiation of commercial paper.

TRANSFER AND NEGOTIATION

The creation of a perfect negotiable instrument means nothing until that document is "issued" or "transferred" to another. An "issuance" requires a proper delivery to the holder. A basic rule is that the issuance must be voluntary. A completed check that is stolen by another would not be a lawful issuance.

In most instances, the document is handed to or mailed to the other. In a few instances, it may be retained by the drawer or maker and issued by "constructive delivery." A note, for example, may be placed into escrow until a certain undertaking is completed or until a certain event occurs.

Once an instrument has been properly issued, one of four basic things may be done with it:

1. It may be deposited to the account of the person to whom it was issued if it is a check or draft.
2. It may be cashed by the one to whom it was issued if it is a check or draft.
3. If it is payable to bearer, it may be delivered to anyone, usually in satisfaction of an existing debt.

4. If payable to order, it must be indorsed before it can be deposited, cashed, or delivered to a third party.

Items 1, 2 and 4 require that the instrument be "indorsed" in some manner by the one to whom it is payable. In item 3, an indorsement is *not* required, although most persons request an indorsement in order to create extra "warranties." Warranties will be examined later.

"Indorsement" is defined as the signing or marking of an instrument, with or without qualifying words, with the intent to make a transfer. An indorsement may be on the instrument itself or an attachment to it called an "allonge."[8] Examine Figure 10-1.

FIGURE 10-1
"An Allonge"

(When making a special indorsement, it is not necessary to use the words "pay to the order of". "Pay to" is sufficient).

There are five types of indorsements.

TYPES OF INDORSEMENTS

BLANK INDORSEMENT

This is the most common type and comes into being when the indorser signs his or her name only and does not use additional words. For example, a check is issued payable to the order of Mark Stevens. Mark turns the check over and on the left hand end of the check writes "Mark Stevens." Such an indorsement changes an order instrument into a bearer instrument and is dangerous for that reason. If it is lost, another may claim rights to it by the mere possession and "presumption of delivery." This indorsement is commonly used at the tellers window as one prepares to cash a check.

SPECIAL INDORSEMENT

This type of indorsement names the person or firm to whom the indorser wants the instrument paid. That person or firm can then name another person or firm. What this does is change the document from the order of the first indorser to the order of the second one who holds it. Technically this process could continue through the hands of dozens of persons and firms. As space runs out on the document, an "allonge" can be glued to it. In theory, one negotiable instrument can be used to settle a hundred different debts. In practice, an instrument is usually "curbed" while still relatively new. This is done by cashing it or by adding a restrictive indorsement.

RESTRICTIVE INDORSEMENT

If the first holder wants to obtain cash from the instrument, it is simply cashed. If one wants the instrument deposited, it is stamped or marked "For Deposit Only." This is the most common type of restrictive indorsement. Another form would be "Pay Bill Jones Only." This restricts further negotiation. The U.C.C. defines a restrictive indorsement as one that is either

    (a) conditional;

    (b) purports to prohibit further transfer of the instrument;

    (c) includes the words "for collection", "for deposit", "pay any bank" or like terms signifying a purpose of deposit or collection;

    (d) otherwise states that it is for the benefit or use of the indorser or of another person. [9]

EFFECT OF RESTRICTIVE INDORSEMENT

(1) No restrictive indorsement prevents further transfer or negotiation of the instrument.

(2) An intermediary bank, or a payor bank which is not the depositary bank, is neither given notice nor otherwise affected by a restrictive indorsement of any person except the bank's immediate transferor or the person presenting for payment.

(3) Except for an intermediary bank, any transferee under an indorsement which is conditional or includes the words "for collection", "for deposit", "pay any bank", or like terms must pay or apply any value given by him for or on the security of the instrument consistently with the indorsement and to the extent that he does so he becomes a holder for value.

(4) The first taker under an indorsement for the benefit of the indorser or another person must pay or apply any value given by him for or on the security of the instrument consistently with the indorsement and to the extent that he does so he becomes a holder for value. A later holder for value is neither given notice nor otherwise affected by such restrictive indorsement unless he has knowledge that a fiduciary or other person has negotiated the instrument in any transaction for his own benefit or otherwise in breach of duty.[10]

CONDITIONAL INDORSEMENT

Such an indorsement conditions the payment upon the happening of an event. They are not widely used and can be troublesome in practice if they are used.

QUALIFIED INDORSEMENT

A typical qualified indorsement is "Without Recourse." The indorser is saying, "if the instrument is dishonored, do not look to me under the rules of express warranties." Such an indorsement does not in any manner impair negotiability.

One who indorses a negotiable instrument and then later "reacquires" that same document, is in an interesting position.

REACQUISITION

Where an instrument is returned to or reacquired by a prior party, he or she may cancel any indorsement which is not necessary to his or her title and reissue or further negotiate the instrument. But any intervening party is discharged as against the reacquiring party and subsequent holders not in due course, and if his or her indorsement has been canceled, that person is discharged as against subsequent holders in due course as well.[11] Examine Figure 10-2.

Turning from indorsements, it becomes important to gain a general understanding of the doctrine of "holders in due course." This is a preferred status and one of great importance to business persons.

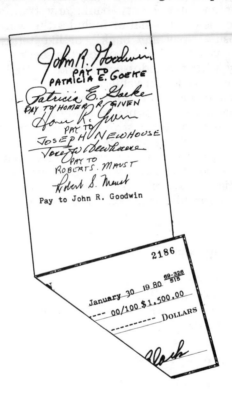

FIGURE 10-2

HOLDERS IN DUE COURSE

The doctrine of holders in due course (HDC) developed as part of the basic principles of commercial paper. By 1950, this was one of the better established areas of law, but the consumer movement changed that somewhat. Because of this, we must examine the HDC doctrine as it relates to both business persons and consumers.

BUSINESS PERSONS AND THE HDC DOCTRINE

For one to be a holder in due course, that person must have taken an instrument for value, in good faith and without notice of a claim against it or a defense to it.

The definition of "value" parallels the definition of "consideration" under contract law. An exception lies in "antecedent debts." An existing debt will not provide consideration in a contract—while it will provide value within the HDC doctrine.

Second, the instrument must be taken in good faith, which the U.C.C. tells us means "honest in fact." If a payee of an instrument is so closely intertwined with a later holder that it can be presumed that the latter knows the business practices of the former, good faith may not exist.

Finally, a holder must not have notice of any claim or defense against the instrument by any other person. The U.C.C. provides that one has notice of a claim or defense " . . . if the instrument is so incomplete, bears such visible evidence of forgery or alteration, or is otherwise so irregular as to call into question its validity, terms of ownership or to create an ambiguity as to the party to pay."[12]

The U.C.C. further sets forth classes of persons who cannot be an HDC, such as one who acquires an instrument at a judicial sale; one who acquires it by taking over an estate, and one who acquires it in a "bulk sale" that is not in the regular course of business of the transferor.

If one qualifies as an HDC, with limited exceptions, that person is entitled to be paid on the instrument regardless of claims, defenses or other matters unknown to the HDC. The status is much like one who receives a $1,000 bill in a transaction. That person need not worry if the bill had been stolen in a robbery sometime in the past.

CONSUMERS AND THE HDC DOCTRINE

Under the Federal Trade Commission Act, the FTC was given a broad grant of authority in consumer credit matters.

First, since May 14, 1976, it has been unlawful for any "sellers" to take a consumer credit contract unless it contains the following notice printed in ten-point or larger type:

NOTICE

ANY HOLDER OF THIS CONSUMER CREDIT CONTRACT IS SUBJECT TO ALL CLAIMS AND DEFENSES WHICH THE DEBTOR COULD ASSERT AGAINST THE SELLER OF GOODS OR SERVICES OBTAINED (PURSUANT HERETO OR) WITH THE PROCEEDS HEREOF. RECOVERY HEREUNDER BY THE DEBTOR SHALL NOT EXCEED AMOUNTS PAID BY THE DEBTOR HEREUNDER.

In addition, if a seller has a continuing relationship with a lender, and refers customers to the lender, or is affiliated in some manner with that lender, then the seller must make certain that the note contains the following notice;

NOTICE

AND HOLDER OF THIS NOTE IS SUBJECT TO ALL CLAIMS AND DEFENSES WHICH THE DEBTOR COULD ASSERT AGAINST THE SELLER OF GOODS OR SERVICES OBTAINED WITH THE PRO-CEEDS HEREOF. RECOVERY HEREUNDER BY THE DEBTOR SHALL NOT EXCEED AMOUNTS PAID BY THE DEBTOR HEREUNDER.

Under this FTC rule, a seller is defined as " . . . a person who, in the ordinary course of business, sells or leases goods or services to consumers." This would seem to exclude consumer related real estate transactions from the coverage of the FTC rule. One who breaches the FTC rule is guilty of an unfair and deceptive act and violates Section 5 of the Federal Trade Commission Act, becoming liable for the penalties thereunder.

Turning from the HDC doctrine, it becomes necessary to examine checks and notes as they are encountered in practice.

CHECKS IN USE

A check is an instrument signed by the drawer which orders the *drawee* (bank) to pay the sum stated to the *payee* or *holder* of the document. The check has three basic parties, the holder, or holders simply being an extension of the payee. A check represents a present obligation to pay, unless it is dated ahead—then it is a promise to pay later. A check contains no recitation of consideration such as "For Value Received", and may be taken by another as a gift.

Provided that a check meets the requirements of negotiability, it is a true negotiable instrument and the most common found in business. Because of its widespread, constant use, problems arise more frequently in the use of checks than in the use of notes. On the other hand, the standarized form of checks makes them the easiest to create.

RIGHTS AND LIABILITIES OF THE DRAWEE

A bank (drawee) may refuse to pay a check if it lacks proper indorsements; if it is drawn against insufficient funds, and if it is presented for payment more than six months after its date. In the latter instance, the check is said to be "stale."

A drawee can be held liable for improper payment when the signature of the drawer is forged; if the check has been altered, and when an indorsement is missing. A drawee is also liable if it pays a check upon which a proper "stop-order" has been made.

STOP-ORDERS

One who draws a check may stop payment by notifying the drawee, giving the check number, date and other relevant data. The stop-order may be made by phone and is good for 14 days. If reduced to writing within that time period, it is good for 6 months, which takes the check into the "stale" rule. The stop-order can also be renewed. There is a considerable body of law on stop-orders and, in general, the stop-order must come at a time that gives the drawee a reasonable time to act upon it. The burden of proving loss for payment on a "stopped item" is upon the drawer-not the drawee. All that is required is that the drawee act in good faith.

DISHONORED CHECKS

If a check is dishonored, the holder-payee must give notice and protest to parties liable on the instrument. After that, it can be treated as a "collection item". One who holds a dishonored check should try to redeposit it, since it might clear the second time.

WARRANTIES

DRAWERS

A drawer warrants that upon notice of dishonor or protest, the drawer will pay the amount of the check to the holder. The drawer also admits the existence of the payee and the capacity of the payee to indorse the check.

INDORSERS

Every indorser warrants that upon dishonor, followed by notice, that he or she will pay the check "according to its tenor" at that time, to the holder or later indorser. Unless otherwise agreed, indorsers are liable to one another in the order in which they sign. (See Figure 10-1.) An exception would be found where a reacquirer strikes out previous indorsements.

An indorser may escape warranty liability if a qualified indorsement was used, and also if that person is a mere "accomodation indorser".

NOTES IN USE

A note is a two party item created by the *maker* and is payable to the *payee*. It must meet the test of negotiability as to form and it is most often a promise to pay in the future. Notes are widely used in real estate and personal property financing. See Figure 10-3.

If notes meet the requirements of negotiability, they may be transferred from one to another by indorsement, just as checks can be transferred. The principles of indorsements discussed above apply to notes.

WARRANTIES

A maker promises to pay the note as it was made or as it was completed, if completed as the maker instructed. The maker warrants the existence of the payee and the capacity of that person to indorse.

STATUTES OF LIMITATIONS

All states have a limit of time in which a note that is due can be collected. In New York this time is six years. A maker made a note in 1967 "payable thirty days after demand." Demand for payment was made in 1974. The court ruled that the note had no value since the six years began to run on the date of the note-not from the date that demand was made.[13] The error of the holder was in not recognizing that this was a demand note-not a time instrument.

CERTIFICATES OF DEPOSIT IN USE

The interest payments on CD's are higher than on savings accounts

FIGURE 10-3

Fayette City, Ohio   January 15, 1979

     FOR VALUE RECEIVED, I promise to pay to the
order of The Westover Bank, Holland Avenue, Westover, Ohio,
the full and just sum of Five Thousand ($5,000.00) Dollars
together with interest thereon at the rate of Ten (10%) per
annum.

     This note shall be paid in equal, consecutive
monthly installments of not less than Two Hundred ($200.00)
Dollars which payments shall first be applied to interest
and the balance to principal. The first payment shall be
made on the 15th day of February, 1979, and a like payment
on the same day of each month thereafter until the full
principal balance plus interest is fully paid and satisfied.

     This note is secured by a mortgage on certain
real estate situate in Lyons District, King County, Ohio,
this day conveyed in trust to John Sterling.

     WITNESS the following signatures and seals:

                       J. Robert Losh (SEAL)
                       J. Robert Losh

                       Jean L. Losh (SEAL)
                       Jean L. Losh

---

and attract depositors because of this. Since CD's are actually a form
of a note payable at a fixed future time, the bank is free to make
use of the funds in the meantime. Being negotiable, they can be
used by the owner to pay obligations before their due date. They can
also be used as collateral for loans. CD's are transferred by indorsement, just as checks and notes.

BILLS OF EXCHANGE IN USE

    "Bills of exchange" can take various forms. One is a "bank accep-
tance" which is a time draft drawn on a letter of credit. Bank accep-
tances are widely used in foreign transactions. It is drawn on and
accepted by a bank. The drawer is expected to cover the item by its

maturity date. A bank acceptance is basically a grant of a *banks credit* rather than a grant of its *funds*. Its use enables a seller to collect on the debt due the seller without having to collect the funds first in order to make a covering deposit by the due date.

A "trade acceptance" is drawn by the seller of goods on the *buyer of the goods*. The seller can then discount the acceptance at a bank. Their use enables a seller to be paid at once for goods sold. The buyer must then pay the amount of the draft to the bank on its maturity date.

A "sight draft" is an order by a seller, directed to the buyer's bank to honor the draft. A "bill of lading" is usually attached. When the buyer pays the draft, the bank will release the bill of lading, thus freeing the goods to the buyer.

It can be seen that bills of exchange are different from checks in their creation yet both serve the same functions.

A HOTEL CHECK

Hilton International has entered the commercial paper field in a unique manner. They are issuing "Hilton Cheques" in the sums of $36 or $45. The former is for a single room, the latter for a double. These are honored at any of 28 Hilton Hotels in Europe, North Africa and Israel. This is true no matter what the local rate for the room may be. In the nine of the 28 Hilton Hotels where the room-rates are below these prices, meals are included with the room to make up the price difference. These checks are similar to travelers checks—but their use is limited, of course, as intended by Hilton International. Examine Figure 10-4. It should be observed that they *could* be used to pay debts to those who would be willing to accept them. Thus they would be treated to that extent as any other commercial paper.

FIGURE 10-4

QUESTIONS

1. What reason can you suggest for the anticipated wide acceptance of "electronic money" not becoming a reality?
2. Why must a check be unconditional?
3. Why doesn't costs of collection on a note disturb the sum certain?
4. How does Article 3 treat "Pay to the Order or Bearer"?
5. Give an example of a check payable in the alternative.
6. T. or F. Printed terms on a note are superior to written terms on it.
7. Does a restrictive indorsement prevent further negotiation of an instrument?
8. Why can a "reacquirer" strike out certain indorsements?
9. What are the three requirements to make one an HDC?
10. When a check is dishonored, what must one do and how quickly should it be done?

ENDNOTES

1. *Sterling Nat'l Trust Co. v. Fidelity Mort. Investors,* 510 F. 2d 870, 16 U C.C. Rep. 157 (2d Cir. 1975).
2. U.C.C. 3-111 (2).
3. U.C.C. 3-112 (1).
4. U.C.C. 3-115.
5. U.C.C. 3-116.
6. U.C.C. 3-117.
7. U.C.C. 3-118.
8. U.C.C. 3-202 (2).
9. U.C.C. 3-205.
10. U.C.C. 3-206.
11. U.C.C. 3-207.
12. U.C.C. 3-304 (1) (a).
13. *Environics, Inc., v. Pratt,* 18 U.C.C. Rep. 143 (1975).

11

Informal Hospitality Organizations

The vast majority of travel-lodging business organizations are corporations. Some are partnerships and a few may be proprietorships. The latter are rare today—although this was not the case 20 years ago. In this chapter, for purposes of achieving a balanced understanding of legal forms of business, we will first examine proprietorships, and then examine the legal principles of partnerships. And in the following chapter, a close look will be taken at corporations, how they are formed, their legal nature, and how they operate.

PROPRIETORSHIPS

A proprietorship is a business which is owned and most often operated by one person. The ownership is vested in that person only. No one else has any legal interest in the business. A proprietor may hire a manager and employees to run the business, and the sole ownership retains intact. If a husband and wife jointly own a business, it could not be a proprietorship because the single ownership requirement would not be present.

The conduct of a business in this form carries no limitations on liability; the owner always faces unlimited liability. The continuance of the business depends upon the ability of the proprietor to continue its operation. If a proprietor becomes incapacitated, or dies, the business must undergo some change or transformation for it to survive. A father, as a sole owner, can will his motel to his son, but upon the father's death, the priprietorship of the father has ended.

Some business persons see advantages in conducting business in this form, mostly from the standpoint of maintaining absolute control. But as a practical matter, the proprietor of today is going the way of the cigar-store Indian and the five-cent glass of beer.

A more common form of business is found in the partnership.

PARTNERSHIPS

The Uniform Partnership Act (UPA) defines a partnership as ". . . an association of two or more persons to carry on as co-owners of a business for profit."[1] This definitions tells us several things:

1. Two or more "persons" must be involved. (A corporation can be a "person" within the meaning of the UPA).
2. These persons must be co-owners. (A proprietor and an employee would not be partners for this reason.)
3. There must be continuity of business. (It cannot be a single business venture that ends at the completion of some specific undertaking).
4. The business activity must be carried on with the objective of making a profit. (A firm that *tries* to make a profit but loses money would still meet the requirement of this provision).

All businesses or firms that meet this definition are partnerships. In practice, it is often difficult to establish the existance of a partnership as will be illustrated later.

There are various types of partnerships that should be examined.

TYPES OF PARTNERSHIPS

"Commercial partnerships" are firms engaged in "trading"—buying and selling. "General" firms are those " . . . in which the parties carry on their trade or business, whatever it may be for the joint benefit and profit of all of the parties concerned, whether the capital be limited or not, or the contributions thereto be equal or unequal."[2] A "limited partnership" is one " . . . consisting of one or more general partners, jointly and severally responsible as ordinary partners, and by whom the business is conducted, and one or more special partners, contributing in cash payments a specific sum as capital, and who are not liable for the debts of the partnership beyond the fund so contributed."[3] A "partnership at will" would be one set to continue for no fixed period of time. A "special partnership" is one created to pursue a special branch of business as contrasted with a general partnership. A "subpartnership" is one in which one partner in a firm takes another person as a partner with him in relation to his share of the profits of the primary firm. Partnerships in these various forms are encountered in the travel-lodging industry.

It is helpful to become acquainted with the various terms and definitions set out in the UPA.

TERMS AND DEFINITIONS

"Court" includes every court and judge having jurisdiction in a partnership case. "Business" includes every trade, occupation or profession. "Persons" includes individuals, partnerships, corporations, and other associations. (Thus two corporations could be partners under the UPA). "Conveyance" includes assignments, leases, mortgages and encumberances.

Next, the Act contains provisions relating to knowledge and notice.

INTERPRETATION OF KNOWLEDGE AND NOTICE

(1) A person has "knowledge" of a fact not only when he has actual knowledge thereof, but also when he has knowledge of such other facts as in the circumstances shows bad faith.

(2) A person has "notice" of a fact when the person who claims the benefit of the notice:

(a) States the fact to such person,
(b) Delivers through the mail, or by other means of communication, a written statement of the fact to such person or to a proper person at his place of business or residence.[4]

Thus under the UPA, one can have notice of a fact when an employee receives notice. This can become important in the determination of various legal rights as we have seen and as we shall see.

The Act contains rules of construction to assist the courts in deciding partnership disputes. These are quoted from Part 1, sections 4 and 5 of the UPA.

RULES OF CONSTRUCTION

(1) The rule that statutes in derogation of the common law are

to be strictly construed shall have no application to this act.

(2) The law of estoppel shall apply under this act.

(3) The law of agency shall apply under this act.

(4) This act shall be so interpreted and construed as to effect its general purpose to make uniform the law of those states which enact it.

(5) This act shall not be construed so as to impair the obligations of any contract existing when the act goes into effect, nor to affect any action or proceedings begun or right accrued before this act takes effect.

RULES FOR CASES NOT PROVIDED FOR

In any case not provided for in this act the rules of law and equity, including the law merchant, shall govern.

As mentioned previously, it is often difficult for a court to determine if in fact a partnership exists. If it does not, then the UPA does not apply. The Act sets forth the following rules to assist the courts in this regard.

RULES FOR DETERMINING THE EXISTENCE OF A PARTNERSHIP

In determining whether a partnership exists, these rules shall apply:

(1) Except as provided by section 16 persons who are not partners as to each other are not partners as to third persons.

(2) Joint tenancy, tenancy in common, tenancy by the entireties, joint property, common property, or part ownership does not of itself establish a partnership, whether such co-owners do or do not share any profits made by the use of the property.

(3) The sharing of gross returns does not of itself establish a partnership, whether or not the persons sharing them have a joint or common right or interest in any property from which the returns are derived.

(4) The receipt by a person of a share of the profits of a business is *prima facie* evidence that he is a partner in the business, but no such inference shall be drawn if such profits were received in payment:

  (a) As a debt by installments or otherwise,
  (b) As wages of an employee or rent to a landlord,
  (c) As an annuity to a widow or representative of a deceased partner,
  (d) As interest on a loan, though the amount of payment vary with the profits of the business,

(e) As the consideration for the sale of a good-will of a business or other property by installments or otherwise.[5]

Turning from these preliminary matters, we must examine the nature of partnership property.

PARTNERSHIP PROPERTY

All property originally brought into the firm, or later acquired for the partnership, is firm property. In addition, all property acquired with firm funds is firm property unless a contrary intention appears. Contrary to the common law rule, title to real property may be acquired in the firm name. If so, it can only be conveyed to others in the firm name. The same is true of personal property. While real and personal property can be acquired in the name of one or all of the partners as individuals, this creates unnecessary legal problems and should be avoided.

PROPERTY RIGHTS OF A PARTNER

Each partner has three distinct property rights:

1. Each has rights in "specific partnership property." To illustrate, A B and C form a partnership. A contributes $1,000, B contributes $4,000 and C contributes nothing but agrees to work for six months without wages. The $5,000 is used to buy a truck which C is to operate for the firm. A B and C each have rights in the truck—it is *specific partnership property.* None of them can claim any right in the truck to the exclusion of the others. This form of ownership is distinct and is referred to as a "tenancy in partnership." A does not have a 1/5 interest nor does B have a 4/5ths interest in the truck. All three have an undivided partnership interest in every square inch of the vehicle. Because of this, individual creditors of the partners have no direct access to firm property. Firm property cannot be attached or levied on by a creditor of one partner because the other partners have rights in that same property.

2. Each partner has a right to his or her "interest" in the firm. Translated, "interest" means earnings and surplus of the firm.

3. Each partner has a right to participate in the management. Unless agreed otherwise, each partner has an equal vote in all firm matters regardless of the amount of capital contribution of each.

Thus we see that the UPA treats partners as equals regardless of the amount each places into the business. This concept is important and will be examined later in detail. The Act now sets forth in detail the nature of the rights in specific property.

NATURE OF A PARTNER'S RIGHT IN SPECIFIC PARTNERSHIP PROPERTY

(1) A partner is co-owner with his partners of specific partnership property holding as a tenant in partnership.

(2) The incidents of this tenancy are such that:

   (a) A partner, subject to the provisions of this act and to any agreement between the partners, has an equal right with his partners to possess specific partnership property for partnership purposes; but he has no right to possess such property for any other purpose without the consent of his partners.

   (b) A partner's right in specific partnership property is not assignable except in connection with the assignment of rights of all the partners in the same property.

   (c) A partner's right in specific partnership property is not subject to attachment or execution, except on a claim against the partnership. When partnership property is attached for a partnership debt the partners, or any of them or the re-representatives of a deceased partner, cannot claim any right under the homestead or exemption laws.

   (d) On the death of a partner his right in specific partnership property vests in the surviving partner or partners, except where the deceased was the last surviving partner, when his right in such property vests in his legal representative. Such surviving partner or partners, or the legal representative of the last surviving partner, has no right to possess the partnership property for any but a partnership purpose.

   (e) A partner's right in specific partnership property is not subject to dower, curtesy, or allowance to widows, heirs, or next of kin.[6]

ASSIGNMENT OF INTEREST

If a partner assigns his or her interest in the firm to a private creditor, this does not dissolve or otherwise disturb the firm. The assignee (the one to whom the assignment is made) has no right to interfere in the management of the business, or to inspect the books of the firm.

If a private creditor of a partner brings suit against a partner and obtains a judgment, the Act provides a means by which the interest of the debtor-partner can be reached.

PARTNER'S INTEREST SUBJECT TO CHARGING ORDER

(1) On due application to a competent court by any judgment

creditor of a partner, the court which entered the judgment, order, or decree, or any other court, may charge the interest of the debtor partner with payment of the unsatisfied amount of such judgment debt with interest thereon; and may then or later appoint a receiver of his share of the profits, and of any other money due or to fall due to him in respect of the partnership, and make all other orders, directions, accounts, and inquiries which the debtor partner might have made, or which the circumstances of the case may require.

(2) The interest charged may be redeemed at any time before foreclosure, or in case of a sale being directed by the court may be purchased without thereby causing a dissolution:

(a) With separate property, by any one or more of the partners, or

(b) With partnership property, by any one or more of the partners with the consent of all the partners whose interests are not so charged or sold.

(3) Nothing in this act shall be held to deprive a partner of his right, if any, under the exemption laws, as regards his interest in the partnership.[7]

The above principles of partnership property are important and should be reviewed until they are understood. This is necessary to gain an effective understanding of relations of partners with third parties and with themselves.

RELATIONS OF PARTNERS WITH THIRD PARTIES

Each partner is treated as being the agent of each of the other partners. They are the legal counterparts of each other. When one does an act for the apparent purpose of carrying on the usual business of the firm, it binds the firm and thus all of the partners. (Examine Figure 11-1).

FIGURE 11-1

ABC Partnership

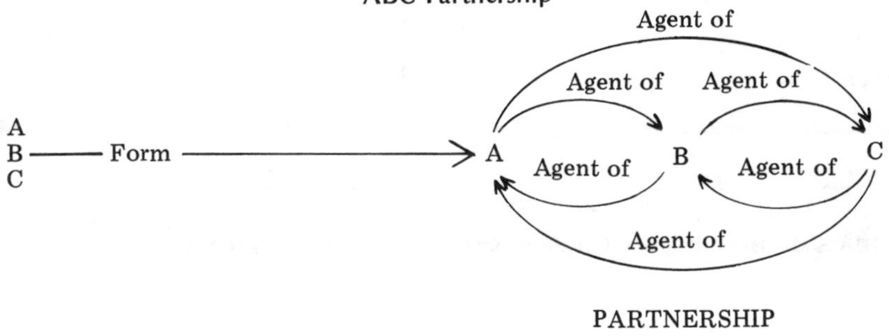

PARTNERSHIP

However, if a third person knows or should know that a proposed act is not for the purpose of carrying on the usual firm business, then that act does *not* bind the firm. Because of this, third parties must use care. If A tries to pledge the credit of the firm in order to obtain funds to buy a tractor-trailer, and the lender knows the firm runs a motel only, it would be obvious that a firm purpose was *not* involved. If the loan is made in spite of this, the lender could not look to the firm for payment of the debt—only to the partner who made the loan.

There are five specific acts that a partner is prohibited from doing with third persons: (1) assigning firm property for creditors, (2) disposing of the goodwill of the firm, (3) any act that would make it impossible for the firm to carry out its usual business, (4) confession of a judgment in court, and (5) submitting a partnership claim to arbitration. It must be observed however, that any of these five items *could* be done with the consent of all of the partners. These principles tells us that a third party must always use care and give some thought to the nature of a pending transaction with one partner.

To illustrate, ABC partnership operates a condominium unit. A offers to sell to the manager of Holy Hotel a truck load of furniture taken from the condominium. This act could well fit into the prohibition (3) above. Faced with such circumstances, a third party must use caution—even if bargain prices are being offered. If the manager buys without inquiry, the firm can recover the furniture since it is partnership property. The act clearly states, "No act of a partner in contravention of a restriction on authority shall bind the partnership to persons having knowledge of the restriction."[8] It must be remembered that "knowledge" can arise from the surrounding circumstances and does not have to be direct knowledge.

ADMISSIONS OF A PARTNER

An admission or representation made by one partner to a third party, that relates to partnership affairs, can be used as evidence against the firm. Because of this, partners tend to be closed-mouth when discussing firm business with tax personnel, bankers and others.

NOTICE OF ONE PARTNER

What one partner knows, or should know, is held to be the knowledge of the firm. This makes it imperative that partners freely communicate knowledge with each other-but not with third parties.

PARTNER'S WRONGFUL ACTS

One partner acting in the ordinary course of business places liability upon the other partners for any act or inaction that harms or causes loss to a third party, because they are agents of each other. The liability of the partners for such wrongs are "joint—or several." That is, the injured party can sue them all, or only one. Liability for breach of contract is "joint"—so they must all be sued.

LIABILITY OF INCOMING PARTNER

A person admitted as a partner into an existing partnership is liable for all the obligations of the partnership arising before his admission as though he had been a partner when such obligations were incurred, except that this liability shall be satisfied only out of partnership property.[9] This provision gives one quite a few things to think about when contemplating becoming a partner in an existing firm. It must be noted, however, that a new partner cannot be taken in without the consent of all other partners.

RELATION OF PARTNERS TO EACH OTHER

Partners share equally in profits regardless of their contributions. They can agree otherwise, but this is unwise, since one must contribute equally toward any losses," . . . according to his share in the profits."[10] To illustrate, assume the following contributions.
   A. $1,000
   B. $2,000
   C. $3,000

They agree that all profits shall be shared as follows:
   A. 1/5 th
   B. 2/5 ths
   C. 3/5 ths

The firm now earns $10,000 "interest". It will be distributed as follows:
   A. $2,000
   B. $4,000
   C. $6,000

Now assume that the firm *loses* $6,000. Each must contribute the following toward the loss.

 A. $1,000
 B. $2,000
 C. $3,000

This is the reason that equal sharing of profits is generally the best idea.

If a firm is "dissolved," and "wound up," then each partner is entitled to have his or her capital contributions returned in full before surplus or interest is shared. This provides even better reason for equal sharing.

INDEMNIFICATION

The firm must indemnify (make whole) any payment made by one partner out of personal funds for firm business. If a delivery of food arrives at the restaurant after hours and A pays the delivery charges out of pocket, the firm must indemnify A.

INTEREST

If one partner makes a loan or advance above the agreed contribution to capital, then that partner is a creditor of the firm and is entitled to interest on those funds. Once a partnership is dissolved, wound-up and terminated, each partner is entitled to be paid interest on capital contributions until they are paid. With these two exceptions, partners are *not* entitled to interest on funds they place in a partnership.

SALARIES

As a general rule, partners are not entitled to be paid wages for their services. They gain by their sharing of profits and surplus (interest). However, a surviving partner is entitled to reasonable compensation in winding up the partnership affairs.

The following sections from UPA, Part 4, spells out the final obligations of partners to each other.

PARTNERSHIP BOOKS

The partnership books shall be kept, subject to any agreement between the partners, at the principal place of business of the partnership, and every partner shall at all times have access to and may inspect and copy any of them.

DUTY OF PARTNERS TO RENDER INFORMATION

Partners shall render on demand true and full information of all things affecting the partnership to any partner or the legal representative of any deceased partner or partner under legal disability.

PARTNER ACCOUNTABLE AS A FIDUCIARY

(1) Every partner must account to the partnership for any benefit, and hold as trustee for it any profits derived by him without the consent of the other partners from any transaction connected with the formation, conduct, or liquidation of the partnership or from any use by him of its property.

(2) This section applies also to the representatives of a deceased partner engaged in the liquidation of the affairs of the partnership as the personal representatives of the last surviving partner.

RIGHT TO AN ACCOUNT

Any partner shall have the right to a formal account as to partnership affairs:

(a) If he is wrongfully excluded from the partnership business or possession of its property by his co-partners,

(b) If the right exists under the terms of any agreement,

(c) As provided by section 21,

(d) Whenever other circumstances render it just and reasonable.

CONTINUATION OF PARTNERSHIP BEYOND FIXED TERM

(1) When a partnership for a fixed term or particular undertaking is continued after the termination of such term or particular undertaking without any express agreement, the rights and duties of the partners remain the same as they were at such termination, so far as is consistent with a partnership at will.

(2) A continuation of the business by the partners or such of them as habitually acted therein during the term, without any settlement or liquidation of the partnership affairs, is *prima facie* evidence of a

continuation of the partnership.

The final topic that we will examine is that of "dissolution," "winding up" and "termination."

Since partnerships are normally made up of human beings whose lives must of necessity end in time, this topic is of importance. One should understand at the beginning of a partnership what is going to happen at the end of it.

DISSOLUTION

The dissolution of a partnership is " . . . the change in the relation of the partners caused by any partner ceasing to be associated in the carrying on . . . of the business."[11] Death, imprisonment, bankruptcy, insolvency, walking out, court decree, disability and many other things that can occur to one partner can "dissolve" the partnership. But we must hasten to point out that the word only refers to a preliminary condition. The firm still exists for business purposes—but the relationship between the parties is not the same after dissolution.

Thus a partnership is not terminated by dissolution and continues until the winding up stage. If the partners had created a buy-and-sell agreement funded by life insurance, then upon the death of A, B and C buys out the share of A, and the firm continues as the B and C partnership. If not, then the business must proceed to the winding up stage.

If dissolution is caused by the wrongful act of a partner, such as theft or breach of fiduciary responsibility, then the Act provides rules that can determine liability and distribution. For our purposes, we will assume that A, B and C have operated a motel for a number of years as a partnership, and A has passed away.

EFFECT OF DEATH

The liability of A continues in spite of the death and it does not discharge the liabilities of the others toward A. In addition, the individual assets of A are liable for A's firm obligations, subject to the claims of the individual creditors of A to those assets. That is, the individual estate of each partner is subject to both private and business debts, with the former having first claim against them.

DISTRIBUTION

For purposes of distribution, the assets of a firm are found in two places: (1) partnership property (this is why it is important to identify firm property) and (2), contributions of the partners needed to pay off all firm liabilities. Here is found the reason why a partner faces unlimited liability to third persons.

ORDER OF PAYMENT

The liabilities of the firm are ranked as follows:

1. Those owing to creditors other than partners.
2. Those owing to partners other than for capital and profits.
3. Those owing to partners in respect of capital.
4. Those owing to partners in respect of profits (interest).[12]

TO ILLUSTRATE

Two examples are set out to illustrate these principles in use. First, assume these facts: A, B and C form a partnership with capital contributions as follows:

A - $1,000
B - $2,000
C - $3,000

The agreement is silent on sharing of profits (losses) so they share equally. They transact business for years, make a profit, and divide the interest at the end of each year. The firm files an "informational partnership tax form" each year and each partner reports the interest received as personal income.

This month, A dies. At that time, the ownership of A immediately passes to B and C—but for *partnership purposes.* There is no buy-and-sell agreement in effect since they never created one. So B and C recognize that this dissolution must be carried to the winding up and termination stages. This is due to the fact that the widow of A wants no part in the firm and is demanding that she be paid the share of A. B and C complete existing contracts, avoid new business, and carefully liquidate all assets, real and personal, and this brings $98,000. The debts owed to firm creditors total $50,000. Applying the order of distribution, it works out this way:

1. $50,000 is paid to firm creditors.
2. The capital is returned as follows:

A - $1,000
B - $2,000
C - $3,000

3. The excess, or $42,000, is then divided into three parts or $14,000 to each partner and $14,000 to A's widow.

The total distribution is as follows:

A's Estate (widow)	$15,000
B	$16,000
C	$17,000

(For purposes of simplicity, it was assumed that B and C made no charge for their services in winding up. If they had, it would simply have been paid first.)

ANOTHER EXAMPLE

All facts remain the same except, (1) A had made a loan to the firm of $10,000 with interest, and (2) after liquidation, only $64,000 was realized. The distribution will now be as follows:

1. $50,000 to firm creditors leaving $14,000.
2. $10,000 plus interest due of $1,000 to the estate of A - (his widow), leaving $3,000.

This leaves $3,000 with which to pay off the capital contributions, which total $6,000, or an operating loss of $3,000. This loss must be shared equally, or $1,000 to each partner.

CAPITAL CONTRIBUTIONS	SHARE OF LOSS
A $1,000	1,000
B $2,000	1,000
C $3,000	1,000
	$3,000

The distribution to A's Estate, and B and C, is then as follows in respect to capital:

A's Estate	.000
B	1,000
C	2,000
	$3,000

The distribution of the $3,000 in this manner leaves the former partners in an equal relationship with each other.

The recap of the distribution follows:

Firm Creditors	$50,000
A's Estate	11,000
B.	1,000
C.	2,000
	$64,000

If the operating loss had been greater the individual assets of each partner would have been looked to - subject to the prior claim of individual creditors.

If the individual assets of one partner are exhausted before the partnership share is paid, then the solvent partners must absorb that additional amount, sharing it equally. The solvent partners would then have a cause of action against the insolvent partner, or his or her estate.

It should be understood that the steps illustrated here are simplified. In practice the determination is made according to standard accounting procedures.

The Act contains provisions that relate to those who continue a partnership after dissolution and spell out the rights of the retiring partner, or the estate of the deceased partner. These are complex and beyond the scope of our discussion.

The UPA contains a section that relates to "limited partnerships".

LIMITED PARTNERSHIPS

As we have observed, a general partner faces unlimited liability as a member of a firm. The Act sets forth provisions by which one can join a firm, but not be subjected to this unlimited liability. This portion of the Act requires three things:

1. A document must be prepared and placed on record to give notice of the limit on liability.
2. The limited partner's name cannot be used in the firm name.
3. The limited partner cannot take an active voice in the management of the firm business. A limited partner must be a true "silent partner."

However, if a firm is in financial trouble, a limited partner may be consulted for advice. In *Trans-Am Builders, Inc. v. Woods Mill, Ltd.*,[13] the court said it would be unreasonable to hold that a " . . . . limited partner may not advise the general partner and visit the partnership business, particularly when the project (a building in progress) is confronted with severe financial crisis."

Following is a partnership-hospitality case:

TAYLOR v. LEWIS
553 S.W. 2d 153 (Texas 1977)

ON MOTION FOR REHEARING

REYNOLDS, Justice.

In affirming the trial court's judgment on original consideration, we held that the record failed to reflect that certain of appellant's points of error were preserved for review. Accompanying appellant's motion for rehearing is appellees' concession of a procedural correctness that, together with our erroneous computation as to the time the judgment became final, causes us to withdraw our 18 April 1977 opinion, together with the resulting judgment, and to substitute the following:

Plaintiff Alton R. Taylor failed to convince a jury that he became a partner with defendants H. C. Lewis, Harold Chapman and Ray Chapman in a motel venture or that the defendants had breached his employment agreement. Because no reversible error is presented, we affirm the trial court's take-nothing judgment.

Harold Chapman and Ray Chapman owned land in Lubbock, Texas, on which contractor H. C. Lewis was to construct the Lubbock Inn Motel. Considering the land and construction at cost, the Chapmans were to own fifty per cent and Lewis was to own the other one-half of their partnership venture.

As the construction was beginning in November of 1971, Alton R. Taylor expressed to Harold Chapman his interest in managing the motel. After a series of meetings, it was orally agreed that Taylor would manage the motel. For his management services, Taylor was to be furnished an automobile, was to receive a salary of $800 each month during the construction, a $1,000 monthly salary after the motel opened, and at such time as there were profits, Taylor was to receive ten per cent of the profits to be applied toward the purchase of a ten per cent interest in the motel as determined by the cost of the land and the construction.

Taylor began his services in January of 1972. The Lubbock Inn Motel became operational in September of that year. The operation had not produced any net profits up to 21 May 1973 when, upon execution of an agreement between the parties, Taylor ceased to manage the motel. The agreement, reciting that a dispute has arisen whether Taylor is a partner and has properly managed the Inn and that defendants demand that Taylor relinquish management, provides that Taylor, upon receipt of his accrued salary and without recognizing the propriety of the demand, shall peacefully relinquish management without waiving any of his rights.

Thereafter, Taylor filed this suit against H. C. Lewis, individually and as independent executor of the estate of Elaine Lewis, deceased, and the Chapmans to establish the existence of a partnership and for an accounting, settlement and winding up of the partnership affairs. Alternatively, he sought damages for breach of his employment agreement.

The litigants are in accord with respect to their basic understanding, which is merely an executory agreement to form a partnership in the future when the condition precedent—i.e., the realization of net profits—is fulfilled. Notwithstanding, Taylor contends, and the defendants deny, that they intended, as shown by their expressions and implied from their conduct and the surrounding circumstances, to enter into a relationship which included the essential elements of a partnership so that, in fact, their association became a partnership.

To evince the partnership, Taylor produced evidence that he left a job of long standing to go with defendants at a sacrifice in regular monthly income, hoping and expecting to make some money in the new venture. He went to Chicago to purchase furniture with the defendants, who publicly referred to

him on occasions in Lubbock as a partner. He and defendants signed applications for a beverage cartage permit, a mixed beverage permit, a mixed beverage late hours permit, a sales tax permit and a caterer's permit in which he was
listed as a partner as well as in the permits issued pursuant thereto. Taylor was
shown as an owner in an application for a store license. Three newspaper items
referred to him and the defendants as either the builders or operators of the
motel and none of the defendants voiced any objection. He, together with the
defendants, executed a bank renewal note in the sum of $200,000 for interim
financing of the motel. He was listed on a certificate of assumed name supplement as one of the parties conducting the business of The Lubbock Inn. An
insurance policy issued to the Lubbock Inn as a partnership showed Taylor to
be one of the partners. Although he was reported on the quarterly employer's
reports for 1972 as an employee, he was not so reported for 1973. In the United
States Partnership Return of Income for 1972, he was listed as a partner with a
ten per cent interest in the net operating loss of The Lubbock Inn. The general
ledger of the motel showed him as a partner and the stubs for the checks issued
to him in 1973 were marked "Partner's Withdrawal."

Taylor acknowledged that the agreement failed to provide what should be
done in the event of a loss instead of a profit and failed to provide a date for the
conveyance of his ten per cent interest. Although he said it was "discussed"
that he might "buy in" by assuming ten per cent of the indebtedness if defendants were able to borrow the money for the entire project, he did not testify
that such was a part of the agreement between the litigants.

It was the defendants' position that their basic agreement was never changed;
that there was no agreement, and no testimony by Taylor, or anyone else, that
he could become a partner simply by assuming ten per cent of the partnership
debts; and that the relationship never ripened into a partnership with Taylor.
Their testimony was that Taylor was included on the liquor applications because
they were advised the Liquor Control Board required everyone with an interest,
direct or indirect, to be shown, and Lewis was of the opinion that Taylor had
the applications for the liquor permits, as well as the applications for the store
license and sales tax permit, filled out. The county clerk prepared the certificate
of assumed name supplement. The accountant who prepared the tax return
stated he never was told by defendants that Taylor was a partner, and he prepared the return showing Taylor as an income tax partner without any concern
whether he was a legal partner. There was testimony that Taylor signed the bank
renewal note at the request of the banker; that no one told the banker that
Taylor was a partner; that the designation "partner," which was adjacent to the
signatures of the signing defendants, was not placed by Taylor's signature on the
note; that the bank note was paid, but that Taylor made no payment on the
note; and that Taylor did not execute the original bank note or the final note
for $1,550,000 to finance the motel venture.

It was the testimony of Harold Chapman that he and Taylor never used the
word "partnership" and Taylor never claimed to be a partner before May of
1973. He further said that neither he nor, so far as he knew, any of the other
defendants, had any knowledge that the motel books showed, or authorized
the books to be changed to show, Taylor's salary as a partner's withdrawal
account. Ray Chapman's summary of the relationship was: "We assumed that
sometime down the road that when we got the thing finished we would establish
a purchase price and by the time he [Alton Taylor] would either give us a note
for a hundred and fifty or sixty-five thousand, 10 per cent of whatever the
thing cost, or have something to work into to let his bonus apply on the purchase of, but a partnership was never mentioned, it wasn't thought of in that
sense."

Alternatively, Taylor pleaded a "wrongful discharge" generally; he did not plead that his employment was for a definite period of time or that there were specific contractual limitations on discharge. Taylor acknowledged that nothing had been said in the pre-employment discussions about defendants' right to fire him at any time or his right to quit at any time. After mentioning some problems of operation of the motel, Taylor stated that on or about 15 or 16 May 1973, Ray Chapman made objections to the operation and finally said, "If this thing isn't changed, we want you to leave;" and then added, "The fact of the business, we do want you to leave." Taylor asked, "When?" He was told, "The sooner the better." When asked by his counsel, Taylor responded that he did not quit, but that he was fired.

The Chapmans testified that no term of Taylor's employment was discussed or agreed on. Harold Chapman, with whom Taylor first discussed management employment but who was not present when the relationship was terminated stated that, regardless of the recitations in the 21 May 1973 agreement, Taylor was not discharged, but that he quit. On this issue, Lewis' testimony was that, although there was cause to discharge Taylor, he gave no ultimatum to Taylor, that he neither demanded nor participated in making any demand that Taylor leave, and that Taylor was not fired. Ray Chapman reported that in the 14 or 15 May 1973 conversation with Taylor about Taylor's management shortcomings, Taylor became irritated and said, "If you think you can get somebody else to run this place better, you ought to do it." Ray Chapman testified that he did not reply that Taylor was fired, but said, "I think it's come to that point, Alton," adding that some time would be needed to find a replacement.

Taylor failed to convince the eleven jurors who signed the verdict that be became a partner with Lewis and the Chapmans. Although these jurors found that Lewis and the Chapmans agreed to employ Taylor, they found there was no specific period of employment and failed to find that Taylor was discharged from his employment. From the trial court's take-nothing judgment Taylor has appealed, designating six points of error.

By his points three and five, Taylor respectively contends that the court erred in failing to direct a verdict as to the existence of a partnership and that he was discharged by defendants. Because Taylor had the burden of proof on these two issues, an instructed verdict would have been proper only if he established a partnership or a wrongful discharge as a matter of law; otherwise, if there is any conflicting evidence of a probative nature, the determination of the issues was for the jury.

With respect to point three, the Texas Uniform Partnership Act, Vernon's Ann. Civ.St. art. 6132b (1970), defines, in § 6(1), a partnership as an association of two or more persons to carry on as co-owners a business for profit, and sets forth, in § 7, the rules that shall apply for determining the existence of a partnership. Clearly, from these requisites, persons who intend to do the things that constitute a partnership are partners whether their expressed purpose was to create or avoid the relationship.

In connection with both points, Taylor argues that the acts, words and conduct of the parties establish as a matter of law the intent of the parties that he be a partner, and that the 21 May 1973 agreement establishes conclusively that he was discharged. For the reason that we must indulge every inference that properly may be drawn from the evidence against the instruction of a verdict, we cannot say that the issues were established as a matter of law. The evidence upon the issues, which has been previously summarized, was conflicting and resulted in fact issues which were properly submitted to the jury for determination. Points three and five are overruled.

The jury answered "No" to the first special issue asking whether Taylor

became a partner with Lewis and the Chapmans at some point in time after
his employment and prior to 21 May 1973. In submitting this issue, the court,
as a part of its instruction, advised the jury that:

By the term "partnership" is meant a relationship between two or more
persons where there is a common enterprise and a community of interest as
co-owners therein, a prosecutuion of the common enterprise for the joint
benefit of the parties, and a right of each of the parties to participate to some
extent in the profits as such and an obligation of each of the parties to bear
some portion of the losses, if any, sustained in the business (Emphasis added.)

During its deliberation, the jury submitted to the court this question: "Would
an expansion or definition on 'Co-Owners' be possible?" Counsel for Taylor
requested the court to clarify the term by instructing the jury that "it was not
limited to those who contributed property but included also those who became
Co-Owners by reason of contribution of services." The court declined to so
instruct, but instead instructed the jury that "no further definition would be
given."

These actions by the court prompt Taylor's first point of error, a multifarious
one. It embrances, as shown by his argument and an examination of the cited
authorities, two contentions: first, the court erred in including the words "as
co-owners" in the definitional instruction without certain qualifications of its
meaning; second,the court erroneously refused to define "co-owners" at the
jury's request.

Taylor is not in a position to complain that the court did not define the
word "co-owners" in its charge. When the court did not define the word, Taylor
was required by Rule 279 to tender in writing a substantially correct definition
to preserve his complaint. Rather than submitting a substantially correct definition, Taylor merely asserted that the court should clarify the distinction between ownership of assets belonging to the partnership and ownership of an
interest in the partnership itself that was implied by use of the word "co-owners." Under these circumstances, the failure to tender a substantially correct
definition as a part of the requested instruction waived the complaint now made.

Moreover, it was not incumbent upon the court, and especially so in the
absence of a valid predicate, to define the term "co-owners" in its charge. While
the court is obligated by Rule 277 to "submit such explanatory instructions and
definitions as shall be proper to enable the jury to render a verdict," the rule
ordinarily operates to require a definition of only those words or phrases given
a distinctive meaning by law. The word "owner" is one of common use having
no special legal or technical meaning apart from its ordinary acceptation and,
therefore it need not be defined. The prefix "co-" is, according to Webster's
New International Dictionary (2nd Ed.), used with nouns to mean "with;
together; joint." The combination of the two, then, has no meaning other than
the common meaning of joint owners or owners together. So, generally, the
term needs no definition for the juror of average intelligence, who would be
presumed to construe the use of the word in its usual and ordinary sense.

Rule 286 does provide that the jury, after it retires, "may receive further
instructions of the court touching any matter of law" at its request. The reason
for the jury's request for an expansion or for a definition of the word "co-
owners" is neither apparent from the wording of its request as was the situation
in *Stacks v. Rushing*, 518 S.W.2d 611, 613 (Tex.Civ.App.—Dallas 1974, no writ),
nor stemmed from an error obvious on the face of the charge as was the circumstance in *Missouri Pacific Railroad Company v. Cross*, 501 S.W.2d 868,
870 & 873 (Tex.1973). Nevertheless, once the jury made its request, it indicated
the jury was seeking guidance in rendering a verdict and, consistent with the
rules, it became proper—i.e., suitable, right, appropriate—for the court to affirm-

atively, and not negatively, respond. The court could have responded, as the court did in *Southwestern Greyhound Lines, Inc. v. Dickson*, 219 S.W.2d 592, 594 (Tex.Civ.App.—Austin 1949, no writ), that the term was used in the issue in its usual and ordinary meaning, or the court could have given the definition of the term.

The refusal to affirmatively respond to the jury's request invokes the inquiry whether the error amounted to such a denial of Taylor's rights as was reasonably calculated to cause and probably did cause the rendition of an improper judgment. As the only evidence thereof, Taylor refers to the affidavits of jurors attached to his motion for judgment non obstante veredicto. Those instruments show, so Taylor says, that when the court refused to expand upon the meaning of "co-owners," at least three jurors who had originally voted to answer special issue no. 1 "Yes," accepted the interpretation of some jurors that one could not become a co-owner simply by reason of services when others had contributed property, and voted to answer the issue "No." We may not consider the affidavits. They are hearsay and are not evidence of the matters stated therein, but only serve to particularize the evidence to be elicited on a hearing before the court. The record is devoid of any hearing at which the affiants testified to the matters stated in the affidavits.

The most that can be said is that the refusal to affirmatively instruct left the jury free to misconstrue the usual and ordinary meaning of the phrase "as co-owners." It is settled, however, that a misconstruction of the court's charge does not of itself authorize the setting aside of the court's judgment. The jury's failure to find that Taylor became a partner is not, as later discussed, so against the great weight and preponderance of the evidence as to be clearly wrong and unjust. Accordingly, it does not reasonably appear from this record that the court's failure to affirmatively respond to the jury's request was such an error that was reasonably calculated to cause and probably did cause the rendition of an improper judgment. Rule 434. The first point is overruled.

During the pendency of the cause, Taylor directed requests for admissions of fact "within ten days after service" to each defendant individually and, on the same day, submitted the same requests to all defendants jointly. Primarily, the requests were for admissions concerning the defendants' states of mind in making and filing federal income tax returns for 1972 allocating a loss to Taylor as a partner, and in designating him as a partner in a sales tax permit application. More than half of the admissions sought in each request were conditioned on answers that might be made to other admission requests.

Each defendant filed answers to the requests directed to him individually on the twenty-first day after he was served and approximately two and one-half years before trial. The defendants did not file a reply to the requests directed to them jointly.

After the trial commenced, Taylor orally moved the court to deem admitted all requests because the individual responses were not made within the time he specified and the request for joint admissions was unanswered. The trial court overruled the motion and refused to deem the matters admitted. This action is the subject matter of Taylor's second point, the crux of his argument being that Rule 169 requires the admissions requested.

Rule 169 was designed, not as a trap to prevent the presentation of the truth in a full hearing but as a tool for the fair disposition of litigation with a minimum of delay. Thus, the court has considerable discretion whether to apply the sanctions authorized by Rule 169, and the ruling of the court will be disturbed only upon a showing of a clear abuse of that discretion. Under this record and aside from the fact that deeming all of the requests admitted would result in contradictory admissions, we perceive no abuse of discretion sufficient to disturb the court's ruling.

Rule 169 allows "not less than ten days after delivery" of the request from a response; consequently, Taylor's demand for responses "within ten days after service" was defective for not following the requirements of the rule. *Bynum v. Shatto, supra*, at 810-12. Absent his allowance of at least the minimum time mandated by the rule for a response, Taylor has not shown the court clearly abused its discretion in refusing to deem admitted the requests answered twenty-one days after service and some two and one-half years before trial.

The unanswered requests directed to the defendants jointly to secure admissions as to the state of mind of the defendants consisted of the identical admissions, albeit with some variation in wording, which were requested of, and answered by, each defendant individually. Because admissions serve as evidence in lieu of the testimony of witnesses, 2 McDonald, Texas Civil Practice § 10.06 (1970), the demand should be for admissions of relevant and material evidentiary facts within the knowledge of the opposing party and not for inadmissible opinions. While a witness may testify to his own intention and state of mind where the same is material, *Hamburg v. Wood*, 66 Tex. 168, 18 S.W. 623, 625 (1886), the courts uniformly exclude the offer of testimony by a witness as to another person's state of mind where the conduct and other circumstances from which the witness would draw his inference of the other's state of mind could be so communicated to the jury that they would be equally well equipped to draw the inference. See 2 C. McCormick & R. Ray, Texas Law of Evidence § 1428 (2d ed. 1956), and authorities there cited. Here, the same requests made to the defendants individually were answered, the documentary evidence was introduced and the witnesses testified before the jury. The request for joint admissions bearing on the state of mind of others runs afoul of legal principles and, particularly under the circumstances of this cause, should not be deemed admitted facts. *White v. Watkins, supra*. It follows that we cannot say that the court clearly abused its discretion if refusing to deem admitted the admissions requested but unanswered. The second point is overruled.

Taylor utilizes his fourth point of error to submit that the jury's failure to find he became a partner with the defendants is against the great weight and preponderance of the evidence. The particulars of the documentary evidence and the testimony earlier noticed, together with related testimony by other witnesses, were before the jury. It was for the jury, as the finder of facts, to judge the credibility of the witnesses, to assign the weight to be given their testimony, and to resolve the conflicts and inconsistencies in the testimony. To this end, the jury was privileged to believe all or part or none of the testimony of any one witness. We have, as *Traylor v. Goulding*, 497 S.W.2d 944, 945 (Tex.1973), directs we must, weighed all of the evidence. Given the controlling legal principles, we cannot say, with due deference to the jury's prerogative, that the jury's failure to find that Taylor became a partner is so against the great weight and preponderance of the evidence as to be manifestly unjust. The fourth point is overruled.

Point six is drafted to complain of error in submitting special issue no. 8, one of the issues submitted relative to Taylor's cause of action for wrongful discharge. It was the issue inquiring whether, and the one in response to which the jury found that, the litigants did not agree on a specific period as the duration of Taylor's employment.

The point lists three grounds for the error, but Taylor, citing *Gulf Insurance Company v. Hodges*, 513 S.W.2d 267 (Tex.Civ.App.—Amarillo 1974, no writ), argues only that the issue should not have been submitted because it is an inferential rebuttal issue. *Hodges* does hold that an inferential rebuttal issue should not be submitted, but Taylor did not voice this objection to the trial court in his objections to the court's charge. Therefore, the point, as it is briefed and argued, was not preserved for appellate review. Rules 272 and 274; *Marino v. Vigilant Insurance Company*, 523 S.W.2d 518, 520 (Tex.Civ.App.—Houston [14th Dist.] 1975, no writ). Moreover, it is unnecessary to resolve the validity of the point. When Taylor failed to convince the jury that he was discharged and did not attack the answer as being against the great weight and preponderance of the evidence, his cause of action for wrongful discharge was at an end and the error, if any, in submitting special issue no. 8 became immaterial.

Taylor's motion for rehearing is overruled. The judgment of the trial court is affirmed.

QUESTIONS

1. Could two corporations be partners under the UPA definition?
2. How can one know something that he in fact does *not* know?
3. Does the law of agency apply in partnership legal matters?
4. Write out a description of "specific partnership" property.
5. What is the legal effect of the assignment to another of a partners interest in the firm?
6. What is the legal effect of one partner submitting a partnership claim to arbitration?
7. What does "joint or several" liability mean?
8. Distinguish "dissolution" from "termination" giving an example of each.
9. T. or F. If partners have a workable buy-and-sell agreement, the dissolution stage can be avoided.
10. The assets of a partnership may well include *private* assets of a partner. Why?

ENDNOTES

1. UPA Sec. 6 (1).
2. *Elridge v. Troost*, 3. Abb. Prac. N.S. (N.Y.) 23.
3. *Moorhead v. Seymour* (City CT. N.Y.) 77 N.Y.S. 1054.
4. UPA, Part 1, sec. (3).
5. UPA, Part 2, sec. (7).
6. UPA, Part 5, sec. (25).
7. UPA, Part 5, sec. (28).
8. UPA, Part 3, sec. (4).
9. UPA, Part 3, sec. (17).
10. UPA, Part 4, sec. (18) (a).
11. UPA, Part 6, sec. (29).
12. UPA, Part 6, sec. (40) (b) (i) to (iv).
13. (Ga APP.) 210 S.E. 2d. 866 (1974).

Formal Hospitality Business Organizations

By far, the majority of travel and lodging activities are carried out by use of the corporate form. For example, it is unlikely that any of the major public air lines are owned and operated by partnerships or proprietorships. The risk of loss would prevent it if nothing else. In addition, almost all modern lodging facilities are corporate owned. Of course, we must recognize that a corporation may have but one stockholder. But even in that event, the assets of the business are still owned by the corporation. The stockholder simply owns the stock—*not* the corporate assets. This introduces us to the basic corporate concept—the separation of ownership from management. This will be developed in detail as we proceed. First, just what *is* a corporation?

A DEFINITION

A corporation has been defined as "an artificial person or legal entity created by or under the authority of the laws of a state or nation, composed in some . . . instances, of a single person and his successors, being the incumbents of a particular office, but ordinarily consisting of an association of numerous individuals, who subsist as a body politic under a special denomination, which is regarded in law as having a personality and existence distinct from its several members, and which is, by the same authority, vested with the capacity of continuous succession, irrespective of changes in its membership, either in perpetuity or for a limited term of years, and of acting as a unit or single individual in matters relating to the common purpose of the association, within the scope of the powers and authorities conferred upon such bodies by law."[1]

This definition, though lengthy, contains the legal features of the corporation and can be broken down for study purposes.

1. It is an entity in itself.
2. It is a "person" - but it is *an artificial person*, and can be taxed. It is also extended some, but not all constitutional rights.
3. It is created by a grant from a state or nation.
4. It can be owned by one or more persons.
5. It can have continuous existence, meaning theoretically that it can never die.
6. Its life can be set for a prescribed number of years.
7. It will have powers and authorities conferred upon it by law.

Corporations can be classed in various ways and these help orient one to the corporate concept.

CLASSIFICATIONS

DOMESTIC AND FOREIGN

As this classifications relates to our states, a "domestic" corporation is one that is transacting business in the state where it was formed. A "foreign" corporation is operating out of the state of formation. One corporation can be both domestic and foreign if it operates in two or more states.

PARENT AND SUBSIDIARY

A subsidiary corporation is one in which a parent corporation owns at least a majority of the shares, and thus has control of the subsidiary.

SOLE AND AGGREGATE

A sole corporation would have one stockholder, an aggregate, two or more.

DEFACTO AND DEJURE

A defacto corporation is one in which a good faith attempt has been made to bring the corporate form into existence, but some defect has occurred. It in fact lacks legal authority to act as a corporation, but a court may hold that it does exist under "color of law". That is, while it was not perfectly formed, corporate protection is still extended to the stockholder or holders. A dejure corporation is one that " . . . exists by reason of full compliance by incorporators with requirements of an existing law permitting organization of such corporation; it is impregnable to assault in the courts from any source."[3]

CLOSE AND OPEN

A close corporation is one in which the officers and directors have the power to fill vacancies in their ranks without allowing other stockholders to have a voice in the matter. An open corporation is one in which all stockholders have a vote in the filling of such vacancies.

BUSINESS AND NON-PROFIT CORPORATIONS

A "business corporation" is one formed for the purpose of transacting business in the widest sense of that term, including not only trade and commerce, but manufacturing, mining, banking, insurance, transportation, and practically every form of commercial or industrial activity where the purpose of the organization is pecuniary profit; contrasted with religious, charitable, educational, and other like organizations, which are sometimes grouped in the statutory law of a state under the general designation of corporations not for profit.[4]

While there are other classifications, it is helpful to examine other *types* of corporations and the terminology that is used in relation to them.

TYPES AND TERMINOLOGY

Corporations can be "migratory" (moving about), "moneyed" (deals in money), "public-service oriented" (electric and gas companies), "quasi - public" ("almost public," such as a telegraph office), "spiritual" (churches), and "tramp corporations" (organized in one state but operating wholly elsewhere).

The word "company" is understood to be synomous with "corporation." In some states, partnerships cannot use the words "company" or the symbol "co." This is to keep others from believing they are incorporated. "Corporate opportunity" refers to business situations that can be of benefit to the company. If a director or officer makes personal use of such an opportunity, that act could create a "conflict of interest." The "charter" is the document by which a firm is created. "By-laws" are the written regulations of conduct to guide the officers and directors. An "ultra-vires" act is one that is beyond the scope of the corporate powers. "Minutes" are written records made of meetings of officers, directors and stockholders, and will contain "resolutions" made at those meetings. A "resolution" is a formal act of a corporate body, created when important business is transacted, such as the decision to construct a new facility.

Turning from classifications, types and preliminary terminology, let's see how corporations are formed and examine some of the factors that must be considered at the time of formation. This is an important point in corporate history because it is here that the later character of a corporation is determined. One who is employed by a corporation today should keep in mind that the present nature of that entity, can be traced to decisions that were made perhaps decades in the past. An examination of the history of a corporation is essential to an in-depth understanding of it. The history of a corporation can be traced by a study of its charter, bylaws and minutes.

CORPORATE FORMATION

To create a corporation, two steps are encountered; the preliminary stage and the formal stage. Just how well the planning is carried out at the first step will determine the form and perhaps the success of the corporation after its formal creation.

PRELIMINARY STAGE

As with everything, a corporation has to have a beginning. It often begins when one or more persons decide that it would be advantageous to conduct a new business, or perhaps an existing one, by use of the corporate entity. When this happens, preliminary matters must be considered.

First, a formulation of objectives and purposes must be set out. What is the entity to do; what is it to accomplish; what is it *not* going to be able to do? How many stockholders will it have; who will have voting rights; what is the proposed name of the corporation and how will the capital structure of the corporation be set up? These and other questions must be asked and answered. It is customary in corporate formation to use the services of a lawyer, accountant and insurance representative in arriving at answers to many preliminary questions. These persons will provide imput in the form of ideas, suggestions and answers. In small closely held corporations, this preliminary stage may be concluded in a short time; in the case of a major corporation, the process may encompass months of study and analysis.

An important part of this process is the determination of the capital structure. If A wants to build and operate a motel by use of the corporate entity, while remaining the sole stockholder, the capital structure will be simple. Only one class of stock would be necessary, usually "common stock," since only one person will hold it after the firm is created. If A, B, C, D and E want to form a corporate entity to operate an airline, and if each will be making varying contributions to capital, then an entirely different situation is encountered. It may become necessary to structure a second class of stock, normally "perferred," to provide for preferences or disproportinate sharing of earnings. The partnership principle of equal sharing does not apply in corporate operation. A determination must be made as to how voting power is to be distributed. The decision may be made to limit the control of small capital contributors by the issuance of nonvoting, common stock. This could lead to the creation of a close corporation. The classes of stock may be geared to preferences upon the contingency of later distribution of assets. Thought must be given at the outset about rights to redeem classes of stock later on, or to convert them to other classes.

A decision may be made at the outset to make use of "debt" rather than to use "equity" in the corporate capitalization. When stock, common or preferred, is issued to a person, that stock carries with it equity ownership in the firm. If debt is used, the one advancing the funds is treated as a lender, with the firm issuing notes or bonds and not stock. The note or bond holder is then owed a debt by the firm, but does not have an equity ownership in the business.

Tax consequences must be considered. It may be desireable to create a "Subchapter S" corporation,[5] thus permitting the corporation to be taxed once each year just as a partnership. It may be desirable to lease, rather than have the firm own the property that it will be using in the business. Tax wise, it may be a good idea to use a combination of debt and equity even with the major stockholders.

The stock may be qualified to make it "small business stock" so that a later loss on the investment can be deducted against ordinary income to the extent of $100,000 per year on a joint return, or $50,000 on a single return.[6] Many other tax matters must be considered but the above are typical.

At some point, the preliminary or informal stage will be completed. The second or formal stage must now be undertaken. One of the first questions to be decided is "where should the corporation be formed."[2]

WHERE TO INCORPORATE?

In most small businesses, incorporation will be carried out in the state where business is to be transacted. It is less expensive, easier to form and, when done properly, provides all the corporate protection that will be needed.

If one person, or a group of persons, is contemplating a business that may reach into many states and perhaps into foreign countries, such as a proposed motel chain, it would be wise to do some corporate "jurisdiction shopping." This could be done by a comparative study of the features of the respective state laws. It might be well to incorporate where the central office will be located. On the other hand, it might be wise to incorporate in a more liberal legal jurisdiction in order to gain the advantages of liberal court decisions. Some states cater to corporations, such as Delaware, and some offer tax incentives and land concessions for those who incorporate in their states. All of these factors should be taken into consideration. In addition to Delaware, states that offer a favorable corporate climate include Illinois, Indiana, Maryland, Massachusetts, New Jersey, New York, Pennsylvania, Tennessee and West Virginia. As the competition increases between the states to attract new corporations, other states will be added to this list.

Once it is determined where to incorporate, a relatively uniform procedure will be followed by the "promoter"—a term that refers to the one who guides a corporation into existence. In most instances, a lawyer serves as the promoter.

HOW TO INCORPORATE

Drawing upon the preliminary decisions, an application for a charter will be created. In some states this application is called an "Agreement of Incorporation." It will contain the following minimum information:

1. The name. The name will include one of the words "association," "company," "corporation," "club," "incorporated," "society," "union," "syndicate," or one of the abbreviations "co." or

"inc." A name must not be chosen that is the same as or similar to a corporation previously formed in the state or authorized to do business there.

2. The principal office location and place of the "chief works" must be set forth. If the corporation is to have motels in each of a dozen states, this will be specified.

3. The objectives or purposes for which the corporation is being formed shall be set forth. It is here that a corporation obtains the powers to transact business. If these purposes are legal, and if they are approved by the state, then this fictitious entity can do those specified acts through agents and employees. It can also do those acts that can reasonably be implied from the statement of purposes. It will also be able to do those acts that are given to it by law, such as to hold and use a seal, and buy land. But the statement of purposes and objectives is a clear *limitation* on corporate powers—those powers not chosen are eliminated. Thus a corporation formed to operate a restaurant could not mine coal, run a stock brokerage firm or open a dog racing track. Acts outside of the express or implied powers would be "ultra vires"—beyond powers. While such acts would not per se be illegal, they would nevertheless *not* be binding upon the corporation since they would be in excess of corporate powers. Directors or officers who permit ultra vires acts to occur are held personally liable for those acts.

4. The amount of the total authorized capital stock must be set out. This in turn will be given a "par value", or be created as "no par" stock. The latter has no value expressed upon the face of the stock certificates, while the former does have. The amount of the total authorized stock should be large enough to make certain that the financial committments can be met, and yet not so large as to require the excess payment of annual license fees. These fees are based on the total authorized capital, not the actual amount with which a corporation begins business.

To illustrate, A, B & C, incorporate for the express purpose of building and operating a single, 100 unit motel with an attached restaurant. The total authorized capital is set at $500,000, which has a par value of $100 per share, thus creating 5,000 shares. As per their pre-incorporation agreement, each purchases 1,000 shares at $100 per share, for a total of $300,000. This would be their "starting capital." They will be taxed annually however, on the $500,000. The additional 2,000 shares can be issued as more funds are needed. Each party may have the "preemptive right" as new stock is issued. This means that as each additional three shares are issued, each person has a right to buy one share. The preemptive right allows ownership be remain equal as new stock is issued.

Or one or more may have a preference on the issue of new stock, allowing that person to acquire an increased ownership. Or, the original issue may have been common stock with the other 2,000 being preferred stock, which is to be issued to outsiders. Perhaps it will be issued without voting rights. This would allow an additional

$200,000 (or more if the book value increases) to be raised, with control remaining in A, B, and C. The combination and varieties of stock issues are numerous and careful study and analysis should be made at the outset as to what combinations should be created.

5. The names and addresses of the incorporators must be set forth along with a statement of the types and amounts of stock that they have each subscribed to.

6. A corporate life must be stated. It may be for a specified period of time, such as "ten years," but in most cases it will be "perpetual." This avoids having to reincorporate at the end of the specified time period should it be desirable to continue the corporate business.

7. Many states permit the original board of directors to be named in the application. If so, those named will make up the original board and will serve until their successors are appointed or elected.

8. Some states require technical information for future tax purposes. Others only require the first six or seven items above.

The application must now be signed by the incorporators, their signatures will be notarized and the application submitted to the proper state official. Applicable fees must accompany the application.

THE STATE'S ROLE

In many of our states, corporate charter applications are submitted to the Secretary of State. Even in small states, literally dozens of charter applications are received each business day.

The first step taken by the state is to check the proposed name against the index of corporate names. An application containing the name of "Playland Enterprises" would probably be rejected if the index contains the name "Playland, Inc." This is done to prevent confusion later in business operations. The applicants in that case would be asked to submit another name. The corporate objectives would then be screened to see if they state legal purposes. An application to incorporate a casino gambling house in a state other than Nevada and New Jersey would be rejected. An application to create a public school in a state where all public schools are state operated would likewise be rejected. So would an application to create a package liquor business in states that prohibit bulk sales of liquor.

In some instances, the names of the incorporators are screened. If a name appears of a known, or suspected crime figure, the application would be held up for investigation.

If it is found that the application is in order and meets legal form, the state must, as a matter of law, grant the corporate charter. This is done by the issuance of the corporate charter, under the "great seal" of the state and the signature of the proper state official.

A CORPORATION IS BORN

The birthdate of the corporation is the date of the issuance of the charter. At this instant, a new legal entity has come into being. It has no physical existence, it cannot be seen, it has no substance or form outside of legal contemplation, and, as strange as it sounds, it never gains substance in the future. It will remain an invisible, intangible, ficticious entity until such time as it is dissolved, or discontinued. True, it will have stockholders, will own property, will transact business and do many "person-like" activities.

To better understand what has been brought into existence, examine Figure 12-1. The corporation fiction may be thought of as a "bubble" that covers the incorporators as well as the initial board of directors. This "bubble" exists because the state created it. It in turn provides protection for those who fall under its coverage. It represents the corporation itself, and will transact business with third parties, buy and sell property, and can sue and be sued. In the meantime, those under its canopy enjoy limited liability. Their liability is limited to what they invested in the entity in the way of stock purchases, or to what they may still owe for their stock. The balance of each stockholder's personal assets are free from all corporate claims or obligations. What the corporation owes is not owed by them, whether it is a contract or tort obligation.

At this point, our corporation is incomplete because we lack stockholders, bylaws and officers. The organizational meetings must now be held.

FIGURE 12-1

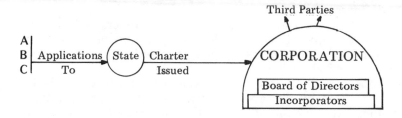

MEETINGS HELD

If an inital board of directors has been named in the charter application, those persons will call a meeting of the board. At that time, bylaws will be drafted, stock issued as it was subscribed for and stock payments collected. The stockholders will then meet, approve the bylaws and elect officers—unless these duties are delegated to the board of directors. A bank account will be authorized and opened.

The incorporators are replaced by the stockholders. The initial board, or one named to replace it will be in existence, along with the officers. The officers in turn will hire employees. The corporate form is now as illustrated in Figure 12-2.

FIGURE 12-2

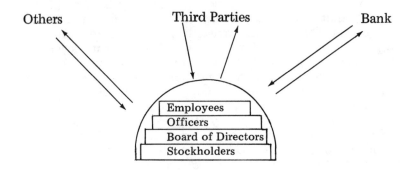

Others   Third Parties   Bank

Employees
Officers
Board of Directors
Stockholders

IN OPERATION

Once the organization is completed, the corporation is free to transact business just as any other business. It can enter into contracts; it can sign notes; it can buy and sell and do all acts necessary to carry forth the corporate purposes—but it must by necessity use agents to do these acts.

The bylaws will set forth the duties of the officers and provide for meetings as required by law. Each corporation must hold an annual meeting of stockholders and special meetings may be called as provided in the bylaws.

Major policies will be set by the stockholders. These policies will be given effect by directives from the directors, which in turn will be implemented by the officers as they supervise the day-to-day operations of the employees.

The corporate entity provides a workable, common-sense way of doing business, as well as protection for those within it. It *can* be subjected to abuse by those who practice "corporate politics." But by and large, it is the most useful, reliable, safest and versatile way in which to transact any modern business, and especially so in the travel - lodging industry.

LEAGUE TO SAVE LAKE TAHOE v. TAHOE REG. PL.
563 P. 2d 582 (Nevada 1977).

THOMPSON, Justice:

This action by League to Save Lake Tahoe was commenced August 16, 1974. Its purpose is to bar construction of resort-hotels in the Tahoe Basin by Oliver Kahle, Ted Jennings, and Harvey's Wagon Wheel, Inc. The League to Save Lake Tahoe is a foreign nonprofit corporation. It does business in Nevada by engaging in activities for which it was incorporated, including the solicitation of memberships and contributions, testifying before legislative committees and governing bodies of political subdivisions, and the holding of public meetings.

When this action was commenced, the League to Save Lake Tahoe was not qualified to do business in Nevada, although doing business here. On May 21, 1975, approximately nine months later, it did qualify to do business in this state.

The district court dismissed the action with prejudice. It reasoned that NRS 80.210 which provides that a foreign corporation" . . . shall not be allowed to commence, maintain, or defend any action or proceeding in any court of this state until it shall have fully complied with the provisions of NRS 80.010 to 80.040, inclusive" mandated dismissal since the League to Save Lake Tahoe had not qualified to do business when suit was commenced.

By this appeal the League to Save Lake Tahoe claims that the court erred in dismissing its case since it later qualified to do business. This contention places in issue the meaning to be accorded the language of NRS 80.210. In any event, the League contends that the dismissal should not have been with prejudice. We turn to address these contentions.

1. A foreign corporation transacting business in Nevada is denied access to the courts of this state unless and until it files with the Secretary of State a certified copy of its charter and obtains from him a certificate authorizing it to do business here. NRS 80.210; 80.010; 80.120; cf. *Peccole v. Fresno Air Serv., Inc.*, 86 Nev. 377, 469 P.2d 397 (1970).

Whether tardy compliance with the filing requirements will allow an unauthorized action to go forward is the issue tendered. The League to Save Lake Tahoe lacked capacity to commence this action. We must decide whether the statute, NRS 80.210, allows curative efforts to revive initial lack of capacity to sue.

The issue has not before been decided by this court. Case authority elsewhere is split and not particularly helpful since statutory language differs. Annot., 6 A.L.R.3d 326 (1966).

The League to Save Lake Tahoe contends that the words "maintain" and "until" in the phrase "shall not be allowed to commence, maintain, or defend any action or proceeding in any court of this state until . . . ." express a legislative intention that an unauthorized action may be "maintained" upon later compliance with statutory filing requirements. The district court did not so view that language. It reasoned that the word "maintain" was meant to apply to a case commenced by a corporation which had qualified to do business here but which subsequently became unqualified because of failure to comply with continuing statutory requirements. This, we think, is a proper application of the statutory language and we approve it.

2. The action was dismissed with prejudice. We presume that the dismissal was so structured because of the court's belief that the statute of limitations would be an available defense to bar another action should it be filed.

According to the complaint, Douglas County granted special use permits for resort-hotels to Jennings, Kahle and Harvey's Wagon Wheel, Inc., on May 7, 1973, April 24, 1973, and June 20, 1973, respectively.

NRS 278.027 requires court action to be commenced within 25 days of the filing of notice of "final action" of the governing body granting any special use or variance, if judicial review is desired.

As to Jennings and Kahle the action of Douglas County thereafter was reviewed by the Nevada Tahoe Regional Planning Agency (NTRPA) and subsequently by the Tahoe Regional Planning Agency (TRPA). The Nevada agency approved their projects. The TRPA did not reach a decision. *California ex rel Younger v. Tahoe Regional Planning Agency*, 516 F.2d 215 (9th Cir. 1975). Consequently, their projects were deemed approved and the decision of Douglas County affirmed. *California ex rel Younger v. Tahoe Regional Planning Agency, supra*, at 219. This automatic approval by reason of TRPA's failure to reach a decision occurred on or about August 12, 1974. The record does not reflect similar agency review of the action of Douglas County with regard to Harvey's Wagon Wheel, Inc.

What is "final action" within the intendment of NRS 278.027? If agency review (NTRPA-TRPA) does not occur, then the action of Douglas County is the "final action" and judicial review, if desired, must be sought within 25 days thereafter. Since such review was not timely sought with regard to Harvey's Wagon Wheel (this action was started approximately one year and seven months after Douglas County acted on Harvey's application for a use permit—if one was ever made) NRS 278.027 is an available defense to bar this action against that defendant-respondent.

If agency review does occur, and TRPA either approves, requires modification of, or rejects the decision of the permit issuing authority, "final action" is taken at that point in time, and judicial review must be sought within 25 days thereafter. If TRPA is unable to decide and does not take "final action" (*California ex rel Younger v. Tahoe Regional Planning Agency, supra*), what date is to be used for the purposes of NRS 278.027? This is what occurred with regard to Jennings and Kahle.

As before noted the failure of TRPA to take "final action" resulted in an automatic affirmance of the decision of the local permit issuing authority, Douglas County. We construe such automatic affirmance to be the equivalent of "final action" within the meaning of NRS 278.027;

The special use permits issued by Douglas County to Jennings and to Kahle were "automatically affirmed" by the TRPA on August 12, 1974. This action was commenced on August 16, 1974, well within the 25 day period specified in NRS 278.027. However, at that time the League to Save Lake Tahoe, for reasons heretofore expressed lacked capacity to commence the action. The League did not qualify to do business in this state until May 21, 1975, some nine months after the special use permit was "automatically affirmed." This belated compliance with the foreign corporation qualification statutes does not defeat the applicability of the statute of limitations during the period of time the corporation was in noncompliance. Institution of suit before compliance with filing requirements does not toll the statute of limitations, nor does later compliance operate retroactively to permit continuation of the action if the statute of limitations had run between filing of the suit and such compliance. Accordingly, we conclude that NRS 278.027 is an available defense to bar this action against Jennings and Kahle.

Therefore, we affirm the dismissals with prejudice, since to do otherwise would be to countenance the filing of another action as to which limitations is a bar.

MOWBRAY, J., and J. CHARLES THOMPSON and BRENNAN, District Judges, concur.

GUNDERSON, Justice, dissenting:

With all respect, it appears to me that in deciding the meaning of NRS 80.-210, the court's decision disposes of a tremendously significant legal issue without exposition of either logic or precedent to support its holding.

The court's interpretation of NRS 80.210, if not later changed in a case perceived as having greater merit, may certainly occasion harsh results. If this court is to adopt a rule apparently countenancing such results, I suggest we should articulate legal or logical reasons sufficient to command the respect and concurrence of the bench and Bar.

SMITH v. BAYOU RENTALS, INC.,
La. App. 345 So. 2d 1229 (1977).

SARTAIN, Judge.

These consolidated suits involve various actions concerning a closely held domestic corporation.

Bayou Rentals, Inc. is a corporation controlled by the heirs of Ted F. Dunham, Sr. which has been the subject of several legal controversies since his death on April 7, 1974. At that time, he owned one hundred twenty-six shares of its stock and his two sons, Ted F. Dunham, Jr. and Richard E. Dunham, owned sixty-two shares each; those three persons also comprised the Board of Directors.

On May 7, 1974, Katharine O. Dunham, his widow and testamentary executrix, called a meeting of the shareholders at which time a new board of directors was elected by acclamation, consisting of Bill J. Alexander, E. L. Peebles, Mrs. Dunham and the two sons. It should be noted, parenthetically, that Article VIII of the corporate charter provides that the board of directors shall be composed of three persons.

Thereafter, dissension apparently arose between these parties and on November 2, 1974, Ted F. Dunham, Jr. and Richard E. Dunham held a special meeting of the board of directors, without notice to the other principals, and took certain action including the election of David L. Smith to the Board, the acceptance of Smith's bill for $15,000.00 for services rendered to the corporation, and the issuance of certain stock to the three of them. This action was justified on the belief of all three that the election of five directors at the May 7th meeting was an absolute nullity and that the Dunham sons, therefore, were the only Board members legally remaining.

Upon notification of this action, Mrs. Dunham initially made certain efforts to nullify it; thereafter, by general agreement of the parties, no further efforts were made to solidify their positions and litigation was begun. That action consisted of the filing of a suit by Smith primarily for the recognition of his stock ownership in the corporation and for the payment of his bill for services. Thereafter, a proceeding for a writ of quo warranto was initiated by Richard E. Dunham in which the opposing faction reconvened for similar relief.

Three hearings were conducted in the trial court concerning the various issues involved therein. In summation, the court dismissed the writ of quo warranto sought by Richard E. Dunham, but maintained that writ on the reconventional demand filed by Mrs. Dunham, Alexander and Peebles; it also dismissed Smith's suit. Only Smith has appealed. We affirm.

The reasons for the action taken by the district court are primarily expressed in an extensive and well reasoned opinion rendered on August 15, 1975. The necessity for a full discussion of that opinion has been obviated because only Smith has appealed. Essentially the court concluded that, although contrary to the corporate charter, the five directors elected at the May 7, 1974 meeting were "de facto" directors and were thus entitled to notice of the November 2 meeting at which time the Dunham sons attempted to proceed on their unilateral course of action. Further, their failure to provide that notice rendered their action null, including the attempted issuance of stock to themselves and to Smith, and that Mrs. Dunham continued as testamentary executrix to retain the voting majority possessed by her late husband. Also applicable to Smith's appeal are later oral reasons for judgment in which it was concluded that the Dunham sons did not have actual or apparent authority to contract with Smith for services to the corporation.

The jurisprudence of this state has recognized "de facto" corporate officers. *St. Bernard Trappers Assn., Inc. v. Michel*, 162 La. 366, 110 So. 617 (1926); *Straughter v. Holy Temple of Church of God and Christ*, 150 So.2d 124 (La. App. 4th Cir. 1963), in the *Matter of Louisiana Investment & Loan Corporation*, 224 F.Supp. 274 (E.D.La.1963). In *Michel*, supra, the court observed:

"'* * * even though the said board was not legally and regularly elected, and even though a majority were ineligible, yet they were de facto officers, acting under color of title and in the open and exclusive possession of the office, and discharging its functions without question or protest and hence that the action of said board in making the assignment was binding on the corporation if such assignment was otherwise legal."

The trial judge correctly found that, although the election of five directors was in violation of the corporate charter, that such action caused those persons to be "de facto" directors. Both Ted F. Dunham, Jr. and Richard E. Dunham, who later attempted to repudiate that action, were present at that election, took part in it, and approved the action taken at that time.

Having assumed the status of "de facto" directors, those five persons remained in that capacity until removed by proper corporate action, which occurred at the next lawfully called meeting on January 9, 1975. The actions at the meetings on November 2 and 5, 1974, which were conducted by the two Dunham sons, without notice to the other three "de facto" directors, were null and void.

The issue of the liability of this corporation for Smith's services is not without difficulty. His involvement began in July, 1974, when he first discussed employment as a management consultant for Bayou Rentals, Inc. with the Dunham brothers. He related that over several previous years, he was employed by the Dunham interests in Louisiana and elsewhere that he had dealt on many prior occasions with those two persons as corporate directors, and that he had no reason to question their status as board members with Bayou. He states that they approached him as directors of that corporation and that they were clothed with the apparent, if not actual, authority to retain him. The legal principle involved is stated in *Harris v. Automatic Enterprises of Louisiana, Inc.*, 145 So.2d 335 (La.App. 4th Cir. 1962), in which the court said:

"* * * The law is clear that a corporation is liable for the acts of its officers, agents, and servants acting within the scope of the actual or apparent authority vested in them. LSA-C.C. Articles 436-439. *Esso Standard Oil Co v. Welsh*, 235 La. 593, 105 So.2d 233."

We find, however, that because of the peculiar facts surrounding this arrangement, that Smith knew or should have known that the authority of the Dunham brothers was not what it seemed to be.

This was clearly not the usual employment relationship. By his own admission, Smith knew very well that Mrs. Dunham controlled the majority of the stock after her husband's death and that Alexander and Peebles were, and had been, actively engaged in the business. Yet, he had absolutely no contact with them concerning the affairs of the corporation for which he was allegedly performing considerable service. He admitted that he discussed the status of the board informally with an attorney during the transitional time period. His close relationship with the persons who hired him and his subsequent action in support of their faction in this dispute compels the conclusion that he knew that the action of his employers had been taken without the approval of the other principals and possibly contrary to their wishes. In short, the depth of his understanding and participation of these events was obviously considerable and it appears that he was not an uninformed bystander who was misled by the authority which the Dunham brothers had.

The remaining three specifications of error by the appellant are directed at procedural rulings made by the district judge in the course of the trial. It is argued that the court erred in ruling that certain stipulations which had been introduced in the quo warranto hearing were binding upon the appellant in the companion suit. However, as correctly point out by the appellee, those stipulations were introduced without objection in the suit being heard prior to the court's ruling.

The appellant also maintains that the trial court's failure to allow an offer of proof or to rehear certain evidence amounted to reversible error. In *Broussard v. State Farm Mutual Automobile Ins. Co.*, 188 So.2d 111 (La.App. 3rd Cir. 1966), writs refused, 249 La. 713, 190 So.2d 233, cert. denied, 386 U.S. 909, 87 S.Ct. 855, 17 L.Ed.2d 783, the court observed:

"In commonlaw states, upon finding prejudicial ruling as to evidence, the case would ordinarily be remanded for new trial. This is not the rule in Louisiana. Under our state constitution, ordinarily appellate review in civil cases is 'on both the law and the facts'. Louisiana Constitution of 1921, Article VII, Section 29. By reason of this constitutional mandate, a Louisiana appellate court will usually decide the appeal on its merits rather than remanding for new trial and new findings by the trier of fact, when the reviewing court is able to make an independent factual determination of the evidence as contained by the complete record of that sought to be introduced at the trial, including that ruled inadmissible by the trial court but nevertheless included in the record for purposes of appellate review, LSA-C.C.P. Art. 1636."

There is sufficient evidence in the record to support the ultimate action of the trial judge and to allow a full review by this court. For these reasons, the judgment of the district court is affirmed. All costs of this appeal are to be borne by the appellant.

AFFIRMED.

QUESTIONS

1. Why does the law extend the status of "person" to a corporation?
2. The defacto principle is found in other areas of law. Why is there a need for such a principle?
3. Name reasons why care should be exercised in the creation of a corporation.
4. Give an example of "debt"—of "equity."
5. Why do our laws require that the corporate name include a suffix that indentifies it as a corporate entity?
6. Explain how a preemptive right works using an example.
7. T. or F. A corporation can be formed that will have a limited existence, such as "two years."
8. What is the birth date of a corporation?
9. List the principal features of a corporation—a partnership.
10. Explain why the corporate device protects those who own it.

ENDNOTES

1. *Nebraska Wheat Growers' Ass'n v. Smith* 115 Neb. 177, 212 N.W. 39.
2. *Wheeler v. New York, N.H. and H.R. Co.*, 112 Conn. 510, 153 A. 159, 160.
3. *Henderson v. School Dist. No. 44*, 75 Mont. 154, 242 P. 979, 980.
4. *Mc Leod v. College*, 69 Neb. 550, 96 N.W. 265.
5. IRC secs. 1371 to 1377.
6. IRC sec. 1244.

13

Hospitality Property

In the travel-hospitality industry, business persons constantly deal with "property contracts" in one form or another. For example, they contract for building sites needed for motel, hotel, or restaurant construction. There is the constant requirement that innkeepers assume obligations for the property of guests both within the inn and while the property is being transported to it. In carrying out such activities, and countless others like them, the law of property comes to the front. It is this body of law that sets forth the rights, duties and liabilities of those who contract for, or who handle the property of others. In this chapter we will identify personal property generally and then discuss real property principles in detail. Personal property principles will be developed further when we examine the rights, duties and liabilities of innkeepers.

HOW IS PROPERTY DEFINED?

One writer tells us that "The right of property is that sole and despotic dominion which one claims and exercises over the external things of the world, in total exclusion of the right of any other individual in the universe. It consists in the free use, enjoyment, and disposal of all a persons acquisitions, without any control or diminution save only by the laws of the land."[1] A court tells us that the word "property" " . . . is also commonly used to denote everything which is the subject of ownership, corporeal or incorporeal, tangible or intangible, visible or invisible, real or personal; everything that has an exchangable value or which goes to make up wealth or estate. It extends to every species of valuable right and interest, and includes real and personal property, easements, franchises, and corporeal hereditaments."[2] This second definition contains multiple words that have the same or similar meaning. Different writers often choose different words and phrases in property matters to mean the same thing. So one must understand the various terms and the distinctions between them.

PROPERTY TERMS

"Corporeal" is an old Anglo-Saxon term that signifies things that have a material existence: something that affects the senses of sight, touch and perhaps smell, and can be handled. Incorporeal property on the other hand, would be things that cannot be seen or handled, existing only in one's mind or in one's contemplation. One must distinguish between "corporeal" and "corporal". The former refers to possessing something material, the latter to something that affects or denotes the exterior of a body, an example being "corporal punishment." An airline owns corporeal property, while the amounts due from travelers on accounts receivables would be incorporeal.

TANGIBLE PROPERTY

Tangible property is "that which may be felt or touched, and it is necessarily corporeal, although it may be real or personal."[3] Intangible property would be the opposite, with copyrights, patents, franchises, and accounts receivable as examples. Conversely, tangible property is "visible" - intangible, "invisible."

The earth (land), everything growing upon it, or affixed inside of it, such as oil and coal, and everything attached to it with the intention of being permanent, is real (corporeal) property. All else is personal (incorporeal) property. Growing crops, turpentine in trees, coal and oil in the ground, are "real". Harvested crops, turpentine in cans, coal in river barges and oil in barrels, would be personal property. Thus we see that what is "real" can be converted to "personal," and the reverse is also true. Bricks are personal property but when used to face a hotel become real property. If later the hotel is dismantled, the bricks would become personal property once again.

What is real and what is personal is of key importance to an understanding of contract law. For example, contracts for the sale of real estate, or any interest therein, must be in writing and signed by the party to be charged on the contract. Contracts for the sale of personal property of $499 or less do not have to be.

EASEMENTS

An easement is "a right in the owner of one parcel of land, by reason of such ownership, to *use* the land of another for a special purpose not inconsistent with a general ownership in the owner.[4] The land against which an easement exists, is the "servient" estate; the land to which the easement is attached, is the "dominant" estate. Easements can be bought, sold, encumbered and conveyed by deeds, deeds of trust and mortgages, just as other real estate. While easements concern land and sometimes passageways in buildings, they are technically incorporeal or invisible since they are not in fact the land or building itself.

As an illustration of an easement, a travel agency finds its parking lot access destroyed by the construction of an interstate highway. (See figure 13-1.) The "state" has the power to take (condemn) private property for public use. The travel agency owner negotiates with an adjoining property owner for an easement or "right-of-way" across the adjoining land. A deed is prepared, payment is made and the travel agency can now use the easement for access. The responsibility for the paving and maintenance of the easement will depend upon the agreement between the parties. It is customary to include the terms of a right-of-way agreement in the deed itself. If the owner of the servient estate is to have the right to use the easement, or if others are to have the same right, this must be spelled out. Easements are routinely acquired for roadways, foot-paths (even through buildings) sewer lines, water mains, and electrical and other transmission lines, both above and below ground.

FIGURE 13-1

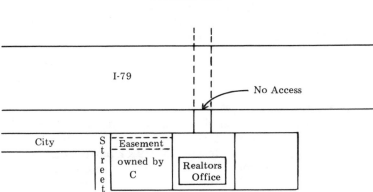

FRANCHISES

Blackstone, in his "Commentaries," tells us that a franchise "... had reference to a royal privilege or branch of the king's prerogative subsisting in the hands of the subject and must arise from the king's grant or be held by prescription". A court said, "But today we understand a franchise to be some special privilege conferred by government on an individual, natural (human being) or artificial (corporation), which is not enjoyed by its (the government) citizens in general."[5] For a group of persons to do business by a corporation, there must be a franchise granted by the state, called a "charter." An insurance company can issue insurance policies because of its franchise; a bank can issue bank-notes because of its franchise, both being state regulated. Franchises can be exclusive, general, personal and secondary. For example, the grant of a charter to a corporation is a primary franchise; the right that the corporation then has to use city streets is secondary.

Today, the word extends to private business dealings, and "franchises" are being bought and sold for fast food outlets, physical fitness gyms, motels, service stations and many more. The presence of franchises usually results in a limitation on the same activities in the same area by others. Holidays Inns of America has many franchises in the hands of private persons and corporations - while it maintains direct ownership of other operations. This corporation will not issue competing franchises for obvious reasons.

HEREDITAMENTS

The term refers to things that can be inherited—that is, pass from one to another upon the death of the former. They can be corporeal or incorporeal and include land, buildings and some forms of personal property. They would be contrasted however, with things that do not pass directly to an heir upon death. For example, stocks of a decedent passes directly to that persons personal representative upon death and not to that person's heirs. The widest expression of hereditaments then, is in relation to real estate.

PUBLIC AND PRIVATE

Public property refers to those things that are *public juris*—"of public right," and is property owned by a city, a county, the state or the federal government. It can be real or personal. Private property would be that owned by individuals, private corporations and other forms of private businesses. This is true even though such businesses may be affected by the public interest, such as banks, insurance companies and telephone companies. In case of "public utilities, fine legal distinctions can arise.

There are many other property terms and these will be explained as they are encountered in the following material. Turning from terms, how does one obtain property rights or ownership, and how is that ownership transferred to others?

OBTAINING AND TRANSFERING OWNERSHIP OF PROPERTY

When one attempts to discuss the acquisition of property, in whatever form, an anomoly exists that must be understood. What one obtains must necessarily be what another has given up. In the absense of the most primative conditions, there is no "original ownership" today. Even the deer that Robin Hood took from Sherwood Forest were the property of the King before they were taken—and even after. Thus to say that A acquired his ownership in the Eden Roc Hotel from the Last Will and Testament of his grandfather, requires that we point out that the ownership of the grandfather thus ended. What one acquires, another must give up. This should be kept in mind as we proceed.

WHAT IS "OWNERSHIP"?

To "own" is to have good legal "title". It is not the same as "acquire," the latter being a process by which the former is obtained. An "owner" is one in whom is vested the title, dominion or ownership of property. One who is an "owner" of property may own less than all of it. In fact it may be the mere *right to use* property. "Ownership" then, is a "collection of rights to use and enjoy property, including the right to transmit it to others."[6] "Title" then, refers to a distinctive mark, such as the title of a king, and in property law means the evidence that a person has of the right of ownership to property. It may be a deed to a house, a probated will, a certificate of title to an automobile, and, in its strict legal sense, implies the right of possession and ownership. Title is *not* the deed, the will or the certificate of title to a car itself. It is the legal right that lies underneath those documents. One can lose the deed to a restaurant - but the legal title remains undisturbed.

HISTORICALLY

The meaning of the words "own", "owner", "ownership," "title" and others, have gone though a long and colorful evolution. This can be expected to continue into the future. At the time of the Norman Conquest in 1066, for example, these words did not have precisely the same meaning as they have for us today. What private ownership meant then could not have been the same as what it means to us today with our elaborate recording systems and refined constitutional protections of property. Looking ahead, it is reasonable to expect that the property laws of 3066 will vary materially from what ours are today and should be more refined.

ROLE OF BROKERS

In the transfer of real property, real estate brokers are encountered. Such brokers have been defined as "persons who procure the purchase or sale of land acting as intermediary between vendor and purchaser, and who negotiate loans on real-estate security and manage and lease estates, . . ."[7]

For many years, the occupation of real estate brokering was a hit and miss proposition, and their services were not used as extensively as they are now. Today, real estate brokers are schooled and licensed and are coming under closer scrutiny because of the increasing role they are assuming in the acquisition of real estate. This, in turn, is forcing greater expertise upon them.

An example of this developing scrutiny is the requirement imposed by the courts that real estate brokers be truthful in their representations to buyers. In a New Mexico case, a broker assured a buyer of a multi-unit building that "there was no problems or inadequacy with the heating and air-conditioning" when in fact there was. After the purchase, the buyer spent over $37,000 for repairs on the heating and air-conditioning. The court held the broker liable for these expenditures because of the false representations.[8] Brokers are also being affected by other new laws. For example, Truth-in-Lending applies to those who extend credit or arranges for the extension of credit and usually it would not apply to a real estate broker. However, if a broker extends credit or arranges for the extension of credit, then TIL applies and the broker should comply by making the required disclosures.

In the acquisition of important tracts of land and buildings, the services of qualified real estate brokers can be invaluable and should be utilized. Many other "brokers" that deal in personal property are encountered in practice, including exchange brokers, stock brokers, ship-brokers and pawnbrokers.

Several methods exist by which legal title and thus ownership may be acquired by one and thus transferred to another, and will now be examined.

BY DEED

The word "deed" basically means "fact" or "act of a party".

In property language, it refers to the document by which one person or firm passes title in property to another person or firm. Most states require that a deed for real estate be sealed. The term "deed" is broad enough to include a mortgage of real estate as well as long-term leases. A deed is distinguishable from a will in that the former passes a present interest and the latter passes no interest at all until the death occurs of the one who executed it.

Deeds can be in various forms. An "indented deed", or indenture, is one that has a saw-tooth pattern cut along its side or top, and is derived from the ancient practice of dividing "chirographs." A chirograph—the "foot of the fine"—was simply an old-time deed. Today, some practitioners follow the practice by use of a wavy line on the deed. A "deed of gift," is one in which property is transferred without consideration. A "deed in fee" is one that conveys the best and most complete title that another can receive. A "deed in less than fee," is one in which something less than the complete title is conveyed. A "deed of trust" is a document used in many states in place of a mortgage.

ESTATE TRANSFERS

Real as well as personal property is routinely transferred from the estate of a deceased person to the heirs of the decedent, or to the ones designated by will to receive the property. One can die "testate—meaning that that person left a will—or "intestate"—meaning that no will was left—or none found.

TESTATE

Upon the death of one who leaves a "last will and testament", title to real property immediately vests in those named in the will. This "inheritance" is subject, however, to the proper administration of the estate.

ESTATE ADMINISTRATION

Upon the death of the "testator," the will is usually read at a meeting called for that purpose. Following this, the estate representative named in the will—Executor if a man, Executrix if a woman—will take the instrument to the proper county office for "probate." Once received by the county official, routine steps follow, including the naming of appraisers and the posting of bond by the estate representative. The bond is usually a sum that equals the value of the personal property of the estate. This is required by law for protective purposes. The will may specify, "no bond shall be required" and if so, only a nominal bond is posted.

It is the job of the appraisers to take an inventory of all property of the decedent, wherever located, and to place values on this property. This is simple enough with cash, checking and savings accounts. In the case of stocks and bonds, values will depend upon (1) the date chosen for evaluation and (2) the market price as of that date. In the case of real estate, tax assessments are often used as a guide. These evaluations are then placed into a proper document and filed as part of probate. Estate taxation is based upon these figures.

Following this, in most states, the estate is advertised for the prescribed period of time. This is done to permit creditors of the decedent to file claims. Many states use a "commissioner of accounts" system, and these persons carry out the advertising requirements.

During this administrative period, the heirs may decide to sell the real estate. This can be done if there is an escrow of funds for estate tax purposes to protect the buyer. If the decedent was owed money by others, this will be collected. Debts owed by the decedent will be paid. In short, the estate continues to transact business just as if the decedent were still alive.

After the period in which to file claims passes, final matters will be settled. State estate and/or inheritance tax forms will be filed and the tax paid. If the estate is large enough, federal estate tax may also be due and this must be paid. Credit is allowed for taxes paid to the state. If the decendent owned real estate in two or more states, then multiple state forms and multiple taxes may be required. After taxes are paid, the state and/or federal government will release the estate to those who inherited it. This "release" now permits stocks and bonds to be transferred out of the estate and will permit final distribution to be made to those who inherited. By this process, real as well as personal property is transferred to others.

If one dies "intestate"—without a last will and testament, the estate passes by the "statutes of descent and distribution." These statutes are based upon the ancient common law order of birth rights and bloodlines. To illustrate, A dies intestate, leaving an only child and a wife. In many states, the child inherits the entire estate, subject to the "dower" interest of the wife. In most states, "dower" is the mere right to use real estate during life and ends upon the death of the wife. Dower also, in some states, includes one-third of personal property. If B dies intestate leaving as his closest relatives two brothers, they will inherit 50% to each. If C dies without heirs, the estate ends and "escheats" to the state. If one dies testate, the bloodlines no longer control - only what the will specifies will be looked to at law. In "community property" states, different provisions control.

Property can be transferred by gift.

GIFTS

A gift is a voluntary transfer of property from one to another without consideration. It may consist of handing an object to another with the intention of transferring present title. It may be in the form of a "deed of gift" when land or large items of personal property are transferred.

The legal requirements of a gift are three in number: (1) capacity on the part of the donor, (2) intention on the part of the donor to make a gift, and (3) completed delivery to the donee. In the case of land, buildings, large machines or the like, delivery is carried out by the delivery of the deed of gift itself. That act passes title to the items listed within it.

Gifts can be absolute or testamentary. An absolute gift is complete upon delivery. A testamentary gift, (causa mortis—in contemplation of death)—is only conditional at the time of delivery. To illustrate, A hands B a diamond ring, believing A's illness is terminal. A recovers. Since the contingency of death did not occur, the gift fails.

By far the most common way that property, real or personal, is transferred, is by sale and purchase.

SALE AND PURCHASE

The sale and purchase of personal property, such as automobiles, inventory and aircraft, was discussed in detail in Chapter 7, Hospitality Sales Contracts. Our discussion from here on, will be limited to real estate sales and purchases.

In the sale and purchase of real estate, the contract and the option are widely used.

REAL ESTATE CONTRACTS

One of the principal functions of the real estate broker, is to create real estate contracts and to see to the execution of them. In this manner, the parties become bound to each other. In addition, the written contract meets the requirements of the statute of frauds. See figure 15-2 for an example, pages 226-27.

In soliciting buyers, real estate brokers use advertisements as well as "for sale" signs at the property itself. Some cities have enacted ordinances that prohibit the use of "for sale" signs on real estate. The U.S. Supreme Court has held that such an ordinance violates the freedom of speech provision of the First Amendment to the United States Constitution.[9]

Once the contract is executed and the down-payment made, the transaction will proceed to "closing." At that time, payment is made, the deed is delivered and the real estate has a new owner. We will examine a real estate closing in detail in chapter 15.

OPTIONS

In some instances, a would-be real estate buyer wants the right to buy—or refuse to buy—the real estate in question, with this right to be firm for a specified time period. This can be accomplished by the use of an "option to buy."

Options must be written, signed and supported by "hand money." The one receiving the option is then free to seek financing and can even contract to sell that same realty to others. Or, if that person should so chose, the property does not have to be bought at all. In the latter event, the hand money is retained by the other as liquidated damages. If the real estate *is* purchased, the hand money is applied to the purchase price.

Once real estate is acquired, the new owner may decide to improve the existing facilities or to construct new ones.

CONSTRUCTION

Another way to acquire property is by the construction of it, using material and labor furnished by others. This too is carried out by the written contract. Construction will be examined in detail in chapter 15.

GRANTS

At the time of the settlement of the American West, huge tracts of public lands were transferred to private hands by land grants— 160 acre tracts being typical. Under the various land-grant acts, one had to "homestead" the tract for a prescribed period of time. Under later acts, a payment per acre was required. The Cherokee Strip in Oklahoma, for example, was settled by a literal footrace of those seeking to establish claims under these acts. Those who staked claims before the official time, ("too soon",) were usually hung on the spot. This resulted in Oklahomans being referred to as "Sooners."

Land is still available in limited quantity by way of grants, particularly in Alaska. Title to personal property is not conveyed by grants—unless one wants to think of food stamps, welfare and other subsidies as a form of grant.

Another way that property can be acquired is by "accession."

ACCESSION

The Roman word "accessio" means to increase or add, and from it we get the word "accession." If a tenant makes permanent improvements to the leased premises, these become the property of the landlord-owner. This assumes of course, that the parties have not agreed otherwise. In river country, the raparian front of A is often washed from A's land and deposited onto the land of B. B has thus acquired new land by accession.

TAX SALES AND FORECLOSURES

If one becomes delinquent in the payment of state taxes on property, and if the delinquency continues for the statutory time period, the property can be sold at public action. The highest bidder thus acquires property. The same is true in sales of property brought about by delinquency on loans which are secured by that property.

DEDICATION TO PUBLIC USE

Although there are other ways of transferring ownership, the last one we will define is "dedication to public use." Developers often do this with streets and park-areas in their subdivisions. It is a means by which transfer is made from private to public hands.

Such dedications may be made with "reversionary clauses"—that is if the city does not maintain the park, it reverts to the party that dedicated it to public use. If no reversionary clause is used, the courts hold that the public entity owns the property and may dispose of it as that body deems best. To illustrate, in 1952, a developer dedicated blocks 1 through 6 in a subdivision to be used as a public park. This was done by the recording of a plat showing this dedication. This in turn was accepted by the city clerk. No provisions were made for reversion. In 1964, the city sold the park to a developer who divided it into lots, built houses on them and then sold the houses. Upon suit by the original owner, the court held that title had been transferred by the dedication and that the city had the legal right to do what it did.[10]

BALZER v. INDIAN LAKE MAINTENANCE, INC.,
346 So. 2d 146 (Florida 1977).

HOBSON, Acting Chief Judge

This case arose in a suit filed by plaintiffs/appellants for a declaratory judgment determining the validity of certain deed covenants providing for the payment of maintenance fees. Plaintiffs particularly assailed the duration of this covenant in that it violated the rule enunciated by this court in *Henthorn v. Tri Par Land Development Corp.*, 221 So.2d 465 (Fla. 2d DCA 1969). The trial court disagreed and entered a final judgment holding the covenants valid and enforceable. We affirm, but for different reasons than given by the trial judge.

The facts in this case are undisputed. Indian Lake Estates is a platted unincorporated subdivision located in Polk County, Florida, consisting of approximately 6,900 acres, divided into 7,287 residential lots, and 665 commercial lots. The plat reflects certain streets, avenues, parks, parkways, and other recreational areas. Title to these areas is vested in the defendant non-profit corporation, Indian Lake Maintenance, Inc., (hereinafter I.L.M.) whose membership is composed of all property owners at Indian Lake Estates. The streets and avenues in the subdivision are not dedicated to the public and are maintained by defendant I.L.M.

Plaintiffs in this cause represent in excess of 1000 nonresident owners of residential lots located in Indian Lake Estates. The Intervenors are 448 owners of residential lots in Indian Lake Estates who currently reside there.

Central to the controversy in this case is the following covenant contained in all deeds and contracts to purchase in the Indian Lake Estates development:

"The purchaser covenants to pay to Indian Lake Estates, Inc., its nominees, successors, or assigns, on January 15 of each year, the sum of $20, for each and every lot purchased, to be used for general maintenance.

"All of the above covenants shall remain in force until January 1, 1966, and shall be automatically renewed for each ten year period thereafter, unless owners of at least two-thirds of the lots in the subdivision known as Indian Lake Estates shall, at least six months prior to any such renewal date, agree in writing to a change in or an abrogation of any of the above covenants, and record such writing so amending the aforesaid covenants."

In a separate legal action referred to by the trial court in the final judgment herein, the Circuit Court of Polk County, Florida, entered a final decree on July 30, 1964, ordering that all maintenance fees collected under the covenant above should be used solely for purposes of maintenance and that quarterly reports should be made to the court showing the amount of maintenance fees collected and how such fees were spent. Thereafter, on February 16, 1966, in the same earlier case, the court entered an order recognizing the defendant I.L.M. as the successor of Indian Lake Estates, Inc., with regard to the covenants concerning maintenance fees. The record shows that I.L.M. has continued to collect and/or attempted to collect this maintenance fee from the individual owners of lots in Indian Lake Estates since that time.

Following submission of the stipulated facts noted above, and oral argument, the trial court entered a final judgment holding the covenant valid and enforceable, subject only to the limitations contained therein. Careful review of the record and briefs filed in this cause require us to frame the issues as follows:

1. Did the trial court err in refusing to apply the rationale of *Henthorn v. Tri Par Land Development Corp.*, 221 So.2d 465 (Fla. 2d DCA 1969) to the case *sub judice*; and

2. If so, is the rule enunciated in *Henthorn, supra*, sufficient to invalidate the maintenance covenant herein?

In *Henthorn* a similar maintenance agreement was attacked by the successor to the developer. The final judgment of the trial court there, reflecting the position of the developer's successor, held the covenant unenforceable because its duration was not ascertainable and thus was a perpetual charge on real property terminable at will under the doctrine of *Collins v. Pic-Town Water Works, Inc.*, 166 So.2d 760 (Fla. 2d DCA 1964). This court reversed and noted the specific limitation in the deed in *Henthorn* distinguished it from *Collins, supra.* Judge Mann went further to state,

"The duration of this agreement is until the first day of January in the year 2000. That is a long time, but by no means indefinite. Thereafter, there is a dependence upon the will of persons then owning the lots and the successor to the developer which is invalid for the same policy reasons which invalidate the remote vesting of property interest, although the interest are distinguishable. See Gray, The Rule Against Perpetuities § § 329 et seq. (4th ed)."

221 So.2d at 466.

Plaintiffs rely exclusively on the third sentence of the quoted paragraph above. They posit that the covenant *sub judice* is not void as it may be perpetual, but that under the language of *Henthorn, supra*, the covenant was valid only until January 1, 1966, at which time it became terminable at will after reasonable notice by any party thereto. Defendant I.L.M. contends that the language contained in *Henthorn*, and relied upon by plaintiffs, was merely *obiter dicta* and without persuasive value. I.L.M. further asserts that the trial court was correct in its finding that the covenant is enforceable because: 1) it is not perpetual since it can be canceled at ten-year intervals; 2) even if considered of infinite duration it is enforceable under the "Continuing Consideration—Continuing Advantage" doctrine; and 3) public policy mandates enforcement of such policies. The latter arguments form the basis of the trial court's judgment in favor of the defendant.

At the outset we hold that *Henthorn* is not sufficiently distinguishable on its facts to have prevented the trial judge from applying the rationale there to the instant case. Moreover, we believe the trial judge mistakenly applied the incorrect legal standard to the facts as stipulated. Nevertheless, we are less than certain that application of the rule in *Henthorn*, with respect to the renewable periods in this case, is a correct statement of the law, i. e., they are invalid.

In the first place this covenant is more nearly akin to a contractual provision than a restriction placed on the use of the land. The fact that the covenant was included in the contracts to purchase, as well as the deeds to lots in Indian Lake Estates, lends support to this proposition. However, whether the covenant is denominated as a restriction or a contract provision will not alter the definite duration of this provision as it is defined in the deeds of all property owners in Indian Lake Estates. As noted in 8 Fla.Jur. Covenants and Restrictions §

27 (1956), "Where the duration of a restrictive covenant is specifically provided for in the covenant, the covenant must espire by its own terms and limitations." General contract law is similar. Thus it is stated at 17 Am.Jur.2d Contracts § 495,

"A contractual provision for termination upon certain conditions can be enforced only in strict compliance with the terms of such conditions.[8] If the contract specifies conditions precedent to the right of cancellation or recission, the conditions must be complied with.[9]" (footnotes omitted)

Aside from *Henthorn* our research has not revealed any case in Florida passing directly on the validity of a covenant involving comparable renewable periods like those contained in the deeds herein. Yet, we think the authorities cited above, in conjunction with those from other jurisdictions, are sufficient to uphold the maintenance covenant. In so holding we reject the trial judge's conclusion that the factual differences in *Henthorn* distinguish it entirely from the factual circumstances here. Instead we submit that the language in *Henthorn*, to wit,

"Thereafter, there is a dependence upon the will of the persons then owning the lots and the successor to the developer which is invalid for the same reasons which invalidate the remote vesting of property interests although the interests are distinguishable."

must be read togehter with the two sentences preceding it,

"The duration of this agreement is until the first day of January in the year 2000. That is a long time but by no means indefinite."

The legal basis for invalidating the renewable periods in *Henthorn* then is that they were so remote as to constitute a perpetual obligation on the land over and above a fixed period contained in the deed. At best there would be no termination of the maintenance agreement until the year 2000.

In contrast, the maintenance covenant herein is specifically subject to modification or cancellation at any time within six months prior to the expiration of any ten-year period beginning January 1, 1966. All that is required for modification or cancellation is an agreement in writing which is recorded. There is no charge on the affected lands which even closely approximates a perpetual obligation incapable of abrogation. For that reason the covenant, whether it be labeled contract or restriction, has definite termination dates which are operable within six months of every January 1 occurring every ten years. Therefore, the provision allowing modification of the maintenance covenant contemplates periodic review by landowners subject to the charge. The only limitation on this power to modify, amend, or cancel is the mobilization of the owners of two-thirds of the lots in the subdivision.

Finally, we would point out that this court has, subsequent to *Henthorn*, upheld the right of developers to provide the furnishing of essential services and bind by covenant owners of subdivision lots to pay for them. *Sloane v. Dixie Gardens, Inc.*, 278 So.2d 309 (Fla. 2d DCA 1973). Moreover, the final judgment below reveals that half, if not more of the funds generated by the maintenance covenant have, since 1966, been expended on necessary items with respect to the general scheme of development. Thus this case falls squarely within the rule enunciated in *Hagan v. Sabal Palms, Inc.*, 186 So.2d 302, 308-9 (Fla. 2d DCA 1966),

"It is undoubtedly the law of Florida that covenants restraining the free use of realty are not favored, but in order to provide the fullest liberty of contract and the widest latitude possible in disposition of one's property, restrictive covenants are enforced so long as they are not contrary to public policy, do not contravene any statutory or constitutional provisions, and so long as the intention is clear and the restraint is within reasonable bounds." (citations omitted)

Accordingly, the final judgment below is affirmed. To the extent that our opinion conflicts with our earlier decision in *Henthorn*, we recede from the positions taken there.

SCHEB and OTT, JJ., concur.

LEAVER v. GROSE
563 P. 2d 773, (Utah 1977).

HALL, Justice:

Plaintiffs appeal from a summary judgment entered by the district court holding that certain restrictive covenants were no longer enforceable, they having expired by their own terms.

Plaintiffs initiated the action to enjoin defendant from altering a single-family residence as a duplex dwelling relying upon "Building Restrictions" filed in the office of the Salt Lake County Recorder on May 12, 1947, which limited properties in Loganview Subdivision to single-family residences. Defendant commenced alterations on her property for the purpose of utilization as a duplex dwelling on June 30, 1975.

The building restrictions in question were enforceable for a period of twenty-five years from the date of their recordation and, thereafter, were automatically extended for successive periods of ten years unless a vote of a majority of the owners of properties therein altered the restrictions. No such vote was ever taken.

The enforcement provisions also contained therein authorized persons owning properties and aggrieved by any violation within the said twenty-five year period to prosecute appropriate actions in law or in equity, but made no provision for any such legal action after the expiration of such time.

The pertinent provisions of the "Building Restrictions" are:

(i)

Each and every lot above described shall be known and is hereby designated as a "Residential Lot" and no structure shall be erected, altered, placed or permitted to remain on any such "Residential Lot" other than one detached single-family dwelling not to exceed two stories in height and a private garage for no more than (3) automobiles.

(xiii)

All covenants and restrictions herein stated and set forth shall run with the land and shall be binding on all the parties and persons claiming any interest in said residential lots hereinbefore described or any part thereof until twenty-five (25) years from the date hereof, at which time the said covenants and restrictions shall be automatically extended for successive periods of ten (10) years unless, by a vote of a majority of the then owners of said residential lots, it is agreed to change the said covenants in whole or in part.

(xiv)

If the parties now claiming any interest in said residential lots hereinbefore described, or any of them, or their heirs, successors, grantees, personal representatives or assigns, *shall violate or attempt to violate any of the covenants and restrictions herein contained prior to twenty-five (25) years from the date hereof*, it shall be lawful for any other person or persons owning any other residential lot or lots in said area to prosecute any proceedings at law or in equity against the person or persons, firms or corporations so violating or attempting to violate any such covenant or covenants and/or restrictions or restriction, and either prevent him or them from so doing or to recover damages or other dues for such violation or violations. [Emphasis added.]

The question before the court below was whether or not the restrictive covenants expired on May 27, 1972, or were-extended by the terms thereof until May 27, 1982. Apparently relying on paragraph (xiv), supra, the court determined that the covenants were not enforceable after the expiration of twenty-five years and dismissed the complaint as a matter of law.

Plaintiffs assert the trial court erred first in not resolving as a matter of law that the restrictive covenants were clear and not ambiguous and that he was entitled to summary judgment and second, even if there was some ambiguity that then a question of the intention of the parties arose which required the taking of evidence. With this latter position we agree.

The ambiguity arises because of the language contained in paragraph (xiv) of the restrictive covenants. There is a specific provision for enforcement for any violation during the twenty-five (25) year period, but no provision for a violation occurring during any automatic ten (10) year period thereafter. It is simply silent on the subject. Consequently, a question of fact arises as to the intention of the parties, i.e., did the framers of the covenants actually intend to provide for prosecution of violations after the expiration of the twenty-five (25) years and merely left out of paragraph (xiv) words such as: . . . twenty-five (25) years from the date hereof of any *automatic extension as provided in paragraph (xiii) hereof.*

It is interesting to note that just such terminology was adopted in paragraph (xv) of the covenants which reads as follows:

Invalidation of any one of the covenants and restrictions hereinbefore set forth by judgment or court order shall in no wise affect any of the other provisions hereof which shall remain in full force and effect until twenty-five years from date hereof subject to automatic extensions as provided in paragraph (xiii) hereof. [Emphasis added.]

In *Reese Howel Co. v. Brown et al.*, cited with approval in *Parrish v. Richards*, this court addressed itself to the question of ambiguous terminology in documents and stated:

We have, however, held, and are firmly committed to the doctrine, that we will have recourse to every aid, rule, or canon of construction to ascertain the intention of the parties . . . . it should be the aim of the courts, as, no doubt, it is their duty, to ascertain and declare the intention of the parties, since that, and nothing else, constitutes their contract, and it is the duty of the courts to enforce, not to make, contracts.

A restrictive covenant cannot be set aside in the absence of clear and convincing evidence. And where covenants are duly executed and recorded the law gives an interested party the right to enforce their terms. Therefore, paragraph xiv appears to be mere surplusage and not a necessary part of the restrictive covenants. In fact, it would appear to be a nullity since it could not prevent a suit from being filed by an aggrieved person to enforce a valid covenant. Such is a constitutional right afforded by Art. I, Sec. 11 which reads in part as follows:

All courts shall be open, and every person, for an injury done to him in his person, . . . shall have remedy by due course of law, . . . and no person shall be barred from prosecuting or defending before any tribunal [of] this State, by himself or counsel, any civil cause to which he is a party.

Reversed and remanded for trial. Costs to plaintiff.

ELLETT, C. J., and CROCKETT, MAUGHAN and WILKINS, JJ., concur.

QUESTIONS

1. What is a "corporeal hereditament"?
2. Give examples of intangible property.
3. What is required to make property "public"?
4. Define "ownership", "title" and "possession."
5. Why must a real estate broker be honest in his or her dealings with customers?
6. Why is a deed often referred to as an "indenture"—and in fact in some states, such as Pennsylvania, is called just that?
7. What is the danger of one passing away intestate?
8. T. or F. The life of a human being has a "legal extension" after death.
9. What are the legal requirements of a binding gift?
10. Why must real estate contracts be in writing?

ENDNOTES

1. *1 Bl. Comm. 138; 2 Bl. Comm. 2 15; Great Northern Ry. Co. v. Washington Elec. Co. 197 Wash. 627, 86 P. 2d 208, 217.*
2. *Samet v. Farmers' & Merchants' Nat. Bank of Baltimore* C.C.A. Md., 247 F. 669, 671; *Globe Indemnity Co. v Bruce,* C.C.A. Okl. 81F. 2d 143, 150.
3. *H.D. & J.K. Crosswell v. Jones,* D.C.S.C. 52 F. 2d. 880, 883.
4. *Hollamon v. Board of Education of Stewart County,* 168 GA. 359, 147 S.E. 882, 884, emphasis added.
5. *State v. Fernandey* 106 Fla. 779, 143 So. 638, brackets added.
6. *Trustees of Phillip Exieter Academy v. Exeters,* 92 N.H. 473, 33 A. 2d 665, 673.
7. *Latta v. Kilbourn,* 150 U.S. 524, 14 S. Ct. 201, 37 L.E.D. 169.
8. *Neff v. Bud Lewis Co.,* 548 P. 2d, 107 (1976).

9. *Linmark Associates Inc., v. Township of Willingboro*, 45 U.S.L. W. 4441 (1977).
10. *Wheeler v. Monroe*, 523 P. 2d 540 (N.M. 1974).

14

Ownership, Control and Management of Hospitality Property

In the last two chapters, we became acquainted with basic matters that relate to both real and personal property. In this chapter we will examine some of those matters in more detail and will take a look at new principles as found in practice. The subject of property is of key importance to those in the travel and lodging industry.

First, we will examine the forms of property ownership, and then we will discuss the ways in which property may be controlled, including the use of liens and encumberances. As we proceed, one should begin to understand that the true nature of property is found in legal rights to that property - not in the physical property itself. This concept is often difficult to grasp at first contact.

FORMS OF PROPERTY OWNERSHIP

Property can be owned in a variety of forms. Because of this, one must examine these in order to increase one's understanding of property. We will examine "sole" and "joint" ownership, "fee simple" and "less than fee simple" ownership, "legal" and "equitable" ownership and "community property."

SOLE AND JOINT OWNERSHIP

One is a sole owner who has legal or equitable title fully vested in that person, and the quality of that ownership is not affected by any condition. To illustrate, A and wife convey fee simple title to B (a single man). Upon the completion of the transfer, B is the sole owner free of conditions or contingencies. Thus B holds fee simple title.

Joint ownership comes into being when title is vested in two or more persons, regardless of how that title was created. To illustrate, Jones, a motel owner, dies intestate (without a will), leaving two children and no wife. These children are joint owners of the motel, each having equal, fully enforcable rights in it. Neither can exclude the other.

Joint ownership creates a "tenancy" of either one or two basic types; a joint tenancy or a tenancy in common. (The word "tenancy" as used here, does not refer to one who leases property from another, rather, it is a common-law form of holding title).

JOINT TENANTS

Smith conveys his motel to his two children as joint tenants and thus each owns an undivided interest in every square inch of the property - neither owns any particular part or segment of it. Joint tenancies can be with "the right of survivorship". Legally both are joint tenants during life, with each owning full legal rights. But upon the death of one, the survivor owns the entire property by virtue of the survivorship clause. Joint tenancies with the right of survivorship are used in stocks and bonds ownership, real estate conveyances and bank accounts. Their use should be preceeded by legal advice, however. Sometimes they are desirable—sometimes they are not.

TENANTS IN COMMON

A conveys a tract of land to B and C, husband and wife. No mention is made in the deed of survivorship between B and C. Thus these two persons hold the land in common, and upon the death of one, the undivided one-half interest of that person passes—not to the survivor—but to the heirs or devisees of the decedent. This can result in what started out to be a dual ownership, ending up in one that may have dozens of people with an interest in the property. To illustrate, A and B holds title to a hotel as tenants in common. There is no right of survivorship. A dies intestate (out of neglect in drafting a will) leaving no wife or children but six brothers and sisters who are all deceased who in turn have left fifteen living children. The hotel is now owned by B—and fifteen other persons—and their husbands and wives. If any of the fifteen are minors, it makes the situation even worse.

The joint tenancy and the tenancy in common have their uses but both can be dangerous, depending upon the circumstances.

FEE SIMPLE TITLE

As mentioned previously, fee simple ownership is the best that one can have in property, and entitles the owner to the entire property, free of all conditions, with the unconditional power to dispose of the property upon death. For example, Jones conveys a tract of land to Smith by fee simple title. Smith owns all of the land and all the rights to it without exception. If prior to the sale to Smith, Jones had sold the Sewickley seam of coal under the land to Brown, Smith would have less than fee simple title to the land. Brown would have fee simple title to the Sewickley coal—but no title to the land itself.

LEGAL AND EQUITABLE OWNERSHIP

The "legal" owner of property is the one who is recognized by law as the owner and who is responsible for it. Legal owners may hold jointly with the right of survivorship or as co-owners as previously discussed.

If legal title to property is vested in one person, *but for the benefit of another*, the second person is the "equitable owner." That person is recognized in equity as the owner even though the bare legal title is vested in the other. The equitable owner has the right to the beneficial use of the property. To illustrate, A conveys land to B to manage, rent, farm, and otherwise produce income from it, for the benefit of C. B has legal title, but C has equitable title. B is the trustee and C is the beneficiary, a "trust" arrangement. Trusts are widely used in both business and personal affairs.

A final form of property ownership has limited application since it applies in only eight states, yet it should be understood.

COMMUNITY PROPERTY

When husband and wife acquire property during marriage, it is "community property" and is held by them as a form of "marital partnership." If, during marriage, property is titled in the name of the husband, it is still held as community property with the wife.

Property acquired by either person before marriage, or after divorce, would not have this classification. This form of property ownership is a product of civil (French) law, and is found in Louisiana, Texas, Arizona, California, Idaho, New Mexico, Nevada and Washington. Such ownership protects the interests of a non-working wife in property acquired by a working husband. The theory is that the wife contributed to the acquisition by services performed in the maintenance of the household.

Turning from the forms of ownership, it is important to understand the ways in which property can be controlled. Basically it is controlled by the owners and by the state.

CONTROL OF PROPERTY

CONTROL BY OWNERS

One who has legal title to property has the right to use, occupy, change, modify and sell that property. If these rights are infringed upon by others, the courts can restore those rights. In addition, the owners of property can control their property by the use of the contract.

Two examples will be examined: restrictive clauses in land sales contracts and deeds, and condominium management regulations. Control of property by owners however, is not necessarily limited to these two examples. In practical usage, there are many ways that property can be controlled. We will also take a look at control by the state, and examine liens and encumberances of property. When reading this material, you should keep in mind that liens and encumberances are another form of control of property. A "lien holder" is always in a position to demand rights against the property in question.

RESTRICTIVE CLAUSES

A owns ten acres of land. The land is divided into lots, streets are laid out and utilities are provided. A offers these lots to others, but with restrictions. A requires that all houses built upon these lots must cost over $50,000; not have detached buildings; be brick faced; contain a minimum of 1,800 square feet of ground space; and cannot exceed two stories in height. The restrictions specify how the building will be placed on the lot and prohibits construction of certain buildings, such as service stations and factories.

This is an effective control and will be upheld by the courts, provided the control will end at a reasonable time, such as 25 years from the date of sale. These restrictions can be spelled out in the deed to the buyer, or reference may be made in the deed to another deed that contains the restrictions.

Thus, one purchasing land on which to build a restaurant, must make certain that the land is not so controlled by the seller—or a prior seller. A preliminary title search (see page 230) will permit this information to be uncovered.

This in effect, is a form of private zoning, as opposed to public zoning. Review the cases on pages 200 and 203.

A form of private control of property is found in the rules and regulations for the management of condominiums that are drafted and placed into being by the owners of the condominimum units.

CONDOMINUIM MANAGEMENT

In the past twenty years, the condominuim form of property ownership has found wide acceptance. Basically it is a form of joint ownership as discussed previously. However, it goes beyond mere joint ownership and requires that a workable system of control be brought into being, so that the lives and the affairs of the joint owners can proceed as smoothly as possible.

What we see in condominiums is the creation of controls that have great similarity to the laws that regulate citizens as they live in a city. These laws have hospitality aspects, and condominiums are often directed by a condominium manager or overseer.

Many states have adopted statutes that contain provisions whereby the owners of such unit properties can provide for control of those who purchase the units within each condominium. Thus the controls come from the owners, even though the state legislature provides the laws around which they are drafted. A typical state "Condominum and Unit Property" statute is found in Appendix B.

The condominium concept is not limited to apartment living. It is used today in warehousing, professional buildings, store facilities, and in any property ownership situation in which more than one person shares a common property interest but in which those persons do not want to pay rent.

Now we will examine control of property by the state and by third parties. It is here that we become aware that "ownership" of property is never an absolute. In fact, all ownership is qualified by the rights of the state and by those who obtain liens, or who place encumberances against it. Included here is the right of control by zoning; the right to condemn property for public use; the right of third parties to place "liens" against property and the right of third parties to place encumberances aginst property.

CONTROL BY THE STATE

Each state, by common law and statutes, places controls upon the owners of property. For example, the power of each state to lay and collect property taxes on property, real and personal, tangible and intangible, is in fact a control. Failure to pay taxes has the same legal effect as when one fails to meet mortgage payments: the property can be lost because of it.

In addition, the states and the federal government have the right of "eminent domain"—the power to take private property for public use. This power was used to build our interstate system and is widely employed in the construction of public parking garages and other public structures.

When property is acquired in this manner, or if an acquisition is imminent (such as when public funds are appropriated for the taking), the owner faces problems and one of them is in the taxation on the proceeds. If a partnership has property, the appropriation of which is imminent, that firm should not acquire replacement property in a corporate name. If this is done, tax advantages under Section 1033 of the Internal Revenue Code may be lost. While the state can take such property, it cannot do so without the payment of "just compensation." It is in the application of these proceeds that care must be exercised.

If A and B, who are partners, have their motel condemned for road building, or other public purposes, they should not buy land on which to build a new motel with those funds under their corporate name. The new acquisition should be a replacement of the one lost, and using the corporate entity would defeat their tax advantages.[1]

One problem inherent in threatened condemnation is that the government agency, (city, county, state or federal), may decide to abandon the condemnation. The courts recognize this right, so an owner must exercise care. However, if a governmental agency is unreasonable, some courts will provide relief under the idea that the agency should have "played fair."[2]

Another form of state control of property, and not always the most popular with land owners, is found in zoning laws.

"ZONING"

Zoning has been defined as "the division of a city by legislative regulation into districts and the prescription and application in each district of regulations having to do with structual and architectual designs of buildings and of regulations prescribing use to which buildings within designated districts may be put."³ The effect of these laws is to control the use to which land and buildings can be placed in the zoned districts.

In recent years, zoning has been extended from the cities (where it found its first application) into the counties, thus making it state-wide in some states.

One who wants to build a hospitality facility, must determine if the desired location is subject to zoning. If not, it must then be determined if other controls may affect the land.

NONCONFORMING USES

Because of the *ex post facto* provision of the U.S. Constitution, a zoning law enacted in one year, can not alter a use of property that existed prior to passage of that law. Thus if one operated a travel agency in a neighborhood that was later zoned for "single family dwellings," that "nonconforming use" could continue. In addition, the agency could be sold to others and the use would still continue. However, most zoning laws provide that if the use is discontinued for a specified time period (one year is typical), the use is abandoned, and the property becomes subject to the zoning.

VARIANCES

Zoning laws contain provisions for granting "variances." Upon proper application and satisfactory proof, the zoning can be changed to a different classification. This gives flexibility to these laws. Public hearings are required to do this.

Zoning laws have been the subject of many court battles since their inception. Two examples will illustrate.

"SLOW GROWTH"

A California community adopted a zoning plan that provided for the issuance of only 500 home building permits for the next five years. The law was challenged as a constitutional violation of travel rights. The lower court struck it down, but upon appeal, the upper court upheld the law as " . . . an exclusionary zoning device de-signed solely to insulate Petaluma (the California town) from the urban complex in which it finds itself."⁴ Other courts have held the opposite, as the following demonstrates.

ANOTHER CASE

One acre zoning in New Jersey was struck down because it denied land to the poor and was thus "patently discriminatory."[5]

Directly related to zoning is the requirement that before repairs can be made to buildings, or before new buildings can be constructed in the zoned areas, a "building permit" must be obtained.

BUILDING PERMITS

By requiring permits before repairs can be made or before new construction can be started, a helpful control device is provided. The application for a permit gives the governmental agency a chance to do several things: (1) to see if the proposed building meets the zoning requirements; (2) to see if the plans and specifications submitted with the application meet the electrical, heating and other building code requirements, and (3) to alert the various inspectors so that construction can be monitored as it progresses.

Also, the requirement of obtaining permits allows the government to refuse them as a means of getting rid of dangerous buildings. Since they cannot be repaired, they can be ordered destroyed.

One contemplating hospitality construction is well advised to seek all information possible about zoning and related requirements.

FEDERAL LAWS

Many other laws affect the use of property, including the Interstate Land Sales Disclosures Act.[6] This law requires certain developers to submit detailed information to the department of Housing and Urban Development.

The National Environmental Policy Act,[7] requires an environmental-impact statement (EIS) to be made on proposed legislation that will affect the quality of the human environment. The effect is to curb the creation of control-laws on property, but its long range effect might just be the opposite.

The final topic is that of "liens" and "encumberances."

LIENS AND ENCUMBERANCES

A "lien" is a charge, or security, or encumberance on property. It may be a claim for the payment of money; it may be restrictions placed on use by a prior owner. A lien (pronounced "lee-enn") is *not* a right to the property itself but rather is a claim that attaches to it. To illustrate, Ace Corporation gives security in its factory to Zero Bank to secure a loan of $100,000. Ace Corporation owns the factory but the bank has a lien against it. Upon payment of the debt plus interest, the bank will "lift" the lien by the execution of a "release". (See page 236). The property is then free of the lien.

Liens can be voluntary or involuntary.

VOLUNTARY LIENS

When Ace Corporation made the $100,000 loan from the bank, it agreed to the lien against the warehouse and thus it was a voluntary lien. Voluntary liens are used to borrow money, buy land, construct buildings, finance inventory and countless other business related uses. Where real estate is involved, the lien is created by a "mortgage" or "deed of trust". If personal property is involved, the "security agreement" is in wide spread use. Voluntary liens against real estate will be examined in Chapter 15.

INVOLUNTARY LIENS

There are various ways in which liens can be placed involuntarily against both real and personal property. That is, the liens are "attached" without the agreement of the property owner. Such liens are dangerous, since they may lead to the loss of the property to which the lien attaches. Three types of liens will be discussed here; failure to pay taxes, mechanics liens, and lawsuit judgments.

FAILURE TO PAY TAXES

If one fails to pay legitimate taxes assessed by a governmental agency, a lien will arise by operation of law and will be attached to, and can be enforced against, the property upon which the tax is delinquent. If one fails to pay personal property taxes, a lien attaches to that property. If the default continues for the statutory period, the property can be seized and then sold to satisfy the obligation. The same is true of real estate, only here there is no need to "seize" the property. If one owes federal income tax, and if this claim is placed on record, a lien attaches to all of the real estate of the debtor. In addition, the IRS can assert the claim against the bank and savings account of the debtor, and against any sums that may be due the debtor from others.

MECHANICS' LIENS

A contracts with B to construct a moter-hotel for A. B hires employees and buys materials from suppliers with which to do the job. If B fails to pay the employees or the suppliers, these persons have the right to file a "laborers'" or "mechanics' (suppliers) lien" against the property of A. This means that if A should pay B in full for the construction, the property will still be subject to the unpaid claims. These claims, when properly perfected, become liens against the motel-hotel. The structure can then be sold by the lien holders to satisfy their claims.

Mechanics' lien laws are statutory—there was no such thing at common law— and the time periods in which they can be enforced are short. The typical statute permits laborers and suppliers to file their liens within 60 or 90 days after "the last labor is provided or the last materials delivered."

Thus, one engaged in a construction project must be mindful of such liens, and be prepared to guard against them. The principal method is to make payments as the construction progresses, but only upon proof of payment of labor and materials. Or invoices for labor and material might be paid direct by the property owner. The use of performance bonds is also in order. Another technique is to deal only with reputable builders. But unfortunately this is not adequate, since even honest builders can go bankrupt.

LAWSUIT JUDGMENTS

A builder completes the construction of a parking lot for Holy Hotel. All suppliers and laborers are paid—and the hotel owner refuses to make payment. The builder may have mechanics' lien rights, but let's assume that the hotel owner stalls the builder for 120 days so the lien right is lost. The builder must then turn to the courts for recovery.

First, suit is filed. Since a valuable piece of real estate is involved, a notice of the pending litigation—"lis pendens"—should be prepared and placed on record in the county where the hotel is located. This creates an instant lien against the hotel in the states that permit its use. The amount sued for will, of course, be the sum due. In due course, the builder will obtain judgment for the sum due plus interest at the legal rate of interest from the date of judgment. This judgment should also be recorded.

Now the builder can proceed on the judgment to enforce the lien. This is done by "execution". If payment is not made, the judgment creditor can bring a "creditors' suit." This will ultimately result in the sale of the hotel. The proceeds of the sale will be applied to costs and the debt plus interest.

The following cases discuss some of the principles covered in this chapter.

CANDIB v. CARVER
Fla. App. 344 So. 2d 1312 (1977).

PER CURIAM.

Murray Candib, owner of a condominium on the 23rd floor of Palm Bay Towers Condominium, brought an action for injunctive relief to enjoin Roy J. Carver from violating (Article X, Subsection 5) the Declaration of Condominium by causing excessive noise; from continuing to unreasonably annoy Candib and his family, and to enjoin Carver from landing his helicopter on or around the condominium. The complaint sought both actual and punitive damages. At the initial hearing on the complaint, it was determined that the request to enjoin Carver from landing his helicopter on or around the Palm Bay Club was moot, because a permanent injunction had been entered enjoining the Palm Bay Club from granting, permitting, or conducting any and all helicopter flying, landing, or parking on the premises.

At the hearings for injunctive relief, it was determined that the condominiums owned by Carver were directly above the condominium owned by Candib. The Declaration of Condominium of the Palm Bay Towers Condominium, Article X, Section 5, relating to nuisances, was admitted into evidence. The trial court, after hearing all the evidence, entered an order denying the injunctive relief, finding that a legal nuisance did not exist; that there being no legal nuisance, Candib's request for damages was also denied.

It appears from the judgment the denial of injunctive relief or damages was based on the conclusion of the trial court that the plaintiff had not established the existence of a legal nuisance and, further, that the court cited authority for the proposition that "mere disturbance and annoyance, as such, do not in themselves necessarily give rise to an invasion of a legal right". While that proposition may be correct in the abstract, it does not have application by which a legal right is conferred for the protection of one against such activity by another.

That is the situation here, where the contract [Declaration of Condominium], after providing "no nuisance shall be allowed upon the condominium property", also separately provided that a unit owner should not so use his property as to be an unreasonable source of annoyance to unit owners or so as to interfere with the peaceful and proper use of the property by any condominium owner. Thus, not only does the contract protect against a nuisance but also confers a right of protection against a degree of annoyance, which may be less than a legal nuisance. If the intent of the contract had been to protect against only a legal nuisance, the contract provision could have so stated and stopped there without adding the other provision prohibiting the use as referred to above.

Law is cited to the effect that annoyance and interference with one's peaceful and proper use of his property, short of a legal nuisance, is not an invasion or violation of a legal right of the offended party. As pointed out above, that proposition of law does not apply here, where a legal right against such disturbance [short of legal nuisance] was expressly conferred on the unit apartment owners by the contract.

It was shown in the record that the main noise interference emanating from the defendant's condominium units, which were directly above the plaintiff's, was brought about by a type of flooring covering a certain area which had been installed by the defendant unit owner, without being insulated or soundproofed in a manner necessary to obviate excessive noise below and also without prior specification approval of the association, as provided for in the condominium documents. As owner of such a condominium unit, the plaintiff-appellant is entitled to the benefit of the rights conferred on him by the contract for protection against unreasonable noise and annoyance emanating from the apartment of another unit owner, particularly where the annoyance is the result of a construction or renovation feature created by the other unit owner.

The plaintiff made a case for enforcement of his contract right in that regard, for relief by way of injunction or damages. In this connection, see *Sterling Village Condominium, Inc. v. Breitenbach*, 251 So.2d 685 (Fla. 4th D.C.A. 1971), wherein the Fourth District Court of Appeal said the following in upholding the rights under condominium documents:

*   *   *   *   *   *   *   *   *   *

"Daily in this state thousands of citizens are investing millions of dollars in condominium property. Chapter 711, F.S.A., 1967, the Florida Condominium Act, and the Articles or Declaration of Condominiums provided for thereunder ought to be construed strictly to assure these investors that what the buyer sees the buyer gets. *Every man may justly consider his home his castle and himself as the king thereof; nonetheless his sovereign fiat to use his property as he pleases must yield, at least in degree, where ownership is in common or cooperation with others.* The benefits of condominium living and ownership demand no less. The individual ought not be permitted to disrupt the integrity of the common scheme through his desire for change, however laudable that change might be." [emphasis added]

*   *   *   *   *   *   *   *   *   *

See also the opinion of the Fourth District Court of Appeal in *Hidden Harbour Estates, Inc. v. Norman*, 309 So.2d 180 (Fla. 4th D.C.A. 1975), wherein the court again upheld condominium documents and said the following, in part:

*   *   *   *   *   *   *   *   *   *

"* * * In its final judgment in the trial court further held that any resident of the condominium might engage in any lawful action in the club house or on any common condominium property unless such action was engaged in or carried on in such a manner as to constitute a nuisance.

"With all due respect to the veteran trial judge, we disagree. It appears to us that inherent in the condominium concept is the principle that to promote the health, happiness, and peace of mind of the majority of the unit owners since they are living in such close proximity and using facilities in common, each unit owner must give up a certain degree of freedom of choice which he might otherwise enjoy in separate, privately owned property. Condominium unit owners comprise a little democratic sub society of necessity more restrictive as it pertains to use of condominium property than may be existent outside the condominium organization. *The Declaration of Condominium involved herein is replete with examples of the curtailment of individual rights usually associated with the private ownership of property.* It provides, for example, that no sale may be effectuated without approval; no minors may be permanent residents; no pets are allowed.

*   *   *   *   *   *   *   *   *   *

"* * * *It is not necessary that conduct be so offensive as to constitute a nuisance in order to justify regulation thereof.* Of course, this means that each case must be considered upon the peculiar facts and circumstances thereto appertaining.

Finally, restrictions on the use of alcoholic beverages are widespread throughout both governmental and private sectors; there is nothing unreasonable or unusual about a group of people electing to prohibit their use in commonly owned areas.

"Accordingly, the judgment appealed from is reversed and the cause is remanded with directions to enter judgment for the appellant." [emphasis added]

After the trial judge found no nuisance, he terminated the proceedings. We therefore return the matter to him to consider whether the plaintiff was entitled to an injunction enjoining the defendant from any use or practice which is an unreasonable source of annoyance or which interferes with the peaceful and proper use of his unit by the plaintiff. The court may make this determination either upon the record as made or by considering this record and such other evidence as may be offered. The trial judge should also, if he finds the defendant has violated the provision of the Declaration of Condominium [referred to in footnote 1], award such damages as he deems appropriate under the pleadings and evidence.

The final judgment here under review be and the same is hereby reversed and remanded to the trial court for further proceedings.

Reversed and remanded, with directions.

CORAL ISLE WEST ASS'N, INC., v. CINDY REALTY, INC.
430 F. Supp. 396 (1977)

ATKINS, District Judge

This matter is before the Court on defendants' motion to discharge the notice of lis pendens. Upon reviewing memoranda of counsel and the relevant authorities, it is hereby ORDERED AND ADJUDGED that defendants' motion to discharge the notice to lis pendens is GRANTED.

This is an action for treble damages and injunctive relief brought under Section 4 of the Clayton Act, 15 U.S.C. § 15, and § 1 of the Sherman Act, 15 U.S.C. § 1. The gravamen of the complaint is that the defendants unlawfully obligated plaintiffs to a 99-year recreation lease, which is binding upon all successors in title to the individual condominium apartments.

Upon filing the complaint, the plaintiffs also filed a notice of lis pendens against the entire condominium complex. Defendants now move for a Court Order discharging the lis pendens.

The law is well-settled that lis pendens is notice of all facts apparent on the face of the pleadings and such other facts as would put the purchaser on inquiry. Furthermore, Fla.Stat. 48.23, the statute governing the effect and procedure of filing a notice of lis pendens, is not restricted to actions in which the title to real property or some interest therein is involved, but it applies to both real and personal property. It follows, then, that in the instant proceedings the disputed leasehold may be the basis for the issuance of a notice of lis pendens.

The problem, however, focuses on what property is affected by the leasehold agreement. The plaintiff contends that the dispute over the leasehold embraces the entire condominium complex, i. e., all the units and the common areas. The defendant asserts that the leasehold is personalty and in no way affects any portion of the complex.

There are only a few Florida cases which help shed light on this problem. The most helpful decision interpreting the applicable statute is *Beefy King Int'l v. Veigle*, 464 F.2d 1102 (5th Cir. 1972). There, the Fifth Circuit, in affirming the lower Court's order discharging the notice of lis pendens, noted that:

> The purpose of a lis pendens is to notify prospective purchasers and encumbrancers that any interest acquired by them in the property in litigation is subject to the decree of the court. It is simply a notice of pending litigation. The effect of a lis pendens on the owner of property, however, is constraining. For all practical purposes, it would be virtually impossible to sell or mortgage the property because the interest of a purchaser or mortgagee would be subject to the eventual outcome of the lawsuit. Thus the Florida statute provides that the court may control the lis pendens as if it were an injunction unless the pleading shows "that the action is founded on a duly recorded instrument, or on a mechanic's lien," which was not the case here. Since the statute must mean that the court may discharge a notice of lis pendens in the same manner that it dissolves injunctions, it was not improper for the district court to hold a hearing and receive evidence on the motion to discharge.

The Court further pointed out that:

> We find no such abuse of discretion. The court determined that the suit does not directly affect the real property. A thorough reading of the complaint, review of the evidence, and study of the brief and supplemental brief of the appellants do not convince us otherwise. Assuming the solvency of the defendants, it appears clear that the plaintiffs can be afforded complete relief on any claim that they make in this lawsuit without reference to the title to the real property covered by the lis pendens. Under the Florida cases a lis pendens is proper only when the required relief might specifically affect the property in question. There is no other justification for burdening the alienability of the property pending the outcome of the lawsuit. (Emphasis added.)

In the instant proceedings, the complaint, in Paragraph 7, avers that:

"7) Association is the lessee under the subject Ninety-Nine Year Lease. Each unit owner, simultaneous with his purchase of a unit at the Coral Isle West Condominium, is required to enter into a Pledge Agreement, agreeing to be bound by the Ninety-Nine Year Lease, having the effect of in fact then being sub-lessee. Said lease provides for a lien which may be enforced against an individual apartment unit in case the owner of said apartment defaults in payment of the rent prescribed by the lease, as well as a lien upon the assets and common surplus of the Association, said lien being a first lien paramount and superior to all others upon any right, title, and interest of the Lessees in and to the lease and the demised premises therein. The provisions of the lease are made binding on all successors in title to the individual condominium apartments, and the lien provisions constitute a covenant running with the land, even if the condominium itself is terminated." (Emphasis added.)

We can throw light upon the issue before us by analogizing the interests subsisting under a leasehold agreement with those under a mortgage. In their complaint, plaintiffs allege that the failure to comply with the terms of the leasehold operates to create a "lien which may be enforced against the *individual* apartment units." (Emphasis added.) As discussed in note 1, supra, a mortgage interest likewise creates a lien on the property which secures the promissory note. Plaintiffs' reasoning, if applied to a default situation during mortgage foreclosure proceedings, would lead one to conclude that a mortgagee of "one individual apartment unit" may file a complaint and lis pendens against the condominium complex in the aggregate, that is against all the units and the common areas.

This analogy assists the Court in piercing the veneer of reasonableness that disguises the fallacy of plaintiffs' reasoning. Verily, our hypothetical mortgagee would be entitled to file a complaint and lis pendens against an "individual apartment unit" when attempting to enforce his security; he would not be permitted to bind, via a lis pendens, the entire complex. This is the precise policy justification underlying the principle that a lis pendens neither affects property not embraced within the description of the pleadings nor does its operation extend beyond the prayer for relief. If the rule were otherwise, an overbroad description in the notice of lis pendens would, in effect, encumber more security than the lien embraces, and as such would unnecessarily deprive the owners of such financial benefits as selling unencumbered property or mortgaging out their equity.

In the instant case, the property description in the plaintiffs' lis pendens is so broad as to encompass all condominium units and common areas. This, to be sure, exceeds the property which might be affected if plaintiffs were to succeed in this lawsuit.

Admittedly (as plaintiffs urge) prospective purchasers and lessees should be notified of the pending suit. Nevertheless, a judgment in this action can only be binding upon actual class members. Hence, if plaintiffs are concerned about notice, the plaintiffs should file a lis pendens against their units and those of actual class members. (The Association has been dropped as a party to this litigation.) The "notice" policy underlying the doctrine of lis pendens can thereby be effectuated without emasculating the countervailing policy of protecting the owners' property interest against an overbroad notice of lis pendens. To be sure these seemingly conflicting interests can be harmonized by plaintiffs' filing of notices of lis pendens against units of class members, and not against the condominium in the aggregate.

Accordingly, it is hereby ORDERED & ADJUDGED that the notice of lis pendens is discharged. The Court is mindful of plaintiffs' concern to notify prospective purchasers and lessees of affected condominium units of the pending proceedings. Plaintiffs may therefore file notices of lis pendens against their units as well as those of actual class members.

QUESTIONS

1. What is "fee simple" ownership and to what extent does it go at law?
2. Give an example of equitable title and explain why that title is not "legal".
3. Write out restrictions that you would want on land that you are going to subdivide. Would you want to exclude motels? Why?
4. In Condominum management, what is a "council" and what do they do? (See Appendix B).
5. What is the purpose of a condominuim "declaration"?
6. Why do the condominium statutes contain provisions that regulate recording of documents?
7. T. or F. The method of taxation of condo-units is provided in the statutes.
8. Why are mechanics' liens suits dangerous to condo-owners?
9. What is the source of the power to take private property for public use?
10. What are "non-conforming" uses and how are they provided for? Can exceptions be made to them? How?

ENDNOTES

1. Rev. Rul. 72-27, 1972-4 (I.R.B. 9.)
2. *City of Torrance v. Superior Court of Los Angeles County*, 545 P. 2d 1313 (Cal. 1976)
3. *Miller v. Board of Public Works of City of Los Angeles*, 195 Cal. 477, P. 381, 38 A.L.R. 1479.
4. *Construction Indies. Ass'n of Sonoma County v. City of Petaluma*, No. 74 - 2100 (9th Cir., 1975).
5. *South Burlington County N.A.A.C.P. v. Mount Laurel*, 336 A. 2d. 713 (N.J. 1975).
6. 15 U.S.C. sections 1701 et. seq.
7. 43 U.S.C. sect. 4321 et. seq.

15

Hospitality Construction and Mortgage Financing

One of the most important legal phases of the travel - hospitality business is encountered in the construction, remodeling and removal of facilities involved in that industry, A hotel has to be constructed initially; it must be maintained and remodeled as time goes by; and at some point it will be removed so that the construction cycle may begin anew. Only in rare cases can management provide cash funds to accomplish such purposes. In most instances, resort must be made to funds held by banks, insurance companies, or others engaged in construction—remodeling and destruction lending. In this chapter, we will examine how such lending is carried out. It is important to note that our discussion will be confined to the acquisition of land, and the construction, remodeling and replacement of hospitality facilities. Financing of equipment, inventory and other personal property with which to *furnish* a facility is another problem.

To facilitate orderly discussion, the following facts will be assumed.

FACTS

On October 12, 1942, James S. Everly and Elaine C. Everly, husband and wife, conveyed 12.3 acres of land in Star District, at the intersection of Interstate 79 and U.S. 48, to John B. Wilson and Sara J. Wilson, husband and wife. The deed is recorded in King County in Deed Book 595 at page 721. This deed contained the right of survivorship. John B. Wilson passed away on November 17, 1975 and by operation of the survivorship clause, this tract of land became the sole property of his wife, Sara. Wilson's estate, in due course, was settled and all taxes were paid.

William B. Koval and Stephen J. Koval, D/B/A Koval Enterprises, are the owners of three motor-hotels and are laying the groundwork for the construction of a restaurant. The brothers do business as a partnership under the laws of their state. Mrs. Wilson listed her 12.3 acres with Jerry Deal, Realtor, who in turn took a "listing contract" from Mrs. Wilson. This contract follows in Figure 15-1.

REALTOR'S ROLE

After the realtor and Mrs. Wilson executed the contract, Deal erected a "for sale" sign at the land location. In addition, a series of ads were placed in local papers. The Koval brothers saw the ads and made inquiry. After a visit to the site, negotiations began between Mrs. Wilson and the Kovals. The attorney for the Kovals, John C. Calhoun, then entered the picture. Mrs. Wilson's attorney was James C. Terry, 205 High Street, Gladhand.

The Koval's had previously hired a university professor to do a feasibility study, and those findings were that the area surrounding Gladhand would support a new, high quality, restaurant facility. It was the study that had prompted the Kovals to look for a building site in the first place.

FORMAL OFFER MADE

After making preliminary arrangements with the bank that had financed their other motels, the Koval brothers decided to make a formal offer for the purchase of the 12.3 acres.

The offer they made was $10,000 down, with the price to be $100,000. The down payment was to be applied to the purchase price if closed within sixty days. If the sale was not consumated, the $10,000 was to be retained by Mrs. Wilson as liquidated damages. The Realtor prepared and offered to Mrs. Wilson, a formal offer, as in Figure 15-2.

After examination of the offer, and being satisfied that it would serve her purposes, Mrs. Wilson accepted within the prescribed time period. Thus a binding buy-and-sell contract was in operation between the parties.

FIGURE 15-1
(Courtesy of Jerry Deal, Broker, Morgantown, West Virginia)

REAL ESTATE LISTING CONTRACT

OWNER Sara J. Wilson, Widow

ADDRESS OF OWNER 123 Jackson Lane, Gladhand, USA 26505

ADDRESS OF PROPERTY TO BE SOLD Intersection I-79 and US Rt. 48

TO

REALTOR GLADHAND BOARD OF REALTORS
Gladhand, USA

ADDRESS OF REALTOR 471 Inglewood Boulevard, Morgantown, West Virginia, 26505

DATE July 1, 19—

In consideration of your acceptance of this agreement and of your promise to list, to offer for sale and to endeavor to sell my property herein above specified, to advertise the same in such manner as you may deem advisable and further, to enlist in this behalf the best effort of your organization in its ordinary course of business, I hereby give and grant you, for a period of 90 days from the date of this instrument the exclusive right and authority to sell the property, hereinafter described for the price and upon the terms hereinafter set forth.

You are hereby authorized to accept a deposit on the purchase price of said property and in my name or as my agent execute and deliver a binding written contract for the sale and conveyance of said property during the life of this contract.

I hereby warrant that I am the owner of said property and that the information given on the reverse side hereof is true, that my title to said property is good and marketable, free from all encumbrances except as stated.

I hereby further agree (upon the considerations hereinabove mentioned) to pay you a commission of

__Six (6)%__
of the firm sales price of said property for your services, whether such sale be made by you or by me or by any person acting for me in my behalf, upon the terms hereinafter mentioned, or upon any other terms acceptable to me; or if the property is afterwards sold within __90 days__ from the termination of this Agency to a purchaser to whom it was submitted by you during the continuance of said Agency, and whose name has been disclosed to me.

I hereby further agree that should you accept an earnest money deposit and the prospective purchaser fails to complete the transaction, you may keep said earnest money deposit up to the amount of the full commission and any residue thereof will be turned over to me.

PRICE for which said property is to be sold is __$123,000.00__ Dollars.

TERMS OF SALE: The sum of __$10,000.00__ dollars is to be paid by the purchaser upon the signing of Agreement of Sale, as earnest money; said agreement and earnest money are to be held by you in escrow and paid to me upon the delivery of deed to purchaser.

The further sum of __$113,000.00__ Dollars to be paid as follows: __cash at closing.__

MORTGAGES: Held by __Farmers' and Merchants' Bank__
Payment plan __Monthly__

I grant you exclusive "For Sale" sign privilege on said described property and agree to refer to you all inquiries which I may receive during the continuance of this agency.

In any exchange of the aforesaid described property, permission is hereby given to you in negotiating such exchange to collect commissions on all properties involved in the transaction.

It is understood that should some other licensed broker furnish you with a customer who purchases the property through you, the division of the commission shall be in accordance with the usual custom among real estate brokers.

Singular pronouns of the first person shall be read as plural when this agreement is signed by two or more persons.

This agency shall be binding upon and inure to the benefit of the heirs, administrators and assigns of the respective parties hereto.

Sara J. Wilson Owner
_____ Wife

FIGURE 15-2

Uniform Purchase Contract

GLADHAND BOARD OF REALTORS
Gladhand, U.S.A.

REALTOR

1. The undersigned **William B. Koval and Stephen J. Koval, Partners**
whose principal place of residence is **Garndville, USA 26506**
hereinafter referred to as the VENDEE, hereby offers and agrees to purchase from **Sara J. Wilson, Widow,** , whose principal place of residence is
123 Jackson Lane, Gladhand, USA 26505 , hereinafter
referred to as the VENDOR, the following described property:
Situated in the **District** of **Star,**
County of **Queen** , and State of **Any State**
, and known as **12.3 acres, Star District**
together with a lot approximately

(Here followings a metes and bounds description)

This offer is made contingent upon the offerors being
able to obtain proper building permits to construct a restaurant
on said real estate.

2. PURCHASE PRICE
The Vendee agrees to pay to the Ven r for above described property the sum of **One Hundred Thousand**------------------------------------- Dollars ($ **100,000**) payable as follows:
Ten Thousand ----------------------------------- Dollars (**$10,000**)
earnest money accompanying this offer and to apply on the purchase price when this sale is consummated;
Ninety Thousand ------------------------------ Dollars ($ **90,000**)
additional cash payment upon consummation of sale;
n/a Dollars ($)
by the execution of a promissory note or notes and deed of trust or other satisfactory instrument upon
said premises, which said notes or notes shall bear interest at the rate of (%) per cent
per annum. Payable at the rate of ($) per month (including
principal and interest). Said promissory note or notes, deed of trust or other instruments, other than the
deed of conveyance, shall be prepared at the expense of the vendee. The Vendee will pay the fees for recording the deed and deed of trust. The Vendor shall pay for the necessary state and federal documentary
stamps.

3. DEED
Upon the acceptance of this offer by the Vendor and the performance of all conditions stipulated here-
in, to be performed by the Vendee, the Vendor shall convey a clear title to said premises to
William B. Koval, and Stephen J. Koval, Partners, dba Koval Enterprises

FIGURE 15-2 (continued)

4. RISK OF LOSS BEFORE CONSUMMATION OF SALE

After acceptance of this offer and until consummation of sale by delivery of deed, the risk of loss by fire and other casualty shall be borne by vendor, and all policies of insurance thereon shall be endorsed to cover both vendor and vendee. In the event of such loss vendee shall have the option to accept any insurance money paid upon such loss, crediting same upon the purchase price and paying the remainder as set forth in this contract, or to be released from all obligation to purchase said property and have the right to the immediate repayment of his earnest money.

5. INSURANCE — TAXES AND ASSESSMENTS

Insurance policies in sufficient amount to protect the interest of the Vendor shall be obtained by the Vendee in accordance with the terms of the deed of trust or other instrument mentioned in Paragraph 2. above. The Vendee shall pay all premiums for such insurance as they may become due. The Vendee shall assume and pay taxes and other assessments for the   last quarter of 19_

of the year   and subsequent years on said property.

6. RENTS

Rents shall be apportioned as of the date of consummation of the sale.

7. POSSESSION

                                        vacant
Possession of the property as then̶x̶e̶x̶x̶x̶x̶x̶ shall be delivered to the Vendee on the date of the consummation of the sale, or on or before   January 16, 19_

8. TITLE

The Vendee shall be permitted to inspect any and all the indicia of title in possession of the Vendor and also deed, note, deed of trust or other instrument prepared by the Vendor for the Vendee but before such papers have been signed by the Vendor, and if the Vendee desires further evidence of title he shall obtain it at his own expense.

9. TIME OF PERFORMANCE — DEFAULT

This offer shall be open for acceptance for a period of   twenty   (20) days from the date hereof. This offer shall be accepted by delivery to the Vendee of a duplicate of this instrument executed by the Vendor, or by the Realtor. If the offer is not accepted within said period, the earnest money deposited herewith shall be returned immediately to the Vendee. If the offer is accepted within said period the Vendor and Vendee shall have   sixty   (60) days from date of acceptance in which to consummate the sale. If the Vendee defaults in performance of any of the obligations imposed by the terms hereof, the Vendor may, at his option, treat the contract as null and void and retain the earnest money deposited herewith as liquidated damages for failure of the Vendee to perform the contract. In the event the Vendor is unable to convey to the Vendee clear title by a General Warranty Deed within a period of   sixty   (60) days from the date of the acceptance, the Vendee, may at his option treat the contract as null and void and the Vendor must immediately return said earnest money to the Vendee without any liability upon the Vendor for failure to convey the premises.

The sale shall be consummated at a place in   Gladhand, USA 26505, or as designated by the REALTOR herein named upon the terms and conditions stated herein. No other representations of Vendor or Vendee other than contained in this agreement shall be binding upon either party.

Dated this   20th   day of   August , 19_

                                                                    Vendee
Accepted for Submission
To   Vendor
                                      Realtor

                            ACCEPTANCE BY VENDOR

        At
this   day of   19
                                                                    Vendor

herein (or by his authorized REALTOR)
hereby accepts the above offer with all the conditions and provisions therein contained.

                                                    Vendor
                                                      or
                            By:
                                              Authorized Realtor

CONTRACT WITH ARCHITECT

An architect's contract was entered into by the Kovals, and the design work and cost estimates proceeded promptly. The Koval's then made another visit to their banker.

BANK'S ROLE

The bank took a formal application from the partners and a current financial statement was provided. It is essential that a financial statement be truthful and not mislead the bank. If the bank is misled, liability may later arise, both civil and criminal, on the grounds of fraud or misrepresentation. The Koval's requested a committment from the bank on land acquisition and construction costs. The real estate appraiser for the bank then made an appraisal of the 12.3 acres and submitted his findings to the bank as follows:

Hey, Hay and Hayes
Appraisers
Gladhand
August 30, 19___

Traveler's National Bank
1500 Center Avenue
Gladhand

Att: Charles Newman, Loan Officer.

Dear Mr. Newman:

I have made an appraisal of the 12.3 acres of land owned by Sara J. Wilson, widow, located in Star District at the Intersection of I-79 and U.S. 48, described as follows:

(Here follows the legal description by meters and bounds).

Based upon comparables found in the adjacent areas, it is my opinion that the real estate in question has a market value of $105,000.00. This evaluation is subject however, to the site meeting applicable zoning and health restriction laws.

Sincerely,
s/s Jim Hayes

COMMITTMENT LETTER

The bank now committed itself to a loan as follows:

September 15, 19___

Dear William and Stephen:

At the meeting of our loan committee last evening, we agreed to make you a loan of $73,500.00, at 9% interest, for a seven year period, and will take as security, the 12.3 acres that you have under contract with Sara J. Wilson. This loan is 70% of the appraised value per our loan policies on vacant land.

Upon receipt of a copy of the building contract, we will grant you an additional loan of 80% of the construction price of the proposed restaurant, subject to our usual pay-out, construction policies. We are enclosing a preliminary estimate of closing costs for your information, in the sum of $3,000.00.

We are pleased to be able to serve you.

Sincerely,
s/s Charles Newman
Loan Officer.

At this point, the Kovals have a contract to buy the land; they have a committment on the land and the proposed building and they have $10,000 invested. By their estimates, applying the 70% and 80% lending limits, they will need $130,000 additional to cover the fees, the 30% on the land, and the 20% on the cost of the building which has been estimated at $500,000. These funds can be raised from assets of the partnership, so they decide to proceed with the project. It now becomes necessary to enter into a construction contract.

ADVERTISING FOR BIDS

Using the plans, specifications and cost estimates of the architect, bids are asked for. This is done by publication in the legal notices of various newspapers spelling out how copies of the plans may be obtained. Upon advice of counsel, they require that each bid be accompained by a 10% bid bond, in cashiers check form. The purpose of this is to give their CPA an adequate opportunity to examine the bids received before a final decision is made.

In the meantime, the brothers are faced with a time limit.

TIME IS RUNNING

The contract to buy expires shortly and time is passing. Since the financing has been approved but they do not yet have a construction contract, they must act quickly or abandon the project, and thus forfeit the $10,000 down payment. They decide to proceed since others are now indicating to Mrs. Wilson that they are willing to pay up to $150,000 for the 12.3 acres. This competition arose because of other projects that have been started at the I-79 intersection.

LAWYER'S ROLE

The Koval's then instructed John C. Calhoun, Esq., to give notice that they were ready to proceed with the closing. A date was agreed upon by the parties. In the meantime, Calhoun has work to do.

TITLE SEARCH

The bank will require proof that the legal title of the real estate is "good and marketable". This proof can be provided by "title insurance"—or by a title search certificate from an attorney.

It is customary to place conditions in the contract of sale as was done in the present case. If the title search uncovers defects that violate these conditions, the contract is void and the down payment must be returned.

How is a title search carried out?

"TITLE CHAIN"

Attorney Calhoun established the source of title of John B. and Sara J. Wilson by examaning the deed by which they obtained title from James C. Everly and wife. This led him to the source of title of Everly's grantor; and to the grantor of *their* grantor. It is customary to continue this process to the first conveyance before 1900. After the chain of title is complete, it will be "adversed."

ADVERSING THE CHAIN

It is now necessary to establish what happened to the property while title to it was vested in all of those in the chain. Were any portions of it sold: were minerals sold? Were easements granted or leases given? Were any prior owners sued, and if so, were judgments recorded against them? Was the realty pledged as security for a loan? After all of this, and anything else uncovered, Calhoun will make his title report to the Kovals and the Traveler's National Bank.

TITLE REPORT

This report, in part, follows:

"I have examined the record title to the following described real estate, (description follows), and as of December 15, 19—, submit the following report:

TAXES

Taxes are both halves of 19—, in the sum of $326.31 per half have not been paid. There is no fire fee since the acreage contains no structures. These taxes must be prorated at closing.

LIENS

Deed of trust given by John B. and Sara J. Wilson, husband and wife, dated the 15th day of March, 1963, of record in the Office of the Clerk of Star District, in Deed of Trust Book No. 323 at page 781, to secure the Farmers' and Merchants' Bank of Fayette City, in the original sum of $20,000.

ZONING

This tract is zoned by the county as commercial and is thus available for restaurant use without further change.

SANITATION REQUIREMENTS

There are no sanitary facilities available and the land is subject to standard percolation tests for septic tank fields.

OUT CONVEYANCES

In 1906, a right-of-way was granted to West End Power Company for purposes of the construction and maintenance of a power transmission line across this real estate.

In 1910, an easement was granted to the Eureka Pipe Line Company for the construction and maintenance of an oil transmission live across the larger tract from which the 12.3 acres was later subdivided.

Both of these easements cross the 12.3 acres tract at the points indicated on the attached survey plat. (Copy attached).

ENCUMBERANCES

This real estate is subject to a life estate reserved in James S. Everly. The records do not indicate whether Mr. Everly is alive or not.

This tract is further subject to an oil and gas lease to Hopeless Gas Company, dated July 7, 1955. This lease has a "10 year production" clause and could be in effect if production had been started within the first 10 years.

In 1928, a prior owner of this tract made plans to subdivide the land and to construct houses. In preparing to do this, building restrictions were created and placed on record as follows: (these are set out in detail). Because of a 25 year limit on these restrictions, and since no housing was ever constructed, these restrictions are no longer in effect.

It is my opinion that Sara J. Wilson has good and marketable title to this real estate, subject to:

1. The above.
2. What a careful visual inspection of the land would disclose.
3. The accuracy of the records in the Clerk's Office.

Dated this 15th day of
December, 19—

John C. Calhoun

s/s John C. Calhoun
Attorney at law.

Calhoun then prepared to do the following:

1. Pro-rate the taxes for closing as of January 15, 19—.
2. Obtain a pay-off figure on the deed of trust from the Farmers' and Merchants' Bank as of the same date.
3. Make application for the percolation test for purposes of installation of the septic tank field.
4. Determine the date of death of James S. Everly, who died in a neighboring state.

5. Determine if the gas lease was in effect.

The brothers decided that the two right-of-ways would not inter-fere with the construction—which now included long-range plans for a motel in addition to the restaurant.

CLOSING

A definite date and time for closing was set and the parties noti-fied. The parties will be present with their respective counsel. Some lenders use "house counsel"—others use the services of the lawyers for the parties. Prior to closing, the lawyer for the seller will have; prepared the deed and forwarded a copy to the lawyer for the buyer; (see figure 15-3) obtained, or made arrangements to obtain, releases needed, if any; and pro-rated the taxes. The lawyer for the buyer will have completed the title search; determined pay-offs needed to clear title; and coordinated financial matters with the loan officer. The loan officer will have prepared the HUD disclosure forms and will have given a copy of the HUD booklet to the buyers. Truth-in-Lend-ing disclosure forms will also have been prepared along with a settle-ment sheet. See Figure 15-4.* The closing is then ready to be carried out.

The deed of trust, note, and disclosure forms will be signed by the buyers. Copies of the disclosures are given to the parties. The seller will sign the deed and other documents required. Both parties will examine the settlement figures and, if they are in agreement, the pro-ceeds will be distributed by drafts made payable to the parties as indicated.

The lawyer for the buyer will obtain releases (see Figure 15-5) needed by payment to the lien holders (here only one). The lawyer will then proceed to the recording point.

RECORDING

First releases (here only one) will be recorded to extinguish prior liens. Next, the deed from the seller to the buyer will be placed on record. Third, the deed of trust (mortgage) is recorded, thus perfect-ing the bank's security interest in the property. The recording lawyer will examine title once again and, if no other claim or lien has inter-vened, will issue a final title report to the buyers and lenders.

*The HUD and TIL disclosures are normally made in consumer—not business loans. They are mentioned here for educational purposes.

FIGURE 15-3

THIS DEED, Made this 15th day of January, 19—, by and between Sara J. Wilson, Widow, Grantor and party of the first part, and William B. Koval and Stephen J. Koval, Partners, dba Koval Enterprises, a partnership, Grantees and parties of the second part.

WITNESSETH: That for and in consideration of the sum of One Hundred Thousand ($100,000.00) Dollars this day cash in hand paid, the receipt of which is hereby acknowledged, the Grantor, Sara J. Wilson, does grant and convey unto the Grantees as partners, William B. Koval and Stephen J. Koval, dba Koval Enterprises, with covenants of General Warranty, all of the following described parcel of real estate, situate in Star District, Gladhand, USA and being more particularly described as follows:

(Here follows a metes and bounds description of the 12.3 acres).

And being the same real estate that was conveyed to John B. Wilson and Sara J. Wilson, husband and wife, from James S. Everly et ux, by deed dated the 12th day of October, 1942, of record in the Office of the County Clerk of Star District in Deed Book 595 at page 721. John B. Wilson departed this life on the 17th day of November, 1975, and left as his sole heir at law, the Grantor herein,

Under penalties of fine and imprisonment as provided by law, the Grantor certifies that the total consideration for the real estate herein conveyed is $100,000.00.

WITNESS the following signature and seal:

Sara J. Wilson (SEAL)
Sara J. Wilson

(Acknowledgment follows)

FIGURE 15-4
(Complete the above two blanks)

CLOSING STATEMENT
January 15, 19—

BUYER: William B. Koval and Stephen J. Koval,
                Partners, d/b/a/ Koval Enterprises

SELLER: Sara J. Wilson, Widow

LOCATION: 12.3 Acres, Star District

MORTGAGEE: Traveler's National Bank

SELLER		BUYER	
Consideration:	$100,000.00	Consideration:	$100,000.00
Less Hand Money:	10,000.00	Less Hand Money:	10,000.00
Balance:	90,000.00	Balance:	90,000.00
Less:		Add:	
Attorney fee:	Paid direct	Attorney fee:	Paid direct
Realtor Commission	6,000.00	Recording fee, Deed,	3.75
Transfer Stamps	330.00	Deed of trust	2.75
Real Estate Taxes,		Appraisal fee	100.00
pro-rated	679.91		
Payoff Farmers' and		Less:	
Merchants' Bank	7,366.42	Proceeds of deed of	
Release	1.00	trust loan	73,500.00
NET DUE SELLER $_____		NET DUE FROM BUYER: $_____	

If the land had contained a structure, fire insurance would have been arranged before closing. The buyer would produce proof of this coverage before title passed from one to the other. This is necessary to prevent a lapse of coverage. The insurance of the seller *will not* cover the buyer once title passes.

Upon completion of the recording legal title is vested in the buyers, subject only to the lien of the lending bank. Any subsequent claims or liens would be subordinate to the lender.

Now that the Koval brothers own the 12.3 acres, they will turn their attention to the construction bids.

BIDS

It is customary to open construction bids in the presence of the bidders. Once the bids are opened, the Kovals will want them analyzed so that they will be certain to accept the best bid—which is not always the lowest one. At this point, the bid bonds prevent any of

FIGURE 15-5

FARMERS' and MERCHANTS' BANK
                To: } RELEASE, DEED OF TRUST
SARA J. WILSON, Widow

The Farmers' and Merchants' Bank, ... a corporation
hereby releases a deed of trust executed by ..John B. Wilson and Sara J. Wilson, husband.....
.and wife, ... to.. David W. Zinn ...., Trustee
dated the ...15th.... day of ..March ...., 19.63., recorded in the office of the Clerk of the
County Court of Monongalia County, West Virginia in DEED OF TRUST BOOK No. .323........, page 781....
the obligation secured thereby having been fully paid and satisfied.

....

IN WITNESS WHEREOF, the said corporation has caused its corporate name to be hereto subscribed and
its corporate seal hereto affixed by ..Robert A. Weimer..........................
its .Vice. President, by authority duly given, this ....14th............... day of
(SEAL)   January, ..., 19. —..

                                        Robert A. Weimer

                                By .Robert A. Weimer.................................
                                                            Vice   President

STATE OF WEST VIRGINIA, TO-WIT
COUNTY OF MONONGALIA,
   I, ...Sidney DelRio..................... a Notary Public of the County aforesaid, do certify
that ....Robert A. Weimer ...., who signed the writing above (or hereto annexed,) bearing
date the ..14th..... day of ..January........ 19—... for .The Farmers' and Merchants'....
.Bank............. (name of Corporation) has this day in my said county, before me, acknowledged the said
writing to be the act and deed of said Corporation.

   Given under my hand this .14th....... day of January...................., 19—.
                                        William A. Jones
My commission expires ..March .1........., 19 —.   Notary Public

STATE OF WEST VIRGINIA
MONONGALIA COUNTY, TO-WIT:
   I, TOM JACKSON Clerk of the County Court of the county aforesaid, do certify that the foregoing writing
together with the certificate thereto attached, was this day, presented to me in my office, and was admitted to
record therein at .... o'clock ....M.
Given under my hand this .... day of ...., 19....
                                        Tom Jackson
                                                            Clerk

the bidders from withdrawing their bids. This could happen when one bidder discovers that his bid was unreasonably lower than the others. If they withdraw they forfeit the bid bond.

BID ACCEPTED

In due course, the Kovals will accept the bid of their choice, thus bringing into play the construction contract.

The terms of the contract, including, price, materials to be used, time of completion, liquidated damage clause and others, will be the terms upon which the bid was made. This is why caution is in order in accepting a bid. One must be certain that terms were not altered or left out. For example, a low bidder may want a longer time in which to complete the work. Thus a higher bid, but one with a shorter completion time, might be more desirable. Now the Koval brothers must complete the financial arrangements for payment of the costs of construction.

BACK TO THE BANK

Now that the land is owned by the Kovals, and now that the bank has a valid first lien on it, the additional financing is not so complex.

The lender will create, or have created in advance, a construction payment schedule. The contractor will be paid as work is completed. For example, one-eighth of the contract will be paid when grading and foundations are completed; one-fourth when all outside walls are up; one-fourth when the structure is under roof, and the balance upon completion. These schedules vary from lender to lender.

Before construction begins, the lender needs assurance of two things: (1) that no work has been started on the land and (2) that no other claims or liens have intervened against the Koval brothers. Once these are established, a second note will be executed by the Kovals and a second mortgage will be given on the 12.3 acres. In some instances, the lender may combine both loans and cover them by one mortgage.

CONSTRUCTION BEGINS

It is the duty of the contractor to obtain building permits; to provide liability insurance for the work site and to cover employees with workman's compensation coverage.

As the work progresses, city or county inspectors will watch the construction, as will agents from the lender. At prescribed times, payments will be made to the contractor, making certain that all suppliers and laborers have been paid to date. This is done to guard against mechanics' or laborers' liens, which, in some states, take priority over security interests of lenders.

If all proceeds well, the restaurant will be completed on schedule; the contractor will be paid, and the Kovals can begin business operations. If construction is delayed, the contractor will forfeit the sum provided in the liquidated damage clause in the contract. It is customary to withhold final payment to the builder for one year so that "punch list" items can be observed for that time. Such lists include those things that may be found to be defective after construction, such as septic tank fields, water and toilet facilities and the like. Punch list items are small when compared with the over-all construction and the sum held in escrow (held back), are usually minor.

FORECLOSURE

The Kovals have assumed a major obligation to their lender and they must meet this obligation as agreed. If they fail to do so, the lender may declare default on the note or notes, and order the mortgage foreclosed. This means the real estate will be sold to satisfy the outstanding obligation. Foreclosure procedures are dictated by the terms found in the deed-of-trust or mortgage, and include notice to the debtors, public advertising of the foreclosure, and public sale by auction.

A good faith buyer at a foreclosure sale obtains good title to the real estate sold. It is well to observe that when *personal property* is financed and default occurs, it is "repossessed". One cannot repossess a restaurant, so the remedy of "foreclosure" is used.

HOSTETTER v. INLAND DEV. CORP. OF MONTANA
561 P. 2d 1323 (1977).

HATFIELD, Chief Justice.

This is an appeal from the district court, Gallatin County, denying appellants' foreclosure on a mechanic's lien.

On April 22, 1974, appellants, doing business as Dutch Touch, entered into a contract with Inland Development Corporation of Montana, a subsidiary of Inland Construction Corporation of Minnesota. Inland Development was the primary contractor responsible to Big Sky of Montana, Inc. for the Glacier Condominium Project located in Meadow Village at Big Sky, Montana. The project consisted of 14 buildings which housed 64 condominium units. The Dutch

Touch contract involved the construction of ceramic bathtub enclosures in each individual unit, with no work on the common areas to be performed. This was a single contract, the basis of payment to be the total number of square feet of tile laid. Dutch Touch commenced work on this contract during April 1974.

On August 20, 1974, Big Sky filed and recorded a declaration of unit ownership covering the Glacier Condominiums. During September, October, and November, 1974, Big Sky sold 18 of the 64 condominium units to third parties.

Dutch Touch completed the tile work on March 24, 1975, claiming the amount due for labor, material, and supplies to be $14,554.60. As of June 18, 1975, Dutch Touch had received $13,038.12 leaving $1,516.48 unpaid. On June 18, 1975, Dutch Touch filed a single mechanic's lien for the unpaid balance upon the real property and premises encompassing the 14 buildings and 64 units of the Glacier Condominiums.

On August 19, 1975, Dutch Touch initiated a foreclosure action in district court seeking a personal judgment against Inland Development on the contract and enforcement of its lien against the interest of Big Sky in the Glacier Condominiums. A lis pendens was also filed at this time.

A third party action was filed by Big Sky against Inland Construction on the primary contract. The trial on this third party complaint was suspended until the determination of the lien foreclosure.

The district court, sitting without a jury, entered judgment against Dutch Touch upon the following conclusions of law: 1) That the Glacier Condominium Project became subject to the provisions of the Montana Unit Ownership Act, sections 67-2301 et. seq., R.C.M.1947, by reason of the filing of the delcaration by Big Sky on August 20, 1974, 2) that a lien covering the entire project was invalid under section 67-2324, R.C.M.1947; and 3) that Dutch Touch failed to establish a lien against any individual unit in the Glacier Condominium Project.

Two issues are presented for review: 1) Was Dutch Touch's single lien rendered invalid when Big Sky filed the declaration? 2) Was Dutch Touch entitled to foreclose against only those units owned by Big Sky for the entire amount of the lien?

This is a case of first impression, the interpretation of section 67-2324, R.C.M.1947, as it relates to a subcontractor's lien arising from work performed and materials supplied during the initial construction of a condominium project.

The interest in unit ownership legislation was generated by federal legislation making Federal Housing Administration insurance available for condominiums, provided that state law concerning unit ownership existed. 12 U.S.C.S. § 1715 y(a). FHA then provided a Model Act which many states, including Montana, followed. The primary purpose of this condominium legislation is to insure the compatability of such housing projects with pre-existing law. 77 Harvard L.Rev. 777 (1964).

Under the pre-existing lien law of Montana, Dutch Touch would be entitled to a blanket lien effective against the entire condominium project. This is so since the work was performed under one contract, and not a series of separate contracts for each unit.

We must now determine what effect subjecting the property to the Montana Unit Ownership Act has upon the lien of Dutch Touch.

Section 67-2324, R.C.M.1947, states:

"(1) Subsequent to recording a declaration and while the property remains subject to sections 67-2302 to 67-2342; no lien shall arise or be effective against the property. During such period liens or encumbrances shall arise or be created only against each unit and the undivided interest in the common elements appertaining thereto, in the same manner and under the same conditions as liens or encumbrances may arise or be created upon or against any other separate parcel of real property subject to individual ownership.

"(2) No labor performed or materials furnished with the consent or at the request of a unit owner, his agent, contractor or subcontractor, shall be the basis for the filing of a mechanic's or materialman's lien against the unit of any other unit owner not consenting to or requesting the labor to be performed or the materials to be furnished, except that consent shall be considered given by the owner of any unit in the case of emergency repairs thereto performed or furnished with the consent or at the request of the manager.

"(3) If a lien becomes effective against two or more units, the owner of each unit subject to such a lien shall have the right to have his unit released from the lien by payment of the amount of the lien attributable to his unit. The amount of the lien attributable to a unit and the payment required to satisfy such a lien, in the absence of agreement, shall be determined by application of the percentage established in the declaration. Such partial payment, satisfaction or discharge shall not prevent the lienor from proceeding to enforce his rights against any unit and the undivided interest in the common element appertaining thereto not so released by payment, satisfaction or discharge."

This is one section of the entire Unit Ownership Act and it is the duty of this Court to interpret it in such a manner as to insure coordination with the other sections of the Act, and fulfill legislative intent.

Reading the Act in its entirety, it becomes apparent that there are safeguards to insure that builders, mechanics, and materialmen involved in the initial construction of a project are to be fully compensated before individual units are sold. Furthermore, Big Sky failed to comply with these safeguards.

Section 67-2303.1 allows the sale of units prior to the completion of construction of the "building", which the Act defines as a multiple unit building. However, the money from such sales must be placed in escrow. Disbursements cannot be made from this escrow fund until completion of the building and common elements or compliance with section 67-2303.2 through 2303.6, whichever occurs first. In any event, such disbursements are to be only for cost of construction, legal, architectural and financial fees, and other incidental costs of the project. Section 67-2303.1(4) then specifically states:

"* * * The balance of the moneys remaining in the fund shall be disbursed *only* upon completion of the building, *free and clear of all mechanic's and materialmen's liens. * * *"* (Emphasis added.)

Big Sky did sell 18 units prior to completion of construction, however, it failed to deposit the moneys from these sales in an escrow account as required, and failed to pay this lien.

Section 67-2323 states:

"*Blanket mortgages and other blanket liens affecting unit at time of first conveyance or lease.* At the time of the first conveyance or lease of each unit following the recording of the declaration, every mortgage and other lien affecting such unit including the undivided interest of the unit in the common elements, *shall be paid and satisfied* of record, or the unit being conveyed or leased and its interest in the common elements *shall be* released therefrom by partial release duly recorded." (Emphasis added.)

Again Big Sky failed to comply with this provision. At the time of its first sale Big Sky had not satisfied this lien nor did it obtain a partial release as required.

The lien of Dutch Touch arose, attached and became effective against the property when work was commenced, the filing merely perfects the lien. *Conti-*

nental Supply Co. v. White, 92 Mont. 254, 266, 12 P.2d 569, 574 (1932) states:

"* * * The lien constitutes an interest in the property; 'the filing extends its life and preserves it.'

"The lien attaches to the structure as the labor is performed or the material is furnished and exists with all of its force at all times between the beginning of the performance of labor or the furnishing of material until the expiration of the time within which notices of lien may be filed.' (Citation omitted.)

"The true function of the lien is to *prevent* subsequent alienations and incumbrances, except in subordination to itself."

See also *Blose v. Havre Oil & Gas Co.*, 96 Mont. 450, 461, 31 P.2d 738 (1934). Furthermore, this lien was originally effective as a blanket lien against the entire project under the *Caird* case. We disagree that this lien was rendered invalid by the filing of the declaration, as held by the district court. Instead, we adhere to the rationale of the Wisconsin Supreme Court when they faced the issue in *Stevens Const. Corp. v. Draper Hall, Inc.*, 73 Wis.2d 104, 242 N.W.2d 893, 898 (1976). The Wisconsin court was also confronted with a mechanic's lien based upon work performed during initial construction and a Unit Ownership Act with a provision the same as our section 67-2324, R.C.M.1947. The Wisconsin statute, § 703.09 W.S.A., is identical to our section 67-2324, with their § 703.09(2) the same as our section 67-2324(3).

Their decision in *Stevens* states:

"Stevens and The Bruce Company argue that their liens arose and became effective when the excavations began in September of 1971. They contend that no distinction should be made between when a lien arises and when a lien becomes effective. We agree with this proposition but it makes no difference in terms of the rights of the claimant-appellants in this case. The word "effective,' in the context of construction liens, should be interpreted to mean 'capable of bringing about an effect.' A construction lien is capable of bringing about an effect at the time it arises, that is, when 'substantial excavation for the foundations' of the new project begin, as provided in sec. 289.-01(4), Stats. The later events of giving notice and filing, as required by sec. 289.06, merely preserve and perfect a lien which is already effective in the sense of being capable of having an effect upon the liened land.

"Acceptance of this position of appellants does not mean that sec. 703.09(2), Stats., is inapplicable to the facts of this case. On the contrary, we conclude that this subsection still governs, even though the claimants' liens were first 'effective' in September of 1971, before the condominium declaration was recorded.

"Subsection (2) provides that a proportional lien occurs whenever 'a lien becomes effective against 2 or more units.' Obviously the most frequently occurring situation in which a lien will become effective against two or more units is when repairs are made to the common areas of the condominium unit, and left unpaid. But we conclude that a lien, originally effective as a blanket lien against the whole property, becomes effective against two or more units within the meaning of sec. 703.09(2), Stats., when the property is made subject to the provisions of ch. 703 by the filing of a condominium declaration before the initiation of foreclosure proceedings against the property as a whole.

"Thus it is not critical that the filing of the lien claims came after the condominium declaration was filed, as the trial court decided. Even if the claims were filed before the condominium declaration was recorded, only proportional liens would attach to the individual units. On the other hand, if foreclosure proceedings are begun before the condominium declaration is recorded, and a lis pendens filed, the situation is frozen so that the subsequent recording of a declaration does not transform the blanket lien into a proportional lien on individual units."

Likewise, the mechanic's lien filed by Dutch Touch was not rendered invalid when Big Sky filed its declaration, but remained a valid single lien, which was proportionately effective against each unit, pursuant to section 67-2324(3), R.C.M.1947.

The second issue presented involves the *enforcement* of the lien once it is established. The foreclosure of a mechanic's lien is governed by the rules of equity. *Cole v. Hunt* 123 Mont. 256, 211 P.2d 417 (1949). The general rule is that a blanket construction lien against an entire property consisting of several parcels cannot be enforced in toto against less than all of such parcels. Annot. 68 A.L.R.3d 1300. The reason is that it would be inequitable to burden some lesser portion of the liened premises with charges for labor and materials which were not actually furnished to that particular parcel. Consequently, this single lien, proportionately effective against each unit, would only be enforceable against each unit proportionately. It is the duty of those purchasing, or taking liens on, property under construction or on which improvements are being made, to make inquiry to ascertain whether or not the property is encumbered by mechanics' or materialmen's liens, and such parties, having knowledge of the fact that the work is going on, are charged with constructive, if not actual, notice of any such lien as has attached to the premises. *Continental Supply Co. v. White*, supra.

However, any unit owners, other than Big Sky, whose property is subject to Dutch Touch's mechanic's lien, were put into that position by Big Sky's total disregard of the provisions of the Unit Ownership Act concerning mechanics' liens and pre-completion sales.

Big Sky failed to place the proceeds of these sales, made prior to completion of construction, into an escrow account, as required by section 67-2303.1, R.C.M.1947. Therefore, the mechanics' liens, effective against each unit so sold, were not satisfied from the escrow fund as contemplated by section 67-2303.1. Big Sky further ignored section 67-2323, R.C.M.1947, whereby every blanket lien or blanket mortgage must be satisfied before the first conveyance or lease of a unit, or a partial release for such unit obtained and recorded.

Equity will grant the relief sought when in view of all circumstances to deny it would permit one of the parties to suffer a gross wrong at the hands of the other party who brought about the condition. This Court cannot ignore the fact that this situation would never have occurred, had Big Sky fully complied with the Unit Ownership Act.

Equity demands that Dutch Touch be allowed to satisfy the entire amount of its lien first from those units retained by Big Sky.

Thereafter, should any amount of the lien remain unsatisfied, Dutch Touch may seek proportionate enforcement of such balance against the 18 units previously sold by Big Sky after the owners of these units are made parties to the action. In the record there is a motion by Big Sky to join these unit owners as parties defendant pursuant to Rule 19, M.R.Civ.P. This motion was never ruled upon by the district court. The Committee Note to Rule 19 states that it is clear that whenever feasible the persons materially interested in the subject of an action should be joined as parties so that they may be heard and a complete disposition made. Such is the case of these unit owners should Dutch Touch have to enforce any portion of the lien against their units in the event the units retained by Big Sky do not satisfy the lien. For this reason the motion of Big Sky should have been granted.

This judgment of the district court is vacated and this cause remanded to rehear the foreclosure action in compliance with this decision.

HASWELL, DALY, HARRISON and SHEA, JJ., concur.

COURSON v. TIL
La. App. 344 So. 2d 719 (1977).

BOLIN, Judge.

This suit involves a question of ranking between a mortgagee on one hand and various contractors and materialmen holding privileges against the mortgaged property on the other hand. TIL executed a mortgage to First Mortgage Investors (FMI) for $1,100,000 as security for money advanced and to be advanced by FMI to TIL for the construction by TIL of an apartment complex. Subsequently FMI foreclosed on the mortgage and the property was sold at a sheriff's sale for $600,000. The mortgagee (FMI) and the various lien holders each claim entitlement to satisfaction out of the proceeds. The trial court ruled in favor of the mortgagee and we affirm.

The primary issue is whether a mortgage to secure simultaneous or future advances, which is recorded prior to the recordation of a written construction contract, primes privileges granted to contractors, subcontractors or furnishers of material involved in the construction.

The construction mortgage on the property was recorded on June 8, 1973. The note was delivered to FMI and some disbursements of funds were also made on that date. The construction contract was signed on June 8 but was not recorded until June 12. The contract provides, "No work shall commence until after the recordation of this contract."

There is voluminous and contradictory testimony concerning when work was begun and material delivered to the site of this construction. The timeliness of the filing of the various liens is not in dispute.

Pertinent to the question on appeal are several sections of Title 9, Louisiana Revised Statutes. Subsection A of § 4801 grants a privilege against immovable property and any improvements thereon to contractors, subcontractors, laborers, and materialmen involved in construction on that property. Subsections B and C each purport to rank the privileges but list different criteria for that purpose.

Subsection B provides that the privileges enumerated in Subsection A are superior to all other claims against the land and improvements "except: . . . mortgages if the . . . mortgages exist and have been recorded before the work or labor has begun or any material has been furnished."

Subsection C provides that where mortgages are executed to secure simultaneous or future advances, these advances are secured in preference to any other claims if the mortgage has been recorded "before any work or labor has begun or material has been furnished, *or before the recordation of a building contract*, . . ." (Emphasis ours)

Citing the above italicized language as well as R.S. 1:9 which provides that the term "or" as used in the revised statutes is used in the disjunctive unless otherwise specified, the trial judge held that a mortgage was superior to the privileges created by 9:4801(A) if it was recorded *either* before materials were supplied or work begun *or* before the building contract was recorded. Since the mortgage was recorded on June 8, and the building contract not until June 12, the trial judge found the mortgage to be superior regardless of when materials were delivered or work begun. We find a reasonable interpretation of 4801, C, supports the result reached by the trial judge.

Appellants contend the trial court's interpretation of subsection C distorts the general purpose of the Private Works Act. They envision a situation whereby a mortgagee who failed to record his mortgage until several weeks after material had been delivered or work had begun so that the mortgage was inferior to the privileges, could elevate his mortgage to a superior rank by subsequently causing the building contract to be recorded. This situation could not arise since Section 4802 provides that a building contract "shall be recorded . . . before the date fixed on which the work is to commence and not more than thirty days after the date of said contract."

We find that the language of Subsection C providing that a mortgage is superior to other claims against the property if it is recorded prior to the recordation of the building contract refers only to a *timely* recorded building contract as defined by 9:4802.

If a building contract is not recorded *timely*, then the controlling provision as to ranking is not Section 4801, C, but rather Section 4812. That section creates a privilege against property in those instances in which there is no building contract "or when a contract has been entered into but has not been recorded, *as and when required* . . ." (Emphasis ours) The phrase "as and when required" must be read to refer to requirements set forth in Section 4802. If the building contract is not recorded timely, Section 4812 states that with certain exceptions the privileges are superior to any claims against the property except when the mortgage exists and is recorded before work has begun or materials furnished.

The building contract in this case provides, ". . . No work shall commence until after the recordation of this contract." The contract was signed on June 8 and recorded on June 12. Therefore this contract was timely recorded as measured by the specifications of Section 4802, and Section 4812 is not applicable.

This mortgage to secure future advances with a timely recorded building contract is specifically governed by 9:4801 C, and under this Subsection a mortgage recorded prior to recordation of the building contract is superior to all other privileges against the property except laborer's privilege, regardless of when materials were supplied or work begun.

The judgment is affirmed at appellants' cost.

HALL, J., concurs in the result.

QUESTIONS

1. What does the listing contract on page 225 have to say about signs?
2. What is "hand money" and why is it important? How can it be forfeited?
3. What happens if realty is lost because of foreclosure prior to a sale?

4. Why does a bank required a title search before making a loan against real estate?
5. What does "adversing" mean in title work?
6. What does it mean to "pro-rate" taxes at a real estate closing?
7. T. or F. At a real estate closing, all outstanding liens will first be paid out of proceeds.
8. A deed tells you how the present owner acquired realty. Why is this important to the title searcher?
9. Describe the legal role played by a "release."
10. Distinguish "foreclosure" from "repossession."

16

Duties of Innkeepers and Guests

An estimated 4,589 Bibles were
stolen from New York hotel
rooms in one year. It is not
rare, experts say, for motel
rooms to be stripped of color-
television sets or for an ice-
making machine to be missing.

—U.S. News and World Report. June 16, 1975

The business of innkeeping is public in nature and because of this, duties arise on the part of the innkeeper that are influenced by the public need. These include the duty to receive guests and the property of guests; the duty to provide suitable accomodations; the duty to treat all guests with a reasonable standard of care and courtesy; the duty to care for the person as well as the property of guests and the duty to comply with applicable health laws. Conversely, the guest has duties to the innkeeper, the principal of these being to conduct oneself with reasonable decorum and to pay for services received. These and other duties of the innkeeper, as well as the guest, will be examined in a preliminary manner in this chapter.

PUBLIC DUTIES

It has long been recognized that when one enters the innkeeping business, duties of a public nature have been assumed by that person.

Thus what may have been private property at the outset, assumes a public character. This means that one no longer retains customary personal rights in the property involved, since it has now become affected by the public interest. If A inherits $500,000 from his grandfather, that money is private and can be controlled solely by A. If A invests the money in a small motel, the character of the money (property) has been changed in two ways: (1) personal property has been converted to real, and (2) the property is now affected by the public interest, need, and control. It follows that the former private control has now been replaced with a relatively high degree of public control for the general good of those of the public affected by, or entitled to, the use of that property. One can withdraw such property and regain private control, but so long as the public use continues, the control is mandated by public needs.

DUTY TO RECEIVE GUESTS

It has long been recognized that, as a matter of law, those engaged in the public venture of innkeeping must receive all guests who seek their accomodations, up to the limits of their capacity. The duty is almost, but not quite, absolute, for there are some exceptions. But the exceptions do not change the basic rule.

An important point however, is that the duty extends to *travelers* only, and does not necessarily extend to "locals" who may use services provided at the inn. However, a local *could* be a traveler and it has been so held.[1] The test applied to determine whether one is a "traveler" is the transient nature of the stay. One who lives in Gary, Indiana, and stays at a Quality Court on Lakeshore Drive, Chicago, just 5 miles away for one night to attend a meeting, would be a "traveler"—and could thus become a "guest."

This classification is important because, as a general rule, an innkeeper does not owe special duties to those who are not "travelers." A lodger, border or tenant at a hotel or motel, would not be a traveler in the legal sense because the stay is not transient or temporary in nature.

The duty to receive guests extends to those who are normally unable to contract, such as those under 18 years of age. An innkeeper would, however, have the right to determine if the infant is capable of paying for the services. There is no requirement that one furnish lodging to an infant at no cost. The infant would be liable for the reasonable value of necessities furnished and would not be able to repudiate the contract later on the grounds of infancy.

TIME OF DAY OR NIGHT?

Must an innkeeper be prepared to receive guests 24 hours a day? In the *Rex v. Ivens* case that follows, Williams, a law clerk (called 'prosecutor' in the case), tried to gain admission at the Bell Inn, at Chepstow, at a time when the husband and wife who operated the inn had retired for the night. What happened after that is spelled out in the courts' opinion.

Rex v. Ivens[2]

". . . With respect to the non-tender of the money by the prosecutor, it is now a custom so universal with innkeepers to trust that a person will pay before he leaves an inn, that it cannot be necessary for a guest to tender money before he goes into an inn; indeed, in the present case, no objection was made that Mr. Williams did not make a tender; and they did not even insinuate that they had any suspicion that he could not pay for whatever entertainment might be furnished to him. I think, therefore, that that cannot be set up as a defense. It however remains for me next to consider the case with respect to the hour of the night at which Mr. Williams applied for admission; and the opinion which I have formed is, that the lateness of the hour is no excuse to the defendant for refusing to receive the prosecutor into his inn. Why are inns established? For the reception of travellers, who are often very far distant from their own homes. Now, at what time is it most essential that travellers should not be denied admission into the inns? I should say when they are benighted, and when, from any casualty, or from the badness of the roads, they arrive at an inn at a very late hour. Indeed, in former times, when the roads were much worse, and were much infested with robbers, a late hour of the night was the time, of all others, at which the traveller most required to be received into an inn. I think therefore, that if the traveller conducts himself properly, the innkeeper is bound to admit him, at whatever hour of the night he may arrive. The only other question in this case is, whether the defendant's inn was full. There is no distinct evidence on the part of the prosecution that it was not. But I think the conduct of the parties shews that the inn was not full; because, if it had been, there could have been no use in the landlady asking the prosecutor his name, and saying, that if he would tell it, she would ring for one of the servants."

The verdict under the misdemeanor (Criminal) statute under which this case was brought, was "guilty" thus clearly pointing out the duty of an innkeeper to receive even in the "wee hours" of the morning—so long as space is available.

TODAY

It is the usual practice in hotels and motels that are located in high crime areas to lock outside doors at designated times of the night. Yet admittance is always possible by the use of a bell or other device to alert the one on duty. An innkeeper must readmit a quest who has left the inn and then returns—even if that return is at 3:00 AM. The duty to receive guests remains regardless of the time of day of night and even more so, if one has an advance reservation.

STATE LAWS

Many states have criminal statutes that provide that an innkeeper who wrongfully refuses to receive a guest can be indicted and brought to trial for violation of the statute. *(Rex v. Ivens* shows us the early English view). In addition, in most states an action may be brought in instances of refusal of admission of a guest, for the civil wrong.

Refusing to receive a guest who has a seeing-eye dog would not be a good excuse—even if the inn does not have facilities for the animal. The refusal might be justified if the animal might cause harm in some manner to others. A seeing-eye dog *could* be refused at a hotel where the national Siamese Cat Convention was in progress. Yet even in that instance, the innkeeper would do well to lend assistance to that person—and his dog— and assist in finding suitable lodging accomodations elsewhere. The duty to receive is too strong to be dismissed lightly. However, there are times when an innkeeper can refuse to receive—and indeed, in some of these instances *there is a duty not to receive.*

EXCUSES

If all of the rooms of an inn are occupied, this in itself is reason enough to refuse to receive . Yet, if the inn is full and one presents himself with a valid reservation for that night, the inn must still receive the guest. This will be developed later in the chapter. If a potential guest appears in an intoxicated, filthy condition, then this is a valid excuse not to receive. If one with a communicable disease attempts to register, that person must be refused. But in many instances, one seeking a lodging room may well be sick and in need of assistance. In such instances, the innkeeper may refuse to receive but should seek outside help for that person.

There are other reasons why one can refuse to receive a guest, and one is the absense of baggage, which will be discussed in the next paragraph. But as a general rule, when rooms are available, or when they will be available after being cleaned, the innkeeper should receive guests, so long as it is determined that the would-be guest will be able to pay for services. It is no longer legal to refuse on the grounds of race, color or national origin—and it is unwise to refuse on the grounds of "lack of apparent stature." For example, a well groomed traveler dressed in blue jeans should not be refused admittance at the resort hotel—even though this was common practice in the immediate past. A soldier should not be turned away because other soldiers had caused problems at the inn. Neither can a member of a certain race by refused for the same reason. Selective discrimination is unwise today.

ABSENCE OF BAGGAGE

In the modern motel as contrasted to hotel, the innkeeper is seldom concerned about guests traveling without baggage. In fact, to even make this determination would place an undue burden upon the staff of the inn. Yet if it is determined that a person, or a group of persons, is or are traveling without baggage, the innkeeper would have the right to make discreet inquiry, and perhaps refuse to admit on those grounds. There is the ever present danger of one planning on making up his or her new spring wardrobe at the expense of other guests. In refusing on these grounds, care would still be in order. In the case of hotels that have a check-in service, the absence of baggage would be more noticable and easier to detect. Yet one must remember that even those of substance can travel quite nicely with a minimum of personal effects today—and quite often do so.

TO RECEIVE GOODS

Since an innkeeper has a duty to receive guests, it follows that the goods of a guest must also be received. This is a general statement and would have limitations. For example a guest must be permitted to bring in baggage and other items customarily taken into inns. A more difficult quesiton arises in reference to pets and perhaps excess goods, such as a truck load of circus equipment that a quest wants placed inside of the inn. In the latter instance, the duty to receive goods would not extend to the circus equipment and those goods could be refused.

Some states have laws prohibiting animals in inns, others permit them but require that special accomodations be provided for them. Many travelers simply place their pets into rooms unknown to the innkeeper. This seems unfair to future guests who will occupy those rooms. But pet owners often have more regard for their animals than they do for their children, so one must treat such matters as delicately as possible. A firm inn policy on pets would be in order. Notice to guests should be provided of this policy.

What is the innkeepers duty to receive those who are invited to the inn by a guest—an invited nonguest?

INVITED NONGUESTS

If a guest invites one to an inn who is not a guest, an innkeeper should use care and caution before excluding that person. The duties of the innkeeper might well extend to one who is there to *visit* the guest. Care and diplomacy would be in order. If the invited nonguest was there for immoral or illegal purposes, or if the invited nonguest engages in obnoxious or undesirable conduct, the innkeeper could exclude on those grounds. A guest of a guest does not have rights beyond those extended by law to guests.

In the following case, an innkeeper wound up in court because of the refusal to admit the wife of a guest to the guest's room. The court spells out the law quite nicely and the innkeeper prevailed in the end. But it might have been better to have admitted the wife after it had been determined that the husband was expecting her. Still, caution is in order. If the wife had been admitted and if she had removed property of the husband, the innkeeper might have been held responsible for that property. It should be observed that this case was decided in a "community property" state—Louisiana. Under community property law, husbands and wives are deemed to jointly own all property acquired during marriage. It makes no difference who pays for it. While community property rights are mentioned in the case, they have no effect on the outcome.

CAMPBELL v. WOMACK
La. App., 345 So. 2d 96 (No. 11120, 1977)

EDWARDS, Judge.

This suit was brought be Elvin Campbell and his wife for damages resulting from breach of contract and embarrassment, humiliation and mental anguish, sustained by Mrs. Campbell as a result of the defendants' refusal to admit Mrs. Campbell to her husband's motel room. The defendants' motion for summary judgment was granted and the action was dismissed. From this dismissal, plaintiffs have appealed.

Plaintiff, Elvin Campbell, is engaged in the sand and gravel business. Since the nature of his business often requires his absence from his home in St. Francisville, Mr. Campbell generally obtains temporary accommodations in the area in which he is working. For this purpose, Mr. Campbell rented a double room on a month to month basis at the Rodeway Inn, in Morgan City, Louisiana. The room was registered in Mr. Campbell's name only.

From time to time, Mr. Campbell would share his room with certain of his employees; in fact he obtained additional keys for the convenience of these employees. It also appears that Mr. Campbell was joined by his wife on some weekends and holidays, and that they jointly occupied his room on those occasions. However, Mrs. Campbell was not given a key to the motel room. On one such weekend, Mrs. Campbell, arriving while her husband was not at the motel, attempted to obtain the key to her husband's room from the desk clerk, Barbara Womack. This request was denied, since the desk clerk found that Mrs. Campbell was neither a registered guest for that room nor had the registered guest, her husband, communicated to the motel management, his authorization to release his room key to Mrs. Campbell. Plaintiffs allege that this refusal was in a loud, rude, and abusive manner. After a second request and refusal, Mrs. Campbell became distressed, left the Rodeway Inn, and obtained a room at another motel. Mr. Campbell later joined his wife at the other motel, and allegedly spent the weekend consoling her. Shortly thereafter, suit was filed against the motel and the desk clerk, Barbara Womack.

Plaintiffs' main contention is that Mrs. Campbell was entitled to a key to her husband's room since she had acquired the status of a guest from her previous stays with her husband in the motel room. The leading pronouncement in Louisiana on the creation of a guest status is found in *Moody v. Kenny*, 153 La. 1007, 97 So. 21 (1923). There it is stated at page 22:

". . . a mere guest of the registered occupant of a room at a hotel, who shares such room with its occupant without the knowledge or consent of the hotel management, would not be a guest of the hotel, as there would be no contractual relations in such case between such third person and the hotel . . ."

Plaintiffs would have us conclude from this statement that once the motel management gained knowledge on the previous occasions that Mrs. Campbell was sharing the motel room with the registered occupant, the motel was thereafter estopped to deny Mrs. Campbell the key to that room. The fallacy of this argument is apparent, since under it even a casual visitor to a hotel guest's room would be entitled to return at a latter time and demand a key to the guest's room, so long as the hotel management had knowledge of the initial visit.

The motel clerk was under no duty to give Mrs. Campbell, a third party, the key to one of its guest's rooms. In fact, the motel had an affirmative duty, stemming from a guest's rights of privacy and peaceful possession, not to allow unregistered and unauthorized third parties to gain access to the rooms of its guest. (cf. LSA—C.C. art. 2965-67). This duty is the same regardless of whether we consider the contractual relationship one of lessor-lessee or motel-guest.

The additional fact that Mrs. Campbell offered proof of her identity and her marital relation with the room's registered occupant does not alter her third-party status; nor does it lessen the duty owed by the motel to its guest. The mere fact of marriage does not imply that the wife has full authorization from her husband at all times and as to all matters, (LSA—C.C. art. 2404). Besides, how could Mrs. Campbell prove to the motel's satisfaction that the then present marital situation was amicable? This information is not susceptible of ready proof.

The plaintiffs further contend that since the rental contract was entered into during the existence of their marriage it was therefore a community asset, and that Mrs. Campbell was entitled to the use of the motel room based on her rights in the community. We need not reach the issue of Mrs. Campbell's community property rights in the motel room, since under the clear language of LSA—C.C. art. 2404, she had no right to enforce the rental contract.

Having found that Mrs. Campbell was not entitled to demand a key to the motel room, and further that no authorization to admit her was communicated to the motel by her husband, there was no breach of contract.

In view of the foregoing, we need not reach the defendants' contention that there was another occupant in the room, whose rights they were protecting.

The summary judgment procedure is designed to avoid the delays and expenses of a trial on the merits when no genuine issue exists as to material fact and the moving party is entitled to judgment as a matter of law. LSA—C.C.P. art. 966. The burden is on the mover to show that there is no dispute regarding facts material to the suit. And since the motion for summary judgment is not a substitute for a trial on the merits, any doubt regarding the existence of genuine issues of material fact should be resolved in favor of trial on the merits.

The affidavits submitted by each side demonstrate that the only issues in dispute are, did Mrs. Campbell share her husband's motel room, and did the motel have knowledge of this? Neither issue is material to this suit since regardless of how they are resolved, the plaintiffs cannot prevail. When the evidence submitted on the motion leaves no relevant, genuine issue of fact, and when reasonable minds must inevitably conclude that the mover is entitled to judgment on the facts before the court, the motion for summary judgment should be granted.

Accordingly, the trial court properly granted defendants' motion for summary judgment.

For the reasons assigned the judgment of the trial court is affirmed at appellants' cost.

AFFIRMED.

Not only does an innkeeper have a duty to receive guests and their property, there is a duty to provide suitable accommodations and services thereafter.

SUITABLE ACCOMMODATIONS

An innkeeper must furnish accommodations for lodging and food and other services that could reasonably be expected to be found at that particular inn. In addition, an innkeeper is held at law to have direct control of the rooms of the inn. Because of this, other ancillary duties are imposed such as the duty to keep the rooms clean and toilets sanitized; to provide suitable fire escapes and fire protection devices, and many others. Failure to provide proper accommodations and services, could result in liability on the part of the innkeeper. This brings into focus the standard of care expected of the innkeeper.

STANDARD OF CARE

An innkeeper *is not an insurer* of the safety of guests or their property. If this were so, an innkeeper would be responsible for *all* injuries or losses regardless of cause.

Rather, the standard applied is that of a "reasonable innkeeper" who possesses that standard of skill and knowledge that could reasonably be expected of one who occupies that positoin at that particular location, and who so acts in a given situation.

If one does not measure up to this standard, then that person may be guilty of negligence. If so, legal liability may attach. Negligence is a tort and *could* give rise to damages for mental injury and anquish in addition to actual losses sustained.

It is a jury question whether what a particular innkeeper did under given circumstances, is what a reasonable innkeeper with the same knowledge and skill would have done under like or similar circumstances. The *reasonable innkeeper* test is flexible and its existence at law tends to make one measure up to it.

COURTEOUS TREATMENT

A guest at an inn has the right to receive courteous treatment from the innkeeper, the employees and agents of the inn as well. This is true even though an innkeeper is *not* an insurer of the guest. The duty of courteous treatment is as old as the law of innkeeping and will be implied by the guest-innkeeper relationship. Any substantial breach of this duty can lead to civil liability. An innkeeper must constantly school employees and agents on the need to be courteous to guests when arriving and leaving, and while in, as well as outside, of the inn.

PHONE CALLS AND MESSAGES

A byproduct of innkeeping is the flow of phone calls, telegrams, mail and other messages for guests. Most inns handle such matters in a routine fashion and seldom do problems arise. Telegrams, letters, and written messages can be maintained at the front desk in the customary "pigeon-hole" key holders. Phone messages for absent guests should be reduced to writing and placed there also. This would require guests to check periodically at the front desk for messages.

Receipt of registered mail for an absent guest should be handled with more caution. The requirement of signing before delivery would give notice that the mail contains something of more than just passing interest. Such mail should be locked in a safe with a notice being promptly given to the guest, wherever that guest might be.

HOLDING MAIL

An innkeeper must use care in agreeing to hold the mail of a guest after the guest has departed. Guidelines should be sought from the local post office and carefully followed.

DUTIES OF GUESTS

The principal duty that a guest owes to an innkeeper is to conduct himself or herself in a courteous, reasonably dignified manner at all times. Guests should, but do not always do so, refrain from riding the tops of outside elevators; throwing furniture into pools; stealing towels; hanging from balconies and running through the inn with abandon. Such conduct on the part of guests goes a long way toward relieving the innkeeper of his or her duties to such guests, and can be used as a defense against actions that one may attempt to bring against the innkeeper.

Another duty is to pay for accommodations and services provided by the innkeeper. Failure to do so is a criminal act and can result in trial and conviction. In the following case, a nonpaying guest had his problems magnified by his lawyer *after* he was convicted of leaving a motel without paying his bill.

FULLER v. STATE
Ala. Cr. App., 344 So. 2d 216 (1977)

BOWEN W. SIMMONS, Retired Circuit Judge.

This is an appeal from an order of the Circuit Court denying appellant's petition for a write of error coram nobis.[3]

It appears that appellant was indicted and judgments entered (1) for forgery and (2) leaving a motel without paying his bill. The separate judgments were entered on separate pleas of guilty. Appeals were taken to this court and both judgments were affirmed without opinions.

Appellant now complains in his pro se petition, that "(he) was advised by his defense attorney to plead guilty, due to witnesses for the defense being out of state, and could not be subpoenaed, and without those witnesses present there was almost no chance for an acquittal, and would receive the maximum if the plea bargain offer was refused".

It is true defendant was entitled to reasonable opportunity to obtain process for the attendance of his witnesses residing within the jurisdiction of the court. But here is appears that the witnesses were not within the jurisdiction of the court and its attendance process.

Nowhere does it appear in the petition here under consideration that the aid of the court was invoked by appellant to procure process for witnesses within the court's jurisdiction, nor for a continuance of the cases.

The petition is faulty in failing to assert, and so far as the record reveals appellant did not have any grounds for a writ of error coram nobis.

It is said in *Butler v. State*, 279 Ala. 311, 184 So.2d 823, that a writ of error coram nobis is not intended to relieve party of his own negligence.

We also observed in *Creel v. State*, 53 Ala.App. 226, 298 So.2d 647, that it is not the office of a writ of error coram nobis to retry indictments and its mission is to root out egregious fraud or collusion leading to judgment.

Coram nobis relates to matters of fact which had they been pursued in the original trial would have prevented judgment and conviction.

We have said that the function of writ of error coram nobis is not to relieve party of his own negligence in not raising issue at the time of trial where he had full knowledge of facts.

We see nothing in the petition that entitled appellant to relief in writ of error coram nobis.

The trial court was justified in denying relief and dismissing petition.

The action of this trial court is due to be affirmed and it is so ordered.

The foregoing opinion was prepared by the Honorable BOWEN W. SIMMONS, Retired Circuit Judge, serving as a judge of this Court under § 2 of Act No. 288, July 7, 1945, as amended; his opinion is hereby adopted as that of the Court.

AFFIRMED.

PUBLIC HEALTH DUTIES

Each state by statute, provides health requirements that must be met by those who serve the public in travel, lodging and other hospitality functions, including restaurants.

In most instances, these statutes are quite old, often having been adopted at the time of the formation of our states. While some of these appear quaint by modern standards, they make up an important part of the duties that fall upon innkeepers, restaurant operators and others.

The statutes that follow are from the Virginias. (They are old.)

HOTELS AND RESTAURANTS.

HOTEL INSPECTOR.

The governor shall appoint a hotel inspector at a salary provided by law, to hold office at the will and pleasure of the governor. He shall, before entering upon the duties of his office, take the oath of office prescribed by the Constitution, and give bond in the penalty of five thousand dollars, which bond, when approved by the governor, shall be filed and recorded in the office of the secretary of state. The hotel inspector shall have had at least five years' experience in conducting a first class American or European hotel. He shall keep an accurate itemized account of expenses and shall file the same quarterly with the secretary of the board of health, together with an account of all fees collected from applicants for hotel and restaurant inspection certificates and of other moneys coming into his hands by virtue of his office.

REGULATIONS BY STATE BOARD OF HEALTH; ENFORCEMENT OF ORDERS AND LAWS RESPECTING PURE FOOD.

The board of health shall make such rules and regulations, not inconsistent with law, as in their judgment are necessary to carry out the provisions of this article, which rules and regulations shall take effect when approved by the attorney general and the governor. The health inspector shall assist in the enforcement of any orders made by the board of health, and of the laws of the State respecting pure food, so far as they relate to hotels and restaurants.

HOTEL AND RESTAURANT DEFINED; HOTELS SUBJECT TO PROVISIONS OF ARTICLE.

For the purpose of this article, every building where food and lodging are usually furnished to guests and payment required therefor shall be deemed a hotel, and every place where food without lodging is usually furnished to guests and payment required therefor shall be deemed a restaurant. But the provisions of this article, except those of sections twenty and twenty-two, shall not apply to any hotel wherein there are fewer than ten bed chambers, nor to any hotel known as a "summer hotel" which is not open for guests from November fifteenth to May fifteenth.

APPLICATION FOR INSPECTION OF HOTEL OR RESTAURANT; TEMPORARY PERMIT; CERTIFICATE OF INSPECTION; FEE.

Every person, firm or corporation proposing to conduct a hotel or restaurant shall apply to the hotel inspector for an inspection and certificate thereof, and said inspector shall inspect the premises described in such application as soon thereafter as may be; but if it be impracticable to do so within ten days after receiving such application, said inspector may issue to such applicant a temporary permit which shall be valid until a regular inspection is made. Only one certificate or permit shall be issued where a hotel and restaurant are combined and conducted in the same building and under the same management. Each certificate or permit shall expire on the thirtieth day of June next following its issuance, and no hotel or restaurant shall be maintained and conducted in this State without the certificate of inspection thereof as herein prescribed, which certificate shall be posted in the main public room of such hotel or restaurant, and shall show the date of each inspection and the notations relating thereto by the hotel inspector. No such certificate shall be transferable. The fee for such inspection and certificate or permit shall be, for a hotel, two dollars, and twenty-five cents additional for each bedroom in excess of seven; and for a restaurant, two dollars, and twenty-five cents additional for each five chairs or stools, or spaces where persons are fed, in excess of ten, but no fee shall exceed ten dollars. Such inspector shall, on the first of each month, pay into the State treasury all fees collected for inspections during the preceding month. Every certificate of inspection or permit under this article shall be made and issued in duplicate.

FORM AND CONTENT OF APPLICATION FOR INSPECTION; PAYMENT OF FEE.

The applicant for inspection of a hotel or restaurant shall file with the hotel inspector a written application, in form to be prescribed by the board of health, which shall set forth the name and address of the owner of the building or property to be occupied, and of the agent of any such owner; the name and address of the lessee and manager, if any, of the hotel or restaurant; the location of such hotel or restaurant and a full description of the building or property to be occupied by it, and such other matters as may be required by the board of health. The fee for inspection shall be paid to the hotel inspector when the application is filed with him.

CONTENTS OF CERTIFICATE AND PERMIT; POSTING.

Every such certificate shall show that the hotel or restaurant is equipped and conducted according to law, and shall be kept posted in some conspicuous place in such hotel or restaurant. Every such permit shall show according to the fact, why it is granted, and that the hotel or restaurant is, according to law, permitted to be kept, and it shall be kept posted in like manner.

CERTIFICATE OR PERMIT PREREQUISITE TO LICENSE.

No license to keep a hotel or restaurant, and no certificate for such license, shall hereafter be authorized or issued unless there be first filed, in the county court to which application therefor is made, a certificate of inspection or permit, granted by the hotel inspector as provided in this article. Every such license shall bear on its face a reference to such certificate of inspection or permit.

ANNUAL INSPECTION OF HOTELS AND RESTAURANTS; POWERS AND DUTIES OF HOTEL INSPECTOR.

The hotel inspector shall inspect, or cause to be inspected, at least once annually, every hotel and restaurant in the State. For that purpose he, or any person designated by him, shall have the right of entry and access at any reasonable time to inspect kitchens where food is prepared, pantries and storage rooms pertaining thereto, dining rooms, lunch counters, and every place where articles pertaining to the serving of the public are kept or prepared. The said inspector shall prohibit the use of any article not in keeping with cleanliness and good sanitary conditions. He shall also have the right to enter any and all parts of a hotel at all reasonable hours to make such inspection, and every person in the management or control thereof shall afford free access to every part of the hotel and render all assistance necessary to enable the inspector to make full, thorough and complete examination thereof, but the privacy of any guest in any room occupied by him shall not be invaded without his consent.

ALTERATIONS AND CHANGES BY OWNER; PENALTY FOR REFUSAL OR FAILURE TO MAKE.

Whenever, upon such inspection, it shall be found that any such hotel or restaurant is not equipped, or being conducted, in the manner and under the conditions required by the provisions of this article, the hotel inspector shall notify the owner, manager or agent in charge of such hotel or restaurant of such changes or alterations as, in the judgment of the hotel inspector, may be necessary to effect a complete compliance with said provisions. Such owner, manager or agent shall thereupon make such alterations or changes as may be necessary to put such buildings and premises in a condition, and conduct it in a manner, that will fully comply with the requirements of this article: Provided, however, that due time after receiving such notice shall be allowed for conforming to the requirements hereof, which time shall be specified in the notice. Should the changes or alterations directed by such notice not be made in the time specified therein, the said inspector shall proceed against the person or persons in default in any court having jurisdiction to enforce the provisions of this article against him or them. Every person, firm or corporation which shall fail or refuse to comply with the provisoins of this section shall be guilty of a misdemeanor, and, on conviction thereof, shall be fined five dollars for and every day such failure or refusal may continue. If such failure or refusal shall continue for thirty days after the time specified in the notice from the hotel inspector for conforming to the requirements thereof, the inspector may proceed in the circuit court of the county wherein such hotel or restaurant is, for an order closing it. After such order is issued, the building or property shall not again be used as a hotel or restaurant until a certificate or permit therefor shall have been issued by the hotel inspector, and any disobedience of such order shall be punished as other contempts of court. Reasonable notice shall be given of the application for such order.

NOTICES BY HOTEL INSPECTOR.

All notices given by the hotel inspector shall be in writing and shall either be delivered in person or sent by registered mail.

LIGHTING; PLUMBING; VENTILATION.

Every hotel and restaurant in this State shall be properly lighted by day and by night, shall be properly plumbed and ventilated, and shall be conducted in every department with strict regard for the health, comfort and safety of its guests. Such proper plumbing and ventilating shall be done and maintained according to approved sanitary principles. Such proper ventilation shall be construed to require at least one door and one window in every sleeping room, which window shall permit easy access to the outside of the building, light well or court. No room shall be used as a sleeping room which does not open to the outside of the building or light wells, air shafts or courts.

WATER CLOSETS.

In every city, town or village where a system of waterworks and sewerage is maintained for public use, every hotel therein shall be equipped with suitable water closets for the accommodation of guests, which water closets shall be connected by proper plumbing with such sewer system, and so constructed that they may be flushed with water in such manner as to prevent sewer gas or effluvia arising therefrom. All lavatories, bathtubs, sinks, drains, closets and urinals in such hotels shall be furnished and equipped in similar manner.

WASHROOMS; TOWELS.

All hotels in this State shall be provided with a general washroom convenient and of easy access to guests, and in each bedroom and general washroom there shall be furnished for each registered guest clean, individual towels, of cotton or linen, so that no two or more registered guests will be required to use the same towel, unless it has first been washed. Such individual towel shall not be less than twelve inches wide and eighteen inches long after being washed.

BEDS AND FLOOR COVERINGS.

Every hotel shall provide each bed, bunk, cot, or other sleeping place for the use of guests with pillow slips and under and top sheets, the under sheet to be of sufficient size to completely cover the mattress and springs, and the top sheet to be of like width and at least ninety-nine inches long and not to be less than ninety inches in length after having been laundered. Such sheets and pillow slips shall be made of white cotton or linen, and all such sheets and pillow slips, after being used by one guest, shall be washed and ironed before being used by another guest, a clean set being furnished each succeeding guest. All bedding, including mattresses, quilts, blankets, pillows, and all carpets and floor covering used in any hotel in this State, shall be thoroughly aired, disinfected and kept clean.

EMPLOYMENT OF PERSON HAVING COMMUNICABLE DISEASE.

No person, firm or corporation engaged in conducting a hotel or a restaurant shall knowingly have in its employ any person who has an infectious or communicable disease.

DISINFECTION OF ROOMS AND BEDS; PENALTY.

Every person keeping or conducting a hotel shall see that every room or bed, which has been occupied by any person known to have an infectious or communicable disease at the time of such occupancy, is thoroughly disinfected by methods to be prescribed by the board of health before such room or bed shall be occupied by any other person. Any person violating the provision of this section shall be subject to a fine not exceeding three hundred dollars, and to confinement in jail not exceeding six months, or both, at the discretion of the court.

HALLWAYS; FIRE ESCAPES.

Whenever it shall be proposed to erect a building three stories or more in height, intended for use as a hotel in this State, it shall be the duty of the owner or proprietor of such hotel to construct the same so that one main hallway on each floor above the ground floor shall run to an opening in the outside wall of the building. Every building used as a hotel shall comply with the provisions of this Code pertaining to fire escapes. All fire escapes shall be indicated by a red light and a placard in each hallway leading to such fire escapes.

FIRE EXTINGUISHERS.

Every hotel shall be provided with one fire extinguisher, of style and size approved by the national board of fire underwriters, on each floor containing twenty-five hundred square feet of floor area; and one additional fire extinguisher on each floor for each additional twenty-five hundred square feet of floor area, or fraction thereof. Every such extinguisher shall be placed in a convenient location in the public hallway, outside of sleeping rooms, at or near the head of stairs, and shall always be in condition for use.

LIABILITY OF HOTEL OR RESTAURANT KEEPER FOR LOSS OF PROPERTY; DEPOSIT OF VALUABLES.

It shall be the duty of the keepers of hotels and restaurants to exercise due care and diligence in providing honest servants and employees, and to take every reasonable precaution to protect the persons and property of their guests and boarders, but no such keeper of any hotel or restaurant shall be held liable in a greater sum than two hundred and fifty dollars for the loss of any wearing apparel, baggage or other property, not hereinafter mentioned, belonging to a guest or boarder, when such loss takes place from the room or rooms occupied by said guest or boarder; and no keeper of a hotel or restaurant shall be held liable for any loss on the part of any guest or boarder of jewelry, money or other valuables of like nature, provided such keeper shall have posted in a conspicuous place in the room or rooms occupied by such guest or boarder, and in the hotel office and public reception room of such hotel or restaurant, a notice stating that jewelry, money and other valuables of like nature must be deposited in the office of such hotel (or restaurant), unless such loss shall take place from such office after such deposit.

OFFENSES.

Any person, firm or corporation who shall operate a hotel or a restaurant in this State, or who shall let a building to be used for such purposes, without first having complied with the provisions of this article, shall be guilty of a misdemeanor and, upon conviction thereof, shall be fined five dollars for each day such failure to comply shall continue.

PROSECUTION

The prosecuting attorney of each county in this State is hereby authorized and required, upon complaint under oath of the hotel inspector, or any person or persons, to prosecute to termination before any court of competent jurisdiction in the name of the State, a proper action or proceeding against any person or persons violating the provisions of this article.

The following cases represent situations that arose out of the innkeeper-guest relationship yet are variations of the rights and duties that we have been discussing. They are included because of their novelty. In the first, an insurance company brought a negligence suit against a guest for fire loss. In the second, a phone call of a guest resulted in the conviction of a criminal.

FIREMAN'S FUND AM. INS. COMPANIES v. KNOBBE
562 P. 2d 825 (Nevada 1977).

MOWBRAY, Justice:

The sole issue presented is whether the doctrine of res ipsa loquitur may be invoked to recover damages from a hotel's guests for a fire that originated in one of the guests' rooms. The district judge on a motion for summary judgment held that under the facts presented the doctrine was not applicable. We agree and affirm.

1. A fire was discovered in a hotel room in Las Vegas. The cause of the fire was determined to be a cigarette. On the night of the fire, the room was occupied by Respondents John and Marilyn Doherty. The Dohertys were traveling in the company of Respondents Andrew and Geraldine Knobbe, who occupied an adjoining, connecting room.

2. A complaint was filed by appellant insurance company against respondents, claiming subrogation to the rights of the hotel and alleging negligence predicated both on a standard evidentiary negligence theory and on the doctrine of res ipsa loquitur. Respondents moved for summary judgment. The court denied the motion, on the ground that there was a conflict of material fact under the

standard evidentiary theory; however, the court granted the motion as to the res ipsa loquitur theory of liability. Appellant then stipulated that there was insufficient evidence to establish negligence without the aid of res ipsa loquitur. This appeal followed.

3. In *Bialer v. St. Mary's Hosp.*, 83 Nev. 241, 243, 427 P.2d 957, 958 (1967), this court said:

> For the doctrine of res ipsa loquitur to apply, three conditions must be met: (1) the event must be of a kind which ordinarily does not occur in the absence of someone's negligence; (2) the event must be caused by an agency or instrumentality within the exclusive control of the defendant; and (3) the event must not have been due to any voluntary action or contribution on the part of the plaintiff.

Evidence was presented that the hotel had 18 keys to the room where the fire occurred. The staff was not questioned to determine whether anyone had entered the room after the four respondents had departed and before the discovery of the fire. Further, appellant failed to demonstrate that respondents had exclusive control or joint control of the instrumentality causing the damage. Taken in the light most favorable to the appellant, the evidence established that all four respondents were smoking in the room. While each had exclusive control of his or her own cigarette, there is no evidence as to which cigarette started the fire. Traditionally, such a failure defeats the plaintiff's case. There have been cases, however, in which res ipsa loquitur has been applied to multiple defendants, thereby shifting the burden to each individual defendant to present exculpating evidence. Appellant relies upon the leading case of *Ybarra v. Spangard*, 25 Cal.2d 486, 154 P.2d 687 (1944), in urging this theory in this case. In *Ybarra*, an appendectomy patient who awoke with a shoulder injury was permitted to invoke the doctrine of res ipsa in whose care he had been while unconscious. No showing had been made as to which defendant or what instrumentality had caused the injury. The court concluded this did not bar the doctrine, holding, however, that the ruling was limited to the fact situation presented.

The rule has also been applied, upon occasion, in a variety of other fact situations: *Smith v. Claude Neon Lights, Inc.*, 110 N.J.L. 326, 164 A. 423 (1933) (plaintiff injured by falling sign sued owner of building and light company which erected and maintained sign); *Schroeder v. City & County Sav. Bank*, 293 N.Y. 370, 57 N.E.2d 57 (1944) (plaintiff injured by collapse of construction barricade sued owner of building and two construction companies); *Bond v. Otis Elevator Co.*, 388 S.W.2d 681 (Tex. 1965) (plaintiff injured when elevator went into free fall sued owner of building and company which installed and maintained elevator); *Burr v. Sherwin-Williams Co.*, 258 P.2d 58 (Cal.App.1953) (plaintiff whose cotton crop was damaged by insecticide spray sued manufacturer of spray, spraying company, and local cooperative which advised use of spray); *Raber v. Tumin*, 36 Cal.2d 654, 226 P.2d 574 (1951) (plaintiff injured by a falling ladder sued lessee of premises and carpenter doing repairs on premises). In the foregoing cases, the instrumentality causing the damage was known. While the plaintiff had not established which defendant had been negligent, he had established that each was at some time or to some extent responsible for that instrumentality. Only the cases involving unconscious patients lack direct evidence as to both the particular defendant and the particular instrumentality responsible, as does the instant case.

More commonly, it has been held that when any of several defendants wholly independent of each other may be responsible for plaintiff's injury, the doctrine of res ipsa loquitur cannot be applied. *See, e.g., Estes v. Estes*, 127 S.W.2d 78

(Mo.App. 1939); *Gerber v. Faber*, 54 Cal.App.2d 674, 129 P.2d 485 (1942); *Wolf v. American Tract Soc'y*, 164 N.Y. 30, 58 N.E. 31 (1900). In *Wolf* the plaintiff had been injured by a brick falling from a building under construction in which 19 independent contractors were at work. The court rejected the lower court's application of res ipsa loquitur to two of these contractors, which would have required them to come forward with proof of their innocence. It concluded, at 32, that:

> Cases must occasionally happen where the person really responsible for a personal injury cannot be identified or pointed out by proof, as in this case; and then it is far better and more consistent with reason and law that the injury should go without redress, than that innocent persons should be held responsible, upon some strained construction of the law developed for the occasion.

Clearly, the doctrine has no application in this case, where there is lacking even a scintilla of evidence indicating which respondent had control of the cigarette that started the fire.

The order granting summary judgment is affirmed.

STATE v. BEAL
344 So. 2d 1012 (Louisana 1977).

SUMMERS, Justice.

Zyronne Beal, appellant, was charged by bill of information with simple burglary of the building and structure belonging to Travelodge Motel located at 2200 Westbank Expressway, Room 255, Harvey, Louisiana, in violation of Article 62 of the Criminal Code. In a trial by jury appellant was found guilty and sentenced to seven and one-half years at hard labor with credit for time served.

The evidence discloses that on August 26, 1975 Glenn Trotter, the night desk clerk of the Travelodge Motel in Harvey, received a phone call from a female motel guest in room 253. She was on the verge of hysteria, saying she was alone in her room and sounds and noises from the next room led her to believe someone was breaking in. Trotter immediately checked the housekeeping sheet and learned that the adjoining room 255 was vacant. He left the office and approached room 255 cautiously. Finding the door ajar, he looked through the slightly open window curtains and saw appellant Beal lift the motel T.V. from the stand and put it on the bed.

When Beal walked toward the door Trotter retreated around the corner. From the vantage point he watched Beal leave the room. Trotter then returned to the front office, heard the alarm system for room 255 sounding and instructed someone to call the police.

Trotter then returned to look into room 255 where he saw Beal wrap the television set in a bedspread in preparing to leave the room. Again Trotter retreated around the corner and as Beal approached, Trotter shouted for him to halt. Surprised, Beal started to run, slipped, got up and started to run again when

Trotter shouted, "Halt, or I'll blow your head off." Whereupon Beal "spread eagle on the ground."

One ruling of the trial judge is relied upon by appellant Beal for reversal of the conviction and sentence.

During the trial Trotter testified on behalf of the State. He stated that he was called on the office telephone by a woman who was a guest in room 253. She reported that it sounded like someone was breaking into room 255 next door. Thereafter, on cross-examination by the defense, Trotter was asked for the name of the lady who called him. When he replied that he could not reveal that information, the trial judge ruled that the woman's name was irrelevant.

Appellant argues that he had a constitutional and statutory right to the name of the woman who called because he was entitled to confront and cross-examine the witnesses against him under Article I, Section 16, of the Louisiana Constitution and Section 273 of Title 15 of the Revised Statutes. Trotter's testimony concerning what the unnamed woman said during the phone conversation was hearsay, and, accordingly, the defendant argues, the accused was deprived of the right to confront her and cross-examine her.

In our view the testimony of the unnamed woman who alerted Trotter to the burglary that was taking place in the adjoining room was unneccessary to the State's case. Her statement on the phone served only to explain how Trotter was alerted to the intruder and why he went to room 255. Her statements did not serve to establish the facts which implicated appellant in the burglary. The relevant facts were confirmed by Trotter's eyewitness account. Trotter observed the defendant moving the television set in room 255; he halted the defendant in the act of departing, apprehending him at the scene with the T.V. and a number of motel keys. There was also testimony by Deputy Jerry Hall that an automobile parked in the vicinity with the trunk open was registered in appellant's name.

The defense offered no evidence at the trial, relying on the presumption of innocence. The evidence presented by the State was therefore overwhelming and the ruling of the trial judge that the name of the woman who sounded the alarm was irrelevant did not prejudice the defense. La. Code Crim.Pro. art. 921.

For the reasons assigned, the conviction and sentences are affirmed.

QUESTIONS

1. Why is the "duty to receive" so strong in the lodging industry?
2. Name three times when an innkeeper can lawfully refuse to receive.
3. Name two legal reasons why lodging facilities must be properly maintained.
4. What does "coram nobis" mean?
5. What is the function of a hotel inspector in the Virginias?
6. Why did the insurance company lose its case on page 263?
7. What does "res ipsa loquitor" mean as it was used in the case of page 263?
8. In *State v. Beal*, why did Trotter refuse to give the name of the woman who called him from room 253?
9. Why did *Beal* lose his appeal that was based on the grounds that he was entitled to the name of the woman who had called from 253?

10. T. or F. it can be expected that other novel suits will arise in the future out of the innkeeper-guest relationship.

ENDNOTES

1. *Walling v. Potter*, 35 Conn. 183, 185 (1868).
2. 7 Car. & P. 213, 173 Eng. Rep. 94 (1835).
3. Coram nobis—"Before us ourselves". Applied to writs of error directed to another branch of the same court.

17

Reservations and Check In

"Making a reservation" is the act of contacting a lodging facility in advance of arrival and gaining in return the assurance that accommodations will be available on the date at the time requested. The making of reservations has become routine and reliable. It is a rare case indeed when a traveler feels concern about whether or not his or her room will be available upon arrival at that destination. Yet, problems often arise. In many instances the problems are legal in nature. To illustrate, does a phone reservation for a motel room, not accompanied by an advanced payment, create a binding contract on the part of the innkeeper to hold that room as promised? Conversely, does there even have to be a binding contract to hold either of the parties to their promises: the one to hold the room and the other to occupy it as promised? Problems arise in practice and it is our purpose to look at some of them and see how the courts have handled them in the past.

A good way to begin is by equating the six requirements of a convential contract with the steps that take place in making of reservations both with, and without, advance deposits. The six requirements are offer, acceptance, mutuality, consideration, competent parties and legal purpose. (See Chapter 6 for a review).

RESERVATIONS

The contractual elements of a reservation would appear to be as follows:

1. Offer—Made by the traveler. "I will need a room on August 3, 4, 5, 19—, double beds, down and out." (It is communicated, made in good faith and is definite).
2. Acceptance—The agreement of the hotel to provide and hold the room upon payment of a one day's deposit in advance.
3. Consideration—The payment of the deposit.
4. Mutuality—Apparent.
5. Legal purpose—Presumed. (If not, the contract would fail).
6. Competent parties—An innkeeper has a duty to receive infants as well as adults as a matter of law.

Now assume that the reservation is by teletype, 6:00 P.M. guaranteed arrival, by giving one's American Express Card number, made on the morning of the day of arrival. Is there *now* a contract?

1. Offer—Made by the traveler.
2. Acceptance—An indication of the willingness of the inn to be bound. If the traveler is told "sorry, we are full," the matter ends there.
3. Consideration—The traveler has promised to take the room and the inn has promised to provide it. These mutual promises would provide the consideration—"quid pro quo."
4. Mutuality—Apparent.
5. Legal purpose—Presumed.
6. Competent parties—No problems, as indicated previously.

In both instances, it would appear that a binding contract has resulted. Sales principles would *not* apply because a *service* is involved. This would also be true of airline reservations.

If the room is not available when the guest arrives, there would be a breach of contract by the inn. If the traveler does not cancel by 6:00 and does not show, that would be a breach of contract by the traveler. A duty would then arise upon the part of the inn to "mitigate"—keep down—the damages of the traveler. This would be done by attempting to fill the room for that night. If this is accomplished, and the inn fills up that night, no loss results to the inn because of the breach by the traveler.

CONTRACT COUNTERPART

Thus the *common law duty* that innkeepers must receive all guests has a counterpart in the law of contract, where under the facts, there is a *contractual duty* to receive. In the latter, the innkeeper cannot use the normal excuses *not* to receive because to do so would breach the contract. In the case of the common law duty to receive, the usual excuses, such as a full house, would be valid.

The distinction between the common law duty to receive and the contractual duty was recognized by a leading author on the subject of contracts: "The obligations of an innkeeper arising from the common-law relation of innkeeper and guest are imposed by law irrespective of contract, and may arise when no contract is or can be made. There is, nevertheless, frequently a contract between the parties fixing the terms of their relation within the limit which the law allows."[1] This distinction becomes important in the material that follows.

EXCUSE

Under contract rules, once a contract is in being, there are few excuses for nonperformance that will be accepted by a court. A "mutual mistake" might be one excuse. Another might be "impossibility." What is impossible at law, however, is not the same as an impossibility in the normal sense. If an inn is full, it would be "impossible" to grant a room to a late arrival who has a reservation. Yet this would not be a *legal impossibility* and could not be used as an excuse for nonperformance. If one is scheduled for a 2:00 P.M. flight and the plane is destroyed by terrorists at 1:30 P.M., *that* might constitute an impossibility, unless another craft is available. The sealing off of a motel by police agencies because of poisonous gas railroad car derailment would provide an excuse at law. So would the destruction of a lodging unit by fire.

If there is a breach of a contractual relationship, the guest must allege and prove the existence of the contract. A complaint that fails to do so would be defective. The guest would also have the burden of proving the nature and extent of the damages (losses), if any, that were suffered.

ADVANCE PAYMENT

If an inn requests that the reservation be paid in advance, the guest has a duty to comply. In addition, it is practice for desk personnel to require the credit card that will be used for payment to be tendered at check-in so that an imprint may be made of it on a charge slip. This is reasonable and few travelers question it. One *might* object on the grounds that it is similar to releasing a blank check.

Upon checking out, the guest is asked to sign after the charge amount has been added. If the guest should leave without checking out, the inn would at law, have implied permission to enter the charges and sign the guests name to the charge slip. By taking the credit card impression in advance, the inn has ample time to determine if the charge will be accepted by the card company, or if the card has been cancelled or stolen. This practice will be continued in the future and is contractually sound.

ACCEPTABLE CONDITION

Even though a traveler may have a contract with an inn or hotel, that person would still have the duty to present himself or herself in a presentable condition. If not, that person could be denied admittance in spite of the contract. This would be tantamount to a breach of contract on the part of the traveler. If the inn cannot sell the room for that night to another, there would be liability on the part of the traveler to make up that loss. The advance deposit could be applied to this loss. However, once confronted with such a situation, upon denial of admittance because of drunkedness, disorderly conduct or the like, the management might do well to return the advance deposit in order to encourage the traveler to seek accommodations elsewhere. Such persons are often prone to blame their problems upon others and to use the courts in an attempt to do so.

LATE ARRIVALS

The duty to receive extends to late arrivals, and especially so if there is a contract. There have been cases where travelers have sued innkeepers for breach of this duty, (see *Rex v. Ivens*, page 249). But today, with proper reservations late arrivals present few problems. If facilities are available for the late arrival who does not have a reservation, then the duty to receive would require that a room be provided regardless of the hour.

FALSE REGISTRATION

It is not uncommon for persons to register at inns under fraudulent names. What effect does this have on an innkeepers liability, contractual and common law, if injury or loss occurs to such persons?

RAPEE v. BEACON HOTEL CORPORATION
293 N.Y.S. 196, 56 N.E. 2d 548 (1944).

LOUGHRAN, Judge.

Plaintiff and his fiancee registered at the defendant's hotel as husband and wife under an assumed name and then went out for the evening. On their return at an early hour the next morning, there was no response to his repeated ringing of the elevator bell at the ground floor, because the elevators were not operated below the mezzanine at that time of day. Eventually the plaintiff leaned against the shaft door of an elevator to listen more closely for what seemed to be the sound of an approaching car. His weight caused the door to slide open and he fell into a pit below. A judgment for his damages has been affirmed and is now challenged by the defendant in this court.

In his charge the Trial Judge said to the jury: "It was the duty of the defendant to see that the elevator doors were properly closed. The gates or doors leading to the shafts of the elevator were required to be locked or bolted or securely fastened on the shaft side, that is, from the inside. * * * The duty which I have charged you the law imposes upon the defendant in the maintenance and operation of passenger elevators is not diminished by the fact that the plaintiff may have intended to occupy a room with a female not his wife or that he imposed upon the hotel authorities by misrepresenting some person to be his wife, or by making use of an assumed name. I charge you that for the purposes of your consideration of this case the plaintiff was a guest of the hotel and that the obligation of due care as I have charged it to you was applicable to this plaintiff in the same manner as to other guests and to other persons lawfully on the premises." To these instructions counsel for the defendant took the following exception: "I respectfully except to that part of your Honor's charge in which you stated that the plaintiff was a guest of the hotel and the same duty which was owing to any guest of the hotel was due and owing to him."

On the strength of this exception, the defendant argues that the plaintiff's fraudulent misrepresentation of his personality made him a trespasser on the hotel premises. We cannot assent to that argument. The misstatement of their names and status by the plaintiff and his companion certainly did not prove that the defendant's one and only purpose in their case was to treat with other particular individuals who were not present at the time. Foremost on the defendant's part was an intention to contract with the man and the woman who had put signatures on the register and, that being so, the plaintiff became a guest of the hotel, though the defendant may perhaps have been deceived as to his identity.

Whether the plaintiff's trickery was nevertheless enough to disable him from maintaining this action was an additional question. (See Beale on Innkeepers and Hotels, § 136.) The defendant insists there was error in the negative answer that was given thereto in the passage we have quoted from the charge of the Trial Judge. But so much of that excerpt as asserted the plaintiff's position as a guest was sound,—or so we have said; and a general exception to an instruction that is correct in part cannot be sustained. For that reason, the defendant's exception to the charge is of no avail at this point. The defendant did not in its answer set up the plaintiff's imposture as a defense. More than that, the motion for dismissal of the complaint made by the defendant at the close of the case did not mention that matter at all. Thus there is no formal warrant in this record for the defendant's demand that the plaintiff forfeit his recovery for his misconduct.

The defendant invokes the statute against keeping houses of ill-fame, Penal Law, § 1146, Consol.Laws, c. 40. The provisions thereof have not persuaded us that we should dismiss this complaint on some theory of public policy.

The judgment should be affirmed, with costs.

LEHMAN, C. J., RIPPEY, LEWIS, CONWAY, DESMOND, and THACHER, JJ., concur.

Judgment affirmed.

In the making of reservations, it is important to understand something about "over-booking" and the legal consequences that may flow from this activity.

OVERBOOKING

"Economic necessity" in the case of airlines may justify overbooking so long as alternative service is available. However, it is not so clear that the same should be true in hotel and motel reservations.

In airline travel, the traveler is renting *transportion on personal property*. The purpose is to achieve movement from one point to another. In the case of lodging, one is *renting space inside of real property*—something that by necessity cannot be moved. In the latter, substitution of other accommodations may be unacceptable, undesirable or both.

Yet, due to the problem of "no-shows", management tends to compensate by "overbooking." While it is true that a no-show guest will be liable for a room that remains empty, as a practical matter little can be done about enforcing the collection. The use of "in-chain" VIP cards or the taking of the numbers of major credit cards as part of the reservation tend to assure that notice of cancellation will be received from the no-shows.

Yet, the contract obligation remains to hold the room if the traveler arrives at the last minute—or even later. Thus a serious problem exists and the legal solution to it is not clear. The following is a leading case on hotel overbooking and contains points of concern and interest to those in the travel and lodging industry.

DOLD v. OUTRIGGER HOTEL
501 P. 2d 368 (S. Ct. Haw. 1972).

KOBAYASHI, JUSTICE.

This is an appeal by the plaintiffs, Mr. and Mrs. D. F. Dold and Mr. and Mrs. Leo Manthei, from a judgment in their favor. Plaintiffs' amended complaint prayed for actual and punitive damages and alleged three counts for recovery, breach of contract, fraud, and breach of an innkeeper's duty to accommodate guests. (Count II for fraud was voluntarily dismissed at trial.) Though the judgment was favorable to them, the plaintiffs contend that the trial judge erred in not allowing an instruction on the issue of punitive damages. This is the issue before the court.

FACTS

The plaintiffs, mainland residents, arranged for hotel accommodations from February 18 to February 23, 1968, through the American Express Company, the agent of the defendant, Outrigger Hotel, hereinafter referred to as "Outrigger". Hawaii Hotels Operating Company, Ltd., managed and operated the Outrigger. Both are Hawaii corporations.

Upon arrival at the Outrigger on February 18, 1968, the plaintiffs were refused accommodations and were transferred by the Outrigger to another hotel of lesser quality because the Outrigger lacked available space. On February 19 and 20 the plaintiffs again demanded that the defendants honor their reservations but they were again refused.

Though the exact nature of the plaintiffs' reservations is in dispute, the defendants claim that since the plaintiffs made no cash deposit, their reservations were not "confirmed" and for that reason the defendants justifiably dishonored the reservations. Plaintiffs contend that the reservations were "confirmed" as the American Express Company had guaranteed to Outrigger a first night's payment in the event that the plaintiffs did not show up. Further, the plaintiffs claim that this guarantee was in fact the same thing as a cash deposit. Thus, plaintiffs argue that the defendants were under a duty to honor the confirmed reservations. Although the jury awarded $600 to the Dolds and $400 to the Mantheis, it is not known upon which count the recovery was based.

An examination of the record in the instant case shows the following:

(1)   It was the policy of the Outrigger that a reservation was deemed confirmed when either a one night's cash deposit was made or the reservation was made by a booking agent which had established credit with the Outrigger.

(2)   The plaintiffs made their reservations through the American Express Company, which had established credit with the Outrigger.

(3)   In lieu of a cash deposit, the Outrigger accepted American Express Company's guarantee that it would pay the first night's deposit for the plaintiffs.

(4)   On February 18, 1968, the Outrigger referred 29 parties holding reservations at the Outrigger to the Pagoda Hotel which deemed these referrals "over-flows."

(5)   On February 18, 1968, the Outrigger had 16 guests who stayed beyond

their scheduled date of departure.

(6) From February 15 to 17 and 19 to 22, 1968, the Outrigger also had more reservations that it could accommodate. Plaintiffs' exhibits Nos. 23 to 29 indicate the number of overflows and referrals of the above-mentioned reservations made by the Outrigger to the Pagoda Hotel on the following dates:

February	15	20 referrals
"	16	20 "
"	17	32 "
"	19	44 "
"	20	9 "
"	21	9 "
"	22	20 "

(7) Evidence was adduced that the Outrigger made a profit from its referrals to the Pagoda Hotel. Upon advance payment for the rooms to American Express who in turn paid Outrigger, the plaintiffs were issued coupons representing the prepayment for the accommodations at the Outrigger. On referral by the Outrigger, the Pagoda Hotel's practice was to accept the coupons and bill the Outrigger for the actual cost of the rooms provided. The difference between the coupon's value and the actual value of the accommodations was retained by the Outrigger.

The plaintiffs prevented a profit from being made by the Outrigger by refusing to use the coupons and paying in cash for the less expensive accommodations.

MAY PLAINTIFFS RECOVER PUNITIVE DAMAGES FOR BREACH OF CONTRACT?

The question of whether punitive damages are properly recoverable in an action for breach of contract has not been resolved in this jurisdiction.

In the instant case, on the evidence adduced, the trial court refused to allow an instruction on the issue of punitive damages but permitted an instruction on the issue of emotional distress and disappointment.[2]

In a case involving a similar pattern of overbooking of reservations the court in Wills v. Trans World Airlines, Inc., 200 F.Supp. 360 (S.D.Cal.1961), stated that the substantial overselling of confirmed reservations for the period in question was a strong indication that the defendant airline had wantonly precipitated the very circumstances which compelled the removal of excess confirmed passengers from its flights.

In Goo v. Continental Casualty Company, 52 Haw. 235, 473 P.2d 563 (1970), we affirmed the public policy considerations behind the doctrine of punitive damages where the breach of contract is accompanied by some type of contemporaneous tortious activity. However, the Goo case did not afford the proper factual setting for this court to consider the propriety of an assessment of punitive damages in contract actions.

Various jurisdictions have adopted their own rules regarding the nature of the tortious activity necessary to recover punitive damages in a contract action. Some require that the breach be accompanied by an independent willful tort or by a concurrent breach of a common law duty.

We are of the opinion that the facts of this case do not warrant punitive damages. However, the plaintiffs are not limited to the narrow traditional contractual remedy of out-of-pocket losses alone. We have recognized the fact that certain situations are so disposed as to present a fusion of the doctrines of tort and contract. Though some courts have strained the traditional concept of compensatory damages in contract to include damages for emotional distress and disappointment, we are of the opinion that where a contract is breached in a wanton or reckless manner as to result in a tortious injury, the aggrieved person is entitled to recover in tort. Thus, in addition to damages for out-of-pocket losses, the jury was properly instructed on the issue of damages for emotional distress and disappointment.

MAY PLAINTIFFS RECOVER PUNITIVE DAMAGES FOR BREACH OF AN INNKEEPER'S DUTY TO ACCOMMODATE?

We now consider count III of plaintiffs' complaint. It has long been recognized that an innkeeper, holding himself out to the public to provide hotel accommodations, is obligated, in the absence of reasonable grounds for refusal, to provide accommodations to all persons upon proper request. This duty traditionally extended to the traveller who presented himself at the inn. However, where the innkeeper's accommodations had been exhausted, the innkeeper could justly refuse to receive an applicant. It is well recognized that punitive damages are recoverable for breach of an innkeeper's duty to his guest where the innkeeper's conduct is deliberate or wanton. We are not aware of any jurisdiction that renders an innkeeper liable on his common law duty to accommodate under the circumstances of this case. Consequently, plaintiffs are not entitled to an instruction on punitive damages on count III of their complaint.

Judgment is affirmed.

MARUMOTO, Justice, concurring in which ABE, Justice, joins.

I concur in the result, but cannot agree with the reasoning in the opinion of the court nor with the statement that the contract here was breached in a wanton or reckless manner so as to result in a tortious injury entitling the plaintiffs to recover in tort.

The plaintiffs in the trial below requested and were refused instructions for punitive damages. They appealed that question and that question alone to this court. The issues presented were two in number: first, whether defendants breached a general, i. e. tort, duty owed plaintiffs in a willful and wanton manner so as to entitle them to the traditional instruction for punitive damages; and second, whether there was a contract between the parties and a subsequent breach, and if so, should punitive damages be permitted in such a situation.

In relation to the first issue, this court decided fifty years ago that it was "* * * too well established to admit of argument that in actions of tort punitive damages may, under certain circumstances, be awarded * * *." Bright v. Quinn, 20 Haw. 504, 511 (1911). There, and in subsequent cases, it was determined that such circumstances existed where the tort injury resulted from defendant's willful, wanton, malicious, or oppressive conduct. In Goo v. Continental Casualty Co., 52 Haw. 235, 473 P.2d 563 (1970), we decided that the record of the case must clearly support a finding of the conduct proscribed by the earlier holdings.

Nowhere, however, have we intimated that a defendant's conduct might be considered as the sole factor determinative of the issues of a case. When one acts, he acts with impunity, unless his actions violate a legal duty imposed upon him by society or assumed by him in agreement with another. Therefore, it is mandatory that the actions of the defendants in this case be examined in relation to the violations alleged or proven by the plaintiffs.

The common law duty of a hotel to accommodate all persons who present themselves to it is ancient and well settled in Anglo-American law. The duty is general, owed to the public at large, and seems to have been laid upon the inn-keeper only where no special assumpsit to the same effect existed.[3] The inn-keeper was not obligated to provide the guest with the precise room selected but only with "reasonable and proper" accommodation. Fell v. Knight, 8 M. & W. 268, 275 (Ex. 1841); and there must have been room available at the time of the prospective guest's presentation.

Considering that there was a contract in existence between the parties here, that the Outrigger arranged to accommodate the plaintiffs at the Pagoda, and that the Outrigger had no vacant rooms at the time of the plaintiffs' presentation, I see no violation by the defendants of their duty to accommodate. This, therefore, completes my examination of all tortious conduct alleged by the plaintiffs to have been committed by the defendants. I use the term "tortious conduct" in accordance with the overwhelming weight of authority to "* * * denote the fact that conduct whether of act or omission is of such a character as to subject the actor to liability under the principles of the law of torts." Restate-ment of Torts § 6, Kuhn v. Bader, 89 Ohio App. 203, 213, 101 N.E.2d 322, 328 (1951).

As to the second issue, I encounter no difficulty in finding that a contract for accommodations existed between the opposing parties. Furthermore, I construe the contract as including both an aesthetic expectation on the part of the plain-tiffs and a particular type of accommodation, namely, one in a hotel located on the beach as is the Outrigger. Nor am I hesitant to express my outrage at the greed and lack of consideration exhibited by the hotel.

At this point, however, I must draw the line. Save in actions for breach of a promise to marry, Johnson v. Travis, 33 Minn. 231, 22 N.W. 264 (1885), no other state of this union has ever approved an award of punitive damages in an action ex contractu. See Annot., 84 A.L.R. 1345 (1933). The Restatement of Contracts § 342, reflecting this overwhelming view, flatly prohibits such a recovery. This is so even where the breach is willful, or where the parties have stipulated to such damages.

Rather than denying contractual punitive damages solely on the facts of this case, I would join with the other courts of this nation and prohibit them in all contract actions. This would overcome the confusion and doubt engendered by the majority opinion in this case and preserve a freedom of contract unclouded by uncertain legal penalties. It would be better in my opinion to agree with one of the foremost authorities on the subject when he states that "* * * it is of doubtful wisdom to add to the risks imposed on entering a contract this liability to an acrimonious contest over whether a breach was malicious or fraudulent * * *." Cf. McCormick, Hornbook Series on Damages § 81 at 291 (1st ed. 1935).

Of course where the breach is intertwined with a tort then punitive damages may be given. There seem to be two classes of such situations. The first is where the breach of contract is accompanied by a fraudulent act, Wellborn v. Dixon, 70 S.C. 108, 49 S.E. 232 (1904), and the second is where the breach is accom-panied by an independent tort. Simpson, Punitive Damages for Breach of Contract, 20 Ohio St. L.J. 284, 287 (1959). Neither of those situations exist in this case.

Also, the question of damages for emotional distress is not before us today; yet, it has been decided. It seems far more preferable to me to strain the tradi-tional concept of compensatory damages than to rupture the foundations of tort and contract liability. Accordingly, I would adopt the approach of Kellogg v. Commodore Hotel, 187 Misc. 319, 64 N.Y.S.2d 131 (1960), and label the damages received by plaintiffs as compensatory.

ABE, J. joins.

The *Dold* case tells us that an overbooked hotel may provide a good defense to the common law duty to receive, yet this defense is not good as to the contract liability. In the *Thomas* case that follows, we see another example of an innkeepers contract liability for a breached reservation.

THOMAS v. PICK HOTELS CORPORATION
244 F. 2d 664 (US Ct. App. 10th Cir. 1955).

MURRAH, Circuit Judge.

Earl D. Thomas, a Negro, sued The Pick Hotels Corporation and others for damages resulting from a denial of hotel accommodations.

The trial court sustained a motion to dismiss the amended complaint on the grounds that the action against the appellee was barred by the Kansas two-year statute of limitations, Kansas G.S.1949, 60—306(3), as one "for injury to the rights of another, not arising on contract * * *."

As we understand appellant's contentions on appeal, they are to the effect that his claim is governed by the Kansas three-year statute of limitations, Kansas G.S.1949, 60—306(2), as (1) one upon a contract, express or implied, or (2) one based upon the common law duty of an innkeeper to provide nondiscriminatory accommodations to all, or (3) as one upon a claim, the liability for which is created by the Kansas Civil Rights Statute, Kansas G.S.1949, 21—2424.

The second section of the Kansas statute of limitations provides that "an action upon contract, not in writing, express or implied; an action upon a liability created by statute, other than a forfeiture or penalty" can only be brought within three years after accrual. Kansas G.S. 1949, 60—306(2).

The action against this appellee hotel corporation based on diversity of citizenship and requisite amount in controversy, was commenced within three years from the accrual of the asserted claim. And if by a liberal interpretation of the pleadings, they can be said to state a claim or claims upon which relief, not barred by the three-year statute of limitations, can be granted, it is our duty to so construe them, although they may be alternatively or inconsistently stated.

The pleadings are prolix and redundant and the asserted claim or claims not readily discernible. But as we summarize them they are intended to state that the defendant hotel agreed first in writing and later by telephone to provide hotel accommodations on a specified date; that when the appellant and his wife presented themselves to the hotel on the reservation date they were refused accommodations solely because of their race. The pleadings refer to an enforceable contract express or implied, and the common law duty of an innkeeper to accommodate all members of the general public without discrimination. They also invoke the Kansas Civil Rights Statute providing for a civil action in damages for the denial of hotel accommodations because of race or color. Kansas G.S.1949, 21—2424.

Contracts for hotel accommodations are usually treated as the means for the inducement or establishment of the common law innkeeper-guest relationship which when established creates a common law relational duty on the part of the innkeeper, the breach of which is redressible in tort. Treating the claim then as one arising out of the common law duty of an innkeeper to provide accommodations without discrimination, the case clearly sounds in tort, does not arise out of a contract, and is therefore clearly barred by the two-year statute of limitations.

The Kansas Civil Rights Statute in substance forbids hotel owners or innkeepers from making any distinction on account of race or color and provides that the offending person shall be liable in damages to the person or persons injured thereby. Kansas G.S.1949, 21-2424. But the statute is merely declaratory of the common law. And it is settled that a right of action created by statute within the meaning of subsection two of the Kansas statute of limitations is one which must not have existed at common law when the statute was adopted. To be created by the statute, the action must not exist but for the statute.

While the common law duty of an innkeeper to provide accommodations may have been dormant or stale in Kansas, it has never been abrogated and undoubtedly existed prior to the adoption of the statute. Indeed the complainant invokes it and relies upon it here. Moreoover, we have construed the comparable Federal Civil Rights Act as giving a right of action sounding in tort, as to which the Kansas two-year statute of limitations is applicable. See Wilson v. Hinman, 10 Cir., 172 F.2d 914. It is therefore plain that treating the claim either as one arising at common law or one under the statute, it is barred by the two-year statutue of limitations.

But there is nothing in the common law or the statute to preclude the parties from entering into a valid and enforceable contract for hotel accommodations. Certainly a contract of this kind is not against public policy of the State of Kansas. Indeed the statute and the common law sanction the contract by forbidding the innkeeper from making any distinction on account of race or color.

The complaint pleads a written contract to provide hotel accommodations on a given date subsequently modified by a telephone conversation, and it pleads an arbitrary refusal to provide such accommodations. The prayer is for damages, compensatory and punitive. But if the demand or prayer is for relief in tort, it in no way affects the right to recover on the contract, for the dimensions of a lawsuit are measured by what is pleaded and proven, not what is demanded.

We conclude that the complaint states a claim on an express contract to provide hotel accommodations and a breach of that contract. The claim is therefore governed by the Kansas three-year statute of limitations as one arising under a contract express or implied.

The judgment is accordingly reversed.

Our discussion of innkeepers liability requires understanding of the types of liability (damages) that one may encounter.

CONSEQUENTIAL DAMAGES

Consequential damages are those that arise ancillary to a breach of contract. For example, after being told of the importance of the reservation being kept,[4] an innkeeper breaches the contract, forcing the traveler to rent a room at a $20 higher rate. The $20 would be a loss directly attributable to the breach. But what if, as a consequence of the breach, the traveler fails to make a planned contact at the inn, and as a result loses a $100,000 contract? If that loss is a direct consequence of the innkeeper's breach, the traveler can also ask a court for those losses, or damages. (The loss would not be the full amount of the lost contract, but the loss of profits on that contract).

A second type of damages is designed to make an example of one under certain conditions.

PUNITIVE DAMAGES

Punitive or exemplary damages are awarded to punish one for oppressive, deliberate, wanton acts against another, and are frequently encountered in tort cases. However, in *contract* situations, the common law rule is that compensatory, and consequential damages, if justified, are adequate without allowing damages to punish. This rule prevails today, as the prior cases indicate.

However, if a breach of a reservation contract is accompanied by foul language, physical threats or other overt acts that are unjustified, punitive or exemplary damages might be sought by the traveler.[5] If a traveler brings a *tort* action for mental suffering caused by the overt acts of an innkeeper, in many states punitive damages could be sought and perhaps recovered.

In the *Dold* case, page 275, the plaintiff's were allowed recovery of punitive damages, but the court based the recovery in tort and not contract. The concurring opinion, page 277, would have allowed for recovery for the breach of contract—compensatory damages only—but not punitive damages.

While an innkeeper may be able to avoid punitive damages because of the breach of a reservation contract, who can afford the litigation?

BREACH OF TRAVELER

Non-showing travelers is a day-to-day matter and one for handling by desk personnel. But what if a reservation is for a block of rooms to accommodate a football team or an orchestra? In that event, an innkeeper should treat the matter with greater formality.

First, it would be well to have prepared in advance a form contract to cover large bookings. This contract should expressly provide for the contingency of cancellation at a date too late to re-let to others, setting forth how damages will be measured. Next, the contract should be signed by someone of the traveling party that has authority to do so.

By taking these steps, collection of compensatory losses due to breach by travelers would be greatly simplified when group booking is involved.

SET PERIODS

It is the custom of resort and other lodging facilities to require that reservations be made for minimum time periods, such as three days, even if only a one day advance payment is requested. This is true in Florida during certain months and at lodging facilities close to major racing events. What is the contractual obligations of a guest who checks out before the minimum time period has expired?

If the accommodations can be rented to others at the same rate, then no loss has been sustained and the matter is closed. If the accommodations cannot be rented, which is often the case because travelers soon know what is or isn't available, the original traveler would have a contractual obligation to make up the loss.[6]

Thus we see that the reservation contractual obligaton rests on *both* parties and either can be looked to for breach of that contract, as the following illustrates.

FREEMAN v. KIAMESHA CONCORD, INC.,
76 Misc. 2d 915, 351 N.Y.S. 2d 541 (1974).

SHANLEY N. EGETH, Judge.

Determination of the issues in this Small Claims Part case requires a present construction of the meaning of language contained in Section 206 of the General Business Law as it applies to current widespread and commonplace practices and usages in the hotel and resort industry. Although the pertinent statutory provision has essentially been in effect since its original enactment ninety years ago there appears to be no reported decision which directly construes or interprets its meaning and applicability.

THE STATUTORY LANGUAGE

The relevant portion of Sec. 206, reads as follows:

". . . no charge or sum shall be collected or received by any . . . hotel keeper or inn keeper for any service not actually rendered or for a longer time than the person so charged actually remained at such hotel or inn . . . provided such guest shall have given such hotel keeper or inn keeper notice at the office of his departure. For any violation of this section the offender shall forfeit to the injured party three times the amount so charged, and shall not be entitled to receive any money for meals, services, or time charged."

THE FACTS

Plaintiff, a lawyer, has commenced this action against the defendant,the operator of the Concord Hotel (Concord), one of the more opulent of the resort hotels in the Catskill Mountain resort area, to recover the sum of $424.00. Plaintiff seeks the return of charges paid at the rate of $84.80 per day for two days spent at the hotel ($169.60) plus three times said daily rate ($254.40) for a day charged, and not refunded after he and his wife checked out before the commencement of the third day of a reserved three day Memorial Day weekend. Plaintiff asserts that he is entitled to this sum pursuant to the provisoins of Sec. 206, General Business Law.

The testimony adduced at trial reveals that, in early May, 1973, after seeing an advertisement in the New York Times indicating that Joel Gray would perform at the (Concord) during the forthcoming Memorial Day weekend, plaintiff contacted a travel agent and solicited a reservation for his wife and himself at the hotel. In response he received an offer of a reservation for a "three night minimum stay" which contained a request for a $20.00 deposit. He forwarded the money confirming the reservaton, which was deposited by the defendant.

While driving to the hotel the plaintiff observed a billboard, located about 20 miles from his destination which indicated that Joel Gray would perform at the Concord only on the Sunday of the holiday week?nd. The plaintiff was disturbed because he had understood the advertisemen' to mean that the entertainer would be performing on each day of the weekend. He checked into the hotel notwithstanding this disconcerting information claiming that he did not wish to turn back and ruin a long anticipated weekend vacation. The plaintiff later discovered that two subsequent New York Times Advertisements, not seen by him before checking in, specified that Gray would perform on the Sunday of that weekend.

After staying at the hotel for two days, the plaintiff advised the management that he wished to check out because of his dissatisfaction with the entertainment. He claims to have told them that he had made his reservation in reliance upon what he understood to be a representation in the advertisement to the effect that Joel Gray would perform throughout the holiday weekend. The management suggested that, since Gray was to perform that evening, he should remain. The plaintiff refused and again asserted his claim that the advertisement constituted a misrepresentation. The defendant insisted upon full payment for the entire three day guaranteed weekend in accordance with the reservation. Plaintiff then told the defendant's employees that he was an attorney and that they had no right to charge him for the third day of the reserved period if he checked out. He referred them to the text of Sec.206, General Business Law, which he had obviously read in his room where it was posted on the door, along with certain other statutory provisions and the schedule of rates and charges. The plaintiff was finally offered a one day credit for a future stay, if he made full payment. He refused, paid the full charges under protest and advised the defendant of his intention to sue them for treble damages. This is that action.

SUBSIDIARY ISSUE: THE CLAIMED MISREPRESENTATION

I find that the advertisement relied upon by the plaintiff did not contain a false representation. It announced that Joel Gray would perform at the hotel during the Memorial Day weekend. Gray did actually appear during that weekend. The dubious nature of the plaintiff's claim is demonstrated by the fact that when he checked in at the hotel he had been made aware of the date of Gray's performance and remained at the hotel for two days and then checked out prior to the performance that he had allegedly travelled to see.

THE CLAIMED VIOLATION OF SEC. 206

We now reach plaintiff's primary contention. Simply put, plaintiff asserts that by requiring him to pay the daily rate for the third day of the holiday weekend, (even though he had given notice of his intention to leave and did not remain for that day), the defendant violated the provisions of Sec. 206, General Business Law and thereby became liable for the moneys recoverable thereunder.

Plaintiff contends that the language of the statute is clear, and that under its terms he is entitled to the relief sought irrespective of whether he had a fixed weekend, week, or monthly reservation, or even if the hotel services were available to him.

It must be noted at the outset that the plaintiff checked into the defendant's hotel pursuant to a valid, enforceable contract for a three day stay. The solicitation of a reservation, the making of a reservation by the transmittal of a deposit and the acceptance of the deposit constituted a binding contract in accordance with traditional contract principles of offer and acceptance. Unquestionably the defendant would have been liable to the plaintiff had it not had an accommodation for plaintiff upon his arrival. The plaintiff is equally bound under the contract for the agreed minimum period.

The testimony reveals that the defendant was ready, willing, and able to provide all of the services contracted for, but that plaintiff refused to accept them for the third day of the three day contract period. These services included lodging, meals, and the use of the defendant's recreational and entertainment facilities. In essence, plaintiff maintains that under the terms of the statue, his refusal, for any reason, to accept or utilize these facilities for part of the contract period precludes the defendant from charging him the contract price.

Section 206 is silent as to its applicability to circumstances which constitute a breach of contract or a conscious refusal to accept offered services. This is one of those instances in which, upon analysis, a statute which appears to be clear and unambiguous is sought to be applied to a situation not envisioned by its framers. Nothing contained in the statute provides assistance in answering the question presented in this case, i. e., may a resort hotel hold a guest to his contract for a stay of fixed duration when that guest has, without cause breached his contract.

There is no legislative history available to assist in determining the intention of the legislature, nor are there any reported decisions construing the statute which can be of assistance in this regard. Recourse must therefore be had to general principles of statutory construction.

Plaintiff argues that Section 206 must be strictly construed against the hotel. In support of this position he cites a number of decisions construing Sections 201 and 202 of the General Business Law. These cases all deal with construction of the statutory right of hotels to limit their monetary liability for the loss of a guest's property. They are inapplicable to the instant situation. The statutory right of a hotel to limit its liability to its guests is in derogation of its unlimited pre-statutory common law liability.

The decisions thereunder universally and appropriately mandate a strict construction of the statutes. However, this case presents the converse situation. Section 206 limits the prior common law unlimited right of a hotel to contract to charge its guests for services and facilities. The statutory restriction upon the hotel is in derogation of the common law. Such a statute must be strictly construed in favor of the hotel and against any expansion of the restriction of its common law right.

The requirement of strict construction in favor of the hotel is buttressed by the penal-like treble damage penalty contained in the statute. A statute which is quasi-penal in nature should be strictly construed against the extension of its application to areas not expressly mandated or contemplated by the legislature.

It is not sufficient to merely conclude that the statute must be strictly construed in favor of the hotel. The construction to be accorded the statute must also harmonize with the other general principles which have evolved to assist Courts in arriving at a determination of legislative intent. Consideration must be given to the "mischief sought to be remedied by the new legislation". (Matter of

Hamlin, 226 N.Y. 407, 124 N.E. 4; McKinney's Statutes, Sec. 95).

Statutory construction must be sought which is . . . "consistent with achieving [the statute's] purpose and with justice and common sense." (McKinney's Statutes, supra, Sec. 96; see Abood v. Hospital Service, 30 N.Y.2d 295, 332 N.Y.S.2d 877, 283 N.E.2d 754; Mtr. of N. Y. Post Corp. v. Liebowitz, 2 N.Y.2d 677, 143 N.E.2d 256). Consideration must be given to the customs, usages and history prevalent at the time of enactment, to present customs and usages not then prevalent, and to the avoidance of "objectionable consequences", "inconvenience", "hardship or injustice", "mischief", or "absurdity". (McKinney's Statutes, supra, Secs. 141, 142, 145, 146, 148).

Contemporaneous exposition ". . . practical construction which has received the acquiescence of the public . . . will . . . be given considerable weight" . . .

In 1883, the year of statutory enactment, transportation in our nation was slow and limited. Few persons travelled great distances for the sole purpose of recreation and pleasure. Small inns proliferated the countryside, frequented by travellers requiring rest and sustenance during the course of long and arduous journeys. Such travellers might briefly stay at a convenient inn along their route, refresh themselves, and continue on to their destination. Too often, they had limited choices en route and frequently the traveller would be easy prey to unscrupulous innkeepers, who might exact unreasonable charges and enforce collection via a friendly constable and utilization of the innkeepers' lien.

Section 206 was enacted to provide some protection against such exploitation.

The automobile, fast trains, and air transportation, a developing affluent and mobile society in which an increasing number of people began to seek diversion and recreational regeneration in utilizing their expanded leisure time, have resulted in a total transformation of the nature of modern hotels.

A vast hotel and recreation industry has since developed to meet the expanding needs of our citizenry. Major resort complexes were created to cater to various recreation inclinations. Our countryside is presently dotted with countless enterprises ranging from the simple and primitive campsite or bungalow to the most luxurious and opulent hotel, providing a quality of accommodation, food and recreational facilities unavailable to even the very rich of ninety years ago. All of these enterprises compete for public patronage. Even the most expensive are frequented by persons of modest means who find they can afford to indulge themselves for periods of limited duration.

In most instances the industry is seasonal in nature. Its facilities are most sought during vacation and holiday periods. Hotels such as the one operated by the defendant have developed techniques to provide full utilization of the facilities during periods of peak demand. One such method is the guaranteed minimum one week or weekend stay, which has gained widespread public acceptance. Almost all of these enterprises have offered their facilities for minimum guaranteed periods during certain times of the year by contracting with willing guests who also seek to fully utilize their available vacation time. These minimum period agreements have become essential to the economic survival and well being of the recreational hotel industry. The public is generally aware of the necessity for them to do so, and accepts the practice.

Adoption of plaintiff's statutory construction in this case would have far-reaching consequences with impact well beyond this case or this defendant. Changes during the past 90 years have transformed the conditions which required urgent redress by statutory enactment in 1883, into a rarity in the year 1973. Absurd results would follow were the statute to be literally and strictly construed in the manner urged by plaintiff. The statute could then become an instrumentality for the infliction of grave harm and injustice, rather than a buffer or shield against the activities of rapacious hotelmen. Plaintiff's construction would create the anomoly of rendering a proper contract illusory while unjustly continuing to obligate only one of the parties to the performance of the contract. The defendant, and most similarly situated hotel keepers have utilized their minimum reservation contracts as a means of achieving economic survival. Chaos and financial disaster would result from the invalidation of such agreements.

A hotel such as the defendant's, services thousands of guests at a single time. The maintenance of its facilities entails a continuing large overhead expenditure. It must have some means to legitimately ensure itself the income which its guests have contracted to pay for the use of its facilities. The minimum period reservation contract is such a device. The rooms are contracted for in advance and are held available while other potential guests are turned away. A guest who terminates his contractual obligations prior to the expiration of the contract period will usually deprive the hotel of anticipated income, if that guest cannot be held financially accountable upon his contract. At that point, replacement income is virtually impossible. Indeed, on occasion, some hotels contract out their entire facilities to members of a single group for a stipulated period many months in advance. No great imagination is required to comprehend the economic catastrophe which would ensue if all such guests were to cancel at the last minute or to check out prior to the end of their contract period without continuing contractual liability. I cannot believe that the public policy of the state sanctions such contractual obliteration.

The construction sought by the plaintiff could result in other consequences which are equally bizarre. The defendant has contracted to supply the plaintiff with a room, three meals a day, and access to the use of its varied sports, recreational or entertainment facilities. As long as these are available to the plaintiff the defendant has fulfilled its contractual commitment. If the plaintiff's construction of the statute is tenable, he might also argue with equal force that unless a guest receives an appropriate rebate or adjustment of bill, the defendant would incur statutory liability, if such guest visited a friend in the vicinity, slept over and failed to use his room for one or more nights of his contracted stay; became enmeshed in an all-night game of cards and failed to use his room; was dieting and failed to avail himself of all the offered meals; did not play tennis, golf, or swim, or became sick and made no use of the available recreational or entertainment facilities.

I conclude that plaintiff may not recover because he has not proved a cause of action based upon a violation of Section 206 of the General Business Law. The evidence does not prove the existence of the type of wrong for which redress was provided in the 1883 enactment. The statute was not intended to prevent a hotel from insisting that its guests comply with the terms of a contract for a fixed minimum stay. There can be no statutory violation by a hotel which fulfills its part of the contract by making its services and facilities available to a guest who refuses to accept them. Such act of refusal by the guest does not justify imposition of the penalties set forth in the statute.

Judgment is accordingly awarded to the defendant with costs.

RECOVERY

In a surprisingly large number of hotel, motel, restaurant, tavern and common carrier cases, the one bringing the suit fails in whole or in part to recover damages. This is usually due to the failure of the plaintiff to bring the facts in line with the applicable law.

Yet in every lawsuit in which a plaintiff loses, the travel or lodging facility has been placed to the expense and time of defense, and has suffered undesirable publicity in the process. For these reasons those in this industry are advised to be "liability conscious" and to conduct their affairs with the dangers posed by potential litigation in mind.

QUESTIONS

1. Do you know why mutual promises provide "consideration?" If not, ask.
2. What legal problems might one face in overbooking?
3. Why did the court refuse to allow the false registration in the *Rapee* case to be used as a reason to deny recovery?
4. What was the point that the concurring judge wanted to make in the *Dold* case?
5. Set out the difference between "consequential" and "punitive" damages.
6. Why has the law refused to allow punitive damages in contract cases in the past?
7. Explain how a breach of contract could develop into a tort situation using an example.
8. T. or F. Group bookings at an inn can be handled with the same informality as customary bookings.
9. Why did the plaintiff fail to recover in the *Freeman* case?
10. Can you think of problems that may arise when taking an unsigned impression of a guest's credit card at check-in?

ENDNOTES

1. *Williston on Contracts*, Vol 5 sec. 1070.
2. Plaintiffs' requested instruction No. 5, as modified, was given as follows: [If you find in favor of the plaintiffs] you must determine the amount of damages the plaintiffs are entitled to recover. [If you find in favor of the plaintiffs,] [p]laintiffs have a right to recover all damages which they have suffered and which the defendants or a reasonable person in the defendants' position should have foreseen would result from their acts or omissions. Such damages may include reasonable compensation for emotional distress and disappointment, if any, which plaintiffs have suffered as a proximate result of the defendants' conduct. There is no precise standard by which to place a monetary value on emotional distress and disappointment nor is the opinion of any witness required to fix a reasonable amount. In making an award of damages for emotional disappointment, you should determine an amount which your own experience and reason indicates would be sufficient in light of all of the evidence.

3. The Restatement of Torts, both the original and the tentative draft of the Second, at § 866, appear to reflect this latter assumption, for it does not include within the scope of its coverage parties who are under a contractual duty to each other.

4. *Hadley v. Bavendale*, 9 EX. 341 (1854).

5. *Frank v. Justine Caterers, Inc.*, 271 APP. DIV. 980, 68 N.Y.S. 2d 193 (1947).

6. *Freeman v. Klamesha Concord, Inc.*, 351 N.Y.S. 2d 541 (1974).

18

Rights of Innkeepers and Guests

Once a guest has been received and is registered, certain rights of the innkeeper come to the front. These include the right to move a guest to a new room; the right to enter the room of the guest under certain conditions; the right to take extreme actions in the event of emergencies; the right to eject guests under certain conditions, and others. After an examination of these rights of the innkeepers, we will examine the rights of guests. In both we will see a delicate legal balance. If this balance is disturbed, complaints and often lawsuits follow. In the end, it is a matter of learning that these rights are as inviolate in one direction as they are in the other. First, a look at some of the rights of inn-keepers.

ASSIGNING NEW ROOMS

The nature of the legal rights that a guest receives when assigned to a room, is peculiar to the law of innkeeping. It is not a lease in the sense of one who leases a house to a tenant. In that case, the tenant gains an almost absolute legal right to occupy the house for the rental period. In the case of guest at an inn, the right gained is closer to a mere license or privilege to occupy.

Thus an innkeeper retains the right to move a guest from one room to another. This should only be done, however, upon a showing of good cause. It would be a duty of the guest to cooperate in the change. The innkeeper should provide assistance to minimize the inconvenience of the guest.

ENTRY OF ROOMS

Once a guest is assigned a room, that room is considered to belong to the guest for the rental period. (This is subject to the right to move the guest to another room). As a rule, the innkeeper has now lost the right to enter that room until the rental period ends. This is qualified by the need to clean the room.

EFFECT OF EMERGENCIES

In the event of an emergency, such as a fire or escaping gas from a nearby derailed train, or a broken water line in the room itself, the innkeeper is given wide latitude. It then becomes a matter of acting as a reasonable innkeeper would act under like or similar circumstances. The innkeeper can, and must, enter to warn of outside dangers. Further, his or her agents can enter to stop further damage. Common sense controls. Under such circumstances, it would do a guest little good to try to convince a court that his or her right to occupy the room had been disturbed because of the emergency actions taken.

EJECTING GUESTS

Once one is received as a guest, it is presumed that both the keeper of the house as well as the guest will observe reasonable standards of conduct toward each other. If the innkeeper does otherwise, the guest has a cause of action in court. If the guest does otherwise, then the innkeeper has the right to eject.

However, in exercising the right to eject, one must make careful inquiry and make certain that the grounds are solid. Two cases will illustrate.

McHUGH v. SCHLOSSER ET. AL.
292 A. 291 (S. Ct. Penna. 1894).

WILLIAMS, J. The defendants are hotel keepers in the city of Pittsburgh. McHugh was their guest, and died in an alley appurtenant to the hotel on the 2d day of February, 1891. Mary McHugh, the plaintiff, is his widow, and she seeks to recover damages for the loss of her husband, alleging that it was caused by the improper conduct of the defendants and their employes. An examination of the testimony shows that McHugh came to the Hotel Schlosser late on Friday night, January 30th, registered, was assigned to, and paid for, a room for the night, and retired. On Saturday and Sunday he complained of being ill, and remained most of both days in bed. A physician was sent for at his request, who prescribed for him. He also asked for and obtained several drinks during the same time, and an empty bottle or bottles remained in his room after he left it. During the forenoon of Monday he seemed bewildered, and wandered about the hall on the floor on which his room was. About the middle of the day the housekeeper reported to Schlosser that he was out of his room, and sitting half dressed on the side of the bed in another room. Schlosser and his porter both started in search of McHugh, and Schlosser seems to have exhibited some excitement or anger. He was found, and the porter led him to his room. While this was being done Schlosser said to him, "You can't stay here any longer;" to which McHugh replied, "I'll git." The porter, on reaching his room, put his coat, hat, and shoes on him, and at once led him to the freight elevator, put him on it, and had him let down to the ground floor. He then took him through a door, used for freight, out into an alley some four or five feet wide, that led to Penn avenue. Rain was falling, and the day was cold. A stream of rain water and dissolving snow was running down the alley. McHugh was without overshoes, overcoat, or wraps of any description. When the porter had gotten him part way down the alley he fell to the pavement. While he was lying in the water, and the porter standing near him, a lady passed along the sidewalk on Penn Avenue and saw him. She walked a square, found Officer White, and reported to him what she had seen. He went to the alley to investigate, and when he arrived McHugh had been gotten to his feet, but was leaning heavily against the wall of the hotel, apparently unable to step. The porter was behind him with his hands upon him, apparently urging him forward. What followed will be best told in the officer's own words. He says: "I asked, 'What's the matter with this man Mr. Powers?'" He says, 'He's sick.' I says 'He ought to have something done for him, and at that time he fell right in the alley on his back. He had his coat open, no vest, and his shoes were untied. He had strings in his shoes, but not tied." The officer was asked if the man spoke after he reached the place where he was, and he replied thus: "He spoke to me. Somebody said he was drunk. He rolled his eyes up, and says: 'Officer, I am not drunk. I am sick. I wish you would get an ambulance and have me taken to the hospital.' Then I ran to the patrol box." It required about 20 minutes to get an ambulance on the ground. During all this time the man continued to lie on the pavement in the alley. At length, after an exposure of about half an hour in the storm, and on the pavement, the ambulance came. He was placed on a stretcher, lifted into the ambulance,and taken to police headquarters, and thence to the hospital; but all signs of life had disappeared when he was laid on the hospital floor. The post mortem examination disclosed the fact that the immediate cause of death was valvular disease of the heart. The theory of the plaintiff was that the shock from exposure to wet and cold in the alley had, in his feeble and unprotected condition, brought on the heart failure from which he died; and, as the exposure resulted from the conduct or directions of the defendants, they were responsible for his death. Three principal questions were thus raised: First. What duty does an innkeeper owe to his guest? Second. What connection was there between the defendants' disregard of their duty, if they did disregard it in any particular, and the death of Mr. McHugh? Third. If the plaintiff be entitled to recover, what is the measure of her damages?

The attention of the court was drawn to the first of these questions by the defendants' third point, in which the learned judge was asked to instruct the jury, in substance, that if the deceased was troublesome to the defendants, and annoying to their guests, they might rightfully put him out of their house, if they used no unnecessary force or violence. This point was refused as framed, but the learned judge proceeded to state the rule thus: "If the annoying acts were willful, the defendants could remove decedent in the manner stated in point. If, however, they were the result of sickness, although they might, under certain circumstances, remove him, such removal must be in a manner suited to his condition." This was saying that if McHugh was intoxicated, and the disturbances made by him were due to his intoxication, he might be treated as a drunken man; but if he was sick, and the disturbances caused by him were due to his sickness, he must be treated with the consideration due to a sick man. This is a correct statement of the rule. In the delirium of a fever a sick man may become very troublesome to a hotel keeper, and his groans and cries may be annoying to the occupants of rooms near him; but this would not justify turning him forcibly from his bed into the street during a winter storm. What the condition of the decedent really was went properly to the jury for determination. If they found the fact to be that he was suffering from sickness, then the learned judge properly said that, if his removal was to be undertaken, it should be conducted in a manner suited to one in his condition. The second question was raised by the defendants' fourth point, which was as follows: "If McHugh died of heart disease, and defendants had no reason to believe that he was so sick that his removal from the house would cause his death, they cannot be held responsible in this action, even though the mere incident of his removal from the house may have in some degree contributed to bring it on at that time." This was refused. It could not have been affirmed without qualification; but its refusal, without more, left the jury without any rule whatever upon the subject. The question which the defendants were bound to consider before putting the decedent out in the storm was not whether such exposure "would surely cause death, but what was it reasonable to suppose might follow such a sudden exposure of the decedent in the condition in which he then was. What were the probable consequences of pushing a sick man, in the condition the decedent was in, out into the storm, without adequate covering, and, when he fell, from inability to stand on his feet, leaving him to lie in the stream of melting ice and snow that ran over the pavement of the alley for about a half hour in all, in the condition in which Officer White found him? The third question was raised by the defendants' first point. No evidence was given tending to show the earning powers or the habits of industry and thrift of the deceased. For this reason the court was asked to instruct the jury that "nothing more than nominal damages can be recovered in this action." This was refused, and the jury was told in the general charge that, as the evidence fixed his age, and gave information about his health and habits, they might from this data estimate his earning capacity, and the pecuniary loss of the plaintiff. Now, it is true, as said in Railroad Co. v. Keller, 67 Pa. St. 300, that since the acts of 1851 and 1855 life has a value which the law will recognize, and which the survivors who are entitled to sue may recover at law. It is true that this value is to be fixed by the jury in view of all the circumstances, and it is not necessarily limited to what is known as "nominal damages." But it is also true that when the probable earnings of the deceased are to be taken into account in fixing the damages it is the duty of the plaintiff to show the earning power of the deceased, or give such evidence in regard to his business, business habits, and past earnings, as may afford some basis from which earning capacity may be fairly estimated. The true measure of damages is the pecuniary loss suffered, without any solatium for mental suffering or grief; and the pecuniary loss is what the deceased would probably have earned by his labor, physical or intellectual, in his business or profession, if the injury that caused death had not befallen him, and which would have gone to the support of his family. In fixing this amount consideration should be given to the age of the deceased, his health, his ability and disposition to labor, his habits of living, and his expenditures. It is very clear that the refusal of the first and fourth points without explanation left the jury without any adequate instruction on the important questions to which these point related. The consequence was a verdict based on earning power of the deceased, which the learned judge felt constrained to reduce, and without some evidence from which the calculation of the pecuniary loss of the plaintiff may be made. The judgment is reversed, and a venire facias de novo awarded.

MORNINGSTAR v. LAFAYETTE HOTEL
211 N.Y. 465, 105 N.E. 656 (1914).

CARDOZO, J. The plaintiff was a guest at the Lafayette Hotel in the city of Buffalo. He seems to have wearied of the hotel fare, and his yearning for variety has provoked this lawsuit. He went forth and purchased some spareribs, which he presented to the hotel chef with a request that they be cooked for him and brought to his room. This was done, but with the welcome viands there came the unwelcome addition of a bill or check for $1, which he was asked to sign. He refused to do so, claiming that the charge was excessive. That evening he dined at the café, and was again asked to sign for the extra service, and again declined. The following morning, Sunday, when he presented himself at the breakfast table, he was told that he would not be served. This announcement was made publicly, in the hearing of other guests. He remained at the hotel till Tuesday, taking his meals elsewhere, and he then left. The trial judge left it to the jury to say whether the charge was a reasonable one, instructing them that, if it was, the defendant had a right to refuse to serve the plaintiff further, and that, if it was not, the refusal was wrongful. In this, there was no error. An innkeeper is not required to entertain a guest who has refused to pay a lawful charge. Whether the charge in controversy was excessive was a question for the jury.

The plaintiff says, however, that there was error in the admission of evidence which vitiates the verdict. In this we think that he is right. He alleged in his complaint that the defendant's conduct had injured his reputation. He offered no proof on that point but the defendant took advantage of the averment to prove what the plaintiff's reputation was. A number of hotel proprietors were called as witnesses by the defendant and under objection were allowed to prove that, in their respective hotels, the plaintiff's reputation was that of a chronic faultfinder. Some of them were permitted to say that the plaintiff was known as a "kicker." Others were permitted to say that his reputation was bad, not in respect of any moral qualities, but as the guest of a hotel. The trial judge charged the jury that they must find for the defendant if they concluded that the plaintiff had suffered no damage, and this evidence was received to show that he had suffered none. It is impossible to justify the ruling. The plaintiff, if wrongfully ejected from the café, was entitled to recover damages for injury to his feelings as a result of the humiliation; but his reputation as a faultfinder was certainly not at issue. The damages recoverable for such a wrong were so less because the occupants of other hotels were of the opinion that he complained too freely. In substance, it has been held that the plaintiff might be refused damages for the insult of being put out of a public dining room because other innkeepers considered him an undesirable guest.

It is no concern of ours that the controversy at the root of this lawsuit may seem to be trivial. That fact supplies, indeed, the greater reason why the jury should not have been misled into the belief that justice might therefore be denied to the suitor. To enforce one's rights when they are violated is never a legal wrong, and may often be a moral duty. It happens in many instances that the violation passes with no effort to redress it—sometimes from praiseworthy forbearance, sometimes from weakness, sometimes from mere inertia. But the law, which creates a right, can certainly not concede that an insistence upon its enforcement is evidence of a wrong. A great jurist, Rudolf von Ihering, in his "Struggle for Law," ascribes the development of law itself to the persistence in human nature of the impulse to resent aggression, and maintains the thesis that the individual owes the duty to himself and to society never to permit a legal right to be wantonly infringed. There has been criticism of Ihering's view, due largely, it may be, to the failure to take note of the limitations that accompany it; but it has at least its germ of truth. The plaintiff chose to resist a wrong which, if it may seem trivial to some, must have seemed substantial to him; and his readiness to stand upon his rights should not have been proved to his disparagement.

The judgment must be reversed, and a new trial granted, with costs to abide the event.

WILLARD BARTLETT, C. J., and WERNER, HISCOCK, CHASE, CUDDE-BACK, and MILLER, JJ., concur.

Judgment reversed, etc.

THE OPPOSITE SEX

The dramatic day of the house detective who discovers the unregistered female in a hotel room at night and takes action to correct that situation has taken its place in history. That is not to say that an innkeeper does not have the power and duty to maintain a decent level of morality at the inn.

But the *methods* of doing so must be carried out in a different manner. The law books are full of cases in which innkeepers have been held liable for damages to guests whose moral conduct came into question. Many of these cases involved married couples who met at an inn at a late hour, with one arriving late, intending to check in in the morning. Yet, the right to question the female nonguest remains. A case illustrates:

RAIDER v. DIXIE INN
248 S.W. 229 (Kentucky 1923)

SAMPSON, C. J. Appellant, Thelma Raider, applied to the Dixie Inn, at Richmond, for entertainment, and paid her board and lodging for a week in advance, saying that her home was in Estill county and she had come to Richmond, at the expense of her mother, to take treatments from a physician. At the end of the week she paid in advance for another week, and so on until the end of a month, when she went down town, and on returning was informed by the proprietor and his wife, who are appellees in this case, that she no longer had a room at that hotel, and remarked to her that no explanation was due her as to why they had requested or forced her removal. Alleging that she was mortified and humiliated by the words and conduct of the proprietors of the hotel, appellant, Raider, brought this action to recover damages in the sum of $5,000. Appellees answered, and denied the averments of the petition in so far as such averments set forth harsh or improper conduct on the part of the proprietors of the hotel, but admitted that they had required appellant to vacate her room and to leave the hotel, and gave as their reason for so doing that she was a woman of bad character, recently an inmate of a house of prostitution in the city of Richmond, and had been such for many years next before she came to the Inn, and was in said city a notoriously immoral character, but that appellees did not know her when she applied for entertainment at their hotel, but immediately upon learning who she was and her manner of life had moved her belongings out of the room intó the lobby of the hotel, and kindly, quietly, and respectfully asked her to leave: that they had in their hotel several ladies of good reputation who were embarrassed by the presence of appellant in the hotel and who declined to associate with her and were about to withdraw from the hotel if she continued to lodge there; that appellant had not been of good behavior since she had become a patron of the hotel. Appellant moved to strike certain of the affirmative averments from the answer, but, without waiving this motion, filed an amended petition in which she set forth substantially the same facts which she had in her original petition, adding the following paragraph:

"Plaintiff says that she is advised that these defendants (the Dixie Inn) had a legal right to remove her, and that she does not question that right, but that she was removed as a guest for hire from said Dixie Inn at a time that was improper and in a manner that was unduly disrespectful and insulting, and that she was greatly mortified and humiliated thereby, and suffered indignity because of the wrongful manner in which she was removed from said Dixie Inn as herein set out and complained of."

To the petition as amended the appellees demurred generally. This the court sustained, and, on the failure of appellant to further plead, dismissed her petition, and she appeals.

As a general rule a guest who has been admitted to an inn may afterwards be excluded therefrom by the innkeeper if the guest refuse to pay his bill, or if he becomes obnoxious to the guests by his own fault, is a person of general bad reputation, or has ceased to be a traveler by becoming a resident.

It appears, therefore, fully settled that an innkeeper may lawfully refuse to entertain objectionable characters, if to do so is calculated to injure his business or to place himself, business, or guests in a hazardous, uncomfortable, or dangerous situation. The innkeeper need not accept any one as a guest who is calculated to and will injure his business. State v. Steele, 106 N.C. 766, 11 S. E.

478, 8 L. R. A. 516, 19 Am. St. Rep. 573. A prize fighter who has been guilty of law breaking may be excluded. Nelson v. Boldt (C. C.) 180 Fed. 779. Neither is an innkeeper required to entertain a card shark (Watkins v. Cope, 84 N. J. Law, 143, 86 Atl. 545); a thief (Markham v. Brown, 8 N. H. 523, 31 Am. Dec. 209); persons of bad reputation or those who are under suspicion (Goodenow v. Travis, 3 Johns. [N. Y.] 427; State v. Steele, supra); drunken and disorderly persons (Atwater v. Sawyer, 76 Me. 539, 49 Am. Rep. 634); one who commits a trespass by breaking in the door (Goodenow v. Travis, supra); one who is filthy or who subjects the guests to annoyance (Pidgeon v. Legge, 5 Week. Rep. 649; see Morningstar v. Hotel Co., 211 N. Y. 465, 105 N. E. 656, 52 L. R. A. [N. S.] 740, and the notes thereto attached).

It therefore appears that the managers of the Dixie Inn had the right to exclude appellant from their hotel upon several grounds without becoming liable therefor, unless the means employed to remove her were unlawful. The petition admits as much by its averment saying:

"She [appellant] is advised that these defendants [appellees] had a legal right to remove her, and that she did not question that right."

It being conceded that appellees had the right to remove appellant from the hotel, the only remaining question is: Did they do so in a proper manner, or did they employ unlawful means to exclude her? The averments of the petition show she was not present at the time they took charge of her room and placed her belongings in the lobby of the hotel, where they were easily accessible to her; that when she came in they quietly told her that they had taken charge of her room, but gave no reason for doing so. We must believe from the averments of the petition that very little was said, and that the whole proceeding was very quiet and orderly. As they had a right to exclude her from the hotel, they were guilty of no wrong in telling her so, even though there were other persons present in the lobby at the time they gave her such information, which is denied.

The averments of the petition as amended "that appellees removed appellant from the hotel in an improper manner and were unduly disrespectful and insulting" are mere conclusions of the pleader, and are not supported by the statement of facts found elsewhere in the petition.

The petition as amended did not state a cause of action in favor of appellant against appellees, and the trial court properly sustained a general demurrer thereto.

Judgment affirmed.

LOCK OUTS

In resort areas, it is common for rooms to be rented on a term basis. At the end of that term, another will be expecting to be granted occupancy. This is usual along the Delaware and Maryland shore line in the summer months. A guest who overstays can be ejected. However, physical force should be avoided. The most common procedure is to lock-out the first guest after all other means have been tried. As a matter of law, the lock-out is in order under these conditions, since the status of the guest would terminate automatically at the end of the agreed period. The fury of a locked-out former guest is however, akin to the woman scorned. It should be avoided if possible.

CRIMINAL SANCTIONS

In the following lock-out case, a court permitted recovery as a matter of criminal law—and not for breach of contract or tort.

PERRINE v. PAULOS
224 P. 2d 41 (1950).

DRAPEAU, Justice.

Two young women were evicted by defendants from a hotel in Los Angeles. Returning from work one evening, they found padlocks on their rooms. They could not get to. any of their personal belongings or clothing. They could not find other accommodations, and had to sleep in their automobiles for three nights. Then on demand of their counsel they were permitted to again occupy their rooms.

The case was tried by the court, with judgment for plaintiffs for $500 each general damages; and $500 more each, exemplary damages.

Defendants argue that there was no relationship of landlord and tenant between the parties, that plaintiffs were merely lodgers; that the proof fails to establish that the manager of the hotel had authority to evict them; that, assuming the agent was so empowered no exemplary damages can be imposed; that, in any event, exemplary damages may not be assessed, because the defendants believed they were acting in accordance with their rights; that plaintiffs failed to minimize their damages; that the complaint presented but one issue, breach of duty by a landlord to a tenant, and did not plead breach of duty by an innkeeper to a guest; and that it was error for the court to permit testimony as to statements of the manager of the hotel of her employment by one of the defendants.

While the complaint may not be a model of pleading, it states a cause of action predicated on the duty of an innkeeper to his guest. It alleges that defendants were owners of the hotel; that plaintiffs were tenants on a weekly basis; and that they were unlawfully evicted.

With reference to the question of evidence: Several witnesses testified that one of the defendants stated she owned the hotel, and that title to it was in the other defendant "for convenience." This testimony, together with the presence of the manager in the hotel, and the admitted fact that the manager padlocked plaintiffs' rooms, collected the rents, and took care of the place, was sufficient to support the judgment. No prejudice to defendants is apparent from the admission of the questioned testimony.

All the rest of defendants' objections are disposed of by the record. Applying elementary rules on appeal relative to the effect and value of evidence, the evidence supports the findings of the trial court.

The evidence establishes without contradiction that defendants owned the hotel and that plaintiffs were guests.

At common law innkeepers were under a duty to furnish accommodations to all persons in the absence of some reasonable grounds. Sections 51 and 52 of the Civil Code declare the rule in this State.

Whether a person is a guest or a boarder at an inn is a question of fact to be determined from the evidence.

An innkeeper who refuses accommodations without just cause is not only liable in damages, but is guilty of a misdemeanor.

Is such cases exemplary damages may be assessed.

In this case no showing whatever was made by defendants in excuse or in justification of their treatment of plaintiffs. They just locked them out.

The judgment is affirmed, and the appeal from the order denying motion for a new trial is dismissed.

WHITE, P. J., and DORAN, J., concur.

Hearing denied; SHENK and EDMONDS, JJ., dissenting.

EJECTION OF NONGUESTS

In this case, a nonguest was requested to leave the lobby of a hotel.

JENKINS v. KENTUCKY HOTEL
261 Ky. 419, 87 S.W. 2d 951 (1935).

STITES, Justice.

Appellant, Ellen Jenkins, brought this action against the appellee, Kentucky Hotel, Inc., to recover damages for an alleged assault claimed to have arisen from a request of the house detective, about 9 o'clock in the evening of June 21, 1934, that she leave the lobby of the hotel. Upon the trial of the case, the court peremptorily instructed the jury to find a verdict for the appellee at the close of the testimony for the appellant. On the night in question, appellant says that she went to the Kentucky Hotel for the purpose of meeting her brother and sister-in-law, who where attending a meeting then in progress on the fourth floor of the hotel. She inquired of the clerk if the meeting was still going on, and, on being told that it was, she took a seat in the lobby, at a place near the elevators, where she could see who came down. While thus seated, the house detective approached her and asked what she was doing there. She told him the object and purpose of her visit, and she says that the detective told her, in a rude and insulting manner, that no such meeting as she claimed was being held in the hotel, and ordered her to leave the premises. She says that his manner and demeanor were so menacing and threatening that she believed that unless she followed his instructions he would use force bodily to evict her. Rather than be subjected to physical force, she says she left the premises and went out into the rain, where she remained for some minutes, and later came back into the hotel and went up to the meeting on the fourth floor, where she joined her brother and sister-in-law.

It is admitted that appellant was at most a mere licensee, and that if she had been requested in a proper manner to leave the lobby and had failed to do so, reasonable force could lawfully have been used to eject her. It is contended, however, that the rude and insulting manner accompanying the request to leave was an assault. With this we cannot agree. Howsoever culpable may have been the words or attitude of the detective, there was no unlawful offer of injury by force, and nothing, so far as the evidence discloses, from which a reasonable person might anticipate the exercise of more force than the law permitted. This court has approved the following definition: "An assault is an unlawful offer of corporeal injury to another by force, or force unlawfully directed toward the person of another, under such circumstances as create a well-founded fear of immediate peril." Smith v. Gowdy, 196 Ky. 281, 244 S. W. 678, 679, 29 A. L. R. 1353. The words used by the detective, as recited by appellant, contained no offer of force whatever, either lawful or unlawful. While his manner, according to appellant, was rude and highly objectionable, it was nothing more. He had the right to eject appellant if she refused to leave as requested. Bad manners are not actionable. However unfortunate this affair may have been, from the standpoint of both appellant and appellee, there was nothing in the acts or conduct complained of that constituted an assault. There was no breach of any legal duty owed to appellant.

Judgment affirmed.

INNKEEPERS' LIEN

One of the rights of an innkeeper is the right to claim a lien upon the property of guests for the room and other charges. This right existed at common law but today is provided by statute in most states. These statutes set forth the procedures that must be followed to enforce the lien. Before enforcing the innkeepers lien, legal advice should be sought.

RIGHTS OF GUESTS

The word "right" is a noun and taken in an obstruct sense, refers to ". . . justice, ethical correctness, or consonance with the rules of law or the principles of morals. In this signification it answers to one meaning of the Latin 'jus', and serves to indicate law in the abstract, considered as the foundation of all rights or the complex of underlying moral principles which impart the character of justice to all positive law, or give it an ethical content."[1]

Taken in a concrete sense, a right is ". . . a power, privilege, facility, or demand, inherent in one person and incident upon another."[2]

Constitutional law provides us with four basic rights. These can be classified as personal, natural, political and civil. Our primary concern is with the latter.

CIVIL RIGHTS

These are rights ". . . as belong to every citizen of the state or country, or, in a wider sense, to all its inhabitants, and are not connected with the organization or administration of government. They include the rights of property, marriage, protection of laws, freedom of contract, trial by jury . . ." and others.[3] "Or, as otherwise defined, civil rights are rights appertaining to a person in virtue of his citizenship in a state or community. Rights capable of being enforced or redressed in a civil action. Also a term applied to certain rights secured to citizens of the United States by the thirteenth and fourteenth amendments to the constitution, and by various acts of congress made in pursuance thereof."[4]

Following is section 201, Title II of the Civil Rights Act of 1964:

Section 201. *Establishments Covered*

(a) All persons shall be entitled to the full and equal enjoyment of the goods, services, facilities, privileges, advantages, and accommodations of any place of public accommodation, as defined in this section, without discrimination or segregation on the ground of race, color, religion, or national origin.

(b) Each of the following establishments which serves the public is a place of public accommodation within the meaning of this title if its operations affect commerce, or if discrimination or segregation by it is supported by State action:

(1) any inn, hotel, motel, or other establishment which provides lodging to transient guests, other than an establishment located within a building which contains not more than five rooms for rent or hire and which is actually occupied by the proprietor of such establishment as his residence;

(2) any restaurant, cafeteria, lunchroom, lunch counter, soda fountain, or other facility principally engaged in selling food for consumption on the premises, including, but not limited to, any such facility located on the premises of any retail establishment; or any gasoline station;

(3) any motion picture house, theater, concert hall, sports arena, stadium or other place of exhibition or entertainment; and

(4) any establishment (A) (i) which is physically located within the premises of any establishment otherwise covered by this subsection, or (ii) within the premises of which is physically located any such covered establishment, and (B) which holds itself out as serving patrons of such covered establishment.

(c) The operations of an establishment affect commerce within the meaning of this title if (1) it is one of the establishments described in paragraph (1) of subsection (b); (2) in the case of an establishment described in paragraph (2) of subsection (b), it serves or offers to serve interstate travellers, or a substantial portion of the food which it serves, or gasoline or other products which it sells, has moved in commerce; (3) in the case of an establishment described in paragraph (3) of subsection (b), it customarily presents films, performances, athletic teams, exhibitions, or other sources of entertainment which move in commerce; and (4) in the case of an establishment described in paragraph (4) of subsection (b), it is physically located within the premises of, or there is physically located within its premises, an establishment the operations of which affect commerce within the meaning of this subsection. For the purposes of this section, "commerce" means travel, trade, traffic, commerce, transportation, or communication among the several States, or between the District of Columbia and any State, or between any foreign country or any territory or possession and any State or the District of Columbia, or between points in the same State but through any other State or the District of Columbia or a foreign country.

(d) Discrimination or segregation by an establishment is supported by State action within the meaning of this title if such discrimination or segregation (1) is carried on under color of any law, statute, ordinance, or regulation; or (2) is carried on under color of any custom or usage required or enforced by officials of the State or political subdivision thereof; or (3) is required by action of the State or political subdivision thereof.

(e) The provisions of this title shall not apply to private club or other establishment not in fact open to the public, except to the extent that the facilities of such establishment are made available to the customers or patrons of an establishment within the scope of subsection (b).

In the recent past, those races other than caucasian were not provided inn or restaurant accommodations. They had to do without.

TODAY

Today, because of federal and state laws, the question has become academic at best. It is a clear duty of those in the travel and lodging industry to provide accommodations on an equal basis without discrimination of any sort—with one exception: sex. But even this is changing with the times.

Title II nullifies all laws that are inconsistent with it. A classic example of such prior laws is the South Carolina ordinance discussed in *Peterson v. Greenville*.

PETERSON ET AL. v. CITY OF GREENVILLE

373 U.S. 244 (1962).

Mr. CHIEF JUSTICE WARREN delivered the opinion of the Court.

The petitioners were convicted in the Recorder's Court of the City of Greenville, South Carolina, for violating the trespass statute of that State. Each was sentenced to pay a fine of $100 or in lieu thereof to serve 30 days in jail. An appeal to the Greenville County Court was dismissed, and the Supreme Court of South Carolina affirmed. 239 S. C. 298, 122 S. E. 2d 826. We granted certiorari to consider the substantial federal questions presented by the record. 370 U. S. 935.

The 10 petitioners are Negro boys and girls who, on August 9, 1960, entered the S. H. Kress store in Greenville and seated themselves at the lunch counter for the purpose, as they testified, of being served. When the Kress manager observed the petitioners sitting at the counter, he "had one of [his] . . . employees call the Police Department and turn the lights off and state the lunch counter was closed." A captain of police and two other officers responded by proceeding to the store in a patrol car where they were met by other policemen and two state agents who had preceded them there. In the presence of the police and the state agents, the manager "announced that the lunch counter was being closed and would everyone leave" the area. The petitioners, who had been sitting at the counter for five minutes, remained seated and were promptly arrested. The boys were searched, and both boys and girls were taken to police headquarters.

The manager of the store did not request the police to arrest petitioners; he asked them to leave because integrated service was "contrary to local customs" of segregation at lunch counters and in violation of the following Greenville City ordinance requiring separation of the races in restaurants:

"It shall be unlawful for any person owning, managing or controlling any hotel, restaurant, cafe, eating house, boarding-house or similar establishment to furnish meals to white persons and colored persons in the same room, or at the same table, or at the same counter; provided, however, that meals may be served to white persons and colored persons in the same room where separate facilities are furnished. Separate facilities shall be interpreted to mean:

"(a) Separate eating utensils and separate dishes for the the serving of food all of which shall be distinctly marked by some appropriate color scheme or otherwise;

"(b) Separate tables, counters or booths;

"(c) A distance of at least thirty-five feet shall be maintained between the area where white and colored persons are served;

"(d) The area referred to in subsection (c) above shall not be vacant but shall be occupied by the usual display counters and merchandise found in a business concern of a similar nature;

"(e) A separate facility shall be maintained and used for the cleaning of eating utensils and dishes furnished the two races." Code of Greenville, 1953, as amended in 1958, § 31-8.

The manager and the police conceded that the petitioners were clean, well dressed, unoffensive in conduct, and that they sat quietly at the counter which was designed to accommodate 59 persons. The manager described his establishment as a national chain store of 15 or 20 departments, selling over 10,000 items. He stated that the general public was invited to do business at the store and that the patronage of Negroes was solicited in all departments of the store other than the lunch counter.

Petitioners maintain that South Carolina has denied them rights of free speech, both because their activity was protected by the First and Fourteenth Amendments and because the trespass statute did not require a showing that the Kress manager gave them notice of his authority when he asked them to leave. Petitioners also assert that they have been deprived of the equal protection of the laws secured to them against state action by the Fourteenth Amendment. We need decide only the last of the questions thus raised.

The evidence in this case establishes beyond doubt that the Kress management's decisions to exclude petitioners from the lunch counter was made because they were Negroes. It cannot be disputed that under our decisions "private conduct abridging individual rights does no violence to the Equal Protecttion Clause unless to some significant extent the State in any of its manifestations has been found to have become involved in it."

It cannot be denied that here the City of Greenville, an agency of the State, has provided by its ordinance that the decision as to whether a restaurant facility is to be operated on a desegregated basis is to be reserved to it. When the State has commanded a particular result, it has saved to itself the power to determine that result and thereby "to a significant extent" has "become involved" in it, and, in fact, has removed that decision from the sphere of private choice. It has thus effectively determined that a person owning, managing or controlling an eating place is left with no choice of his own but must segregate his white and Negro patrons. The Kress management, in deciding to exclude Negroes, did precisely what the city law required.

Consequently these convictions cannot stand, even assuming, as respondent contends, that the manager would have acted as he did independently of the existence of the ordinance. The State will not be heard to make this contention in support of the convictions. For the convictions had the effect, which the State cannot deny, of enforcing the ordinance passed by the City of Greenville, the agency of the State. When a state agency passes a law compelling persons to discriminate against other persons because of race, and the State's criminal processes are employed in a way which enforces the discrimination mandated by that law, such a palpable violation of the Fourteenth Amendment cannot be saved by attempting to separate the mental urges of the discriminators.

Reversed.

The case that upheld the constitutionality of Title II was *Atlanta Motel v. United States.* This case is set out in full in Appendix C.

QUESTIONS

1. What practical matters should be considered in deciding to move a guest to a new room?
2. Name three instances when an innkeeper can lawfully enter the room of a guest without notice.
3. In the *McHugh* case, might the hotel personnel have been acting in good faith? Was there any negligence on the part of the police officer?
4. Under what conditions would the "lock-out" be considered?
5. What are the rights of innkeepers in keeping non-guests out of lobbies?
6. What is the "innkeepers lien"?
7. Define "civil rights."
8. T. or F. Civil rights were ignored by our courts for a relatively long period of time.
9. Does the Civil Rights Act of 1964 apply to private clubs? Why?
10. What might be one explanation for the length and detail of the *Atlanta Motel* case as set out in Appendix C?

ENDNOTES

1. *Black's Law Dictionary*, 4th Edition.
2. Id
3. *Winnett v. Adams*, 71 Neb. 817, 99 N.W. 681.
4. *State v. Powers* 51 N.L. 432, 17 A. 969.

19

Property of Guests and Third Parties

At common law, an innkeeper was responsible for the loss of money or goods (property) of the guest, unless the loss was caused by "default of the traveler himself, the act of God, or the Queen's enemies." Thus an innkeeper, much like a common carrier, became the insurer of the goods of guests. Further, liability extended to damage to the goods as well as physical harm to the guests themselves.

These rules of the common law were based upon realities of another age and were grounded in fairness to the traveler. One traveling on horseback for long distances was in a constant position of peril. This was especially so if one lost his means of transportation, or had clothing stolen. One on such a journey who lost his or her belongings could have been literally stranded. As time passed and we entered the age of rapid transportation, the need for the traveler to be safeguarded faded and has reached a point where the need is not nearly as great. Yet remnants of the common law remain.

During the transition referred to, it became obvious that the common law rules were too harsh to be applied in modern times. The movement to provide relief for innkeepers from these rules began slowly, yet noticeably, in the last century. Innkeepers began to use "rules of the house" and contract disclaimers to provide themselves with some measure of relief. The legislatures of England and the states in turn, responded with statutes designed to limit the liability of innkeepers. In this chapter we will be concerned with the loss of property of guests and nonguests—other than automobiles. The latter topic will be discussed in the next chapter.

LIMITATIONS ON LIABILITY

The liability of the modern innkeeper may be limited in three principal ways: 1) by the rules of the inn; 2) by the use of contract disclaimers, and 3) by statutory law.

RULES OF THE INN

An innkeeper is free to develop and place into use reasonable rules to be followed by guests in the inn. Once a guest has notice of such rules, he must obey them. If he fails to do so, and if loss results, then the guest is negligent because of the failure to observe the rules and recovery is barred. However, an innkeeper cannot use such rules to avoid duties imposed by law, such as the duty to receive, the duty to be careful and the duty to be responsible for the loss of the goods of a guest caused by the negligence of the innkeeper.

A common rule found in all inns is that valuables must be deposited at the front desk if the innkeeper is to be responsible for them. If a guest has notice of such a rule, failure to abide by it would relieve the innkeeper of liability for loss. Such rules apply to excessive amounts of cash or jewelry when not being carried by the guest. They would *not* apply to clothes and other items that a guest constantly uses, such as a wrist watch.

NOTICE OF RULES

The notice of such rules must be in a form that a reasonable person could understand. Some examples of these rules would be a sign prohibiting glass at pool-side; notices in parking lots that cars must be locked; the posting of hours on game rooms; or a notice that hats and coats must be checked at the check room. Guests are expected to observe such rules. Failure to do so would be treated as contributory negligence if loss results to the guest.

CONTRACTS TO LIMIT LIABILITY

While an innkeeper may set reasonable rules, the courts frown upon attempts by innkeepers to limit liability by use of contract provisions. In an Oklahoma case, a guest checked baggage at a hotel checkroom and was given a receipt. On the reverse of the receipt were the following words:

> In consideration of the receipt and free storage . . . for which this check is issued, it is agreed . . . that the hotel shall not be liable for loss or damage to said property unless caused by the negligence of the hotel in which event only the hotel shall be liable for a sum not to exceed $25.00. The hotel shall not in any event be liable for loss or damage to said property by fire, theft or moth, whether caused by its own negligence or otherwise.

Following a loss, the hotel appealed the verdict that had been favorable to the guest. The court held that "such alleged contractual limitations . . . in this jurisdiction are contrary to public policy and void."[1]

In many instances, an innkeeper becomes the *bailee* of the goods of a guest. Backing up the Oklahoma case is the general rule of law that a bailee cannot limit his or her liability for negligence that results in the loss of property of the bailor-guest. (A bailee is not liable for loss *that is not his or her own fault* since a bailee is not an insurer of the bailed goods). The *Hallman* case illustrates.

HALLMAN v. FEDERAL PARKING SERVICES
134 A. 2d 382 (1957)

ROVER, Chief Judge.

From an adverse ruling in the trial court appellant brings this appeal to recover the value of personal property removed from his automobile by theft while he was a guest at the New Colonial Hotel.

The facts as developed by the evidence disclosed that on the evening of November 8, 1956, appellant with his wife and daughter stopped for a night's lodging at the hotel, in the course of their journey to Florida. When registering with the desk clerk, appellant asked if the hotel had parking facilities and was assured that the vehicle would be taken care of by the bellboy. The desk clerk testified that it was normal procedure in the hotel for the bellboy to ask an arriving guest if he wanted his car parked. The bellboy would then get a claim check from the hotel, supplied it by appellee parking lot, if the guest desired this service.

The baggage necessary for the use of the parties during their brief stay was transferred to appellant's room and the automobile was delivered for the night by the bellboy to an open parking lot independently managed and controlled by appellee Federal Parking Services, Incorporated. There the automobile was turned over to an attendant who locked it and retained the keys. At the time the vehicle was taken to the lot, it contained pieces of luggage on the rear seat and floor, wearing apparel hung on racks, and the usual items of traveling paraphernalia, some of which had been placed under a seat. On the bellboy's return to the hotel, he gave appellant a claim check bearing the name of the parking lot and the stamped name "New Colonial." The claim check contained a printed notice limiting liability which provided that the parking lot was not responsible for loss due to theft and articles in vehicles were left at the Owner's risk.

The following morning when appellant arrived at the lot for his automobile, he discovered the side window broken. The glove compartment had been forced open and emptied and personal property, including that placed under the seat, valued at approximately $557 had been removed.

From these facts the court concluded as a matter of law (1) that there was no contract of bailment between the hotel and appellant; (2) that the doctrine of *infra hospitium* was inapplicable; and (3) that while a contract of bailment existed between the parking lot and appellant, there was no showing that it failed to exercise the degree of care required. We are unable to agree with these conclusions in whole.

We need not resolve the arrangement between the hotel and the parking lot as to whether the hotel was the agent of the parking lot or vice versa as the paucity of evidence on this point would permit a purely conjectural solution at most. We pass them to a consideration of the relationship existing between appellant and both the hotel and the parking lot and the degrees of liability, if any, to be imposed.

Appellant argues that once the property of a guest is taken into the custody and control of the innkeeper the goods are considered *infra hospitium* and the liability for loss or destruction of the goods imposed is that of an insurer, unless the property is lost or destroyed by an act of God, the public enemy, or by fault of the guest. This is undoubtedly the rule of common law having its source in the ancient case of Calye[2] which dealt with the innkeeper's liability for the loss of a guest's horse put to pasture. The common-law rule is of force in this jurisdiction.[3] The doctrine of *infra hospitium* has been applied in cases where a car or its contents are lost while in the exclusive care and cutody of a hotel.[4] However, where the hotel takes custody of the vehicle, as here, and delivers it to a lot or garage not an integral part of the hotel and thereafter a loss of the property occurs, the better rule imposes the liability of a bailee for hire on the hotel.[5] As such it is required to exercise an ordinary degree of care to protect and return the property of which it assumes custody.

The trial court, sitting without a jury, found as a fact that appellant was informed that the lot was open and that it was not a part of the hotel. We have searched the record thoroughly and concluded that this finding is without evidential support. We find only the undisputed evidence that the hotel as a policy offered its guests parking facilities and informed appellant it would take care of his car. Where a trial court's finding is entirely unsupported by evidence, an appellate court may disregard it. Nolan v. Werth, 79 U.S.App.D.C. 33, 142 F.2d 9.

We conclude that when the bellboy, with actual authority of the hotel to deliver automobiles to the lot, took possession of the keys and the vehicle, both the vehicle and the contents of the automobile were accepted by the hotel into its custody. It had physical control and the intent to control the property; a bailment relationship was therefore created. Accordingly, the trial court's conclusion that there was no contract of bailment between the hotel and appellant was erroneous. That payment for parking was made to the lot and not the hotel is immaterial for the service was incident to this type of a business and a hotel, particularly in a metropolitan area, derives indirect benefits and profits by providing such facilities.

Turning to the hotel's acceptance of the property in the vehicle, appellant and his family were in transit stopping only for the night. They could reasonably be expected to leave luggage, wearing apparel, and other personal belongings in the car not necessary for their night's lodging. Courts have uniformly held that the liability of a bailee for hire for the loss of property in an automobile depends on notice or knowledge of the contents. The notice need not be actual or express; constructive or implied notice may be inferred.[6] Clearly the hotel was put on notice that appellant was a traveler and the apparel hanging from racks was in plain view. Upon entering the car the luggage on the floor and rear seat could easily be seen, and common knowledge and experience could anticipate that the car might contain in its interior other articles normally carried by travelers. On this point appellees rely on Lucas v. Auto City Parking Co., D.C.Mun.App., 62 A.2d 557. That case is distinguishable in that the property there was not in plain view and the claimed acceptance of the goods was based largely on custom which this court held to be of a unilateral nature.

Finally, as to the parking lot, we conclude that there was no privity between appellee lot and appellant. The evidence does not show that the original contract of bailment contemplated a sub-bailment. It neither shows that appellant by express or implied authority authorized a sub-bailment, nor that there was a ratification on his part of a sub-bailment.

This court has often held that whether the bailor's action is based on contract or negligence, proof of delivery and failure of the bailee to return the property make out a prima facie case of liability. The burden of proceeding with evidence shifts to the bailee to explain or justify the loss, or to introduce evidence showing that the loss or damage did not result from want of that degree of care the bailment required.[7]

In substance the evidence in this case simply disclosed that the hotel held itself out to appellant as providing parking facilities for his car. In reliance on the information of the desk clerk the car with most of its contents in plain view was entrusted to the hotel for safekeeping. The vehicle with its property was accepted by the hotel through its bellboy, who by actual authority and hotel practice was empowered to accept it. While the claim check given appellant contained both the names of the hotel and lot, appellant could have reasonably inferred that his car with its contents was still in the care and custody of the hotel.

The bulk of the defense evidence consisted of an attempt to show appellant's contributory negligence in leaving the property in the car and an attempt to show that the lot had exercised due care. We have previously discussed and disposed of the first point. A review of the evidence reveals that no explanation or justification is offered by the hotel for its failure to redeliver the property other than the fact of theft. Some evidence other than the mere allegation of theft is necessary before the burden of proving the bailee's negligence is shifted back to the bailor. The hotel has neither offered proof sufficient in weight and quality to show the loss was not connected with the lack of proper care on its part, nor has it offered any affirmative proof that it exercised the ordinary degree of care required in order to refute the inference of the prima facie case and prevent recovery.

We therefore reverse the judgment of the lower court and remand the case for a determination of the reasonable value of the lost property and the costs of repairs to the automobile, and for entry of judgment for the appellant in such sum against the hotel. In so doing, we are mindful that the court has many times ruled that the printed notice of limitation of liability on the claim check is not binding unless the terms are known to the bailor.[8] The complete absence of testimony as to knowledge of the limitation and agreement to it makes any contention of limited liability untenable.

Reversed with instructions.

By far, the most effective limitations on the liability of inn-keepers is found in statutory laws created to expressly limit that liability.

STATUTORY LIMITATIONS

An examination of various modern state statutes, allows us to arrive at a conclusion: the legislatures felt that the common law liability was no longer realistic. And perhaps as one considers the changes that have taken place in the means of travel and the facilities available, such a conclusion is justified. In addition, these laws create classes of property for guests. Typical are 1) money and valuables, 2) property in transit to and from the inn, 3) property destroyed by fire and 4) all other property of the guests.

MONEY AND VALUABLES

The typical state statute allows an innkeeper to maintain a safe for the deposit of money and valuables. Once a guest is given notice that the safe is available, failure to deposit such items relieves the innkeeper of liability for loss of those items. In addition, the statutes permit the innkeeper to refuse to accept money or valuables above the statutory limit. The innkeeper *may* accept the risk and will then be held liable for the full amount if loss occurs.

TYPICAL NOTICE

The notice is given by placing a copy of the state statute on the back of each unit door and at other places within the confines of the inn. This notice is accompanied by a listing of the rates per day for that particular room (see page 65 for a sample). Most states require that the notice be in the exact words of the statute. Failure to post can result in forfeitures of all charges made by the guests, and, under some statutes, forfeiture of a multiple of those charges, three times being typical.

Such notices have been observed at front doors, in elevators, lobbies and at dining room entrances. Since travelers seem to like to take these notices as souvenirs, they must be replaced on a continuing basis.

EXAMPLES

In Virginia, no innkeeper is liable for loss of baggage or personal property in excess of three hundred dollars. And no innkeeper shall be liable for the loss of jewelry or other valuables if notice is given that they must be deposited in the hotel safe, nor is the innkeeper obliged to accept valuables in excess of five hundred dollars.[9] If locks are provided and notice is given, no liability shall attach if the guest fails to lock the room.[10] Liability in case of fire or similar disaster is limited to two hundred and fifty dollars per guest.[11]

In West Virginia, the statute provides that the liability for loss of property shall be limited to two hundred and fifty dollars. And no liability shall attach to the loss of jewelry or other valuables if notice requiring that such valuables be deposited in the hotel safe is given, unless such valuables are lost after being deposited.[12]

The fact that the guest was intoxicated and was careless with his money, exhibiting it freely and refusing to give it to the innkeeper, or that his door was unlocked, does not establish negligence on the part of the guest so as to relieve the innkeeper from liability for loss caused by theft *by one of his employees*.[13] When merchandise was stolen from an automobile in a parking lot it was held that the use of a parking lot by guests was included in the room rental, and when the innkeeper knew that a guest had left valuable goods stored in his automobile the innkeeper was liable for such loss.[14]

If a guest of a hotel has notice of a requirement that he should deposit his money and jewelry at the office or be personally responsible for its safety, his failure to make such a deposit is negligence, barring a recovery for a loss of such property by theft from his room.[15] But such deposit made on several previous occasions, and the presence of a printed notice of such requirement not shown to have been brought to his attention, are not conclusive evidence of such knowledge. A finding of a jury against it cannot be disturbed by the court.[16]

LOSS BY FIRE

The statutes that limit liability for loss by fire, or loss by other means, are all similar to the money and valuables statutes. A limit is placed on liability unless it appears that the loss was caused by the fault or negligence of the innkeeper. In the case of stored baggage, a double limit on liability is often encountered. If a guest who checks baggage with the innkeepers fails to state a value, the limit on liability is set by statute at a set figure such as $100. If a value *is* declared, the limit on liability is set at another figure such as $500. The statutes that place limits on liability for fire require that the innkeeper be without fault or negligence.

GOODS IN TRANSIT

The statutes that limit liability for the loss of property of a guest while in transit, follow the minimum value declared—maximum pattern, much as stored baggage provisions.

The statutes presuppose that the loss was *not* caused by the negligence of the innkeeper. If it was, the liability would extend to the full value of the goods and not to the statutory limitation. To illustrate, A leaves a valuable watch at a front desk. The watch is sealed in an envelope and locked in a safety deposit drawer. A fire breaks out at the inn and the innkeeper removes the watch intending to protect it from the fire, but then negligently loses it. The liability extends to the full value of the watch. If the watch had remained in the safe and had been destroyed, the statutory limitation would have applied.

Another distinction is found when deposited property is stolen by the innkeeper or by an employee. In the former, liability for the full value would attach. In the latter, the statutory limitation would control. In these illustrations, we are assuming that the value of the deposited property *had not been declared*. If it had been, the innkeeper had the right to refuse the risk. But if the risk had been accepted, the statutory limitation would not apply.

The statutes that limit liability extended originally only to those goods deposited with the innkeeper. Thus an innkeeper could use the statute as a defense to the loss of goods left at the front desk, but not those stolen from a room or hallway. The statutes have been amended to extend to the "confines" of the inn—"infra hospitium."

PROPERTY OF GUESTS

At what point does the responsibility of the innkeeper begin to protect and safeguard the property of guests? Legal rights and duties will depend upon the facts and the timing.

TO ILLUSTRATE

A calls Holidex X, and asks that the motel courtesy car call for him and his baggage at the airport. The driver fails to load a suitcase at the airport and it is subsequently stolen. A checks into the motel and discovers the loss. The innkeeper's duty began at the airport. If the guest decided not to check in, then the innkeeper may escape liability for the lost suitcase. In the latter instance the driver of the courtesy car may be held liabile.

The problems often caused by the transportation of the goods of a potential guest has prompted some states to enact statutes that limit liability for loss of such goods while in transit. In New York, for example, the limit on liability is $500.[17]

GUEST RESPONSIBILITY

There are times when loss of property becomes the sole responsibility of a guest. Three examples will illustrate. (1) The guest gives particular instructions which are followed by the innkeeper or his or her agents or employees. A says, "park my car beside the inn and leave the door unlocked and the keys over the visor." If the car is stolen, the loss falls on the guest. (2) A roommate of a guest steals money from that guest. The innkeeper is not liable. (3) A guest authorizes someone outside of the inn to handle his or her goods. The guest is responsible if that person damages, steals or loses the goods. A guest can incur personal responsibility in another manner.

CONTRIBUTORY NEGLIGENCE

"Negligence" has been defined as ". . . the failure to use such reasonable care and caution as would be expected of a reasonable man."[18] Negligence can result in liability to an innkeeper for loss of both guests and bailors property, but not so if the guests or bailors are guilty of *contributory negligence.*

DEFINED

"Contributory negligence" is ". . . the act or omission amounting to want of ordinary care on part of complaining party, which concurring with (the innkeepers') negligence, is the proximate cause of (the loss) . . ."[19] When goods of a guest are lost, contributory negligence will bar recovery from the innkeeper. It has been traditional to allow a jury to determine if contributory negligence was present. It would be a question of fact—not law.

The burden of proving that an innkeeper was negligent is on the guest. The burden of proving the contributory negligence of the guest is on the innkeeper. But both must be the "proximate cause of the loss." If a guest is negligent, but the innkeeper could have avoided the effect of that negligence, the innkeeper is then liable for his or her negligence. This legal process can be summed up as follows: If the innkeeper is negligent, the guest must prove this in order to recover. If a guest is negligent, the innkeeper must prove this to bar recovery. If the negligence of the guest is *not* the proximate cause of the loss, then the innkeeper is responsible for his or her negligence. To illustrate, a guest leaves valuables lying by the TV in a motel room. This is negligence. The guest is in the process of checking out and an employee of the inn places the valuables in the hall beside the door. This is also negligence. The valuables are now stolen. The negligence of the guest was *not* the proximate cause of the loss so the innkeeper is liable. If the valuables had been stolen from the room, the negligence of the guest would be a good defense to the innkeeper. If the employee had removed the valuables and deposited them at the front desk, liability would have been avoided. However, if this had happened and *then* the goods were lost, the innkeeper would be liable.

STOLEN PROPERTY

An ancient rule of innkeeping was that an innkeeper was responsible for the loss of the goods of a guest that were stolen by others, during those periods of time in which the guest-innkeeper relationship was in being. This duty began when the relationship started and ended when it ended. The rule was a direct outgrowth of the basic purpose of innkeeping—to provide shelter, entertainment and safety for travelers. It logically followed that if one must safeguard the *person* of the traveler when a guest, then the *property* of the traveler must also be safeguarded. The rule is in effect today except as modified by statutory law as we have seen.

While some legal writers have felt that this responsibility of the innkeeper rested upon the law of bailment, it does not in most cases. A bailment requires delivery of goods from a bailor to the bailee. In most motel operations for example, there is *seldom* a delivery of goods to an innkeeper. Rather the guest retains possession, taking the goods to the room to be used there. Therefore the responsibility of the innkeeper rests upon the ancient principles of innkeeping and not upon the principles of bailment.

It should be observed however, that an innkeeper *may become a bailee* of property of a guest as well as property of those who are not guests, if the facts disclose such relationships. As mentioned previously, an innkeeper cannot limit his or her liability for negligence as a bailee.

LOST PROPERTY

In some states, innkeepers are held to be virtual insurers of the safety of the property of guests. The mere loss of the goods raises a presumption of fault on the part of the innkeeper. This presumption can be overcome, however, by proof that the loss was due to an act of God, the public enemy in time of war, or negligence or fraud of the guest. Otherwise the innkeeper is responsible.

This responsibility was held by the courts to be necessary by reason of public policy, and is quite similar to the duties imposed on common carriers.

In a lesser number of states, the courts permit an innkeeper to offer proof that such loss was not his or her fault. If there is such satisfactory proof, the innkeeper is not responsibile for the loss.

But regardless of which view is followed in any particular state, an innkeeper should be aware of the necessity of protecting and safeguarding the property of guests. Some techniques in use include providing temporary storage areas for the goods of guests who are checking in; making available suitable carts so guests can check in in one trip, and the use of personnel to oversee baggage as a guest checks out. Tight control is in order.

LEAVING PROPERTY ONLY AT THE INN

In some instances, a traveler will leave baggage or other personal property at an inn. In the years past, it was often a horse. If the traveler does not then register as a guest, but goes elsewhere, is the innkeeper responsible to the owner for such personal property? The test that has been applied over the years has been that of the intention of the traveler. Did the traveler *intend* to become a guest, even if he or she never became one for one reason or another? If the answer is "yes", then guest liability attaches to the innkeeper for the loss of those goods. In *Alder v. Savory Plaza*, one was held to be a guest at one hotel while in fact registered at another!

ALDER v. SAVORY PLAZA, INC.
279 App. Div. 110, 108 N.Y.S. 2d 80 (1951).

PECK, Presiding Justice.

This is an action to recover for the loss of jewelry and personal effects contained in a suitcase which was delivered by plaintiff to defendant for safekeeping. The claimed value of the jewelry was something over $20,000 and the claimed value of the personal effects about $3300.

The jury returned a verdict in plaintiff's favor for $2,000, which the trial court on plaintiff's motion set aside as a compromise. A new trial was ordered. Defendant appeals from the order setting aside the verdict and ordering a new trial and also from the denial of its motion to reduce the verdict to the sum of $100.

The action was defended principally on the ground that plaintiff was a guest of defendant's hotel and defendant was entitled to the benefit of sections 200 and 201 of the General Business Law. Section 200, which exempts a hotel from liability for the loss of jewelry of a guest who fails to deposit such property in the safe provided for the purpose, was set up as a complete defense. Section 201, which limits a hotel keeper's liability to the sum of $100 for the loss of personal property delivered to the hotel for storage elsewhere than in the room assigned to a guest unless at the time of delivery a value in excess of $100 is stated and a written receipt secured, was asserted as a partial defense.

Defendant's contention on this appeal is that the jury's verdict was not plainly a compromise, but was implicit with the justified finding that plaintiff had not delivered her jewelry for deposit in the safe as she was required to do, and defendant was therefore freed from liability on account of the jewelry. Excepting the jewelry, defendant contends the jury was warranted in placing a value of $2,000 on the other personal effects, principally used clothing, which cost $3,300. Defendant maintains that it was error, therefore, for the trial court to set the verdict aside, but also maintains that the verdict should be reduced to $100, which would be the extent of defendant's liability for the clothing under section 201 of the General Business Law.

We must determine upon the facts and the law whether defendant is entitled to the defenses of sections 200 and 201 and whether there was any basis in the evidence and submission of the case to the jury for the jury's verdict.

The facts are as follows: Plaintiff was accustomed to staying at defendant's hotel whenever she visited New York and had been a guest of the hotel many times. She and her husband had requested reservations for May 15, 1946. Upon their arrival at 10 o'clock that morning, they were advised that their reservation was for the following day, but that the hotel would try to accommodate them, so they registered hoping that a room might be assigned during the day. At the same time, they delivered their luggage to the bell captain, and it was deposited in a section of the lobby set aside for the luggage of arriving and departing guests. Plaintiff's husband attended to business during the day while plaintiff was in and out of the hotel. When both returned to the hotel in the afternoon, they found that a room was still not available, so they whiled away some time in the lounge bar and had dinner in the room of a friend who was a guest of the hotel.

All during the day defendant's manager was seeking accommodations for the couple but was unable to locate them in the hotel. He finally secured accommodations for them for the night at the Sherry Netherlands Hotel where they registered at about 8:00 P.M., taking with them two suitcases and and a cosmetic case, and leaving the suitcase with the valuables and two matching cases at defendant's hotel.

Plaintiff testified that before leaving defendant's hotel for the night she told the bellman that she had better do something about her jewelry which was in the large suitcase, suggesting that it would be necessary to take the jewelry out of its leather box and put it into envelopes which the hotel provided for deposit in its safe. Whereupon, according to plaintiff the bellman replied: "It won't be necessary, we will put the whole suitcaes in the vault." The bellman charged with this assurance testified that he had no such conversation with plaintiff.

When plaintiff returned to defendant's hotel the next morning, to take up a residence for two or three weeks, and requested delivery of her luggage, the large suitcase was missing. During the night the suitcase had been delivered by the night manager of the hotel to an impostor. The circumstances of this delivery are not altogether clear as the night manager was deceased at the time of the trial. Whether there was some complicity on the part of one or more of the hotel employees, as plaintiff suggests, we are not called upon to surmise. It is quite apparent that defendant was negligent, probably grossly negligent, and if the case could be determined simply on a question of negligence, plaintiff would be entitled to recover the amount of her loss.

Unquestionably defendant had given due notice to its guests of the availability of a safe for the deposit of their valuables. If plaintiff was a guest of the hotel, she was bound by the notice so given and obliged to deliver her jewelry to the office for deposit in the safe, or suffer the peril of its loss. That is, unless defendant waived compliance with the statute. The questions as to the jewelry, therefore, where whether plaintiff was a guest of the hotel and whether defendant had waived compliance with the statute.

Any issue as to whether plaintiff was a guest (and it may be noted that in her first cause of action plaintiff alleges that she was a guest and in her second cause of action for the same recovery omits that allegation) was not submitted to the jury in such a way that it is possible to determine whether the jury passed upon or even considered the question. We are prepared to rule, however, as matter of law on the admitted facts, that plaintiff was a guest.

It was, therefore, required of plaintiff, if she wished to give her jewelry hotel protection, to deliver it or at least tender it to the defendant for deposit in its safe. Both as a matter of experience and sense, plaintiff knew that this should be done, and according to her testimony she had the foresight to suggest that such a deposit be made. It was only upon the alleged assurance of the bellman that the entire suitcase would be placed in the vault that she was satisfied.

There may be a question of the bellman's authority or apparent authority under the circumstances, which we do not consider on this appeal. That question will remain for the court or jury on the next trial. Assuming, however, that plaintiff would be justified in relying on the bellman's assurance, the factual question is whether such assurance was given with a consequent waiver of the provisions of section 200 of the General Business Law.

While it is defendnat's contention that the jury could have found, and that the verdict should be interpreted as a finding, that defendant was entitled to the protection of section 200, we are utterly unable to say or guess whether that was the jury's view or whether the question even entered into their consideration. There was no clear submission of the question to the jury and their attention certainly was not focussed on the question. Nor were they told what facts or considerations would bear upon their decision of such a question.

One factual issue which would have to be put to the jury before the court would know their finding, or either could pass on the applicability of section 200, is whether or not plaintiff had the conversation she testified to having with the bellman. If she did not have such conversation, there could be no purported compliance on her part with section 200 or waiver of its protection by defendant. Without that issue being submitted to the jury, we are unable to parse the verdict or give it the interpretation which defendant contends for. The verdict was, therefore, properly set aside.

We will make only one further observation for the guidance of the court on the new trial, and that is in connection with the applicability of section 201 of the General Business Law to the lost property other than jewelry. Plaintiff being a guest, section 201 applies. No value in excess of $100 having been stated or written receipt secured, defendant's liability for the value of the suitcase and its contents, other than the jewelry, was limited to $100. Negligence or even gross negligence on the part of defendnat is no consideration in this connection.

The order appealed from setting the verdict aside and ordering a new trial should be affirmed, with costs.

Order affirmed with costs to respondent.

GLENNON and SHIENTAG, JJ., concur.

COHN and CALLAHAN, JJ., dissent.

COHN, J., dissents in the following memorandum:

I dissent and concur in the result reached by CALLAHAN, J., upon the ground that the jury could properly find, under the court's charge, that the relationship of guest and innkeeper did not exist insofar as this transaction was concerned and that the jury had the right to render a verdict in favor of the plaintiff in the sum of $2,000.

CALLAHAN, J., dissents and votes to reverse and reinstate the verdict, in opinion.

GOODS FROM THIRD PARTIES

The courts have held that the innkeepers liability extends to the goods of a guest that were delivered to the inn by a third party, when it is the practice to receive such goods. Of course, an innkeeper could refuse to accept such goods and would thus not be responsible for them.

Related to this is a situation where goods are left with the innkeeper by a guest, *that in fact belong to a nonguest third party.* In such instances, a true bailment would exist and the innkeeper would be held responsible for the *full value* of such goods that were later lost. The innkeeper could not use as a defense any statute that limited liability. *Such statutes only apply to the property of guests.*

As a variation of this, what if a third party leaves goods at an inn on consignment to a guest? The guest decides not to purchase the property and leaves it with the innkeeper. The third party is to pick it up later, but it is lost in the meantime. Is the innkeeper's liability limited to the duty owed to the guest—or is it unlimited as a bailee to the third party?

The courts have stated that the test would have to be determined by the extent of the knowledge conveyed to the innkeeper. If the innkeeper knew that the goods were those of the third party and not that of the guest, bailment liability would attach. Otherwise only innkeepers liability would attach.

BANQUETS AND OTHER ACTIVITIES

Innkeepers cater to clubs, meetings and all types of organizations and provide meeting rooms and banquet facilities for these purposes.

If those who attend a meeting or a banquet are also registered at the inn, it is clear that they are guests while at the banquet.

If they are "locals" and attend a banquet, they would not be guests. The distinction is important in the case of lost property. If they are guests, the innkeepers statutory liability limits would be applicable. If not, the innkeeper may be responsible for the entire loss as a bailee, or perhaps not at all. In the *Ross* case, the innkeeper was held liable as a bailee for property loss because of the negligence of an agent of the innkeeper.

ROSS v. KIRKEBY HOTELS
160 N.Y.S. 2d 978 (1957)

HOFSTADTER, Justice.

The plaintiffs, husband and wife, recovered below against the defendant, the operator of the Hotel Warwick, in the City of New York, the full value of their luggage and wearing apparel stolen from the husband's automobile. The plaintiffs were to be married at the Warwick on the day of the theft, the arrangements for the ceremony and the reception to follow at the hotel having been made by the bride's mother. The husband, accompanied by his brother, arrived at the hotel in his car the morning of his wedding day.

The trial court was justified in finding on disputed evidence that the car was placed in the care of the hotel doorman, with specific instructions to park it in the hotel garage, so that nothing would go wrong; that the doorman undertook to do so, and told the plaintiff husband to leave the keys in the ignition switch. As the husband entered the hotel with his brother, he saw the doorman drive the automobile away. At the time the value of the car and its contents was not stated, nor was a written receipt of any kind issued by the defendant. Later in the day, when the husband came out of the hotel to arrange for the delivery of his car, he found it in the street and discovered that it had been broken into and that all its contents were missing. The doorman admitted that he had not placed the car in a garage, but had parked it across the street from the hotel.

It is undisputed that the plaintiffs did not register as guests of the hotel, that no room was assigned to them, and that the sole purpose of their visit was to participate in the wedding ceremony and reception.

The delivery of the car to the defendant's doorman to be placed in a garage, in the circumstances stated, constituted a bailment, Galowitz v. Magner, 208 App.Div. 6, 203 N.Y.S. 421, and parking the car on the street instead was a violation of the terms of the bailment, which of itself imposed liability on the defendant irrespective of negligence, Mortimer v. Otto, 206 N.Y. 89, 99 N.E. 189. Leaving the car containing the plaintiffs' wardrobe in the street, especially after the explicit instructions that it be placed in a garage, likewise warranted a finding of negligence, because of the defendant's failure to exercise the care imposed on it by law as a bailee.

The defendant urges, however, that the bailment was an incident of the relation of hotel keeper and guest between it and the plaintiffs and that, because of this relation, it is entitled to the limitation of liability prescribed by section 201 of the General Business Law. This section, so far as here material, provides:

"No hotel keeper except as provided in the foregoing section shall be liable for damage to or loss of wearing apparel or other personal property in the room or rooms assigned to a guest for any sum exceeding the sum of five hundred dollars, unless it shall appear that such loss occurred through the fault or negligence of such keeper, nor shall he be liable in any sum exceeding the sum of one hundred dollars for the loss of or damage to any such property when delivered to such keeper for storage or safe keeping in the store room, baggage room or other place elsewhere than in the room or rooms assigned to such guest, unless at the time of delivering the same for storage or safe keeping such value in excess of one hundred dollars shall be stated and a written receipt, stating such value, shall be issued by such keeper, but in no event shall such keeper be liable beyond five hundred dollars, unless it shall appear that such loss occurred through his fault or negligence, * * *."

Though the plaintiffs' loss is found to have occurred through the defendant's fault or negligence, the impact of the section must nevertheless be considered, for when, as here, no value is stated at the time of the guest's delivery of the property to the hotel keeper, the statutory limitation becomes applicable, notwithstanding the hotel keeper's negligence, Honig v. Riley, 244 N.Y. 105, 155 N.E. 65; Adler v. Savoy Plaza, Inc., 279 App.Div. 110, 115, 117, 108 N.Y.S.2d 80, 84, 86. It, therefore, becomes necessary to determine whether the plaintiffs were guests of the hotel within the purview of section 201.

It is to be noted that section 201 refers at several points to "the room or rooms assigned" to the guest. Thus, the assignment of a room to be occupied is stressed as an element of the relation. The court is aware of the cases relied on by the appellant, in which the relation of hotel keeper and guest has been held to arise before the actual assignmnet of a room, Adler v. Savoy Plaza, Inc., 279 App.Div. 110, 108 N.Y.S.2d 80 or to carry over the limitation after the guest no longer occupies his room, Dilkes v. Hotel Sheraton, Inc., 282 App.Div. 488, 125 N.Y.S.2d 38. In those cases, however, the occupancy of a room was either in definite contemplation or had already occurred, so that the acceptance of the plaintiff's property for safekeeping could fairly be treated as something done in the course of the usual relation between hotel and guest.

This vital element of the relation is totally absent in the case at bar. The plaintiffs did not seek or receive lodging at the defendant's hotel. As stated, they came solely to attend the marriage function. They did not request that a room be assigned to them and neither they nor the defendant at any time had in mind their occupancy of a room. Their presence in the hotel for a purpose other than that of becoming guests did not make them guests within the language or intent of section 201 of the General Business Law, dealing with the relation of hotel keeper and guest in its traditional sense. It follows that the defendant is not entitled to the benefit of the limitation of liability and that the plaintiffs were correctly permitted to recover the full value of their property.

Judgment affirmed, with $25 costs.

STEUER and AURELIO, JJ., concur.

TENANTS

It is not uncommon for certain persons to take up residence at a hotel or motel for an extended period or time, such as six months.

That person loses the classification of "guest" and becomes a tenant, or "lodger" or "boarder." When this happens, the liability of the innkeeper changes. Since the person is no longer a "traveler", the innkeeper does not face the liability protection that the law extends to the traveler.

An innkeeper is *not* liable for loss of goods of a tenant, provided the loss is not caused by the negligence or carelessness of the innkeeper.

For example, if one occupying a motel room for 90 days has goods stolen from that room, the innkeeper is not liable unless it can be shown that there was negligence on the part of the innkeeper or his or her agents or employees. The innkeepers relation to a tenant is akin to that of a bailee to a bailor.

BAILMENT

If a tenant leaves goods with an innkeeper for safekeeping, the innkeeper holds those goods as a bailee—and not as an innkeeper. This means that if the goods are stolen, the tenant cannot recover from the innkeeper, unless the tenant can prove negligence. In addition the tenant must be able to prove freedom from contributory negligence on his or her part.

A bailee must use ordinary, reasonable care with bailed property, but a bailee is *not* an insurer of the goods.

GRATUITOUS BAILEE

In many instances, an innkeeper receives goods of a tenant and makes no charge for holding them. "The obligations of . . . (a) gratuitous bailee are commonly described as involving the exercise of slight care and as being violated where there has been gross negligence. The distinction between 'slight' and reasonable care and between 'ordinary' negligence and 'gross' negligence is often shadowy and unsatisfactory. But the courts, however fortunate or otherwise they may have been in expressing that distinction, do recognize that it exists. . . . A depositor of goods or securities for safekeeping with a gratuitous bailee can only claim that diligence which a person of common sense, not a specialist or expert in a particular department could exercise in such department."[20]

Thus we see an important distinction in the degree of liability between an innkeeper and guest, and an innkeeper and a tenant.

EXCUSES FROM LIABILITY

Finally, an innkeeper is not responsible for loss of any sort, caused by acts of God, "or acts of the public enemy". "Acts of God" include rain, storms, earthquakes, lightning and freezing weather. All of these occur without the intervention of a "human agency." The "public enemy" would include loss caused by an armed invasion or bombing by an enemy. An armed robber would *not* be a "public enemy" in the sense in which those words are used at law. It must be some power with which our government is in war or open controversy.

QUESTIONS

1. T. or F. "Rules of the Inn" could be used to allow an innkeeper to escape all statutory but no common law liability.
2. How do the courts view efforts of innkeepers to limit liability by the use of disclaimers?
3. Sketch a rough-draft disclaimer to absolve an innkeeper from pool-side liability. How would a court view this?
4. What is the responsibility of a bailee when goods are stolen while in the bailee's hands?
5. What does "privity" mean as an old-time contract doctrine?
6. Statutory limitations on innkeepers liability tends to protect whom—the guest or innkeeper? Or do these statutes protect both?
7. What might happen if a statutory notice limiting liability is properly posted and then stolen?
8. What is the legal effect of contributory negligence on the part of a guest who loses property?
9. Explain how the "confines of the inn" might be extended for some distance from the inn by judicial interpretation.
10. What does "proximate cause" mean and what is its importance in an innkeeper-guest, lost property situation?

ENDNOTES

1. *Oklahoma City Hotel v. Levine* 189 Okla. 331, 116 P.2d 997 (1941)
2. Calye's Case, 8 Co.Rep. 32a, 77 Reprint 520.
3. Sections 34-101 and 34-102, Code 1951, have limited application and relate to certain classes of property. These provisions are not relevant to the case under consideration.
4. Park-O-Tell Co. v. Roskamp, 203 Okl. 493, 223 P.2d 375, liability imposes by statute declaratory of the common law; Merchants Fire Assur.

Corp. of New York v. Zion's Sec. Corp., 109 Utah 13, 163 P.2d 319.

5. Campbell v. Portsmouth Hotel Co., 91 N.H. 390, 20 A.2d 644, 135 A.L.R.
1196; Kallish v. Meyer Hotel Co., 182 Tenn. 29, 184 S.W.2d 45, 156
A.L.R. 231; Smith v. Robinson, Tex.Civ.App., 300 S.W. 651. Cf. Bidlake
v. Shirley Hotel Company, 133 Colo. 166, 292 P.2d 749; Zurich Fire Ins.
Co. of New York v. Weil, Ky., 259 S.W.2d 54; Lader v. Warsher, 165 Misc.
559, 1 N.Y.S.2d 160; Weisman v. Holley Hotel Co., 128 W.Va. 476, 37
S.E.2d 94. See Annotation, 156 A.L.R. 233.

6. Campbell v. Portsmouth Hotel Co., supra; Mee v. Sley System Garages,
Inc. 124 Pa. Super. 230, 188 A. 626; Barnette v. Casey, 124 W.Va. 143, 19
S.E.2d 621. See Annotation, 27 A.L.R.2d 796.

7. Shea v. Fridley, D.C.Mun.App., 123 A.2d 358; Smith's Transfer & Storage
Co. v. Murphy, D.C.Mun.App., 115 A.2d 300; National Mortgage & Inv.
Corp. v. Shulman, D.C.Mun.App., 104 A.2d 420.

8. Manning v. Lamb, D.C.Mun.App., 89 A. 2d 882; Lucas v. Auto City
Parking Co., supra; Palace Laundry Dry Cleaning Co. v. Cole, D.C.Mun.
App., 41 A.2d 231.

9. Sec. 1602, Michie's Va. Code (1942); sec. 35-10, Code of Virginia (1950).

10. Sec. 1603, Michie's Va. Code (1942); sec. 3511. Code of Virginia (1950).

11. Sec. 1604, Michie's Va. Code (1942); sec. 35-12, Code of Virginia (1950).

12. Sec. 1366, Michie's W. Va. Code (1943).

13. *Cunningham v. Bucky*, 42 W. Va. 671, 26 S.E. 442, 57 Am. St. Rep. 876,
35 L.R.A. 850.

14. *Weisman v. Holley Hotel Co.*, 128 W.Va. 476, 37 S.E. 2d 94.

15. *Nesben v. Jackson*, 89 W.Va. 470, 109 S.E. 489.

16. *Nesben v. Jackson*, supra.

17. General Business Law, N.Y. Section 203 (a) and (b).

18. *Hamrick v. McCutcheon*. 101 W.Va. 485, 133 S.E. 127, 129.

19. *Honaker v. Crutchfield*. 247 Ky. 495, 57 S.W. 2d 502.

20. *Dalton v. Hamilton Hotel*. 152 N.E. 268 (1926).

Liability for the Automobiles of Guests

An innkeeper has traditionally been held to strict liability for the loss of the guests means of transportation, once such transportation is brought within the "confines of the inn." The old cases were, of course, concerned with horses and carriages.[1] If loss resulted from the negligence of the owner of the transportation however, then liability *did not* extend to the innkeeper. Also, innkeepers were excused from such liability by "acts of God," such as storms, floods, wind and lightning. So we see that while an innkeeper was liable for loss to a guest's means of transportation, he was not an "insurer" of such property.

These early principles have been brought down to us today and apply to automobiles, buses, vans, motorcycles and even helicopters that are within the confines of an inn and owned by a guest of that inn. A "guest", as we have seen, would be one who meets the "transient" test and not one living at an inn on a permanent or a semipermanent basis. The early cases extended the definition of "confines of an inn" to include not only "in house" parking areas, but adjacent parking areas. In an early case, a field near an inn was held to be "within the confines" when the innkeeper placed a traveler's horse there to pasture, and the horse subsequently vanished.[2]

LOSS v. DAMAGE

The degree of liability extended because of loss, has not been applied when there has been mere damage to goods, rather than complete loss. In the latter, most states require some showing of negligence on the part of the innkeeper before recovery may be permitted. However, some states apply the same standard of liability for damaged goods as they do for loss.

PARK-O-TELL CO., v. ROSKAMP
223 P. 2d 375 (1950).

JOHNSON, Justice.

The parties herein occupied reverse positions in the trial court, and they will hereafter be referred to as plaintiff and defendant.

This is an action to recover for loss of an automobile and its contents under innkeepers law.

The plaintiff alleged in his petition that he and his wife registered as guests at the defendant's hotel, known as Park-O-Tell in Oklahoma City on October 15, 1946, that in consideration of the room rent paid defendant furnished a garage in which to park the plaintiff's automobile; that on the afternoon of said day, after registering at the hotel, he turned the custody of his car over to an attendant of the defendant, that plaintiff saw the attendant drive his automobile into the garage and park it; that at the time he turned the car over to the attendant it contained numerous personal belongings of the plaintiff and his wife, a list of which plaintiff attached to his petition; that on October 16 he asked for his car, but defendant failed to deliver the same to plaintiff; that after making search of the garage defendant advised him that the car had been stolen; that the car was of the value of $1,700.00; that the personal property of plaintiff and wife was left in the car placed in custody of defendant was of the value of $935.40; that by reason of the theft of his vehicle he expended $191.00 railroad fare to return home; and prayed judgment for $2,826.40.

Defendant answered denying generally the allegations of the plaintiff's petition, and specifically alleged that it made no charge for parking purposes for the use of said garage and that it makes none to any of its guests; that it took no possession, custody or control of the plaintiff's automobile or any of its contents; that the automobile was not placed in its care or custody; and that it takes no custody of any of the automobiles of its guests, either by servants, agents, employees or otherwise. Defendant further alleged that plaintiff left his keys in his automobile, and was thereby guilty of negligence and that his loss was due to lack of care of plaintiff; and that plaintiff assumed full responsibility of any and all losses.

Upon the issues thus joined, trial was had to a jury. The court instructed the jury that under the facts in the case the defendant was liable to plaintiff and submitted to the jury only the question of the reasonable cash value of the automoble and contents. Verdict was for the plaintiff for $2,500.00, upon which the court rendered judgment accordingly. From this judgment the defendant appeals.

Defendant presents error under two propositions: First, "The innkeepers law does not apply to the automobile or its contents." Second "The question of liability, under proper instructions, should have been submitted to the jury."

It is asserted under proposition one that neither the law of innkeeprs nor the law of bailments applies, and that the only liability, if any, rests upon the law of reasonable care and negligence.

The trial court submitted this case to the jury on the theory that it came within the innkeepers statute, 15 O.S.1941 § 501, which provides: "An innkeeper or keeper of a boarding house is liable for all losses of or injuries to, personal property placed by his guests or boarders under his care, unless occasioned by an irresistible super-human cause, by a public enemy, by the negligence of the owner, or by the act of someone whom he brought into the inn or boarding house, and upon such property the innkeeper or keeper of a boarding house has a lien and a right of detention for the payment of such amount as may be due him for lodging, fare, boarding, or other necessaries by such guest or boarder; and the said lien may be enforced by a sale of the property in the manner prescribed for the sale of pledged property."

That plaintiff was a guest of the hotel is undisputed. It is undisputed that as a guest he turned his car and its contents over to an attendant of the hotel; that this attendant told him that his car and personal property in it would be safe; that the attendant drove his car into the hotel and parked it, leaving the keys in it, as was usually done for the guests; that the next day he asked for his car and that defendant failed to return it; that defendant after making a search advised him that the car had been stolen.

The defendant admits that the Park-O-Tell is a place with a wide, sweeping drive into the center of the hotel, with parking space in the hotel and also space at the back of the hotel, which is enclosed where, when needed, cars of guests are parked; that the parking facilities are advertised as a part of the accommodations furnished to the guests without extra charge. Defendant insists, however, that the hotel did not take possession of the guests' automobiles, but it is undisputed that attendants did take guests' automobiles at the entrance of the hotel, drive them into the hotel and park them, usually leaving the keys in them; that if driven into the hotel by the guest, the guest was instructed where to park; that often it was necessary for the attendants to move the cars from one place to another in the hotel. Defendant to sustain its contention that it did not take or have possession of plaintiff's car suggests that plaintiff retained the right to go and get his automobile or the contents thereof at any time he desired; that plaintiff went into the hotel where his car was parked and took from it some personal items and returned to his room; that by doing so he knew that the keys were left in his car, and when he failed to lock the car and take the keys he was thereby guilty of negligence.

It is asserted by defendant that there was a sharp conflict in the testimony as to the facts under which the automobile was parked, as to whether the automobile and its contents were brought into the hotel, and as to whether or not the property in question was ever placed in the possession of and under the control of the defendant hotel, and as to whether the loss occurred by reason of the negligence of plaintiff. A careful examination of the record does not sustain this assertion. No witness of defendant denied or contradicted the statement of plaintiff as to what happened on the date that he registered at defendant's hotel. One of the attendants testifying as a witness for defendant said that on the date of the loss of the automobile he remembered plaintiff's automobile being parked in the hotel, but did not remember whether or not he talked to plaintiff when the car was brought into the hotel.

A review of the evidence convinces us that the evidence that plaintiff placed his automobile and its contents under defendant's care and that the plaintiff was without negligence is so conclusive that the trial court in the exercise of sound judicial discretion would have beeen compelled to set aside a verdict for the defendant. Under these circumstances the court was justified in its instruction taking from the jury the question of liability and leaving to it the question of damages.

Under the common-law rule an innkeeper, although not negligent, was liable for loss of property of a guest unless the guest was guilty of negligence or the loss was occasioned by an act of God or the public enemy.

This court in Abercrombie v. Edwards, 62 Okl. 54, 161 P. 1084, with reference to the innkeepers statute of Oklahoma, sec. 501, supra, in the fourth syllabus said: "The provision of this statute that the innkeeper is liable for goods of his guests, 'placed under his care,' is declaratory of the common law, not restrictive thereof. Under such provisoin it is not necessary, in order to render the innkeeper liable for their loss, that the goods be placed under his special care, or that notice be given of their arrival. It is sufficient if they are brought into the inn in the usual and ordinary way and are not retained under the exclusive control of the guest, but are under the general and implied control of the innkeeper."

The term "property" as used in this statute, it being declaratory of the common law, is broad enough to cover an automobile and its contents. 43 C.J.S., Innkeepers, § 16.

The trial court in overruling motion for a new trial appropriately stated the issues and law in this case as follows:

"The legal question presented on the trial and on the motion is novel and no case in point on the facts has been found. * * *

"The material facts were undisputed, the Court instructed the jury to find for the plaintiff under the innkeeper statute (O.S. 1941, 15-501), instructed them on the measure of damages (O.S.1941, 12-590), and a verdict was returned for the value of the car, and personal property left in it at the time it was parked with the defendant.

"The defendant contends that its liability, if any, is that of bailee as to the car, and in no event is defendant liable under the facts, for its contents.

"The defendant was an innkeeper and the plaintiff was a guest, when the loss occurred. All the facts and circumstances, including defendant's name, point to the fact that it was an inn having, and holding itself out to the public as providing the facilities peculiar to an inn catering to transients traveling in private automobiles with their baggage and other accessories of travel. The conveniences offered to such travelers by an inn of this nature are well known. Emphasis is placed, as shown by the evidence, on the 'parking' feature, that is, the guest is relieved as a primary part of the services offered, of the burden and necessity of securing a safe parking, that is storage, place for his car and its contents. That latter are not usually all necessary for the enjoyment of the food and lodging provided for a temporary stay in an inn and the storing of the car with contents in it is a decided convenience, and one which was furnished by the defendant.

"The offer of the defendant made to the public was accepted by the plaintiff. It was the intent of the parties that the defendant was furnishing and the plaintiff paying for the above mentioned service. The car and its contents, therefore, were personal property placed under the care of the defendant under the innkeeper statute."

Defendant's proposition two that the question of liability, under proper instructions, should have been submitted to the jury is without merit.

The material facts being undisputed, the loss of plaintiff's property, and the relationship of innkeeper and guest as between defendant and the plaintiff being established, and there being no evidence of negligence of plaintiff, the question of legal liability under the innkeepers law was properly determined by the court, and it was not error under the facts in this case to instruct the jury to return a verdict for the plaintiff.

In this connection it is noted that the trial court in instruction number one said: "In this case the court is of the opinion that under the law you should be instructed to return a verdict for the plaintiff, thus, the sole and only question for your determination will be the amount of damages. * * *"

In addition the court gave the other usual stock instructions, but defendant complains only as to failure to instruct as to legal liability and the negligence of plaintiff.

In view of what has been said, we deem further discussion unnecessary. The judgment is affirmed.

WELCH, CORN, LUTTRELL and HALLEY, JJ., concur.

GIBSON and O'NEAL, JJ., dissent.

BAILMENT

In almost any instance where one's vehicle is parked on in-house lots, a "bailment" exists. In a bailment, goods are left by the "bailor" with the "bailee" who is to return the goods at some point. In the typical auto-bailment, the keys are taken and a receipt issued for later reclamation purposes. In bailment situations, one must prove fault on the part of the bailee before recovery can be had for damages if loss results.

Thus we see that a guest's means of transportation may fall both within the "confines of the inn rule", as well as into the realm of the law of bailments. Recovery for loss and damages have been allowed on both theories.

LOSS OF ITEMS INSIDE VEHICLES

An off-shoot of the problems caused by loss or damage to a guest's means of transportation is found in the theft of goods from *within* those vehicles. An innkeepers responsibility for the goods of a guest *brought into an inn* is quite different than that for goods left in a vehicle. If an innkeeper does not know the goods are in the vehicle, there would probably be no innkeeper's or bailee's liability at all. An example would be diamonds left in a glove compartment and subsequently stolen. This lack of liability would extend to luggage left in a car. While the car may be within the confines of the inn, a court may hold that the luggage is not. If the vehicle is accepted by an attendant, parked, and the keys retained, liability for loss may attach. If the guest self parks the vehicle, it probably would not. If the damages or loss is caused by an agent or employee of the inn, then liability would attach to the inn. The same would be true when the inn uses the services of a parking facility owned by others. The agency relationship with the third party would perpetuate the liability of the inn to the same degree as if the parking lot had been operated by an employee of the inn.

LIMITING LIABILITY

As a general rule, an innkeeper *cannot* limit liabilities that arise out of his various duties. Due to the public nature of his calling, it would be against public policy to do so.

But as to the automobile of a guest, the innkeeper is generally a bailee. In the absense of a statute to the contrary, a bailee can limit liability if it is done properly. The *Rutter* case illustrates.

RUTTER v. PALMER
2 K.B. 87. (1922)

APPEAL from the judgment of Lord Trevethin C.J. on the trial of an action without a jury.

The plaintiff was the owner of a LeGui four-seated motor-car which he had placed in the hands of the defendant, a motor-car dealer who kept a garage at Tooting, for sale on commission either by private treaty or public auction. The car was placed with the defendant on February 7, 1920, on the terms of an agreement in writing which contained the following clauses:—

"Unless you"—i.e., the defendant—"give a receipt for the goods stating the same to have been delivered to you in perfect condition in every respect, you will not be responsible for any damage whatever to the goods whilst in your possession. . . . "

"Customer's cars are driven by your staff at customers' sole risk. . . ."

On February 10, 1920, at about 5:30 P.M. the car was sent out by the defendant in charge of a driver to be shown to a prespective purchaser. It was being driven along Plough Lane, Wimbledon. It was fitted with smooth tyres. The streets were slippery and the car was being driven at an unreasonably fast speed. It skidded along the tram-lines in Plough Lane and came into violent collision with an electric standard belonging to the London United Tramways Co. and the car and the electric standard were both seriously damaged.

The plaintiff claimed 160*l* damages. The defendant denied negligence and pleaded that the car was being driven at the plaintiff's sole risk.

The Lord Chief Justice held that the car was damaged by the negligence of the defendant's driver, and held further that the clause in the contract stipulating that customers' cars were driven at customers' sole risk did not operate to exempt the defendant from liability for the negligence of his driver. He therefore gave judgment for the plaintiff.

The defendant appealed.

Croom-Johnson for the appellant. A bailee may exempt himself from liability for the negligence of his servants. There is no law which forbids him from so doing: *Stewart* v. *London and North Western Ry. Co.* (1); *Lewis* v. *Great Western Ry. Co.* (2); *Travers & Sons* v. *Cooper.* (3) The only question is whether he has used apt words to express the intention. Where his liability is that of a common carrier some skill may be necessary in drafting the exempting clause; but where, as in this case, his liability springs from one source only, for example, from negligence, the same precision is not required and a less elaborate form of words will serve *McCawley* v. *Furness Ry. Co.* (4); *Gibaud* v. *Great Eastern Ry. Co.* (5); *Reynolds* v. *Boston Deep Sea Co.* (6)

In the circumstances of this case the words "at customers' sole risk" can have only one meaning—namely, that the appellant will not be liable for the negligence of his drivers. [He also cited *Cordey* v. *Cardiff Pure Ice Co.* (7)]

(1) (1864) 3 H. & C. 135.	(4) L. R. 8 Q. B. 57.
(2) (1877) 3 Q. B. D. 195.	(5) [1921] 2 K. B. 426, 434.
(3) [1915] 1 K. B. 73.	(6) (1922) 38 Times L. R. 429.

(7) (1903) 88 L. T. 192.

Shakespeare and *Montague Berryman* for the respondent. A bailee who intends to excuse himself from liability for negligence must do so in plain and unambiguous terms. Merely general words will not suffice. In *Price* v. *Union Lighterage Co.* (1) words exempting the defendants "from any loss of or damage to goods which can be covered by insurance" were held not to protect them from the negligence of their servants. In *Travers & Sons* v. *Cooper* (2) the words exempted the defendant from liability "for any damage to goods however caused which can be covered by insurance." Kennedy L.J. said (3): "In the present case . . . . there can be no doubt that the defendant had at least the duty not to be negligent in regard to the carriage of the goods in his lighter, and he was negligent. Is he protected by the terms of the special contract from the consequences of that negligence to the owner of the goods? But for the words 'however caused' I am of opinion that he would not be, and that the decision of this Court in *Price* v. *Union Lighterage Co.* (1) affirming the judgment of Walton J. (4), which is referred to by Pickford J. in his judgment in the present case, would bind us so to hold. In that case, however, there were no such words as 'however caused.' " There are no such words in the present case. *The Pearlmoor* (5) and *James Nelson & Sons* v. *Nelson Line, Ld.* (6), are to the same effect. The distinction relied on by the appellant between the common carrier and the bailee who accepts goods for sale is not borne out by the authorities and was expressly negatived by Phillimore L.J. in *Travers & Sons* v. *Cooper.* (7) The conflict of judicial opinion shows that the words "at customers' sole risk" are not so plain and unambiguous as to relieve the appellant from liability for the negligence of his servants. The clause must be read with some limitation; otherwise it would exempt the appellant from liability if one of his clerks took the car out for his own amusement. It should be read subject to the condition that damage is not caused by the appellant's servants.

Croom-Johnson was not called upon in reply.

BANKS L.J. This appeal raises a question upon the true construction of an owner's risk clause in a garage proprietor's contract. At first sight I thought there was much to be sold in favour of the Lord Chief Justice's decision, supported as it is by a dictum of Kennedy L.J. in *Travers & Sons* v. *Cooper* (1), but further consideration has satisfied me that a contract relating to the driving of a motorcar and the risk therein involved is a contract of a special kind presenting features which distinguish it from a contract of carriage by a railway company or a common carrier. A common carrier is liable for the acts of his servants whether they are negligent or not; an ordinary bailee is not liable for the acts of his servants unless they are negligent. If a common carrier would protect himself from responsibility for all acts of his servants he must use words which will include those acts which are negligent; because words which would suffice to protect him from liability for acts properly done by his servants in the course of their service may fall short of protecting him from their negligent acts. But if an ordinary bailee uses words applicable to the acts of his servants, inasmuch as he is not liable for their acts unless negligent, the words will generally cover negligent acts, although such acts are mentioned, because otherwise the words would have no effect. Moreover it is well known to be the common practice for the owners of motor-cars to insure themselves against all risks in connection with the car, that is to say against damage done not only to the car but by the car, and damage caused not only by negligent acts but by innocent acts as well.

I turn now to the contract; it is a garage proprietor's contract and it contains a number of printed conditions upon which he agrees to receive the goods—in this case a motor-car. One clause is designed to protect the garage proprietor against injury to the car while on his premises. It runs thus: "Unless you give a receipt for the goods stating the same to have been delivered to you in perfect conditon in every respect you will not be responsible for any damage whatever to the goods whilst in your possession." That clause does not apply here; but there is another clause which says: "Customers' cars are driven by your staff at customers' sole risk." The car was taken out by a driver of the appellant to be shown to a prospective purchaser. While it was being so driven it came into collision with a lamp-post, and both the car and the lamp-post were seriously damaged. The Lord Chief Justice found that the accident was caused by negligent driving. In giving judgment for the respondent he remarked that the clause construed literally was wide enough to cover negligent driving by a member of the appellant's clerical staff, and that some limitation must be placed upon its meaning. I agree to this extent, that the words "your staff" must mean "your regular driving staff," and the clause must be read as if it ran: "Customers' cars are driven by your drivers at customers' sole risk." If that is not introduced for the purpose of protecting the garage proprietor from the negligent acts of his driver, it is hard to see what effect it has beyond being a mere statement of the general law. Mr. Shakespeare invited us to read into this clause an exception of damage caused by the driver's negligence. I do not think we could do that, even if it were desirable to do so; but I see no reason for doing it. The clause may well have been inserted in the contract to bring home to the customer that it is for him to insure against accidencts in which the car may be concerned. The principle of the carriers' cases does not apply to bailees of this class, and still less to a bailee of a motor-car for special reasons is unwilling to accept the risk of damage. For these reasons I think the appeal must be allowed.

(1) [1904] 1 K. B. 412.   (4) [1903] 1 K. B. 750.
(2) [1915] 1 K. B. 73.   (5) [1904] P. 286.
(3) [1915] 1 K. B. 93.   (6) [1907] 1 K. B. 769.
           (7) [1915] 1 K. B. 100.

STATUTORY LIMITATIONS IN THE UNITED STATES

All state have statues that limit liability of the innkeeper for loss of the goods of a guest. At the present time, however, these laws are not broad enough to cover automobiles or their contents.

STATUTORY LIMITATIONS

Both England and Nova Scotia have enacted statutes relating to innkeeper's liability for the automobiles and their contents that belong to guests.

The Nova Scotia act (N.S. Laws, c. 28, 1953) reads in part as follows:

8(1) No innkeeper shall be liable for the loss of a vehicle of a guest or of its contents except where the loss occurs when the vehicle is stored or parked in a garage of the inn or in a car park within the precincts of the inn or maintained elsewhere by the innkeeper and where a fee is charged by the innkeeper for the storage or parking or where the innkeeper or his servant accepts the vehicle for handling or safekeeping.

QUESTIONS

1. What policy reason prompted the courts to hold innkeepers responsible for the loss of transportation of guests?
2. Might the "confines of an inn" include a distant parking lot? Under what circumstances?
3. How would you define "reasonable care"? How would this standard be applied in a court?
4. What effect does the negligence of a guest have upon the innkeepers liability for loss of the guests auto?
5. Why would an innkeeper try to claim the status of bailee when an auto is stolen from the inn?
6. Under what conditions may a court take from a jury the question of liability, leaving them to decide only the question of damages?
7. What are the basic rights of a bailor: a bailee?
8. What are the basic duties of a bailor: a bailee?
9. What steps can an innkeeper take in an attempt to limit liability for loss of the auto of a guest?
10. What was the Nova Scotia Legislature attempting to do with the statute, quoted in part, earlier?

ENDNOTES

1. *Hulett v. Swift* 33 N.Y. 571, 88 Am. Dec. 405 (1865).
2. *Cayle's Case*, 8 Coke Rep. 32 (Eng. 1584).

21

Injury to Guests and Others

In this chapter we will examine the principles that become involved when a guest is injured in his or her person, or reputation, as contrasted to the injury to goods of that person. While the law limits the liability of an innkeeper for the loss of injury to *goods* of a guest, here we encounter an area in which there are no limits on liability. Recovery for injuries to a person or one's reputation, is controled (1) by the skill of defense counsel, and (2) reluctance that a jury may have in assessing damages at too high a figure. These are intangibles and one cannot afford to assume that one's counsel will do a good job, or that a jury may be restrained when arriving at a verdict. The opposite is often true. Therefore in *any* business that deals with the public, one must always be "liability conscious" and train employees and agents to feel the same way. This is especially so because of what the law of agency, as we have examined it in Chapter 8, does to the liability of the principal. This topic will be re-examined in Chapter 23, Restaurants and Bars, since the areas of risk there are higher in some ways than in mere innkeeping.

SAFE PREMISES

An innkeeper has a duty to maintain safe premises at all times. Floors, stairways and walkways must be kept clean and free of slippery substances;[1] stairwells must be lighted[2] and elevators must be kept in good repair.[3] Window screens should be adequately fastened[4] and large plate glass spans should be crossed by protective railings. Rooms and furnishings must be inspected constantly to prevent unsafe conditions from occuring, such as loose legs on chairs or unsafe wall mounts on TV sets.[5] Showers must be in good working order to prevent the possibility of scald burns.[6] Baby beds and roll-aways should always be offered in a sanitary, safe condition. Proper vermin control services should be utilized as required.[7]

OUTSIDE OF THE INN

The requirement of furnishing safe premises would extend to the confines of the inn. Walkways must be lighted and kept free of ice and debris. Railings must be provided at elevated portions of walkways, alongside pools, recreation areas and parking lots.

Failure to see that these things are done would be negligence. If injury results from such negligence, a cause of action would exist on the part of the injured guest. Upon a finding of negligence by a jury, and upon proof of loss, the inn could be held liable.

Indeed, if an innkeeper ignores a known dangerous condition, that person may face tort liability as well as prosecution for the criminal wrong. Yet, an innkeeper is *not* an insurer of the safety of guests.

CONTRIBUTORY NEGLIGENCE

An injured guest may be barred from recovery if that person contributed to his or her injury, the same as contributory negligence will bar recovery for loss or damage to goods. In addition, if a guest does an act or takes part in some activity knowing that injury may result, the guest may be barred from recovery because of the "assumption of the risk."

If the proximate cause[8] of the injury is the negligence of the innkeeper or an agent or employee, even if there was contributory negligence or assumption of the risk, the innkeeper may be held liable for the loss sustained. The secret in avoiding liability for injury is to avoid being careless in the operation of the inn. An area in which this is especially true is in the operation and maintenance of swimming pools.

SWIMMING POOLS

For many years, swimming pools at inns were luxuries reserved only for the more affluent resort operations. Today they are common-place and in fact are almost uniformily available.

If one were to devise a way in which guests could be injured in a perpetual fashion, it would be difficult to improve upon the swimming pool. Guests are constantly falling while running, diving into partly filled pools after dark; falling from diving boards; colliding with one another in the water when diving; and in general, maiming and otherwise injuring themselves and others. As strange as it may sound, innkeepers have fared better in swimming pool cases than in other areas of innkeeper's liability.

The cases indicate that one must use reasonable care in maintaining the pool and the surrounding areas. If supervision is provided, it must be adequate. If not, guests should be made aware that the risk is their's alone. The pool and the area around it should be kept free of broken glass. "Roughhousing" should be prohibited and pools should be kept locked after hours.

Otherwise, it is generally accepted that swimming and diving are hazardous activities. Thus when one voluntarily undertakes such activities that person does so at his or her own risk. In spite of this, pool areas should be constantly inspected and properly maintained. While an innkeeper may avoid liability in court, it is much more advantageous to avoid court in the beginning. One should consider a pool as a high risk area and treat it accordingly. If it is beneficial to maintian a pool, then it is mandatory that enough funds be allocated for proper maintenance. For example, what might be the liability of an innkeeper who permits a pool to become unsanitary, which results in serious sickness to those who use it? It must be remembered that the health laws, even though not specifically mentioning swimming pools, would still control. In addition, many states have health laws that *do* regulate swimming pools and so do most larger cities. One must comply with these laws when swimming pools are maintained at the inn.

Next, what is an innkeepers responsibility to protect guests from the employees of the inn as well as from third parties?

PROTECTING FROM EMPLOYEES

Innkeepers have duty to protect guests from the acts of employees and agents that may cause injury. Such injury can result from acts on the part of employees while on or off duty. The duty to protect the guest is a positive one and does not end at the end of the work day of an employee. Employees must be schooled in the necessity of maintaining courteous, safe conduct toward guests at all times, both inside the inn and within the confines of the inn.

Some statutes and case decisions exonerate innkeepers from guest liability for *willful* acts of employees or agents while off duty.

PROTECTING FROM THIRD PERSONS

Innkeepers have a duty to protect guests from injurious acts of third parties. Liability has attached where a patron has become intoxicated and injured a guest.[9] Liability has attached where boistrous banquet patrons have knocked down guests while running in the lobby and while spinning revolving doors. The innkeeper must use reasonable care to control such activities even though, at best, this can be a difficult job. The law does not expect miracles—only that one act as a reasonable innkeeper should under like or similar circumstances.

A particular area of danger is when one, or one's employees or agents, libels or slanders a guest or patron—or as in the *Moricoli* case, a performer at the inn.

MORICOLI v. SCHWARTZ
361 N.E. 2d 74 (1977)

STAMOS, Justice.

Plaintiff, Thomas Lane Moricoli, brought an action to recover damages for slanderous defamation of his character allegedly resulting from certain statements uttered by defendant, James L. Schwartz, and republished by defendant, Barbara T. Reid. Count I of the complaint contained an allegation of slander. Count II prayed for damages allegedly arising from a tortious interference with prospective economic advantage. Count III sought damages allegedly arising from a breach of contract. Plaintiff appeals from that part of an order of the Circuit Cook of Cook County, dated August 8, 1975, as granted defendants' motion to dismiss Count I of plaintiff's complaint for failure to state facts upon which a cause of action may be predicated. The trial court specifically found that the alleged defamatory words upon which the action was predicated are subject to being innocently construed and hence, not actionable.

Plaintiff's complaint alleged *inter alia* that plaintiff is a singer and nightclub entertainer using the name of Tommy Lane for his performances; that he auditioned and contracted with defendant Reid, on behalf of defendant P&S Management, Inc., to appear at two of that corporation's hotels; that on September 16, 1974 at a meeting of the corporation's officers and staff and in the presence of defendant Reid and others, defendant Schwartz maliciously spoke of and concerning plaintiff in the following false and defamatory words: "Tommy Lane is a fag and we don't want any fag working for us."; that defendant Reid, on September 17, 1974, in the presence of plaintiff and others republished the statement of defendant Schwartz in the following false and defamaotry words: "The contract is being cancelled because Mr. Schwartz says Tommy Lane is a fag"; and that thereafter the contract was cancelled. Plaintiff alleges that the aforementioned statements are slanderous *per se* inasmuch as they allege that plaintiff is a homosexual.

According to Webster's Third International Dictionary of the English Language (unabridged ed. 1966), the word "fag" admits of four commonly used meanings:

1

fag / n -s [ME *fagge* flap, knot in cloth]1: FAG END 2: CIGARETTE;

2

fag / vb [obs E *fag* to droop] *vi* 1: to become weary: TIRE, FLAG 2: to work to exhaustion: DRUDGE, TOIL 3a: to be a fag: serve as a fag (*fagging* for older boys during his first year) b: to serve as a fag in the field in British school games; *vt* 1: to compel to serve as a fag 2: to exhause by toil, drudgery or sustained heavy activity—often used with *out* 3: to make (the end of a rope) frayed or untwisted

3

fag / n -s 1: *chiefly British; a fatiguing task; DRUDGERY 2: an English public-school boy who acts as a servant to another boy in a higher form b: MENIAL, DRUDGE, SERVITOR.*

4

fag *or* fag-got / *n* -s [origin unknown] slang: HOMOSEXUAL.

In construing the meaning of the word "fag," we note that Illinois follows the innocent construction rule. That rule holds that the statements in question are to be read as a whole and the words given their natural and obvious meaning, and requires that allegedly defamatory words which are capable of being read innocently must be so read and declared nonactionable as a matter of law. Such words will be given an innocent construction if they are reasonably susceptible of such construction or if the allegedly defamatory matter is ambiguous. Whether language is susceptible of an innocent construction is a question of law for the court, to be resolved by reading the language stripped of innuendo. This doctrine has been held to be applicable to both libel and slander actions.

When the words of the statements uttered in the instant case are given their obvious and natural meaning, we do not see how these words can be given an innocent construction. Although characterized as "slang," the aforementioned published authority indicates that the sole occasion upon which the word "fag" is commonly used in the United States, in the form of a noun and to connote an adult human being, is with reference to a homosexual. To suggest otherwise serves only to further tax the gullibility of the credulous and require this court to espouse a naiveté unwarranted under the circumstances.

Moreover, defendants' reference to plaintiff as a "fag" in conjunction with the assertion that this status served as ground for terminating plaintiff's term of employment may not be characterized as mere objectionable but nonactionable name-calling. At common law words of abuse do not give an action for slander. However, where such words are not reasonably given to various shades of meaning but instead serve to mark their peculiar target as an object of scorn and reproach, they cannot be dismissed as mere terms of general abuse. We conclude that the trial court erred in finding that the statements in question are non-actionable as a matter of law upon application of the innocent construction doc-trine. Therefore, the judgment of the circuit court in this regard must be reversed.

The question with which we are next presented is whether defendants' state-ments are slander *per se*, allowing plaintiff to recover from defendants without allegation or proof of special damages. It is established in Illinois that one of four categories of utterances which are actionable *per se* and do not require proof of special damages is that type of statement which imports commission of a crime. It has been urged that the statements uttered in the case at bar may be fairly categorized as importing the offense of deviate sexual conduct. However, where words do not of themselves import commission of a crime, they may not be so construed by reference to antecedent circumstances or words not part of the language complained of and thus, are not slanderous *per se*. The statements complained of in the instant case do not, of themselves, import commission of a crime in the state of Illinois. Hence, they are not actionable absent allegation and proof of actual damages.

Plaintiff finally urges that this court adopt the view espoused by a noted commentator in the field and approved by a New York court of review. Upon this somewhat novel theory the imputation of homosexuality to an individual of either sex must be construed to constitute a fifth category, actionable without proof of damage. Prosser comments, "Although the question has arisen in only one case, it appears very likely, in view of the popular feeling on the matter, that the imputation of homosexuality to either sex" would be actionable *per se*. We feel that in view of the changing temper of the times such presumed damage to one's reputation, from the type of utterances complained of in the instant case, is insufficient to mandate creation of such a category.

For the aforementioned reasons, that portion of the judgment striking Count I of the complaint is reversed and remanded.

REVERSED AND REMANDED.

DOWNING, P.J., and PERLIN, J., concur.

The *Sands* case illustrates the dangers inherent in slip and fall cases.

MIZENIS v. SANDS MOTEL, INC.,
50 Ohio App. 2d 226, 362 N.E. 2d 661 (1975).

CLIFFORD F. BROWN, Presiding Judge.

This is an appeal from a summary judgment in favor of defendant Balconi and Smith, Inc., operators of the Sands Motel, arising out of an action by the plaintiff, a motel guest, who fell while descending an exterior stairway from a second floor motel room. The stairway was in a slippery and dangerous condition as the result of a natural accumulation of ice and snow.

The stipulation of facts by the parties, considered in reaching a summary judgment, contained, inter alia, the following facts:

"1. The only means of ingress and egress to plaintiff's motel unit consisted of two exterior stairways, of metal construction, located at opposite ends of the motel unit.

"2. Both exterior stairways were in a slippery and dangerous condition due to a failure on the part of the motel to remove snow and ice that accumulated thereon. This slippery and dangerous condition had existed for three or more days prior to plaintiff's being assigned to his room. The accumulated ice and snow on these exterior stairways was made dangerous and slippery by virtue of the fact that it had been subjected to traffic by other persons and the surface had thereby become packed and hard.

"3.   Plaintiff became aware of the dangerous and slippery condition upon first ascending the stairs to enter the motel room which had been assigned to him. Plaintiff immediately phoned the motel desk and complained of the dangerous condition of the stairs and asked that it be remedied.

"4.   Plaintiff considered all other possible means of egress but there were none other than the two exterior stairways. Using great care, on the morning of January 22, 1970, plaintiff descended the stairway. Plaintiff again complained to the motel desk clerk of the condition of the stairways.

"5.   In all it was on the fifth trip on the same stairs on January 22, 1970, that plaintiff fell.

"6.   On all occasions on which the plaintiff used the stairway, plaintiff used great care for his own safety, on all occasions using the hand rails, moving very slowly and watching very carefully where he was going. On his last descent from his motel unit, plaintiff's foot slipped from underneath him, causing him to fall and to sustain an injury to his leg. At the time plaintiff fell, he had hands on both hand rails, was moving cautiously, and was carefully watching where he was going.

"7.   Plaintiff had been a guest of the motel on several other previous occasions during the winter months. On all these prior occasions the motel had removed ice and snow from the stairways."

The plaintiff-appellant sets forth two assignments of error as follows:

"1.   The trial court erred in finding that there is no duty upon a motel operator to remove natural accumulations of snow within a reasonable time from the exterior stairways providing the only means of ingress and egress to the second floor occupants of the motel.

"2.   The trial court erred in finding that the occupant of a second story motel who uses the only means of ingress and egress to his motel room, knowing that said means of ingress and egress is slippery, is charged with assuming the risk as a matter of law."

By granting summary judgment for defendants-appellees, the trial court, by implication, concluded that as a matter of law plaintiff was not entitled to recover for one or both of two reasons, namely: that reasonable minds could come to but one conclusion (1) that there was no duty owing by defendant to plaintiff concerning the accumulation of ice and snow on the exterior metal stairway where plaintiff fell and was injured, and, therefore, no negligence of defendant arose, and (2) plaintiff voluntarily assumed the risk of snowy and icy conditions of the exterior metal stairway which precipitated plaintiff's fall and consequent injuries.

Stated another way, the trial court, by rendering a summary judgment for defendant, determined that pursuant to Civ.R.56(C) there was no genuine issue as to any material fact concerning defendant's negligence—there being no negligence—or concerning plaintiff's assumption of the risk with regard to the snowy and icy condition of the exterior metal stairway—that as a matter of law plaintiff voluntarily assumed the risk and, therefore, defendant was entitled to a judgment in his favor.

A resolution of the question of whether there was a genuine issue of fact concerning defendant's negligence and the existence of plaintiff's voluntary assumption of the risk requires an analysis of the controlling judicial precedents applicable to this case.

Debie v. Cochran Pharmacy-Berwick, Inc. (1967), 11 Ohio St.2d. 38, 227 N.E.2d 603, and *Sidle v. Humphrey* (1968), 13 Ohio St.2d 45, 233 N.E.2d 589, upon which defendants rely, define the obligations of an occupier of premises to a business invitee and stand for the following legal propositions:

1. Where the owner or occupier of business premises is not shown to have notice, actual or implied, that the natural accumulation of snow and ice on his premises has created there a condition substantially more dangerous to his business invitees than they should have anticipated by reason of their knowledge of conditions prevailing generally in the area, there is a failure of proof of actionable negligence.

2. The mere fact standing alone that the owner or occupier has failed to remove natural accumulations of snow and ice from private walks on his business premises for an unreasonable time does not give rise to an action by a business invitee who claims damages for injuries occasioned by a fall thereon.

3. An occupier of premises is under no duty to protect a business invitee against dangers which are known to such invitee or are so obvious and apparent to such invitee that he may reasonably be expected to discover them and *protect himself against them.*

4. The dangers from natural accumulations of ice and snow are ordinarily so obvious and apparent that an occupier of premises may reasonably expect that a business invitee on his premises will discover those dangers and *protect himself against them,* and such occupier has no duty to his business invitee to remove natural accumulations of snow and ice from private walks and steps of his premises.

Even if, for the sake of argument, plaintiff is placed in the same status as the plaintiffs in *Debie* and *Sidle* cases, the first two legal propositions set out above are not applicable. In the present case, unlike *Debie* and *Sidle*, defendants did have actual notice that the ice and snow on the stairway created a condition substantially more dangerous to plaintiff than plaintiff should have anticipated by reason of his knowledge of conditions prevailing generally. Moreover, the failure of defendants as occupiers to remove the natural accumulations of snow and ice does not stand alone.

The third and fourth numbered propositions of law stated above, extracted from the *Sidle* case, raise genuine issues when applied to the record in this case, for these reasons. The obvious and apparent danger of the snowy, icy stairway to plaintiff, as a business invitee, was not, as a matter of law, a danger that he might "reasonably be expected to protect himself against," because the exterior stairways were the only means of ingress and egress from his motel room. Plaintiff sought protection unsuccessfully by asking the motel manager to remedy the icy condition. Plaintiff's only other alternative for protecting himself, too absurd to suggest as a practical remedy, was to stay in his motel room until the spring thaws melted the snow and ice. As a minimum, reasonable minds should determine whether or not plaintiff should have protected himself in this or some other way. Therefore, summary judgment cannot be predicated upon the legal propositions contained in the *Debie* and *Sidle* cases.

Further, both *Debie* and *Sidle* distinguish and explain with approval *Oswald v. Jeraj* (1946), 146 Ohio St. 676, 67 N.E.2d 779, as a case which involves a landlord-tenant situation. *Oswald* is more closely akin to the factual situation and legal relationship of plaintiff as a motel guest of the defendants.

The obligation of a landlord to his tenant, or of an innkeeper to his guests, to keep stairways, entrances and hallways in a reasonably safe condition, does not arise expressly from the lease between landlord and tenant, or from the contract between the innkeeper and guest, but is implied because the use of stairways is necessary to gain access to the premises or to the guest's room, for which he contracted. It is stated in 29 Ohio Jurisprudence 2d 494, Inns & Restaurants, Section 20, that:

"Concerning the duty imposed by law upon an innkeeper to furnish safe premises to his guests and patrons * * * the innkeeper, who is not an insurer, must exercise reasonable care under the circumstances, his liability resting upon the same principles applicable in other cases where persons enter upon premises at the invitation of the owner or occupant and are injured in consequence of the dangerous condition of the premises."

Prosser, Torts (4th ed. 1971), page 407; annotation 49 A.L.R.3d 387, 394; Degraff, *Snow and Ice*, 21 Cornell L.Q. 436, 447-453 (1936); *cf. Roth v. Trakas* (1930), 36 Ohio App. 136, 172 N.E. 847 and *Beaney v. Carlson* (1963), 174 Ohio St. 409, 411, 189 N.E.2d 880 (Shopping Centers); 29 Ohio Jurisprudence 2d, *supra*.

The Restatement of the Law 2d Torts, Para. 496E, has a comment on the necessity of voluntary assumption. The headnote reads:

"1.   A plaintiff does not assume a risk of harm unless he voluntarily accepts the risk.

"2.   The plaintiff's acceptance of a risk is not voluntary if the defendant's tortious conduct has left him no reasonable alternative course of conduct in order to (a) advert harm to himself or another, or (b) exercise or protect the right or privilege of which the defendant has no right to deprive him."

A motel guest's acceptance of a risk is not to be regarded as voluntary where the innkeeper's tortious conduct has forced upon him a choice of courses of conduct which leaves him no reasonable alternative to taking his chances. An innkeeper who, by his own wrong, has constrained the motel guest to choose between two evils cannot be permitted to say that the guest is barred from recovery because he made the wrong choice. The same is also true where the guest is compelled to accept the risk in order to exercise or protect a right or a privilege to deprive him. A motel guest does not assume the risk of his innkeeper's negligence in maintaining a common passageway when it is the only exit from the premises.

A motel guest cannot be said as a matter of law to assume the risk voluntarily, though he knows the danger and appreciates the risk, if at the time he was acting under such exigency or such urgent call of duty, or such constraint of any kind as in reference to the danger deprives his act of its voluntary character.

In some cases the course of danger may be so extreme as to be out of all proportion to the value of the interest to be protected and the plaintiff may be charged with contributory negligence in his own unreasonable conduct. Prosser, *supra* at 452.

A basic element in assumption of the risk is venturousness. In the present case, we cannot conclude that merely because plaintiff Charles Mizenis going back and forth on the icy stairway to his motel room that he was being venturous. However, there may be an element of contributory negligence in his conduct upon which reasonable minds could differ, and thus a jury question of contributory negligence exists. This also raises a jury question as to whether or not defendant, as an innkeeper, acted in a way a reasonably prudent person would have acted; thus, a jury issue of negligence of the defendant arises.

Accordingly, both assignments of error are well taken and the judgment of the Court of Common Pleas is reversed and this cause is remanded.

Judgment reversed and cause remanded.

WILEY and POTTER, JJ., concur.

FALLING OBJECTS

What is the liability of an innkeeper to a third party who is injured by an object that falls from one of the windows of the inn?

CONNOLLY v. NICOLLET HOTEL
95 N.W. 2d 657 (1959)

MURPHY, Justice.

Action by Marcella A. Connolly against The Nicollet Hotel, a copartnership, and Alice Shmikler, as trustee of Joseph Shmikler, and others, doing business as The Nicollet Hotel, for the loss of the sight of her left eye alleged to have been caused by defendants' negligence.

The accident occurred about midnight June 12, 1953, during the course of the 1953 National Junior Chamber of Commerce Convention which had its headquarters at The Nicollet Hotel in Minneapolis. It was occasioned when plaintiff was struck in her left eye by a substance falling from above her as she walked on a public sidewalk on Nicollet Avenue adjacent to the hotel.

The 1953 National Junior Chamber of Commerce Convention, Inc., was joined as a defendant in the action, but at the close of the testimony a verdict was directed in its favor. The jury returned a verdict against The Nicollet Hotel copartnership, which will hereinafter be designated defendants, in the sum of $30,000. This is an appeal from an order of the trial court granting judgment for such defendants notwithstanding the verdict. On appeal plaintiff contends that defendants were negligent in failing to maintain order and control the conduct of their guests with respect to persons using the sidewalk adjacent to the hotel building and that hence the court erred in granting judgment notwithstanding the verdict.

The evidence, presented entirely by plaintiff inasmuch as defendants rested at the conclusion of plaintiff's case, established the following: The easterly side of The Nicollet Hotel is adjacent to Nicollet Avenue. The hotel lies between Washington Avenue to the north and Third Street to the south. It is a 12-story building, but on the Nicollet Avenue side it is limited to eight stories in height. It has a capacity of approximately 490 sleeping rooms on the upper eleven floors. There are no other high buildings in its vicinity. Just south of the hotel on Nicollet Avenue is The Nicollet Hotel garage also operated by defendants. On the east side of Nicollet Avenue opposite the hotel were two 4-story buildings. To the south of these is a parking lot.

Nicollet Avenue in this block is about 50 feet in width. The sidewalks adjacent to it on each side are about 10 feet in width from curb line to building line. At the time of the accident that half of the west sidewalk nearest to the hotel was blocked off by a barricade from the Nicollet Avenue hotel entrance south for about 95 feet, leaving an area about 5 feet in width for pedestrian traffic for such distance. The hotel entrance on Nicollet Avenue is about midway between Washington Avenue and the entrance to the hotel garage.

At the time of the accident there was nothing unusual about the weather. Plaintiff, in company with one Margaret Hansen, had just left the hotel via its Nicollet Avenue entrance and was walking southerly toward Third Street on the west side of Nicollet Avenue. When she had traveled approximately six to ten steps from the canopy extending over such entrance, she observed two people walking toward her. She then heard a noise which sounded like a small explosion and saw something strike the walk in front of her. She observed that one of the persons approaching her was struck on the left shoulder by some substance. She then exclaimed, "We better get off this sidewalk, * * * or somebody is going to get hit." Immediately thereafter she glanced upward and was struck in the left eye by a substance she described as a mud-like substance or a "handful of dirt." Margaret Hansen testified that she also saw the substance falling from eye level to the sidewalk to a step or two in front of her. She described the sound made by the striking object as explosive and accompanied by a splattering. The only place from which the article might have fallen from above was the hotel building.

The blow which struck plaintiff caused her to lose her balance but not to fall. Her knees buckled and she was caught by Margaret Hansen and held on her feet. Following the blow, she stated that she could not open her left eye and the left side of her face and head became numb, and her shoulders, hair, and the left side of her face were covered with dirt. A dark substance which looked like mud was found imbedded in her left eye. After the accident the assistant manager of the hotel attempted to remove a "mud like substance" from plaintiff's eye by using a cotton applicator. As a result of the foregoing accident, plaintiff lost the sight of the injured eye.

As stated above, the 1953 National Junior Chamber of Commerce Convention occupied a substantial portion of the hotel at the time of the accident. In connection therewith various delegates and firms maintained hospitality centers there where intoxicants, beer, and milk were served to guests and visitors. Two of such centers were located on the Nicollet Avenue side of the building.

The assistant manager of the hotel on duty at the time of the accident and in charge of maintaining order had received notice that water bags had been thrown from the hotel during the previous days of the convention. The night engineer testified that on the Hennepin Avenue side of the hotel he had observed liquor and beer bottles and cans on the sidewalk and described the accumulation in this area as greater than he had ever witnessed during the 18-month period he had been employed at the hotel. He also testified that he had found cans and beer bottles upon the fire escape at the third-floor level during the convention.

Arthur Reinhold, an employee of the garage, had been informed that objects had fallen or been thrown from the hotel and that a window screen had fallen from the building, first striking the barricade covering the sidewalk next to the garage, and then falling upon a pedestrian. He also was advised that ice cubes had been thrown from the hotel and that a bottle had been thrown or had fallen therefrom during the course of the convention.

Since in reviewing an order upon a motion granting judgment notwithstanding the verdict we are required to view the evidence in the light most favorable to the verdict, it is material to point out these additional facts: A floral shop was maintained on the premises where potted plants were sold. During the course of the convention a mule was stabled in the lobby of the hotel, and a small alligator was kept on the fourth floor. There was firing of guns in the lobby. Broken bottles and broken glass were found on the sidewalk near the garage adjacent to the building so that it was necessary to clean the sidewalk near the garage as frequently as twice a day during the course of the convention. The doorman at the hotel was equipped with a shovel and broom which he used for this sidewalk maintenance. Property of the hotel was damaged on the third, fourth, fifth, sixth, eighth, ninth, tenth, and eleventh floors. The window of the office of the credit manager was broken. From the testimony of the executive housekeeper of the hotel the damage consisted of wet carpets, broken chairs, broken screens, molding torn loose from connecting doors, and walls spotted with liquor and water. The inspection of the building made after the accident indicated that there were three missing window screens, mirrors pulled off the walls in bathrooms, light fixtures were broken, signs were broken, hall lights were broken, exit lights were broken, the bowl in the men's washroom was torn off the wall, holes were drilled through door panels, and 150 face towels had to be removed from service. Broken glass and bottles were found on landings and stair wells, a condition which existed almost every night at all floor levels. It became apparent to the general manager of the hotel on June 11, 1953, the day prior to the happening of the accident to the plaintiff, that the disorderly behavior of the hotel guests created a hazard to the defendant's property. He issued the following memorandum to his staff:

"WE HAVE ALMOST ARRIVED AT THE END OF THE MOST HARROWING EXPERIENCE WE HAVE HAD IN THE WAY OF CONVENTIONS, AT LEAST IN MY EXPERIENCE! WHEN WE BECAME INVOLVED AND SAW WHAT THE SITUATION WAS, WE HAD NO ALTERNATIVE BUT TO PROCEED AND 'TURN THE OTHER CHEEK.' HOWEVER, IT INVOLVES CERTAIN EXPENSES THAT I DO NOT PROPROSE TO FOREGO WITHOUT AT LEAST AN ARGUMENT—AND MAYBE LEGAL SUIT.

* * * * * * * * * *

"I, OF COURSE, AM SPEAKING OF ANY DAMAGE, WHICH FOR THE MOST PART WILL BE REPORTED BY THE HOUSEKEEPING DEPARTMENT. HOWEVER' THAT I MAY DRAW UP A COMPREHENSIVE CASE, PLEASE HAVE THE INFORMATION IN MY OFFICE NOT LATER THAN NOON, FRIDAY. WE WILL, INCIDENTALLY, START TO TAKE DOWN ALL SIGNS, ETC., AT 9:00 AM, FRIDAY MORNING."

In granting the defendants' motion for judgment notwithstanding the verdict, the trial court was of the view that there was no evidence which would support a finding that the defendants had knowledge of the particular risk of injury to a member of the public and that by the exercise of ordinary care they could not know that a guest's conduct would naturally result in injury to others. The trial court apparently agreed with the defendants' contention that prior to the plaintiff's injury there was no time to ascertain the location of the room from which the object fell or from which it was thrown and to evict therefrom the person or persons responsible therefor.

1. It is generally agreed that a hotel owner of innkeeper owes a duty to the public to protect it against foreseeable risk of danger attendant upon the main-

tenance and operation of his property and to keep it in such condition that it will not be of danger to pedestrians using streets adjacent thereto.

The failure of hotel owner and operator to take reasonable precautions to eliminate or prevent conditions of which he is or should be aware and which might reasonably be expected to be dangerous to the public may constitute negligence.

The plaintiff contends that the act which caused the injury was foreseeable and that the defendants failed in their duty to exercise reasonably care to restrain their guests or to prevent the injury.

2. There are certain controlling principles of law which must be kept in mind in considering the merits of the plaintiff's claims as they are established by the record. It is recognized that one who assembles a large number of people upon his premises for the purpose of financial gain to himself assumes the responsibility for using all reasonable care to protect others from injury from causes reasonably to be anticipated. In the exercise of this duty it is necessary for him to furnish a sufficient number of guards or attendants and to take other precautions to control the actions of the crowd. Whether the guards furnished or the precautions taken are sufficient is ordinarily a question for the jury to determine under all of the circumstances.

3. The common-law test of duty is the probability or foreseeability of injury to the plaintiff. As expressed by Chief Judge Cardozo, "The risk reasonably to be perceived defines the duty to be obeyed, and risk imports relation; it is risk to another or to others within the range of apprehension." In Restatement, Torts, § 348, the same rule is expressed with respect to liability of one who holds out his property for use of the public. It is said that in the exercise of reasonable care the owner of a public place has a "duty to police the premises" and to furnish a sufficient number of servants to afford reasonable protection "if the place is one or the character of the business is such that the utility or other possessor should expect careless or criminal third persons to be thereon either generally or at some particular time." Schubart v. Hotel Astor, Inc., 168 Misc. 431, 438, 5 N.Y.S.2d 203, 210.

4. For the risk of injury to be within the defendants' "range of apprehension," it is not necessary that the defendants should have had notice of the particular method in which an accident would occur, if the possibility of an accident was clear to the person of ordinary prudence.

5. It should further be emphasized that, while the standard of care remains constant, the degree of care varies with the facts and circumstances surrounding each particular case. And, in considering the degree of care to be exercised by the defendants under the circumstances in the case before us, it is relevant to consider authorities dealing with the liability of hotelkeepers and bar operators.

6. Since the defendants are not only hotel operators but are engaged as well in the sale of intoxicating liquor, it is material to point out that they are under the duty to protect guests and patrons from injury at the hands of irresponsible persons whom they knowingly permit to be in and about the premises on which their business is conducted. In Mastad v. Swedish Brethren, 83 Minn. 40, 42, 85 N.W. 913, 914, 53 L.R. A. 803, 805, 85 Am.St.Rep. 446, 448, we said:

> "* * * All who engage in a public business of that nature are bound to protect their guests, both in person and property, from acts and misconduct of wrongdoers permitted to remain upon the premises; and the rules of law applicable to the common carrier are applicable alike to them."

Although it appears from the record that the defendants doubted the wisdom of permitting free liquor and beer to be served upon the premises, they nevertheless permitted it.

It is the policy of the law, both statutory and decisional, to protect the public from social consequences of intoxicating liquor. There is perhaps no field of business activity more hedged about with state and municipal laws and regulations designed to protect the public. When a person engaged in that business permits crowds to gather upon his premises for profit, he must recognize the risks which flow from the nature of the business.

7. In the light of the foregoing observations we may examine the record for the purpose of determining whether or not the act causing the injury was within the range of foreseeability and, if so, whether the defendants exercised the required degree of care to protect the public from the consequences of such an act. Since the act causing the injury must be considered in the light of the circumstances and conditions under which it is alleged to have occurred, it should be observed that the defendants not only furnished room accommodations for from 350 to 400 delegates but also provided their rooms and facilities as headquarters for a convention attended by more than 4,000 young men. This use differed from the ordinary commercial business of the hotel in that its rooms and facilities were turned over the convention for meetings, caucuses, and social purposes. An officer of the convention described the delegates as a group of young men who "work hard and * * * play hard." It may be expected that in the light of human experience the defendants were aware of the fact that among this number, as in any group of young men, would be certain number not concerned with the serious work of the convention. It must have been apparent to the defendants that the ready availability of free intoxicants would not tend to repress the urges of this element. After the convention had been in session for several days, it came to the attention of the management of the hotel that the premises, both inside and out, had been littered with the debris of broken glasses and bottles. They became aware of the considerable damage to their property and received complaints from a pedestrian and policemen that water bags were being thrown from the hotel upon the sidewalk. The accumulated effect of these happenings was to the executive director of the hotel a "harrowing experience." This was all before the accident to the plaintiff occurred. That the dropping of objects from the hotel windows by certain of those occupying the premises was within the range of foreseeability is evidenced by the fact that the hotel company, prior to the convention, took the precaution of cutting the corners out of hotel laundry bags so as to prevent their use as water containers. Moreover, it seems to us that in light of what had happened prior to the accident the management of the hotel must have been aware of the fact that in the indiscriminate throwing of glasses, bottles, and other objects in and about the hotel they might expect as part of that course of conduct that objects might be thrown from the windows to the sidewalk below. It is our view that these facts and circumstances presented a question for the jury to determine as to whether the negligent act which caused the plaintiff's injuries was within the defendants' range of foreseeability.

8. We turn next to inquire as to what precautions were taken by the defendants to protect the plaintiff as a member of the public from such foreseeable risk. It appears from the record that, after the hotel manager received the report that water bags had been dropped to the street, he said they patrolled the house and in rooms where they found "they were doing entertaining we told them to be careful about throwing out anything." He said that it wouldn't have done any good to try to find out the room from which the water bags were thrown, apparently for the reason that the convention was "out of control." He said the loss of control occurred every night "Any time after seven o'clock in the

evening, from seven on." There is this testimony:

"Q. Would you say yes or not that it was the most harrowing experience you had as a hotel operator of that hotel? A. Well, I would say yes.

"Q. And isn't it true that you and the other officers of the hotel were all of that view even before the converstaion was over?

* * * * * * * * * * *

"A. Well, I would say, yes.

* * * * * * * * * * *

"Q. Now, is it true at the conclusion of this convention that you and the other members of the hotel management was shocked by the damage done to your premises during the course of this convention? A. Yes, we were."

The manager of the hotel was asked if, when Miss Connolly was injured, he did not say, "Well, here is another of those incidents. I will be glad when this * * * convention is over." He did not deny making that statement and admitted that he might have made it because that was the way he felt at the time it happened. There is this testimony from the housekeeper:

"Q. But when you have in combination in a matter of a couple days time mirrors broken, recessed lights in the hallway broken, permanent quiet signs attached to the wall torn off, when you have the exit lights damaged, when you have the hall fixtures damaged, when you have the screens damaged, as you described, when you have wash bowls torn off of the wall in the men's room, when you have doors kicked in, when you have mouldings torn off, when you have seven holes drilled into a door of the hotel, wouldn't you say that is a shocking experience over a two day period of time?

* * * * * * * * * * *

"A. Yes, I think it is.

"Q. The like of which you had never seen before in that interval of time with any convention in that hotel. A. That's right. It really is true."

The record establishes that the defendants made no complaint as to the conduct of the guests and invitees to any responsible official of the Junior Chamber of Commerce. Had one been made, it may be assumed that the officers of the convention could have controlled their own members. Neither did the management of the hotel complain to the authorities or ask for additional police protection. On the record we are satisfied that it was plainly a question for the jury to say whether under these unusual circumstances the defendants should have anticipated an accident such as happened and whether they should have taken some precautions by way of securing additional police or watchmen to supervise the conduct of their patrons. It is apparent from the record that, after the hotel management became aware of the disorderly character of the convention, it took no further affirmative action to protect the interests of the public. We are of the view that, once it became apparent to the defendants that the preliminary precautions which had been taken were not sufficient to protect the public from foreseeable risks which might arise from the disorderly character of the convention, the hotel had an affirmative duty to take futher precautions to protect the public. Without undertaking to state precisely what precautions should have been taken by the defendants under the circumstances, we think that evidence of the defendants' failure to hire additional guards, to secure additional police protection, or to appeal to responsible officers of the convention presented a fact question as to whether the defendants exercised due care communsurate with the circumstances. The argument may well be advanced that by "turning the other cheek," to use an expression of the hotel's managing director, the defendants acquiesced in the misuse of their property and became for all practical purposes participants in such misuse.

9. The defendants futher contend that there can be no liability to the plaintiff for the reason that she was neither an invitee nor patron of their establishment. They argue that they cannot be held liable for the unauthorized acts of a third person who, while on their premises, causes injury to an occupant of a public sidewalk. It may be briefly said that, even though the plaintiff was not a patron or a guest of the defendants, a relationship existed between them at the time and place of the injury which gave rise to a legal duty on the part of the defendants. That relationship imposed an affirmative duty upon the defendants to guard the public from danger flowing from the use of their property by their guests and invitees, even though that use was not authorized by the defendants. There was a duty on the part of the defendants to members of the public at large to protect them from injury by forces set in motion as a result of the use which the defendants permitted to be made of their property. Here the plaintiff was a pedestrian within her rights as an occupant of the sidewalk on a street adjacent to the defendants' hotel. There was evidence from which a jury could find that she was injured as a result of disorderly conduct upon the premises, the risk of which was foreseeable and in regard to which the defendants after notice failed to take measures to protect her as a member of the public. In Priewe v. Bartz, 249 Minn. 488, 491, 83 N.W.2d 116, 119, in discussing the rights of a patron of a 3.2 beer establishment we said that such a person "has a right to rely on the belief that he is in an orderly house and that its operator, personally or by his delegated employee, will exercise reasonable care 'to the end that the doings in the house shall be orderly.' " By the same token it may be said that a pedestrian using a sidewalk adjacent to a hotel where intoxicating liquor is sold and dispensed may assume that the owner will exercise reasonable care to the end that the acts and conduct permitted upon the property will not expose a member of the public to the risk of bodily harm.

10. The conclusions we reach are supported by respected authority. In Gore v. Whitmore Hotel Co., 229 Mo.App. 910, 83 S.W.2d 114, a pedestrian was injured in an accident resulting from the throwing of a paper bag containing water from an upper floor of the defendant hotel while a convention of the Veterans of Foreign Wars was in progress. The manager of the hotel admitted that objects had been thrown from the hotel on every night of the convention. It was the contention of the defendant that in order to impose liability it was necessary to establish that the proprietor of the hotel had reason to foresee that the object would be dropped or thrown so that the proprietor would have notice and an opportunity to exercise reasonable care to prevent the occurrence; that the guests to whom the defendant had assigned rooms were entitled to courteous treatment; and that the defendant had no right of access to the rooms of guests. The court held, however, that the guests were under a duty to refrain from unlawful and disorderly conduct which endangered the safety of others; that a willful violation of that duty forfeited the right of the guest to possession of the room; and that when the defendant became aware of the existence of the disorderly conduct of the guest it was its duty to exercise reasonable care to abate the condition. There, as here, there was no evidence to identify the particular room from which the object was thrown. Nevertheless, the court held that it was the duty of the defendant in the exercise of reasonable care to identify the offenders and the rooms used by them in the perpetration of the wrong. In that case the house officer had checked various rooms occupied by the guests and made inquiry as to whether or not they had thrown water into the streets. The

night manager also went across the street and watched windows of the hotel but could not identify any of the rooms from which the objects were thrown. The court there said (229 Mo.App. 916, 83 S.W.2d 118):

"The mere failure of defendant to exercise ordinary care to identify the rioters was not sufficient to fix liability upon it. The defendant was not liable unless it could by the exercise of ordinary care have abated the condition in time to have prevented the injury to plaintiff. The evidence was sufficient to allow the jury to find that the defendant, though it had the right to evict the wrongdoers, negligently failed to identify them and, hence, never attempted to exercise such right. Having the legal right to evict the offenders, this court cannot say as a matter of law that the defendant could not by the exercise of reasonable care have enforced this right prior to the time plaintiff was injured. The question was one for the jury."

Admittedly under the facts in the Gore case there were more frequent incidents of objects having been thrown from the hotel by its occupants. But it does not seem to us that the duration or frequency of the disorderly acts is determinative. The issue is whether the proprietors of the hotel had notice of the disorderly behavior of their guests and, after having had such notice, whether they took such steps as a person of ordinary prudence would take to protect others from foreseeable hazards resulting from the disorderly conduct of their guests.

We think the authorities relied upon by the defendants may be distinguished. Wolk v. Pittsburgh Hotels Co., 284 Pa. 545, 131 A. 537, 42 A.L.R. 1081, where it was held that an innkeeper is not liable for injuries caused by a transient guest's placing of objects on a window sill, which objects fell to the street injuring a person in an automobile, and Larson v. St. Francis Hotel, 83 Cal.App. 2d 210, 211, 188 P.2d 513, 514, where a pedestrian was injured when a guest of the defendant hotel as "the result of the effervescence and ebullition of San Franciscans in their exuberance of joy on V-J Day" tossed an armchair out of a hotel window, may be distinguished in that they deal with instances of sporadic or isolated acts of which the owner did not have notice and in regard to which he had no opportunity to take steps to remove the danger. We think that Holly v. Meyers Hotel & Tavern, Inc., 9 N.J. 493, 89 A.2d 6, may also be distinguished. Under the facts in that case the court concluded (9 N.J. 496, 89 A.2d 7): " * * * there was no occasion for any affirmative action" during the 2-hour period between the time the guests of the hotel who were responsible for the accident were warned by the hotel management and the time the accident occurred. These cases do not deal with facts establishing a course of disorderly conduct continuing over a period of days and under circumstances where the defendants admitted that they had lost control of the orderly management of their property and failed to do anything about it.

11.   The defendants contend that the proof is circumstantial and that there is no evidence that the object which struck the plaintiff came from the hotel. The plaintiff was struck in the eye by a mass of moist dirt or earth. The jury could find that this object was not an accumulation of dirt which fell from the structure. The record indicates that periodic inspections were made of the exterior of the building so that there would be no sizeable collection of dirt on it. Nor was it likely that the mass of dirt or earth came from some other building. From the physical location of the place where the accident occurred and the surrounding structures, there was ample evidence from which the jury could find that the place from which the mass of dirt or earth came would be the Nicollet Hotel property. The record before us indicates that the Nicollet Hotel is a 12-story structure. The accident occurred approximately 100 feet from Washington Avenue and 100 feet from the garage entrance south of the

hotel. Across the street from the hotel on Nicollet Avenue are two 4-story buildings. Nicollet Avenue is 50 feet in width. There was nothing unusual about the weather conditions and no evidence of a wind which might carry a mass of mud from a distant source. There is no evidence to indicate that the mass of mud came from a vehicle or other pedestrian. We think that under the facts in this case the evidence presents inferences which make the question of where the mass of mud came from one for the jury.

We have said many times that the law does not require every fact and circumstance which make up a case of negligence to be proved by direct and positive evidence or by the testimony of eyewitnesses, and that circumstantial evidence alone may authorize a finding of negligence. Negligence may be inferred from all the facts and surrounding circumstances, and where the evidence of such facts and circumstances is such as to take the case out of the realm of conjecture and into the field of legitimate inference from established facts, a prima facie case is made.

Reversed.

QUESTIONS

1. State three reasons why an innkeeper must learn to be "liability conscious."
2. What role does contributory negligence play in liability cases?
3. What was the legal issue in the *Moricoli* case on page 338?
4. What role did "assumption of the risk" play in the *Mizenis* case on page 340?
5. Why is the duty to keep stairways in safe condition *implied* in law?
6. Why does assumption of the risk require "venturousness"?
7. What suggestions might you make about how a convention in a hotel can be controlled?
8. Why does the law place duties on innkeepers to protect those who are not guests?
9. List specific areas of potential danger at a motel that has a swimming pool.
10. Draft a proposed notice to limit liability at a swimming pool that has no life guard on duty.

ENDNOTES

1. *Mizenis v. Sands Motel*, page 340, this text.
2. *Jenkins v. Missouri State Life Ins. Co..* 334 Mo. 941, 69 S.W. 2d 666 (1934)
3. *Trulock v. Willey.* 187 F. 956 (8th Cir. 1911)
4. *Baker v. Dallas Hotel*, 162 Wash. 289, 298 P. 465 (1931).
5. *Lyttle v. Denney*, 222 Pa. 395, 71 A. 841 (1909).
6. *Parson v. Dwightstate Co..* 301 Mass. 324, 17 N.E. 2d 197 (1938).
7. *DeLuce v. Fort Wayne Hotel.* 311 F. 2d 853 (6th Cir. 1962).
8. That which, in a natural and continuous sequence, unbroken by any efficient intervening cause, produces the injury, and without which the result would not have occurred. *Swayne v. Connecticut*, 86 Conn. 439, 85 A. 634, 635.
9. *Reibolt v. Bedient*, page 380, this text.

22

Travel Agencies

A topic of growing interest in the travel and lodging industry is the legal liability of those who serve as "travel conduits", between one who is planning to travel and those who provide the travel, lodging, and entertainment at the destination. Such persons, or firms, are known as "travel agents"—although the use of the word "agents" leaves a lot to be cleared up in the legal sense.

In the customary situation, the traveler (who in most instances is a consumer, yet may be combining business with a pleasure trip) seeks the advice and services of the travel agent. The traveler sets forth the proposed trip, providing a general idea of time, destination and desired price range, and what he or she wants to accomplish on the trip. The travel agent then makes arrangements with a wholesale travel agent, and air, rail or sea carriers; then coordinates with innkeepers at the destination and makes the necessary reservations there. In addition the travel agent often sets up tour plans for the traveler. For these services, the travel agent charges a fee, usually a percentage of the deposits required by wholesale travel agents, inns and others. These deposits are forwarded to the wholesale agent and those at the destination.

Thus we find at least four and perhaps five persons or firms involved in this process:

1. The direct sale travel agent who deals with the traveler face to face.
2. The wholesale travel agent who is contacted by the direct sales agent. (In many instances, wholesale agents are bypassed).
3. The innkeeper.

4. The airline, railroad or shipping line, or a combination of them, that will be referred to as "carrier."

5. Tour operators at the destination, whom we will call "guides."

Obviously in such a multiple-party undertaking, many things can go wrong. Funds may not be forwarded as promised; lodging may not be available upon arrival; guides may fail to materialize as planned; carriers may not meet the required timetables; and worst of all, injury or death may occur to the traveler in the process. It is our purpose in this chapter to explore the ramifications of the legal liability of agents, both direct and wholesale, to the traveler.

SOME BASICS

First, it is helpful to examine some of the legal basics involved in this relationship. We will also look at a variety of cases in which disputes have arisen.

"SALE" OR NOT?

To begin with, does an agent "sell" a traveler a trip package within the "UCC, Sales" meaning of that word? This is an important question. In the absence of the furnishing of food or drink, the preliminary answer appears to be "no." A "service" rather than a "sale" is provided. Next, what standard of care is a travel agent held to?

STANDARD OF CARE

Both direct sale and wholesale travel agents are held by the courts to possess that standard of knowledge and skill that could be expected of the reasonable person who is engaged in that business. Failure to meet these standards could result in legal liability just as in other areas of law.

PRIOR EXPERIENCE

If an agent has had unfavorable experience with those at the destination, that information should be made available to the traveler. If the agent has had no previous experience, a duty exists to make reasonable inquiry about accommodations at the destination as part of the service to the traveler.

DUTY TO ACCEPT

While an innkeeper must accept all guests, the same is not true of the travel agent. A travel agent may turn down potential travelers as he or she may choose.

NOT AN INSURER

In addition, a travel agent is not an insurer of the safety of the traveler—and certainly does not want to be. But as previously mentioned, if the agent knows of risks or has reason to know of them, these should be brought to the attention of the traveler. The failure to do so may create responsibility on the part of the agent to the traveler who suffers a loss because of those risks.

The problems that we have been discussing, have resulted in new regulations on the travel agent business.

REGULATION OF THE INDUSTRY

The travel agent industry came in for some black eyes in the early Nineteen Seventies. The result of this was an increased demand for governmental controls of travel agents. In the past, due to a relatively low demand for such services, there was little regulation. Today there is the American Society of Travel Agents, who has served the industry well for many years and has done all it could to protect travel agents.

At the federal level, the Federal Trade Commission (FTC) and the Civil Aeronautics Board (CAB) and others, had powers—but seldom used them. Both have now become active in controlling the activities of travel agents directly and indirectly. This is a direct outgrowth of the consumer protection movement that became so prevelent in the past decade.

NEW CONTROLS

Late in 1977, the Civil Aeronautical Board issued a proposal that would require the following on all charter travel tours:

1. All payments made in checks, credit card charges or money orders would be made payable to an escrow bank—not to the travel agent or tour operator.
2. Advance payments would be banned.

January 31, 1978, was set as the deadline for filing comments. The long-range effect of these new regulations will be determined by the cases that arise in the coming years.

In the past, travel agents have turned to the law for protection from irate travelers who did not get what they thought they were buying. We will examine the view of the ASTA and then look at some cases that have been decided in recent years.

ASTA

The American Society of Travel Agents has long argued that the direct sale agent is not responsible for the ommissions or wrong-doing of wholesale travel agents and others in the travel chain. It is logical for this organization to take such a position. But the courts often view the matter in a different light, as the following case illustrates.

BUCHOLTZ v. SIROKIN TRAVEL, LTD
80 Misc. 2d 333, 363 N.Y.S. 2d 415 (1974).

Before HOGAN, P. J., and FARLEY and GAGLIARDI, JJ.

PER CURIAM.

Judgment affirmed without costs.

In this Small Claims action, plaintiff seeks to cast defendant travel agency into damages for reservations that went awry. Since it is undisputed that the travel agency had utilized the services of a wholesaler who had put together a "package tour," defendant contends on this appeal that the wholesaler alone is liable for any default in performance.

Allocation of responsibility in the case before us should proceed upon the principles of agency law. In our opinion, where, as here, there is no proof of an independent relationship between the retail travel agent and the wholesaler, the travel agent should be considered the agent of the customer. If, in using a wholesaler to make the travel arrangements, the travel agent acts with the consent, express or implied, of the principal-customer, then, if reasonable diligence has been used in its selection, the travel agent will not be responsible for any dereliction of duty on the part of the wholesaler. If, on the other hand, the travel agent acts without such consent, he will be responsible to the customer for any damage sustained as a result of the acts of the wholesaler.

The court below, in applying these principles, found that the plaintiff did not consent to the employment of the wholesaler. Although its opinion did not so state, the record indicates that the court also declined to hold that knowledge of the practice of employing wholesalers should be imputed to the plaintiff. We see no reason to disturb this determination. The record supports a finding that plaintiff was not informed of the existence of the wholesaler until after the reservations were agreed upon and it cannot be said that knowledge of this practice is so pervasive among the public as to compel a finding of implied consent.

We find no merit in defendant's remaining contention.

All concur.

AGENTS OR NOT?

If a direct sale agent is a true legal "agent" (see Chapter 8), then so long as the identity of the principal (such as a wholesale travel agent, innkeeper, carrier or guide) is disclosed, there is no contractual obligation on the part of the agent. An agent is not responsible for contracts negotiated for the principal so long as the principal is disclosed.

However, as one examines the basic requirements of an agency relationship, it becomes clear that travel agents often do not meet the requirements of a true legal agency. These requirements are four in number:

1. Both the principal or agent must agree to the relationship.
2. The principal must have the right to control the agent.
3. A fiduciary relationship must exist between them.
4. The agent must have the power to bind the principal.

An examination of these requirements makes it clear that in the usual travel situation, at least one and often more of them are not present. Thus the position taken by the ASTA is on shaky legal ground. The cases that have attempted to construe this topic have not been satisfactory to date, as the *Bucholtz* case illustrates.

If a direct sale travel agent does *not* disclose the wholesale agent, then the contract of the traveler and the sales agent would be binding upon the agent. This is an affirmance of the traditional legal liability of an agent who acts for an undisclosed principal.

E.A. McQUADE TRAVEL AGENCY, INC., v. DOMECK
190 So. 2d 3, Dist. Ct. App. Fla. (1966).

ANDREWS, Judge.

The defendant, E. A. McQuade Travel Agency, Inc., appeals final judgment entered for the plaintiffs, Harry L. Domeck and Viola A. Domeck, awarding plaintiffs $2,057.50 plus costs for breach of contract. Plaintiffs filed a cross-assignment of error alleging that the proper amount of damages should be $2,667.50, plus costs.

Plaintiffs filed this suit against defendant to recover damages for breach of contract. Plaintiffs alleged that, in consideration of $2,677.50 paid to defendant, defendant agreed to sell plaintiffs two tickets on a certain cruise to Europe. Defendant answered alleging that it received the monies for the benefit of and transmittal to Caribbean Cruise Lines, Inc., a foreign corporation.

This cause came before the trial court on stipulated statement of facts to the effect that, on May 12, 1964, the defendant agreed to sell plaintiffs two tickets on a European cruise of the M/S Riviera which was to leave on September 11, 1964; that plaintiffs paid defendant the sum of $2,667.50 on or prior to July 23, 1964. All payments were made to E. A. McQuade Travel Agency, but the tickets were not delivered to the plaintiffs. It is also stipulated that there was no discussion between the plaintiffs and the defendant as to the person or corporation for which the defendant acted as agent, if any, or as to what disposition would be made of the money paid to defendant.

Prior to August 15, 1964, defendant forwarded $2,406.75 to Caribbean Cruise Lines, Inc., the company that was offering the cruise to Europe. On or about August 15, 1964, the plaintiffs and the defendant were informed that the M/S Riviera would not be making the scheduled cruise and that Caribbean Cruise Lines, Inc. sought protection under Chapter X of the Bankruptcy Act, 11 U.S.C.A., § 501 et seq.

The plaintiffs requested the defendant to return to them the money which they had paid for the tickets they did not receive. The defendant has offered to pay to plaintiffs $266.75 which was its commisson but declined to pay any additional monies except such amount as it recovered from Caribbean Cruise Lines, Inc. The defendant has been unable to recover from Caribbean Cruise Lines, Inc.

The original complaint contained a prayer for judgment in the amount of $2,057.50 plus costs. Prior to trial plaintiffs amended their complaint to reflect the exact amount they had paid defendant to be $2,667.50.

The trial court held the defendant liable because it failed to disclose its principal and awarded the plaintiffs $2,057.50 plus costs.

The main question presented for our determination is whether the defendant sufficiently disclosed the identity of its principal, Carribbean Cruise Lines, Inc., by merely revealing the name of the cruise ship, M/S Riviera.

In our research we failed to find a Florida decision directly on the question of disclosure of principal by an agent. However, the law in other states is well established that the disclosure of agency is not complete for the purpose of relieving the agent from personal liability unless it embraces the name of the principal. The disclosure of the name of the ship is merely the disclosure of a trade name, and is not a disclosure of the identity of the principal. The liability of an agent acting for an undisclosed principal is fully discussed in Unger v. Travel Arrangements, Inc., 1966, 25 A.D.2d 40, 266 N.Y.S.2d 715, a decision involving the same cruise.

We agree with the trial court that the defense of agency does not relieve the defendant from liability. The record supports the trial court's finding that the defendant was an agent of an undisclosed principal and therefore can be held liable. Hohauser v. Schor, Fla.App.1958, 101 So.2d 169. We hold that there is sufficient evidence to support the trial court's holding that the defendant breached its contract with plaintiffs by failing to furnish the promised tickets.

The court has carefully considered the other points raised on appeal by appellant and finds them without merit.

Accordingly, we affirm as to liability and reverse as to amount of damages with direction that the judgment be amended to award damages to the plaintiffs in the amount of $2,667.50, plus costs.

SMITH, C. J., and WALDEN, J., concur.

DUAL AGENTS

Another legal possibility in determining liability of travel agents, is in treating a traveler-direct sale agent and traveler-wholesale agent as being two agencies, not one. First, there is the agency between the direct sale agent and the traveler. As soon as all legal obligations are met by the first agent, such as contacting the wholesale agent, arranging for tickets and paying over required deposits, the first agency has has been completed and liability ends there for the first agent.

The second agency now comes into being between the traveler and wholesale agent. A case illustrates this view.

LEVINE v. BRITISH OVERSEAS AIRWAYS CORPORATION
66 Misc. 2d 820, 322 N.Y.S. 2d 119 (1971)

BENTLEY KASSAL, Judge.

Plaintiffs move for summary judgment against defendants, British Overseas Airways Coporation ("BOAC") and Leo Lazar d/b/a/ Comet Travel Agency ("Comet") to recover the sum of $86 as a refund for a portion of two airline tickets returned unused to BOAC. Comet failed to appear in this action. BOAC does not dispute that plaintiffs are entitled to the refund, but asserts in opposition to this motion that "pursuant to airline custom and regulation", it paid the claimed amount, less the travel agent's commission, to Comet, as "agent" for plaintiffs, and is thus no longer liable to plaintiffs. BOAC's answer however, does not refer to Comet as plaintiffs' agent but states that BOAC paid the money to Comet pursuant to the said IATA regulations, contract and industry custom.

The essential facts are not in dispute; the issue to be resolved in whether Comet was plaintiffs' agent in this transaction, and, if so, whether payment to Comet discharged BOAC from further liability for the refund.

The facts are these: On September 3, 1970, plaintiffs purchased two round-trip BOAC tickets from Comet for this trip—New York/London/Amsterdam/Copenhagen/Stockholm/London/New York. On September 30, 1970, pursuant to BOAC insturctions, plaintiff Robert Levine sent the two unused portions of the tickets directly to BOAC for a refund. His accompanying letter is as follows: "We are enclosing herewith two (2) tickets (BEA No. 6942777 and No.

6942778), each for a refund in the sum of $43. Kindly forward your check in the sum of $86 to me at your earliest convenience, and oblige."

BOAC, having determined that plaintiffs were entitled to a refund, sent back a form letter acknowledging plaintiffs' request and advising them that the claim had been processed through "your travel agents", who would make the final settlement with them. Simultaneously, BOAC sent a check to Comet, made to Comet's order, for $78.98, the refund due, less Comet's retained commission of $6.02. This check was negotiated by Comet on October 13, 1970, but no payment has ever been received by plaintiffs.

In January, plaintiffs again wrote to BOAC to demand the refund. On January 19, 1971, the day this action was instituted, BOAC wrote Comet enclosing a photocopy of its check and requesting that plaintiffs be paid. Since that time, BOAC has repeatedly contacted Comet to make payment to plaintiffs, without avial.

In its answer BOAC does not cite any specific regulations of the International Air Transport Association, a voluntary association of international air carriers, or any binding custom, to substantiate its claim that it has satisfied its obligation of payment by making the refund to the travel agent. Nor do I have knowledge of any IATA regulations regarding such refunds.

It is understandable, however, that BOAC and other airlines may have adopted this practice for their own benefit as the most convenient and feasible method of repayment since the travel agent retains a commission on the sale. But such practice, established unilaterally, could not bind plaintiffs or exonerate BOAC from liability to plaintiffs, simply on the ground of its being their own usual procedure. Plaintiffs returned their tickets directly to BOAC, not through their travel agent. They were not in the travel business, and no custom existed between them and BOAC or any other airline as to any further involvement of the travel agent beyond the initial purchase and issuance of the original BOAC tickets. Furthermore, the instructions in plaintiffs' letter are explicit to that effect. "Kindly forward your check in the sum of $86 *to me* * * *" (emphasis added). Thus, the fact that BOAC might have followed its usual "custom" will not immunize it from liability to plaintiffs, especially in view of plaintiffs' express instructions.

The other theory on which BOAC relies is one of agency. It claims that its obligation has been discharged because a travel agent is the agent of the traveler and thus payment to the agent constitutes payment to the traveler, his principal. Plaintiffs, on the contrary, consider Comet to be BOAC's agent.

When a person goes to a travel agency to book transportation and other arrangements with a vague request such as "Get me a flight to London on the 15th and hotel reservations", it may very well be in that situation that the travel agent, who is essentially a "broker", becomes the traveler's agent; under those circumstances, he is not the agent of the airline, even though he may have a supply of blank official tickets supplied to them. At most, the travel broker is an agent for an undisclosed principal and the agent alone is responsible to the traveler; the airline only becomes liable if it ratifies the transaction made by the broker.

In the two cases mentioned (omitted), which are relied upon by BOAC as controlling in this action, the plaintiffs-travelers booked all-inclusive tours through their brokers and the airlines which they sued neither had notice of the flight arrangements nor had they received any of the money collected by the travel agencies. Under such circumstances, the respective courts refused to hold the airlines liable. In confining its conclusions to the facts, the Illinois Court further significantly noted that "there undoubtedly are many situations where (the travel broker) could become the agent of (the airline)". It has been recognized that once the travel agent pays over the fare to the carrier, the traveler has a valid claim for restitution against the carrier.

In my opinion, once plaintiffs' initial purchase of the tickets from Comet had been satisfactorily completed, any possible agency relationship which may have existed between them was thereupon terminated. Having used only a portion of their tickets, plaintiffs were entitled to a refund, whether they had purchased their tickets from Comet or across a BOAC counter. They chose to deal directly with BOAC, as a disclosed principal, to ask for a refund. They did not deal with Comet and it was not necessary for plaintiffs to return tickets through the travel agency, as BOAC's acceptance implies; nor was it "necessary" for BOAC to return this money via Comet, except for their own convenience and sole-benefit for accounting purposes to avoid the extra step of having to collect the commission Comet had retained on the ticket sale. Plaintiffs never authorized BOAC to remit the refund in this manner; Comet was not authorized to receive this payment; plaintiffs in no way held out Comet as their agent for this purpose.

Assuming *arguendo* that an agency relationship between plaintiffs and Comet continued after the initial sale of the tickets, this would not *per se* justify BOAC's refund payment since "an agent has no authority to receive payment merely because of the fact that he represented a principal in the transaction out of which the debt arose * * *" Restatement Agency 2d sec. 71, Comment; see also 12 Am.Jur.2d, Brokers sec. 79. Payment to a party who has no authority, actual or apparent, to receive it does not discharge the debtor.

Accordingly, summary judgment is granted against defendant, British Overseas Airways Corporation and against defendant Leo Lazar d/b/a Comet Travel Agency, by default, and judgment may be entered in favor of the plaintiffs for the relief demanded in the complaint.

AS INDEPENDENT CONTRACTORS

More and more direct sale travel agents are taking legal steps to make it clear that they are *not* agents of the wholesale travel agents or those at the destination. This is being done by the use of conspicious disclaimers in the contract with the traveler. Thus the direct sales agent is bound by the contract to make the arrangements agreed upon, but makes no promises or warranties as to performance by others, or quality of accommodations. This limits the legal liability of the direct sales agent, leaving the liability based solely upon the traveler-direct sales agent contract. After all reservations are properly made, failure of those services would be the responsibility of others. On the other hand, if the traveler specifies a specific *quality* of accommodations and the direct sales agent fails to obtain them, or forgets to do so, then contractual liability would exist.

If a direct sale agent makes express promises to the traveler as to quality of service and the like, these promises become part of the contract and would be binding upon the agent. A better practice would be to use the disclaimer rather than shouldering the additional contract burdens. But this is a matter for the direct sales agent to decide.

MEASURE OF DAMAGES

In those cases where liability attaches to a travel agent, the question arises as to what the extent and measure of damages should be.

ODYSSEYS UNLIMITED, INC., v. ASTRAL STAR TRAVEL SERVICE
77 Misc. 2d 502, 354 N.Y.S. 2d 88 (1974).

JOSEPH LIFF, Justice.

Following an earlier practice, in the summer of 1972 the Paterson and Majewski families began to plan a joint vacation over the Christmas holiday. In doing so they relied upon Astral Travel Service ("Astral") an agency with which they had previously dealt. They looked forward to spending a few days with their five children in the Canary Islands, of course not anticipating the discomfort, inconvenience and disappointment they would suffer.

In this action plaintiff Odysseys Unlimited, Inc. ("Odysseys") sues to recover on Astral's two checks in the amounts of $676.80 and $875.90 on which Astral had stopped payment. Astral in one counterclaim alleges that its clients, the interpleaded defendants Majewski and Paterson, demanded a refund because of the breach of the agreement of the trip. In a second counterclaim Astral seeks to recover from Odysseys the sum of $1,345.00 (unrelated to the Majewski-Paterson claim) which represents an advance by Astral for a group tour to the Canary Islands via Iberia Airlines which would have included accommodations at the San Felipe Hotel. Astral, confronted with claims against it by Odysseys and Astral breached agreements with them and demand the return to them of $1,375.90 and $1,076.80, the total cost of their trips. In a second counterclaim they seek $10,000.00 as damages for having "suffered great inconvenience, humiliation, pain and were compelled to spend their vacation in inferior accommodations" (Paragraph 15 of interpleaded defendants' answer). Astral's reply and cross-claim allege that if the interpleaded defendants suffered any damages it was plaintiff Odysseys' fault and asks that Odysseys be compelled to indemnify it against any judgment which may be recovered by the interpleaded defendants.

Astral (a retail travel agent) suggested to Dr. Paterson and Mr. Majewski a package tour prepared by Odysseys (a wholesale agency). The tour, entitled 'Xmas Jet Set Sun Fun/Canary Isle", was scheduled to depart December 26, 1972 by jet for Tenerife, Canary Isles, Puerto de la Cruz, staying at the "delux Semiramis Hotel" and returning on January 1, 1973 by jet. Majewski and Paterson accepted this trip costing $1,375.90 and $1,076.80 respectively and made their down payments to Astral. Astral withheld its commission and forwarded the balance along with the reservations to Odysseys who in turn confirmed the reservations to Astral's Mr. Howard Pollack. Exhibit B is a handsome colored brochure illustrating the Hotel Semiramis, its location, accommodations, etc., etc. designed to excite the eye of any one contemplating a trip abroad. An information sheet (Exhibit A) furnished details of the trip and referred to the accommodations at the "Five-Star Hotel Semiramis".

On December 26, 1972 the group flew off to the Canary Islands. They arrived at the airport in Tenerife at about dawn and waited about two hours (one-half hour was spent in a bus) before they were taken to the Hotel Semiramis. At this point the passengers had been en route some thirty hours. While at the airport they saw Mr. Newton, President of Odysseys, who accompanied the group tour. (The inference may reasonably be drawn that he went along because he anticipated the difficulties which were shortly to be encountered.) Two hundred fifty weary but expectant guests arrived at the Semiramis and were presented with a letter from the hotel (Exhibit C) advising them that there was no space available and that he was looking for others. For about four hours, two hundred fifty people (including bag and baggage except for what was strayed) were in the lobby of the Semiramis until they were divided into groups and directed to other hostelries. The Paterson and Majewski families were brought to the Porto Playa Hotel which was not fully ready for occupancy because it was under construction and without the recreational facilities and conveniencies available at the Hotel Semiramis. Portions of the Porto Playa Hotel were enclosed in scaffolding. Paterson and Majewski testified that work was done in their rooms, water supply uncertain, electric connections incomplete, etc., etc. throughout their stay.

The Court is convinced that prior to the group's departure Mr. Newton was aware that there were no reservations at the Semiramis Hotel for his charges. He testified that on either December 18th or 19th, 1972 he knew of the overbooking at the hotel. Paterson and Majewski stated that Newton told them at the hotel that the reservations were in jeopardy and would not be honored but he did not share his knowledge. In his letter of January 12, 1973 addressed to tour members, Mr. Newton confirms the fact that he had been aware of some "problem with overbooking by that hotel" (Semiramis Hotel) and states that his agent (Viajes Aliados, S. A.) "had the foresight to have arranged for alternate accommodations" (Exhibit 5). He is at the least disingenuous in asserting that he had assurance from the Spanish National Tourist Office that the Semiramis Hotel would have accommodations for the group because that office informed him that the Hotel Semiramis was "instructed to receive all the members of your group for whom reservations were made". However, the reservations for the tour were not confirmed and , therefore, the hotel was not obligated to accommodate the members of the group (Exhibit3).

Odysseys has not demonstrated that it performed the agreement as required and "[a] party who seeks to recover damages from the other party to a contract for its breach must show that he himself is free from fault in respect to performance" (10 N.Y.Jur., Contracts § 385). One of the elements in a breach of contract action is the "performance by plaintiff" (2 N.Y. PJI 868) and because Odysseys did not produce reservations for Paterson and Majewski at the Semiramis Hotel, recovery on the two checks is denied and the complaint is dismissed.

Majewski and Paterson sue in contract and negligence seeking recovery of their payments for their trip and for their ordeal. Their claims spring from a breach of contract by Astral for its failure to furnish the hotel accommodations agreed upon. Majewski and Paterson are entitled to recover from Astral for the breach of contract. Damages in the usual breach of contract action should indemnify a party "for the gains prevented and losses sustained by the breach; to leave him in no worse, but put him in no better, position than he would have been had the breach not occurred" (2 N.Y. PJI 907; see also 13 N.Y.Jur., Damages § 38; 25 C.J.S. Damages § 74). However, when a passenger sues a carrier for a breach of their agreement concerning accommodations the "[i]nconveniences and discomforts which a passenger suffers * * * are to be considered in the assessment of the damages" (N.Y. Damages Law § 624). "[D]amages arising from a breach of the contract to carry, which results in inconvenience and indignity to the passenger while in transit, are not limited to the price of passage" (Lignante v. Panama Railroad Co., 147 App.Div. 97, 99-100, 131 N.Y.S. 753, 754; see also Aplington v. Pullman Co., 110 App.Div. 250, 97 N.Y.S. 329) and "the discomfort and inconvenience to which" a passenger was put by the breach of the carrier's contract "was within the contemplation of the parties and a proper element of damage" (Campbell v. Pullman Company, 182 App.Div. 931, 169 N.Y.S. 1087; see also Owens v. Italia Societa Per Azione, 70 Misc.2d 719, 723, 334 N.Y.S.2d 789 [Civil Court of the City of New York] aff'd 75 Misc.2d 104, 347 N.Y.S.2d 431 [Appellate Term, First Dept.]). Although these cases concerned accommodations with common carriers the principle should be applied to the relationship between travel agent and clients. The agent should be "held responsible to: (a) verify or confirm the reservations and (b) use reasonable diligence in ascertaining the responsibility of any intervening 'wholesale or tour organizer" (Bucholtz v. Sirotkin Travel Ltd., 74 Misc. 2d 180, 182, 343 N.Y.S.2d 438, 442). Because the contract was violated and the accommodations contracted for not furnished a more realistic view for awarding damages to Majewski and Paterson would include not only the difference in the cost of the accommodations but also compensation for their inconvenience, discomfort, humiliation and annoyance.

Odysseys attempted to mitigate the damages to Majewski and Paterson by offering proof as to the difference in value between what they received (at a four-star hotel) and what was agreed upon (a five-star ménage). However, this evidence is without force because the hotel at which they stayed was under construction, its recreational facilities were non-existent and its location was not nearly as desirable as that of the Semiramis. The proverbial expression about a picture being worth a thousand words has particular application to Exhibits B, D—1 and 2, and I—1, 2, 3 and 4 to reveal what Majewski and Paterson expected and what they found. Paterson and Majewski are entitled to return of the total sum each paid for the trip as damages to them and their family for the inconvenience and discomfort they endured.

The tour included a period from December 26th to January 1st. The party landed on its easterly journey on the 27th December. When the Majewskis and Patersons became aware of their predicament they made heroic efforts to return immediately but heavy bookings in the holiday season made that impossible. They were constrained to remain and to suffer the results of Mr. Newton's callousness. Had their dealings been directly with the plaintiff we would have considered the imposition of additional damages. However, their negotiations and dealings were with Astral who might have exerted greater efforts to see that arrangements were properly made.

In all of the circumstances we think that it would be appropriate to make the Patersons and Majewskis whole in pocket. Accordingly, they are awarded judgment against Astral in the amounts of $1,076.80 to Paterson and $1,375.90 to Majewski.

On Astral's cross-claim against Odysseys for breach of contract, concerning the Majewski and Paterson claims if successful, Astral is entitled to a judgment against Odysseys in the amount of $2,452.70 less $308.30 which Astral retained as its commission, because Odysseys failed to perform its contract and it was Odysseys which was responsible for the fate which befell Majewski and Paterson.

In an unrelated matter Astral counterclaimed against Odysseys seeking return of a $1,345.00 deposit for a group tour also to the Canary Islands but via Iberia Airlines and with a stay at the San Felipe Hotel. Astral gave this sum to Odysseys as a deposit for a group tour of fifty persons since it was allegedly required by the San Felipe Hotel to "firm up your confirmation" (Exhibit L). Odysseys indicated that this deposit was non-refundable (Exhibits L and N). Having received cancellations by members of the group that was to take this trip, Astral was unsuccessful in attempts to substitute their vacationers and requested a refund of the deposit paid. Odysseys' proof failed to show that it suffered any loss by the cancellation or that it paid any part of the deposit to the hotel. We also found that Odysseys asked for the deposit because it was required by the hotel but no part of it was ever paid over to the hotel. Accordingly, Astral is entitled to a return of their deposit and may enter judgment against Odysseys for said amount.

DISCLAIMERS

Those engaged in the travel agency business, often use disclaimers of liability in their contracts with their customers. As a principle of law, parties of equal bargaining power can reach any reasonable agreement and the courts tend to uphold those agreements. But in correlation to this is the rule that if the bargaining power of the parties is *not* equal, the courts look with disfavor at the disclaimers of liability. This is illustrated in the *Egan* case.

EGAN v. KOLLSMAN INSTRUMENT CORP.
287 N.Y.S. 2d 14 (1967)

FULD, Chief Judge.

Mrs. Eileen M. Seiter was killed when the American Airlines plane on which she was a passenger crashed as it approached LaGuardia Airport on February 3, 1959. Her administrators have brought this action for wrongful death and American has raised as an affirmative defense the limitation of liability provisions of the Warsaw Convention (49 U.S.Stat., pt. 2, p. 3000, hereinafter referred to as the "Convention"). Two questions are presented by this appeal: Was the final leg of the flight—from Chicago to New York City— to be deemed "international transportation" for purposes of the Convention so as to render it applicable to the present action and, if it was, had the carrier sufficiently complied with the Convention's notice requirements to permit it to limit its liability?

Mrs. Seiter had purchased an airline ticket for a round trip between New York City and Vancouver, Canada. The ticket scheduled her on successive flights of Northwest Airlines and United Airlines with stopovers at Seattle (west and eastbound) and at Chicago (eastbound). On the face of the ticket, below the name of the passenger, the following footnote appeared in exceedingly small, almost unreadable (4½ point) print:

"Carriage/Transportation under this Passenger Ticket and Baggage Check, hereinafter called 'ticket', is subject to the rules relating to liability established by the Convention for the Unification of Certain Rules relating to Internationl Carriage/Transportation by Air signed at Warsaw, October 12, 1929, if such Carriage/Transportation is 'international carriage/transportation' as defined by said Convention."

Mrs. Seiter arrived in Vancouver on January 26, 1959, as scheduled, but, on February 3, when she was ticketed to return to New York, she discovered that all flights out of Vancouver had been cancelled because of inclement weather. Instead of waiting for the next available flight, she proceeded to Seattle by bus, obtaining a refund check from Northwest Airlines for that portion of her journey when she reached that city.

Mrs. Seiter reached Seattle in time to permit her to take off on the Northwest flight to Chicago for which she had been originally scheduled. Reaching Chicago too late to make her scheduled connection to New York City, she presented her ticket to Northwest Airlines and received a new one for passage on an American Airlines flight to LaGuardia Airport. The new ticket—under the heading "COMPLETE ROUTING THIS TICKET AND CONJUNCTION TICKET(S)"—specified the origin and destination as "NY" and expressly recited that it was "ISSUED IN EXCHANGE FOR" the original ticket, the fare being listed at the figure which had initially been paid for the entire round trip. Mrs. Seiter boarded respondent American's aircraft which, as stated above, crashed while attempting to make a landing at La Guardia.

The present action, for wrongful death, was brought against American Airlines and two other defendants—one the manufacturer of an assertedly defective altimeter and the other the assembler of the aircraft. We are, however, concerned solely with the sufficiency of American's (third) affirmative defense which asserts an "exemption from and limitation of liability in accordance with all of the applicable provisions of said Convention". The court at Special Term upheld that defense, denying the plaintiffs' motion to dismiss it, and the Appellate Division unanimously affirmed Special Term's order, granting leave to appeal on a certified question.

As both courts below recognized, answer to the underlying question—whether the flight from Chicago to New York City was "international transportation" under the Convention—depends upon the nature of the contract between the carrier and its passenger.[1] When it provides for "international" transportation, "whether or not there be a break in the transportation" (art. 1, subd. [2]), all flights taken under it are governed by the Convention. In the *Ross* case, our court held that "the Convention becomes the law of the carriage when the 'contract' of the parties provides for passage between certain described termini. When such is the contract, then the Convention has automatic full impact, by its own terms".

The Convention's emphasis on the contract actually "made" appears to have been specifically designed to prevent any subsequent intervening circumstances from affecting the result. The reason is manifest; as one commentator put it, "[t]his prescription possesses, for the parties involved, the appreciable advantage of settling in advance the application of the Warsaw Convention, thus becoming independent of fortuitous events".

The contract embodied in the original ticket issued in this case was undoubtedly for international transportation since, in the words of the Convention (art. 1, subd. [2]), it provided for "an agreed stopping place within a territory * * * of another power". Whether or not Mrs. Seiter might have been able to rescind this contract and enter into a wholly new one of an entirely domestic character in Seattle, the simple fact is that she chose not to do so.[2] The remainder of her journey—from Seattle to Chicago and from Chicago to New York—was performed under the original contract; and since, as already noted, it provided for international transportation, it was subject to the Convention.

The plaintiff contends, however, that in view of the bus trip from Vancouver, the later flights were not performed by "successive air carriers" as required by the Convention (art. 1, subd. [3]) and that, in order for a subsequent domestic flight to be subject to the Convention, the international transportation must be "completely by air". It may well be true—although we need not now consider the matter—that, had the parties initially agreed that the journey from Vancouver to Seattle would be by bus, the Convention would not have been applicable to the later flights. But Northwest was unquestionably named as a successive air carrier on the ticket originally issued pursuant to that contract and, so long as the flight was performed under it, the Convention applies.

Nor can there by any doubt that the American Airlines flight from Chicago to New York was also performed under the original contract. It is to be noted that it was not Mrs. Seiter but the contracting airline, Northwest, which obtained the ticket out of Chicago for her. Examination of that ticket discloses that it was a part of "complete routing" from New York to Vancouver, and back again to New York, at the fare originally paid. The respondent American may not be regarded as an outside party, a stranger to the contract for international carriage in view of the fact that the passenger had agreed in that contract that Northwest "may without notice substitute alternate carriers or aircraft" (Conditions of Contract, Item No. [7]).

It is equally clear that American did not have to be an actual party to such original contract in order to obtain the benefits of the Convention: subdivision (1) of article 30 specifically provides that any successive air carrier who accepts passengers under a contract for international transportation is "subject[ed] to the rules set out in this convention, and shall be deemed to be one of the contracting parties to the contract of transportation".

This brings us to the plaintiffs' further argument that, even if the Warsaw Convention applies, the carrier is not entitled to invoke the provisions limiting its liability because the ticket delivered to Mrs. Seiter did not give sufficient notice that the rules of the Convention relating to the limitation of liability were applicable.

Under article 3 (subd. [1], par. [e]) of the Convention, an airline is required to deliver a passenger ticket which contains a "statement that the transportation is subject to the rules relating to liability established by this convention".[3] The ticket before us did contain, in footnotes on the several coupons, such a statement but, as is apparent from inspection, it is in such exceedingly small and fine print as almost to defy reading.[4] Thus, although there was literal compliance with the prescription of article 3, the question arises whether such compliance satisfies the Convention's demands when viewed in the light of its over-all purposes. We do not believe that it does. In our judgment, a statement which cannot reasonably be deciphered fails of its purpose and function of affording notice and may not be accepted as the sort of statement contemplated or required by the Convention.

In support of its argument to the contrary, the respondent points to Ross v. Pan Amer. Airways, 229 N.Y. 88, 85 N.E.2d 880. The ticket there under consideration, not too unlike the one before us, had been delivered not to the passenger personally but to a third person who had been in charge of all arrangements up to the time of the plane's departure. In holding that delivery to the latter was sufficient, the court observed that, when a ticket provided for international transportation, the Convention applied "by its own terms and not because the parties have so agreed" and that the carrier need show no more than delivery of the ticket (p. 97, 85 N.E.2d p. 885). As already indicated,the sole question presented concerned the adequacy of such delivery. No argument was made by the passenger as to the form of the ticket or the readability of the statement as to liability. And, indeed, in 1964, 15 years later, the court decided Eck v. United Arab Airlines, Inc., 15 N.Y.2d 53, 255 N.Y.S.2d 249, 203 N.E.2d 640, 6 A.L.R.3d 1260 and, despite the carrier's strong reliance on the rationale and language of *Ross*, expressly rejected a "strictly literal reading" of the Convention or any of its provisions. Remarking the changes which had occurred in the years since the Convention had been drafted and stressing the vital canon of construction that, when a treaty is invoked, *"what is to be applied are its principles if its purposes are to be observed"* (emphasis in original), the court declared (p. 59, 255 N.Y.S.2d p. 251, 203 N.E.2d p. 641):

"The reasoning which supports a strictly literal reading of the phrase might not have done violence to the over-all scheme and design of the Convention under the conditions existing when the treaty was drafted. At that time it would have been in harmony with the methods under which the carriers were operating and with the objectives of the Convention. [Case cited.] Now, however, almost a half century later, when the carriers have radically changed their methods of booking passage, the whole scheme of the treaty in relation to international air travel makes it imperative to analyze this self-executing treaty in assigning meaning to any part of it. In doing this it must be recognized that the literal wording of one particularly applicable section of the entire treaty should not set the limits of our interpretive examination."

And, even more recently, the United States Court of Appeals for the Second Circuit, confronted with the precise problem now before us, decided that a ticket, containing a statement (as to the carrier's liability) virtually identical in content and form with that in this case, failed to give passengers the notice required by the Convention. (See Lisi v. Alitalia-Linee Aeree Italiane, 370 F.2d 508, supra, cert. granted, 389 U.S. 926, 88 S.Ct. 281, 19 L.Ed.2d 276.) After observing out that "[t]he Convention's arbitrary limitations on liability—which have been severely and repeatedly criticized—are advantageous to the carrier", the court, in an opinion by Judge KAUFMAN, went on to say that *"the quid pro quo* for this one-sided advantage is delivery to the passenger of a ticket * * * which give[s] him notice" of a "very substantially" limited liabilty and affords him "the opportunity to purchase additional flight insurance or to take such other steps for his self-protection as he sees fit" (pp. 512-513). Pointing out that the statement on the tickets under consideration was printed in such a manner as to be virtually unnoticeable and unreadable, the court concluded, as already noted, that the tickets did not give the passengers the required notice.

Other interpretations of article 3 have also taken into account the fact that a traveler today is likely to undertake international travel quite casually and without realizing the drastically limited protection he is receiving when compared to that provided by domestic flights. (See Mertens v. Flying Tiger Line, 341 F.2d 851 [2d Cir]; Warren v. Flying Tiger Line, 352 F.2d 494 [9th Cir.]; but see Seth v. British Overseas Airway Corp., 329 F.2d 302, 307 [1st Cir.].) In the Mertens case (341 F.2d 851, supra), the court read article 3 "to require that the ticket be delivered to the passenger in such a manner as to afford him a reasonable opportunity to take measures to protect himself against the limitation of liability" (p. 856) and held that the requirement was not met by reason of the fact, among others, that the ticket delivered was "printed in such a manner as to virtually be both unnoticeable and unreadable" (p. 857). In addition, the Civil Aeronautics Board in 1963 adopted a regulation requiring (1) that the statement as to limitation of liability follow the far more clear and specific language specified by the board; (2) that it "be printed in type at least as large as ten point modern type [as contrasted with the 4½ point type in this case] and in ink contrasting with the stock"; and (3) that a similar statement be placed at all ticket counters in letters at least one fourth of an inch high (Code of Fed.Reg., tit. 14, § 221.175.)[5]

These decisions and regulations are suggestive of a national policy requiring that air carriers give passengers clear and conspicuous notice before they will be permitted to limit their liability for injuries caused by their negligence. An examination of the ticket forms which the respondent used, in the light of that policy, can only lead one to conclude that Mrs. Seiter was not sufficiently apprised of the consequences which would result from the fact that her flight happened to carry her outside of the United States. Despite the fact that the Convention was applicable to her journey, the carrier's failure to give the requisite notice prevents it from asserting a limitation of liability. Accordingly, the plaintiff's motion to dismiss the third affirmative defense should have been granted.

The order of the Appellate Division should be reversed, with costs in all courts, and the certified question answered in the negative.

VAN VOORHIS, BURKE, SCILEPPI, BERGAN, KEATING and BREITEL, JJ., concur.

Order reversed, with costs in all courts, and case remitted to Supreme Court, Kings County, for further proceedings in accordance with the opinion herein. Questions certified answered in the negative.

QUESTIONS

1. Why must a travel agent disclose unfavorable prior experiences to new customers?
2. Why did the CAB take the action that it did in 1977 in re travel agents?
3. What was the holding in the *Bucholtz* case on page 356?
4. Why do the laws of agency in their traditional form, fall short in the travel agency business?
5. Disclosure of a ships name in maritime cases is sufficient to identify a principal. Why was the result different in the *McQuade* case on page 357?
6. Why would a travel agent seek to establish an independent contractor relationship with customers?
7. What was the key point on damages in the *Odysseys* case on page 362?
8. What reasons do courts cite in refusing to honor some disclaimers?
9. Reread the disclaimer on page 366. Was the court happy with it?
10. T. or F. Travel agents are probably controlled as much now as they will ever be.

ENDNOTES

1. Article 1 of the Convention, which bears on its applicability, reads as follows:

   "(1) This convention shall apply to all international transportation of persons, baggage, or goods performed by aircraft for hire. It shall apply equally to gratuitous transportation by aircraft performed by an air transportation enterprise.

   "(2) For the purposes of this convention the expression 'international transportation' shall mean any transportation in which, according to the contract made by the parties, the place of departure and the place of destination, whether or not there be a break in the transportation or a transshipment, are situated either within the territories of two High Contracting Parties, or within the territory of a single High Contracting Party, if there is an agreed stopping place within a territory subject to the sovereignty, suzerainty, mandate or authority of another power, even though that power is not a party to this convention. Transportation without such an agreed stopping place between territories subject to sovereignty, suzerainty, mandate, or authority of the same High Contracting Party shall not be deemed to be international for the purposes of this convention.

   "(3) Transportation to be performed by several successive air carriers shall be deemed, for the purposes of this convention, to be one undivided transportation, if it has been regarded by the parties as a single operation, whether it has been agreed upon under the form of a single contract or of a series of contracts, and it shall not lose its international character merely because one contract or a series of contracts is to be performed entirely within a territory subject to the sovereignty, suzerainty, mandate, or authority of the same High Contracting Party."

2. That she took out a $50,000 insurance policy in Seattle has, as Special Term declared, "little bearing on [the passenger's] intent relative to termination of the contract for international transportation or of the character of the trip from Seattle to New York in terms of internal or international passage." Mrs. Seiter may have purchased the $50,000 policy because she desired coverage in addition to the $25,000 of insurance (to cover the round trip) which she had procured before leaving New York, in view of the forecast of bad weather. Its purchase certainly created no inference that she considered the round trip at an end.

3. Article 3 provides:

   "(1) For the transportation of passengers the carrier must deliver a passenger ticket which shall contain the following particulars:

   (a) The place and date of issue;

   (b) The place of departure and of destination;

   (c) The agreed stopping places, provided that the carrier may reserve the right to alter the stopping places in case of necessity, and that if he exercises that right, the alteration shall not have the effect of depriving the transportation of its international character;

   (d) The name and address of the carrier or carriers;

   (e) A statement that the transportation is subject to the rules relating to liability established by this convention.

   (2) The absence, irregularity, or loss of the passenger ticket shall not affect the existence or the validity of the contract of transportation, which shall none the less be subject to the rules of this convention. Nevertheless, if the carrier accepts a passenger without a passenger ticket having been delivered he shall not be entitled to avail himself of those provisions of this convention which exclude or limit his liability."

4. One court has described the notice in this way (Lisi v. Alitalia-Linee Aeree Italiane, D.C., 253 F.Supp. 237, 243, affd. 2 Cir., 370 F.2d 508):

   "The footnotes printed in microscopic type at the bottom of the * * * coupons, as well as condition 2(a) camouflaged in Lilliputian print in a thicket of 'Conditions of Contract' crowded on [the outside back cover], are both unnoticeable and unreadable. Indeed, the exculpatory statements on which defendant relies are virtually invisible. They are ineffectively positioned, diminutively sized, and unemphasized by bold face type, contrasting color, or anything else. The simple truth is that they are so artfully camouflaged that their presence is concealed."

5. The language of the statement which was mandated by the CAB was similar to that provided for in the amendment to article 3 appearing in the so-called Hague Protocol to the Convention executed in 1955. (See 3 CCH Aviation L. Rep., par. 27,106). This Protocol was never ratified by the Senate, apparently because its most significant feature, increasing the maximum liability to $16,000, was considered inadequate. It is of more than passing interest that in 1965 our Government in a Notice of Denunciation declared that it opposed the Convention's low limits on liability and indicated an intention to withdraw from the Convention unless an agreement were reached (among the world's international air carriers) to raise the limit to $75,000 and that in May of 1966 such an agreement was executed. (See 3 CCH Aviation L.Rep., par. 27,130; The Warsaw Convention—Recent Developments and the Withdrawal of the United States Denunciation, 32 J. Air L. & Com. 243.)

23

Restaurants and Bars

A restaurant is a place of public accomodation where food is prepared, sold and consumed on the premises, or in carry-out form. The term is broad enough to include cafeterias, fast-food shops, grills, coffeehouses, cafes and others, but would *not* include eating places at private clubs. The latter do not have the public features of a restaurant. In the past, the term "tavern" meant an inn as well as an eating and drinking place. Today, the term is limited to the latter, since a tavern has more of the characteristics of a restaurant than of an inn. All of the above today *are not inns*, therefore the customary innkeeper's duties and liabilities do not necessarily apply. But there are duties and liabilities of restaurant operators (known as "restaurateurs") distinct from those of innkeepers. Of course, we must recognize that an innkeeper may also keep a restaurant simultaneously with the inn. In that event, dual responsibilities arise. This distinction is made in the cases. It is helpful to begin by an examination of how a court has defined a "restaurant" and then compare this with a statutory definition.

CASE DEFINITION

A restaurant is an establishment where meals and refreshments are served.[1] The distinction between a restaurant and a lodging facility is important because the duties, rights and liabilities are not the same. A restaurant is often included as part of the premises of a hotel or motel. If one is a guest of the hotel, then the innkeeper's duties and liabilities extend to those guests as they use the restaurant. Conversly, one who merely uses the restaurant and is not a guest at the hotel, is not entitled to have all innkeeper duties and obligations extended to him or her.

DEFINITION BY STATUTE

"Everyplace where food without lodging is usually furnished to guests and payment required therefore shall be deemed a restaurant. . . . The provisions of this article shall not apply to temporary food sales, not exceeding two weeks in length, by religious, educational, charitable or nonprofit organizations,"[2] says the West Virginia Code.

The removal by the legislature of temporary food sales not exceeding two weeks in length, by religious, educational, charitable or nonprofit organizations, makes inapplicable the provisions of the West Virginia food service sanitation regulation to such organizations and this would be true when such sales are conducted by the exempt organization in connection with carnivals, church activities, banquets, and fairs, involving the community and public.[3]

RESTAURANT v. INN

As a general principle, a restaurant is a place of entertainment for all. It makes no difference if one is a "local" or a "traveler." As we have seen, an inn is just the opposite.

LIABILITY OF RESTAURATEUR

The liability of a restaurateur for the property of patrons is based upon one of two legal principles: actual bailment in which the restaurant operator, by employees, takes possession of the property of a patron; or where there is constructive possession—that is, possession is not actual yet the restaurant nevertheless has control of the property. The burden of proof of negligence is on the patron. Each case must be decided upon its facts. In a fast-food carry out restaurant, there would hardly ever be a bailment, actual or constructive, of the property of a patron.

LIMITS ON LIABILITY

Statutes limit liability of restaurant operators for the loss of the goods of patrons, much like those of innkeepers. The maximum amount is usually smaller, however, such as $75.00.

LIABILITY TO WHOM?

At common law, one could not be held to warranty liability unless that person was in "privity of contract" with the injured person. That is, the seller must have sold the object to the injured party that caused the harm, and not someone else. This doctrine of privity has been abrogated (abolished) in some of the states by different versions of the UCC that were adopted. It has been abolished by court rulings in other states.

For example, if A invites B to have dinner at Restaurant X, and B is injured by a foreign substance in the food, is Restaurant X responsible even though A intended to pay for the food? The courts tend to answer this question in the affirmative, holding that there is an implied contract to furnish suitable food to *both* of them, even though the actual contract is with A alone.[4]

DUTIES

Contrary to the common law innkeeper rule, a restaurant operator is *not* under an obligation to receive all who seeks service there. However, the restaurateur is subject to federal[5] and state laws that prohibit discrimination on the grounds of race, color, creed or national origin—or sex in the states that have such laws.[6] But it is clear that these anti-discrimination laws apply only to *public*—not private places. A private club can establish its own standards of membership for whatever reason.[7]

However, as with so many long standing rules of law, exceptions seem to be in the making. The trend appears to be toward extending the common law innkeepers duty to receive, to the restaurant operator. This would be particularly so where the refusal was arbitrary, capricious or unreasonable. In such instances, the question of damages to one's reputation would arise, placing the matter in the realm of tort law. The cases that are establishing this trend are basing their findings on tort not contract. One who goes to a restaurant and who does not have a reservation, can not argue that the refusal of service amounted to a breach of contract. Where was the contract?

If one *does* have a reservation and is refused service, that is another matter. The following case illustrates.

HARDER v. AUBERGE DES FOUGERES, INC.
1972[8]

Before HERLIHY, P. J., and GREENBLOTT, SIMONS, KANE and REYNOLDS, JJ.

PER CURIAM.

This is an appeal from an order of the Supreme Court at Special Term, entered March 7, 1972 in Albany County, which granted defendants' motion to dismiss the complaint for failure to state a cause of action.

The first cause of action alleged by appellant states, in part, that respondent "unlawfully, willfully, deliberately, and without just cause, refused to admit or seat plaintiff and his guests for dinner service even though plaintiff and his guests (a) had made a bona fide reservation, (b) requested service, and (c) were ready, willing and able to pay any reasonable charges imposed by defendants for such meal." And further that, "By reason of defendants' actions and failure to furnish plaintiff and his guests with appropriate accommodations in this restaurant, plaintiff and his guests were subjected to great inconvenience, humiliation, and insult and were exposed to public ridicule in the presence of a number of people in such restaurant. As a result of the activities of defendants, its officers, agents, representatives or employees, plaintiff and his guest were forced to leave this restaurant and proceed to another place for their meals. Because of the commotion caused by defendants, plaintiff was injured in his good name and reputation which was absolutely uncalled for and unwarranted * * *."

The complaint must be viewed in the framework of our liberal rules of pleading, and if what is stated is a cause of action cognizable by the courts of this State, the pleading must be sustained.

At common law, a person engaged in a public calling, such as an innkeeper or common carrier, was held to be under a duty to the general public and was obligated to serve, without discrimination, all who sought service. On the other hand, proprietors of private enterprises, such as places of amusement and resort, were under no such obligation, enjoying an absolute power to serve whom they pleased.

The reason for the rule that innkeepers could not refuse service to members of the public was to make travel throughout the King's domain possible. For whatever benefit and purpose the rule once served in ancient times, it has no relevance in the 20th Century, and should not be recognized for the purpose of distinguishing inns from other places of public accommodation. In our view, a restaurant proprietor should be under the same duty as an innkeeper to receive all patrons who present themselves "in a fit condition", unless reasonable cause exists for a refusal to do so.

Moreover, there is some authority indicating that the ancient rule is not well regarded. Blackstone stated that a cause of action would lie against "an innkeeper, or other victualler" who refused to admit a traveler without cause (3 Blackstone's Comm., Sharswood ed., p. 166), and Judge Cardozo found that a "plaintiff, if wrongfully ejected from * * * [a] café, was entitled to recover damages for injury to his feelings as a result of the humiliation". Although in *Morningstar* the plaintiff was a guest in the hotel wherein the cafe from which he was ejected was situated, there is nothing in the opinion to indicate that this was a crucial factor in the court's decision. (211 N.Y. 465, 467, 105 N.E. 656, 657).

Furthermore, a proprietor of an inn or similar establishment, is under a duty to protect his patrons from injury, annoyance, or mistreatment through the acts of his servants or employees. The law imposes an obligation upon him to see that his agents and employees extend courteous and decent treatment to his guests, and holds himself liable in violation of this obligation by the use of insulting and abusive language. For these reasons we conclude that the allegations of the first cause of action adequately plead an intentional tort.

The order should be modified, on the law and the facts, so as to deny the motion to dismiss the first cause of action, and, as so modified, affirmed, without costs.

Order modified, on the law and the facts, so as to deny the motion to dismiss the first cause of action, and, as so modified, affirmed, without costs.

HERLIHY, P. J., GREENBLOTT and KANE, JJ., concur.

SIMONS and REYNOLDS, JJ., dissent and vote to affirm in an opinion by REYNOLDS, J.

REYNOLDS, Justice (dissenting).

We would affirm. The complaint does not state a cause of action under common law or statute. Appellant does not claim or argue a cause of action for an intentional tort. We cannot agree with the dictum discussion which would extend the duty of a hotel owner to that of a restaurant under the case law.

Common sense should dictate that refusals of restaurant service should be handled in a discreet, subdued matter no matter what the reason for the refusal might be.

It may well be true today that outside of private clubs, modern restaurants are becoming more and more true public facilities. If this view is accepted, then the duty to receive, just as with the innkeeper, should be extended. This might well be the case with the fast-food shops that dot our landscapes. Certainly one should not be denied service other than for undesirable physical condition or obnoxious conduct. The right to refuse under those conditions has long been upheld with innkeepers and restaurateurs. As a matter of fact, there would be a *duty* to refuse under such adverse conditions, because to fail to do so would prompt complaints from other customers.

Closely related to the legal question of liability is that of the *quality* of food and service that a restauratuer must provide to the customers who are served.

Article 2, section 314, of the UCC, provides, "Unless excluded or modified, a warranty that the goods shall be merchantable is implied in a contract for their sale if the seller is a merchant with respect to goods of that kind. Under this section, the serving for value of food or drink to be consumed either on the premises or elsewhere is a sale." The Official Comment to this section, item 5, states, "Serving food or drink for value, is a sale, whether to be consumed on the premises or elsewhere. Cases to the contrary are rejected." The warranty that applies to the sale of food is found in the same section in subsection 2 (c) which states: "Goods to be merchantable must be at least such as . . . (c) are fit for the ordinary purposes for which such goods are used . . . "

"The question as to whether an *implied warranty of wholesomeness* attaches in the transaction between a restaurant-keeper and a patron has been the subject of much judicial controversy throughout the country. From a review of the authorities, it may be safely said that the decided weight is in favor of holding that an implied warranty of wholesomeness does attach to the restaurateur-patron relationship. The focal point of the controversy has been whether the transaction should be designated a sale or merely the rendering of a service. The majority view, or the "Massachusetts-New York Rule" as it is called because it originated in those states, classifies the transaction as a sale or, at least, a qualified sale, to which the warranty attaches. Under the minority view, or the "Connecticut-New Jersey Rule," the transaction is held not to be a sale, but is curiously labeled "the uttering of food," to which no warranty attaches. It is the view of the supreme court of appeals of Virginia that the conclusions of those courts which hold the transaction to be a sale are based upon better and sounder reasoning, reflecting a more logical approach to the realities of a simple, everyday relationship. The customer does in fact rely upon a dispenser of food for more than the use of due care. He depends upon the experience and trade wisdom of the dispenser in selecting the articles or ingredients of the food, and upon his skill in the preparation and service thereof. The customer has no effective opportunity to inspect or select so far as wholesomeness is concerned. Thus, in Virginia it is held that the furnishing of food by a restaurant-keeper to a patron is a sale and carries an implied warranty that the food is wholesome and fit for human consumption, for the breach of which the restaurant-keeper is liable for consequential damages. This holding of Virginia accords with the section of the Uniform Commercial Code which provides that "the serving for value of food or drink to be consumed either on the premises or elsewhere is a sale" in which there is implied "a warranty that the goods shall be merchantable . . . if the seller is a merchant with respect to goods of that kind." This provision is, of course, now in effect in both Virginia and West Virginia.

FOREIGN SUBSTANCES

As a rule, objects that are foreign to food served in a restaurant could give rise to a breach of warranty of merchantability under the UCC, or give rise to a tort action for negligence. Such objects would include grass in soup, pebbles in spinach, and a nail in a salad. One has a duty to serve food that does not contain such foreign objects.

But what if an object in food that causes injury is *natural to the food*? This injects a new element and the courts are not so quick to place a legal responsibility upon the seller. Examples would include pits in whole olives, fish bones in fish and chicken bones in fried chicken. One who is injured by such objects must bear some of the responsibility—and perhaps all of it. The same has been held with fish bones found in chowder.[9]

If food or other items for consumption are served in a restaurant or other place of business, the result is just the opposite. In one case, a cherry pit left in ice cream was held to be not what one would reasonably expect to find in ice cream. The question of whether the one who consumed that ice cream, which caused injury, acted reasonably while eating the ice cream, was for a jury to decide and the case was returned to the lower court for that purpose.[10] In a similar case, a court held that a few fish bones in fish chowder could be reasonably expected, thus allowing the restaurant to escape liability.[11]

MICROWAVE OVENS

The advent and current wide usage of microwave ovens for food preparation, has resulted in states enacting statutes to protect those persons who might suffer harm because of their use. The following statute is typical.

Any restaurant, hotel, motel, dining room, hospital, snack bar or any food dispensing facility utilizing a microwave oven shall prominently display a public notice in the following words:

"NOTICE TO PERSONS HAVING HEART PACEMAKERS: This Establishment Uses a Microwave Oven."

The state director of health shall be responsible for administering this section. He may delegate the duties to any county boards of health or combined local boards of health.

The state health department shall purchase such notices assuring a uniform size and color of the notices.

Any person, firm or corporation who shall violate any provision of this section shall be guilty of a misdemeanor, and, upon conviction thereof, shall be fined not less than one hundred dollars nor more than five hundred dollars.

Turning now from the law that controls restaurateurs, let's take a look at what those in the "bar", "tavern" and "lounge" business are confronted with.

TAVERNS

DRAMS SHOP ACTS

Many states have enacted statutes that hold the seller of alcoholic beverages to an intoxicated person, responsible for injuries to third parties caused by the drunkeness of that person.[12] At common law, the opposite was the truth. The courts held that when an intoxicated person injured a third person, it was due to the consumption of the alcohol - not the *sale* of it. This is akin to the old court rulings that held that the serving of a meal in a restaurant was a service and not a sale. Such views have changed, of course, and different results follow today.

In the following case, a tavern customer sued the tavern owner for injuries caused by another customer who became intoxicated and assaulted him.

REIBOLT v. BEDIENT
Wash. App. 562 P. 2d 991 (1977).

SWANSON, Judge

On the evening of Sunday, September 16, 1973, Wilbur Reiboldt, along with several of his friends, journeyed to the Anchor Inn Tavern in the Pioneer Square area of Seattle to enjoy a program of live music. While Reiboldt was engaged in setting up his recording equipment, he was twice approached by an allegedly intoxicated Indian named Half Moon who tried to solicit free drinks from Reiboldt. On each occasion, Reiboldt informed Half Moon that he was not an employee of the tavern but, rather, was merely a patron. After the second attempt at "bumming" free drinks from Reiboldt, Half Moon attacked Reiboldt by striking him alongside the head. As a result of this blow, Reiboldt was thrust to the floor but managed in a dazed condition to stagger to his feet. Immediately upon reaching his feet, Reiboldt was again struck by Half Moon. This second attack caused Reiboldt to fall to the floor unconscious. At this point, Half Moon allegedly kicked Reiboldt causing him to suffer a broken leg. During the entire incident which, according to the witnesses, lasted from approximately 5 to 15 minutes, Albert R. Bedient, the tavern owner, was tending to his duties behind the bar. His testimony adduced at trial indicated that he had no knowledge of the supposed drunken nature of Half Moon, nor did he know of any complaints registered by any patrons concerning potential violence. Bedient testified that as soon as his attention was drawn to the altercation, he immediately went to the scene, but by the time he got there the fight was over. On the other hand, there was testimony introduced on behalf of Mr. Reiboldt that Bedient knew of Half Moon's intoxicated condition prior to the time of the incident and had, in fact, demanded Half Moon's departure from the Anchor Inn Tavern earlier that same day. There was also testimony which the jury could have believed which indicated that Bedient refused to respond to cries for help from the various patrons of the tavern.

Wilbur Reiboldt subsequently brought this action for personal injuries against Albert Bedient and the Anchor Inn Tavern, alleging that he had sustained serious bodily injuries in Bedient's tavern and that Bedient had been negligent in failing to protect his patrons from harm and injury. The jury returned a verdict of $75,000 in Reiboldt's favor. Bedient then timely sought a judgment notwithstanding the verdict or, in the alternative, a new trial, which was granted. Reiboldt appeals from the order granting a new trial, and Bedient cross-appeals.

Turning first to the claims made by appellant Reiboldt, the trial court gave the following reasons for granting a new trial:

1. Defendants' argument on the question of contributory negligence is not valid. There is something to it, but not enough.

2. This is a very thin case of liability. The only evidence whatever on the subject of negligence was that of Janet Charles. [In lower record.]

3. The size of the verdict, although not shocking, was astounding. It was at least five times greater than it should have been.

4. If there is anything to the plaintiff's case, he will have adequate opportunity to present it to another jury.

5. Although the court is hard put to put any single factor down that would warrant the granting of a new trial, it is the feeling of the court that justice has miscarried and that a new trial should be granted.

Reiboldt contends that the reasons stated by the trial court in its order was inadequate to grant a new trial. We agree and reverse.

The entry of a new trial is governed by CR 59. The trial court's order appears to include only two of the possible nine grounds stated in CR 59 for granting a new trial:

(a)(5) Damages so excessive or inadequate as unmistakably to indicate that the verdict must have been the result of passion or prejudice;

.   .   .   .

(a)(9) That substantial justice has not been done.

However, the order itself fails to comply with the requirements of CR 59(f):

In all cases where the trial court grants a motion for a new trial, it shall, in the order granting the motion, state whether the order is based upon the record or upon facts and circumstances outside the record which cannot be made a part thereof. If the order is based upon the record, the court shall give definite reasons of law and facts for its order. If the order is based upon matters outside the record, the court shall state the facts and circumstances upon which it relied.

The order expresses reasons or opinions which provide little or no assistance respecting appellate review of this case. We can only conclude that the trial judge simply disagreed with the jury, and this is not sufficient.

In order to uphold, as a basis for a new trial, a trial court's belief that the verdict is too high, the order must contain a finding that the amount awarded by the jury was "so excessive . . . as unmistakably to indicate that the verdict must have been the result of passion or prejudice". CR 59(a)(5). Such a finding is absent from the order under review. As stated in *James v. Robeck*, 79 Wash. 2d 864, 870, 490 P.2d 878, 882 (1971),

[I]t is our opinion that the rule now and for some time prevailing in this jurisdiction requires that the passion and prejudice be of such manifest clarity as to make it unmistakable.

Our review of the record does not support a conclusion that the jury verdict was so high as unmistakably to indicate passion or prejudice. Moreover, there exists a strong presumption of the adequacy of jury verdicts, see RCW 4.76-.030; *Cox v. Charles Wright Academy, Inc.*, 70 Wash.2d 173, 422, P.2d 515 (1967), and the trial court is precluded, absent a showing of passion or prejudice, from substituting its conclusion for that of the jury on the issue of damages.

With regard to the second reason for granting a new trial stated in the order, "the feeling of the court that justice has miscarried," we are hard pressed to accept such a ground as adequate, especially in light of the provisions of CR 59(f) which require that the order granting a new trial "state, whether the order is based upon the record or upon facts and circumstances outside the record which cannot be made a part thereof." If we assume that the order is based upon matters outside the record, the order fails to contain the facts and circumstances upon which it relied, as required by the rule. On the other hand, if we assume that the order is based upon the record, the rule requires that the court give "definite reasons of law and facts for its order." CR 59(f). We must conclude that the order provides no adequate basis for review of the asserted "failure of substantial justice" as a ground for new trial. See *Knecht v. Marzano, supra.* [Citation omitted.]

Next, we consider the arguments advanced by respondent in his cross-appeal. Essentially, he contends that the trial court erred in failing to direct a verdict in his favor both at the close of the plaintiff's case and at the close of all the evidence. A motion for a directed verdict admits the truth of the evidence of the party against whom the motion is made and all inferences that reasonably can be drawn therefrom. In addition, such a motion therefrom requires that the evidence be interpreted most strongly against the moving party and in the light most favorable to the opposing party. It is also a well-recognized rule in this state that in ruling upon a motion for a directed verdict, no element of discretion is involved and the trial court can grant such a motion only when it can be held as a matter of law that there is no evidence, nor reasonable inference from the evidence, to sustain the verdict. In evaluating the evidence introduced, and all reasonable inferences arising therefrom, the trial court must determine whether the nonmoving party has presented substantial evidence establishing a prima facie case in support of its claim. After carefully reviewing the record, we find sufficient evidence which could, if believed by the jury, support plaintiff Reiboldt's theory that the owner of the Anchor Inn breached his duty to exercise reasonable care and vigilance to protect patrons from reasonably foreseeable injury. We find no error in the trial court's denial of respondent's motion for a directed verdict.

Respondent next contends that the trial court erred when if refused to give a requested instruction on contributory negligence. A careful review of the record indicates no evidence upon which to base an instruction on contributory negligence. We find no error.

Finally, respondent argues that the trial court erred when it refused to grant it motion *in limine*. In *State v. Morgan*, 192 Wash. 425, 430, 73 P.2d 745, 747 (1937), our Supreme Court ruled that

[i]n the exercise of its sound discretion, the [trial] court could refuse to go into the matter in advance of the offer of evidence, in regular course, during the trial, and no error can be predicated upon this ruling.

It is, therefore, a matter of discretion as to whether or not a motion, prior to trial, to limit the evidence will be granted. Furthermore, in the instant case the respondent cross-appellant had ample opportunity to object to testimony as it was presented that he felt was irrelevant to the issue under litigation. Moreover, respondent Bedient has directed us to only four instances where allegedly prejudicial evidence was offered into evidence. After carefully reviewing each occurrence, we note that the cumulative effect of the supposed extraneous evidence was not prejudicial to respondent's case. Furthermore, in all the instances cited to us by the respondent, the trial court sustained objections to the introduction of irrelevant testimony when asked to do so. We cannot say that the trial court abused its discretion in this matter.

The order granting a new trial is reversed, and the cause is remanded for reinstatement of the verdict and entry of a judgment consistent with the verdict.

CALLOW and ANDERSEN, JJ., concur.

What happens when the owner of a tavern hires a security guard who, in turn, shoots a patron? This happened in the *Jax* case.

JAX LIQUORS, INC. v. HALL
Fla. App. 344 So. 2d 247 (1976)

SMITH, Judge

Each appellant raises the privotal question of whether it or they can be held liable for the parking lot shooting of an unruly bar patron of appellant Jax by an armed and uniformed guard, the employee of a security service operated by appellants Clark and Moore.

The firing of the pistol, viewed as an isolated event, was entirely unneccessary to any legitimate purpose of appellants and of the guard's employment. However, both Jax and the security service operated by Clark and Moore were served by the guard's armed presence in the bar. The confrontation began when the guard intervened, as he was expected to do, to prevent the patron from removing one of Jax's drinking glasses from the bar. The altercation grew from the event with unbroken continuity. The wound was inflicted while both parties were still on Jax's property. We conclude that the guard had not departed the scope of his employment when he shot the patron. Compare *Columbia By the Sea, Inc. v. Petty*, 157 So.2d 190 (Fla. App. 2nd, 1963); *Sixty-Six, Inc. v. Finley*, 224 So.2d 381 (Fla.App. 3rd, 1969). Contrast *Reina v. Metropolitan Dade County*, 285 So.2d 648 (Fla.App. 3rd, 1973), cert. disch. 304 So.2d 101 (Fla. 1974).

There being evidence that Jax had and exercised a right of control concerning the manner in which the guard performed his duties, the jury could properly have found that the guard and appellants Clark and Moore were not independent contractors for whose tort Jax would be immune. The same finding forecloses the crossclaim of Jax for indemnity against the guard service.

Each of appellants' points has been reviewed and found unavailing.

Affirmed.

BOYER' C. J., and RAWLS, J., concur.

ON PETITIONS FOR REHEARING

PER CURIAM.

The petitions for rehearing are DENIED.

BOYER, C. J., and RAWLS, J., concur.

SMITH, J., concurs with separate opinion.

SMITH, Judge (concurring):

I join in the court's denial of appellants' petitions for rehearing. Our disposition of those petitions has been delayed by lengthy reconsideration of the basic position advanced by Jax Liquors in this case, that it did not have and exercise a right to control the manner in which Williams, the guard, performed his duties. The court has been unable to agree upon an opinion on rehearing which elucidates further our decision as originally announced. However, I think it appropriate to express in terms of the evidence my own reasons, not approved by the other members of the court, for denying rehearing:

In contrast with the facts of *Williams v. Wometco Ent., Inc.*, 287 So.2d 353 (Fla.3d DCA 1974), cert. den., 294 So.2d 93 (Fla. 1974), and *Brien v. 18925 Collins Ave. Corp.*, 233 So.2d 847 (Fla. 3d DCA 1970), guard Williams was subject to the control of Jax not only in selecting "the result to be obtained" but also in respect to "the means to be employed."

This is not a case in which a merchant simply hired a guard service to patrol his premises. Jax, in order to preserve order and deal with unruly patrons, sought and obtained armed, uniformed guards for its dozen establishments in the Jacksonville area. Jax, not Clark and Moore, was the source of instructions that guard Williams station himself inside the door of the lounge, which Jax's supervisor characterized as the "hot zone," that the guard disperse crowds from the door, that the guard "try to talk" with rowdy or intoxicated patrons, that the guard exclude minors and, most significantly for present purposes, that the guard prevent patrons from walking out of the bar with Jax's glass tumblers. I am satisfied Jax did more than simply requisition law and order from a guard service, and that there was a jury issue whether Jax assumed important aspects of control over the means to be employed by the guard in accomplishing the desired result.

QUESTIONS

1. Why is there a difference between the laws of hotels and those of restaurants?
2. Do you know what "per curium" means? If not, ask.
3. Why is it important to have a legal definition of a restaurant—a hotel?
4. How do statutes limiting liability of a restaurant operator differ from those that limit liability of innkeepers?
5. How does the privity of contract principle come into play in restaurant cases?
6, Why was there no common law duty on restauratuers to receive all who sought their services?
7. Can you see "new law" in the making in the *Harder* case on page 376? In what respect?
8. Why did the drafters of the UCC see the need to include a specific provision to cover the serving of food and drink?
9. If a substance is part of food in nature, injury by it seldoms forms the basis for recovery in court. Why?
10. T. or F. An olive pit in an olive in a martini, would be a "foreign substance."

ENDNOTES

1. *Alpaugh v. Wolverton,* 184 Va. 943, 36 S.E. 2d 906.
2. W.Va. Code, Ch. 16, Art. 6, Sec. 3 (1966).
3. Opinion, West Virginia Attorney General, Jan. 9, 1970.
4. *Conklin v. Hotel Waldorf Astoria Corp.,* 169 N.Y.S. 2d 205 (1957).
5. Title II, Civil Rights Act of 1964, 42 U.S.C. 2000 (1964).
6. New York, McKinney's Supp. 1972, sec. 296 (2).
7. Moose Lodge No. 7 of *Harrisburg v. Irvis,* 407 U.S. 163 (1972). Mr. Irvis, a then member of the Pennsylvania legislature, was denied permission to eat lunch at a Moose Lodge in Harrisburg, Pennsylvania.
8. *Harder v. Auberge Des Fougeres, Inc.* 40 App. Div. 2d 98, 338 N.Y.S. 2d 356 (Third Dept. 1972).
9. *Webster v. Blue Ship Tea Room, Inc.,* 347 Mass. 421, 198 N.E. 2d 309 (1964).
10. *Williams v. Braum Ice Cream Store, Inc.,* 534 P. 2d 700 (Okla. 1974).
11. *Webster v. Blue Chip Tea Room. Inc.,* supra note 9.
12. *Mitchell v. The Shoals, Inc.,* 227 N.Y.S. 2d 113 (1967).

24

Carriers

An important part of travel and lodging law is found in those rules and statutes that regulate cruise ships and airlines. These rules and statutes are principally of recent origin, although rules of cruise ships can be traced back for centuries to when sailing ships plied the oceans. In this chapter we will look at the principles that regulate ship travel and then examine airline cases. It should be noted that the law is in a state of flux and changes will be forthcoming in the future—particularly in air travel. Here we see, for the first time, the matter of subsidies coming into use in travel matters.

In the past the United States has subsidized, with tax dollars, cruise ships operating on the high seas. The Federal Maritime Commission has felt that such ships promoted the national interest. This policy had been created originally to benefit cargo ships but carried over to cruise ships.

Under this act, ships could not be older than 25 years and still receive subsidies, the assumption being that this time span represented the economic life of an ocean going vessel. By 1977, only two cruise ships were receiving these subsidies—and they were both almost 25 years old. Subsidization of our airlines is another story and will not be examined here. First, let's look at the law that regulates cruise ships.

CRUISE SHIPS

CONTRACT OF CARRIAGE

When a breach of contract of common carriage occurs, compensatory damages are available to the traveler who can prove those damages. Punitive damages *cannot* be recovered unless the breach is accompanied by an intentional, wanton and willful act of the carrier or its agents. If a willful act of an employee is outside the scope of employment, then punitive damages cannot be recovered from the common carrier.[1] In most states, punitive damages cannot be recovered in a breach of contract case unless the acts also constitute an independent cause of action in tort.[2]

CONTRACTUAL DUTY

A common carrier has a contractual duty to transport passengers, exercising the highest degree of vigilance and care. This duty extends to employees and agents even when such acts are outside the scope of employment. But observe that we are talking about *contractual* duties—not tort duties, and it must be remembered that the damages recoverable are only compensatory and not punitive when the act of the employee is outside the scope of the employment.

If an employee of a common carrier acts within the scope of his or her employment and insults, or harms a traveler intentionally, then punitive damages can be recovered from the common carrier upon proper proof in court.

The act must be authorized by the carrier or ratified by the carrier later. In other words, the act of the employee must be that of the carrier.[4] As a general principle, a criminal act committed by an employee outside of the scope of employment does not render the employer liable—unless ratification takes place.[5] In some states, employers cannot ratify an unlawful act of an employee. In the following case, the plaintiff brought suit for both compensatory and punitive damages because of an assault by an employee against her during a cruise.

COMMODORE CRUISE LINE LTD, v. KORMENDI
Fla. App. 344 So.2d 896 (1977)

Before HENDRY, C.J., and BARKDULL and NATHAN, JJ.

PER CURIAM

Appellant, defendant below, appeals from a final judgment entered pursuant to a jury verdict which awarded appellees, plaintiffs below, both compensatory and punitive damages for an assault and battery alleged to have been committed upon appellee Ilona Kormendi by an employee of appellant during a cruise on appellant's ship; and from a post judgment "order denying defendant's motion to alter or amend final judgment and/or to set aside the judgment and/or for new trial."

Appellee, traveling without her husband, was allegedly assaulted and battered by an employee of appellant. The incident was alleged to have occurred one evening, during a Carribbean cruise on appellant's ship, while appellee was a passenger. The assailant apparently attempted to rob appellee's cabin, but was taken by surprise by appellee's presence in said cabin. A scuffle ensued after which the knife-wielding individual ran from the scene. This retreat was, however, not taken before appellee identified the person as a black man in crewman's garb. A subsequent investigation by the ship's captain and officers transpired, however, the identity of the assailant was never discovered.

The cause proceeded to trial upon the theory of breach of contract of common carriage. At trial there was ample testimony to suggest that the aforementioned investigation to ascertain the identity of the assailant was far from adequate, as there were no black passengers aboard the ship during the cruise and only two black crewmen.

At trial's conclusion, a jury returned a verdict for appellees and against appellant in the sum of Eighty-five Thousand Dollars ($85,000.00) compensatory damages and Two Hundred Thousand Dollars ($200,000.00) punitive damages. Post trial motions were filed by appellant and denied by the court and this appeal follows.

Appellant raises two points on appeal. The first point challenges the sufficiency of the evidence in support of appellees' claim for assault and battery. After reviewing the record, we are of the opinion that there was substantial competent evidence adduced that would support a verdict for appellees. As such, there was not error in denying either appellant's motion for directed verdict or its post-trial motion for entry of judgment notwithstanding the verdict, properly styled a motion for judgment in accordance with motion for directed verdict.

Appellant's second point concerns the correctness of an award of punitive damages. It is appellant's contention that, pursuant to a cause of action based upon a breach of contract of common carriage, punitive damages are only awardable against an employer when its employee commits an intentional, willful, wanton or malicious act while within the scope of his employment. *Sub judice*, no contention or argument was made by appellees that the assault occurred while within the official duties of the employee and therefore, appellant argues, it was error to allow punitive damages.

For the reasons that follow, we agree with appellant's contention and reverse.

Under Florida Law, punitive damages are not generally recoverable for breach of contract unless the acts constituting the breach also amount to an independent cause of action in tort, sustained by proper allegations and proof of an intentional wrong, insult, abuse or gross negligence.

Furthermore, under Florida law, a contractual duty arises between a passenger and common carrier obligating the carrier to transport the passenger to his or her destination, exercising the highest degree of care and vigilance for the passenger's safety. *Hall v. Seaboard Air Line Ry. Co.*, 84 Fla. 9, 93 So. 151 (1921); 5 Fla. Jur. *Carriers*, § 108. The carrier's duty is transferred by and through its employees and any willful misconduct by its employees are actionable as against the carrier-employer. *Hall*, supra, 14 Am. Jur. 2d *Carriers*, § 1059.

In addition, in comparison to an ordinary master-servant relationship, a common carrier is liable to a passenger for the wrongful acts of his or her employees during the contractual period, notwithstanding the fact that said acts are not within the scope of the employees employment. Compare *Reina v. Metropolitan Dade County*, 285 So. 2d 648 (Fla. 3d DCA 1973), where the contract of carriage had terminated before the employee—bus driver assaulted the former passenger.

The only question, then, for our determination, is whether the expanded liability of a common carrier for damages occasioned by a breach of contractual duty owed by its employee to a passenger includes liability for punitive damages, over and above compensatory damages, notwithstanding the fact that the complained of act or acts were committed by the employee outside the scope of his employment.

While case law and authority for awarding punitive damages against a common carrier and in favor of a passenger for the wrongful acts of an employee done within the scope of the employee's employment are ample, *Miami Transit Co. v. Yellen*, 156 Fla. 351, 22 So. 2d 787 (1945); *Atlantic Greyhound Lines v. Lovett*, 134 Fla. 505, 184 So. 133 (1938); 5 Fla. Jur. *Carriers*, § 144; our research and research of counsel have failed to reveal dispositive authority from within this state for the question posed above.

Research of the law in other jurisdictions which have considered the question does reveal the following. In order for a common carrier to be liable to a passenger for punitive damages, the insulting, abusive or intentional wrong must be committed by the employee while discharging duties within the scope of his employment, or the act must be authorized by the employer or subsequently ratified by him.

In that the assault was not committed by the employee while discharging duties within the scope of his employment, it was therefore incumbent upon appellees to allege and prove at trial that the act was subsequently ratified or initially authorized by appellant. This was never done, however, *assuming arguendo*, that the theory of ratification was attempted by appellees, this would be to no avail. The law is clear that unless the original act under scrutiny is done on the behalf of the employer, no ratification can take place. In addition, the Florida Supreme Court has stated that a criminal act committed outside the scope of a servant's authority cannot be ratified by the master. *Mallory v. O'Neil*, 69 So.2d 313 (Fla.1954).

In conclusion, we hold that where, as here, a passenger injured by an employee of a common carrier files suit based upon a breach of contract of carriage, punitive damages can only be awarded to the passenger upon a proper allegation and proof that the complained of act was committed by the employee while within the scope of his employment or, when the act was initially authorized by the carrier or subsequently ratified by him.

Accordingly, it was error to award punitive damages to appellees and therefore, the judgment appealed must be reversed and remanded with instructions to the trial judge to deduct the award of punitive damages from the total recovery. Once done, the final judgment as modified is affirmed.

Affirmed in part; reversed and remanded in part.

Turning from our brief look at the laws of cruise ships, let's examine the laws that come to the front in the operation of airlines. Two problems have been in the courts: one has to do with "bumping" and the other with "overbooking."

RESERVATIONS—AIRLINES

DAMAGES

When breach of an airline reservation occurs, recoveries have been permitted for compensatory damages (actual losses) as well as punitive or exemplary damages. In one case, a federal judge permitted a "bumped" traveler to recover punitive damages, basing the decision on federal law.[6]

Some overbooking may be justified for pure economic reasons. This assumes that alternate service is made available for all who need it, and within a reasonable time. In that industry, because of the constant no-shows, an exception to the general contract obligation to hold the seat, might, and probably should, be applied by the courts. Yet the courts do not look at the matter this way. As the following case illustrates, recovery has been allowed when confirmed reservation holders are denied seats because of overbooking.

ARCHIBALD v. PAN AMERICAN WORLD AIRWAYS
460 F. 2d 14 (1972)

CHOY, Circuit Judge.

Mr. and Mrs. George B. Archibald appeal a district court order directing a verdict for Pan American World Airways, Inc. (Pan Am). The District Court found that the Archibalds had failed to present a prima facie case of undue or unreasonable preference or unjust discrimination in violation of 49 U.S.C. § 1374(b). We reverse and remand.

On August 2, 1968, the Archibalds made two economy reservations for Pan Am's Flight 801 on August 6 from Tokyo to Guam. Pan Am accepted and confirmed the reservations, and told the Archibalds no further confirmation was necessary. On August 6, the Archibalds checked in at the airport nearly an hour early, and received seat assignments. When they attempted to board the plane, however, they and 28 other passengers were asked to step aside. Many of these passengers eventually enplaned, but the Archibalds and a dozen others did not. Three passengers who did go aboard made their reservations after the Archibalds had made theirs.

Pan Am then told the remaining passengers that the flight had been oversold, and that they would not be able to go. The airline provided hotel accommodations for the bumped passengers, tendered a voucher for payment of denied boarding compensation which Mr. Archibald did not cash, and put the Archibalds on the next available flight to Guam.

49 U.S.C. § 1374(b) reads, in pertinent part:

"No air carrier or foreign air carrier shall make, give, or cause any undue or unreasonable preference or advantage to any particular person . . . in any respect whatsoever or subject any particular person . . . to any unjust discrimination or any undue or unreasonable prejudice or disadvantage in any respect whatsoever."

This section creates a private federal cause of action for unreasonable preferences and unjust discrimination. Fitzgerald v. Pan American World Airways, Inc., 229 F.2d 499 (2nd Cir. 1956). An injuction against prospective or continuing discrimination is usually refused out of deference to administrative remedies before the Civil Aeronautics Board. Mortimer v. Delta Air Lines, 302 F.Supp. 276, 282 (N.D.Ill., 1969); Wills v. Trans World Airlines, Inc., 200 F. Supp. 360, 366 (S.D.Cal., 1961). However, purely nominal compensatory damages are available, including an award for humiliation and hurt feelings when the facts warrant, and the extent and nature of the affront are established. Flores v. Pan American World Airways, Inc., 259 F.Supp. 402, 404 (D.P.R., 1966). See *Wills, supra*, 200 F.Supp. at 366-367, in which the plaintiff received $1.54 for pecuniary loss and $5,000 in punitive damages. Punitive damages over and above actual injury are awardable if the defendant acted "wantonly, or appressively, or with such malice as implies a spirit of mischief or criminal indifference to civil obligations." *Wills, supra*, at 367-368.

Decisional law has not yet clearly established what constitutes a prima facie case under § 1374(b). Actual discrimination or preference must be shown. *Flores, supra*. Other elements of a plaintiff's case are found in the three reported decisions involving passengers with reservations who were not allowed to board planes. In *Mortimer*, an economy passenger was bumped to make room for a first class passenger. While its opinion dealt with jurisdictional issues, the court commented, "In order to succeed in an action under this section, it must be alleged, as it is here, and proven that the plaintiff's right to fair, equal and non-discriminatory treatment has been violated." 302 F. Supp. at 281.

In *Wills*, an economy passenger was sacrificed in favor of a first class passenger with a later reservation in direct violation of the airline's own bumping policy. The courts held that the plaintiff was "entitled to priority in flight accommodations over all passengers who had made later reservations than he and yet were permitted to board the flight. . . . By disregarding plaintiff's priority, the defendent airline unjustly and unreasonably discriminated against him, and thus violated the Act." 200 F. Supp. at 365. And in Stough v. North Central Airlines, Inc., 55 Ill.App.2d 338, 204 N.E.2d 792 (1965), the court affirmed a jury verdict that the airline had not discriminated against two passengers with reserved seats who (in accordance with company safety regulations) were not allowed to board a plane which departed with empty seats.

These three cases demonstrate that while overselling does not per se give rise to a § 1374(b) action, substantial overselling is evidence of malice to be considered in assessing punitive damages. See*Wills, supra*, 200 F.Supp. at 367-368. Some overselling is an economic necessity for an airline in view of inevitable cancellations and no-shows. However, when a flight is thus oversold, the airline must fill the plane in a reasonable and just manner. *Stough* and *Wills* indicate that bumping which is outwardly discriminatory or preferential may be legitimated by proof that the airline adhered to its established policy and that the policy is reasonable. This policy is within the peculiar knowledge of the airline, which is most able to present evidence justifying the selection of one passenger over another. The passenger cannot reasonably be expected to divine at the gate, or discover later, what the airline's policy is and whether it has been obeyed. The passenger is able to prove that he possessed a confirmed reservation and a resultant right to a seat, and that this priority was not honored. This suffices to establish that a preference or discrimination has occurred. It is not unreasonable then to place upon the airline the burden of proving that the discrimination or preference was reasonable by demonstrating company policy and why, in each particular case, one passenger was chosen over another.

The Archibalds proved that they had a priority right to an economy seat because they held confirmed reservations on Flight 801, and that Pan Am allowed three passengers with later reservations to board the plane. With this, they established a prima facie case that Pan Am had unjustly and unreasonably discriminated against them. Since Pan Am had not demonstrated, if it could, the reasonableness of its preference of the three passengers over the Archibalds, a directed verdict for the airline was inappropriate at that stage of the trial.

Reversed and remanded.

These cases, however, are not based on breach of contract, but rather on violations of the Federal Aviation Act, section 414 (b). However, in *Mortimer v. Delta Airlines*, 302 F. Supp. 276 (N.D. Ill. 1969), it would seem that the court is saying that *breach of contract could be* the basis of an action for overbooking.

Other problems arise in the operation of airlines, and three cases have been selected to illustrate the variety of these problems. Perhaps the most common type of case is the one where luggage is lost during travel.

COHEN v. VARIG AIRLINES, ETC.
390 N.Y.S. 2d 515 (1976)

Carriers

In action by airline passengers against airline to recover value of lost baggage checked with airline, there was insufficient evidence to support trial court's finding that airline's refusal to unload all luggage from its plane constituted "willful misconduct," so as to abrogate limitation of liability provision of Warsaw Convention.

Before DUDLEY, P.J., and RICCOBONO and TIERNEY, JJ.

PER CURIAM:

Judgment entered December 15, 1975 (Danzig, J.) modified by decreasing the total recovery to the sum of $700.00, with interest and costs; as modified, affirmed without costs.

There was insufficient evidence in the record to support the trial court's finding that the act of defendant in refusing to unload all luggage from its plane in Rio de Janeiro constituted "willful misconduct" within the purview of Article 25(1) of the Warsaw Convention (*Grey v. American Airlines, Inc.*, 227 F.2d 282 [2d Cir.]).

DUDLEY, P.J., and TIERNEY, J., concur.
RICCOBONO, J., dissents in the following memorandum.

RICCOBONO, Justice (dissenting):

I dissent and vote to affirm for the reasons set forth in the opinion of Danzig, J., at Trial Term, except as indicated at the end of this memorandum.

In my view, there was sufficient evidence in the record for the Trial Court to find in the unique and unusual factual pattern under review that the act of defendant, by its employee, in refusing to remove plaintiff's luggage from its plane in Rio de Janeiro constituted "willful misconduct" within the purview of Article 25(1) of the Warsaw Convention (*Grey v. American Airlines, Inc.*, 227 F.2d 282 [2d Cir.]). Moreover, I agree with Trial Term that New York law governed the elements of damages to be recovered by plaintiffs.

Plaintiffs' recovery was not limited by defendant's filed tariff to the loss of their personal property. Individuals and corporations engaged in quasi public business may not contract to absolve themselves from liability for their own willful misconduct or gross negligence.

Tishman & Lipp, Inc. v. Delta Airlines, 275 F.Supp. 471 (S.D.N.Y.), aff'd 413 F.2d 1401, 2nd Cir., relied on by appellant is not applicable. Plaintiffs' luggage contained the usual apparel and accoutrements of vacationers, not thousands of dollars worth of jewelry.

The award to plaintiff Hermaine K. Cohen, however, was excessive. Contrary to the finding below her medicines were not in the lost luggage; she had them with her. I would therefore reduce her award for distress and inconvenience by $250.00.

In the next case, an airline was sued for scald burns received by a passenger while in flight. Notice how the "directed verdict" was set aside since the court felt that there were questions of fact for a jury to decide.

RUDEES v. DELTA AIRLINES, INC.
553 S.W. 2d. 84 (Tenn.1977)

MATHERNE, Judge.

While riding as a fare-paying passenger on a regularly scheduled flight of the defendant airline, the plaintiff sustained personal injuries when a stewardess spilled scalding coffee on his lap. The plaintiff sued for damages, and the trial judge, at the conclusion of the plaintiff's proof, directed a verdict for the defendant. The plaintiff appeals, assigning that action of the trial judge as error.

The plaintiff boarded the defendant's DC-9 airplane at Memphis for a flight to Atlanta, Georgia. The passengers were asked to keep their seat belts fastened due to the possibility that the plane might encounter air turbulence. At a point approximately 100 miles from Atlanta, a stewardess came down the aisle of the airplane carrying at waist level an open tray which contained several cups of scalding coffee. The plaintiff was seated on an aisle seat with his seat belt fastened; he had not ordered coffee. The airplane apparently hit some clear air turbulence which made the stewardess sway in the aisle and ill the contents of the cups on the plaintiff's lap. This resulted in rather sev e burns to the plaintiff's thighs and groin area.

The defendant, on motion for directed verdict, argued that the plaintiff had not proved any negligence on its part. Counsel for the defendant argued, and the trial judge apparently agreed, that the plaintiff could not recover because he failed to prove that the pilot was negligent or that the defendant knew or should have known about the air turbulence.

The foregoing argument overlooks the basis of the lawsuit. The plaintiff alleged that the stewardess was negligent: (1) in spilling the coffee; (2) in her manner of carrying scalding coffee down the aisle of the plane; (3) in carrying the coffee in uncovered containers; and (4) in attempting to serve scalding coffee during flight. The issue is the negligence of the stewardess; therein lies the lawsuit.

Facts were proved from which the jury could have found the proximate cause of the plaintiff's injuries was the negligence of the stewardess as charged. We hold that reasonable minds could well differ on this issue and that the trial judge erred in directing a verdict for the defendant.

The judgment of the trial court is reversed, and this lawsuit is remanded for a new trial. The accumulated costs in the trial court and in this Court are adjudged against the defendant-appellee. The cost of the new trial will be there adjudged.

CARNEY, P. J., and NEARN, J., concur.

Those in the travel and lodging business will often call upon the airlines to make deliveries of equipment and other personal items. The following involves a bank that shipped bank notes by air. The principles are worth noting since they would have application in other travel and lodging functions when goods are shipped by air. Again, the rules of the Warsaw Convention become involved.

MFRS. HANOVER TRUST CO. v. ALITALIA AIRLINES
429 S F. Supp. 964 (1977)

CONNER, District Judge:

On January 4, 1974, a Wells Fargo truck delivered a parcel of nondescript appearance to Cargo Building No. 86 [Building 86], the export operations facility of Alitalia Airlines at John F. Kennedy International Airport, Jamaica, New York. Within two hours of its delivery to Building 86 pending transport aboard Alitalia flight 611, the parcel—containing bank notes in the sum of $200,000 consigned to the Umma Bank of Tripoli, Libya—was to make an unscheduled landing in the hands of three gunmen. The latter, together with their prize, have to date escaped capture or recovery. What the gunmen gained, Manufacturers Hanover Trust Company lost, as shipper of the notes. Ultimate liability for that loss was the subject of a four-day, non-jury trial that began on June 8, 1976. This Opinion incorporates the Court's findings of fact and conclusions of law pursuant to Rule 52(a) F.R.Civ.P.

I.

At approximately one o'clock in the afternoon of January 4, 1974, James

Brown, a security guard then employed by Beatty Protective Service, was dispatched to Building 86 on assignment, outfitted with street clothes, a .38 caliber police special, and the knowledge that he had been hired to guard high-value cargo of otherwise unidentified nature. Guided by Alitalia's assistant cargo manager and its deputy supervisor down a corridor fronted by offices, Brown was directed to a chair adjacent to an unmarked, locked door in view of a number of female typists. Thus stationed, Brown was instructed to, "Sit in this chair and watch the pretty girls." However pleasurable that initial scene according to Brown's subjective lights, the view became surely less agreeable shortly before 3:00 P.M., when Brown abruptly found himself looking into the barrel of a loaded revolver. Rather shakily holding the weapon was a man bearing the outward trappings of a Telephone Company repairman, accompanied by another similarly garbed.

Thus addressed by a gun, gripped as it was in an unsteady hand, and by the electrifying announcement, "This is a stick-up," Brown—chosing wisdom's course—eschewed the weapon in his shoulder holster and speedily retreated, with several Alitalia secretaries also in tow, through the corridor and into a men's room, obedient to directions of the gunmen.

Scant minutes earlier, the gunmen's initial contact with Nicola Amoruso, Alitalia's cargo operations manager, had been far more placid. Having proceeded into Building 86 through one of its unguarded entryways, and apparently having gained unchallenged access from the outer public area to the inner office area through a door marked "Authorized Personnel Only," the two had chanced upon Amoruso in their search for the Building 86 supervisor. After Amoruso had identified himself as the manager of operations, the pair explained that a communications problem had been traced to Building 86 and asked to be led to the building's telephone panel. The three-man procession down the corridor from Amoruso's office was suddenly halted, however, when—with revolvers freshly drawn and levelled at Amoruso—the gunmen declared their actual purpose, i. e., to get "the shipment of money." Initially frozen in terror, and eventually achieving movement only by force of the gunmen's prodding, Amoruso—attempting to remain at least visibly calm—followed his assailants' order to instruct other Alitalia employees not to use their telephones pending "repairs," the gunmen meanwhile secreting their weapons beneath their jackets. That done, Amoruso and a secretary were herded into a ladies' room, soon to be involuntarily joined in the approximately 5' x 5' area by a contingent of some ten or more co-workers.

Shortly thereafter, one of the gunmen reclaimed Amoruso from the ladies'-room crush and ordered him to "open up the strong room." The sole key to the Building 86 "valuables room" was contained, Amoruso knew, in a cabinet—itself normally locked—in the assistant cargo manager's office. Impelled by the gunman's apparent determination and impatience as well as by his weapon, Amoruso made his way to his assistant's office and discovered, to his relief, that the cabinet holding the valuables-room key had fortuitously been left open. With the key in his possession and the gunman at his heels, repeatedly threatening death if he triggered an alarm, Amoruso hastily repaired to the door of the valuables room—the post from which Brown had only moments before been unceremoniously relieved. The door was thereupon unlocked, revealing on the shelves within two lone packages. One, the parcel containing the bank notes, was promptly passed from Amoruso to the gunman. The second package, thereafter reported to have contained gold dental alloy worth some $60,000, apparently was ignored. Having served his fleeting purpose, and again being pushed toward the confines of the ladies' room, Amoruso noted that his two assailants had been joined by a third, a hooded figure without the Telephone Company gear of the others, but no less potently equipped with a gun.

Redeposited in the ladies' room, Amoruso joined his dozen or so colleagues resignedly awaiting deliverance. Their release came about five minutes later, when the door to the ladies' room was opened by Anthony Baldi, then the assistant cargo manager at Alitalia. During the major portion of the robbery's course, Baldi had been occupied by business that had taken him happily beyond Building 86 and that had kept him wholly unsuspecting of the drama within. Less happily, however, Baldi was to become a momentary participant in that drama upon his return to Building 86, when, accosted by the third gunman, he was first ordered to "freeze" and then to "turn around." Apparently dissatisfied with the execution of those commands, the gunman pistol-whipped Baldi before fleeing through one of the building's exits. Bleeding and dizzy, Baldi summoned enough wit to telephone the airport police. Sounds from the lavatories nearby eventually brought Baldi to the aid of his colleagues within. By this time, all of the gunmen had quit the premises.

Their ten-to-fifteen-minute capitivity ended, the Alitalia employees eagerly emerged en masse from the lavatory, only to encounter five or six strangers with guns drawn, order them to "freeze." Assuming this new group to be a fresh wave of robbers, the former captives turned on their heels and ran "instinctively" back to the lavatory, a proven safe retreat. The armed men, however, were subsequently identified as members of the Port Authority police, dressed in civilian clothes, summoned scarcely minutes earlier by Baldi. Beyond the battery of police questions that inevitably would follow and the administration of necessary medical aid to the wounded Baldi, normalcy had returned to Building 86.

II.

As noted at the outset, the bank notes stolen from Building 86 on January 4, 1974 have never been retrieved. The parties herein agree, as does this Court, that the extent of Alitalia's liability, if any, for that loss must be determined by reference to the Warsaw Convention [the Convention], as reproduced in its English translation at 49 Stat. 3000 (1934). See Article 1(1)-(2) of the Convention.

Articles 18 and 20(1) of the Convention set the measure of plaintiff's present claim, the former in relevant part providing that "[t]he carrier shall be liable for * * * loss of * * * any goods * * * during [the period in] which the * * * goods are in charge of the carrier * *," the latter providing that "[t]he carrier shall not be liable if he proves that he and his agents have taken all necessary measures to avoid the damage or that it was impossible for him or them to take such measures." Both parties herein apparently concede that Articles 18 and 20 in tandem operate to establish a presumption of carrier liability, in the event of a loss within the Convention's terms, that, in the present context, may be rebutted only by defendant's persuasive proof that it took "all necessary measures" to prevent the loss at issue. See *Wing Hang Bank, Ltd. v. Japan Air Lines Co., Ltd.*, 357 F.Supp. 94 (S.D.N.Y.1973); *Rugani v. K.L.M. Royal Dutch Airlines*, 4 Avi. 17,257 (N.Y.Ct. of City of N.Y.), *aff'd*, 285 App.Div. 944, 139 N.Y.S.2d 899 (1st Dep't), *aff'd*, 309 N.Y. 810, 130 N.E.2d 1013 (1954); *Kraus v. Koninklijke Luchtvaart Maatschappij, N. V.*, 92 N.Y.S.2d 315 (Sup.Ct.N.Y.Co.1949); cf. *Grey v. American Airlines*, 227 F.2d 282 (2d Cir. 1955); Lowenfeld & Mendelsohn, The United States and the Warsaw Convention, 80 Harv.L.Rev. 497, 500 (1967).

Both plaintiff and defendant have devoted considerable efforts to explain and support their respective constructions of the phrase "all necessary measures."

But, in the end, a common-sense reading serves best. Thus, notwithstanding plaintiff's argument to the contrary, this Court concludes that the phrase "all necessary measures" cannot be read with strict literality, but must, rather, be construed to mean "all *reasonable* measures." After all, there could scarcely be a loss of goods—and consequently no call for operation of Article 20—were a carrier to have taken every precaution literally necessary to the prevention of loss. Nor, on the other hand, may a carrier escape liability under Article 20, as Alitalia suggests, by demonstrating no more than its recourse to some—as opposed to all—reasonable measures. In short, Article 20 requires of defendant proof, not of a surfeit of preventatives, but rather, of an undertaking embracing all precautions that in sum are appropriate to the risk, *i. e.*, measures reasonably available to defendant and reasonably calculated, in cumulation, to prevent the subject loss. Such construction finds implicit support in the few precedents squarely on point, see *Wing Hang Bank, Ltd. v. Japan Air Lines Co., Ltd. supra; Rugani v. K.L.M. Royal Dutch Airlines, supra,* and in the leading treatise on the Convention, see D. Goedhuis, National Airlegislations and the Warsaw Convention 217-38 (The Hague 1937).

With so much determined, the question of Alitalia's liability in the present case need not detain us long. Alitalia, the record makes clear, did undertake a number of measures, each intrinsically reasonable, to secure high-value cargo held in its custody. The existence and structure of the Building 86 valuables room; the armed guard hired specially to obstruct illicit access thereto; the log-book record of high-value cargo, conscientiously maintained; Alitalia's refusal to accept high-value cargo deliveries until an armed guard's arrival; certain precautions taken by Alitalia to prevent undue circulation of documents reflecting a shipment of high-value cargo—all combined to demonstrate that defendant had not been wholly unmindful of nor unmoved by considerations of security. But such precautions would be, predictably enough, likely unavailing in the circumstance of an armed robbery, as witness the scenario at Building 86 on the afternoon of January 4, 1974. To preserve against such eventuality, more could—and should—have been done. With unrestricted access into Building 86 and through it, the armed guard stationed on a chair at the valuables-room entrance was positioned no more securely than the proverbial sitting duck. As Alitalia'a own witnesses agreed, restrictions on access to and through Building 86—or, at least, an enclosure about the valuables-room and its guard—might have discouraged or frustrated robbery, if not insured against it. Moreover, armed robbery might have been prevented—or ultimately stymied—had a silent alarm system, with a direct connection to the Port Authority police station, been installed on the premises of Building 86. The costs involved in the installation and annual maintenance of such a system, *i. e.*, $200 and $300, respectively, would have been more than reasonable in light of its robbery-prevention value.

We cannot say, of course, that such precautions would necessarily have averted the loss upon which the instant suit is based. Nor, for that matter, can we say that Alitalia's employees, under the circumstances in which they found themselves on January 4, 1974, could and should have acted otherwise for the sake of thwarting their assailants' purpose. We conclude only—but nontheless fatally for the defense—that Alitalia did not take all reasonable measures that prudent foresight would have envisioned for the securing of high-value cargo.

Alitalia's reference to the fact that the January 4, 1974 incident at Building 86 was the first instance of armed robbery involving an airline cargo warehouse at Kennedy Airport is mentioned if only to demonstrate that it has not be overlooked. That armed robbers had so far spared such facilities could hardly have insulated the reasonably prudent airline carrier from the knowledge that an armed robbery of a cargo warehouse was a likely future contingency. Of no greater moment is defendant's observation that plaintiff had, within the space of some eighteen months preceding the robbery at Building 86, shipped without incident sixteen consignments of currency to the Umma Bank via Alitalia.

Equally unavailing to the defense is Alitalia's insistence that it necessarily be held to a standard of care no more rigorous than that observed by the majority of airlines at Kennedy Airport in 1974. In this respect, it is perhaps enough to note the following observations from Judge Learned Hand:

> "There are, no doubt, cases where courts seem to make the general practice of the calling the standard of proper diligence; we have indeed given some currency to the notion ourselves. * * *. Indeed in most cases reasonable prudence is in fact common prudence, but strictly it is never its measure, a whole calling may have unduly lagged in the adoption of new and available devices. It never may set its own tests, however persuasive be its usages. Courts must in the end say what is required * * *." *The T. J. Hooper*, 60 F.2d 737, 740 (2d Cir. 1932).

Other airlines at Kennedy Airport, at least until January 1974, may well have been less security conscious than was Alitalia; few, if any, may have been more so. Nevertheless, if other airline cargo facilities might have been as, or more, awkwardly situated in the face of an armed robbery than was Building 86, that fact cannot confer added grace to Alitalia's posture herein.

III.

Under Article 22(2) of the Convention, carrier liability for the loss of freight must be limited to the sum of 250 francs per kilogram "unless the consignor has made, at the time when the package was handed over to the carrier, a special declaration of the value at delivery and has paid a supplementary sum if the case so requires." Appearing on the face of Air Waybill No. 055-3807-7830, the contract of carriage covering the bank notes now at issue, is plaintiff's special declaration of value in the amount of $200,000. Plaintiff has paid all charges imposed by the defendant carrier in connection with the air waybill, including a supplemental valuation charge of $200. In such event, the measure of plaintiff's damages is determined by the amount of value thus declared.

In accordance with the foregoing, plaintiff shall have judgment in the amount of $200,000, with interest thereon at the rate of six per-cent per annum computed from January 4, 1974, plus costs.

Submit judgment order on notice.

QUESTIONS

1. Why are certain cruise ships subsidized by the federal government?
2. What does the law require before one can recover punitive damages?
3. What was the main legal issue in the *Commodore* case on page 388?
4. What was the "Warsaw Convention"? What was its purpose?
5. Why was "willful misconduct" so important in the *Cohen* case on page 393?
6. What is a "directed verdict"? What is it used for?
7. Can there be a directed verdict in a case where there is in fact a jury question? Why?
8. Why is the question of negligence one that a jury must determine?

9. What is an "affirmative defense"? If you do not know, ask.
10. T. or F. The Warsaw Convention was designed to protect airlines only.

ENDNOTES

1. *Commodore Cruise Line, Ltd. v. Kormendi,* see page 388.
2. *Country Club of Miami Corporation v. McDaniel,* 310 So. 2d 436 (Fla. 3d. DCA 1975).
3. *McManigal v. Chicago Motor Coach Company,* 18 Ill. App. 2d 183, 151 N.E. 2d 410 (1958).
4. *Pullman Co. v. Hall* 46 F. 2d 399 (4th Cir. 1931); *Saucy v. Greyhound Corporation,* 27 A. 2d 112, 276 N.Y.S. 2d 173 (1967); *Sullivan v. Yellow Cab Company,* 212 A. 2d 616 (D.C. App. 1965).
5. *G. & M. Restaurants Corp v. Tropical Music Service Inc.,* 161 So. 2d 566 (Fla. 2d DCA 1964).
6. Civil Aeronatics Act of 1938, section 8404 (b). "No air carrier shall, . . . cause any undue . . . preference . . . to any person . . . in any respect whatsoever" (in the granting of air seats). Also see *Nader v. Allegheny Airlines,* civ. act No. 1346-72 (D.C. 1973).

Appendix A

TITLE VII of the CIVIL RIGHTS ACT OF 1964 as AMENDED BY
THE EQUAL EMPLOYMENT OPPORTUNITY ACT*

DEFINITIONS

Sec. 701. For the purpose of this title—

(a)   The term "person" includes one or more individuals, governments, governmental agencies, political subdivisions, labor unions, partnerships, associations, corporations, legal representatives, mutual companies, joint-stock companies, trusts, unincorporated organizations, trustees, trustees in bankruptcy, or receivers. (As amended by P.L. No. 92-261, eff. March 24, 1972.)

(b)   The term 'employer' means a person engaged in an industry affecting commerce who has fifteen or more employees for each working day in each of twenty or more calendar weeks in the current or preceding calendar year, and any agent of such a person, but such term does not include (1) the United States, a corporation wholly owned by the Government of the United States, an Indian tribe, or any department or agency of the District of Columbia subject by statute to procedures of the competitive service (as defined in section

* Civil Rights Act of 1964, As amended, 42 U.S.C. secs. 2000e- 2000e (15).

2102 of title 5 of the United States Code), or (2) a bona fide private membership club (other than a labor organization) which is exempt from taxation
under section 501(c) of the Internal Revenue Code of 1954, except that during
the first year after the date of enactment of the Equal Employment Opportunity
Act of 1972, persons having fewer than twenty-five employees (and their agents)
shall not be considered employers. (As amended by P.L. No. 92-261, eff. March
24, 1972.)

(c)   The term "employment agency" means any person regularly undertaking with or without compensation to procure employees for an employer or
to procure for employees opportunities to work for an employer and includes
an agent of such a person. (As amended by P.L. No. 92-261, eff. March 24,
1972.)

(d)   The term "labor organization" means a labor organization engaged in
an industry affecting commerce, and any agent of such an organization, and
includes any organization of any kind, any agency, or employee representation
committee, group, association, or plan so engaged in which employees participate and which exists for the purpose, in whole or in part, of dealing with employers concerning grievances, labor disputes, wages, rates of pay, hours, or
other terms or conditions of employment, and any conference, general committee, joint or system board, or joint council so engaged which is subordinate to
a national or international labor organization.

(e)   A labor organization shall be deemed to be engaged in an industry
affecting commerce if (1) it maintains or operates a hiring hall or hiring office
which procures employees for an employer or procures for employees opportunities to work for an employer, or (2) the number of its members (or, where
it is a labor organization composed of other labor organizations or their representatives, if the aggregate number of the members of such labor organization)
is (A) twenty-five or more during the first year after the date of enactment of
the Equal Employment Opportunity Act of 1972, or (B) fifteen or more thereafter. (As amended by P.L. No. 92-261, eff. March 24, 1972)

(1)   is the certified representative of employees under the provisions of the
National Labor Relations Act, as amended; or the Railway Labor Act, as amended;

(2)   although not certified, is a national or international labor organization
or a local labor organization recognized or acting as the representative of employees of an employer or employers engaged in an industry affecting commerce; or

(3)   has chartered a local labor organization or subsidiary body which is
representing or actively seeking to represent employees of employers within
the meaning of paragraph (1) or (2); or

(4)   has been chartered by a labor organization representing or actively
seeking to represent employees within the meaning of paragraph (1) or (2)
as the local or subordinate body through which such employees may enjoy
membership or become affliated with such labor organization; or

(5)   is a conference, general committee, joint or system board, or joint
council subordinate to a national or international labor organization, which
includes a labor organization engaged in an industry affecting commerce within
the meaning of any of the preceding paragraphs of this subsection.

(f)   The term "employee" means an individual employed by an employer,
except that the term "employee" shall not include any person elected to public office in any State or political subdivision of any State by the qualified

voters thereof, or any person chosen by such officer to be on such officer's personal staff, or an appointee on the policy making level or an immediate adviser with respect to the exercise of the constitutional or legal powers of the office. The exemption set forth in the preceding sentence shall not include employees subject to the civil service laws of a State government, governmental agency or political subdivision. (As amended by P.L. 92-161, eff. March 24, 1972)

(g)   The term "commerce" means trade, traffic, commerce, transportation, transmission, or communication among the several States; or between a State and any place outside thereof; or within the District of Columbia, or a possession of the United States; or between points in the same State but through a point outside thereof.

(h)   The term "industry affecting commerce" means any activity, business, or industry in commerce or in which a labor dispute would hinder or obstruct commerce or the free flow of commerce and includes any activity of industry "affecting commerce" within the meaning of the Labor-Management Reporting and Disclosure Act of 1959, and further includes any governmental industry, business, or activity. (As amended by P.L. No. 92-261, eff. March 24, 1972)

(i)   The term "State" includes a State of the United States, the District of Columbia, Puerto Rico, the Virgin Island, American Samoa, Guam, Wake Island, the Canal Zone, and Outer Continental Shelf Lands Act.

(j)   The term 'religion' includes all aspects of religious observance and practice, as well as belief, unless an employer demonstrates that he is unable to reasonably accommodate to an employee's or prospective employee's religious observance or practice without undue hardship on the conduct of the employer's business. (As amended by P. L. 92-261, eff. March 24, 1972)

EXEMPTION

Sec. 702. This title shall not apply to an employer with respect to the employment of aliens outside any State, or to a religious corporation, association, educational institution, or society with respect to the employment of individuals of a particular religion to perform work connected with the carrying on by such corporation, association, education institution, or society of its activities. (As amended by P.L. 92-261, eff. March 24, 1972)

DISCRIMINATION BECAUSE OF RACE, COLOR, RELIGION, SEX, OR NATIONAL ORIGIN

Sec. 703. (a) It shall be an unlawful employment practice for an employer—

(1)   to fail or refuse to hire or to discharge any individual, or otherwise to discriminate against any individual with respect to his compensation, terms, conditions, or privileges of employment, because of such individual's race, color, religion, sex, or national origin; or

(2)   to limit, segregate, or classify his employees or applicants for employment in any way which would deprive or tend to deprive any individual of employment opportunities or otherwise adversely affect his status as an employee, because of such individual's race, color, religion, sex, or national origin. (As amended by P.L. 92-261, eff. March 24, 1972)

(b)   It shall be an unlawful employment practice for an employment agency to fail or refuse to refer for employment, or otherwise to discriminate against, any individual because of his race, color, religion, sex, or national origin, or to classify or refer for employment any individual on the basis of his race, color, religion, sex or national origin.

(c)   It shall be an unlawful employment practice for a labor organization—

(1)   to exclude or to expel from its membership, or otherwise to discriminate against, any individual because of his race, color, religion, sex, or national origin;

(2)   to limit, segregate, or classify its membership or applicants for membership or to classify or fail or refuse to refer for employment any individual, in any way which would deprive or tend to deprive any individual of employment opportunities, or would limit such employment opportunities or otherwise adversely affect his status as an employee or as an applicant for employment, because of such individual's race, color, religion, sex, or national origin; or

(3)   to cause or attempt to cause an employer to discriminate against an individual in violation of this section.

(d)   It shall be an unlawful employment practice for any employer, labor organization, or joint labor-management committee controlling apprenticeship or other training or retraining, including on-the-job training programs to discriminate against any individual because of his race, color, religion, sex, or national origin in admission to, or employment in, any program established to provide apprenticeship or other training.

(e)   Notwithstanding any other provision of this title, (1) it shall not be an unlawful employment practice for an employer to hire and employ employees, for an employment agency to classify, or refer for employment any individual, for a labor organization to classify its membership or to classify or refer for employment any individual, or for an employer, labor organization, or joint labor-management committee controlling apprenticeship or other training or retraining programs to admit or employ any individual in any such program, on the basis of his religion, sex, or national origin in those certain instances where religion, sex, or national origin is a bona fide occupational qualification reasonably necessary to the normal operation of that particular business or enterprise, and (2) it shall not be an unlawful employment practice for a school, college, university, or other educational institution or institution of learning to hire and employ employees of a particular religion if such school, college, university, or other educational institution or institution of learning is, in whole or in substantial part, owned, supported, controlled, or managed by a particular religion or by a particular religious corporation, association, or society, or if the curriculum of such school, college, university, or other educational institution or institution of learning is directed toward the propagation of a particular religion.

(f)   As used in this title, the phrase "unlawful employment practice" shall not be deemed to include any action or measure taken by an employer, labor organization, joint labor-management committee, or employment agency with respect to an individual who is a member of the Communist Party of the United States or of any other organization required to register as a Communist-action or Communist-front organization by final order of the Subversive Activities Control Board pursuant to the Subversive Activities Control Act of 1950.

(g)   Notwithstanding any other provision of this title, it shall not be an unlawful employment practice for an employer to fail or refuse to hire and employ any individual for any position, for an employer to discharge an individual from any position, or for an employment agency to fail or refuse to refer any individual for employment in any position, or for a labor organization to fail or refuse to refer any individual for employment in any position, if—

(1)   the occupancy of such position, or access to the premises in or upon which any part of the duties of such position is performed or is to be performed, is subject to any requirement imposed in the interest of the national security of the United States under any security program in effect pursuant to or administered under any statute of the United States or any Executive order of the President; and

(2)   such individual has not fulfilled or has ceased to fulfill that requirement.

(h)   Notwithstanding any other provision of this title, it shall not be an unlawful employment practice for an employer to apply different standards of compensation, or different terms, conditions, or privileges of employment pursuant to a bona fide seniority or merit system, or a system which measures earnings by quantity or quality of production or to employees who work in different locations, provided that such differences are not the result of an intention to discriminate because of race, color, religion, sex, or national origin; nor shall it be an unlawful employment practice for an employer to give and to act upon the results of any professionally developed ability test provided that such test, its administration or action upon the results is not designed, intended, or used to discriminate because of race, color, religion, sex, or national origin. It shall not be an unlawful employment practice under this title for any employment practice under this title for any employer to differentiate upon the basis of sex in determining the amount of the wages or compensation paid to employees of such employer if such differentiation is authorized by the provisions of Section 6(d) of the Fair Labor Standards Act of 1938 as amended (29 USC 206(d)).

(i)   Nothing contained in this title shall apply to any business or enterprise on or near an Indian reservation with respect to any publicly announced employment practice of such business or enterprise under which a preferential treatment is given to any individual because he is an Indian living on or near a reservation.

(j)   Nothing contained in this title shall be interpreted to require any employer, employment agency, labor organization, or joint labor-management committee subject to this title to grant preferential treatment to any individual or to any group because of the race, color, religion, sex, or national origin of such individual or group on account of an imbalance which may exist with respect to the total number of precentage of persons of any race, color, religion, sex, or national origin employed by any employer, referred or classified for employment by any employment agency or labor organization, admitted to membership or classified by any labor organization, or admitted to, or employed in, any apprenticeship or other training program, in comparison with the total number or percentage of persons of such race, color, religion, sex, or national origin in any community, State, section, or other area, or in the available work force in any community, State, section, or other area. (As amended by P.L. 92-261, eff. March 24, 1972)

OTHER UNLAWFUL EMPLOYMENT PRACTICES

Sec. 704. (a) It shall be an unlawful employment practice for an employer to discriminate against any of his employees or applicants for employment, for an employment agency or joint labor-management committee controlling apprenticeship or other training or retraining, including on-the-job training programs, to discriminate against any individual, or for a labor organization to discriminate against any member thereof or applicant for membership, because he has opposed any practice, made an unlawful employment practice by this title, or because he has made a charge, testified, assisted, or participated in any manner in an investigation, proceeding, or hearing under this title. (As amended by P.L. No. 92-261, eff. March 24, 1972)

(b)   It shall be an unlawful employment practice for an employer, labor organization, employment agency, or joint labor-management committee controlling apprenticeship or other training or retraining, including on-the-job training programs, to print or cause to be printed or published any notice or advertisement relating to employment by such an employer or membership in or any classification or referral for employment by such a labor organization, or relating to any classification or referral for employment by such an employment agency, or relating to admission to, or employment in, any program established to provide apprenticeship or other training by such a joint labor-management committee indicating any preference, limitation, specification, or discrimination, based on race, color religion sex or national origin, except that such a notice or advertisement may indicate a preference, limitation, specification, or discrimination based on religion, sex or national origin when religion, sex, or national origin is a bona fide occupational qualification for employment. (As amended by P.L. No. 92-216, eff. March 24, 1972)

EQUAL EMPLOYMENT OPPORTUNITY COMMISSION

Sec. 705. (a) There is hereby created a Commission to be known as the Equal Employment Opportunity Commission, which shall be composed of five members, not more than three of whom shall be members of the same political party. Members of the Commission shall be appointed by the President by and with the advice and consent of the Senate for a term of five years. Any individual chosen to fill a vacancy shall be appointed only for the unexpired term of the member whom he shall succeed, and all members of the Commission shall continue to serve until their successors are appointed and qualified, except that no such member of the Commission shall continue to serve (1) for more than sixty days when the Congress is in session unless a nomination to fill such vacancy shall have been submitted to the Senate, or (2) after the adjournment sine die of the session of the Senate in which such nomination was submitted. The President shall designate one member to serve as Chairman of the Commission for the administrative operations of the Commission, and, except as provided in subsection (b), shall appoint, in accordance with the provisions of title 5, United States Code, governing appointments in the competitive service, such officers, agents, attorneys hearing examiners, and employees as he deems necessary to assist it in the performance of its functions and to fix their compensation in accordance with the provisions of chapter 51 and subchapter III of chapter 53 of title 5, United States Code, relating to classification and General Schedule pay rates: Provided, That assignment, removal, and compensation of hearing examiners shall be in accordance with sections 3105, 3344, 5362, and 7521 of title 5, United States Code.

(b)   (1) There shall be a General Counsel of the Commission appointed by the President, by and with the advice and consent of the Senate, for a term of four years. The General Counsel shall have responsibility for the conduct of litigation as provided in sections 706 and 707 of this title. The General Counsel shall have such other duties as the Commission may prescribe or as may be provided by law and shall concur with the Chairman of the Commission on the appointment and supervision of regional attorneys. The General Counsel of the

Commission on the effective date of this Act shall continue in such position and perform the functions specified in this subsection until a successor is appointed and qualified.

(2)   Attorneys appointed under this section may, at the direction of the Commission, appear for and represent the Commission in any case in court, provided that the Attorney General shall conduct all litigation to which the Commission is a party in the Supreme Court pursuant to this title. (As amended by P.L. No. 92-261, eff. March 24, 1972)

(c)   A vacancy in the Commission shall not impair the right of the remaining members to exercise all the powers of the Commission and three members thereof shall constitute a quorum.

(d)   The Commission shall have an official seal which shall be judicially noticed.

(e)   The Commission shall at the middle and at the close of each fiscal year report to the Congress and to the President concerning the action it has taken; the names, salaries, and duties of all individuals in its employ and the moneys it has disbursed; and shall make such further reports on the cause of and means of eliminating discrimination and such recommendations for further legislation as may appear desirable.

(f)   The principal office of the Commission shall be in or near the District of Columbia, but it may meet or exercise any or all its powers at any other place. The Commission may establish such regional or State offices as it deems necessary to accomplish the purpose of this title.

(g)   The Commission shall have power—

(1)   to cooperate with and, with their consent, utilize regional, State, local, and other agencies, both public and private, and individuals;

(2)   to pay to witnesses whose depositions are taken or who are summoned before the Commission or any of its agents the same witness and mileage fees as are paid to witnesses in the courts of the United States;

(3)   to furnish to persons subject to this title such technical assistance as they may request to further their compliance with this title or an order issued thereunder;

(4)   upon the request of (i) any employer, whose employees or some of them, or (ii) any labor organization, whose members or some of them, refuse or threaten to refuse to cooperate in effectuating the provisions of this title, to assist in such effectuation by conciliation or such other remedial action as is provided by this title:

(5)   to make such technical studies as are appropriate to effectuate the purposes and policies of this title and to make the results of such studies available to the public;

(6)   to intervene in a civil action brought under section 706 by an aggrieved party against a respondent other than a government, governmental agency or political subdivision. (As amended by P.L. No. 92-261, eff. March 24, 1972)

(h)   The Commission shall, in any of its educational or promotional activities, cooperate with other departments and agencies in the performance of such educational and promotional activities.

(i)   All officers, agents, attorneys and employees of the Commission, including the members of the Commission, shall be subject to the provisions of section 9 of the act of August 2, 1939, as amended (Hatch Act), notwithstanding any exemption contained in such section.

PREVENTION OF UNLAWFUL EMPLOYMENT PRACTICES

Sec. 706. (a) The Commission is empowered, as hereinafter provided, to prevent any person from engaging in any unlawful employment practice as set forth in section 703 or 704 of this title.

(b) Whenever a charge is filed by or on behalf of a person claiming to be aggrieved, or by a member of the Commission, alleging that an employer, employment agency, labor organization, or joint labor-management committee controlling apprenticeship or other training or retraining including on-the-job training programs, has engaged in an unlawful employment practice, the Commission shall serve a notice of the charge (including the date, place and circumstances of the alleged unlawful employment practice) on such employer, employment agency, labor organization, or joint labor-management committee (hereinafter referred to as the 'respondent') within ten days and shall make an investigation thereof. Charges shall be in writing under oath or affirmation and shall contain such information and be in such form as the Commission requires. Charges shall not be made public by the Commission. If the Commission determines after such investigation that there is not reasonable cause to believe that the charge is true, it shall dismiss the charge and promptly notify the person claiming to be aggrieved and the respondent of its action. In determining whether reasonable cause exists, the Commission shall accord substantial weight to final findings and orders made by State or local authorities in proceedings commenced under State or local law pursuant to the requirements of subsections (c) and (d). If the Commission determines after such investigation that there is reasonable cause to believe that the charge is true, the Commission shall endeavor to eliminate any such alleged unlawful employment practice by informal methods of conference, conciliation, and persuasion. Nothing said or done during and as a part of such informal endeavors may be made public by the Commission, its officers or employees, or used as evidence in a subsequent proceeding without the written consent of the persons concerned. Any person who makes public information in violation of this subsection shall be fined not more than $1,000 or imprisoned for not more than one year, or both. The Commission shall make its determination on reasonable cause as promptly as possible and, so far as practicable, not later than one hundred and twenty days from the filing of the charge or, where applicable under subsection (c) or (d), from the date upon which the Commission is authorized to take action with respect to the charge.

(c) In the case of an alleged unlawful employment practice occurring in a State, or political subdivision of a State, which has a State or local law prohibiting the unlawful employment practice alleged and establishing or authorizing a State or local authority to grant or seek relief from such practice or to institute criminal proceedings with respect thereto upon receiving notice thereof, no charge may be filed under subsection (a) by the person aggrieved before the expiration of sixty days after proceedings have been commenced under the State or local law, unless such proceedings have been earlier terminated, provided that such sixty-day period shall be extended to one hundred and twenty days during the first year after the effective date of such State or local law. If any requirement for the commencement of such proceedings is imposed by a State or local authority other than a requirement of the filing of a written and signed statement of the facts upon which the proceeding is based, the proceeding shall be deemed to have been commenced for the purposes of this subsection at the time such statement is sent by registered mail to the appropriate State or local authority.

(d)   In the case of any charge filed by a member of the Commission alleging an unlawful employment practice occurring in a State or political subdivision of a State which has a State or local law prohibiting the practice alleged and establishing or authorizing a State or local authority to grant or seek relief from such practice or to institute criminal proceedings with respect thereto upon receiving notice thereof, the Commission shall, before taking any action with respect to such charge, notify the appropriate State or local officials and, upon request, afford them a reasonable time, but not less than sixty days (provided that such sixty-day period shall be extended to one hundred and twenty days during the first year after the effective day of such State or local law), unless a shorter period is requested, to act under such State or local law to remedy the practice alleged.

(e)   A charge under this section shall be filed within one hundred and eighty days after the alleged unlawful employment practice occurred and notice of the charge (including the date, place and circumstances of the alleged unlawful employment practice) shall be served upon the person against whom such charge is made within ten days thereafter, except that in a case of an unlawful employment practice with respect to which the person aggrieved has initially instituted proceedings with a State or local agency with authority to grant or seek relief from such practice or to institute criminal proceedings with respect thereto upon receiving notice thereof, such charge shall be filed by or on behalf of the person aggrieved within three hundred days after the alleged unlawful employment practice occurred, or within thirty days after receiving notice that the State or local agency has terminated the proceedings under the State or local law, whichever is earlier, and a copy of such charge shall be filed by the Commission with the State or local agency.

(f)   (1) If within thirty days after a charge is filed with the Commission or within thirty days after expiration of any period of reference under subsection (c) or (d), the Commission has been unable to secure from the respondent a conciliation agreement acceptable to the Commission, the Commission may bring a civil action against any respondent not a government, governmental agency, or political subdivision named in the charge. In the case of a respondent which is a government, governmental agency, or political subdivision, if the Commission has been unable to secure from the respondent a conciliation agreement acceptable to the Commission, the Commission shall take no further action and shall refer the case to the Attorney General who may bring a civil action against such respondent in the appropriate United States district court. The person or persons aggrieved shall have the right to intervene in a civil action brought by the Commission or the Attorney General in a case involving a government, governmental agency, or political subdivision. If a charge filed with the Commission pursuant to subsection (b) is dismissed by the Commission, or if within one hundred and eighty days from the filing of such charge or the expiration of any period of reference under subsection (c) or (d), whichever is later, the Commission has not filed a civil action under this section or the Attorney General has not filed a civil action in a case involving a government, governmental agency, or political subdivision, or the Commission has not entered into a conciliation agreement to which the person aggrieved is a party, the Commission, or the Attorney General in a case involving a government, governmental agency, or political subdivision, shall so notify the person aggrieved and within nenety days after the giving of such notice a civil action may be brought against the respondent named in the charge (A) by the person claiming to be aggrieved or (B) if such charge was filed by a member of the Commisssion, by any person whom the charge alleges was aggrieved by the alleged unlawful employment practice. Upon application by the complainant and in such circumstances as the court may deem just, the court may appoint an attorney for such complainant and may authorize the commencement of the action without the payment of fees, costs, or security. Upon timely application, the court may, in its discretion, permit the Commission, or the Attorney General in a case involving a government, governmental agency, or political subdivision, to intervene in such civil action upon certification that the case is of general public importance. Upon request, the court may, in its discretion, stay further proceedings for not more than sixty days pending the termination of State or local proceedings described in subsections (c) or (d) of this section or further efforts of the Commission to obtain voluntary compliance.

(2) Whenever a charge is filed with the Commission and the Commission concludes on the basis of a preliminary investigation that prompt judicial action is necessary to carry out the purpose of this Act, the Commission, or the Attorney General in a case involving a government, governmental agency, or political subdivision, may bring an action for appropriate temporary or preliminary relief pending final disposition of such charge. Any temporary restraining order or other order granting preliminary or temporary relief shall be issued in accordance with rule 65 of the Federal Rules of Civil Procedure. It shall be the duty of a court having jurisdiction over proceedings under this section to assign cases for hearing at the earliest practicable date and to cause such cases to be in every way expedited.

(3) Each United States district court and each United States court of a place subject to the jurisdiction of the United States shall have jurisdiction of actions brought under this title. Such an action may be brought in any judicial district in the State in which the unlawful employment practice is alleged to have been committed, in the judicial district in which the employment records relevant to such practice are maintained and administered, or in the judicial district in which the aggrieved person would have worked but for the alleged unlawful employment practice, but if the respondent is not found wihin any such district, such an action may be brought within the judicial district in which the respondent has his principal office. For purposes of sections 1404 and 1406 of title 28 of the United States Code, the judicial district in which the respondent has his principal office shall in all cases be considered a district in which the action might have been brought.

(4) It shall be the duty of the chief judge of the district (or in his absence, that acting chief judge) in which the case is pending immediately to designate a judge in such district to hear and determine the case. In the event that no judge in the district is available to hear and determine the case, the chief judge of the district, or the acting chief judge, as the case may be, shall certify this fact to the chief judge of the circuit (or in his absence, the acting chief judge) who shall then designate a district or circuit judge of the circuit to hear and determine the case.

(5) It shall be the duty of the judge designated pursuant to this subsection to assign the case for hearing at the earliest practicable date and to cause the case to be in every way expedited. If such judge has not scheduled the case for trial within one hundred and twenty days after issue has been joined that judge may appoint a master pursuant to rule 53 of the Federal Rules of Civil Procedure.

(g) If the court finds that the respondent has intentionally engaged in or is intentionally engaging in an unlawful employment practice charged in the complaint, the court may enjoin the respondent from engaging in such unlawful employment practice, and order such affirmative action as may be appropriate, which may include, but is not limited to, reinstatement or hiring of employees, with or without back pay (payable by the employer, employment agency, or labor organization, as the case may be, responsible for the unlawful employment practice), or any other equitable relief as the court deems appropriate. Back pay liability shall not accrue from a date more than two years prior to the filing of a charge with the Commission. Interim earnings or amounts earnable with reasonable diligence by the person or persons discriminated against shall operate to reduce the back pay otherwise allowable. No order of the court shall require the admission or reinstatement of an individual as a member of a union, or the hiring, reinstatement, or promotion of an individual as an employee, or the payment to him of any back pay, if such individual was refused admission, suspended, or expelled, or was refused employment or advancement or was suspended or discharged for any reason other than discrimination on account of race, color, religion, sex, or national origin or in violation of section 704(a). (As amended by P.L. No. 92-261, eff. March 24, 1972)

(h)   The provisions of the Act entitled "An Act to amend the Judicial Code and to define and limit the jurisdiction of courts sitting in equity, and for other purposes," approved March 23, 1932 (29 U.S.C. 101-115), shall not apply with respect to civil actions brought under this section.

(i)   In any case in which an employer, employment agency, or labor organization fails to comply with an order of a court issued in a civil action brought under this section the Commission may commence proceedings to compel compliance with such order. (As amended)

(j)   Any civil action brought under this section and any proceedings brought under subsection (j) shall be subject to appeal as provided in sections 1291 and 1292, title 28, United States Code. (As amended by P.L. 92-261, eff. March 24, 1972)

(k)   In any action or proceeding under this title the court, in its discretion, may allow the prevailing party, other than the Commission or the United States, a reasonable attorney's fee as part of the costs, and the Commission and the United States shall be liable for costs the same as a private person.

Sec. 707. (a) Whenever the Attorney General has reasonable cause to believe that any person or group of persons is engaged in a pattern or practice of resistance to the full enjoyment of any of the rights secured by this title, and that the pattern or practice is of such a nature and is intended to deny the full exercise of the rights herein described, the Attorney General may bring a civil action in the appropriate district court of the United States by filing with it a complaint (1) signed by him (or in his absence the Acting Attorney General), (2) setting forth facts pertaining to such pattern or practice, and (3) requesting such relief, including an application for a permanent or temporary injunction, restraining order or other order against the person or persons responsible for such pattern or practice, as he deems necessary to insure the full enjoyment of the rights herein described.

(b)   The district courts of the United States shall have and shall exercise jurisdiction of proceedings instituted pursuant to this section, and in any such proceeding the Attorney General may file with the clerk of such court a request that a court of three judges be convened to hear and determine the case. Such request by the Attorney General shall be accompanied by a certificate that, in his opinion, the case is of general public importance. A copy of the certificate and request for a three-judge court shall be immediately furnished by such clerk to the chief judge of the circuit (or in his absence, the presiding circuit judge of the circuit) in which the case is pending. Upon receipt of such request it shall be the duty of the chief judge of the circuit or the presiding circuit judge, as the case may be, to designate immediately three judges in such circuit, of whom at least one shall be a circuit judge and another of whom shall be a district judge of the court in which the proceeding was instituted, to hear and determine such case, and it shall be the duty of the judges so designated to assign the case for hearing at the earliest practicable date, to participate in the hearing and determination thereof, and to cause the case to be in every way expedited. An appeal from the final judgment of such court will lie to the Supreme Court.

In the event the Attorney General fails to file such a request in any such proceeding, it shall be the duty of the chief judge of the district (or in his absence, the acting chief judge) in which the case is pending immediately to designate a judge in such district to hear and determine the case. In the event that no judge in the district is available to hear and determine the case, the chief judge of the district, or the acting chief judge, as the case may be, shall certify this fact to the chief judge of the circuit (or in his absence, the acting chief judge) who shall then designate a district or circuit judge of the circuit to hear and determine the case.

It shall be the duty of the judge designated pursuant to this section to assign the case for hearing at the earliest practicable date and to cause the case to be in every way expedited.

(c)   Effective two years after the date of enactment of the Equal Employment Opportunity Act of 1972, the functions of the Attorney General under this section shall be transferred to the Commission, together with such personnel, property, records, and unexpended balances of appropriations, allocations, and other funds employed, used, held, available, or to be made available in connection with such functions unless the President submits, and neither House of Congress vetoes, a reorganization plan pursuant to chapter 9 of title 5, United States Code, inconsistent with the provisions of this subsection. The Commission shall carry out such functions in accordance with subsections (d) and (e) of this section.

(d)   Upon the transfer of functions provided for in subsection (c) of this section, in all suits commenced pursuant to this section prior to the date of such transfer, proceedings shall continue without abatement, all court orders and decrees shall remain in effect, and the Commission shall be substituted as a party for the United States of America, the Attorney General, or the Acting Attorney General, as appropriate.

(e)   Subsequent to the date of enactment of the Equal Employment Opportunity Act of 1972, the Commission shall have authority to investigate and act on a charge of a pattern or practice of discrimination, whether filed by or on behalf of a person claiming to be aggrieved or by a member of the Commission. All such actions shall be conducted in accordance with the procedures set forth in section 706 of this Act. (As last amended by P.L. No. 92-261, eff. March 24, 1972)

EFFECT OF STATE LAWS

Sec. 708. Nothing in this title shall be deemed to exempt or relieve any person from any liability, duty, penalty, or punishment provided by any present or future law of any State or political subdivision of a State, other than any such law which purports to require or permit the doing of any act which would be an unlawful employment practice under this title.

INVESTIGATIONS, INSPECTIONS, RECORDS, STATE AGENCIES

Sec. 709. (a) In connection with any investigation of a charge filed under section 706, the Commission or its designated representative shall at all reasonable times have access to, for the purposes of examination, and the right to copy any evidence of any person being investigated or proceeded against that relates to unlawful employment practices covered by this title and is relevant to the charge under investigation.

(b)   The Commission may cooperate with State and local agencies charged with the administration of State fair employment practices laws and, with the consent of such agencies, may, for the purpose of carrying out its functions and duties under this title and within the limitation of funds appropriated specifically for such purpose, engage in and contribute to the cost of research and other projects of mutual interest undertaken by such agencies, and utilize the services of such agencies and their employees, and, notwithstanding any other provision of law, pay by advance or reimbursement such agencies and their employees for services rendered to assist the Commission in carrying out this title. In furtherance of such cooperative efforts, the Commission may enter into written agreements with such State or local agencies and such agreements may include provisions under which the Commission shall refrain from processing a charge in any cases or class of cases specified in such agreements or under which the Commission shall relieve any person or class of persons in such State of locality from requirements imposed under this section. The Commission shall rescind any such agreement whenever it determines that the agreement no longer serves the interest of effective enforcement of this title.

(c)   Every employer, employment agency, and labor organization subject to this title shall (1) make and keep such records relevant to the determinations of whether unlawful employment practices have been or are being committed, (2) preserve such records for such periods, and (3) make such reports therefrom as the Commission shall prescribe by regulation or order, after public hearing, as reasonable, necessary, or appropriate for the enforcement of this title or the regulation or orders thereunder. The Commission shall, by regulation, require each employer, labor organization, and joint labor-management committee subject to this title which controls an apprenticeship or other training program to maintain such records as are reasonably necessary to carry out the purposes of this title, including, but not limited to, a list of applicants who wish to participate in such program, including the chronological order in which applications were received, and to furnish to the Commission upon request, a detailed description of the manner in which persons are selected to participate in the apprenticeship or other training program. Any employer, employment agency, labor organization, or joint labor-management committee which believes that the application to it of any regulation or order issued under this section would result in undue hardship may apply to the Commission for an exemption from the application of such regulation or order, and, if such application for an exemption is denied, bring a civil action in the United States district court for the district where such records are kept. If the Commission or the court, as the case may be, finds that the application of the regulation or order to the employer, employment agency, or labor organization in question would impose an undue hardship, the Commission or the court, as the case may be, may grant appropriate relief. If any person required to comply with the provisions of this subsection fails or refuses to do so, the United States district court for the district in which such person is found, resides, or transacts business, shall, upon application of the Commission, or the Attorney General in a case involving a governmental agency or political subdivision, have jurisdiction to issue to such person an order requiring him to comply.

(d)   In prescribing requirements pursuant to subsection (c) of this section, the Commission shall consult with other interested State and Federal agencies and shall endeavor to coordinate its requirements with those adopted by such agencies. The Commission shall furnish upon request and without cost to any State or local agency charged with the administration of a fair employment practice law information obtained pursuant to subsection (c) of this section from any employer, employment agency, labor organization, or joint labor-management committee subject to the jurisdiction of such agency. Such information shall be furnished on condition that it not be made public by the recipient agency prior to the institution of a proceeding under State or local law involving such information. If this condition is violated by a recipient agency, the Commission may decline to honor subsequent requests pursuant to this subsection. (As amended by P.L. 92-261, eff. March 24, 1972)

(e)   It shall be unlawful for any officer or employee of the Commission to make public in any manner whatever any information obatined by any proceeding under this title involving such information. Any officer or employee of the Commission who shall make public in any manner whatever any information in violation of this subsection shall be guilty of a misdemeanor and upon conviction thereof, shall be fined not more than $1,000, or imprisoned not more than one year.

INVESTIGATORY POWERS

Sec. 710. For the purpose of all hearings and investigations conducted by the Commission or its duly authorized agents or agencies, section 11 of the National Labor Relations Act (49 Stat. 455; 29 U.S.C. 161) shall apply. (As amended by P.L. 92-261, eff. March 24, 1972)

NOTICES TO BE POSTED

Sec. 711. (a) Every employer, employment agency and labor organization, as the case may be, shall post and keep posted in conspicuous places upon its premises where notices to employees, applicants for employment and members are customarily posted a notice to be prepared or approved by the Commission setting forth excerpts from or, summaries of, the pertinent provisions of this title and information pertinent to the filing of a complaint.

(b)   A willful violation of this section shall be punishable by a fine of not more than $100 for each separate offense.

VETERANS' PREFERENCE

Sec. 712. Nothing contained in this title shall be construed to repeal or modify any Federal, State, territorial, or local law creating special rights or preference for veterans.

RULES AND REGULATIONS

Sec. 713. (a) The Commission shall have authority from time to time to issue, amend, or rescind suitable procedural regulations to carry out the provisions of this title. Regulations issued under this section shall be in conformity with the standards and limitations of the Administrative Procedure Act.

(b)   In any action or proceeding based on any alleged unlawful employment practice, no person shall be subject to any liability or punishment for or on account of (1) the commission by such person of an unlawful employment practice if he pleads and proves that the act of omission complained of was in good faith, in conformity with, and in reliance on any written interpretation or opinion of the Commission, or (2) the failure of such person to publish and file any information required by any provision of this title if he pleads and proves that he failed to publish and file such information in good faith, in conformity with the instructions of the Commission issued under this title regarding the filing of such information. Such a defense, if established, shall be a bar to the action or proceeding, notwithstanding that (A) after such act or omission, such interpretation or opinion is modified or rescinded or is determined by judicial authority to be invalid or of no legal effect, or (B) after publishing or filing the description and annual reports, such publication or filing is determined by judicial authority not to be in conformity with the requirements of this title.

FORCIBLY RESISTING THE COMMISSION OR ITS REPRESENTATIVES

Sec. 714. The provisions of sections 111 and 1114, title 18, United States Code, shall apply to officers, agents, and employees of the Commission in the performance of their official duties. Notwithstanding the provisions of sections 111 and 1114 of title 18, United States Code, whoever in violation of the provisions of section 1114 of such title kills a person while engaged in or on account of the performance of his official functions under this Act shall be punished by imprisonment for any term of years or for life. (As amended by P.L. 92-261, eff. March 24, 1972)

SPECIAL STUDY BY SECRETARY OF LABOR

Sec. 715. There shall be established an Equal Employment Opportunity Coordinating Council (hereinafter referred to in this section as the Council) composed of the Secretary of Labor, the Chairman of the Equal Employment Opportunity Commission, the Attorney General, the Chairman of the United States Civil Service Commission, and the Chairman of the United States Civil Rights Commission, or their respective delegates. The Council shall have the responsibility for developing and implementing agreements, policies and practices designed to maximize effort, promote efficiency, and eliminate conflict, competition, duplication and inconsistency among the operations, functions and jurisdictions of the various departments, agencies and branches of the Federal Government responsible for the implementation and enforcement of equal employment opportunity legislation, orders, and policies. On or before July 1 of each year, the Council shall transmit to the President and to the Congress a report of its activities, together with such recommendations for legislative or administrative changes as it concludes are desirable to further promote the purposes of this section. (As amended by P.L. No. 92-261, eff. March 24, 1972)

EFFECTIVE DATE

Sec. 716. (a) This title shall become effective one year after the date of its enactment. (The effective date thus is July 2, 1965.)

(b)   Notwithstanding subsection (a), sections of this title other than sections 703, 704, 706, 707 shall become effective immediately.

(c)   The President shall, as soon as feasible after the enactment of this title, convene one or more conferences for the purpose of enabling the leaders of groups whose members will be affected by this title to become familiar with the rights afforded and obligations imposed by its provisions, and for the purpose of making plans which will result in the fair and effective administration of this title when all of its provisions become effective. The President shall invite the participation in such conference or conferences of (1) the members of the President's Committee on Equal Employment Opportunity, (2) the members of the Commission on Civil Rights, (3) representatives of State and local agencies engaged in furthering equal employment opportunity, (4) representatives of private agencies engaged in furthering equal employment opportunity, and (5) representatives of employers, labor organizations, and employment agencies who will be subject to this title.

NON DISCRIMINATION IN FEDERAL GOVERNMENT EMPLOYMENT

Sec. 717. (a) All personnel actions affecting employees or applicants for employment (except with regard to aliens employed outside the limits of the United States) in military departments as defined in section 102 of title 5, United States Code in executive agencies (other than the General Accounting Office) as defined in section 105 of title 5, United States Code (including employees and applicants for employment who are paid from nonappropriated funds), in the United States Postal Service and the Postal Rate Commission, in those units of the Government of the District of Columbia having positions in the competitive service, and in those units of the legislative and judicial branches of the Federal Government having positions in the competitive service, and in the Library of Congress shall be made free from any discrimination based on race, color, religion, sex, or national origin.

(b) Except as otherwise provided in this subsection, the Civil Service Commission shall have authority to enforce the provisions of subsection (a) through appropriate remedies, including reinstatement or hiring of employees with or without back pay, as will effectuate the policies of this section, and shall issue such rules, regulations, orders and instructions as it deems necessary and appropriate to carry out its responsibilities under this section. The Civil Service Commission shall—

(1) be responsible for the annual review and approval of a national and regional equal employment opportunity plan which each department and agency and each appropriate unit referred to in subsection (a) of this section shall submit in order to maintain an affirmative program of equal employment opportunity for all such employees and applicants for employment;

(2) be responsible for the review and evaluation of the operation of all agency equal employment opportunity programs, periodically obtaining and publishing (on at least a semi-annual basis) progress reports from each such department, agency, or unit; and

(3) consult with and solicit the recommendations of interested individuals, groups, and organizations relating to equal employment opportunity.

The head of each such department, agency, or unit shall comply with such rules, regulations, orders, and instructions which shall include a provision that an employee or applicant for employment shall be notified of any final action taken on any complaint of discrimination filed by him thereunder. The plan submitted by each department, agency, and unit shall include, but not be limited to—

(1) provision for the establishment of training and education programs designed to provide a maximum opportunity for employees to advance so as to perform at their highest potential; and

(2)   a description of the qualifications in terms of training and experience relating to equal employment opportunity for the principal and operating officials of each such department, agency, or unit responsible for carrying out the equal employment opportunity program and of the allocation of personnel and resources proposed by such department, agency, or unit to carry out its equal employment opportunity program.

With respect to employment in the Library of Congress, authorities granted in this subsection to the Civil Service Commission shall be exercised by the Librarian of Congress.

(c)   Within thirty days of receipt of notice of final action taken by a department, agency, or unit referred to in subsection 717(a), or by the Civil Service Commission upon an appeal from a decision or order of such department, agency, or unit on a complaint of discrimination based on race, color, religion, sex or national origin, brought pursuant to subsection (a) of this section, Executive Order 11478 or any succeeding executive orders, or after one hundred and eighty days from the filing of the initial charge with the department, agency, or unit or with the Civil Service Commission on appeal from a decision or order of such department, agency, or unit until such time as final action may be taken by a department, agency, or unit, an employee or applicant for employment, if aggrieved by the final disposition of his complaint, or by the failure to take final action on his complaint, may file a civil action as provided in section 706, in which civil action the head of the department, agency, or unit, as appropriate, shall be the defendant.

(d)   The provisions of section 706 (f) through (k), as applicable, shall govern civil actions brought hereunder.

(e)   Nothing contained in this Act shall relieve any Government agency or official of its or his primary responsibility to assure nondiscrimination in employment as required by the Constitution and statutes or of its or his responsibilities under Executive Order 11478 relating to equal employment opportunity in the Federal Government. (As amended by 92-261, eff. March 24, 1972)

SPECIAL PROVISION WITH RESPECT TO DENIAL, TERMINATION AND SUSPENSION OF GOVERNMENT CONTRACTS

Sec. 718. No Government contract, or portion thereof, with any employer, shall be denied, withheld, terminated, or suspended, by any agency or officer of the United States under any equal employment opportunity law or order, where such employer has an affirmative action plan which has previously been accepted by the Government for the same facility within the past twelve months without first according such employer full hearing and adjudication under the provisions of title 5, United States Code, section 554, and the following pertinent sections: Provided, That if such employer has deviated substantially from such previously agreed to affirmative action plan, this section shall not apply: Provided further, That for the purposes of this section an affirmative action plan shall be deemed to have been accepted by the Government at the time the appropriate compliance agency has accepted such plan unless within forty-five days thereafter the Office of Federal Contract Compliance has disapproved such plan. (As added by P.L. 92-261, eff. March 24, 1972)

Appendix B

====

UNIT PROPERTY ACT

====

DEFINITIONS

The following words or phrases as used in this chapter shall have the meanings ascribed to them in this section, unless the context of this chapter clearly indicates otherwise:

(a)   "Building" means any multi-unit building or buildings or complex thereof, whether in vertical or horizontal arrangement, as well as other improvements comprising a part of the property and used or intended for use for residential, commercial or industrial purposes or for any other lawful purpose or for any combination of such uses.

(b)   "Code of regulations" means such governing regulations as are adopted pursuant to this chapter for the regulation and management of the property, including such amendments thereof as may be adopted from time to time.

(c)   "Common elements" means and includes:

(i)   The land on which the building is located and portions of the building which are not included in a unit;

(ii)   The foundations, structural parts, supports, main walls, roofs, basements, halls, corridors, lobbies, stairways and entrances and exits to the building;

(iii)   The yards, parking areas and driveways;

(iv)   Portions of the land and building used exclusively for the management, operation or maintenance of the common elements;

(v)   Installations of all central services and utilities;

(vi)   All apparatus and installations existing for common use;

(vii)   All other elements of the building necessary or convenient to its existance, management, operation, maintenance and safety or normally in common use; and

(viii)   Such facilities as are designated in the declaration as common elements.

(d)   "Common expenses" means and includes:

(i)   Expenses of administration, maintenance, repair and replacement of the common elements;

(ii)   Expenses agreed upon as common by all the unit owners; and

(iii)   Expenses declared common by provisions of this chapter, or by the declaration or the code of regulations.

(e)   "Council" means a board of natural individuals of the number stated in the code of regulations who are residents of this State, who need not be unit owners and who shall manage the business, operation and affairs of the property on behalf of the unit owners and in compliance with and subject to the provisions of this chapter.

(f)   "Declaration" means the instrument by which the owner of property submits it to the provisions of this chapter as hereinafter provided, and all amendments thereof.

(g)   "Declaration plan" means a survey of the property prepared in accordance with section two, article four, of this chapter.

(h)   "Majority" or "majority of the unit owners" means the owners of more than fifty per cent in the aggregate in interest of the undivided ownership of the common elements as specified in the declaration.

(i)   "Person" means a natural individual, corporation, partnership, association, trustee or other legal entity.

(j)   "Property" means and includes the land, the building, all improvements thereon, all owned in fee simple, and all easements, rights and appurtenances belonging thereto, which have been or are intended to be submitted to the provisions of this chapter.

(k)   "Recorded" means that an instrument has been duly entered of record in the office of the clerk of the county court of the county in which the property is situate.

(l)   "Clerk" means the clerk of the county court of the county in which the property is situate.

(m)   "Revocation" means an instrument signed by all of the unit owners and by all holders of liens against the units by which the property is removed from the provisions of this chapter.

(n)   "Unit" means a part of the property designed or intended for any type of independent use, which has a direct exit to a public street or way, or to a common element or common elements leading to a public street or way, or to an easement or right of way leading to a public street or way, and includes the proportionate undivided interest in the common elements which is assigned thereto in the declaration, or any amendments thereof.

(o)   "Unit designation" means the number, letter or combination thereof designating a unit in the declaration plan.

(p)   "Unit owner" means the person or persons owning a unit in fee simple.

(q)   "Mortgage" means either mortgage or deed of trust.

APPLICATION OF CHAPTER

The provisions of this chapter shall be applicable only to real property, the sole owner of all the owners of which submit the same to the provisions hereof by a duly recorded declaration.

STATUS OF UNITS; OWNERSHIP

Each unit, together with its proportionate undivided interest in the common elements is for all purposes real property and the ownership of each unit, together with its proportionate undivided interest in the common elements, is for all purposes the ownership of real property.

COMMON ELEMENTS

The percentage of undivided interest in the common elements assigned to each unit shall be set forth in the declaration and such percentage shall not be altered except by recording an amended declaration duly executed by all of the unit owners affected thereby. The undivided interest in the common elements may not be separated from the unit to which such interest pertains and shall be deemed to be conveyed, leased or encumbered with the unit even though such interest is not expressly referred to or described in the deed, lease, mortgage or other instrument. The common elements shall remain undivided and no owner may exempt himself from liability with respect to the common expenses by waiver of the enjoyment of the right to use any of the common elements or by the abandonment of his unit or otherwise, and no action for partition or division of any part of the common elements shall be permitted, except as provided in section two [§ 36A-8-2], article eight of this chapter. Each unit owner or lessee thereof may use the common elements in accordance with the purpose for which they are intended. The maintenance and repair of the common elements and the making of any additions or improvements thereto shall be carried out only as provided in the code of regulations.

INVALIDITY OF CONTRARY AGREEMENTS

Any agreement contrary to the provisions of this chapter shall be void and of no effect.

ADMINISTRATIVE PROVISIONS

ADMINISTRATION GOVERNED BY CODE OF REGULATIONS

The administration of every property shall be governed by a code of regulations, a true and correct copy of which, and all duly adopted amendments of which, shall be duly recorded.

ADOPTION, AMENDMENT OR REPEAL OF CODE OF REGULATIONS

The council has authority to make, alter, amend and repeal the code of regulations, subject to the right of a majority of the unit owners to change any such actions.

CONTENTS OF CODE OF REGULATIONS

The code of regulations shall provide for at least the following and may include other lawful provisions:

(a) Identification of the property by reference to the place of record of the declaration and the declaration plan;

(b) The method of calling meetings of unit owners and meetings of the council;

(c) The number of unit owners and the number of members of council which shall constitute a quorum for the transaction of business;

(d) The number and qualification of members of council, the duration of the term of such members and the method of filling vacancies;

(e) The annual election by the council of a president, secretary and treasurer and any other officers which the code of regulations may specify;

(f) The duties of each officer, the compensation and removal of officers and the method of filling vacancies;

(g) Maintenance, repair and replacement of the common elements and payment of the cost thereof;

(h) The manner of collecting common expenses from unit owners; and

(i) The method of adopting and of amending rules governing the details of the use and operation of the property and the use of the common elements.

COMPLIANCE BY OWNERS WITH CODE OF REGULATIONS, ADMINISTRATIVE PROVISIONS, ETC

Each unit owner shall comply with the code of regulations and with such rules governing the details of the use and operation of the property and the use of the common elements as may be in effect from time to time, and with the covenants, conditions and restrictions set forth in the declaration or in the deed to his unit or in the declaration plan.

REMEDY FOR NONCOMPLIANCE WITH CODE OF REGULATIONS, ADMINISTRATIVE PROVISIONS, ETC

Failure to comply with the code of regulations and with such rules governing the details of the use and operation of the property and the use of the common elements as may be in effect from time to time and with the covenants, conditions and restrictions set forth in the declaration or in deeds of units or in the declaration plan shall be grounds for an action for the recovery of damages or for injunctive relief, or both, maintainable by any member of the council on behalf of the council or the unit owners or, in a proper case, by an aggrieved unit owner or by any person who holds a mortgage lien upon a unit and is aggrieved by any such noncompliance.

DUTIES OF COUNCIL

The duties of the council shall include the following:

(a) The maintenance, repair and replacement of the common elements;

(b) The assessment and collection of funds from unit owners for common expenses and the payment of such common expenses;

(c) The adoption and amendment of the code of regulations and the promulgation, distribution and enforcement of rules governing the details of the use and operation of the property and the use of the common elements, subject to the right of a majority of the unit owners to change any such actions; and

(d) Any other duties which may be set forth in the declaration or code of regulations.

POWER OF COUNCIL

Subject to the limitations and restrictions contained in this chapter, the council shall on behalf of the unit owners:

(a) Have power to manage the business, operation and affairs of the property and for such purposes to engage employees and appoint agents and to define their duties and fix their compensation, enter into contracts and other written instruments or documents and to authorize the execution thereof by officers elected by the council; and

(b) Have such incidental powers as may be appropriate to the performance of their duties.

WORK ON COMMON ELEMENTS

The maintenance, repair and replacement of the common elements and the making of improvements or additions thereto shall be carried on only as provided in the code of regulations.

CERTAIN WORK PROHIBITED

No unit owner shall do any work on his unit or the common elements which would jeopardize the soundness or safety of the property or impair any easement or hereditament without the unanimous consent of the unit owners affected thereby.

EASEMENTS FOR WORK

The council shall have an easement to enter any unit to maintain, repair or replace the common elements, as well as to make repairs to units if such repairs are reasonably necessary for public safety or to prevent damage to other units or to the common elements.

COMMON PROFITS AND EXPENSES

The common profits of the property shall be distributed among, and the common expenses shall be charged to, the unit owners according to the percentage of the undivided interest of each in the common elements as set forth in the declaration and any amendments thereto.

VOTING BY UNIT OWNERS

At any meeting of unit owners, each unit owner shall be entitled to the same number of votes as the percentage of ownership in the common elements assigned to his unit in the declaration and any amendments thereto.

RECORDS OF RECEIPTS AND EXPENDITURES; EXAMINATION BY OWNERS; RECORDS OF ASSESSMENTS

The treasurer shall keep detailed records of all receipts and expenditures, including expenditures affecting the common elements, specifying and itemizing the maintenance, repair and replacement expenses of the common elements and any other expenses incurred. Such records shall be available for examination by the unit owners during regular business hours. In accordance with the actions of the council assessing common expenses against the units and unit owners, he shall keep an accurate record of such assessments and of the payment thereof by each unit owner.

DECLARATIONS, CONVEYANCES, MORTGAGES AND LEASES

CONTENTS OF DECLARATION

The declaration shall contain the following:

(a)　A reference to this chapter and an expression of the intention to submit the property to the provisions of this chapter;

(b)　A description of the land and building;

(c)　The name by which the property will be known;

(d)　A statement that the property is to consist of units and common elements as shown in a declaration plan;

(e)　A description of the common elements and the proportionate undivided interest, expressed as a percentage, assigned to each unit therein, which percentages shall aggregate one hundred per cent;

(f)　A statement that the proportionate undivided interest in the common elements may be altered by the recording of an amendment duly executed by all unit owners affected thereby;

(g)　A statement of the purposes or uses for which each unit is intended and restrictions, if any, as to use;

(h)　The names of the first members of council;

(i)　Any further details in connection with the property which the party or parties executing the declaration may deem appropriate.

DECLARATION PLAN

The declaration plan shall bear the verified statement of a registered architect or licensed professional engineer certifying that the declaration plan fully and accurately (i) shows the property, the location of the building thereon, the building and the layout of the floors of the building, including the units and the common elements and (ii) sets forth the name by which the property will be known, and the unit designation for each unit therein.

CONTENTS OF DEEDS OF UNITS

Deeds of units shall include the following:

(a)　The name by which the property is identified in the declaration plan and the name of the political subdivision and the ward, if any, and the name of the county in which the building is situate, together with a reference to the declaration and the declaration plan, including reference to the place where both instruments and any amendments thereof are recorded;

(b)　The unit designation of the unit in the declaration plan and any other data necessary for its proper identification;

(c)　A reference to the last unit deed if the unit was previously conveyed;

(d)　The proportionate undivided interest, expressed as a percentage, in the common elements which is assigned to the unit in the declaration and any amendments thereof;

(e)　In addition to the foregoing, the first deed conveying each unit shall contain the following specific provision:

"The grantee, for and on behalf of the grantee and the grantee's heirs, personal representatives, successors and assigns, by the acceptance of this deed covenants and agrees to pay such charges for the maintenance of, repairs to, replacement of and expenses in connection with the common elements as may be assessed from time to time by the council in accordance with the Unit Property Act of [this state], and further covenants and agrees that the unit conveyed by this deed shall be subject to a charge for all amounts so assessed and that, except insofar as section five, article seven of said Unit Property Act may relieve a subsequent unit owner of liability for prior unpaid assessments, this covenant shall run with and bind the land or unit hereby conveyed and all subsequent owners thereof"; and

(f)   Any further details which the grantor and grantee may deem appropriate.

MORTGAGES AND OTHER LIENS OF RECORD AFFECTING PROPERTY AT TIME OF FIRST CONVEYANCE OF EACH UNIT

At the time of the first conveyance of each unit following the recording of the original declaration, every mortgage and other lien of record affecting the entire building or property or a greater portion thereof than the unit being conveyed shall be paid and satisfied of record, or the unit being conveyed shall be released therefrom by partial release duly recorded.

SALES, CONVEYANCES OR LEASES OF OR LIENS UPON SEPARATE UNITS

Units may be sold, conveyed, mortgaged, leased or otherwise dealt with in the same manner as like dealings are conducted with respect to real property and interests therein. Every written instrument dealing with a unit shall specifically set forth the name by which the property is identified and the unit designation identifying the unit involved.

RECORDING

INSTRUMENTS RECORDABLE

All instruments relating to the property or any unit, including the instruments provided for in this chapter, shall be entitled to be recorded, provided that they are acknowledged or proved in the manner provided by law.

RECORDING A PREREQUISITE TO EFFECTIVENESS OF CERTAIN INSTRUMENTS

No declaration, declaration plan or code of regulations, or any amendments thereto, shall be effective until the same have been duly recorded.

PLACE OF RECORDING

The clerk shall record declarations, deeds of units, codes of regulations, and revocations in the same records as are maintained for the recording of deeds of real property. Mortgages relating to units shall be recorded in the same records as are maintained by the clerk for the recording of real estate mortgages. Declaration plans, and any and all amendments thereto, shall be recorded in the same records as are maintained for the recording of subdivision plans.

INDEXING BY RECORDING OFFICER

The clerk shall index each declaration against the maker thereof as the grantor and the name by which the property is identified therein as the grantee. The clerk shall index each declaration plan and code of regulations and any revocation in the name by which the property is identified therein in both the grantor index and the grantee index. The clerk shall index each unit deed and mortgage and lease covering a unit in the same manner as like instruments are indexed.

RECORDING FEES

The clerk shall be entitled to charge the same fees for recording instruments which are recordable under this chapter as the clerk is entitled to charge for like services with respect to the recording of various similar instruments under the general law.

REMOVAL OF PROPERTY FROM PROVISIONS OF CHAPTER; RESUBMISSION

REMOVAL

Property may be removed from the provisions of this chapter by a revocation expressing the intention to so remove property previously made subject to the provisions of this chapter. No such revocation shall be effective unless the same is executed by all of the unit owners and by the holders of all mortgages, judgments or other liens affecting the units and is duly recorded.

EFFECT OF REMOVAL

When property subject to the provisions of this chapter has been removed as provided in section one of this article, the former unit owners shall, at the time such removal becomes effective, become tenants in common of the property. The undivided interest in the property owned in common which shall appertain to each unit owner at the time of removal shall be the percentage of undivided interest previously owned by such person in the common elements.

RESUBMISSION

The removal of property from the provisions of this chapter shall not preclude such property from being resubmitted to the provisions of the chapter in the manner herein provided.

ASSESSMENTS, TAXATION AND LIENS

ASSESSMENTS AND TAXES

Each unit and its proportionate undivided interest in the common elements as determined by the declaration and any amendments thereof shall be assessed and taxed for all purposes as a separate parcel of real estate entirely independent of the building or property of which the unit is a part. Neither the building, the property nor any of the common elements shall be assessed or taxed separately after the declaration and declaration plan are recorded, nor shall the same be subject to assessment or taxation, except as the units and their proportionate undivided interests in the common elements are assessed and taxed pursuant to the provisions of this section.

ASSESSMENT OF CHARGES

All sums assessed by resolutions duly adopted by the council against any unit for the share of common expenses chargeable to that unit shall constitute the personal liability of the owner of the units so assessed and shall, until fully paid, together with interest thereon at the rate of six per cent per annum from the thirtieth day following the adoption of such resolutions, constitute a charge against such unit which shall be enforceable as provided in section three of this article.

METHOD OF ENFORCING CHARGES

Any charge assessed against a unit may be enforced by a civil action by the council acting on behalf of the unit owners, provided that each suit when filed shall refer to this chapter and to the unit against which the assessment is made and the owner thereof and shall be indexed by the clerk of the county court of the county in which the unit is situate as lis pendens. Any judgment against a unit and its owner shall be enforceable in the same manner as is otherwise provided by law.

MECHANICS' LIENS AGAINST UNITS

Any mechanics' liens arising as a result of repairs to or improvements of a unit by a unit owner shall be liens only against such unit. Any mechanics' liens arising as a result of repairs to or improvements of the common elements, if authorized in writing pursuant to a duly adopted resolution of the council, shall be paid by the council as a common expense and until so paid shall be liens against each unit in a percentage equal to the proportionate share of the common elements relating to such unit.

UNPAID ASSESSMENTS AT TIME OF VOLUNTARY SALE OF UNIT

Upon the voluntary sale or conveyance of a unit, the purchaser shall be jointly and severally liable with the seller for all unpaid assessments for common expenses which are a charge against the unit as of the date of the sale or conveyance, but such joint and several liability shall be without prejudice to the purchaser's right to recover from the seller the amount of any such unpaid assessments which the purchaser may pay, and until any such assessments are paid they shall continue to be charged against the unit which may be enforced in the manner set forth in section three of this article: Provided, however, that any person who shall have entered into a written agreement to purchase a unit shall be entitled to obtain a written statement from the treasurer setting forth the amount of unpaid assessments charged against the unit and its owners, and if such statement does not reveal the full amount of the unpaid assessments as of the date it is rendered, neither the purchaser nor the unit shall be liable for the payment of an amount in excess of the unpaid assessments shown thereon. Any such excess which cannot be promptly collected from the former unit owner may be reassessed by the council as a common expense to be collected from all of the unit owners, including the purchaser, his successors and assigns.

MISCELLANEOUS

INSURANCE

The council shall, if required by the declaration, the code of regulations or by a majority of the unit owners, insure the building against loss or damage by fire and such other hazards as shall be required or requested, without prejudice to the right of each unit owner to insure his own unit for his own benefit. The premiums for such insurance on the building shall be deemed common expenses.

REPAIR OF RECONSTRUCTION

Except as hereinafter provided, damage to or destruction of the building or of one or more of several buildings which comprise the property shall be promptly repaired and restored by the council using the proceeds of insurance held by the council, if any, for the purpose, and the unit owners directly affected thereby shall be liable for assessment for any deficiency in proportion to their respective undivided ownership of the common elements: Provided, however, that if there is substantially total destruction of the building or of one or more of several buildings which comprise the property, or if seventy-five per cent of the unit owners directly affected thereby duly resolve not to proceed with repair or restoration, then, and in the event, the salvage value of the property or of the substantially destroyed building or buildings shall be subject to partition at the suit of any unit owner directly affected thereby, in which event the net proceeds of sale, together with the net proceeds of insurance policies held by the council, if any, shall be considered as one fund and shall be divided among all the unit owners directly affected thereby in proportion to their respective undivided ownership of the common elements, after discharging, out of the respective shares of unit owners directly affected thereby, to the extent sufficient for the purpose, all liens against the units of such unit owners.

SEVERABILITY

If any provision of this chapter, or any section, sentence, clause, phrase or word, or the application thereof in any circumstance is held invalid, the validity of the remainder of the chapter and of the application of any such provision, section, sentence, clause, phrase or word in any other circumstances, shall not be affected thereby.

Appendix C

ATLANTA MOTEL v. UNITED STATES
379 U.S. 241 (1964)

Mr. Justice Clark delivered the opinion of the Court.

This is a declaratory judgment action, 28 U. S. C. § 2201 and § 2202 (1958 ed.), attacking the constitutionality of Title II of the Civil Rights Act of 1964, 78 Stat. 241, 243. In addition to declaratory relief the complaint sought an injunction restraining the enforcement of the Act and damages against appellees based on allegedly resulting injury in the event compliance was required. Appellees counterclaimed for enforcement under § 206 (a) of the Act and asked for a three-judge district court under § 206 (b). A three-judge court, empaneled under § 206 (b) as well as 28 U. S. C. § 2282 (1958 ed.), sustained the validity of the Act and issued a permanent injunction on appellees' counterclaim restraining appellant from continuing to violate the Act which remains in effect on order of Mr. Justice Black, 85 S. Ct. 1. We affirm the judgment.

The Factual Background and Contentions of the Parties.

The case comes here on admissions and stipulated facts. Appellant owns and operates the Heart of Atlanta Motel which has 216 rooms available to transient guests. The motel is located on Courtland Street, two blocks from downtown Peachtree Street. It is readily accessible to interstate highways 75 and 85 and state highways 23 and 41. Appellant solicits patronage from outside the State of Georgia through various national advertising media, including magazines of national circulation; it maintains over 50 billboards and highway signs within the State, soliciting patronage for the motel; it accepts convention trade from outside Georgia and approximately 75% of its registered guests are from out of

State. Prior to passage of the Act the motel had followed a practice of refusing to rent rooms to Negroes, and it alleged that it intended to continue to do so. In an effort to perpetuate that policy this suit was filed.

The appellant contends that Congress in passing this Act exceeded its power to regulate commerce under Art. I, § 8, cl. 3, of the Constitution of the United States; that the Act violates the Fifth Amendment because appellant is deprived of the right to choose its customers and operate its business as it wishes, resulting in a taking of its liberty and property without due process of law and a taking of its property without just compensation; and, finally, that by requiring appellant to rent available rooms to Negroes against its will, Congress is subjecting it to involuntary servitude in contravention of the Thirteenth Amendment.

The appellees counter that the unavailability to Negroes of adequate accommodations interferes significantly with interstate travel, and that Congress, under the Commerce Clause, has power to remove such obstructions and restraints; that the Fifth Amendment does not forbid reasonable regulation and that consequential damage does not constitute a "taking" within the meaning of that amendment; that the Thirteenth Amendment claim fails because it is entirely frivolous to say that an amendment directed to the abolition of human bondage and the removal of widespread disabilities associated with slavery places discrimination in public accommodations beyond the reach of both federal and state law.

At the trial the appellant offered no evidence, submitting the case on the pleadings, admissions and stipulation of facts; however, appellees proved the refusal of the motel to accept Negro transients after the passage of the Act. The District Court sustained the constitutionality of the sections of the Act under attack (§ § 201 (a), (b) (1) and (c) (1)) and issued a permanent injunction on the counterclaim of the appellees. It restrained the appellant from "[r]efusing to accept Negroes as guests in the motel by reason of their race or color" and from "[m]aking any distinction whatever upon the basis of race or color in the availability of the goods, services, facilities, privileges, advantages or accommodations offered or made available to the guests of the motel, or to the general public, within or upon any of the premises of the Heart of Atlanta Motel, Inc."

The History of the Act.

Congress first evidenced its interest in civil rights legislation in the Civil Rights or Enforcement Act of April 9, 1866. There followed four Acts, with a fifth, the Civil Rights Act of March 1, 1875, culminating the series. In 1883 this Court struck down the public accommodations sections of the 1875 Act in the *Civil Rights Cases*, 109 U. S. 3. No major legislation in this field had been enacted by Congress for 82 years when the Civil Rights Act of 1957 became law. It was followed by the Civil Rights Act of 1960. Three years later, on June 19, 1963, the late President Kennedy called for civil rights legislation in a message to Congress to which he attached a proposed bill. Its stated purpose was

> "to promote the general welfare by eliminating discrimination based on race, color, religion, or national origin in . . . public accommodations through the exercise by Congress of the powers conferred upon it . . . to enforce the provisions of the fourteenth and fifteenth amendments, to regulate commerce among the several States, and to make laws necessary and proper to execute the powers conferred upon it by the Constitution." H. R. Doc. No. 124, 88th Cong., 1st Sess., at 14.

Bills were introduced in each House of the Congress, embodying the President's suggestion, one in the Senate being S. 1732 and one in the House, H. R. 7152.

However, it was not until July 2, 1964, upon the recommendation of President Johnson, that the Civil Rights Act of 1964, here under attack, was finally passed.

After extended hearings each of these bills was favorably reported to its respective house, H. R. 7152 on November 20, 1963, H. R. Rep. No. 914, 88th Cong., 1st Sess., and S. 1732 on February 10, 1964, S. Rep. No. 872, 88th Cong., 2d Sess. Although each bill originally incorporated extensive findings of fact these were eliminated from the bills as they were reported. The House passed its bill in January 1964 and sent it to the Senate. Through a bipartisan coalition of Senators Humphrey and Dirksen, together with other Senators, a substitute was worked out in informal conferences. This substitute was adopted by the Senate and sent to the House where it was adopted without change. This expedited procedure prevented the usual report on the substitute bill in the Senate as well as a Conference Committee report ordinarily filed in such matters. Our only frame of reference as to the legislative history of the Act is, therefore, the hearings, reports and debates on the respective bills in each house.

The Act as finally adopted was most comprehensive, undertaking to prevent through peaceful and voluntary settlement discrimination in voting, as well as in places of accommodation and public facilities, federally secured programs and in employment. Since Title II is the only portion under attack here, we confine our consideration to those public accommodation provisions.

Title II of the Act.

This Title is divided into seven sections beginning with § 201 (a) which provides that:

"All persons shall be entitled to the full and equal enjoyment of the goods, services, facilities, privileges, advantages, and accommodations of any place of public accommodation, as defined in this section, without discrimination or segregation on the ground of race, color, religion, or national origin."

There are listed in § 201 (b) four classes of business establishments, each of which "serves the public" and "is a place of public accommodation" within the meaning of § 201 (a) "if its operations affect commerce, or if discrimination or segregation by it is supported by State action." The covered establishments are:

"(1) any inn, hotel, motel, or other establishment which provides lodging to transient guests, other than an establishment located within a building which contains not more than five rooms for rent or hire and which is actually occupied by the proprietor of such establishment as his residence;

"(2) any restaurant, cafeteria . . . [not here involved];

"(3) any motion picture house . . . [not here involved];

"(4) any establishment . . . which is physically located within the premises of any establishment otherwise covered by this subsection, or . . . within the premises of which is physically located any such covered establishment . . . [not here involved]."

Section 201 (c) defines the phrase "affect commerce" as applied to the above establishments. It first declares that "any inn, hotel, motel, or other establishment which provides lodging to transient guests" affects commerce *per se.* Restaurants, cafeterias, etc., in class two affect commerce only if they serve or offer to serve interstate travelers or if a substantial portion of the food which they serve or products which they sell have "moved in commerce." Motion picture houses and other places listed in class three affect commerce if they customarily present films, performances, etc., "which move in commerce." And the establishments listed in class four affect commerce if they are within, or include within their own premises, an establishment "the operations of which affect commerce." Private clubs are excepted under certain conditions. See § 201 (e).

Section 201 (d) declares that "discrimination or segregation" is supported by state action when carried on under color of any law, statute, ordinance, regulation or any custom or usage required or enforced by officials of the State or any of its subdivisions.

In addition, § 202 affirmatively declares that all persons "shall be entitled to be free, at any establishment or place, from discrimination or segregation of any kind on the ground of race, color, religion, or national origin, if such discrimination or segregation is or purports to be required by any law, statute, ordinance, regulation, rule, or order of a State or any agency or political subdivision thereof."

Finally, § 203 prohibits the withholding or denial, etc., of any right or privilege secured by § 201 and § 202 or the intimidation, threatening or coercion of any person with the purpose of interfering with any such right or the punishing, etc., of any person for exercising or attempting to exercise any such right.

The remaining sections of the Title are remedial ones for violations of any of the previous sections. Remedies are limited to civil actions for preventive relief. The Attorney General may bring suit where he has "reasonable cause to believe that any person or group of persons is engaged in a pattern or practice of resistance to the full enjoyment of any of the rights secured by this title, and that the pattern or practice is of such a nature and is intended to deny the full exercise of the rights herein described . . . ." § 206 (a).

A person aggrieved may bring suit, in which the Attorney General may be permitted to intervene. Thirty days' written notice before filing any such action must be given to the appropriate authorities of a State or subdivision the law of which prohibits the act complained of and which has established an authority which may grant relief therefrom. § 204 (c). In States where such condition does not exist the court after a case is filed may refer it to the Community Relations Service which is established under Title X of the Act. § 204 (d). This Title establishes such service in the Department of Commerce, provides for a Director to be appointed by the President with the advice and consent of the Senate and grants it certain powers, including the power to hold hearings, with reference to matters coming to its attention by reference from the court or between communities and persons involved in disputes arising under the Act.

Application of Title II to Heart of Atlanta Motel.

It is admitted that the operation of the motel brings it within the provisions of § 201 (a) of the Act and that appellant refused to provide lodging for transient Negroes because of their race or color and that it intends to continue that policy unless restrained.

The sole question posed is, therefore, the constitutionality of the Civil Rights Act of 1964 as applied to these facts. The legislative history of the Act indicates that Congress based the Act on § 5 and the Equal Protection Clause of the Fourteenth Amendment as well as its power to regulate interstate commerce under Art. I, § 8, cl. 3, of the Constitution.

The Senate Commerce Committee made it quite clear that the fundamental object of Title II was to vindicate "the deprivation of personal dignity that surely accompanies denials of equal access to public establishments." At the same time, however, it noted that such an objective has been and could be readily achieved "by congressional action based on the commerce power of the Constitution." S. Rep. No. 872, *supra*, at 16-17. Our study of the legislative record, made in the light of prior cases, has brought us to the conclusion that Congress possessed ample power in this regard, and we have therefore not considered the other grounds relied upon. This is not to say that the remaining authority upon which it acted was not adequate, a question upon which we do not pass, but merely that since the commerce power is sufficient for our decision here we have considered it alone. Nor is § 201 (d) or § 202, having to do with state action, involved here and we do not pass upon either of those sections.

The Civil Rights Cases, 109 U. S. 3 (1883), and their Application.

In light of our ground for decision, it might be well at the outset to discuss the *Civil Rights Cases, supra*, which declared provisions of the Civil Rights Act of 1875 unconstitutional. 18 Stat. 335, 336. We think that decision inapposite, and without precedential value in determining the constitutionality of the present Act. Unlike Title II of the present legislation, the 1875 Act broadly proscribed discrimination in "inns, public conveyances on land or water, theaters, and other places of public amusement," without limiting the categories of affected businesses to those impinging upon interstate commerce. In contrast, the applicability of Title II is carefully limited to enterprises having a direct and substantial relation to the interstate flow of goods and people, except where state action is involved. Further, the fact that certain kinds of businesses may not in 1875 have been sufficiently involved in interstate commerce to warrant bringing them within the ambit of the commerce power is not necessarily dispositive of the same question today. Our populace had not reached its present mobility, nor were facilities, goods and services circulating as readily in interstate commerce as they are today. Although the principles which we apply today are those first formulated by Chief Justice Marshall in *Gibbons v. Ogden*, 9 Wheat. 1 (1824), the conditions of transportation and commerce have changed dramatically, and we must apply those principles to the present state of commerce. The sheer increase in volume of interstate traffic alone would give discriminatory practices which inhibit travel a far larger impact upon the Nation's commerce than such practices had on the economy of another day. Finally, there is language in the *Civil Rights Cases* which indicates that the Court did not fully consider whether the 1875 Act could be sustained as an exercise of the commerce power. Though the Court observed that "no one will contend that the power to pass it was contained in the Constitution before the adoption of the last three amendments [Thirteenth, Fourteenth, and Fifteenth]," the Court went on specifically to note that the Act was not "conceived" in terms of the commerce power and expressly pointed out:

> "Of course, these remarks [as to lack of congressional power] do not apply to those cases in which Congress is clothed with direct and plenary powers of legislation over the whole subject, accompanied with an express or implied denial of such power to the States, as in the regulation of commerce with foreign nations, among the several States, and with the Indian tribes . . . . In these cases Congress has power to pass laws for regulating the subjects specified in every detail, and the conduct and transactions of individuals in respect thereof." At 18.

Since the commerce power was not relied on by the Government and was without support in the record it is understandable that the Court narrowed its inquiry and excluded the Commerce Clause as a possible source of power. In any event, it is clear that such a limitation renders the opinion devoid of authority for the proposition that the Commerce Clause gives no power to Congress to regulate discriminatory practices now found substantially to affect interstate commerce. We, therefore, conclude that the *Civil Rights Cases* have no relevance to the basis of decision here where the Act explicitly relies upon the commerce power, and where the record is filled with testimony of obstructions and restraints resulting from the discriminations found to be existing. We now pass to that phase of the case.

The Basis of Congressional Action.

While the Act as adopted carried no congressional findings the record of its passage through each house is replete with evidence of the burdens that discrimination by race or color places upon interstate commerce. See Hearings before Senate Committee on Commerce on S. 1732, 88th Cong., 1st Sess.; S. Rep. No. 872, *supra;* Hearings before Senate Committee on the Judiciary on S. 1731, 88th Cong., 1st Sess.; Hearings before House Subcommittee No. 5 of the Committee on the Judiciary on miscellaneous proposals regarding Civil Rights, 88th Cong., 1st Sess., ser. 4; H. R. Rep. No. 914, *supra.* This testimony included the fact that our people have become increasingly mobile with millions of people of all races traveling from State to State; that Negroes in particular have been the subject of discrimination in transient accommodations, having to travel great distances to secure the same; that often they have been unable to obtain accommodations and have had to call upon friends to put them up overnight, S. Rep. No. 872, *supra,* at 14-22; and that these conditions had become so acute as to require the listing of available lodging for Negroes in a special guidebook which was itself "dramatic testimony to the difficulties" Negroes encounter in travel. Senate Commerce Committee Hearings, *supra,* at 692-694. These exclusionary practices were found to be nationwide, the Under Secretary of Commerce testifying that there is "no question that this discrimination in the North still exists to a large degree" and in the West and Midwest as well. *Id.,* at 735, 744. This testimony indicated a qualitative as well as quantitative effect on interstate travel by Negroes. The former was the obvious impairment of the Negro traveler's pleasure and convenience that resulted when he continually was uncertain of finding lodging. As for the latter, there was evidence that this uncertainty stemming from racial discrimination had the effect of discouraging travel on the part of a substantial portion of the Negro community. *Id.,* at 744. This was the conclusion not only of the Under Secretary of Commerce but also of the Administrator of the Federal Aviation Agency who wrote the Chairman of the Senate Commerce Committee that it was his "belief that air commerce is adversely affected by the denial to a substantial segment of the traveling public of adequate and desegregated public accommodations." *Id.,* at 12-13. We shall not burden this opinion with further details since the voluminous testimony presents overwhelming evidence that discrimination by hotels and motels impedes interstate travel.

The Power of Congress Over Interstate Travel.

The power of Congress to deal with these obstructions depends on the meaning of the Commerce Clause. Its meaning was first enunciated 140 years ago by the great Chief Justice John Marshall in *Gibbons v. Ogden,* 9 Wheat. 1 (1824), in these words:

> "The subject to be regulated is commerce; and . . . to ascertain the extent of the power, it becomes necessary to settle the meaning of the word.

The counsel for the appellee would limit it to traffic, to buying and selling, or the interchange of commodities . . . but it is something more: it is intercourse . . . between nations, and parts of nations, in all its branches, and is regulated by prescribing rules for carrying on that intercourse. [At 189-190.]

.   .   .   .   .

"To what commerce does this power extend? The constitution informs us, to commerce 'with foreign nations, and among the several States, and with the Indian tribes.'

"It has, we believe, been universally admitted, that these words comprehend every species of commercial intercourse . . . . No sort of trade can be carried on . . . to which this power does not extend. [At 193-194.]

.   .   .   .   .

"The subject to which the power is next applied, is to commerce 'among the several States.' The word 'among' means intermingled . . . .

.   .   .   .   .

". . . [I]t may very properly be restricted to that commerce which concerns more States than one. . . . The genius and character of the whole government seem to be, that its action is to be applied to all the . . . internal concerns [of the Nation] which affect the States generally; but not to those which are completely within a particular State, which do not affect other States, and with which it is not necessary to interfere, for the purpose of executing some of the general powers of the government. [At 194-195.]

.   .   .   .   .

"We are now arrived at the inquiry—What is this power?

"It is the power to regulate; that is, to prescribe the rule by which commerce is to be governed. This power, like all others vested in Congress, is complete in itself, may be exercised to its utmost extent, and acknowledges no limitations, other than are prescribed in the constitution. . . . If, as has always been understood, the sovereignty of Congress . . . is plenary as to those objects [specified in the Constitution], the power over commerce . . . . is vested in Congress as absolutely as it would be in a single government, having in its constitution the same restrictions on the exercise of the power as are found in the constitution of the United States. The wisdom and the discretion of Congress, their identity with the people, and the influence which their constituents possess at elections, are, in this, as in many other instances, as that, for example, of declaring war, the sole restraints on which they have relied, to secure them from its abuse. They are the restraints on which the people must often rely solely, in all representative governments. [At 196-197.]"

In short, the determinative test of the exercise of power by the Congress under the Commerce Clause is simply whether the activity sought to be regulated is "commerce which concerns more States than one" and has a real and substantial relation to the national interest. Let us now turn to this facet of the problem.

That the "intercourse" of which the Chief Justice spoke included the movement of persons through more States than one was settled as early as 1849, in the *Passenger Cases*, 7 How. 283, where Mr. Justice McLean stated: "That the transportation of passengers is a part of commerce is not now an open question." At 401. Again in 1913 Mr. Justice McKenna, speaking for the Court, said: "Commerce among the States, we have said, consists of intercourse and traffic between their citizens, and includes the transportation of persons and property." *Hoke v. United States*, 227 U.S. 308, 320. And only four years later in 1917 in *Caminetti v. United States*, 242 U.S. 470, Mr. Justice Day held for the Court:

> "The transportation of passengers in interstate commerce, it has long been settled, is within the regulatory power of Congress, under the commerce clause of the Constitution, and the authority of Congress to keep the channels of interstate commerce free from immoral and injurious uses has been frequently sustained, and is no longer open to question." At 491.

Nor does it make any difference whether the transportation is commercial in character. *Id.*, at 484-486. In *Morgan v. Virginia*, 328 U.S. 373 (1946), Mr. Justice Reed observed as to the modern movement of persons among the States:

> "The recent changes in transportation brought about by the coming of automobiles [do] not seem of great significance in the problem. People of all races travel today more extensively than in 1878 when this Court first passed upon state regulation of racial segregation in commerce. [It but] emphasizes the soundness of this Court's early conclusion in *Hall v. DeCuir*, 95 U.S. 485." At 383.

The same interest in protecting interstate commerce which led Congress to deal with segregation in interstate carriers and the white-slave traffic has prompted it to extend the exercise of its power to gambling, *Lottery Case*, 188 U. S. 321 (1903); to criminal enterprises, *Brooks v. United States*, 267 U. S. 432 (1925); to deceptive practices in the sale of products, *Federal Trade Comm'n v. Mandel Bros., Inc.*, 359 U. S. 385 (1959); to fradulent security transactions, *Securities & Exchange Comm'n v. Ralston Purina Co.*, 346 U. S. 119 (1953); to misbranding of drugs, *Weeks v. United States*, 245 U. S. 618 (1918); to wages and hours, *United States v. Darby*, 312 U. S. 100 (1941); to members of labor unions,*Labor Board v. Jones & Laughlin Steel Corp.*, 301 U. S. 1 (1937); to crop control, *Wickard v. Filburn*, 317 U. S. 111 (1942); to discrimination against shippers, *United States v. Baltimore & Ohio R. Co.*, 333 U. S. 169 (1948); to the protection of small business from injurious price cutting, *Moore v. Mead's Fine Bread Co.*, 348 U. S. 115 (1954); to resale price maintenance, *Hudson Distributors, Inc. v. Eli Lilly & Co.*, 377 U. S. 386 (1964); *Schwegmann v. Calvert Distillers Corp.*, 341 U. S. 384 (1951); to professional football, *Radovich v. National Football League*, 352 U. S. 445 (1957); and to racial discrimination by owners and managers of terminal restaurants, *Boynton v. Virginia*, 364 U. S. 454 (1960).

That Congress was legislating against moral wrongs in many of these areas rendered its enactments no less valid. In framing Title II of this Act Congress was also dealing with what it considered a moral problem. But that fact does not detract from the overwhelming evidence of the disruptive effect that racial discrimination has had on commercial intercourse. It was this burden which empowered Congress to enact appropriate legislation, and, given this basis for the exercise of its power, Congress was not restricted by the fact that the particular obstruction to interstate commerce with which it was dealing was also deemed a moral and social wrong.

It is said that the operation of the motel here is of a purely local character. But, assuming this to be true, "[i]f it is interstate commerce that feels the pinch, it does not matter how local the operation which applies the squeeze." *United*

States v. Women's Sportswear Mfrs. Assn., 336 U. S. 460, 464 (1949). See *Labor Board v. Jones & Laughlin Steel Corp.*, *supra*. As Chief Justice Stone put it in *United States v. Darby, supra*:

"The power of Congress over interstate commerce is not confined to the regulation of commerce among the states. It extends to those activities intrastate which so affect interstate commerce or the exercise of the power of Congress over it as to make regulation of them appropriate means to the attainment of a legitimate end, the exercise of the granted power of Congress to regulate interstate commerce. See *McCulloch v. Maryland*, 4 Wheat. 316, 421." At 118.

Thus the power of Congress to promote interstate commerce also includes the power to regulate the local incidents thereof, including local activities in both the States of origin and destination, which might have a substantial and harmful effect upon that commerce. One need only examine the evidence which we have discussed above to see that Congress may—as it has—prohibit racial discrimination by motels serving travelers, however "local" their operations may appear.

Nor does the Act deprive appellant of liberty or property under the Fifth Amendment. The commerce power invoked here by the Congress is a specific and plenary one authorized by the Constitution itself. The only questions are: (1) whether Congress had a rational basis for finding that racial discrimination by motels affected commerce, and (2) if it had such a basis, whether the means it selected to eliminate that evil are reasonable and appropriate. If they are, appellant has no "right" to select its guests as it sees fit, free from governmental regulation.

There is nothing novel about such legislation. Thirty-two States now have it on their books either by statute or executive order and many cities provide such regulation. Some of these Acts go back fourscore years. It has been repeatedly held by this Court that such laws do not violate the Due Process Clause of the Fourteenth Amendment. Perhaps the first such holding was in the *Civil Rights Cases* themselves, where Mr. Justice Bradley for the Court inferentially found that innkeepers, "by the laws of all the States, so far as we are aware, are bound, to the extent of their facilities, to furnish proper accommodation to all unobjectionable persons who in good faith apply for them." At 25.

As we have pointed out, 32 States now have such provisions and no case has been cited to us where the attack on a state statute has been successful, either in federal or state courts. Indeed, in some cases the Due Process and Equal Protection Clause objections have been specifically discarded in this Court. *Bob-Lo Excursion Co. v. Michigan*, 333 U. S. 28, 34, n. 12 (1948). As a result the constitutionality of such state statutes stands unquestioned. "The authority of the Federal Government over interstate commerce does not differ," it was held in *United States v. Rock Royal Co-op., Inc.*, 307 U. S. 533 (1939), "in extent or character from that retained by the states over intrastate commerce." At 569-570. See also *Bowles v. Willingham*, 321 U. S. 503 (1944).

It is doubtful if in the long run appellant will suffer economic loss as a result of the Act. Experience is to the contrary where discrimination is completely obliterated as to all public accommodations. But whether this be true or not is of no consequence since the Court has specifically held that the fact that a "member of the class which is regulated may suffer economic losses not shared by others . . . has never been a barrier" to such legislation. *Bowles v. Willingham*, *supra*, at 518. Likewise in a long line of cases this Court has rejected the claim that the prohibition of racial discrimination in public accommodations interferes with personal liberty. See *District of Columbia v. John R. Thompson Co.*, 346 U. S. 100 (1953), and cases there cited, where we concluded that Congress had delegated law-making power to the District of Columbia "as broad as the police power of a state" which included the power to adopt "a law prohibiting discriminations against Negroes by the owners and managers of restaurants in the District of Columbia." At 110. Neither do we find any merit in the claim that the Act is a taking of property without just compensation. The cases are to the contrary.

We find no merit in the remainder of appellant's contentions, including that of "involuntary servitude." As we have seen, 32 States prohibit racial discrimination in public accommodations. These laws but codify the common-law innkeeper rule which long predated the Thirteenth Amendment. It is difficult to believe that the Amendment was intended to abrogate this principle. Indeed, the opinion of the Court in the *Civil Rights Cases* is to the contrary as we have seen, it having noted with approval the laws of "all the States" prohibiting discrimination. We could not say that the requirements of the Act in this regard are in any way "akin to African slavery." *Butler* v. *Perry*, 240 U. S. 328, 332 (1916).

We, therefore, conclude that the action of the Congress in the adoption of the Act as applied here to a motel which concededly serves interstate travelers is within the power granted it by the Commerce Clause of the Constitution, as interpreted by this Court for 140 years. It may be argued that Congress could have pursued other methods to eliminate the obstructions it found in interstate commerce caused by racial discrimination. But this is a matter of policy that rests entirely with the Congress not with the courts.

Appendix D

Does Title II of the Civil Rights Act of 1964, apply to restaurants?

KATZENBACH, ACTING ATTORNEY GENERAL, ET AL. v. McCLUNG, ET AL.
379 U. S. 294 (1964).

MR. JUSTICE CLARK delivered the opinion of the Court.

This case was argued with No. 515, *Heart of Atlanta Motel* v. *United States*, decided this date, *ante*, p. 241, in which we upheld the constitutional validity of Title II of the Civil Rights Act of 1964 against an attack by hotels, motels, and like establishments. This complaint for injunctive relief against appellants attacks the constitutionality of the Act as applied to a restaurant. The case was heard by a three-judge United States District Court and an injunction was issued restraining appellants from enforcing the Act against the restaurant. 233 F. Supp. 815. On direct appeal, 28 U. S. C. §§ 1252, 1253 (1958 ed.), we noted probable jurisdiction. 379 U. S. 802. We now reverse the judgment.

The Motion to Dismiss.

The appellants moved in the District Court to dismiss the complaint for want of equity jursidiction and that claim is pressed here. The grounds are that the Act authorizes only preventive relief; that there has been no threat of enforcement against the appellees and that they have alleged no irreparable injury. It is true that ordinarily equity will not interfere in such cases. However, we may and do consider this complaint as an application for a declaratory judgment under 28 U. S. C. §§ 2201 and 2202 (1958 ed.). In this case, of course, direct appeal to this Court would still lie under 28 U. S. C. § 1252 (1958 ed.). But even though Rule 57 of the Federal Rules of Civil Procedure permits declaratory relief although another adequate remedy exists, it should not be granted where a special statutory proceeding has been provided. See Notes on Rule 57 of Advisory Committee on Rules, 28 U. S. C. App. 5178 (1958 ed.). Title II provides for such a statutory proceeding for the determination of rights and duties arising thereunder, §§ 204—207, and courts should, therefore, ordinarily refrain from exercising their jurisdiction in such cases.

The present case, however, is in a unique position. The interference with governmental action has occurred and the constitutional question is before us in the companion case of *Heart of Atlanta Motel* as well as in this case. It is important that a decision on the constitutionality of the Act as applied in these cases be announced as quickly as possible. For these reasons, we have concluded, with the above caveat, that the denial of discretionary declaratory relief is not required here.

The Facts.

Ollie's Barbecue is a family-owned restaurant in Birmingham, Alabama, specializing in barbecued meats and homemade pies, with a seating capacity of 220 customers. It is located on a state highway 11 blocks from an interstate one and a somewhat greater distance from railroad and bus stations. The restaurant caters to a family and white-collar trade with a take-out service for Negroes. It employs 36 persons, two-thirds of whom are Negroes.

In the 12 months preceding the passage of the Act, the restaurant purchased locally approximately $150,000 worth of food, $69,683 or 46% of which was meat that it bought from a local supplier who had procured it from outside the State. The District Court expressly found that a substantial portion of the food served in the restaurant had moved in interstate commerce. The restaurant has refused to serve Negroes in its dining accommodations since its original opening in 1927, and since July 2, 1964, it has been operating in violation of the Act. The court below concluded that if it were required to serve Negroes it would lose a substantial amount of business.

On the merits, the District Court held that the Act could not be applied under the Fourteenth Amendment because it was conceded that the State of Alabama was not involved in the refusal of the restaurant to serve Negroes. It was also admitted that the Thirteenth Amendment was authority neither for validating nor for invalidating the Act. As to the Commerce Clause, the court found that it was "an express grant of power to Congress to regulate interstate commerce, which consists of the movement of persons, goods or information from one state to another"; and it found that the clause was also a grant of power "to regulate intrastate activities, but only to the extent that action on its part is necessary or appropriate to the effective execution of its expressly granted power to regulate interstate commerce." There must be, it said, a close and substantial relation between local activities and interstate commerce which requires control of the former in the protection of the latter. The court concluded, however, that the Congress, rather than finding facts sufficient to meet this rule, had legislated a conclusive presumption that a restaurant affects interstate commerce if it serves or offers to serve interstate travelers or if a substantial portion of the food which it serves has moved in commerce. This, the court held, it could not do because there was no demonstrable connection between food purchased in interstate commerce and sold in a restaurant and the conclusion of Congress that discrimination in the restaurant would affect that commerce.

The basic holding in *Heart of Atlanta Motel*, answers many of the contentions made by the appellees. There we outlined the overall purpose and operational plan of Title II and found it a valid exercise of the power to regulate interstate commerce insofar as it required hotels and motels to serve transients without regard to their race or color. In this case we consider its application to restaurants which serve food a substantial portion of which has moved in commerce.

The Act As Applied.

Section 201 (a) of Title II commands that all persons shall be entitled to the full and equal enjoyment of the goods and services of any place of public accommodation without discrimination or segregation on the ground of race, color, religion, or national origin; and § 201 (b) defines establishments as places of public accommodation if their operations affect commerce or segregation by them is supported by state action. Sections 201 (b) (2) and (c) place any "restaurant . . . principally engaged in selling food for consumption on the premises" under the Act "if . . . it serves or offers to serve interstate travelers or a substantial portion of the food which it serves . . . has moved in commerce."

Ollie's Barbecue admits that it is covered by these provisions of the Act. The Government makes no contention that the discrimination at the restaurant was supported by the State of Alabama. There is no claim that interstate travelers frequented the restaurant. The sole question, therefore, narrows down to whether Title II, as applied to a restaurant annually receiving about $70,000 worth of food which has moved in commerce, is a valid exercise of the power of Congress. The Government has contended that Congress had ample basis upon which to find that racial discrimination at restaurants which receive from out of state a substantial portion of the food served does, in fact, impose commercial burdens of national magnitude upon interstate commerce. The appellees' major argument is directed to this premise. They urge that no such basis existed. It is to that queston that we now turn.

The Congressional Hearings.

As we noted in *Heart of Atlanta Motel* both Houses of Congress conducted prolonged hearings on the Act. And, as we said there, while no formal findings were made, which of course are not necessary, it is well that we make mention of the testimony at these hearings the better to understand the problem before Congress and determine whether the Act is reasonable and appropriate means toward its solution. The record is replete with testimony of the burdens placed on interstate commerce by racial discrimination in restaurants. A comparison of per capita spending by Negroes in restaurants, theaters, and like establishments indicated less spending, after discounting income differences, in areas where discrimination is widely practiced. This condition, which was especially aggravated in the South, was attributed in the testimony of the Under Secretary of Commerce to racial segregation. See Hearings before the Senate Committee on Commerce on S. 1732, 88th Cong., 1st Sess., 695. This diminutive spending springing from a refusal to serve Negroes and their total loss as customers has, regardless of the absence of direct evidence, a close connection to interstate commerce. The fewer customers a restaurant enjoys the less food it sells and consequently the less it buys. S. Rep. No. 872, 88th Cong., 2d Sess., at 19; Senate Commerce Committee Hearings, at 207. In addition, the Attorney General testified that this type of discrimination imposed "an artificial restriction on the market" and interfered with the flow of merchandise. *Id.*, at 18-19; also, on this point, see testimony of Senator Magnuson, 110 Cong. Rec. 7402-7403. In addition, there were many references to discriminatory situations causing wide unrest and having a depressant effect on general business conditions in the respective communities. See, *e. g.*, Senate Commerce Committee Hearings, at 623-630, 695-700, 1384-1385.

Moreover there was an impressive array of testimony that discrimination in restaurants had a direct and highly restrictive effect upon interstate travel by Negroes. This resulted, it was said, because discriminatory practices prevent Negroes from buying prepared food served on the premises while on a trip, except in isolated and unkempt restaurants and under most unsatisfactory and often unpleasant conditions. This obviously discourages travel and obstructs interstate commerce for one can hardly travel without eating. Likewise, it was said, that discrimination deterred professional, as well as skilled, people from moving into areas where such practices occurred and thereby caused industry to be reluctant to establish there. S. Rep. No. 872, *supra*, at 18-19.

We believe that this testimony afforded ample basis for the conclusion that established restaurants in such areas sold less interstate goods because of the discrimination, that interstate travel was obstructed directly by it, that business in general suffered and that many new businesses refrained from establishing there as a result of it. Hence the District Court was in error in concluding that there was no connection between discrimination and the movement of interstate commerce. The court's conclusion that such a connection is outside "common experience" flies in the face of stubborn fact.

It goes without saying that, viewed in isolation, the volume of food purchased by Ollie's Barbecue from sources supplied from out of state was insignificant when compared with the total foodstuffs moving in commerce. But, as our late Brother Jackson said for the Court in *Wickard* v. *Filburn*, 317 U. S. 111 (1942):

> "That appellee's own contribution to the demand for wheat may be trivial by itself is not enough to remove him from the scope of federal regulation where, as here, his contribution, taken together with that of many others similarly situated, is far from trivial." At 127-128.

We noted in *Heart of Atlanta Motel* that a number of witnesses attested to the fact that racial discrimination was not merely a state or regional problem but was one of nationwide scope. Against this background, we must conclude that while the focus of the legislation was on the individual restaurant's relation to interstate commerce, Congress appropriately considered the importance of that connection with the knowledge that the discrimination was but "representative of many others throughout the country, the total incidence of which if left unchecked may well become far-reaching in its harm to commerce." *Polish Alliance* v. *Labor Board*, 322 U. S. 643, 648 (1944).

With this situation spreading as the record shows, Congress was not required to await the total dislocation of commerce. As was said in *Consolidated Edison Co.* v. *Labor Board*, 305 U. S. 197 (1938):

> "But it cannot be maintained that the exertion of federal power must await the disruption of that commerce. Congress was entitled to provide reasonable preventive measures and that was the object of the National Labor Relations Act." At 222.

The Power of Congress to Regulate Local Activities.

Article I, § 8, cl. 3, confers upon Congress the power "[t]o regulate Commerce . . . among the several States" and Clause 18 of the same Article grants it the power "[t]o make all Laws which shall be necessary and proper for carrying into Execution the foregoing Powers . . . . " This grant, as we have pointed out in *Heart of Atlanta Motel* "extends to those activities intrastate which so affect interstate commerce, or the exertion of the power of Congress over it, as to make regulation of them appropriate means to the attainment of a legitimate end, the effective execution of the granted power to regulate interstate commerce." *United State* v. *Wrightwood Dairy Co.*, 315 U.S. 110, 119 (1942). Much is said about a restaurant business being local but "even if appellee's activity be local and though it may not be regarded as commerce, it may still, whatever its nature, be reached by Congress if it exerts a substantial economic effect on interstate commerce . . . . " *Wickard* v. *Filburn, supra*, at 125. The activities that are beyond the reach of Congress are "those which are completely within a particular State, which do not affect other States, and with which it is not necessary to interfere, for the purpose of executing some of the general powers of the government." *Gibbons* v. *Ogden*, 9 Wheat. 1, 195 (1824). This rule is as good today as it was when Chief Justice Marshall laid it down almost a century and a half ago.

This Court has held time and again that this power extends to activities or retail establishments, including restaurants, which directly or indirectly burden or obstruct interstate commerce. We have detailed the cases in *Heart of Atlanta Motel*, and will not repeat them here.

Nor are the cases holding that interstate commerce ends when goods come to rest in the State of destination apposite here. That line of cases has been applied with reference to state taxation or regulation but not in the field of federal regulation.

The appellees contend that Congress has arbitrarily created a conclusive presumption that all restaurants meeting the criteria set out in the Act "affect commerce." Stated another way, they object to the omission of a provision for a case-by-case determination—judicial or administrative—that racial discrimination in a particular restaurant affects commerce.

But Congress' action in framing this Act was not unprecedented. In *United States* v. *Darby*, 312 U.S. 100 (1941), this Court held constitutional the Fair Labor Standards Act of 1938. There Congress determined that the payment of substandard wages to employees engaged in the production of goods for commerce, while not itself commerce, so inhibited it as to be subject to federal regulation. The appellees in that case argued, as do the appellees here, that the Act was invalid because it included no provision for an independent inquiry regarding the effect on commerce of substandard wages in a particular business. (Brief for appellees, pp. 76-77, *United States* v. *Darby*, 312 U. S. 100.) But the Court rejected the argument, observing that:

> "[S]ometimes Congress itself has said that a particular activity affects the commerce, as it did in the present Act, the Safety Appliance Act and the Railway Labor Act. In passing on the validity of legislation of the class last mentioned the only function of courts is to determine whether the particular activity regulated or prohibited is within the reach of the federal power." At 120-121.

Here, as there, Congress has determined for itself that refusals of service to Negroes have imposed burdens both upon the interstate flow of food and upon the movement of products generally. Of course, the mere fact that Congress has said when particular activity shall be deemed to affect commerce does not preclude further examination by this Court. But where we find that the legislators, in light of the facts and testimony before them, have a rational basis for finding a chosen regulatory scheme necessary to the protection of commerce, our investigation is at an end. The only remaining question—one answered in the affirmative by the court below—is whether the particular restaurant either serves or offers to serve interstate travelers or serves food a substantial portion of which has moved in interstate commerce.

The appellees urge that Congress, in passing the Fair Labor Standards Act and the National Labor Relations Act, made specific findings which were embodied in those statutes. Here, of course, Congress has included no formal findings. But their absence is not fatal to the validity of the statute, see *United States* v. *Carolene Products Co.*, 304 U.S. 144, 152 (1938), for the evidence presented at the hearings fully indicated the nature and effect of the burdens on commerce which Congress meant to alleviate.

Confronted as we are with the facts laid before Congress, we must conclude that it had a rational basis for finding that racial discrimination in restaurants had a direct and adverse effect on the free flow of interstate commerce. Insofar as the sections of the Act here relevant are concerned, §§ 201 (b) (2) and (c), Congress prohibited discrimination only in those establishments having a close tie to interstate commerce, *i. e.*, those, like the McClungs', serving food that has come from out of the State. We think in so doing that Congress acted well within its power to protect and foster commerce in extending the coverage of Title II only to those restaurants offering to serve interstate travelers or serving food, a substantial portion of which has moved in interstate commerce.

The absence of direct evidence connecting discriminatory restaurant service with the flow of interstate food, a factor on which the appellees place much reliance, is not, given the evidence as to the effect of such practices on other aspects of commerce, a crucial matter.

The power of Congress in this field is broad and sweeping; where it keeps within its sphere and violates no express constitutional limitation it has been the rule of this Court, going back almost to the founding days of the Republic, not to interfere. The Civil Rights Act of 1964, as here applied, we find to be plainly appropriate in the resolution of what the Congress found to be a national commercial problem of the first magnitude. We find it in no violation of any express limitations of the Constitution and we therefore declare it valid.

The judgment is therefore

Reversed.

Index to Charts, Figures, and Statutes

An *allonge,* 139
A.B.C. partnership, 157
Appraisal letter, 228

Closing statement, 235
Commitment letter, 229
Corporations, 181
Creation of a government, 22

Deed, 234

Economic Impact of Foreign Travelers
  to the U.S., 2

General Business Law, N.Y. Section
  203 (a) and (b), 323

Hotel Check, 148
How U.S. Travelers Spend Their
  Travel Dollars, 4

Indorsements, 142

Limited Partnerships, 165

New York, McKinney's Supp. 1972,
  Sec. 296(2), 385
No Access, 191

Opinion, West Virginia Attorney
  General, January 9, 1970, 385
Organization of a Corporation, 182
Origins of International Travelers to
  the U.S., 9

Real Estate Listing Contract, 225
Release of Deed of Trust, 237

Selected Tourism Related Organizations, 5
Sharing Profits and Losses, 164

Title II, Civil Rights Act of 1964,
  42 U.S.C. 2000 (1964), 385
Title Report, 231, 232

Uniform Purchase Contract, 226, 227

W. Va. Code, Ch. 16, Art. 6, Sec. 3
  (1966), 385

Index to Cases

Note: Text page numbers in this index are indicated by boldface type.

Aaron v. Ward, 203 N.Y. 351 (1911), **83**

Aaron v. Wolden, 84 Ala. 502, 4 So. 672, **56**

Alber v. Savory Plaza, Inc., 279 App. Div. 110, 108 N.Y.S. 2d 80 (1951), **315**

Alpaugh v. Wolverton, 184 Va. 943, 36 S.E. 2d 906, **385**

American Banana Co. v. United Fruit Co., 213 U.S. 347 (1909), **31**

Archibald v. Pan American World Airways, 460 F. 2d 14 (1972), **391**

Baker v. Dallas Hotel, 162 Wash., 289, 298 P. 465 (1931), **352**

Balzer v. Indian Lake Maintenance, Inc., 346 So. 2d 146 (Florida 1977), **200**

Barlow v. Scott, Mo. Sup., 85 S.W. 2d 504, 517, **56**

Barnette v. Casey, 124 W.Va. 143, 19 S.E. 2d 621, **323**

Barre v. Hong Kong Restaurant, Inc., La. App., 346 So. 2d 318 (1977), **127**

Becker v. Volkswagen of Am., Inc., 18 U.C.C. Rep. 135 (Cal. App. 1975), **105**

Bott. v. Wheller, 183 Va. 643, 33 S.E. 2d 184, **90**

Bright v. Turner, 205 Ky. 188, 265 S.W. 627, 628, **56**

Bucholtz v. Sirokin Travel, LTD, 80 Misc. 2d 333, 363, N.Y.S. 2d 415 (1974), **356**

Bullock v. Bullock, 52 N.J. Eq. 561, 30 A. 676, 27 L.R.A. 216, **56**

Burke v. Shaver, 92 Va. 345, 23 S.E. 749, **90**

Campbell v. Portsmouth Hotel Co., 91 N.H. 390, 20 A. 2d 644, 135 A.L.R. 1196, **323**

Campbell v. Womack, La. App., 345 So. 2d 96 (No. 11120, 1977), **252**

Candib v. Carver, Fla. App., 344 So. 2d 1312 (1977), **217**

Cayle's Case, 8 Coke Rep. 32 (Eng. 1584), **322, 334**

City of Torrance v. Superior Court of Los Angeles County, 545 P. 2d 1313 (Cal. 1976), **222**

Clock v. Missouri-Kansas-Texas Railroad Co. v. Crawford, 407 F. Supp. 448 (E.D. Mo. 1976), **104**

Cohen v. Varig Airlines, etc., 390 N.Y.S. 2d 515 (1976), **393**

Commodore Cruise Line LTD, v. Kormendi, Fla. App. 344 So. 2d 896 (1977), **388, 400**

Condado Aruba Caribbean Hotel v.

Tickel, Colo. App., 561 P. 2d 23 (1977), **43**

Conklin v. Hotel Waldorf Astoria Corp., 169 N.Y.S. 2d 205 (1957), **385**

Connolly v. Nichollet Hotel, 95 N.W. 2d 657 (1959), **344**

Construction Indies, Ass'n of Sonoma County v. City of Petaluma, No. 74-2100 (9th Cir., 1975), **222**

Contractors Ass'n of Eastern Pa. v. Hodgson, 3rd Civ. 1971, 3 FEP Cases 395; Cert. denied U.S. Sup. Ct., 3 FEP Cases 1030 (1971), **129**

Coral Isle West Ass'n Inc., 430 F. Supp. 396 (1977), **219**

County Club of Miami Corporation v. McDaniel, 310 So. 2d 436 (Fla. 3d DCA 1975), **400**

Courson v. Til, La. App., 344 So. 2d 719 (1977), **243**

Cox v. Cox, 289 So. 2d 609, 14 U.C.C. Rep 330 (1974), **104**

Cunningham v. Bucky, 42 W.Va. 671, 26 S.E. 442, 57 Am. St. Rep. 876, 35 L.R.A. 850, **323**

Dalton v. Hamilton Hotel, 152 N.E. 268 (1926), **323**

Dangerfield v. Marhel, 222 N.W. 2d 373, 15 U.C.C. Rep. 915 (N.D. 1974), **104**

Dapierlla v. Arkansas Louisiana Gas Co., 225 Ark. 150, 12 U.C.C. Rep. 468 (1976), **104**

Deck House, Inc., v. Scarborough, Sheffield & Gastin, Inc., 228 S.E. 2d 142, 20 U.C.C. Rep. 278 (Ga. App. 1976), **105**

DeLuce v. Fort Wayne Hotel, 311 F. 2d 853 (6th Cir. 1962), **352**

Dold v. Outrigger Hotel, 501 P. 2d 368 (S. Ct. Haw. 1972), **275**

Double E. Sportswear Corp. v. Girard Trust Bank, 488 F. 2d 292 (3d Cir. 1973), **104**

Dunn v. Dunn Vincent, Inc., 562 P. 2d 972 (Oregon 1977), **86**

E.A. McQuade Travel Agency, Inc., v. Domeck, 190 So. 2d 3, Dist. Ct. App. Fla. (1966), **357**

Eastern Airlines, Inc., v. McDonnell Douglas Corp., 532 F. 2d 957, 19 U.C.C. Rep. 353 (5th Cir. 1976), **104**

Egan v. Kollsman Instrument Corp., 287 N.Y.S. 2d 14 (1967), **365**

Elridge v. Troost, 3. Abb. Prac. N.S. (N.Y.), 77 N.Y.C. 1054, **172**

Environics, Inc., v. Pratt, 18 U.C.C. Rep. 143 (1975), **149**

ExParte Chesser, 93 Fla. 590, 112 So. 87, 90 (1920), **72**

F.A. D'Andrea, Inc., v. Dodge, 15 F. 2d 1003, **90**

Fireman's Fund A.M. Ins. Companies v. Knobbe, 562 P. 2d 825 (Nevada 1977), **263**

Frank v. Justine Caterers, Inc., 271 App. Div. 980, 68 N.Y.S. 2d 193 (1947), **288**

Freeman v. Klamesha Concord, Inc., 76 Misc. 2d 915, 351 N.Y.S. 2d 541 (1974), **282, 288**

Fuller v. State, Ala. Cr. App., 344 So. 2d 216 (1977), **256**

G.&M. Restaurants Corp. v. Tropical Music Service, Inc., 161 So. 2d 566 (Fla. 2d DCA 1964), **400**

Goldfarb v. Virginia State Bar, 421 U.S. 773 (1975), **56**

Griggs v. Duke Power Co., U.S. Sup. Ct., 3 FEP Cases 175 (1971), **129**

Hadley v. Bavendate, 9 E.X. 341 (1854), **288**

Hallman v. Federal Parking Services, 134 A. 2d 382 (1957), **307**

Hamrick v. McCutcheon, 101 W.Va. 485, 133 S.E. 127, 129, **323**

Harder v. Auberge Des Fougeres, Inc., 40 App. Div. 2d 98, 338 N.Y.S. 2d 356 (Third Dept. 1972), **376, 385**

H.D. & J.K. Crosswell v. Jones, D.C. S.C. 52 F. 2d 880, 883, **205**

Henderson v. School Dist. No. 44, 75 Mont. 154, 242 P. 979, 980, **188**

Hollamon v. Board of Education of Stewart County, 168 Ga. 359, 147 S.E. 882, 884, **205**

Honaker v. Crutchfield, 247 Ky. 495, 57 S.W. 2d 502, **323**

Hostetter v. Inland Dev. Corp. of Montana, 561 P. 2d 1325 (1977), **328**

Hulett v. Swift, 33 N.Y. 571, 88 Am. Sec. 405 (1865), **334**

In re Carter's Estate, 254 Pa. 518, 99 A. 58, **72**

Insurance Co. of North America v. Rodiant Elec. Co., 222 N.W. 2d 323, 15 U.C.C. Rep. 261 (Mich. App. 1974), **105**

Isbill v. Stoval, Tex. Civ. App., 92 S.W. 2d 1067, 1070, **72**

Jazel Corp. v. Sentinel Enterprises, Inc., 20 U.C.C. Rep. 837 (N.Y. Sup. Ct. 1976), **105**

Jenkins v. Kentucky Hotel, 261 Ky. 419, 87 S.W. 2d 951 (1935), **298**

Jenkins v. Missouri State Life, Inc., 334 Mo. 941, 69 S.W. 2d 666 (1934), **352**

John P. Agnew Co., Inc., v. Hooge, 69 App. D.C. 116, 99 F. 2d 349, 351, **72**

Johnson v. Richmond & D.R. Co., 86 Va. 975, 11 S.E. 829, **90**

Krikorian v. Dailey, 171 Va. 16, 197 S.E. 442, **90**

Landry v. Gillory, 344 So. 2d 1138 (La. App. 1977), **88**

Lantx v. B-1202 Corporation d/b/a/ Bonanza Restaurant, 429 F. Supp. 421 (1977), **125**

Latta v. Kilbourn, 150 U.S. 524, 148 Ct. 201, 37 L.E.D. 169, **205**

League to Save Lake Tahoe v. Tahoe, Reg. Pl., 563 P. 2d 582 (Nevada 1977), **183**

Leaver v. Grose, 563 P. 2d 773 (Utah 1977), **203**

Levine v. British Overseas Airway Corporation, 66 Misc. 2d 820, 322 N.Y.S. 2d 119 (1971), **359**

Lewis v. Hughes, 346 A. 2d 231, 18 U.C.C. Rep. 52 (Md. App. 1975), **104**

Linmark Associates, Inc., v. Township of Willingboro, 45 U.S.L. W. 4441 (1977), **206**

Lyttle v. Denney, 222 Pa. 395, 71 A. 841 (1909), **352**

Manning v. Lamb, D.C. Mun. App., 89 A. 2d 882, **323**

Markantonatos v. Oregon Liquor Control Commission, Or. App., 562 P. 2d 570 (1977), **28**

McCulloch v. Maryland, Wheat, 316 407 (1819), **31**

McHugh v. Schlosser et al., 292 A. 291 (S. Ct. Penna. 1894), **290**

McLeod v. College, 69 Neb. 550, 96 N.W. 265, **188**

McManigal v. Chicago Motor Coach Company, 18 Ill. App. 2d 183, 151 N.E. 2d 410 (1957), **400**

Mfrs. Hanover Trust Co. v. Alitalia Airlines, 429 S.F. Supp. 964 (1977), **395**

Miller v. Board of Public Works of City of Los Angeles, 195 Cal. 477, 38 A.L.R. 1479, **222**

Mitchell v. The Shoals, Inc., 227 N.E. 2d 21, 280 N.Y.S. 2d 113 (1967), **385**

Mizenis v. Sands Motel, Inc., 50 Ohio App. 2d 226, 362 N.E. 2d 661 (1975), **340, 352**

Moorhead v. Seymour, (City Ct. N.Y.) 77 N.Y.S. 1054, **172**

Moose Lodge No. 7 of Harrisburg v. Irvis, 407 U.S. 163 (1972), **385**

Moricoli v. Schwartz, 361 N.E. 2d 74 (1977), **338**

Morningstar v. Lafayette Hotel, 211 N.Y. 465, 105 N.E. 656 (1914), **293**

Myers v. United States, 272 U.S. 52, 240, 293, **31**

Nebraska Wheat Grower's Ass'n v. Smith, 115 Neb. 177, 212 N.W. 39, **188**

Neff v. Bud Lewis Co., 548 P. 2d 107 (1976), **205**

Nesben v. Jackson, 89 W.Va. 470, 109 S.E. 489, **323**

O'Dell v. Appalachian Hotel Corp., 153 Va. 283, 149 S.E. 487, 68 A.L.R. 629, **90**

Odysseys Unlimited, Inc., v. Astral Star Travel Service, 77 Misc. 2d 502, 354 N.Y.S. 2d 88 (1974), **362**

Oklahoma City Hotel v. Levine, 189 Okla. 331, 116 P. 2d 997 (1941), **322**

Oskay Gasoline & Oil Co. v. Continental Oil Co., 19 U.C.C. Rep. 61 (1976), **104**

Owen v. Burn Const. Co., 563 P. 2d 91 (1977), **39**

Page v. Sloan, **60**

Park-O-Tell Co. v. Roskamp, 203 Okl. 493, 223 P. 2d 375, **322, 326**

Parson v. Dwight State Co., 301 Mass. 324, 17 N.E. 2d 197 (1938), **352**

Perrine v. Paulos, 224 P. 2d 41 (1950), **297**

Peterson et al. v. City of Greenville, 373 U.S. 244 (1962), **302**

Pullman Co. v. Hall, 46 F. 2d 399 (4th Cir. 1931), **400**

Raider v. Dixie Inn, 248 S.W. 229 (Kentucky 1923), **295**

Reibalt v. Bedient, page 380 this text, **352**

Rhode Island Exch. Bank v. Hawkins, 6 R.I. 206, **56**

Roller v. McGraw, 63 W.Va. 462, 60 S.E. 410, **90**

Ross v. Kirkeby Hotels, 160 N.Y.S. 2d 978 (1957), **319**

Rudees v. Delta Airlines, Inc., 553
S.W. 2d 84 (Tenn. 1977), **394**
Rutter v. Palmer, 2 K.B. 87 (1922), **330**

Sale v. Railroad Commission, 15 Cal.
2d 612, 140 P. 2d 38, 41, **72**
Samet v. Farmers' & Merchants' Nat.
Bank of Baltimore, C.C.A. Md., 247
F. 669, 671, **205**
Shafer Motor Freight Service, 4 N.Y.S.
2d 526, 167 Misc. 681, **56**
Shea v. Fridley, P.C. Mun. App., 123
A. 2d 358, **323**
Smith v. Bayou Rentals, Inc., La.
App., 345 So. 2d 1229 (1977), **185**
South Burlington County N.A.A.C.P.
v. Mount Laurel, 336 A. 2d 713 (N.J.
1975), **222**
State v. Beal, 344 So. 2d 1012 (Louisi-
ana 1977), **265**
State v. Fernandey, 106 Fla. 779, 143
So. 638, **205**
State v. McDonough, 129 Conn. 483,
29 A. 2d 582, 584, **72**
State v. Powers, 51 N.L. 432, 17 A.
969, **304**
Sterling Nat'l Trust Co. v. Fidelity
Mort. Investors, 510 F. 2d 870, 16
U.C.C. Rep. 157 (1975), **149**
Swayne v. Connecticut, 86 Conn. 439,
85 A. 634, 635, **352**

Takko v. Peter Pan Seafoods, 563 P.
2d 710 (Oregon 1977), **102**
Taylor v. Lewis, 553 S.W. 2d 153
(Texas 1977), **165**
Tearney v. Marmison, 103 W.Va. 394,
137 S.E. 543, **90**
Thomas v. Pick Hotels Corporation,
244 F. 2d 664 (U.S. Ct. App. 10th
Cir. 1955), **279**
Trulock v. Willey, 187 F. 956 (8th Cir.
1911), **352**
Trustees of Phillip Exeter Academy v.
Exeters, 92 N.H. 473, 33 A. 2d 665,
673, **205**

Webster v. Blue Ship Tea Room, Inc.,
347 Mass. 421, 198 N.E. 2d 309
(1964), **385**
Weisman v. Holley Hotel Co., 128
W.Va. 476, 37 S.E. 2d 94, **323**
Wheeler v. Monroe, 523 P. 2d 540
(N.M. 1974), **206**
Wheeler v. New York, N.H. and H.R.
Co., 112 Conn. 510, 153 A. 159, 160,
188
Williams v. Board of Education, 45
W.Va. 199, 31 S.E. 985, **90**
Williams v. Braum Ice Cream Store,
Inc., 534 P. 2d 700 (Okla. 1974), **385**
Winnett v. Adams, 71 Neb. 817, 99
N.W. 681, **304**

Index to Words and Topics

Acceptance, 77, 284
  revoking, 98
  See also Contracts
Accession, 198
Administrative agencies, 22, 28, 47
Administrative law, 3, 27
Admissions, 171
Aer Lingus, 3
Age Discrimination Employment Act, 9
Agency, 8
  defined, 8
  estoppel, 110
  express, 109
  formation of the relationship, 109
  implied, 110
  notice, 115
  ratification, 112
  scope of agent's authority, 110
  servants, 108
  termination of the relationship, 115
Agents, 112
  duties, rights, and liabilities, 112
Airlines, 354
  lost baggage, 393 *et seq.*
  overbooking, 393
  reservations, 391
    damages, 391
  scald burns, 394, 395
American Bar Association, 4
American Express, 275
Antecedent debts, 143
Architect's contract, 228
Aruba, Netherlands Antilles, 43
Assault, 86

Back pay, 126
Bailee, 321
  gratuitious, 321
Bailment, 308, 321, 329
Banquets, 318
Bars (taverns), 373, 374, 380, 383
  defined, 373, 374
  dram shop acts, 380
  protection from customers, 380 *et seq.*
  protection from guards, 383 *et seq.*
Bathhouses, 84
Bid bonds, 229
Bids, 235
  See also Mortgage financing
Bill of lading, 148
Bills of exchange, 147
Board of directors, 181
Breach, 80
  anticipatory, 80
Brokers, 194
Boarding house, 7
  boarder, 8
Building permits, 214
Building restrictions, 203
Burden of proof, 168
By-laws, 176

California, 132
Capital structure, 177
Case of first impression, 25
Cases, 5
  briefs, 64
  citation example, 60

lawsuit, 5
Caterer, 89
Certificates of deposit, 146-47
C.I.F. (cost of goods, insurance, and
    freight), 97
City council, 20
Civil law, 34
Civil Rights Act, 9, 122
Charging order, 156, 157
Check in, 65, 269
    false registration, 272, 273
    late arrivals, 272
    See also Reservations
Clayton Act, 219
Closing, 233
    See also Title search
Coal mining, 3
C.O.D. (cash on delivery), 97
Code of Hammurabi, 20
Code of Professional Responsibility, 46
Colorado, 44
Commercial paper, 137 *et seq.*
    ambiguous terms, 137
    incomplete instruments, 136-37
    some history, 131
    transfer and negotiation, 138-39
    types of, 132-33
    See also Indorsements; Reacquisi-
        tions; Warranties
Commitment letter, 229
    See also Mortgage financing
Common carriers, 305, 384, 387
    assault on guests, 388 *et seq.*
    carriers contract, 364, 388
    contract of carriage, 387, 388
    cruise ships, 387
    guards, 395 *et seq.*
    subsidies, 387
Common law, 25, 34
Common stock, 177
Community property, 252
    See also Hospitality property
Condominium management and condo-
        miniums, 211, 217, 239
    condominium declarations, 241
Condominium, 8
Coney Island, 84
Consideration, 78
Constitutions, 21, 26
    amendments, 21
    equal rights, 21
    treaties, 21
Contempt of court, 82
Continental Congress, 22
Contracts, 6
    against public policy, 83
    bilateral or unilateral, 74
    breach, 79, 276, 280, 390
    classifications, 74
    competent parties, 79

definition, 6
    executory and executed, 75
    express or implied, 75
    form of, 76
    joint and several, 74
    illegal, 82
    implied, 82
    legal purpose, 79
    performance and breach, 79
    requirements of, 76
    to limit liability, 306
    void, voidable, and unenforceable, 75
Constructive delivery, 138
Contributory negligence, 309, 382
Convention of 1787, 23
Co-owners, 169
Coram nobis, 256
Corporate charter, 180
Corporate life, 180
Corporate opportunity, 176
Corporations, 173
    board of directors, 181-82
    classifications, 174-75
    corporate charter, 180
    de facto directors, 186
    defined, 173
    formation of, 176 *et seq.*
    types of, 175-76
County courts, 70
Court reporter, 20
Courts, 66
    classification of, 66
    clerks, 69
    definition of, 66
    limited jurisdiction, 69
    terms of, 68
Covenants, 200
Crime, 36
Cross-examination, 40, 42
Cure, 98
Customs, 301
    local, 302

Damaged goods, 326
Damages, 80, 87
    compensatory, 84
    consequential, 280
    liquidated, 80, 237
    nominal, 292
    punitive, 217, 275, 281, 390
Debt, 177
Dedication to public use, 199
Deeds, 194
De facto directors, 186
Definition
    corporation, 12
Deleware, 178
Demurrer, 102
Deposition, 62
Disability, 128

Discretion, 220
  See also Judges
Discrimination, 9
Dishonored checks, 145
Disturbance, 217
  annoyance, 217
  disappointment, 362 *et seq.*
  mental anguish, 252, 284
  nuisance, 217
  See also Torts
Domestic holiday makers, 6
Douglas, William O., Justice, 31
  Eighth Annual Benjamin Cardozo
    Lectures, 31
Dram shop act, 380
  See also Bars
Drawee, rights and liabilities, 144
  See also Commercial paper

Easements, 191
ECOA, 47
Egypt, 20
  Pharaoh, 20
Elevators, 273
Employee relations, 9
Equal Employment Opportunity Act, 9
Equal Pay Act, 9
Equity, 37
  Chancellor, 38
  contempt of court, 38
  divorces, 38
  injunctions, 38
  rescission, 38
  specific performance, 38, 81
  Writ System, 37
Escrow fund, 240
Estate administration, 195-96
Estate transfers, 195
Excursionists, 6
Executive privilege, 22
Express warranties, 141
  commercial paper, 141

Falling objects, 344-52
Federal Reporters, 59
Federal Trade Commission, 28, 143
Florida, 3, 54
Food, 377 *et seq.*
  foreign substances, 378-79
  quality of, 377-78
  warranties, 377-78
Foreclosure, 238
Forgery, 143
Franchising, 192
Fraud, 275
Frauds, 75, 81
  the statute of, 75
Future advances, 243
  See also Mortgage financing

Gambling debts, 43
Gambling houses, 44
Gifts, 197
Goods, 96
  conforming, 96
  improper delivery, 97
  nonconforming, 97
  of third parties, 318
  perishable, 97
  recapture of rights in, 99
  rejected, 97
  risk of loss, 99
Grants, 198
Guests, 7, 86, 248
  absence of baggage, 251
  advance payment, 271
  civil rights, 300
  duties of, 247
  false registration, 272-73
  holding mail of, 255
  late arrivals, 272
  lodging, 7
  phone calls to, 255
  responsibility, 313
  rights of, 299-300
  sick, 292
  transient, 7
  See also Innkeepers; Nonguests
Guests, injury to, 335
  contributory negligence, 336
  outside of the inn, 336
  protecting from employees, 337
  safe premises, 335-36
  swimming pools, 337
Guests, property of, 305, 312
  automobiles of, 325
  contributory negligence, 313
  damaged goods, 326
  goods in transit, 312
  leaving property at inn, 315
  lost property, 314
  money and valuables, 310
  stolen property, 314

Hearsay, 42
Hereditaments, 192
Hilton International, 148
Holders in due course, 142
Holmes, Oliver Wendell, Justice, 2
Hospitality property, 207
  ownership of, 207
    sole, 207
    joint, 207
    joint tenants, 208
    tenants in common, 200
  title, 209
    fee simple, 209
    legal and equitable, 209
  control of, 210

by owners, 210
Hotel check, 148
Hotel inspectors, 257
    See also Innkeepers
Hotels, 7
Humiliation, 86

Independent contractor, 63, 116
Indorsements, 139
    blank, 140
    conditional, 141
    qualified, 141
    restrictive, 140
    special, 140
Injunction, 217
In limine, 382
Innkeeper, in general, 7, 86
Innkeepers, duties of, 247
    contract disclaimers, 306-7
    courteous treatment, 350
    duty to receive, 248, 250, 279, 376
    excuses, 251
    limits on liability, 316
    loss of property, 328
        from automobiles, 329
    money and valuables, 310
    nondiscriminatory accommodations, 279
    public duties, 247, 284
    public health duties, 257
    rules of house, 305
    standard of care, 254, 255
    statutory limitations, 310
    suitable accommodations, 254
    to receive goods, 251
Innkeepers, rights of, 289 *et seq.*
    assign new rooms, 289, 290
    eject guests, 289, 290
    emergencies, 290
    enter rooms, 290
    lien, 299
    limiting liability, 330, 333
    lock-outs, 296
    opposite sex, 294
    See also Innkeepers, duties of
Inspection, hotel, 97
Instructions, 287
Integrated service, 302
    discrimination, 84
Interest (partnership law), 155
International Air Transport Association, 4
Interstate Commerce Commission, 28
Intoxicating liquor, 347

Judges, 52
    appellate, 52
    judex, 52
    schools of thought, 53

Judgment, 25
    confession of, 52
    consent, 53
    default, 53
    deficiency, 53
    final, 53
    in personam, 53
    interlocutory, 53
    judgment N.O.V., 39, 42
    lien, 53
    summary, 253
    "take-nothing," 166
Juries, 54
    in court, 55
"Jurisdiction shopping," 178
Jury, 55
    trial, 55
    verdict, 56

Kansas Civil Rights Act, 280

Lafayette, Louisiana, 88
LaGuardia, 366
Lake Tahoe, 183
Landlord and tenant, 7
Las Cruces, 39
Law, 2
    American Law Institute, 2
    classifications of, 3
    contract, 35
    definition of, 2
    enforced, 2
    history, 20
    human-made, 55
    judge-made, 52
    "justiciable controversies," 21
    private, 34
    property, 35
    procedural, 34
    public, 34
    Roman, 52
    sources of, 20
    substantive, 34
    tort, 36
    uniform, 24
    written, 20
Lawyers, 4
    bar, 4
    barristers, 4
    paralegal, 47
    services, 47
    solicitors, 4
    trial, 4
Legal profession, 46
    fee schedules, 46
    price fixing, 46
Legal research, 59
    TAP rule, 59
Liens and encumbrances, 214, 240

failure to pay taxes, 215
involuntary, 215
mechanics liens, 216
voluntary, 215
Limited partnerships, 165
Limiting liability, 330
Liquor Control Board, 167
Lis Pendens, 219
See also Liens and encumbrances
Locals, 319
Louisiana, 132
Lubbock Inn Motel, 166

Maintenance agreement, 201
Marshall, John, 23
Mechanics liens, 117, 216, 238
See also Liens and encumbrances
Mental anguish, 252, 284
Microwave ovens, 379
Minimum reservations, 286
See also Reservations
Misrepresentation, 81
Mortgage financing, 223
See also Hospitality property
Motel, 7
Motorist, 7
Mutuality, 78

National Conference of Commissioners
on Uniform State Laws, 24, 132
National Tourism Resources Review
Commission, 10
Negligence, 307, 320
Negotiable Instruments Law, 24, 132
Negotiability, 132
requirements of, 133
See also Commercial paper
Nevada, 183
Nonguests, 251
invited, 251
ejection of, 298
Nonsuit, 102
North Carolina, 60
No-shows, 274
Notes, 146, 147
statutes of limitations, 147

Ocean Isle Motel, 60
Offer, 76, 95, 284
revocation of, 95
Options, 198
Oregon, 132
Organizational meetings, 181
Organization for Economic Cooperation
and Development (OECD), 2
Orthopedic surgery, 128
O.S.H.A., 47
Out conveyances, 232
See also Title search

Overbooking, 274
no-shows, 274
Overtime compensation, 125, 126
Ownership, 193
historically, 193-94

Parol evidence rule, 94
Partners,
as a fiduciary, 161
books, 160
contributions, 159
indemnification, 160
information, 161
interest, 160
right to accounting, 161
salaries, 160
sharing p/1, 159 *et seq.*
See also Partnerships
Partnerships, 152
admissions of partners, 158
continuation of, 161-62
contributions to, 159
definition of, 152
dissolution of, 162 *et seq.*
incoming partner of, 159
notice to, 158
property of, 155-56
sharing profits and losses, 159 *et seq.*
types of, 152-53
Uniform Partnership Act, 152
See also Partners
Permits, 167 *et seq.*
beverage cartage, 167
caterers, 167
late hours, 167
mixed beverage, 167
sales tax, 167
Physical impairment, 128
Portland, 29
Precedent, 25
Prima facie, 309
Principals, 114
duties of P to T, 114
liability of, 116
Private Works Act, 244
Property, hospitality, 189 *et seq.*
definition of, 189
obtaining, 193
public and private, 193
terms, 190 *et seq.*
transfering, 193
See also Liens and encumbrances
Proprietorships, 151
Public expulsion, 86
Punch list, 238
See also Mortgage financing

Quo warranto, 187

Real estate contracts, 197-98
Recording, 233
    See also Title search
Records, 47
Recreation services, 11
    liability of those delivering, 11
Reporter system, 58
Reservations, 269, 270
    advance payment, 271
    contract counterpart, 270-71
    excuses, 271
    late arrivals, 272
    overbooking, 274
    See also Check-in
Res ipsa loquitur, 62
Resolution, 5, 176
Restatement, Second, Torts, 63
Restaurants, 7, 127
    defined, 373-74
    duties, 375-76
    injuries, 127
    liability of owner, 375
    quality of food, 377
    warranties, 377-78
    Zorba the Greek, 29
Restrictive clauses, 210
Restrictive covenants, 203
Rome, 52
Rooms assigned, 370
Rovelstad, James M., 16
Royal Catering, 88
Rules of Civil Procedure, 61

Sale and purchase of personal property, 197
Sales contracts, 7
    buyer, 7
    definitions, 92, 100
    existing and identified, 92
    formation of, 93
    goods, 92
    merchants, 7
    modification, 93, 95, 102
    offer and acceptance, 95
    rescission, 95
    seller, 7
    Statute of Frauds, 93, 100
    Statute of Limitations, 100
    usage or trade, 95
    waiver, 93, 95
Sales v. service, 101
Second mortgage, 237
    financing, 223
    See also Mortgages
Secretary of Labor, 126
Separation of powers, 22
Sherman Act, 219
Sight draft, 148
Slip and fall, 340-44

Small business stock, 177
Specific partnership property, 155
    See also Partnerships
Stare Decisis, 22
    rejecting, 22
Statute of Frauds, 94
    avoiding, 94
Statute of Limitations, 103, 279
Statutes, 23, 64
    standard, 23
    uniform, 23, 24
Statutory construction, 285
Stop orders, 145
Subchapter S, 177
Subdivision lots, 202
Summary judgment, 62
Summer hotel, 8
Surface water, 25

Tangible property, 190
Tavern, 87
Tax sales and foreclosures, 199
Tenants, 320, 321
Testate, 195
Texas Uniform Partnership Act, 168
Thoracic outlet syndrome, 127
Title, 98
    passing of, 98
Title search, 230
    advertising, 231
    title chain, 230
    title report, 231-32
    See also Mortgage financing
Torquere, 36
Tort, 36, 278, 280, 281
    negligence, 37
    nuisance, 37
    trespass, 37
Tourists, 6
Tour operators, 354
Trade acceptance, 148
Trade usage, 101
Travel agencies, 353
    disclaimers, 365
    duty to accept, 355
    not an insurer, 355
    prior experiences, 354
    regulation of, 355-56
    standard of care, 354
Travel agents, 353, 360
    as independent contractors, 361
    dual agents, 359
    measure of damages, 362
    wholesale, 353-54
Travel and Lodging Industry, 1
    annual sales, 1
    Discover America Travel Organization, 5

flag carriers, 2
foreign visitors, 1
impact of, 1
institutions and organizations, 3
legal environment of, 1
Traveler, 5, 10, 248, 249, 277, 281, 283, 285, 301, 305
  arrivals, 9
  custom or usage, 301
  definition of, 5
  need for special legal attention, 5
  "white water" trips, 9
Trespass, 38
  viet armis, 38
Truth in Lending, 118

Ultra Vires Acts, 176
Uniform Commercial Code, 24, 132, 137
Uniform Land Transfer Act, 24
Uniform Partnership Act, 152
  See also Partnerships
Uniform Sales Act, 24
United States Constitution, 5

United States Department of Interior, 10
United States Travel Service, 3
U.S. Army Corps of Engineers, 4
U.S. Congress, 3
U.S. Travel Data Center, 16

Virginia, Richmond, 65

Warranties, commercial paper, 145 *et seq.*
Warsaw Convention, 368-69, 370-71
Water heater, 60
West Virginia, 3, 16
Without recourse, 141
Worker's Compensation, 127
Wrongful discharge, 168

Zoning, 212
  nonconforming uses, 213
  slow growth, 213
  variances, 213